NIXON

The Fifth Year of His Presidency

CONGRESSIONAL QUARTERLY

1414 22ND STREET, N.W., WASHINGTON, D.C. 20037

49820

Congressional Quarterly Inc.

Congressional Quarterly Inc., an editorial research service and publishing company, serves clients in the fields of news, education, business and government. It combines specific coverage of Congress, government and politics by Congressional Quarterly with the more general subject range of an affiliated service, Editorial Research Reports.

Congressional Quarterly was founded in 1945 by Nelson and Henrietta Poynter. Its basic periodical publication was and still is the CQ *Weekly Report*, mailed to clients every Saturday. A cumulative index is published quarterly.

The CQ *Almanac*, a compendium of legislation for one session of Congress, is published every spring. *Congress and the Nation* is published every four years as a record of government for one presidential term.

Congressional Quarterly also publishes paperback books on public affairs. These include the twice-yearly *Guide to Current American Government* and such recent titles as *Supreme Court, Justice and the Law* and *Watergate: Chronology of a Crisis.*

CQ Direct Research is a consulting service which performs contract research and maintains a reference library and query desk for the convenience of clients.

Editorial Research Reports covers subjects beyond the specialized scope of Congressional Quarterly. It publishes reference material on foreign affairs, business, education, cultural affairs, national security, science and other topics of news interest. Service to clients includes a 6,000-word report four times a month bound and indexed semi-annually. Editorial Research Reports publishes paperback books in its fields of coverage. Founded in 1923, the service merged with Congressional Quarterly in 1956.

Book Service Editor: Robert A. Diamond

Contributors: Thomas J. Arrandale, Kim W. Brace, Mary Cohn, Oliver W. Cromwell, Diantha Johnson, Andrea Loewenstein, Carolyn S. Mathiasen, Peg O'Hara, Donald Smith.

Editorial Assistant and Index: Robert E. Healy.

Cover Design: Howard Chapman, Art Director.

Production Supervisor: Richard C. Young. Assistant Production Supervisor: Richard Butler.

Library of Congress Cataloging Data

Nixon, Richard Milhous, 1913-
    Nixon: the fifth year of his Presidency.

    1. United States—Politics and government—1969- 2. United States—Social policy. 3. United States—Foreign relations—1969- I. Congressional Quarterly, inc. II. Title.
E855.N475   320.9'73'0924   74-4270
ISBN 0-87187-052-5

TABLE OF CONTENTS

NIXON'S FIFTH YEAR: FROM TRIUMPH TO NATIONAL DOUBT

Richard M. Nixon began his fifth year as President in triumph. He ended American involvement in the Indochina war and brought home American prisoners of war. He continued to strengthen ties with both the Soviet Union and Red China, reducing prospects of other wars. Domestically, the country's economy prospered. For a fleeting moment early in 1973, Nixon rode as high a crest of public popularity as he had experienced at any time since entering the White House.

The triumph was short-lived. Nixon proved unable to cope with congressional opposition to most of his legislative proposals, and the year 1973 saw the virtual dismantling of his New Federalism plan for decentralizing federal spending. A ripsaw series of economic maneuvers failed to halt persistent inflation, and—despite two major bureaucratic reformations—an incipient energy crisis burst upon an unprepared populace.

But these setbacks for the White House paled in comparison to other events. By the end of the year, Nixon's support in Congress and in the public opinion polls had dropped to all-time lows as scandal and embarrassment rocked the administration.

As 1973 passed into history, the House Judiciary Committee was launching a formal investigation into impeachment charges against the President. Most observers predicted that an impeachment vote in the House would never succeed without the support of the electorate. And the public opinion polls showed that, though impeachment sentiment was growing steadily, the American people were not yet ready to stand behind so drastic a climax to the Watergate scandal and its aftermath.

Measuring the Fall. The polls were impressive indices of Nixon's fall from favor, however. A Gallup Poll published Feb. 6, shortly after Nixon announced the Vietnam cease-fire, showed 68 per cent of the American public approving of the way Nixon was handling his job as president. That figure equaled Nixon's previous peak of popularity, which occurred early in the first year of his presidency. By early November 1973, Nixon's public support as reported by Gallup had dropped to an all-time low of 27 per cent. And a Harris Survey published in mid-December showed that 45 per cent thought they would respect Nixon more if he resigned and let his new vice president, Gerald R. Ford, take over the Oval Office.

In another Harris poll, published on Christmas Eve, respondents rejected by a razor-thin margin of 45 to 44 per cent the proposition that Nixon "has reached the point where he can no longer be an effective President and should resign for the good of the country." According to Louis Harris, "The majority of the American people has been badly shaken by the Watergate episode. Yet the public draws back from the critical 'impeach or resign' position. Mr. Nixon is somewhat sustained by his reputation on foreign affairs and the public belief that he enjoys the training and experience necessary in a President."

The fact that 1974 was a congressional election year presented a hazard to the Nixon presidency. The year carried with it the possibility that Nixon would find himself being deserted by members of his own party who were up for re-election and who feared loss at the polls by association. A Nov. 11 Gallup Poll showed support for Republicans in the House had sunk to its lowest level in 38 years. Sen. Barry Goldwater, whom many consider the party's elder statesman, seemed to be pointing to an escape route when, in an interview published Dec. 17 in the *Christian Science Monitor*, he declared that Nixon had left doubts about his honesty and his ability to govern.

Whatever lay in the future, 1973 had many of the qualities of a roller coaster ride for the Nixon presidency—and most of it was downhill. *(Chronology, next page)*

Foreign Affairs

Nixon's major 1973 achievements lay in the field of foreign affairs, in which he has long considered himself an expert. Through adviser Henry A. Kissinger, whom he later named secretary of state, Nixon masterminded the Jan. 23 Vietnam peace agreement, the withdrawal of American troops and the return of American prisoners of war. Under another agreement negotiated by Kissinger, the United States and China on Feb. 22 announced the establishment of "liaison offices" in each others' capital cities and the expanding of trade and cultural ties. The agreement, along with Nixon's 1972 trip to China, marked the first formal diplomatic contact the United States had had with China since 1949.

After months of being buffeted by Watergate scandals, the week of June 17-22 was one Nixon could be pleased with. The visit of Soviet leader Leonid I. Brezhnev and the signing of several pacts, including one on nuclear arms, boosted Nixon's image as a statesman. In addition to the nuclear arms agreement, Soviet and U.S. officials initialed pacts broadening cooperation in the fields of cultural exchange, transportation, oceanography, agriculture, income taxation and the peaceful uses of atomic energy. On June 21, Nixon accepted Brezhnev's invitation to visit Moscow in 1974 for another round of summitry.

Nixon also claimed victory for handling the Middle East crisis when on Oct. 25 he placed American forces on alert to signal to the Soviets that the United States would not accept the unilateral introduction of Soviet troops in the area as a peace-keeping force. United Nations Security Council action later that day defused the emerging crisis.

Nixon's foreign affairs victories were not unqualified, however. Congress upstaged his Vietnam performance by decreeing an Aug. 15 cut-off of all combat activities in Indochina. And, though American forces had left, the

(Continued on p. 4)

The Nixon Record: From Vietnam Peace Agreement . . .

JANUARY

8th. The trial of the seven Watergate defendants begins.

11th. Nixon announces Phase III, relaxing wage and price controls except in the food, health and construction industries.

20th. Nixon inaugurated for second term.

23rd. Nixon announces the Vietnam peace agreement and plans for POW return.

29th. Nixon sends to Congress his fiscal 1974 budget, cutting social welfare programs.

FEBRUARY

7th. Senate creates the Watergate committee.

17th. Nixon nominates L. Patrick Gray III as FBI director.

22nd. U.S. and China announce establishment of "liaison offices" and cultural and trade exchanges.

MARCH

6th. Gray tells the Senate Judiciary Committee that White House counsel John W. Dean III attended all FBI interviews of White House staff regarding the Watergate break-in, prompting calls for Dean to testify.

12th. In a major policy announcement, Nixon claims executive privilege in refusing to allow Dean or any other members or former members of his personal staff to testify before a congressional committee.

23rd. Judge John J. Sirica postpones sentencing of Watergate defendant James W. McCord pending his cooperation in testifying about the incident.

29th. In a policy reversal, Nixon orders price ceiling on beef, lamb and pork.

APRIL

5th. Nixon withdraws Gray's nomination for FBI director.

5th. The Labor Department reports the wholesale price index for all commodities rose 2.2 per cent during March—the highest monthly rise since 1951.

11th. A federal judge orders the Nixon administration to cease dismantling the Office of Economic Opportunity.

17th. In a dramatic reversal, Nixon agrees to allow all members of the White House staff to testify before the Senate Watergate committee. The President said he was investigating "serious charges which have come to my attention." Press Secretary Ronald L. Ziegler characterizes all previous statements from the White House regarding Watergate as "inoperative."

18th. Nixon delivers to Congress an energy message, proposing methods to increase fuel imports and stimulate domestic production.

27th. U.S. District Court Judge W. Matthew Byrne discloses that E. Howard Hunt and G. Gordon Liddy had burglarized the files of Daniel Ellsberg's psychiatrist.

30th. In an address to the nation, Nixon says he takes responsibility for Watergate, and announces the resignations of White House aides H. R. Haldeman and John D. Ehrlichman, Attorney General Richard G. Kleindienst and Dean. Nixon promises a full investigation and says, "There can be no whitewash at the White House."

MAY

4th. A Gallup Poll finds that 40 per cent of the 456 persons questioned did not think Nixon told the whole truth in his April 30 speech. Fifty per cent said they thought he had participated in a coverup.

10th. Former Attorney General John N. Mitchell and former Secretary of Commerce Maurice H. Stans are indicted in New York in connection with a $200,000 cash contribution to the Nixon campaign from financier Robert L. Vesco.

18th. On the second day of Senate Watergate committee hearings, McCord implicates Nixon in alleged offers of executive clemency in return for a guilty plea during the Watergate trial.

22nd. In a written statement, Nixon admits there was a White House coverup of Watergate but asserts his innocence of planning or knowledge.

23rd. The Senate Judiciary Committee endorses Elliot L. Richardson's selection of Archibald Cox as special Watergate prosecutor and reports favorably Richardson's nomination as attorney general.

JUNE

13th. Again reversing himself on economic policy, Nixon orders a 60-day price freeze. The action is seen as a tacit admission that his previous economic policies had failed.

21st. Soviet leader Leonid I. Brezhnev concludes a visit to Washington that includes the signing of a nuclear arms pact.

25th. Dean tells the Senate Watergate committee that he believes Nixon was aware of the Watergate coverup as early as September 1972.

29th. Nixon accepts a congressionally imposed Aug. 15 deadline for the ending of combat activities in Indochina.

29th. Nixon appoints Gov. John A. Love (R Colo.) to head the newly created Energy Policy Office and announces a $10-billion, five-year energy research and development effort.

. . . to Watergate Revelations and 'I Am Not a Crook'

JULY

12th. Nixon treated for viral pneumonia.

16th. FAA Administrator Alexander P. Butterfield, a former White House aide, surprises the Senate Watergate committee with the information that Nixon routinely recorded conversations in the White House.

18th. Conceding that inflation is beyond the federal government's immediate control, Nixon lifts the freeze on food prices and lays out complex plans for toughened Phase IV controls on the economy.

22nd. A Gallup Poll shows Nixon's popularity at 40 per cent—a 28-point decline since January.

23rd. The Senate Watergate committee and Archibald Cox subpoena White House tapes and documents. Nixon refuses to comply, setting into motion a three-month legal battle.

AUGUST

1st. Maryland U.S. Attorney General George Beall informs Agnew's lawyers that the Vice President is under investigation for conspiracy, extortion, bribery and tax evasion.

6th. The administration discloses that total spending on Nixon's California and Florida homes is close to $10-million instead of an original $39,000 estimate.

15th. In a response to the Senate Watergate hearings, Nixon asserts his innocence and asks a national television audience not to stay "mired in Watergate."

20th. A reported plot to assassinate Nixon causes the Secret Service to re-route the President's motorcade through New Orleans. Nixon shoves Press Secretary Ronald L. Ziegler.

22nd. During his first televised meeting with the press in 14 months, Nixon fields hostile questions about Watergate.

29th. Sirica orders Nixon to turn over to him for his private inspection the nine tapes subpoenaed July 23 by Cox.

SEPTEMBER

5th. Congress reconvenes after a month at home. Members report constituents talk more about the cost of living than about Watergate.

10th. Nixon sends a supplementary state of the union message to Congress, complaining of inactivity on his proposals.

OCTOBER

10th. Agnew resigns, pleads "no contest" to charge of tax evasion.

12th. During a televised ceremony, Nixon announces Gerald R. Ford as his vice presidential nominee.

19th. In a bargain struck with Cox, Dean pleads guilty to a single felony count of conspiracy to obstruct justice and agrees to testify for the prosecution in future trials of other White House officials, perhaps against Nixon himself.

20th. Nixon fires Cox after the special prosecutor refuses a White House offer to compromise on the Watergate tapes delivery. Richardson and Ruckleshaus resign.

23rd. In a dramatic reversal, Nixon agrees to turn over the Watergate tapes to Sirica.

25th. Nixon places U.S. armed forces on alert, reportedly in response to a Soviet threat to unilaterally supervise the Arab-Israeli truce.

26th. In a stormy news conference, Nixon lashes out at the press for its "outrageous, vicious, distorted reporting" of the Cox firing.

31st. White House special counsel J. Fred Buzhardt tells Sirica that two of the subpoenaed Watergate tapes do not exist.

NOVEMBER

7th. In a televised message, Nixon outlines a long-range program to curb fuel consumption in face of growing shortages.

7th. Congress enacts into law over Nixon's veto a bill to restrict the President's warmaking powers.

12th. Buzhardt informs Sirica that a third relevant White House tape does not exist.

17th. In response to questions about his finances, Nixon tells an Associated Press Managing Editors meeting, "I am not a crook."

26th. Nixon's secretary, Rose Mary Woods, in a return appearance before Sirica, says she may have accidentally erased an 18½-minute June 20, 1972, Watergate conversation between Nixon and Haldeman.

DECEMBER

4th. Nixon abolishes Love's office and appoints Deputy Treasury Secretary William E. Simon to head a new energy office.

8th. Nixon releases a sweeping personal financial report.

17th. Sen. Barry Goldwater (R Ariz.) declares that Nixon has left doubts about his honesty and his ability to govern.

19th. The Senate Watergate committee subpoenas nearly 500 White House tape recordings and documents.

20th. The House Judiciary Committee sets a target date of April 1974 for completion of a staff investigation concerning possible charges of impeachment.

fighting continued. The President's ultimate foreign policy tool—his warmaking powers—were curtailed over his veto. And Nixon's promised "Year of Europe" failed to materialize.

Economy

With the value of the dollar continuing its downturn in the world market and with inflation soaring, Nixon vascillated between employing economic controls and honoring the conservative concept of allowing free market forces to regulate the economy. After less than three months of Phase III voluntary wage and price guidelines, Nixon March 29 imposed price ceilings on beef, lamb and pork for an indefinite period. The move came in the midst of shoppers' boycotts of meat as protests against record high prices.

Similarly, after months of posturing against high prices and the President's refusal to control them, Congress granted the President blank-check extension of his authority to impose controls.

Nixon again reversed his policy June 13 by ordering a 60-day freeze on prices. As on Aug. 15, 1971, when he imposed Phase I, Nixon resorted to a freeze as shock treatment for an inflation-plagued economy. And, as in 1971, the action was a tacit admission that his previous economic policies had failed. He promised in the interim to devise "a new and more effective system of controls...to contain the forces that have sent prices so rapidly upward in the past few months."

On July 18, Nixon acknowledged that the 60-day freeze had aggravated food supply problems and lifted the freeze on most food prices. Most other prices remained frozen until Aug. 12, when Phase IV, a selective but tough price control system went into effect.

Prices continued to rise in Phase IV, and one of the few bright spots was a strengthening of the dollar on international monetary markets. By the end of the year, Democrats in Congress were blaming the administration for inflation but were not agreed on an alternate program.

Energy

The October 1973 oil export embargo by Arab nations was the final event that dramatized the nation's need for new domestic energy sources, and by the winter of 1973-74, the energy crisis had intruded into almost every facet of American life.

Between policy statements, bureaucratic reshufflings and blame-trading, Congress and the administration generated only limited action on the energy crisis in 1973. Nixon reorganized his machinery for dealing with the crisis twice, first setting up Gov. John A. Love (R Colo.) to head a newly created Energy Policy Office June 29, and then on Dec. 4 replacing both man and agency with Deputy Treasury Secretary William E. Simon as head of the new Federal Energy Administration.

The President achieved one of his major energy goals Nov. 16 by signing legislation enabling the construction of a trans-Alaskan pipeline as part of his general goal of making the United States self-sufficient in energy.

Other steps urged by Nixon at various times during the year were: federal legislation to regulate strip mining, construction of deepwater port facilities to increase oil

imports, deregulation of natural gas prices, tax incentives for oil exploration, streamlining of procedures for the siting of electric power plants, increasing oil production on outer continental shelf lands, speed-up of nuclear power plant development, providing funds for energy research and development, development of production at naval petroleum reserves, revision of federal mineral leasing laws, relaxation of clean air standards for coal conversion, conversion to year-round daylight savings time (which was signed into law Dec. 15), and tapping of the federal Highway Trust Fund for aid to mass transit.

Through various spokesmen at various times, the administration disagreed with itself and with Congress over two major issues: fuel allocation and gasoline rationing. After several administration reversals, a mandatory allocation program signed by Nixon went into operation Dec. 27. By late December the administration was undecided on gasoline rationing but seemed to be leaning toward voluntary rationing or an alternative to rationing —imposing substantially increased taxes on gasoline.

Congressional Relations

President Nixon took a beating in Congress in 1973, with Watergate providing theme music but evidently having little substantive effect. Congress opposed Nixon more often in the first seven months of the year than it had opposed any President in the past 20 years. A Congressional Quarterly special study of presidential support showed that Nixon won 43 per cent of the recorded votes on which he took a position during Jan. 3 to Aug. 3, 1973. It was the first time since the study began in 1953 that any President had ever lost more often than he had won.

Though Watergate seemed an obvious factor, many members insisted that they were reacting to presidential impoundments, vetoes and the threatened demolition of long-standing social programs, not to Watergate.

Faced with an unruly Democratic majority, Nixon's tool for shaping legislation in 1973 was the veto, and he used it effectively eight times. The Nov. 4 override of the war powers veto evidently had less to do with loss of support because of Watergate than it did a long-standing congressional attempt to reassert its powers and the desire of some members to be firmly on record as opposing future Vietnam quagmires. Still, since Nixon took office in 1969, he had had more vetoes overridden than any president since Harry S Truman.

The reassertion of powers movement, which gained momentum before Watergate became an issue, continued in the areas of anti-impoundment legislation and congressional insistence that the Senate be given the right to confirm future directors and deputy directors of the Office of Management and Budget.

Impoundment took a nearly unanimous drubbing in the courts as well as undergoing heavy fire from members of Congress. As of early September, the administration could claim victory in only five of 30 cases decided; and on April 11 a federal judge ordered the administration to cease dismantling the Office of Economic Opportunity.

Spending continued as a general source of friction between the administration and Congress, with congressional Democrats criticizing Nixon's $268.7-billion fiscal 1974 budget for neglecting social welfare programs. The Democratic position on the New Federalism was sounded by Senate Majority Leader Mike Mansfield (Mont.). Revenue sharing does not work, he said, and "will not work in the future"; cities and states are being "led down the garden path" by the Nixon administration. Republican sentiment was summed up by Senate Minority Leader Hugh Scott (Pa.): "Asking the Democrats to hold down spending is like asking an alcoholic to be your bartender."

Ironically, Watergate had something of a spin-off effect in actually improving White House-Capitol Hill relations by causing the departure of unpopular presidential aides H. R. Haldeman and John D. Ehrlichman and the arrival of familiar congressional hands Melvin R. Laird and Bryce N. Harlow.

Agnew, Ford

The resignation of Vice President Spiro T. Agnew and his plea of no contest to a single count of tax evasion paved the way for the appointment and confirmation of House Minority Leader Gerald R. Ford of Michigan, who immediately became the front-runner for the 1976 Republican presidential nomination.

Finances

Reacting to a barrage of damaging press reports of Nixon's personal finances, the President Dec. 8 released a sweeping financial statement, including summaries of his tax returns during his years in office. The statement raised further questions, however, about tax deductions for the gift of his vice presidential papers, the low level of federal income taxes he had paid, the sale of part of his San Clemente property, and his failure to pay state income taxes in either California or the District of Columbia.

Watergate

When the year 1973 is put into historical perspective, it may turn out that the three critical dates for Nixon were March 6, March 19 and July 16. March 6 was the first day of L. Patrick Gray III's confirmation hearings for permanent FBI director, when Gray told the Senate Judiciary Committee of White House counsel John W. Dean III's involvement in the FBI investigation of Watergate. On March 19, Watergate defendant James W. McCord Jr. agreed to tell all he knew of the incident in return for a promise from federal Judge John J. Sirica of leniency in sentencing. And July 16 was the date that Federal Aviation Administrator Alexander P. Butterfield surprised the Senate Watergate committee with his testimony that Nixon had taped conversations in his White House office during the whole Watergate period.

Through it all, Nixon maintained his innocence of the planning and coverup of Watergate. At the end of 1973, Nixon's fate seemed to hang more than anything else on the question that had haunted the nation throughout the year: Was the President telling the truth?

VIETNAM: REACHING AGREEMENT ON 'PEACE WITH HONOR'

The longest war in United States history drew to a close on Jan. 23, 1973, when President Nixon in a nationally televised speech announced an agreement "to end the war and bring peace with honor in Vietnam and Southeast Asia." *(Excerpts of speech, box p. 7)*

Formal signing of the agreement by representatives of the United States, South Vietnam, North Vietnam and the Viet Cong's provisional revolutionary government took place on Jan. 27. At 7 p.m. (EST) that day, an internationally supervised cease-fire went into effect.

Under the terms of the agreement, all U.S. prisoners of war in Indochina would be returned home within 60 days from the start of the cease-fire. During that same period, the 25,000 American troops remaining in South Vietnam would be returned.

The agreement was initialed in Paris by Henry A. Kissinger, then Nixon's national security adviser, and chief negotiator Le Duc Tho of North Vietnam, ending three months of intensive negotiating. Anticipation that a settlement was finally nearing had been kindled Oct. 26, 1972, with Kissinger's statement that "peace is at hand." But hopes were dashed during the week of Dec. 16-22, 1972, when the United States announced a suspension of the Paris peace talks with Hanoi and a resumption of full-scale bombing of all of North Vietnam.

Details of Agreement

On Jan. 24, the day after Nixon's announcement, the text of the agreement was released. Kissinger, at a lengthy press conference, went into the details of the document, which contained 23 articles, and of the four protocols that went with it. He predicted the settlement of hostilities in Cambodia and Laos soon after the Vietnam agreement had been signed. Following are highlights of the agreement and of Kissinger's comments:

Cessation of Hostilities. At the time of the cease-fire, both sides were to stop all military activities. The United States agreed to remove, deactivate or destroy the mines it had planted in North Vietnamese ports.

Removal of American and other foreign troops and dismantlement of military bases would be completed within 60 days of the signing. North Vietnamese troops already in South Vietnam would be allowed to remain in place but not to be replaced. Replacement of arms, munitions and other war materials—but not men—would be permitted for both sides on a one-for-one basis but would not be allowed to increase.

Kissinger pointed out that U.S. economic advisers and civilian technicians, some attached to military units, would be allowed to stay in Vietnam.

Personnel Return. Captured military personnel and foreign civilians would be returned in 60 days. Lists of these personnel were to be exchanged by the two sides at the time of the signing. The two sides would cooperate in

getting information about persons missing in action. On the basis of an agreement signed in 1954, the North and South Vietnamese would resolve the question of repatriating captured Vietnamese civilians within 90 days.

South Vietnam Self-Determination. One article of the agreement stated that the right of South Vietnamese to self-determination is "sacred, inalienable, and shall be respected by all countries." The people shall decide their political future "through genuinely free and democratic general elections under international supervision."

To help the South Vietnamese achieve self-determination, a National Council of National Reconciliation and Concord was to be established, within 90 days if possible. The council, with members appointed equally by the two sides, was to be responsible for setting up the elections called for in the agreement.

One significant part of this section of the agreement, said Kissinger, "is that the United States has consistently maintained that we would not impose any political solution on the people of South Vietnam." The Saigon government would remain in office, he said, but the political future remained to be worked out between the two sides in Vietnam.

A second significant provision in the section was the requirement for a reduction and demobilization of Vietnamese armed forces, Kissinger said.

Reunification. South and North would set their own timetable for reunification, "without coercion or annexation by either party, and without foreign interference," the agreement stated. The demilitarized zone at the 17th parallel was, in accordance with the 1954 Geneva agreement, "only provisional and not a political or territorial boundary."

Enforcement Machinery. Two international commissions were to oversee the peace agreement. Supervising the cease-fire and withdrawal of troops would be the Four-Party Joint Military Commission. It would have a ceiling of 3,300 members, divided equally among the United States, the South Vietnamese, the North Vietnamese and the Viet Cong. This commission would cease to exist after withdrawals were completed in 60 days. It would be replaced by a Two-Party Joint Military Commission comprised of South Vietnamese and Viet Cong troops.

Assisting in the supervision of the cease-fire would be a 1,160-member International Commission of Control and Supervision (ICCS). Its members would be from Canada, Poland, Hungary and Indonesia. (Canada July 21 ended its role on the ICCS. It charged that the Hungarians and Poles had obstructed ICCS operations and that North Vietnamese infiltration into South Vietnam continued on a "massive" scale. Iran replaced Canada on the commission.)

Within 30 days after the signing of the agreement, an international peace conference would be held to, among other things, "contribute to and guarantee peace in Indochina." Invited to participate, besides the four parties involved in the Paris negotiations, would be China, France, Russia, Great Britain, the four countries on the international supervisory commission and the secretary general of the United Nations. (The conference convened Feb. 26 in Paris, and an accord was signed March 2.)

Cambodia, Laos. The seventh of the agreement's nine chapters was devoted to Cambodia and Laos—protection of their "fundamental rights," respect for their neutrality. The Paris conference participants pledged not to use the two countries "to encroach on the sovereignty and security of one another and of other countries."

Other parts of the chapter required an end to foreign military activities in Laos and Cambodia and self-determination for their people. "It is our firm expectation that within a short period of time there will be a formal cease-fire in Laos which, in turn, will lead to a withdrawal of all foreign forces from Laos and, of course, to the end of the use of Laos as a corridor of infiltration," said Kissinger. He said the situation in Cambodia was more complex but that "it is our expectation that a de facto cease-fire will come into being over a period of time relevant to the execution of this agreement."

Kissinger's Observations

Kissinger, the United States' chief negotiator in Paris and the man who had had to live with his erroneous report of Oct. 26, 1972, that "peace is at hand," said at his Jan. 24 news conference that this country "is seeking a peace that heals. We have had many armistices in Indochina. We want a peace that will last."

He recalled his Dec. 16 report of a stalemate in Paris. The deadlock applied to the protocols, he said. There was disagreement over the demilitarized zone and the role of South Vietnam in the settlement, he added. When the negotiators returned on Jan. 8, the atmosphere was cool, but by the next day it was apparent that both sides wanted to break the deadlock, said Kissinger.

On Oct. 26, according to Kissinger, he did not want to provide a complete check list against which both sides could be measured. The "substantial adaptations" the United States asked for on Oct. 26 had been achieved, he said. "We did not increase our demands after Oct. 26, and we substantially achieved the clarifications which we sought...it is obvious that a war that has lasted for 10 years will have many elements that cannot be completely satisfactory to all the parties concerned."

He was asked if the heavy 12-day bombing of the north in December was the key to achieving the agreement.

He replied that he would not speculate on North Vietnamese motives, "but I will say that there was a deadlock which was described in the middle of December, and there was a rapid movement when negotiations resumed.... These facts have to be analyzed by each person for himself."

A reporter asked Kissinger how the agreement differed from one that might have been reached four years earlier.

At that time, he answered, the North Vietnamese refused to separate military and political issues and

Nixon Jan. 23 Speech Excerpts

Good evening. I have asked for this radio and television time tonight for the purpose of announcing that we today have concluded an agreement to end the war and bring peace with honor in Vietnam and in Southeast Asia....

Throughout the years of negotiations, we have insisted on peace with honor. In my addresses to the nation from this room of January 25th and May 8th, I set forth the goals that we considered essential for peace with honor.

In the settlement that has now been agreed to, all the conditions that I laid down then have been met. A cease-fire, internationally supervised, will begin at 7 p.m. this Saturday, January 27th, Washington time. Within 60 days from this Saturday, all Americans held prisoners of war throughout Indochina will be released. There will be the fullest possible accounting for all of those who are missing in action.

During the same 60-day period, all American forces will be withdrawn from South Vietnam.

The people of South Vietnam have been guaranteed the right to determine their own future, without outside interference....

The United States will continue to recognize the Government of the Republic of Vietnam as the sole legitimate government of South Vietnam.

We shall continue to aid South Vietnam within the terms of the agreement and we shall support efforts by the people of South Vietnam to settle their problems peacefully among themselves.

We must recognize that ending the war is only the first step toward building the peace. All parties must now see to it that this is a peace that lasts, and also a peace that heals, and a peace that not only ends the war in Southeast Asia, but contributes to the prospects of peace in the whole world....

As this long and very difficult war ends, I would like to address a few special words to each of those who have been parties in the conflict.

First, to the people and Government of South Vietnam: By your courage, by your sacrifice, you have won the precious right to determine your own future and you have developed the strength to defend that right....

To the leaders of North Vietnam: As we have ended the war through negotiations, let us now build a peace of reconciliation. For our part, we are prepared to make a major effort to help achieve that goal; but just as reciprocity was needed to end the war, so, too, will it be needed to build and strengthen the peace.

To the other major powers that have been involved even indirectly: Now is the time for mutual restraint so that the peace we have achieved can last.

And finally, to all of you who are listening, the American people: Your steadfastness in supporting our insistence on peace with honor has made peace with honor possible....

Now that we have achieved an honorable agreement, let us be proud that America did not settle for a peace that would have betrayed our allies, that would have abandoned our prisoners of war, that would have ended the war for us but would have continued the war for the 50 million people of Indochina.

Let us be proud of the 2-1/2 million young Americans who served in Vietnam, who served with honor and distinction in one of the most selfless enterprises in the history of nations. And let us be proud of those who have sacrificed, who gave their lives so that the people of South Vietnam might live in freedom and so that the world might live in peace....

The Basic Elements of the Vietnam Agreement

MILITARY PROVISIONS

Cease-fire

• Internationally-supervised cease-fire throughout South and North Vietnam, effective at 7:00 pm EST, Saturday, January 27, 1973.

American Forces

• Release within 60 days of all American servicemen and civilians captured and held throughout Indochina, and fullest possible accounting for missing in action.

• Return of all United States forces and military personnel from South Vietnam within 60 days.

Security of South Vietnam

• Ban on infiltration of troops and war supplies into South Vietnam.

• The right to unlimited military replacement aid for the Republic of Vietnam.

• Respect for the Demilitarized Zone.

• Reunification only by peaceful means, through negotiation between North and South Vietnam without coercion or annexation.

• Reduction and demobilization of Communist and Government forces in the South.

• Ban on use of Laotian or Cambodian base areas to encroach on sovereignty and security of South Vietnam.

• Withdrawal of all foreign troops from Laos and Cambodia.

POLITICAL PROVISIONS

• Joint United States—Democratic Republic of Vietnam statement that the South Vietnamese people have the right to self-determination.

• The Government of the Republic of Vietnam continues in existence, recognized by the United States, its constitutional structure and leadership intact and unchanged.

• The right to unlimited economic aid for the Republic of Vietnam.

• Formation of a non-governmental National Council of National Reconciliation and Concord, operating by unanimity, to organize elections as agreed by the parties and to promote conciliation and implementation of the Agreement.

INDOCHINA

• Reaffirmation of the 1954 and 1962 Geneva Agreements on Cambodia and Laos.

• Respect for the independence, sovereignty, unity, territorial integrity and neutrality of Cambodia and Laos.

• Ban on infiltration of troops and war supplies into Cambodia and Laos.

• Ban on use of Laotian and Cambodian base areas to encroach on sovereignty and security of one another and of other countries.

• Withdrawal of all foreign troops from Laos and Cambodia.

• In accordance with traditional United States policy, U.S. participation in postwar reconstruction efforts throughout Indochina.

• With the ending of the war, a new basis for U.S. relations with North Vietnam.

CONTROL AND SUPERVISION

• An International Commission of Control and Supervision, with 1160 international supervisory personnel, to control and supervise the elections and various military provisions of the Agreement.

• An International Conference within 30 days to guarantee the Agreement and the ending of the war.

• Joint Military Commissions of the parties to implement appropriate provisions of the Agreement.

---

insisted on the dismemberment of the South Vietnamese government as a prelude to negotiation.

Later Developments

Implementation of the cease-fire agreement was not without setbacks and threats of disintegration. There were several impasses over the timetable for releasing prisoners of war and other issues; but in each case the stalemate was broken and on March 29, American military involvement in Vietnam came to an end. On that day, the remaining 67 American prisoners held by North Vietnam were freed in Hanoi, and the United States withdrew its remaining 2,500 troops from South Vietnam.

Between Jan. 27 and March 29, a total of 587 American military and civilian prisoners had been released and 23,500 U.S. troops withdrawn from South Vietnam. The war had cost 45,929 U.S. combat casualties from 1960-72 and an officially estimated $135.5-billion from fiscal 1965 through fiscal 1973.

With the termination of direct U.S. military involvement in Vietnam and the signing of a cease-fire in Laos Feb. 21, attention shifted to the continuing war in neighboring Cambodia. The President's decision to keep up heavy U.S. bombing over that country sparked the beginning of the 1973 congressional challenge to presidential war-making powers, as members of Congress began increasingly to question Nixon's constitutional authority to continue the bombing without obtaining explicit congressional authorization.

The congressional challenge met with dramatic success, exemplified in passage of legislation ordering a Cambodian bombing halt by Aug. 15 and more far-reaching legislation, passed over Nixon's veto, that limited presidential war-making powers in the future.

DETENTE: SUCCESS BASED ON FORM MORE THAN SUBSTANCE

Soviet Communist Party leader Leonid I. Brezhnev left the United States June 25 after a week of talks with President Nixon, members of Congress and business executives. During his visit to Washington June 17-22, Brezhnev and Nixon signed several agreements, including a declaration of principles to guide arms limitation negotiations and an agreement on prevention of nuclear war. After leaving Washington, Brezhnev met with the President for two days in San Clemente, Calif.

Brezhnev's trip to the United States repaid a visit Nixon made to Moscow in May 1972, when the two signed several unprecedented agreements, including one on nuclear arms. Nixon June 21 accepted an invitation for a third summit meeting in Moscow in 1974.

The success of the 1973 summit meeting between the leaders of the two superpowers appeared to have been based more on form than substance. While a number of agreements were signed during Brezhnev's visit, they generally were minor in nature.

Rather than concrete results, the meeting between U.S. and Soviet leaders was marked by a new spirit of detente—a feeling promoted by the two leaders that the cold war in fact had ended.

That spirit was pointed out by Dr. Henry Kissinger, President Nixon's national security adviser, at a June 25 press briefing in San Clemente, Calif.

Commenting on the joint communique released the same day, Kissinger observed: "One good way of assessing the results of the summit is to compare last year's comminique with this year's communique."

Quoting from the 1972 document, Kissinger concluded that the meeting that year in Moscow had been designed to affirm the concept of peaceful coexistence, while "this year we are speaking of a continuing relationship."

But he added that "as relations between the Soviet Union and United States proceed along the course that was charted last May (1972)...we cannot expect that these meetings...will produce a dramatic new departure."

Although Nixon and Brezhnev did not spend much time discussing the lesser agreements signed during the week-long talks, Kissinger said, "the fact that they have determined to give a symbolic expression to this relationship, gives an impetus to negotiations that otherwise would drag on for months, and permits the quick resolution of particular issues which, if left to the expert level, could produce extended stalemate...."

Communique

The tenor of the joint communique issued just before Brezhnev's June 25 departure from the United States for France was reflective of the amicable—almost jovial—mood pervading the entire Brezhnev visit.

Accentuating the positive, the communique stressed the prospects of decreasing the dangers of nuclear war, limiting the nuclear arsenals of both countries and increasing U.S.-Soviet trade.

Trade. The communique did not mention President Nixon's proposal that the Soviet Union be granted most-favored-nation tariff status. That proposal—part of the President's trade bill—had been held up in both the House and Senate over the controversy concerning Soviet emigration policies for Russian Jews.

At a June 19 luncheon with 25 members of Congress, Brezhnev contended that almost all Soviet Jews were free to leave the country and that the cases of those who could not were being reviewed. But Sen. Henry M. Jackson (D Wash.), the leading Senate critic of Soviet emigration policies, charged the next day that statistics cited by the Russian leader in his talk to the congressional delegation were "wrong and misleading."

Increased trade obviously had been central to Brezhnev's hopes from the beginning of the summit. At a June 22 meeting with 60 U.S. businessmen, Soviet Foreign Trade Minister Nikolai Patolichev—accompanying Brezhnev—quipped, "Contacts are good, but contracts are better." The final communique stated that both countries would work toward a modest increase in trade to between a total of $2-billion and $3-billion in the next three years.

Middle East and Europe. The communique indicated some progress in the area of European affairs, but little in the Middle East.

The document revealed that for the first time the Russians had agreed to convene the East-West talks on mutual force reductions in Europe on Oct. 30 in Vienna.

On the Middle East, the communique indirectly admitted that Nixon and Brezhnev were unable to produce any realistic solution. Kissinger told his June 25 press conference that although the two leaders could not agree on any resolution of the problem, they both understood the need to avoid a conflict between the two superpowers there. *(October Middle East crisis, p. 11)*

Agreements

The following agreements were signed during Brezhnev's U.S. visit:

Nuclear War. Pledged both countries to avoid actions that could lead them into a nuclear confrontation with each other or a third nation. In key provisions, both nations agreed "to refrain from the threat or use of force...in circumstances which may endanger international peace and security" and to enter into "urgent consultations" should the risk of a nuclear conflict occur. No enforcement machinery was provided.

Peaceful Uses of Atomic Energy. Agreed to increased cooperation in developing peaceful uses of atomic energy, including construction of joint research facilities "at all stages up to industrial-scale operations."

Transportation. Pledged cooperation in solving problems related to air, sea and land transportation. The agreement would last five years.

Oceanography. Agreed on cooperation in studying the world's oceans. The five-year agreement would extend previous cooperative research and set up a joint committee to implement information exchange and convene annual conferences and seminars.

Cultural Exchange. Agreed to expanded scientific, cultural, technological and educational contacts and exchanges. The agreement expanded the existing two-year renewable accords, begun in 1958, to a general accord to last through 1979.

Agriculture. Agreed to cooperate in agricultural research, trade, development, production and processing. The agreement was to remain in force for five years.

Commercial Relations. Agreed to discuss the desirability of establishing a U.S.-Soviet chamber of commerce and to expand and improve commercial facilities in Moscow and Washington.

Air Travel. Agreed to expand air passenger service between the United States and the Soviet Union.

Taxes. Agreed to eliminate double taxation of citizens and companies of one country living or working in the other. This was a treaty requiring Senate ratification. The United States had similar treaties with a number of non-communist nations.

Arms Limitation Guidelines

Nixon and Brezhnev June 21 signed a declaration of principles to accelerate the Strategic Arms Limitation Talks (SALT) so that a permanent treaty limiting each side's offensive missile and bomber capability could be reached by the end of 1974. The permanent treaty would replace the five-year interim agreement signed in Moscow in 1972. *(Text of declaration, box this page)*

The declaration, to serve as guidelines for U.S. and Soviet negotiators at the SALT talks in Geneva, said the permanent agreement could apply both to the number and quality of offensive weapons but specified that modernization and replacement of strategic weapons would be permitted under negotiated conditions. Implementation would be subject to verfication by "national technical means." The United States previously had insisted on on-site inspection.

Both sides expressed willingness to sign interim agreements in certain areas pending completion of a permanent agreement.

The SALT agreements signed by Nixon and Brezhnev in Moscow in 1972 consisted of a defensive treaty limiting anti-ballistic missile (ABM) sites and a five-year agreement freezing the number of land- and sea-based offensive missiles at roughly existing levels.

Offensive Arms Limitation Text

Following is the White House text of the agreement signed June 21 by President Nixon and Communist Party General Secretary Leonid I. Brezhnev concerning the limitation of strategic offensive weapons.

The President of the United States of America, Richard Nixon, and the General Secretary of the Central Committee of the CPSU, L. I. Brezhnev,

Having thoroughly considered the question of the further limitation of strategic arms, and the progress already achieved in the current negotiations,

Reaffirming their conviction that the earliest adoption of further limitations of strategic arms would be a major contribution in reducing the danger of an outbreak of nuclear war and in strengthening international peace and security,

Have agreed as follows:

First. The two Sides will continue active negotiations in order to work out a permanent agreement on more complete measures on the limitation of strategic offensive arms, as well as their subsequent reduction, proceeding from the Basic Principles of Relations between the United States of America and the Union of Soviet Socialist Republics signed in Moscow on May 29, 1972, and from the Interim Agreement between the United States of America and the Union of Soviet Socialist Republics of May 26, 1972 on Certain Measures with Respect to the Limitation of Strategic Offensive Arms.

Over the course of the next year the two Sides will make serious efforts to work out the provisions of the permanent agreement on more complete measures on the limitation of strategic offensive arms with the objective of signing in 1974.

Second. New agreements on the limitation of strategic offensive armaments will be based on the principles of the American-Soviet documents adopted in Moscow in May 1972 and the agreements reached in Washington in June 1973; and in particular, both Sides will be guided by the recognition of each other's equal security interests and by the recognition that efforts to obtain unilateral advantage, directly or indirectly, would be inconsistent with the strengthening of peaceful relations between the United States of America and the Union of Soviet Socialist Republics.

Third. The limitations placed on strategic offensive weapons can apply both to their quantitative aspects as well as to their qualitative improvement.

Fourth. Limitations on strategic offensive arms must be subject to adequate verification by national technical means.

Fifth. The modernization and replacement of strategic offensive arms would be permitted under conditions which will be formulated in the agreements to be concluded.

Sixth. Pending the completion of a permanent agreement on more complete measures of strategic offensive arms limitation, both Sides are prepared to reach agreements on separate measures to supplement the existing Interim Agreement of May 26, 1972.

Seventh. Each Side will continue to take necessary organizational and technical measures for preventing accidental or unauthorized use of nuclear weapons under its control in accordance with the Agreement of September 30, 1971 between the United States of America and the Union of Soviet Socialist Republics.

MIDDLE EAST: A POSSIBLE CONFRONTATION AVERTED

Barely four months after Soviet Communist Party leader Leonid I. Brezhnev's visit to the United States, the U.S.-Soviet rapprochment was put to a severe test by another Middle East crisis. *(Brezhnev visit, p. 9)*

A near confrontation between the United States and the Soviet Union appeared to be averted Oct. 25 when the Soviets agreed to the creation of an international peacekeeping force for the Middle East without U.S., Soviet or other big power participation.

U.S. armed forces had been placed on alert in the early morning hours of Oct. 25, reportedly in response to the possibility of a unilateral Soviet movement of troops into the Mideast to supervise the truce. In a press conference later that day, Secretary of State Henry A. Kissinger told reporters that the U.S. alert was "precautionary" and "not in any sense irrevocable." He said that U.S. forces had been alerted because of the "ambiguity" of the situation, after it had been learned that Soviet units had been alerted.

In the wake of the events, President Nixon postponed a press conference that had been scheduled for the evening of Oct. 25. It was rescheduled for the following day.

The issue of the peacekeeping force arose just as the Middle East truce appeared to be taking hold. On Oct. 24, the Soviet Union proposed to the United States that the two powers join together to supervise the truce—a proposal rejected by the United States.

"The United States does not favor and will not approve the sending of a joint Soviet-U.S. force into the Middle East," Kissinger told reporters. Instead, the United States backed the creation of a United Nations observer force without the participation of personnel from any of the permanent members of the UN Security Council—which would automatically preclude the United States and the Soviet Union.

The crisis was eased the afternoon of Oct. 25, when Soviet Ambassador Yakov Malik told the United Nations that his country would accept a proposal made by a group of nonaligned nations for the creation of a supervisory force without big power participation. The U.N. Security Council voted to accept the resolution 14-0, with China not participating.

After the vote, John A. Scali, U.S. ambassador to the United Nations, said: "We believe that the resolution before us will, if faithfully implemented by all concerned, result in the prompt and effective establishment of a true cease-fire in the Middle East. Nothing could be more important as a step toward peace."

Jackson Announcement. The sense of crisis which had gripped the capital earlier in the day had been heightened by an announcement by Sen. Henry A. Jackson (D Wash.) that the Soviet Union had sent a "brutal" note to the United States warning that Russian forces

would be sent unilaterally to the Middle East if the United States refused to join in a peacekeeping operation. "We're right at the brink again," Jackson declared.

However, Kissinger in his press conference dismissed Jackson's remarks by saying that the senator had not participated in the White House deliberations. The secretary of state refused to provide any details on the communications between the United States and the Soviet Union.

Throughout his press conference, Kissinger attempted to play down the emerging sense of a national crisis. "We do not consider ourselves to be in a confrontation with the Soviet Union," he repeated several times. He said that up to that point the Soviet Union had not taken any irrevocable action and that "It is our hope that no such action will be taken."

Kissinger stressed the need for restraint by the two nuclear powers and their "special duty" to avoid confrontation. He called it inconceivable that U.S.-Soviet rivalry might be transplanted to the Middle East.

Congressional Leaders. On the morning of Oct. 25, President Nixon and Kissinger met for 90 minutes with Republican and Democratic congressional leaders to discuss the Middle East situation. After the meeting, House Speaker Carl Albert (D Okla.) told reporters that "there's only a precautionary alert and the overwhelming emphasis is on diplomacy at this time." Albert said also that he had not heard of any "brutal" Soviet note during the White House briefing. Jackson did not attend the meeting.

Senate Foreign Relations Committee Chairman J. W. Fulbright (D Ark.) refused to give any specifics on the meeting, but he told reporters that he was "very hopeful that action in the Security Council today will resolve the problem." Sen. George D. Aiken (R Vt.) called the alert "a pressure tactic by the United States."

Later in the day, on the House floor, Majority Leader Thomas P. O'Neill Jr. (D Mass.), who attended the White House session, insisted that there had been "nothing political" about it. He said that the nation was going through a very serious 24 to 48 hours and told his Democratic colleagues: "In time of crisis, we stay together."

Domestic Politics. Kissinger abruptly dismissed any suggestion that the crisis over the Middle East had been created by the Nixon administration as a smokescreen for its Watergate scandal troubles. He called the suggestion a "symptom" of what has happened to the country. "There has to be a minimum of confidence that senior officials of the American government are not playing with the lives of the American people," Kissinger insisted.

However, the secretary of state did admit that the Soviets may have been encouraged by recent events in

Chronology of Events in Middle East Crisis

Oct. 6. War breaks out when Egyptian and Syrian troops cross into Israeli-occupied territory in the Sinai Peninsula and the Golan Heights.

Oct. 15. The United States announces it is resupplying Israel with military equipment to counterbalance a "massive airlift" to Egypt by the Soviet Union.

Oct. 17. President Nixon meets with the foreign ministers of Kuwait, Morocco, Algeria and Saudi Arabia in Washington. Soviet Premier Alexei Kosygin holds secret talks in Cairo with Egyptian President Anwar Sadat.

Arab oil-producing announce a five per cent monthly reduction in the flow of oil to the United States and other nations supporting Israel. Subsequently Arab nations announce a total cut-off of oil exports to the United States.

Oct. 22. The United Nations Security Council approves a resolution calling for a cease-fire in the Middle East. Israel and Egypt accept the resolution, but sporadic fighting continues. Syria does not agree to the truce until Oct. 24.

Oct. 25. Nixon puts American forces on a world-wide military alert in response to the possibility of a Soviet movement of troops into the Middle East to supervise a truce. Later in the day Moscow agrees to a U.N. resolution establishing an international peacekeeping force without big power participation.

Oct. 29. Secretary of State Henry A. Kissinger meets in Washington with Egypt's acting foreign minister, Ismail Fahmy.

Nov. 1. Nixon and Kissinger meet with Israeli Premier Golda Meir in Washington.

Nov. 7. Kissinger meets in Cairo with Egyptian President Sadat. The two countries announce that they will resume diplomatic relations that were broken off during the June 1967 war in the Middle East.

Nov. 11. Israel and Egypt sign a six-point cease-fire agreement worked out by Kissinger.

Nov. 12. Kissinger says in Peking that the United States is considering a mutual security treaty with Israel.

Nov. 14. The first face-to-face encounter between Israeli and Egyptian negotiators is held at a United Nations tent on the Cairo-Suez Road. The meeting results in an agreement providing for an exchange of prisoners of war and the lifting of an Israeli seige of the city of Suez and the Egyptian Third Army.

Nov. 15. The first exchange of Egyptian and Israeli prisoners takes place.

Nov. 26. An Arab summit conference opens in Algeria. The heads of state of Libya, Iraq and Jordan do not attend during the three-day meeting. Attending Arab leaders conditionally endorse the moves toward a Middle East peace agreement and recognize the Palestine Liberation Organization as the sole legitimate representative of the Palestinian people.

Dec. 13. Kissinger begins a visit to several Middle East capitals.

Dec. 21. The first Arab-Israeli peace conference opens in Geneva. Kissinger and Soviet Foreign Minister Andrei A. Gromyko urge that a permanent peace settlement be worked out to avoid another Middle East war. Participants include Israel, Egypt, Jordan, the United States, the Soviet Union and the United Nations. Syria boycotts the conference.

Dec. 22. The first round of the peace conference ends with an agreement to begin talks on separating Israeli and Egyptian forces along the Suez Canal.

Dec. 27. Kissinger tells a news conference that improved U.S. relations with Russia depend on Moscow's behavior in the Middle East. He concedes that Soviet action at the Geneva conference "has been constructive and has been recognized to be constructive by all the parties there."

Washington. "One cannot have a crisis of authority for a period of months without paying the price along the line," Kissinger said in response to a reporter's question.

Nixon Press Conference. At his Oct. 26 news conference, Nixon outlined the chronology of U.S.-Soviet negotiations on the Middle East.

A "very significant and potentially explosive crisis developed" on Oct. 24, Nixon said. "We obtained information which led us to believe that the Soviet Union was planning to send a very substantial force into the Mideast —a military force."

As a result, the President continued, he ordered a "precautionary" world-wide military alert for American forces shortly after midnight to signal to the Soviets that the United States "could not accept any unilateral move on their part to move military forces into the Mideast." Shortly thereafter, Nixon sent Soviet Communist Party

Leader Leonid I. Brezhnev "an urgent message" asking him not to send troops, and urging instead that the Soviets join the United States in supporting a United Nations resolution that would exclude major powers from participating in a peacekeeping force.

During the "several exchanges" that followed, Nixon said, "we reached the conclusion that we would jointly support the resolution, which was adopted in the United Nations."

The "outlook for a permanent peace is the best that it has been in 20 years" as a result of the two powers having agreed to "participate in trying to expedite the talks between the parties involved," Nixon said.

In response to questions, Nixon denied inferences that he had orchestrated the crisis to take attention away from public and congressional criticism of his firing of Watergate special prosecutor Archibald Cox on Oct. 20. "It was a real crisis," he said. "It was the most difficult crisis we've had since the Cuban confrontation in 1962."

SPREADING WATERGATE AFFAIR CAST CLOUD OVER NIXON

At the beginning of 1973 "Watergate" was thought of primarily as the name of the Washington, D.C., apartment-office complex where a break-in of Democratic National Committee Headquarters had taken place in June 1972. By the end of 1973 the term was broadly used to connote an astonishing variety of unsavory matters including a cover-up of criminal activities, political sabotage and kick-backs, spending on presidential properties and even the President's income taxes.

The Watergate revelations dominated the year's news. They fundamentally changed the relationship between Nixon and Congress and brought considerable doubt as to whether he would serve out his term. Many observers talked of the emergence of a new public attitude toward the conduct of politics that could bring changes in the way political campaigns were financed and conducted. The scandals also forced an overhaul of the White House staff with the result that much of the power to manage the executive branch shifted back from the White House to the Office of Management and Budget (OMB).

The burglary had taken place June 17, 1972. Five men had been caught, and two others were linked to the operation and subsequently arrested. The break-in appeared to have been the brainchild of G. Gordon Liddy, counsel to the Committee to Re-elect the President (CRP), and not to have involved higher-ups. During the 1972 presidential campaign the Democrats tried unsuccessfully to stir up public moral indignation over the affair, but it was largely ignored. White House Press Secretary Ronald L. Ziegler dismissed it as a "third-rate burglary." Of the news media, only the *Washington Post* relentlessly pursued the story. Months later, when it had been fully established that Watergate involved much more than burglary, two young *Washington Post* reporters (Bob Woodward and Carl Bernstein) received the Pulitzer prize for their investigative efforts.

The trial of the seven Watergate burglars ran quietly from Jan. 8-30, 1973, and ended without any higher-ups being implicated. At its end, Judge John J. Sirica complained that it had not succeeded in bringing out the motive behind the burglary. He expressed hopes that a Senate investigation might be more successful. The Senate established the Select Committee on Presidential Campaign Activities—later to become famous as the Watergate Committee—to look into the 1972 presidential campaign, but few of its creators at that time expected major revelations.

FBI Involvement, McCord Letter

Watergate began to appear more frequently in the news during March when the Senate Judiciary Committee held hearings on Nixon's nomination of L. Patrick Gray III, acting director of the FBI, to be permanent director.

Gray admitted that the White House had kept a tight hand on the FBI's 1972 Watergate investigation and had insisted that White House counsel John W. Dean III attend all FBI interviews of White House personnel. Gray also said that Dean had "probably lied" at one point during the investigation. Gray's nomination did not survive the hearings; after a wave of bad publicity he resigned as acting FBI director.

The suspicions which were building during the Gray hearings were substantiated March 23 when Judge Sirica unexpectedly postponed sentencing of one of the Watergate burglars—James W. McCord Jr. Sirica announced that he had received a March 19 letter from McCord which said, "There was political pressure applied to the defendants to plead guilty and remain silent. Perjury occurred during the trial in matters highly material to the very structure, orientation and impact of the government's case and to the motivation and intent of the defendants." The letter broke loose an avalanche of revelations, charges and countercharges that continued through 1973. The essence of McCord's charges was substantiated— perjury had been committed at the trial, the burglars' legal expenses had been paid with CRP funds, a cover-up had been developed to keep the facts behind the burglary secret. Moreover, the burglary turned out to have been but a small part of a larger campaign of political sabotage.

After the McCord letter broke, most of the early news came from leaks from "unidentified sources." Among the leaks were reports that McCord had identified White House counsel Dean and the former deputy director of the Committee to Re-Elect the President (CRP), Jeb Stuart Magruder, as having had prior knowledge of the break-in and having participated in an effort to cover up the facts surrounding the incident. For a month, the White House flatly denied the stories. Ziegler March 25 said: "Mr. Dean had absolutely no prior knowledge or any awareness whatsoever of the Watergate incident. The story is flatly incorrect."

The White House denials were met with increasing skepticism and calls for openness by Republicans as well as Democrats. For a while the White House continued to insist that these had been no cover-up, and a presidential position refusing to let top aides testify before the Senate Watergate Committee on grounds of executive privilege seemed to put the administration and Congress on a collision course.

White House Resignations

Then on April 17 the White House began to switch position. President Nixon told a brief news conference that "all members of the White House staff will appear voluntarily when requested by the (Watergate) committee." He also told reporters he had begun "intensive new inquiries into the Watergate affair on March 21 "as a result of serious charges which came to my attention."

The White House switch came against a background of more news leaks linking John N. Mitchell, former attorney general and chairman of CRP, to the break-in, planning and cover-up. Other news reports indicated that Dean's resignation was imminent; Dean released a statement April 19 asserting that he would not be a "scapegoat."

After nearly two more weeks of rumors, the President April 30 went on nationwide television to announce the resignations under pressure of Dean, as well as the resignations of top aides John D. Ehrlichman and H. R. Haldeman and Attorney General Richard G. Kleindienst. He denied that the latter three were resigning because of wrongdoing. He promised that "justice will be pursued fairly, fully and impartially" in determining misconduct during the 1972 campaign. He appointed Defense Secretary Elliot L. Richardson as attorney general in charge of the investigation and gave him the option of appointing a special prosecutor.

Mitchell, Stans Indictments. The resignations were followed shortly by more bombshells. On May 10 Mitchell and former Commerce Secretary Maurice H. Stans were indicted in New York and charged with obtaining a secret cash campaign contribution in return for arranging government favors for financier Robert L. Vesco.

Ellsberg Trial. In Los Angeles, all charges of theft and conspiracy against Daniel Ellsberg in the Pentagon Papers trial were dismissed on May 11 on grounds of government misconduct. Judge W. Matthew Byrne said White House officials, including a Watergate conspirator, had tapped Ellsberg's phone and burglarized his psychiatrist's office. Byrne later revealed that Ehrlichman had approached him with a tentative offer of the job of FBI director during the conduct of the trial.

Watergate Hearings

The Senate Watergate hearings got underway May 17 and were the major focus of Watergate developments during the summer. A parade of clean-cut, young, contrite former CRP and White House aides appeared, some to admit perjury during earlier investigations. They drew a picture of political sabotage that went far beyond Watergate, motivated by extreme loyalty to Nixon and by a belief that any tactics against people who had supported anti-Vietnam war demonstrations were acceptable.

The hearings brought forth details of a special White House investigative unit known as the "plumbers" which had been responsible for acts such as the harassment of Ellsberg. Among the other highlights was the four-day appearance of Dean in July. Dean turned over a number of documents to the committee, including the White House "enemies' list" and stood as the only witness to directly implicate the President in the cover-up. He was matched by a tough, aggressive four-day appearance by Ehrlichman, who steadily denied that there had been any wrongdoing on his part or the President's.

White House Tapes. Perhaps the most important revelation of the committee hearings came as a result of

closed-session questioning of Federal Aviation Agency Administrator Alexander P. Butterfield. Butterfield, a former aide to Haldeman, July 13 acknowledged under direct questioning that the President's offices were equipped with a special voice-activated system which tape recorded all conversations. The information became public when Butterfield appeared before the committee July 16 and the White House confirmed the existence of the tapes. The existence of the tapes entirely changed the Watergate case; presumably the evidence existed to prove or disprove Dean's allegations.

The Special Prosecutor

The Senate Judiciary Committee in May was unexpectedly tough in dealing with the confirmation of Richardson as attorney general. It refused to send the nomination to the floor until Richardson had appointed a special prosecutor to handle the Watergate investigation.

After reportedly being rebuffed by several choices, Richardson May 18 announced the appointment of former Solicitor General (1961-65) and Harvard law professor Archibald Cox. Richardson promised Cox complete independence and Cox promised the Judiciary Committee that he would not hesitate to follow the trail of any Watergate-related crime, even if it led to the Oval Office of the White House.

Cox assembled a large team of lawyers, many of whom were young Democrats, which set to work with little fanfare. Unlike the Senate Watergate Committee, which was plagued by news leaks, the prosecutor's staff was characterized by discretion. During the summer, its existence was hardly noticed by the general public except for the issue of the Watergate tapes.

Both the Watergate committee and the special prosecutor's office went to court to get the White House to turn over tapes of presidential conversations they believed they needed for their investigations. The White House had rejected subpoenas as a violation of the separation of powers. The committee was rebuffed, but Judge Sirica Aug. 28 in essence upheld Cox's request for nine recordings with a modification that the tapes be given initially to him for private review. In a 5-2 decision the U.S. Circuit Court of Appeals Oct. 12 upheld Sirica's ruling.

In a nationwide address on Watergate Aug. 15 the President had told the nation, "The time has come to turn Watergate over to the courts, where the question of guilt or innocence belongs." But on Oct. 19 he unexpectedly released a statement that he would not seek Supreme Court review of the appeals court ruling on the tapes. He said he was "confident" that the appeals court dissenting opinions would be sustained by the Supreme Court but that it was "not in the national interest to leave this matter unresolved for the period that might be required for a review by the highest court." Therefore, he said, he would turn over written summaries of the tapes to the court and the accuracy of the summaries would be verified by Sen. John C. Stennis (D Miss.). He said Cox had been directed "to make no further attempts by judicial process to obtain tapes, notes, or memoranda of presidential conversations." Cox the same day refused to accept the plan, which he said would "defeat the fair administration of criminal justice."

'Saturday Night Massacre'

Cox followed up his refusal with a defiant press conference on Saturday afternoon Oct. 20. That night at 8:25, Ziegler announced that the President had ordered Richardson to fire Cox; Richardson refused and resigned; the President then ordered Deputy Attorney General William D. Ruckelshaus to fire Cox; Ruckelshaus refused and was fired; the President then ordered Solicitor General Robert H. Bork as acting attorney general to fire Cox and Bork complied. The special prosecutor's office was to be abolished.

The "Saturday night massacre" let loose an enormous outpouring of public rage. Reaction was almost entirely negative, and constituent protest led 84 congressmen to introduce legislation calling for impeachment of the President. On Oct. 23 the White House, clearly recognizing its miscalculation, reversed itself and announced it would hand over the nine tapes to the court. The special prosecutor's office was not abolished and on Nov. 1 Bork announced the selection of Texas trial lawyer Leon Jaworski as Cox's replacement. Jaworski got down to work with most of Cox's staff intact and congressional liberals put aside a bill to establish an independent special prosecutor.

But the reversal on the tapes and reappointment of a prosecutor did not undo the damage Nixon had done to his case by the firing of Cox. For one thing, the calls for impeachment led the House Judiciary Committee to move into a full-scale impeachment inquiry. A report was expected sometime in spring 1974. Moreover, once the tapes were released, it developed that two of the tapes had never existed. The White House said the tape had run out on one of the conversations; it said the other conversation had taken place on a telephone in the Nixon's private quarters which was not hooked up to the recording system. Still more damaging to the President was the Nov. 26 revelation that a tape of a June 20, 1972, conversation contained an 18-minute gap. The gap covered the entire period of a conversation between Nixon and Haldeman which was considered crucial evidence in proving whether or not Nixon knew of the Watrgate cover-up. The tape was turned over to a six-man panel of electronics specialists. The panel told Judge Sirica Jan. 15, 1974, that the gap had been caused by at least five separate, manual erasures. Judge Sirica referred the matter to a federal grand jury.

ITT Influence

As it became clear that Watergate involved much more than one burglary, the special prosecutor's staff was divided into five task forces which were known as "Watergate," "Political Espionage," "Plumbers," "Campaign Contributions" and "ITT." The latter dealt with a complicated situation which grew out of an antitrust suit against the International Telephone and Telegraph Corp. (ITT).

The Justice Department in 1969 began a suit to force ITT to divest itself of two small companies—the Canteen Corporation (vending machines) and the Grinnell Corporation (manufacturing) and a major company, the Hartford Fire Insurance Corporation. A major purpose of the suit was to get a Supreme Court ruling on the applicability of the Clayton Antitrust Act to conglomerate-type mergers.

In 1971 the suit was settled out of court in a manner generally considered favorable to ITT. It was able to keep the Hartford company if it gave up the smaller companies. In February 1972 columnist Jack Anderson printed a memo allegedly written by ITT lobbyist Dita B. Beard indicating that the Justice Department had agreed to the relatively favorable settlement in return for a promise from an ITT subsidiary to help defray the costs of the 1972 Republican National Convention. The memo also indicated that President Nixon and former Attorney General Mitchell had played important roles in the deal. The memo was a major issue during confirmation hearings of Attorney General Kleindienst.

The Senate Watergate Committee Aug. 1 released a 1972 internal White House memo warning of the existence of documents that could "directly involve the President" in the ITT case. The special prosecutor's task force was seeking to find out if the allegation in the case were true and, if so, who had been involved. After Cox was fired, newspaper reports said his office's digging into the ITT case was a major source of White House dissatisfaction with him. The White House Jan. 8, 1974, released a background paper denying the charges in the case. Rather, it said the President "had concluded the ITT litigation was inconsistent with his own views of antitrust policy because it was an attack on 'bigness' rather than an attempt to insure corporate competition."

Campaign Contributions

The special prosecutor's office also looked into illegal contributions made during the 1972 campaign. By the end of the year, eight corporations had admitted making illegal donations to the Nixon campaign. They were: American Airlines ($55,000), Ashland Oil ($100,000), Braniff Airways ($40,000), Goodyear Tire and Rubber ($40,000), Minnesota Mining and Manufacturing ($30,000), the Carnation Company ($7,900) and Phillips Petroleum ($100,000).

Milk Fund. There was apparently no evidence that the illegal contributions were made in response to promises of government favors. But in another area there were such charges. A public interest law firm in 1973 filed suit against dairy interests on behalf of consumer advocate Ralph Nader alleging that an administration decision to approve higher milk price supports in March 1971 was guided by the promise of large campaign contributions from the dairy industry. The special prosecutor's office was also looking into the milk deal. The White House Jan. 8, 1974, issued another background paper denying the allegations. It said the price supports were raised largely because Democrats in Congress were threatening to pass a bill that would have raised them even more.

Another controversial campaign contribution publicized during 1973 was $100,000 in cash given by financier Howard Hughes to President Nixon's close friend Charles G. "Bebe" Rebozo in 1969 and 1970. Rebozo said the money was an advance contribution for the President's 1972 campaign and that he held it in a safe deposit box because a finance chairman had not been appointed. He returned the money to Hughes in June 1973.

Nixon's Finances

Other issues loosely tied in with Watergate actually had nothing to do with the 1972 presidential campaign.

One of these was spending on the Nixon residences. An Aug. 6 General Services Administration (GSA) report revealed that at least $10-million in federal funds had been spent at the President's homes in San Clemente, Calif., and Key Biscayne, Fla. The President's income tax payments also came into question. Rumors about the President's taxes led him to make an unprecedented release of financial records Dec. 8. In early 1974 both the Internal Revenue Service (IRS) and Joint Committee on Internal Revenue Taxation were looking into the payments, particularly the question of whether Nixon had acted properly in claiming a $576,000 deduction for the gift of his vice presidential papers to the United States.

Nixon Stance. During the year, Nixon shuttled publicly between an attitude of trying to set the record straight on Watergate and an effort to show that he was a man involved in running the country who had put Watergate behind him. Neither attitude helped him very much with the U.S. public. During the year his standing in the Gallup Poll dropped from 68 per cent approval Feb. 6 (after the Vietnam cease fire) to 27 per cent in November. The 27 per cent figure was registered during "Operation Candor," a White House attempt to make the President more visible to Congress and to the public and to end once and for all the doubts raised by Watergate.

The President held only three regular news conferences between the time the Watergate story broke and the end of January 1974 on Aug. 22, Sept. 5 and Oct. 26. The last of these was a particularly stormy session during which he characterized media coverage of the Cox firing as the most "outrageous, vicious, distorted reporting" he had seen "in 27 years of public life." The President criticized the press for blowing Watergate out of proportion and for ignoring the achievements of his administration. At the Aug. 22 press conference he complained: We have had 30 minutes of this press conference. I have yet to have, for example, one question on the business of the people."

In his Jan. 30, 1974, State of the Union message Nixon reiterated earlier statements that he would not resign and asked for an end to the Watergate investigation: "One year of Watergate is enough." But with the impeachment investigation underway and more indictments expected shortly from the special prosecutor's office, it seemed unlikely that Watergate would go away.

Following is a background of the events leading up to McCord's March 19 letter to Judge Sirica.

BACKGROUND

As the details emerged in 1973, the background of the Watergate burglary and cover-up appeared immensely complicated. It involved not only the break-in, and trial, but such elements as the complex money maneuvers used to pay the burglars and revelations of other "dirty tricks" that were part of the approach to politics that led to the break-in.

THE BURGLARY

About 1 a.m. on June 17, 1972, Frank Wills, a security guard at the Watergate Office Building, found the locks on two garage-level doors taped open. Thinking the tapes had been left by maintenance men, Wills removed them.

About one-half hour later, making his rounds, Wills found the doors retaped and locks jimmied. He called the police.

A few minutes later, the police apprehended five rubber-gloved men at Democratic National Committee headquarters on the sixth floor. The men were James W. McCord Jr., security coordinator for the Committee to Re-elect the President (CRP) and four Miami-based Cuban-Americans: Bernard L. Barker, Virgilio R. Gonzalez, Eugenio R. Martinez and Frank A. Sturgis. They carried on an array of sophisticated housebreaking and wiretapping equipment.

The five men were booked at the second district station house. The police found $1,300 in $100 bills on their persons and subsequently discovered $3,200 more in the two hotel rooms they had rented at the Watergate Hotel next to the office building. In the rooms they also found two address books containing E. Howard Hunt's name and phone numbers and a check made out by Hunt. Next to Hunt's name was the notation "White H."

Within a week, investigators had established that Hunt, a former CIA agent, had been hired by the White House after a recommendation from Nixon adviser Charles W. Colson. Questioned by FBI agents about the Watergate break-in, Hunt refused to speak. Investigators discovered a loaded pistol, diagrams of the Democratic National Committee headquarters and electronic eavesdropping devices in Hunt's office at the old executive office building next to the White House.

On June 28 the name of G. Gordon Liddy publicly entered the case. Liddy, finance counsel to the CRP, was fired by re-election committee chairman John N. Mitchell for refusing to answer FBI questions relating to the break-in. On July 8 Mitchell himself resigned "to devote more time to my wife and family."

During the summer there was a series of newspaper leaks but little public outcry about the Watergate case. A Justice Department investigation of the break-in proceeded under the leadership of Henry E. Peterson, assistant attorney general in charge of the criminal division. A grand jury began talking testimony shortly after the break-in.

On Sept. 15 the grand jury indicted the five burglars, Liddy and Hunt. (*Indictment details, 1972 Almanac, p. 91*)

The following day, news sources identified Alfred C. Baldwin III, an ex-FBI agent and alleged participant in the Watergate bugging incident, as a major source of information on the operation who had linked Liddy and Hunt to the burglars. Baldwin became a key witness in the trial and in a separate civil case filed by the Democrats June 20, 1972, against CRP. He was given immunity from prosecution. He had been stationed at the Howard Johnson motel across from Watergate with a walkie-talkie to watch the Watergate Office Building and be in a position to report to Hunt and Liddy, who were waiting in Barker's hotel room in the Watergate Hotel. He had seen the police reach the sixth floor and warned Hunt and Liddy to get away from the area.

"DIRTY TRICKS" TIE-IN

On Oct. 10 *The Washington Post* added a new dimension to the Watergate case with a story charging that "the Watergate bugging incident stemmed from a massive campaign of political spying and sabotage conducted on behalf of President Nixon's re-election." It said the operation was financed by a secret fund that fluctuated between $350,000 and $700,000. It alleged that the recruiter for sabotage operations was Donald H. Segretti, a young California lawyer and former Treasury Department attorney.

Segretti was tied to such activities as throwing campaign schedules into disarray, leaking false items to the press, planting provocateurs at rallies and spreading false stories about the sexual misconduct of Democratic candidates. One of the activities was widely considered damaging or even fatal to the presidential campaign of Sen. Edmund S. Muskie (D Maine)—a publication of a fake letter alleging Muskie's use of the pejorative word "Canuck" to describe Americans of French-Canadian descent.

THE MONEY MORASS

The details of the Watergate break-in seeped slowly to the public, largely through *The Washington Post.*

Among the first to come to light were the confusing stories of how Bernard L. Barker and the three other Cuban-Americans were paid for their part in the break-in.

The *Post* in late July reported that it had traced Republican campaign funds to the bank account of Barker. One source of payment came to be known as the Dahlberg check. Dwayne Andreas, a Minnesota grain executive, April 9 had given $25,000 in cash to Kenneth Dahlberg, chairman of the Minnesota Committee to Re-elect the President. Dahlberg gave a cashier's check for the $25,000 to the president's chief fund raiser, Maurice Stans. It eventually was passed to Liddy and turned up in the bank account of Barker.

Other money which turned up in Barker's bank account had been routed through Mexico. Robert H. Allen, a major Republican fund raiser in Texas, April 3 transferred $100,000 from Gulf Resources Corporation in Houston to the account of a subsidiary in Mexico City. The subsidiary turned the money over to its Mexican attorney, Manuel Ogarrio Daguerre, who converted $89,000 into four cashier's checks. Those checks also passed to the treasurer of CRP, then to Liddy and then to Barker.

Other Funds. The history of the activities of CRP was replete with stories of large sums of money, often in cash. Altogether, Stans in 1972 raised $55-million, the largest amount of money ever spent in a political campaign. Of this, $20-million came in before new explicit campaign reporting laws went into effect April 7 and $1.7-million of that was in cash.

The money was handled by finance committee treasurer Hugh Sloan. According to his subsequent testimony before the Senate Watergate committee, Sloan was instructed to hand out cash to a variety of Republicans. He gave a total of $250,000 to the President's personal lawyer, Herbert Kalmbach, $250,000 to Liddy, $350,000 to H.R. Haldeman and $100,000 to CRP official Herbert L. Porter. The last money was reportedly for "dirty tricks."

It was variously estimated that between $423,000 and $548,000 was paid to the defendants for support and legal fees after the arrests. This apparently included the $350,000 given to Haldeman and additional funds raised by Kalmbach.

The Vesco Case. One of the cash campaign contributions was $200,000 (supplemented by a subsequent $50,000 check) from New Jersey financier Robert L. Vesco. The money was handed to the finance committee three days after the cutoff date for anonymous contributions, but Stans told Sloan it was to be regarded as "pre-April 7 funds" because it had been promised before that date.

An indictment handed down May 10, 1973, charged that the $200,000 had been obtained by Stans and Mitchell in return for promises to intercede with the Securities and Exchange Commission on behalf of Vesco. Vesco was under investigation for allegedly swindling investors in IOS Ltd., an overseas mutual fund corporation.

The $250,000 contribution had been returned to Vesco in January 1973, and Vesco that spring fled the country. The trial of Mitchell and Stans was repeatedly postponed as the issue became involved with the Watergate tapes.

THE TRIAL

The trial of the seven Watergate defendants began Jan. 8, 1973 before federal district court, Washington, D.C. A jury was chosen in two days and was sequestered.

Within a few days the seven defendants had been reduced to two. On Jan. 11, Judge John J. Sirica accepted a guilty plea from Hunt and on Jan. 15 Barker, Sturgis, Martinez and Gonzalez pleaded guilty. Gerald Alch, McCord's attorney, made a motion for a mistrial after the guilty pleas had been made. He said the absence of the five men from the courtroom would lead the jurors to conclude that guilty pleas had been made and would prejudice the rights of McCord and Liddy to a fair trial. Sirica denied Alch's motion.

During the trial, Baldwin was a key government witness, testifying that wiretapping apparatus had been set up in a motel room across from the Watergate. Hugh Sloan testified that as finance committee chairman he had given $199,000 in cash to Liddy on the instructions of Jeb Stuart Magruder, deputy campaign chairman for the President. Magruder testified that the committee budgeted about $235,000 for intelligence activities directed by Liddy, but that he knew nothing about illegal bugging.

During the trial, Sirica several times personally questioned witnesses and defendants in an effort to get to the bottom of the Watergate affair. He was critical of the prosecution for failing to ask more questions about the motivation of the men. On Feb. 2, at the end of the trial, Sirica said, "I am still not satisfied that all of the pertinent facts that might be available have been produced before an American jury." He set March 23 as the day for sentencing.

GRAY CONFIRMATION

Indications that the Watergate affair had not ended with the trial came during Senate Judiciary Committee hearings on the confirmation of L. Patrick Gray III, Nixon's nominee to succeed J. Edgar Hoover as chief of the FBI. The hearings began Feb. 28 and ended with the

(Continued on p. 19)

Summer Phase Of Public Hearings Drew Wide TV Audience

For a time during the summer of 1973, the public hearings by the Senate Select Committee on Presidential Campaign Activities—the Watergate committee—were one of the most talked about events in the country. This was during the first phase of the hearings, dealing with the burglary and cover-up, which ran intermittently from May 17 through Aug. 7. The public watched the story unfold on live television and the seven members of the committee became famous.

When the hearings resumed Sept. 24 with an investigation of other political "dirty tricks," much of the interest in the proceedings quickly evaporated. Live television ceased and even the senators who were committee members quit attending regularly. When the first session of the 93rd Congress adjourned, it was unclear if public hearings would resume in 1974.

Committee Established. In early February 1973, Judge John J. Sirica complained in court that the trial of the Watergate burglars had not succeeded in bringing forth all the facts of the case. He expressed hopes that a Senate investigation would ferret out the motive for the burglary.

Legislation to set such an investigation in motion was approved by the Senate Feb. 7 when it voted 77-0 to establish a select committee to look into the break-in. The resolution (S Res 60) provided that an investigation was to be conducted by a select committee of seven senators which would have broad authority, including the power to subpoena witnesses. A final report was to be filed no later than Feb. 28, 1974. *(Vote 13, p. 4-S)*

Named chairman of the committee Feb. 8 was Sen. Sam J. Ervin Jr. (D S.C.), author of S Res 60. Other Democrats appointed were Herman E. Talmadge (Ga.), Daniel K. Inouye (Hawaii) and Joseph M. Montoya (N.M.). The three Republicans named were Howard H. Baker Jr. (Tenn.), Edward J. Gurney (Fla.) and Lowell P. Weicker (Conn.).

The majority chose Samuel Dash, 48, a Georgetown University criminal law professor, as majority counsel. Dash, director of Georgetown's Institute of Criminal Law and Procedure, was considered a leading authority on wiretapping. The committee's minority counsel was Fred D. Thompson, 30, a Nashville lawyer. Thompson was a former U.S. attorney for Tennessee's middle district and served as Sen. Baker's campaign manager for that area in 1972.

Phase One. The faces, voices and personalities of these nine men became well known to many of the American people during the summer of 1973. The hearings got under way May 17 in the pillared, chandeliered, marble-walled caucus room of the Russell Senate Office Building.

At first the hearings were televised by all three major networks. Early newspaper reports told of viewers' complaints that they were being deprived of favorite daytime shows and that the country would suffer from overexposure to Watergate. But the telecasts continued, sometimes rotated by the networks, and surveys found that the daytime television audience had increased. Many housewives apparently found the real-life drama more exciting than soap operas. Public Television also provided popular gavel-to-gavel rebroadcasts beginning at eight p.m., and weary Watergate addicts watched faithfully. The television coverage continued until the first phase of the hearings ended in September.

Part of the public fascination with the hearings came from watching the interplay of the personalities of the seven senators. The hearings made 76-year-old Chairman Ervin almost a folk hero. He spiced the proceedings with biblical quotations and bits of country wit while revealing a sharp legal mind. Sam Ervin T-shirts became a best seller. Ervin traded country stories with Vice Chairman Baker often enough so that in July the *New York Times* affectionately referred to the hearings as the Sam and Howard show. Baker also proved to be an able and attractive questioner, and was talked of as a 1976 Republican presidential possibility as a result of his performance on the committee.

Of the other senators, Talmadge and Inouye were both tough interrogators. Gureny was generally considered to be the strongest Nixon supporter on the committee, and his questioning often sought to bring out the administration position. Weicker, a liberal freshman Republican, one of the first members of his party to call for a full Watergate investigation, was a vigorous questioner and sharp critic of the administration.

A visit to the Watergate hearings became one of the capital's major tourist attractions during the summer of 1973. Lines started forming before 6 a.m. and the large room was almost always packed during the first phase of the investigation. The audience was strongly anti-Nixon, and in the early months of the hearings made its feelings known with laughter and applause. Chairman Ervin received a standing ovation when he entered the room. Finally, during the testimony of John D. Ehrlichman in July, the audience became so abusive that the chairman put an end to demonstrations of opinion.

Phase Two. The committee recessed for vacation Aug. 7. By the time the hearings resumed Sept. 24 much of the public fascination had evaporated. The big witnesses had testified and the excitement the hearings had generated seemed to vanish. The commercial networks dropped their coverage after a few September sessions. The "dirty tricks" phase two hearings were held intermittently between Oct. 3 and Nov. 15, but public interest in Watergate turned away from the Senate investigation to such other elements of the case as the missing presidential tapes and the firing of special Watergate prosecutor Archibald Cox.

(Continued from p. 17)

withdrawal of the nomination, at Gray's request, April 5. Confirmation of the nominee had become increasingly unlikely as disclosures relating to Watergate emerged. These were some of the statements from FBI files submitted to the committee:

• Herbert Kalmbach, Nixon's personal attorney, told the FBI he and Dwight Chapin, then the President's appointments secretary, arranged to pay between $30,000 and $40,000 to Donald Segretti, the alleged saboteur.

• Re-election committee officials tried to impede an FBI investigation of the Watergate.

• Dean, the President's counsel, sat in on all interviews of White House personnel conducted by FBI investigators. Gray told the committee on March 6 that he had opposed Dean's presence at the interviews but had permitted him to be present because the alternative would have been to have no interviews.

• Liddy and Hunt, two former White House consultants, "traveled around the United States contacting former CIA employees for the purpose of setting up a security organization for the Republican Party dealing with political espionage."

• An unnamed official of the Republican re-election committee told the FBI that Hugh Sloan "allegedly disbursed large sums to various committee officials for unknown reasons." The disbursements included $50,000 to Jeb Stuart Magruder, $100,000 to Herbert Porter and $89,000 to Liddy.

Among the factors that damaged Gray's chances were accusations that he had made campaign speeches for the president, his testimony before the committee that he had turned over FBI files to John Dean and his March 22 statement to the committee that Dean had probably lied to the FBI in saying he did not know that E. Howard Hunt had a White House office. Gray also was damaged by Dean's refusal to testify before the committee, claiming executive privilege.

Nixon April 5 announced that he was withdrawing Gray's nomination at his request. He praised the nominee as an "able, honest and dedicated American" who had been exposed to "totally unfair innuendo and suspicion" because he had cooperated with Dean. The Judiciary Committee had scheduled a vote on the nomination for April 9, and Gray's opponents were predicting a tie vote, which would have killed it.

AGNEW: SECOND VICE PRESIDENT IN U.S. HISTORY TO RESIGN

Spiro T. Agnew Oct. 10, 1973, became the second vice president in history to resign. Under investigation for multiple charges of alleged conspiracy, extortion and bribery, Agnew agreed to resign and avoided imprisonment by pleading *nolo contendere* (no contest) to a single charge of federal income tax evasion. *(Box, p. 23)*

The plea was the result of a month of White House-initiated plea bargaining between the Justice Department and Agnew's attorneys in which the Justice Department agreed to request a lenient sentence in exchange for the vice president's resignation and plea of guilty to a single charge. A 40-page document outlining other instances of alleged misconduct by Agnew was submitted to the court by the Justice Department without pressing charges. *(Box on charges, p. 24)*

Following disclosure in early August 1973 of a federal investigation into alleged payoffs he had accepted while executive of Baltimore county, governor of Maryland and later as vice president, Agnew made a three-pronged effort to curb the probe. First, he charged that news leaks about the investigation jeopardized his civil rights and requested Attorney General Elliot L. Richardson to investigate the leak of information to the Justice Department.

Second, citing precedent for congressional investigation of alleged vice presidential misconduct, Agnew unsuccessfully urged the House to take over the probe into his earlier activities. Finally, Agnew's attorneys petitioned the special grand jury in Baltimore to halt the inquiry on the grounds that a vice president could not be indicted while in office.

Two days after Agnew's resignation President Nixon nominated House Minority Leader Gerald R. Ford (R Mich.) as his successor. The 25th Amendment, ratified in 1967, required that the President nominate a vice presidential successor to take office upon confirmation by both houses of Congress. In the interim, Speaker of the House Carl Albert (D Okla.) stood next in line for the presidency. In the past, the vice presidency had been vacated 16 times, but before Agnew, only one vice president, John C. Calhoun, had resigned. *(Story on Ford, p. 26)*

Letters of Resignation. As required by law, Agnew's resignation came in a letter to Secretary of State Henry A. Kissinger, delivered Oct. 10. Similar letters were sent to President Nixon and congressional leaders. Agnew had informed Nixon of his decision the evening of Oct. 9.

Minutes after the arrival of the letters, Agnew appeared in U.S. District Judge Walter E. Hoffman's Baltimore courtroom, pleaded *nolo contendere* to charges of failing to report $29,500 in 1967 income and was sentenced to three years unsupervised probation and fined $10,000.

The court action rendered moot the litigation of two other issues raised by his case—the constitutional questions of whether a vice president could be indicted while in office and whether newsmen, claiming the protection of the First Amendment, were obliged to divulge their sources.

Plea Bargaining. Agnew's fine and probationary sentence on the tax evasion charge were the result of the complicated plea bargaining process between the White House, the Justice Department and Agnew's attorneys. Under the final agreement, Agnew waived his right to a trial, agreed to resign from office and agreed to accept sentencing on the single tax charge. Judge Hoffman advised Agnew that the plea of *nolo contendere* was the "full equivalent to a plea of guilty."

In return, the Justice Department agreed to drop all but one pending charge against Agnew and to request leniency on the sentencing. Publication of the department's 40-page summary outlining other charges was also part of the final agreement.

At a news conference Oct. 11, Richardson disclosed that the White House had initiated the plea bargaining process. He told reporters that White House counsel J. Fred Buzhardt Jr. had telephoned him in early September to ask if he would meet with Agnew's attorneys. Richardson described Buzhardt's role in the plea bargaining process as one of "facilitating communications."

The attorney general said that Nixon had been kept "fully informed at all times," and that he had "fully approved each of the major steps" in the Justice Department's action against Agnew. But he added that Nixon had felt "it was not appropriate for him to be informed of the details of the case." Deputy White House Press Secretary Gerald L. Warren had said Aug. 14 that Nixon was not being given reports on the case and would not intervene.

Agnew's attorney Judah Best Oct. 11 contradicted Richardson's statement that Buzhardt had served merely in "facilitating communications." Best said he had met with Buzhardt in Miami Oct. 5-6 and their meeting was critical to the final agreement between Agnew and the Justice Department.

CQ References on Agnew

1972 Almanac: biography, p. 1064; 1972 campaign, p. 1064; nomination acceptance speech, p. 1054. *1970 Almanac*: on anti-war amendments, p. 397; campaign efforts, p. 1071, 1072, 1076; campus unrest commission report, p. 1028. *1969 Almanac*: campus disorders, p. 724, 731; excerpts of speeches, p. 1198; role in Nixon administration, p. 1197; speeches, p. 108. *1968 Almanac*: biography, p. 1004; convention activities and public record, p. 1003; Nixon support, p. 977; nomination and election, p. 944, 952, 979, 980.

Agnew Profile

Spiro Agnew was a nationally unknown "Spiro Who?" when Richard Nixon picked him as his running mate in 1968, but he went on to become perhaps the nation's best-known, most controversial and most quoted Vice President.

Nixon had plucked Agnew from virtual obscurity in 1968, to the surprise of Republican leaders and the nation. Agnew had been elected governor of Maryland in 1966 largely because many Democrats, in a state with 3-1 Democratic registration, refused to vote for their party's nominee, an outspoken opponent of open-housing legislation. Agnew was perceived as a moderate on racial issues.

In 1967 and 1968, Agnew was a leading supporter of New York Gov. Nelson A. Rockefeller for the presidency. He repeatedly urged Rockefeller to declare his candidacy, and did not endorse Nixon until the first day of the 1968 Republican national convention. Nixon then asked Agnew to make the speech placing his name in nomination, and to the surprise of almost everyone, selected him as his running mate.

Agnew's famous knack for phrase-making catapulted him into public attention, and into controversy, in the 1968 campaign. He called Democratic nominee Hubert H. Humphrey "soft on communism," referred to a reporter of Japanese ancestry as a "fat Jap," called persons of Polish ancestry "Polacks," and remarked, "If you've seen one city slum, you've seen them all."

When Agnew criticized war protesters and the press with vigorous and colorful invective, he caught the attention of the media and the public. His 1969 denunciation of "an effete corps of impudent snobs who characterize themselves as intellectuals" and encourage a "spirit of national masochism" opened a flood of rising rhetoric and alliterative Agnewisms which ebbed and flowed for the next several years.

Agnew's campaign speeches in 30 states in the 1970 congressional elections brought forth such language that many observers accused him of polarizing the American people, slandering and pandering to fear. He became a popular speaker, however, as he took a hard line against war protesters, students, welfare recipients, criminals and "radiclibs." In addition to raising $5.5-million for the Republican coffers, he earned the gratitude of party leaders and the following of millions who liked his slam-bang attacks on society's dissenters.

In his first year in office, he was named one of the nation's most admired men in the annual Gallup Poll. He was number three, an unusual showing for a vice president. In 1970 he ranked fourth, in 1971 sixth and in 1972 seventh.

He weathered a period of "Will Nixon dump Agnew?" speculation, but not until July 22, 1972, did Nixon announce that he would retain Agnew on the ticket. Agnew was quiet and low-key in the 1972 campaign, following the lead of the President, who sought to remain above the battle and let surrogates do the politicking.

The *New York Times* reported Oct. 12 that Agnew was prepared to resign as early as mid-September when negotiations first began with the Justice Department. According to sources, Agnew's resignation was delayed because of disagreement over the amount of evidence against him that was to be made public. Other sources cited by the *Times* estimated that the 40-page document submitted to the court contained about ten per cent of the evidence accumulated against Agnew.

Disclosure of Investigation

On Aug. 1, 1973, U.S. Attorney George Beall informed Agnew's lawyer Judah Best that the vice president was under investigation for alleged violations of conspiracy, extortion and bribery and tax statutes.

The allegations concerned reported kickbacks from private architectural and engineering firms that had been improperly awarded state and federal contracts during Agnew's years as executive of Baltimore county, Maryland governor and later as vice president. The prosecutor's office asked Agnew to turn over a number of documents, including bank records and income tax returns. Ironically, the investigation had begun in October 1972 as an inquiry into reported kickbacks to Democratic officials in Maryland.

The story of the Agnew investigation was first made public Aug. 6 by the vice president as the first printed account, to appear in the *Wall Street Journal*, was going to press. Informed of the forthcoming article, Agnew released a brief statement saying, "I am innocent of any wrongdoing...and I am equally confident that my innocence will be affirmed."

Agnew disclosed at a nationally televised news conference Aug. 8 that he had heard rumors in February 1973, that investigators had repeatedly turned up his name in that probe. He denied any misconduct on his part. He told reporters he was defending himself, instead of "spending my time looking around to see who's supporting me."

Responding to questions from a packed auditorium of newsmen, Agnew called the charges "damned lies." He said he had "no expectation of being indicted" and that he had given no consideration to leaving the post of vice president, even temporarily. He indicated his willingness to cooperate with the investigators, a move he followed up on Aug. 14 when he turned over subpoenaed records to the authorities.

Richardson's Decision. Responsibility for the Agnew investigation rested with the Justice Department. Attorney General Richardson said Aug. 19 that he would personally decide whether evidence gathered by federal prosecutors in the investigation should be presented to a grand jury. In making that decision, he said, he also bore the responsibility for the "ultimate resolution" of the key constitutional issue of whether a vice president could be indicted for a crime while he was still in office.

On Sept. 28, Agnew's attorneys petitioned the Baltimore federal district court to halt the grand jury investigation on the grounds that a vice president was immune to prosecution while in office. The Justice Department twice filed responses, but the immunity issue was never decided because of Agnew's resignation.

In its first reply, filed Oct. 5, the Justice Department claimed that a vice president could be indicted in office. It said it would wait a "reasonable time" to allow the House to impeach and the Senate to try Agnew if he were impeached. The department argued that while indictment of a President in office would "incapacitate" the government, a vice president's functions were not "indispensible to the orderly operation of government."

The department Oct. 8 filed its second reply. It termed "frivolous" Agnew's accusations that prosecutors had deliberately leaked information to the press to undermine his position. Furthermore, the reply charged, Agnew's lawyers were engaging in a "fishing expedition" by an Oct. 5 move subpoenaing newsmen to question them about sources for stories on the investigation.

Charges of News Leaks

Riled by the fact that reports to the media on the status of the investigation had continued following his Aug. 8 news conference, Agnew Aug. 21 held a second nationally televised news conference at which he charged that "some Justice Department officials have decided to indict me in the press whether or not the evidence supports their position." It had "become clear" he said, "that the 'sources close to the investigation' so frequently quoted were just that—persons involved in the investigatory process."

The Vice President called on Attorney General Richardson to investigate possible leaks from the department indicating that Agnew was about to be indicted.

Noting that Richardson had denied that any leaks had emanated from the Justice Department and had pledged to investigate the suggestion of such leaks, the Vice President revealed that he had "communicated with the attorney general today and [had] asked that he fulfill that promise and pursue such an investigation vigorously."

Richardson responded quickly with a statement of his own. He denied any leaks as coming from government investigators, but promised that "any plausible lead" implicating Justice officials as the sources of news stories would be "pursued vigorously."

Beall also denied his office was the source of the leaks, and added that Agnew was wrong in saying that he did not want to meet with the Vice President. "We have not reached a conclusion (on a meeting), and this is under study," he said.

At his press conference Oct. 11, Richardson denied that the information could only have come from the Justice Department. Rather, he said, there were strong similarities between the information in the press and that given by the Justice Department to the White House and the vice president's attorneys.

Nixon Statements

Throughout the two-month ordeal leading to his resignation, Agnew met periodically with President Nixon. Although Nixon's public statements concerning the vice president consistently contained at least a measure of support, many Agnew backers felt the President's failure to lend all-out endorsement undercut Agnew's position.

On Aug. 7, the day after the investigation was publicly disclosed, Nixon and Agnew met for nearly two hours. Speaking to reporters afterwards, the vice president said Nixon "unequivocally" supported him. On Aug. 8 Nixon issued a statement saying that the investigation of Agnew was "no reason for the President to change his attitude about the vice president or his confidence in the vice president."

When Agnew made his personal financial records available to the federal prosecutors Aug. 14, Deputy White House Press Secretary Gerald L. Warren was asked how the President felt about the action. Warren replied that Nixon was "interested in making sure that all appropriate steps" were taken. Warren denied news reports that Nixon had asked Agnew not to provide the material lest a precedent was set for Nixon to produce documents for the Watergate prosecutors. He stressed that Nixon was not intervening in the case and was not getting reports on it from the Justice Department.

At a news conference Aug. 22, the day after Agnew had denounced Justice Department officials for leaking information to the press, Nixon emphatically said that anyone found leaking information concerning the case would be "summarily dismissed from government service." With respect to his confidence in Agnew, Nixon said he retained the confidence he had in 1968 when he

---

Precedents: Calhoun, Colfax

Resignation. Before Spiro T. Agnew, the only U.S. Vice President to resign from office was John C. Calhoun of South Carolina, who stepped down on December 28, 1832. After well-publicized policy disputes with President Andrew Jackson, Calhoun opted to return to the Senate to take part in consideration of the repeal of the tariff act of 1832. A shift of a South Carolina senator to the governor's mansion provided the Senate vacancy which Calhoun filled.

House Investigations. Two former vice presidents before Agnew were the targets of House investigations regarding alleged illegal activities: Calhoun and Ulysses S. Grant's vice president, Schuyler Colfax.

In Calhoun's case, he requested the investigation himself, after charges were published in a newspaper in 1826 that he had profited from a war contract while serving as secretary of war. The select investigating committee found him innocent.

In 1872, Colfax's name came up during a congressional investigation of possible attempts to bribe members of Congress as part of the Credit Mobilier scandal. Colfax owned stock in the dummy corporation set up to pocket appropriations intended for the building of the Union Pacific railroad. A special investigating committee appointed to look into the scandal did not clearly establish Colfax's guilt or innocence. However, the House Judiciary Committee concluded no impeachment action should be taken because the alleged illegal activities had occurred before Colfax became vice president.

"Nolo Contendere"

A plea of *nolo contendere* is entered in criminal proceedings with the same legal effect as a plea of guilty. Translated from Latin, it means: "I will not contest it." It admits for the purposes of the case at issue that all the facts are well pleaded, but it may not be cited in other proceedings as an admission of guilt. In contrast to a plea of guilty which restricts a defendant's civil rights, a plea of *nolo contendre* allows him to continue to exercise his full civil rights, including the right to vote and to hold office.

selected Agnew as a running mater, and that it had been "strengthened by (Agnew's) courageous conduct and ability."

Public attention heightened when President Nixon flew back to Washington from San Clemente, Calif. to meet with Agnew Sept. 1. No aides were present at the session.

After the meeting, Warren told journalists "the vice president brought the President up to date on the matters concerning himself." Warren called the session "a good discussion." Agnew's press secretary said the vice president was "utterly relieved" and that he and Nixon had held a "relaxed discussion."

The Agnew story subsided in early September during a three-week lay-off in the special federal grand jury investigation into political corruption in Maryland. But by mid-month, speculation mounted that Agnew was considering resigning under pressure from Nixon officials.

David S. Broder reported in the *Washington Post* Sept. 18 that Agnew had discussed resignation at great length with friends. According to the report, Agnew was intent on resigning due to the pressure the controversy had exerted on his family and due to "the plain indication that the White House—and apparently the President himself—wants Agnew out." A similar report appeared in the *New York Times* Sept. 19.

On Sept. 19, a White House statement on Agnew's status branded as "false" stories alleging that "there is a disposition on the part of the White House or the people in the White House to force the Vice President to resign." The same day, spokesmen for Agnew denied that he was considering offering his resignation.

Appeal to the House

Agnew, apparently deciding not to resign, but to fight the charges, asked the House Sept. 25 to conduct a full inquiry into allegations that he had accepted bribes and kickbacks from Maryland contractors.

His request was made formally in a meeting with House leaders late in the afternoon. It came just as Attorney General Richardson ended weeks of rumors with an announcement that on Sept. 27 the Justice Department would begin presenting evidence to a federal grand jury involving Agnew's role in alleged bribery and extortion.

Agnew's move was interpreted as an effort to block the grand jury proceedings. He said he would fight any criminal proceedings against him, contending that it was constitutionally impermissible for criminal prosecution to be begun against a sitting president or vice president. But, Agnew, said, he would cooperate fully if the House, as he asked, undertook a full inquiry into the charges. As a precedent, he cited the 1827 investigation by the House which cleared Vice President John C. Calhoun of charges of wrongdoing. The House, said Agnew, was the proper authority to undertake such an investigation because it had constitutionally granted power to investigate charges and decide if they warranted impeachment.

President Nixon's role in the decision made by Richardson and Agnew was unclear. He had met with both separately the morning of Sept. 25. That afternoon, after both made their announcement, he issued a statement urging that Agnew be accorded "basic consideration and the presumption of innocence."

House Rejection. At noon Sept. 26 after further leadership meetings during the morning, Albert announced a decision: "The Vice President's letter relates to matters before the courts. In view of that fact, I, as Speaker, will not take any action on the matter at this time." "They made a Democratic decision," said House Minority Leader Ford, "I don't think there's anything we can do since we are in the minority."

Appeal to the Public

Agnew's efforts to forestall the Maryland probe failed. Speaker Albert's rejection of Agnew's bid for a House investigation foreclosed possibilities that Congress would relieve the pressure of the imminent court proceedings. The Justice Department Sept. 27 began presentation of evidence against Agnew to the special federal grand jury in Baltimore. In the middle of it all, refusing to take sides—and thus in the view of many Agnew sympathizers tacitly contributing to the vice president's political destruction—was President Nixon. Agnew appeared an isolated man with dwindling options. On Sept. 29 he attempted to mobilize public opinion in his favor by renewing his charges of news leaks in an emotional speech in Los Angeles.

Agnew, before a wildly cheering audience of 2,000 delegates to the National Federation of Republican Women convention in Los Angeles, accused top Justice officers of attempting to destroy him with "malicious and outrageous" news leaks. Clearly referring to assistant attorney general Henry A. Peterson without naming him, Agnew offered the theory that Petersen and others in the department were trying to recover reputations, which he said had been lost through "ineptness and blunder" in the Watergate affair and other criminal investigations.

"I'm their big trophy," Agnew said. "Well, I'm not going to fall down and be his victim, thank you." Though he had made it clear that he regarded his political career as being beyond redemption, the vice president vowed not to resign even if indicted.

Agnew's charges brought an immediate rebuttal by Richardson. And, during his Oct. 3 news conference, Nixon supported the job Petersen was doing. However, he also declared that he respected Agnew's decision

Excerpts From Grand Jury Criminal Information Against Agnew

Following are excerpts, as published in the Oct. 11 *New York Times,* of the statement submitted to the court in Baltimore on Oct. 10 by the government at the arraignment of Vice President Agnew. The presentation of the 40-page statement was a material condition, requested by the Justice Department, pursuant to the plea bargaining agreement reached between federal prosecutors and Agnew.

I. The Relationship of Mr. Agnew, I. H. Hammerman II and Jerome B. Wolff.

In the spring of 1967, shortly after Mr. Agnew had taken office as Governor of Maryland, he advised Hammerman that it was customary for engineers to make substantial cash payments in return for engineering contracts with the state of Maryland. Mr. Agnew instructed Hammerman to contact Wolff, then the new chairman-director of the Maryland State Roads Commission, to arrange for the establishment of an understanding pursuant to which Wolff would notify Hammerman as to which engineering firms were in line for state contracts so that Hammerman could solicit and obtain from those engineering firms cash payments in consideration therefore.

Hammerman, as instructed, discussed the matter with Wolff, who was receptive but who requested that the cash payments to be elicited from the engineers be split in three equal shares among Agnew, Hammerman and Wolff. Hammerman informed Mr. Agnew of Wolff's attitude; Mr. Agnew informed Hammerman that the split of the cash monies would be 50 per cent for Mr. Agnew, 25 per cent for Hammerman and 25 per cent for Wolff. Hammerman carried that message to Wolff, who agreed to that split.

The scheme outlined above was then put into operation. Over the course of the approximately 18 months of Mr. Agnew's remaining tenure as Governor of Maryland, Hammerman made contact with approximately eight engineering firms. Informed periodically by Wolff as to which engineering firms were in line to receive state contracts, Hammerman successfully elicited from seven engineering firms substantial cash payments pursuant to understandings between Hammerman and the various engineers to whom he was talking that the substantial cash payments were in return for the state work being awarded to those engineering firms. The monies collected in that manner by Hammerman were split (among Hammerman, Agnew and Wolff) in accordance with the understanding earlier reached....

Wolff, as chairman-director of the Maryland State Roads Commission, made initial tentative decisions with regard to which engineering firms should be awarded which state contracts. These tentative decisions would then be discussed by Wolff with Governor Agnew. Although Governor Agnew accorded Wolff's tentative decisions great weight, the Governor always exercised the final decision-making authority....

Hammerman also successfully solicited, at Governor Agnew's instruction, a substantial cash payment from a financial institution in return for that institution's being awarded a major role in the financing of a large issue of state bonds.

II. The Relationship between Mr. Agnew and Allen Green.

Shortly after Mr. Agnew's election in November 1966 as Governor of Maryland, he complained to Allen Green, principal of a large engineering firm, about the financial burdens to be imposed upon Mr. Agnew by his role as Governor. Green responded by saying that his company had benefited from state work and had been able to generate some cash funds from which he would be willing to provide Mr. Agnew with some financial assistance. Mr. Agnew indicated that he would be grateful for such assistance.

Beginning shortly thereafter, Green delivered to Mr. Agnew six to nine times a years an envelope containing between $2,000 and $3,000 in cash. Green's purpose was to elicit from the Agnew administration as much state work for his engineering firm as possible. That purpose was clearly understood by Governor Agnew....

Green continued to make cash payments to Vice President Agnew three or four times a year up to and including December 1972. These payments were usually about $2,000 each. The payments were made both in Mr. Agnew's vice presidential office and at his residence in the Sheraton-Park Hotel, Washington, D.C. The payments were not discontinued until after the initiation of the Baltimore County investigation by the United States Attorney for the District of Maryland in January 1973.

III. The Relationship between Mr. Agnew and Lester Matz.

Lester Matz, a principal in another large engineering firm, began making corrupt payments while Mr. Agnew was County Executive of Baltimore County in the early 1960s. In those days, Matz paid 5 per cent of his fees from Baltimore County contracts in cash to Mr. Agnew through one of Mr. Agnew's close associates.

After Mr. Agnew became Governor of Maryland, Matz decided to make his payments directly to Governor Agnew. He made no payments until that summer of 1968 when he and his partner calculated that they owed Mr. Agnew approximately $20,000 in consideration for the work which their firm had already received from the Governor's administration. The $20,000 in cash was generated in an illegal manner and was given by Matz to Governor Agnew in a manila envelope in Governor Agnew's office on or about July 16, 1968....

Matz made no further corrupt payments to Mr. Agnew until shortly after Mr. Agnew became Vice President, at which time Matz calculated that he owed Mr. Agnew approximately $10,000 more from jobs and fees which the Matz firm had received from Governor Agnew's administration since July 1968. After generating $10,000 in cash in an illegal manner, Matz met with Mr. Agnew in the Vice President's office and gave him approximately $10,000 in cash in an envelope....

In or around April 1971, Matz made a cash payment to Vice President Agnew of $2,500 in return for the awarding by the General Services Administration of a contract to a small engineering firm in which Matz had a financial ownership interest. An intermediary was instrumental in the arrangement for that particular corrupt payment.

not to resign, thereby preserving the appearance of not taking sides in the issue. In commenting on the charges leveled against Agnew, Nixon would only say they were "serious and not frivolous."

Newsmen Subpoenaed. In combatting the news leaks, Agnew's lawyers were successful in gaining power Oct. 3 to subpoena journalists to question them on their sources.

U.S. District Judge Walter E. Hoffman issued a court order authorizing Agnew's lawyers to subpoena sworn testimony from anyone they believed had knowledge about leaks to the press concerning the Agnew probe. The judge also warned members of the grand jury to disregard news accounts of the investigation. Shortly thereafter, the jurors received testimony from five witnesses under conditions of tight security at the Baltimore courthouse.

Final Negotiations

On Oct. 1, the White House confirmed reports that Buzhardt was involved in a "direct and indirect way" in negotiations between Agnew's lawyers and the Justice Department over plea bargaining.

In court, the Justice Department continued to hit hard at the arguments raised in Agnew's defense. The department contended Oct. 5 that a vice president could be indicted and tried on criminal charges while in office. Government prosecutors Oct. 8 attacked Agnew's claim of a calculated campaign of news leaks and criticized his efforts to subpoena newsmen.

Buzhardt and Agnew's lawyer Judah Best conferred in Miami Oct. 5-6. They reached a secret final agreement on the terms under which Agnew would resign and accept sentencing on the single charge of income tax evasion. According to Agnew's attorneys, two provisions were crucial to the final agreement: Agnew would be free to deny in court the information contained in the Justice Department's outline of other alleged misconduct, and he would be able to review the evidence compiled against him.

On Oct. 10, Agnew made public his decision to resign, pleaded no contest to the single tax charge and was sentenced by Judge Hoffman to 3 years unsupervised probation and fined $10,000. Agnew said in a brief statement to reporters upon leaving the courtroom that he would address the nation about his case in several days. He also criticized prosecutors for granting immunity to former associates in exchange for information about him.

Farewell Speech

Agnew bade farewell to the American people via national television Oct. 15, still protesting his innocence and blaming news leaks for the legal troubles that led to his resignation.

In his television address, Agnew said he did not want to bow out "in a paroxysm of bitterness," but he unleashed an attack against those who "improperly and unconscionably" leaked details of the grand jury investiga-

tion of Agnew and against the news media that published the "scurrilous and inaccurate reports. All this was done with full knowledge that it was prejudicial to my civil rights."

Agnew repeated his earlier denials of wrong-doing. Even his court plea of no contest, which Judge Walter E. Hoffman called the "full equivalent of a plea of guilty," Agnew said was made "because it was the only quick way to resolve the situation...not an admission of guilt, but a plea of 'no contest' to still the raging storm."

Agnew "flatly and categorically" denied the "assertions of illegal acts on my part made by the government witnesses." He attacked the former friends and colleagues who testified to Agnew's involvement in a long-standing contractors' kickback scheme as "self-confessed bribe brokers, extortionists and conspirators," and blasted government prosecutors for offering his accusers full or partial immunity from prosecution in return for their testimony.

Despite his professed innocence, Agnew said "the American people deserve to have a vice president who commands their unimpaired confidence and trust. For more than two months now, you have not had such a vice president." For that reason, and so as not to "subject the country to a further agonizing period of months without an unclouded successor for the presidency," particularly "at this especially critical time, with a dangerous war raging in the Middle East and with the nation still torn by the wrenching experiences of the past year," he decided to resign, Agnew said.

Tributes to Nixon. Agnew denied that President Nixon asked him to quit or that their meetings were "unfriendly" or "vitriolic." To the contrary, Agnew said. He paid tribute to Nixon "for the restraint and the compassion he has demonstrated in our conversations about this difficult matter." The President did his best "to accommodate human decency without sacrificing legal rectitude," Agnew said.

'Post-Watergate Morality.' While denying any guilt in the kickback scheme detailed in the Justice Department statement, Agnew did admit that "perhaps, by the new, post-Watergate morality," he did permit "my fund-raising activities and my contract dispensing activities to overlap in an unethical and an unlawful manner." But he contended that accepting contributions to office-holders from contractors seeking state business was a widespread, long-standing practice and that the witnesses against him were "long experienced and' aggressive in Maryland politics."

CONGRESS APPROVED FORD NOMINATION FOR VICE PRESIDENT

With a pledge to do "the very best that I can for America," Gerald R. Ford of Michigan became the 40th vice president of the United States Dec. 6, an hour after the House of Representatives voted 387-5 to confirm him. The Senate had approved the nomination Nov. 27 by a 92-3 vote.

Ford was the first vice president to be selected under the 25th Amendment to the Constitution, which governs presidential and vice presidential succession. Ratified in 1967, the amendment required confirmation of the nominee by a majority of both houses of Congress.

The country had been without a vice president for eight weeks, since Spiro T. Agnew resigned Oct. 10. He was sentenced on a charge of federal income tax evasion.

Ford, the 60-year-old Republican minority leader of the House, took the oath of office before a joint session of Congress, as President Nixon, his cabinet, the entire Supreme Court, members of the diplomatic corps and galleries packed with friends and visitors looked on. It was the first time a vice president was sworn in separately from a president.

Ford's wife held the Bible as Chief Justice Warren E. Burger administered the oath in the chamber of the House, which Ford called his home for 25 years. A "man of Congress," like 30 of his 39 predecessors, Ford was first elected in 1948. He frequently said his life's ambition was to be speaker of the House. Since his nomination by Nixon Oct. 12, he had said repeatedly he did not seek the presidency and did not intend to run in 1976. However, his confirmation heightened speculation that he would become president—that Nixon would resign or be impeached. *(For's House career, voting record, p. 35)*

Nixon accompanied Ford to the swearing in but did not speak. In his speech, Ford pledged "dedication to the rule of law and equal justice for all Americans."

After the swearing-in ceremony, Ford led senators back to the Senate chamber and addressed them briefly.

Confirmation Procedure

In considering the nomination of Gerald Ford, Congress was establishing precedent as it went along.

In 1965, in approving the measure which became the 25th Amendment, Congress staked out a role for itself in filling a vacant vice presidency. Both chambers approved language stating that "whenever there is a vacancy in the office of the Vice President, the President shall nominate a Vice President who shall take office *upon confirmation by a majority vote of both Houses of Congress." (Italics added)* However that amendment failed to specify a procedure to follow in confirming a vice presidential nominee. Discussion of the legislation that became the 25th Amendment focused almost exclusively on presiden-

tial disability; little thought was given to the details of vice-presidential replacement.

The major procedural question to be worked out was what committee would handle the nomination in each chamber. In the House it was quickly decided that the Judiciary Committee would have jurisdiction. In the Senate there was vigorous debate between members who wanted to set up a special committee to consider the nomination and those who wanted to refer it to the Rules Committee. The conflict was resolved when Senate Republicans joined with the Democratic leadership and gave the Rules Committee jurisdiction.

Each committee held separate hearings, rather than holding one set of hearings under a special joint committee, as had been suggested by some, including former Vice President Hubert H. Humphrey (D Minn.).

The nine member Senate Rules Committee, chaired by Howard W. Cannon (D Nev.), opened hearings Nov. 1. Chairman Peter W. Rodino Jr. (D N.J.) opened House Judiciary Committee hearings Nov. 15.

Because of the cloud of scandal under which former Vice President Agnew resigned, and the growing speculation that Ford might succeed to the presidency, members of both houses and both parties asked for a thorough investigation of his background.

Indicating the sweeping nature of the investigation, William M. Cochrane, Senate Rules Committee staff director, said that in addition to a full FBI check, the committee had:

• Asked Nixon to order the Internal Revenue Service to turn over Ford's federal income tax returns filed since 1965 and to conduct detailed audits of his returns for the past five years.

• Asked the Library of Congress to compile a complete record of Ford's positions on issues during his 25 years in the House.

In the House the Judiciary Committee voted to give Rodino power to issue subpoenas for witnesses and documents.

The hearings moved along quickly in both houses. The Senate committee in its questioning of Ford dealt mainly with how he would act if he were President. Other questions dealt with charges of influence-peddling and his record on civil rights, which some members considered poor. In the House Judiciary Committee there were several members who objected to confirming Ford on the grounds that Nixon should not be allowed to pick his own successor. However, a motion by Elizabeth Holtzman (D N.Y.) to table the nomination was defeated.

After the committee hearings were completed in each chamber the nomination was brought to the floor for consideration by the full House and Senate where a simple majority was needed to confirm.

A White House Extravaganza for Ford's Nomination

President Nixon made a gala state ceremony of his nationally televised announcement Oct. 12 that Rep. Gerald R. Ford (R Mich.) was his vice presidential nominee. Cabinet officers, congressional leaders and members of the diplomatic corps filed into the East Room of the White House promptly at 9 p.m., as did the President's family—Patricia Nixon, Tricia Cox and Julie and David Eisenhower. "Hail to the Chief" was played as the President entered.

Nixon, smiling and jovial, appeared to relish the suspense he had created about the selection. Making no mention of former Vice President Agnew, he said, "...it is vital that we turn away from the obsessions of the past.... This is a time for a new beginning for America."

A few minutes into his speech, Nixon let out his carefully guarded secret when he revealed that the nominee was "a man who has served for 25 years in the House of Representatives with great distinction." The audience then knew that Ford was the President's choice, and it burst into enthusiastic applause. Nixon, laughing, cautioned, "...there's several here who have served 25 years in the House of Representatives." Four sentences later he mentioned Ford by name.

Ford, who had been sitting between House Speaker Carl Albert (D Okla.) and Majority Leader Thomas P. O'Neill Jr. (D Mass.), joined the President at the podium. The two placed their arms around each other's shoulders in the manner of nominees at a national political convention. The microphone picked up some off-stage whispers. Nixon: "They like you." Ford: "I have a couple of friends out there."

Bipartisan Cooperation. Nixon had emphasized that his new vice president should be able to work with members of both parties in Congress "at this particular time when we have the executive in the hands of one party and the Congress controlled by another party ...." Speaker Albert had advised Nixon that Ford would have little difficulty in being confirmed by Congress.

In accepting the nomination, Ford promised to "do my utmost to the best of my ability to serve this country well and to perform those duties that will be my new assignment as effectively and efficiently and with as much accomplishment as possible."

Absentees. The justices of the Supreme Court had been invited to the ceremony, but none came. A court spokesman declined comment when asked why by Congressional Quarterly. Just three hours before the ceremony, the U.S. Court of Appeals had announced a ruling that Nixon must turn over disputed White House tape recordings related to the Watergate scandal to U.S. District Judge John J. Sirica. An appeal by the White House would take the case to the Supreme Court.

Senate Majority Leader Mike Mansfield (D Mont.) told the Senate Oct. 13 that he was perhaps the only member of Congress who did not know whom the President had nominated until 5:30 that morning, when he turned on the radio. Mansfield, who had been invited to the ceremony, explained, "It had been a pretty tough week, so far as I was concerned personally. I went to bed rather early, took the phone off the hook and had a good night's sleep." Senate Assistant Majority Leader Robert C. Byrd (D W.Va.) attended the ceremony.

Nixon's Decision-Making. Nixon reportedly had narrowed his list of possible vice presidential nominees to five when he went to Camp David, Md., late Oct. 11 to ponder his decision. Besides Ford, the list was said to include Gov. Nelson A. Rockefeller (R N.Y.); Gov. Ronald Reagan (R Calif.); former Texas Gov. John B. Connally, and Attorney General Elliot L. Richardson.

The President returned to the White House at 8:30 a.m. Oct. 12 and told his staff he had arrived at a decision. Afterward, he met with Ford and Senate Minority Leader Hugh Scott (R Pa.) to talk about procedural matters related to the nomination but not about his selection. Ford was said not to have been told that he was the man until 90 minutes before the East Room ceremony. However, one report indicated he had been informed before noon Oct. 12.

Not even Mrs. Nixon knew about the choice until the ceremony, according to reports from the White House. Secret Service agents were told to stand by but were not given the identity of the nominee.

Senate Action

Hearings

The Senate Rules and Administration Committee held hearings Nov. 1-14 on the nomination of Rep. Gerald R. Ford (R Mich.) to be vice president of the United States.

NOV. 1

Ford walked a tightrope in his nationally-televised opening appearance before the committee—supporting the views and policies of President Nixon, who nominated him, without alienating the Democratic-controlled Congress, which confirmed him.

Committee members probed repeatedly into Ford's views on executive privilege, presidential obedience of the law, separation of powers, impoundment of funds appropriated by Congress, the independence of a new special Watergate prosecutor and the President's right to withhold information which could conceal criminal activity in the executive branch.

They also questioned Ford about allegations of irregularities in his personal and campaign finances and reports that he had been treated by a psychiatrist.

Ford denied all the allegations in vigorous terms— "total fabrications," "way out," "asinine," "unreliable" and "lies." He came prepared to answer all charges; there were no surprises. Ford already had undergone the most thorough investigation of any candidate for any office in the nation's history, and the press had reported old and new allegations widely.

Committee chairman Howard W. Cannon (D Nev.) and ranking Republican member Marlow W. Cook (Ky.) had been given a 1,400-page "raw file" of data compiled by the FBI, and summarized it for the other committee members. Ford also gave the committee copies of his income tax returns for the past seven years and a statement of his financial holdings. He declined to make the tax returns public, as requested by committee member Claiborne Pell (D R.I.) and Common Cause, but said the committee could do so if it wished.

Chairman Cannon opened the hearing with a pledge not to hold Ford's nomination "hostage" to domestic political warfare over the Watergate tapes and related issues. He said the committee should not consider Ford's voting record—even though members might disagree with it—since Congress should not deny the President the right to choose a man "whose philosophy and politics are virtually identical to his own." What it should consider, Cannon said, were Ford's views of the presidency itself and what he would do if he were president.

Ford, in his opening statement, said his public life was "an open book—carefully reread every two years by my constituents." Since his nomination Oct. 12 his private life had been opened as well, he said. He pledged to follow the late President Eisenhower's "simple rule for people in public office...do what's best for America."

His strongest point as Vice President, he said, would be his ability to serve as "a ready conciliator and calm communicator between the White House and Capitol Hill, between the re-election mandate of the Republican President and the equally emphatic mandate of the Democratic 93rd Congress."

His 25 years of experience in Congress, including nine as minority leader, and his 25-year friendship with President Nixon would help him bridge the gap, Ford said. He called that "the greatest single need of our country today," since many people "are beginning to worry about our national government becoming seriously weakened by partisan division."

Ford said his announced decision not to seek the presidency in 1976 if he was confirmed as vice president should help in that respect. "Nobody could accuse me of seeking personal political aggrandizement," he said.

Ford characterized his own political philosophy as "moderate in domestic affairs, conservative in fiscal affairs, and dyed-in-the-wool internationalist in foreign affairs." He said he considered national security the nation's top spending priority.

While Ford apparently made a favorable impression on the committee in his first round of questioning, as committee member Robert C. Byrd (D W.Va.), Senate majority whip, indicated to newsmen, he obviously did not satisfy some of them with his answers to questions regarding the sticky issues of executive privilege, impoundment and appointing a new Watergate prosecutor.

Executive Privilege. "I don't think any president has unlimited authority in the area of executive privilege," Ford said. "On the other hand, I don't think Congress, or the public generally, has any right to all personal and confidential conversations and documents of the presi-

dent.... We just have to take each case as it comes and do what is in the best interest of the country."

Ford agreed with Byrd that concealment of information where criminal behavior is involved would be obstruction of justice. "Where you have serious allegations of criminal behavior," Ford said, "where documents have an impact on the guilt or innocence of an individual, they should be made available."

National Security. On non-national security matters, he said, "there should be cooperation" in making information available to Congress or the courts. However, he defended the President's right to withhold information where national security is involved.

Watergate Prosecutor. Ford said he recognized the "constitutional and legal problems involved" in President Nixon's original refusal to turn over Watergate tapes to the special prosecutor on court orders. However, he said for political reasons he urged Nixon to do so, and was pleased Nixon eventually agreed.

He also stuck to the administration position that a new special prosecutor should be appointed by the attorney general, not by Congress or the courts, and said Nixon had agreed not to fire the prosecutor without the concurrence of a majority of an eight-member congressional group set up for the purpose.

"You can't prevent by law the dismissal of a person appointed by the President," Ford contended. He said he hoped the new Nixon proposal would satisfy demands for guarantees of independence.

Impoundment. Ford also defended a president's right to impound funds appropriated by Congress for programs. "A president shouldn't have to spend every dime Congress makes available for a program," Ford contended. "If we forced the president to do that, you'd have to have a tax increase of astronomical proportions." He said all presidents he had served with had impounded funds. "Impoundment could be the only way a president could get a program straightened out," he said.

If he were president and faced with a program he didn't agree with, Ford said "I hope my good judgment would tell me I should carry out the law" and appoint as administrator a person who would carry out at least the intent of the legislation.

Impeachment. In answer to a question by Mark O. Hatfield (R Ore.), Ford said he did not think Nixon's impoundment policies were grounds for impeachment, or that there were any other grounds for impeaching the President. However, he said the House Judiciary Committee's current inquiry into impeachment should continue, "to clear the air."

NOV. 5, 7

The only source of major allegations against Ford—former Washington lobbyist and author Robert N. Winter-Berger—testified under oath in closed session Nov. 7. After his appearance Committee Chairman Howard W. Cannon (D Nev.) said the committee did not consider Winter-Berger a credible witness and might refer his testimony to the Justice Department for investigation on perjury charges.

Virtually every committee member praised Ford's cooperation and candor in answering questions. Ten members of the House of Representatives testified Nov. 5 on his behalf, and the committee appeared ready to act favorably, perhaps unanimously, on the nomination. Cannon said he would be "very surprised if we find any roadblocks" to Ford's nomination.

The questions Nov. 5 dealt mainly with how Ford would act if he were president. The committee sought to ascertain Ford's views on foreign affairs, the energy crisis, the Supreme Court, busing, the press, selecting advisers, and his understanding of the characteristics of presidential leadership.

Foreign Affairs. Ford approved U.S. initiatives toward detente with China and Russia, and said he would favor moving closer to the Arab states, Cuba and Sweden if areas of dialogue were found.

Ford emphasized his strong support of Israel and of Nixon's $2.2-billion request for aid to Israel. However, he said he did not think the United States should "guarantee" Israel's borders.

Watergate. Ford said he did not think a president should try to prevent or obstruct an investigation into the executive branch, and said he thought Nixon should turn over all tapes and documents necessary to clear up the question of his involvement in the Watergate scandals, to help "save his presidency." Ford personally believed the President was innocent of any involvement, he reiterated.

If the president resigned, could the vice president halt or prevent an investigation into the president's affairs, Ford was asked. "I don't think the public would stand for it," he replied. Ford also said he understood why former Attorney General Elliot L. Richardson resigned rather than fire Special Watergate Prosecutor Archibald Cox on Nixon's demand. Ford said if he were in Richardson's position he probably would have done the same.

Energy Crisis. Ford said it was "almost incomprehensible" to him why the United States was so "negligent" for so long about developing cleaner coal-burning capability. He urged greater spending for research into development of domestic fuel resources to help avoid dependence on foreign oil.

Presidential Advisers. Ford said he would seek "strong input" from members of the House and Senate if he were president and needed advice. "There is a great reservoir of knowledge and good judgment there," he said. As for picking staff advisers, Ford said "to my knowledge, no person I've ever employed has made any mistakes; I've never had to fire anyone." With evidence of illegal or unethical conduct, he would fire any staff member, he said.

The Courts. "Even though I have strong differences of opinion with some members of the Supreme Court and other federal courts," Ford said he opposed proposals to require periodic reappointment or reconfirmation of judges. That would "undercut the independence of the judiciary," Ford said. "I think that independence is important even though I don't always agree with them."

Busing. "If the federal courts persist in trying to have forced busing to achieve racial balance in the public schools and there is no other way we could remedy that," Ford said he would favor a constitutional amendment prohibiting busing. However, he said he felt the courts were beginning to recognize that busing is not the answer to improved education. He preferred compensatory educa-

tion for the disadvantaged instead, Ford said. "Forced busing has caused more trouble and more tension where it has happened than almost anything else in our society."

Presidential Qualities. A president "has to be a person of great truth, and the American people have to believe that he's truthful," Ford said. "...A man of thought, not impetuous. People have to have faith that he's thoughtful and won't shoot from the hip. He has to live his life by the standards, moral and ethical, by which most people live their lives." It is difficult for a president to appear humble; he has to appear to be forceful and strong, Ford said. But he said it is not a sign of weakness to acknowledge mistakes, and a president should be willing to do so.

The Media. "I can't imagine me going out and attacking the press" as former Vice President Spiro T. Agnew did, Ford said. He said he had good relations with the press and did not share what Cannon called "Nixon's blanket condemnation of the media." He agreed the media were the "most significant contributors" in exposing the Watergate scandal.

Winter-Berger Allegations. The Rules Committee members questioned Ford almost apologetically about what one called the "only diversion" in otherwise "constructive" hearings: the allegations of Robert Winter-Berger. They interrogated Winter-Berger for an entire day behind closed doors.

Winter-Berger claimed in a 1972 book, *The Washington Payoff,* and in a sworn affidavit that Ford granted favors in return for campaign contributions, "laundered" campaign contributions, accepted $15,000 in cash from Winter-Berger, and was treated "for at least a year" by a New York psychotherapist, Dr. Arnold Hutschnecker, for irritability, nervousness and depression resulting from the pressures of his job as House minority leader.

Although Winter-Berger told newsmen he stood behind his charges, Cannon said he offered no documentation to prove any of them. He said Winter-Berger could not have "loaned" Ford $15,000 from his personal income between 1966 and 1969, one of the committee's principal concerns, because Winter-Berger's subpoenaed tax returns showed he listed gross income of only $14,076, $7,615, $1,643 and $4,912 for those years. Confronted with the returns, Cannon said, Winter-Berger changed his story and said 90 per cent of the $15,000 paid to Ford was "borrowed" from another lobbyist, the late Nathan Voloshen.

Ford, in his testimony, pointed out that Winter-Berger himself said in his book that he "never knew Ford to accept cash from anybody." Ford also produced records to show that Ford's insurance paid most of his wife's medical bills between 1966 and 1969, which Winter-Berger had said caused Ford's need for money.

Ford said he always did what any congressman does in assisting constituents and friends, but denied that he ever accepted payments for favors. He said he knew of only one Winter-Berger "client" he helped, a well-known Dutch doctor seeking immigrant status. Ford said records showed Winter-Berger made only one $500 contribution to any of his campaigns. Ford also denied he covered up campaign contributions or violated any campaign finance laws.

As for Dr. Hutschnecker, Ford testified he dropped in at the psychotherapist's office once for a 15-minute social chat, at Winter-Berger's insistence, and the doctor may have dropped in at Ford's office once. He denied he ever needed or received psychiatric treatment, since he is "disgustingly sane" and his "mental attitude gets better under pressure."

Hutschnecker also denied he ever treated Ford, and called Winter-Berger's charges "lies" or "fantasies." Winter-Berger also said Hutschnecker had treated President Nixon for several years. The friend who introduced Ford to Winter-Berger, Alice Boter Weston Schowalter, denied she was paid $1,000 to do so.

NOV. 14

The committee Nov. 14 heard five witnesses. Three, for differing reasons, urged that Ford not be confirmed, one supported him, and one cited his "narrow-gauge approach" to civil rights.

Rauh. Joseph L. Rauh, Jr., national vice chairman of Americans for Democratic Action (ADA), made the strongest attack of the hearings on Ford's record and character. He urged Congress to reject Ford and let Nixon nominate a better candidate.

Rauh said Ford's record on civil rights was as bad as the records of Clement F. Haynsworth Jr. and G. Harrold Carswell, Nixon nominees to the Supreme Court who were rejected by the Senate. Indeed, Rauh said, Ford "compares unfavorably...when one considers his northern surroundings."

In addition, Rauh charged, Ford's overall voting record was "much worse than the Nixon administration record generally, not to mention his total lack of experience in foreign affairs, his attack on the judiciary (in his impeachment effort against Supreme Court Justice William O. Douglas), and his pre-judgment (in Nixon's favor) of the Watergate scandal."

Rauh called Ford "a divisive influence who has fought civil rights legislation at every turn." He said Ford was a "final passage man" in civil rights and social legislation—consistently seeking to gut or cripple bills in early stages, then voting for them in final form after passage became certain.

Mitchell. Clarence Mitchell, director of the Washington bureau of the National Association for the Advancement of Colored People, made the same assessment. In addition, he said, Ford had "associated himself with groups in Michigan and across the country who want to turn back the clock on civil rights."

The two black witnesses, Mitchell and Maurice Dawkins, and two Republican committee members, Mark O. Hatfield (Ore.) and Hugh Scott (Pa.), expressed hope Ford would "grow" in his views on civil rights if he became vice president or president, as they said President Lyndon B. Johnson did.

Abzug. Rep. Abzug called for a special election for vice president, and George Washington University law professor John F. Banzhaf III said Ford should not be confirmed until "the suspicious and highly questionable circumstances surrounding (former Vice President) Spiro T. Agnew's forced resignation" were investigated.

Dawkins, speaking for Opportunities Industrialization Centers (OIC), a manpower development organization, endorsed Ford for his support of OIC and other "good work."

Committee Action

The nine-member Rules and Administration Committee after three days of public hearings, nine closed sessions and what it called the most exhaustive FBI investigation in U.S. history of a candidate for public office, concluded unanimously Nov. 20 that it "found no bar or impediment which would disqualify" Ford for the office of vice president. The committee's report (Exec Rept 93-26) was issued Nov. 23.

Not all members agreed with Ford's voting record, political philosophy or public actions in his 25 years in the House. Nor did they necessarily agree he was the best Republican Nixon could have chosen, they noted in the report. But after exploring Ford's philosophy, character, personal and financial integrity, they found that "in these critical areas he fully met reasonable tests."

The committee considered its job "no less important than the selection of a potential president," said Chairman Howard W. Cannon (D Nev.), and members, taking into account public calls for Nixon's impeachment or resignation, did question Ford as if he were a nominee for president rather than vice president.

Areas of Concern. In addition to Ford's views on foreign and domestic policy, executive privilege, impoundment of congressionally appropriated funds, the Watergate affair and other controversial topics, the committee sought information in four principal areas of concern: Ford's personal finances, charges of irregularities in financing his re-election campaigns in 1970 and 1972, allegations of influence-peddling, and a report that Ford had been treated by a psychotherapist because the pressures of his job as House minority leader had allegedly caused him to become nervous, irritable and depressed.

Committee Findings. No violations of law or irregularities were found by the FBI or the committee in Ford's personal or political financial affairs, the report said. The other allegations against him were denied by Ford and other persons involved, and since no evidence was produced to support the charges, the committee said it could not accept them. Ford's principal accuser, former Washington lobbyist Robert N. Winter-Berger, made contradictory statements under oath and failed to produce documents, as promised, to prove his charges, the committee said. The committee labeled Winter-Berger "not a credible witness" and agreed unanimously to submit his testimony to the Justice Department for possible prosecution for perjury and contempt of Congress.

Ford's Finances. Because Agnew's resignation from the vice presidency resulted from improper financial dealings, the committee delved especially deeply into Ford's finances. His income tax returns were examined and audited, but the committee decided not to make them public since other public officials had not been required to disclose theirs.

Records from Ford's tax accountant showed Ford's gross income had averaged more than $75,000 a year since 1967. His salary as minority leader was $49,500 a year, with the remainder coming mainly from honoraria for speeches and appearances, Ford testified. He listed honoraria of $32,000 in 1967, $30,000 in 1968, $28,000 in 1969, $47,000 in 1970, $22,000 in 1971 and $18,000 in 1972.

Previous Vacancies in the Vice Presidency

Vice President	Term Elected	Date of Vacancy	Reason	President
George Clinton (R)	1809-1813	4/20/1812	Death	James Madison
Elbridge Gerry (R)	1813-1817	11/23/1814	Death	James Madison
John C. Calhoun (D)	1829-1833	12/28/1832	Resignation	Andrew Jackson
John Tyler (Whig)	1841-1845	4/ 6/1841	Succeeded to presidency on death of President Harrison	William Henry Harrison
Millard Fillmore (Whig)	1849-1853	7/10/1850	Succeeded to presidency on death of President Taylor	Zachary Taylor
William King (D)	1853-1857	4/18/1853	Death	Franklin Pierce
Andrew Johnson (R)	1865-1869	4/15/1865	Succeeded to presidency following assassination of President Lincoln	Abraham Lincoln
Henry Wilson (R)	1873-1877	11/22/1875	Death	Ulysses S. Grant
Chester A. Arthur (R)	1881-1885	9/20/1881	Succeeded to presidency following assassination of President Garfield	James A. Garfield
Thomas Hendricks (D)	1885-1889	11/25/1885	Death	Grover Cleveland
Garrett A. Hobart (R)	1897-1901	11/21/1899	Death	William McKinley
Theodore Roosevelt (R)	1901-1905	9/14/1901	Succeeded to presidency following assassination of President McKinley	William McKinley
James S. Sherman (R)	1909-1913	10/30/1912	Death	William Howard Taft
Calvin Coolidge (R)	1921-1925	8/ 3/1923	Succeeded to presidency on death of President Harding	Warren G. Harding
Harry S Truman (D)	1945-1949	4/12/1945	Succeeded to presidency on death of President Roosevelt	Franklin D. Roosevelt
Lyndon B. Johnson (D)	1961-1965	11/22/1963	Succeeded to presidency following assassination of President Kennedy	John F. Kennedy

Ford's (and Mrs. Ford's) net worth was $256,378 on Sept. 30, the records showed. Of that, $162,000 was in real estate (the family home in Alexandria, Va., a vacation condominium in Vail, Colo., and a two-family rental dwelling in Grand Rapids, Mich.) and $13,570 was from stocks.

The Internal Revenue Service audit of Ford's tax returns turned up one "business expense" deduction which it disallowed: $871.44 for clothing Ford bought for the 1972 Republican national convention, over which he presided. As a result, Ford paid $435.77 in additional tax, without penalty, on Nov. 9.

Allen View. Committee member James B. Allen (D Ala.) said the committee should have taken a more affirmative approach in its report. Rather than simply saying it found no reasons not to approve Ford, Allen said it should have stressed Ford's reputation as "a man of honor and high principle, a man of ability and dedication, a man of noble purpose and unimpeachable integrity."

He called Ford "an excellent choice."

Floor Action

The Senate Nov. 27, by a 92-3 roll-call vote, approved the nomination.

The overwhelming vote for Ford came one week after the Rules and Administration Committee unanimously recommended his confirmation, and six and a half weeks after his nomination Oct. 12 by President Nixon to replace former Vice President Spiro T. Agnew.

The only votes against Ford were cast by three Democrats: Gaylord Nelson (Wis.), Thomas F. Eagleton (Mo.) and William D. Hathaway (Maine). Five senators were absent: George McGovern (D S.D.), Stuart Symington (D Mo.), Paul J. Fannin (R Ariz.), Edward J. Gurney (R Fla.) and James A. McClure (R Idaho).

Symington, Fannin and Gurney would have voted for Ford if present, it was announced.

Debate on Ford's nomination Nov. 26 and 27 brought many statements of praise for his honesty, integrity and candor. A number of Democrats stressed that their votes to confirm Ford did not imply endorsement of his political philosophy or voting record. But they felt the President had a right to nominate a man who shared his views, and that Ford had successfully met the tests of character demanded by the office.

Several senators expressed the belief or hope that Ford would grow in stature in the vice presidency and that his views on civil rights, criticized in the hearings, would broaden.

"Frankly, I am astonished to hear myself, a lifelong Democrat, support a Republican for vice president," said Alan Cranston (D Calif.). Cranston said Nov. 26 he had surveyed several hundred persons about Ford and found only five who opposed him, and none who questioned his honesty. Cranston was impressed with the "almost startling consensus of conciliation" developing around Ford, who he said "has come into focus as someone who appears to offer the nation a steadiness and a dependability for which it yearns."

"I doubt if there has ever before been a time when integrity has so surpassed ideology in the judging of a man for so high an office in our land," Cranston said.

Philip A. Hart (D Mich.) said Nov. 27 he disagreed with Ford's voting record but maintained the nominee "would be a steady, decent and believable chief executive. And those attributes, I believe, are what this nation needs most at this particular moment in history."

Robert Taft Jr. (R Ohio): "When questioned (at the committee hearings) about matters such as executive privilege, separation of powers, presidential immunity, the (Watergate) special prosecutor and the missing tapes, Mr. Ford demonstrated a respect for not only the letter of the law but the spirit of the law."

Gaylord Nelson, however, found his philosophical differences with Ford too fundamental to compromise, he said Nov. 27. He cited Ford's record on human and civil rights and the war in Vietnam, and said he did not believe Ford could provide "the kind of inspirational leadership this nation will need should he succeed to the presidency."

Eagleton also questioned Ford's leadership ability.

Hathaway said Nov. 26 his negative vote was not based on Ford's character or qualifications but on his view that a president undergoing impeachment investigation should not be allowed to appoint a successor, and that the country should not be governed for a prolonged period by an appointed chief executive. If Nixon left office, Ford would be the first non-elected president in U.S. history, and a "dangerous constitutional precedent" would be set, Hathaway said. He urged the Senate to withhold confirmation and pass his bill (S 2678) providing for a special election when both the presidency and the vice presidency were vacant.

House Action

Hearings

The House Judiciary Committee held hearings Nov. 15-26 on the Ford nomination.

NOV. 15-16

Before Ford could give his opening statement, Rep. John Conyers Jr. (D Mich.) objected to proceeding on the nomination. Robert W. Kastenmeier (D Wis.) and Don Edwards (D Calif.) expressed the same view.

"It is totally inappropriate for the Congress to expedite action on a nomination submitted by a President who is the subject of a serious impeachment inquiry and whose credibility has been so irretrievably damaged that even members of his own party are calling on him to resign," Conyers said.

Committee Schedule. It appeared the House committee would have difficulty finishing its hearings by Nov. 21, the deadline set by Rodino. He planned evening sessions if necessary. With 38 members on the committee, 21 Democrats and 17 Republicans, all lawyers, it took hours to complete a single round of questions.

In addition, there were occasional eruptions of the committee infighting which had preceded the opening of the hearings. Conyers and Rep. Jerome R. Waldie (D Calif.) were incensed that only eight members of the committee had been allowed to read the 1,700-page FBI "raw files" of data collected in the investigation of Ford—especially when Rep. Thomas F. Railsback (R Ill.) read at length laudatory statements made to the FBI in praise of Ford including remarks by Sens. George McGovern (S.D.), Edmund S. Muskie (Maine), United Auto Workers President Leonard Woodcock, and Ford's opponent in his last election.

Rodino ruled out of order a Conyers motion to make the entire FBI file part of the record of the hearings.

Ford Statement. Ford reiterated his beliefs in looking forward rather than backward, in truthfulness and in "friendly compromise." He stated his continued support for President Nixon, but pledged to be his own man and to tell the President when he thought he was wrong. He agreed Nixon was having credibility problems, and said he had advised him to release the Watergate tapes, meet with members of Congress, hold more press conferences and get out among the people to try to restore public confidence.

Ford said he thought his 25 years of service in Congress were "fine training" for the presidency, if he should succeed to that office; Presidents Johnson, Kennedy and Truman came from Congress and "will go down in history as better-than-good presidents. I would think my odds might be the same," Ford said. He said his background in foreign affairs was at least equal to that of previous vice presidents.

NOV. 19-21

The Senate committee's unanimous vote for Ford came as some Democratic members of the House panel continued to demonstrate their concerns about the nominee, who would be "one heartbeat, or one impeachment, away from the presidency," as Rep. Charles B. Rangel (D N.Y.) put it.

Concerns were expressed about Ford's record on civil rights, civil liberties and social programs, and his overall qualifications for leadership, based on the assumption of some members that Ford would succeed to the presidency because of the impeachment or resignation of President Nixon. Said George E. Danielson (D Calif.): "I'm thinking you're going to be president within a year."

Criteria. Several committee members discussed and questioned witnesses as to just what role the House should play in its first vice presidential confirmation proceedings. During the hearings, the committee explored such questions as:

● Should the House follow confirmation procedures similar to those followed by the Senate for routine executive branch nominations? Or does the 25th Amendment (providing for vice presidential selection) give it a broader mandate and responsibility to participate in the choice, as argued on Nov. 19 by Joseph L. Rauh Jr., national vice chairman of Americans for Democratic Action.

● Does the president have the right to nominate his own man—one of his philosophy and principles? Or does the Congress have the mandate to consider and possibly reject the man because of views and voting it disagrees with, as John Conyers Jr. (D Mich.) asked each witness.

● Should Congress approve Ford simply because he had been a member for 25 years, rose to a position of leadership there, and was generally regarded as an honest, decent human being? Or should it demand special qualities of national leadership and excellence that Michael J. Harrington (D Mass.) said Ford lacked.

● Was President Nixon's right to nominate a potential successor clouded, even negated, as some Democrats contended, because he was under threat of impeachment?

Ford Qualifications. Even Jerome R. Waldie (D Calif.), the only committee member to state in hearings that he would vote against Ford, said he was "terribly impressed" with Ford's honesty and candor, summing up what many members of Congress held up as assets of Ford and of a good vice president.

But "in considering the qualifications of a man who stands a greater likelihood of assuming the presidency than any other vice president in our history, honesty and decency are not enough," contended Harrington, the lead-off witness Nov. 19 against Ford.

He said Ford had not demonstrated the "extraordinary leadership capabilities" needed today. He suggested Nixon made an "in-House" nomination because he figured, apparently correctly, that it would be approved easily by Congress. Harrington said he deplored the "Washington-talking-to-Washington" atmosphere of the Ford hearings. Further, he argued that Ford did not measure up to the expectation of the American people, even allowing for the "conservative mandate" of the 1972 presidential election.

Several committee members said the country should not expect a "Messiah," "a superhuman," a "matinee idol" or a "perfect man." They indicated they thought Ford was about as good a choice as Nixon could have made, and suggested, to his detractors, that he might "grow" in the job.

Civil Rights. Several committee members and witnesses attacked Ford's record. Ford defended himself emphatically, saying, "I'm actually proud of my civil rights voting record, and I'm proud of my personal attitude vis-a-vis minority groups."

Clarence Mitchell of the National Association for the Advancement of Colored People (NAACP) said he could not recall any positive or affirmative action Ford ever took as House minority leader for civil rights. He said Nov. 19 that Ford had worked to gut several key civil rights bills, and described him as "restricted," not "committed," on civil rights.

Civil Liberties. Waldie said one of the main reasons he opposed Ford was that Ford's 1970 attempt to impeach Supreme Court Justice William O. Douglas showed Ford was "insensitive" in civil liberties areas and did not understand or accept the independence of the judiciary. That, Waldie said, "could be the most important weakness of all" in a man who could become president and appoint justices to the high court.

Rep. Edward P. Boland (D Mass.), a friend and colleague of Ford's for 21 years, Nov. 19 testified on his behalf, and the National Lawyers Guild opposed the nomination on grounds the 1972 election was illegal and Nixon therefore had no right to appoint Ford.

Committee Action

The House Judiciary Committee Nov. 29 voted 29-8 to report favorably the nomination.

Before voting, Don Edwards (D Calif.) urged rejection of Ford because of his "dismal" record on civil rights, "inappropriate associates," and lack of "high intelligence, great sensitivity and judgment." He and Jerome R. Waldie (D Calif.) criticized Ford for "improper" activities in his 1970 attempt to impeach Supreme Court Justice William O. Douglas.

Jack Brooks (D Texas) urged support for Ford despite political differences. He said Ford was honest, moral and candid, and "if he does become president, he'll be a heck of a lot better than the one we've got." Republicans Lawrence J. Hogan (Md.) and Tom Railsback (Ill.) also praised Ford.

Edward Hutchinson (Mich.), the committee's ranking Republican member, made the motion to report the nomination with the recommendation that the House

Former Member Represents Ford

The constant presence of former Rep. William C. Cramer (R Fla.) with Rep. Gerald R. Ford (R Mich.) at Ford's vice presidential confirmation hearings by the House Judiciary Committee raised the ire of two committee members.

The committee ended its hearings Nov. 26 and approved the nomination Nov. 29.

Reps. Don Edwards (D Calif.) and John Conyers Jr. (D Mich.) expressed their concern that Ford, if he became president, might appoint Cramer to a high position in his administration—possibly attorney general, Edwards suggested.

Conyers said Nov. 26 he was "deeply disturbed" about the sort of people Ford might appoint, based on his conservative associations. Cramer was the only one he mentioned by name. Conyers said Cramer had a well-known anti-civil rights record in Congress from 1955 to 1971.

Edwards pointed out daily during the hearings that Ford was accompanied by Cramer, now a Washington lawyer, and his two law partners. Ford said they were assisting him without compensation, and denied he had made any job commitments. However, Ford said: "I happen to believe he (Cramer) is a very able lawyer and was an extremely competent legislator, and I would have no hesitancy to recommend his appointment to any job in the administration."

Edwards, an old-time foe of Cramer's in congressional civil rights fights, asked a witness at the hearing, Clarence Mitchell of the National Association for the Advancement of Colored People, what he would think of Cramer as attorney general.

"On the Judiciary Committee Mr. Cramer was a very able lawyer. He was always able to come up with a little insertion which would have the effect of nullifying the bill if enacted," Mitchell said. "Each time there was an opportunity to cut off a little bit of civil rights, Mr. Cramer would be for it. It would be most unfortunate if he had a position where he had anything at all to do with civil rights." Mitchell also criticized Ford's civil rights record.

Cramer, from St. Petersburg, Fla., was the first Republican elected to the House from Florida since Reconstruction, and was known as his state's "Mr. Republican." He defeated Federal Judge G. Harrold Carswell for the Republican nomination for the Senate in 1970 but lost the election to Democrat Lawton Chiles.

confirm Ford. Voting fot it were 12 Democrats and all the committee's 17 Republicans:

Democrats: Rodino (N.J.), Donohue (Mass.), Brooks (Texas), Hungate (Mo.), Eilberg (Pa.), Flowers (Ala.), Mann (S.C.), Sarbanes (Md.), Danielson (Calif.), Thornton (Ark.), Owens (Utah) (by proxy) and Mezvinsky (Iowa).

Republicans: Hutchinson, McClory (Ill.), Smith (N.Y.), Sandman (N.J.), Railsback (Ill.), Wiggins (Calif.), Dennis (Ind.), Fish (N.Y.), Mayne (Iowa) (by proxy),

Hogan (Md.), Keating (Ohio), Butler (Va.), Cohen (Maine), Lott (Miss.), Froehlich (Wis.), Moorhead (Calif.) and Maraziti (N.J.).

Those voting against Ford were all Democrats: Kastenmeier (Wis.), Edwards (Calif.), Conyers (Mich.), Waldie (Calif.), Drinan (Mass.), Rangel (N.Y.) (by proxy); Jordan (Texas) and Holtzman (N.Y.).

John F. Seiberling (D Ohio) voted present, saying he had "very serious problems" with the Ford nomination, and would reserve judgment on it until the floor vote, tentatively scheduled for Dec. 6. Joshua Eilberg (D Pa.) voted to report out the nomination but said his vote did not necessarily mean he would vote for Ford on the floor.

Before voting to report the Ford nomination, the committee rejected, 5-33, a motion by Elizabeth Holtzman (D N.Y.) to table the nomination.

Report. The committee filed its report on the nomination Dec. 4 (H Rept 93-695). After reviewing the commitee's investigation, the report concluded: "Finally, not every member of the committee subscribing to this report finds himself in complete agreement with the totality of Mr. Ford's voting record, or even with all aspects of his general philosophy of government. Some, though by no means all, are disturbed with elements of his voting record in the area of civil rights and human rights.

"But looking at the total record, the committee finds Mr. Ford fit and qualified to hold the high office for which he has been nominated pursuant to the Twenty-fifth Amendment."

Each of the eight members who voted against Ford filed dissenting views. Seiberling, who voted present, filed separate views in which he suggested that the proceedings on the Ford nomination had "already brought out sufficient flaws in the 25th Amendment to justify a new search for a better way to handle the problem of presidential succession. Such a search should include consideration as to whether it is necessary even to have a Vice President, since, except as a replacement for the President, it is an unnecessary office."

Floor Action

The House Dec. 6, by a 387-35 recorded vote, approved the nomination of Ford to be vice president of the United States.

The historic vote completing the confirmation process of the nation's 40th vice president came after five hours of floor debate. It was the first time the House of Representatives had participated in a confirmation proceeding, and the first time a vice president was selected under provisions of the 25th Amendment to the Constitution.

The overwhelming 387-35 vote confirming Ford was foreshadowed by the debate. Republican members lined up at the microphones to announce their support for Ford and ask permission to place lengthier statements in the record. They were joined by many Democrats who praised Ford's honesty and integrity even though they had political differences. Some speakers said they expected Ford to become president and that he could help restore the faith of the people in their government.

Main arguments of the opposition were that Ford lacked the qualities of leadership needed in a president, that he was insensitive to the needs of the poor and the black and to the rule of law, and that no nomination should be considered at all until the question of impeaching President Nixon was settled. All the votes against him were cast by Democrats.

Unexpected Votes. The only surprises punctuating the otherwise predictable debate were the announcements by Judiciary Committee Chairman Peter W. Rodino Jr. (D N.J.) that he would vote against Ford, and by Andrew Young (D Ga.) that he would vote for him. Young was the only black member of the House who supported Ford, whose record on civil rights was attacked during his confirmation hearings.

Young was applauded by the heavily pro-Ford House when he broke with "the colleagues I respect most" to support Ford "as an act of faith and hope. I hope and pray he measures up" and can restore public confidence in government through his personal integrity, Young said, although he admitted that "if Ford had had his way on the Voting Rights Act of 1965, I wouldn't be in the House today."

Rodino, who conducted the House hearings on Ford and voted to report his nomination favorably to the floor, had given no indication he planned to vote against Ford. However, having done his duty as Judiciary Committee chairman, Rodino said the needs of his urban constituents "cry out for executive leadership in the area of human rights and the cause of working people.... I vote, not against Gerald Ford's worth as a man of great integrity, but in dissent with the present administration's indifference to the plight of so many Americans."

Nixon Resignation Considered. Despite several last-minute appeals to the House not to put the nation in the position of having a non-elected president and vice president (if Ford should succeed Nixon during his term and then name his own successor), the House became impatient to vote by late afternoon. Several members, however, protested that the debate and their votes were meaningless since the swearing-in ceremony already had been scheduled and television time set.

"This vote will come back to haunt the House just as have past votes based purely on expediency," said Parren J. Mitchell (D Md.), a member of the congressional black caucus. "I can't stop it. A handful of people over here can't stop it.

"We're all going to smile and say Gerald Ford is a good man," said Mitchell, "but can he drag us out of the quagmire we're in? You know he can't." Mitchell said he doubted Ford could provide leadership to the 22 million black Americans who felt "abandoned by this administration" or the million black Americans who "slipped back into poverty" in 1972.

Jerome R. Waldie (D Calif.) said he doubted Ford could measure up to the "incomparably more difficult job" he would have than any vice president in history, "because no presidency will have been left in the shambles that this presidency will have been left in" when the "inevitable" resignation or impeachment of Nixon occurred.

Gerald R. Ford: House Career, Voting Record, 1949-73

Elected to Congress in 1948, Rep. Gerald R. Ford (R Mich.) first won national attention in 1963, when he was elected chairman of the House Republican Conference. That election was a victory for "young Turks" of Republican ranks in the House, who ousted 67-year-old Charles B. Hoeven (R Iowa 1943-65) from the post.

Ford's election was engineered by three representatives who subsequently went widely separate ways: Melvin R. Laird (Wis. 1953-69), a counselor to President Nixon; Charles E. Goodell (N.Y. 1959-68), named a senator in 1968 but defeated in an election bid in 1970, partly because of White House opposition, and Sen. Robert P. Griffin of Michigan.

In 1965, Ford was elected House minority leader, ousting Charles A. Halleck (Ind. 1935-69). Again, Ford's election was engineered by Laird, Goodell and Griffin. The secret ballot vote was close: 73 to 67.

"The southerners really loved Charlie Halleck," Rep. John J. Rhodes (R Ariz.), Ford's successor as minority leader, recalled. "When Jerry came in, there was a kind of stand-offish attitude. For the first few years, he (Ford) didn't have too kindly an attitude toward them. But in recent years, there have been closer relations on some issues."

"I had many sharp differences of opinion with him when he first became minority leader," Rep. James Harvey (R Mich.) said. "In recent years, he has shown more of a mellowness in accepting differences of opinion within the party. Now he knows some people have to vote differently."

The growth of Ford's tolerance for differing opinions also was reflected by the comment of Speaker Carl Albert (D Okla.), who had enjoyed a close personal relationship with Ford. "I think I was the first in Congress to tell the President that Jerry would be the easiest vice-presidential candidate to sell to the House," he said. "He's a very fine man to work with. I think he earned this."

Albert held the job to which, according to many accounts, Ford had long aspired. But he had been mentioned in years past as a possible vice presidential candidate. His name was suggested in 1960, for example, when Nixon ran the first time and settled on Henry Cabod Lodge as his running mate.

Ford remained a strong administration loyalist. In 1971, in response to bitter criticism of Agnew by Rep. William Clay (D Mo.), he defended the then Vice President by denouncing Clay's language in a House speech.

Ford was permanent chairman of the Republican national conventions of both 1968 and 1972.

Voting Record

Ford's voting record during his 25 years in the House was conservative, on some issues even more conservative than the 1973 stance of the Nixon administration. He had been almost unwaveringly loyal to Republican presidents and to the Republican Party.

Ford opposed minimum wage bills in 1960, 1966 and 1973. He voted against Medicare in 1965 and against creation of the Office of Economic Opportunity in 1964. A consistent opponent of farm bills, Ford had a record of

Ford's Biography

Profession: Attorney.
Born: July 14, 1913, Omaha, Neb.
Home: Grand Rapids, Mich.
Religion: Episcopal.
Education: University of Michigan, B. A., 1935; Yale University Law School, LL. B, 1941.
Offices: House of Representatives since 1949.
Military: U.S. Navy in World War II.
Memberships: Interparliamentary Union, U.S.-Canadian Interparliamentary Group, American Legion, VFW, AMVETS, Masons, Elks, Rotary.
Family: Wife, Elizabeth; four children.

Committees: House minority leader since 1965; Appropriations Committee, 1951-65; Public Works Committee, 1949-50.

Career Highlights: Ford was a star of the University of Michigan's undefeated, national championship football teams of 1932 and 1933. In 1934, he was voted the Michigan Wolverines' most valuable player. As a law student at Yale, he served as assistant varsity football coach.

In 1949, the year he entered the House, he was selected by the U.S. Junior Chamber of Commerce as one of the country's 10 outstanding young men.

The American Political Science Association gave Ford its distinguished congressional service award in 1961.

In 1963, he was chosen chairman of the House Republican Conference. In 1965, he was elected minority leader, defeating the incumbent, former Rep. Charles A. Halleck (R Ind.). He was permanent chairman of the 1968 and 1972 Republican national conventions.

Ford was appointed by President Johnson in November 1963 to serve on the Warren Commission to investigate the assassination of President Kennedy. Ford collaborated with John R. Stiles in 1965 to write a book, *Portrait of an Assassin*, about his findings while on the commission.

fiscal conservatism on other matters also. In 1963, for example, he voted against a tax cut pushed by President Kennedy to stimulate the economy.

Presidential Support. Up to the time of his nomination as vice president, Ford was one of only 70 Republicans to vote to sustain all of President Nixon's vetoes in 1973. A Congressional Quarterly tabulation made during Congress' August recess showed Ford had voted with the President 83 per cent of the time during the year. Only Rep. Barber B. Conable Jr. (R N.Y.) had a higher record of presidential support, and that was only 1 per cent higher.

In the 92nd Congress, Ford had an 80 per cent presidential support record. In 1972, he voted to override the President's veto of a $24.7-billion water pollution authorization bill, but there were only 23 votes cast to sustain the President's position.

Split on Transit. Ford's most significant break with the Nixon administration in 1973—a decision apparently related to Ford's residence in the auto-producing state of Michigan—came on mass transit legislation. Ford voted against an administration-supported proposal to permit use of $700-million a year in highway trust fund money for mass transit projects in urban areas.

Vote Ratings. Ford had a high record of voting participation. In 11 of the past 20 years he had taken a position on 90 per cent or more of all House recorded votes.

Predictably, Ford's voting record was rated high by conservative groups and low by liberal organizations. The Americans for Conservative Action gave Ford high marks for every year since 1969, and even in that year he scored 53 per cent with the organization. The Americans for Democratic Action, a liberal group, rated Ford as voting with its positions less than 16 per cent of the time in every year since 1961.

A Congressional Quarterly tabulation showed Ford could be relied upon often by the conservative coalition of southern Democrats and Republicans, when this group formed against Democrats from other parts of the country. But Ford split away from the southern coalition on civil rights issues.

Key Votes. Ford's record on key issues votes in the House, 1949-1973:

Agriculture

1953. Soil Conservation (HR 5227). Amendment to fiscal 1954 agriculture appropriations bill reducing funds for the soil conservation program from $195-million to $140-million. Rejected 196-201 (R 152-54; D 44-146), May 20. Ford VOTED FOR.

1955. Price Supports (HR 12). Bill replacing flexible price supports of 75 to 90 per cent of parity with rigid supports at 90 per cent of parity for five basic farm crops. Passed 206-201 (R 21-172; D 185-29), May 5. Ford VOTED AGAINST.

1958. Price Supports (S J Res 162). Bill preventing reductions in price supports and acreage allotments for all farm commodities below 1957 levels. Passed 211-172 (R 44-41; D 167-31), March 20. Ford VOTED AGAINST.

1959. REA Loans (S 144). Bill transferring from the secretary of agriculture to the administrator of the Rural Electrification Administration (REA) authority to approve or disapprove REA loans. Failed to pass over veto 280-146 (R 6-142; D 274-4), April 30. Ford VOTED AGAINST.

1962. Farm Bill (HR 12391). Conference report on bill authorizing one-year programs to reduce corn, other feed grain and wheat surpluses and to establish a supply management program for wheat. Adopted 202-197 (R 2-160; D 200-37), Sept. 20. Ford VOTED AGAINST.

1963. Cotton Subsidy (HR 6196). Bill authorizing subsidy program for domestic cotton mills in order to eliminate the competitive inequity between raw cotton prices on the world market and those on the domestic market. Passed 216-182 (R 34-134; D 182-48), Dec. 4. Ford VOTED AGAINST.

1970. Farm Bill (HR 18546). Bill providing three-year price support program for wool, wheat, feed grains and cotton. Bill also provided for a dairy program and

limited subsidy payments to $55,000 per crop. Passed 212-171: R 86-88; D 126-85), Aug. 5. Ford VOTED FOR.

1973. Emergency Loans (HR 1975). Amendment to emergency farm loan bill allowing eligible farmers in 555 counties designated by the secretary of agriculture to apply for emergency disaster loans. Adopted 196-190 (R 19-139; D 177-21), Feb. 22. Ford VOTED AGAINST.

1973. Price Supports (HR 8619). Amendment to fiscal 1974 agricultural appropriations bill reducing 1974 price support ceilings from $55,000 per crop to $20,000 per person. Adopted 195-157 (R 109-50; D 86-107), June 15. Ford VOTED AGAINST.

Civil Rights, States' Rights

1949. Poll Tax (HR 3199). Bill outlawing payment of a poll tax as a prerequisite for voting in federal elections. Passed 273-116 (R 121-24; D 151-92), July 26. Ford VOTED FOR.

1956. School Desegregation (HR 7535). Amendment to a school construction aid bill prohibiting allotment of funds to states failing to comply with the 1954 Supreme Court decision on school desegregation. Adopted 225-192 (R 148-46; D 77-146), July 5. Ford VOTED FOR.

1957. Civil Rights Act (HR 6127). Amendment providing for jury trials in any criminal contempt action arising under the legislation. Rejected 158-251 (R 45-139; D 113-112), June 18. Ford VOTED AGAINST.

1959. Pre-emption Doctrine (HR 3). Bill permitting federal courts to strike down state laws under the federal pre-emption doctrine only if Congress specified its intention to pre-empt the field of legislation involved or if a state and a federal law were in irreconcilable conflict, and permitting state enforcement of laws barring subversive activities against the federal government. Passed 225-192 (R 114-30; D 111-162), June 24. Ford VOTED FOR.

1960. Civil Rights Act (HR 8601). Amendment authorizing court-appointed referees to help Negroes register and vote where a "pattern or practice" of discrimination existed. Adopted 295-124 (R 123-24; D 172-100), March 23. Ford VOTED FOR.

1964. Civil Rights Act (HR 7152). Bill enforcing the right to vote; preventing discrimination in access to public accommodations and facilities; expediting school desegregation. Passed 290-130 (R 138-34; D 152-96), Feb. 10. Ford VOTED FOR.

1965. Voting Rights (HR 6400). Bill suspending the use of literacy tests in certain states and areas; authorizing appointment of federal voting examiners to order the registration of Negroes in states and voting districts whose voter activity had fallen below certain specified levels, and imposing a ban on the use of poll taxes in any election. Passed 333-85 (R 112-24; D 221-61), July 9. Ford VOTED FOR.

1966. Civil Rights Act (HR 14765). Amendment deleting the open housing sections of the bill. Rejected 190-222 (R 86-50; D 104-172), Aug. 9. Ford VOTED FOR.

1968. Open Housing (H Res 1100, HR 2516). Resolution agreeing to Senate version of the bill which prohibited discrimination in the sale or rental of housing. Adopted 250-172 (R 100-84; D 150-88), April 10. Ford VOTED FOR.

1969. Voting Rights (HR 4249). Amendment extending nationwide the provisions of the 1965 Voting Rights

Act in place of the committee bill extending the law as enacted, which covered certain states and voting districts. Adopted 208-204 (R 129-49; D 79-155), Dec. 11. Ford VOTED FOR.

1970. School Desegregation (HR 16916). Vote on motion designed to retain provisions of the Office of Education appropriations bill prohibiting use of funds to force busing or closing of schools, and providing for freedom of choice plans. Motion agreed to 191-157 (R 107-35; D 84-122), June 30. Ford VOTED FOR.

1971. EEOC Enforcement (HR 1746). Amendment allowing the Equal Employment Opportunity Commission (EEOC) to bring suit against recalcitrant discriminatory employers in federal court, rather than allowing the EEOC to issue cease and desist orders to such employers. Adopted 200-195 (R 131-29; D 69-166), Sept. 16. Ford VOTED FOR.

1971. Busing (HR 7248). Amendment to the Higher Education Act of 1971 postponing effectiveness of any federal court order requiring busing for racial, sexual, religious or socio-economic balance until all appeals—or the time for all appeals—had been exhausted. Adopted 235-125 (R 129-17; D 106-108), Nov. 4. Ford VOTED FOR.

1972. Busing (HR 13915). Amendment—to a bill prohibiting busing of school children and allowing the reopening of past school desegregation court cases—providing that nothing in the act was intended to be inconsistent with or violate any provision of the Constitution. Rejected 178-197 (R 55-98; D 123-99), Aug. 18. Ford VOTED AGAINST.

Defense

1952. Defense Spending (HR 7391). Amendment to the fiscal 1953 Defense Department appropriations bill limiting military spending to $46-billion. Adopted 220-131 (R 160-11; D 60-120), April 9. Ford VOTED AGAINST.

1969. Draft (HR 14001). Bill amending the Selective Service Act by removing a provision prohibiting the President from instituting a lottery system for induction into the armed forces. Passed 383-12 (R 175-1; D 208-11), Oct. 30. Ford VOTED FOR.

1971. Draft (HR 6531). Amendment providing a one-year extension of the military draft instead of two. Rejected 198-200 (R 65-105; D 133-95), March 31. Ford VOTED AGAINST.

1973. War Powers (H J Res 542). Bill requiring the president to report to Congress within 72 hours any commitment or increasing commitment of U.S. combat troops abroad; requiring the president to terminate any such action within 120 days of his report unless Congress authorized continuation, and allowing Congress to direct the termination of U.S. commitment at any time. Passed 244-170 (R 72-109; D 172-61), July 18. Ford VOTED AGAINST.

Education

1956. School Construction (HR 7535). Bill authorizing $1.6-billion over four years to state educational agencies for school construction. Rejected 194-224 (R 75-119; D 119-105), July 5. Ford VOTED AGAINST.

1961. Emergency School Aid (HR 8890). Motion to consider the emergency education act, authorizing

$325-million for school construction assistance, continuation of National Defense Education Act loan authorizations and impacted areas school aid program. Rejected 170-242 (R 6-160; D 164-82), Aug. 30. Ford VOTED AGAINST.

1962. College Aid (HR 8900). Amendment deleting section of bill authorizing loans and grants to students. Adopted 214-186 (R 130-30; D 84-156), Sept. 20. Ford VOTED FOR.

1963. Medical Schools (HR 12). Bill authorizing a three-year program of matching grants for construction and rehabilitation of teaching facilities for medical schools and providing a six-year loan program for medical students. Passed 288-122 (R 71-99; D 217-23), April 24. Ford VOTED AGAINST.

1963. Higher Education Facilities (HR 6143). Bill providing a five-year program of federal grants and loans for construction or improvement of higher education academic facilities and authorizing $1,195,000,000 for the program for three years. Passed 287-113 (R 107-56; D 180-57), Aug. 14. Ford VOTED FOR.

1965. School Aid (HR 2362). Bill providing a three-year program of grants to states for allocation to school districts with large numbers of children from low-income families and providing grants for purchase of books and library materials. Passed 263-153 (R 35-96; D 228-57), March 26. Ford VOTED AGAINST.

1968. Campus Disorders (HR 15067). Amendment to a higher education aid bill requiring colleges to deny federal funds to students who participated in serious campus disorders. Adopted 260-146 (R 134-43; D 126-102), July 25. Ford VOTED FOR.

1969. Education Funds (HR 13111). Amendment to appropriations bill for the Departments of Labor and Health, Education and Welfare adding $894.5-million for elementary and secondary education, aid to impacted areas, higher education and vocational education. Adopted 294-119 (R 99-81; D 195-38), July 31. Ford VOTED AGAINST.

1970. Office of Education Funds (HR 16916). Bill appropriating $4.4-billion for the Office of Education in fiscal 1971. Passed over veto 289-114 (R 77-101; D 212-13), Aug. 13. Ford VOTED AGAINST.

Foreign Policy

1950. Korean Aid (HR 5330). Bill authorizing $60-million in aid to South Korea. Rejected 191-192 (R 21-130; D 170-61), Jan. 19. Ford VOTED AGAINST.

1951. Trade Act Extension (HR 1612). Amendment directing the Tariff Commission to determine points below which tariffs could not be cut without "peril" to U.S. industries, and to recommend minimum rates to which tariffs should be raised to protect domestic industry. Adopted 225-168 (R 183-4; D 42-163), Feb. 7. Ford VOTED FOR.

1954. Trade Act Extension (HR 9474). Bill extending for one year the President's authority to enter into reciprocal trade agreements. Passed 281-53 (R 126-39; D 154-14), June 11. Ford VOTED FOR.

1951. Foreign Aid (HR 5113). Amendment cutting $350-million from the fiscal 1952 foreign aid bill. Adopted 186-177 (R 149-14; D 37-162), Aug. 17. Ford VOTED FOR.

1956. Foreign Aid. (HR 12130). Bill appropriating $3.4-billion for foreign aid in fiscal 1957. Passed 284-120 (R 124-70; D 160-50), July 11. Ford VOTED FOR.

1957. Foreign Aid (HR 9302). Amendment restoring $715-million in foreign aid appropriations which had been cut from the bill by the House Appropriations Committee. Rejected 129-254 (R 86-83; D 43-171), Aug. 15. Ford VOTED FOR.

1961. Peace Corps (HR 7500). Bill giving the Peace Corps permanent status and authorizing $40-million for it in fiscal 1962. Passed 288-97 (R 82-68; D 206-29), Sept. 14. Ford PAIRED FOR.

1962. Trade Expansion Act. (HR 11970). Bill authorizing the president to negotiate new tariff cuts and compensate injured industries and workers through financial aid or by raising tariffs. Passed 298-125 (R 80-90; D 218-35), June 28. Ford VOTED FOR.

1962. UN Bonds. (S 2768). Bill authorizing the president to match up to $100-million in purchases of United Nations bonds by other UN members. Passed 257-134 (R 66-88; D 191-46), Sept. 14. Ford VOTED FOR.

1964. Foreign Aid (HR 11812). Amendment cutting funds in the fiscal 1965 foreign aid appropriations bill by $247.8-million. Rejected 198-208 (R 143-23; D 55-185), July 1. Ford VOTED FOR.

1965. Foreign Aid (HR 7750). Amendment to the fiscal 1966 foreign aid authorization reducing funds for development loans by $130,958,000 and stipulating that labor unions participating in Latin American housing projects be "non-Communist-dominated" as well as "free." Rejected 178-219 (R 116-14; D 62-205), May 25. Ford VOTED FOR.

1965. Immigration (HR 2580). Bill amending the immigration laws to eliminate the national origins quota system and to set general priorities for the admission of immigrants to the United States. Passed 318-95 (R 109-25; D 209-70), Aug. 25. Ford VOTED FOR.

1970. Cambodia (HR 15628). Motion designed to prevent inclusion in the Foreign Military Sales Act of language which would curb U.S. military operations in Cambodia (Cooper-Church amendment). Agreed to 237-153 (R 138-33; D 99-120), July 9. Ford VOTED FOR.

1972. UN Funds (HR 14989). Amendment restoring $25,103,500 in funds for the United Nations, which was deleted from the fiscal 1973 Department of State appropriations bill by the House Appropriations Committee, and removing a committee provision limiting U.S. contributions to the UN to 25 per cent of their total annual assessment. Rejected 156-202 (R 56-99; D 100-103), May 18. Ford VOTED FOR.

1972. Southeast Asia (HR 16029). Amendment to foreign military aid authorization deleting provision terminating U.S. involvement in the Indochina war by Oct. 1, 1972, subject to release of U.S. prisoners of war, an accounting of men missing in action and a cease-fire to the extent required to protect U.S. withdrawal. Adopted 229-177 (R 149-23; D 80-154), Aug. 10. Ford VOTED FOR.

1973. Cambodia (HR 7447). Amendment to fiscal 1973 supplemental appropriations bill deleting language authorizing the Defense Department to transfer funds from other defense programs for use in Southeast Asia, including the bombing of Cambodia. Adopted 219-188 (R 35-143; D 184-45), May 10. Ford VOTED AGAINST.

1973. Cambodia (HR 7447). Amendment postponing until after Sept. 1, 1973, the prohibition against using any funds in the bill (second supplemental appropriations) or funds in any other previously enacted appropriations bill from being used to carry on military activities in or over Cambodia or Laos. Rejected 204-204 (R 147-37; D 57-167), June 25. Ford VOTED FOR.

1973. Foreign Aid (HR 9360). Bill authorizing $978.9-million in fiscal 1974 for foreign economic assistance, $632-million for Indochina postwar reconstruction, $1.15-billion for foreign military assistance and credit sales, and authorizing $821-million for foreign economic assistance in fiscal 1975. Passed 188-183 (R 69-89; D 119-94), July 26. Ford PAIRED FOR.

Labor, Economic Policy

1952. Steel Strike (HR 8210). Amendment to the Defense Production Act amendments bill requesting the President to invoke the Taft-Hartley Act to enjoin steel workers from striking. Adopted 228-164 (R 146-47; D 82-117), June 26. Ford VOTED FOR.

1959. Labor Regulation (HR 8342). Amendment substituting the Landrum-Griffin bill for the text of an Education and Labor Committee bill. The Landrum-Griffin bill contained curbs on secondary boycotts and organizational and recognition picketing and gave the states power to handle "no man's land" labor disputes. Adopted 229-201 (R 134-17; D 95-184), Aug. 13. Ford VOTED FOR.

1961. Minimum Wage (HR 3935). Amendment to Education and Labor Committee bill reducing from $1.25 to $1.15 an hour the increase in the minimum wage for workers covered by the Fair Labor Standards Act and extending coverage under the act to an additional 1,300,000 workers. Adopted 216-203 (R 142-26; D 74-177), March 24. Ford VOTED FOR.

1962. Manpower Development and Training (HR 8399). Bill authorizing a two-year, $262-million program to train unemployed workers. Passed 354-62 (R 145-22; D 209-40), Feb. 28. Ford VOTED FOR.

1963. Tax Cut (HR 8363). Revenue Act of 1963, lowering personal and corporate income taxes by $11.5-billion. Passed 271-155 (R 48-126; D 223-29), Sept. 25. Ford VOTED AGAINST.

1965. Right-to-Work (HR 77). Bill repealing Section 14 (b) of the Taft-Hartley Act, permitting state right-to-work laws under which the union shop is prohibited. Passed 221-203 (R 21-117; D 200-86), July 28. Ford VOTED AGAINST.

1966. Minimum Wage (HR 13712). Motion designed to delay for one year—until Feb. 1, 1969—the final step of an increase in the minimum wage from $1.25 to $1.60 an hour. Rejected 163-183 (R 101-18; D 62-165), Sept. 7. Ford VOTED FOR.

1968. Tax Surcharge (HR 15414). Conference report on a bill imposing a 10 per cent surcharge on personal and corporate income taxes and imposing a limit on federal spending in fiscal 1969. Adopted 268-150 (R 114-73; D 154-77), June 20. Ford VOTED FOR.

1969. Tax Reform (HR 13270). Bill reducing individual income taxes by an average of 5 per cent, extending the income surtax at 5 per cent through June 30, 1970, repealing the investment tax credit and reducing mineral and oil depletion allowances. Passed 395-30 (R 176-10; D 219-20), Aug. 7. Ford VOTED FOR.

1971. Lockheed Loan (HR 8432). Bill authorizing a federal guarantee of bank loans for failing major businesses (Lockheed Aircraft Corporation). Passed 192-189 (R 90-60; D 102-129), July 30. Ford VOTED FOR.

1972. Revenue Sharing (HR 14370). Bill providing assistance payments totaling $29.6-billion over five years to states and local governments for high-priority expenditures, encouraging states to broaden their tax systems and authorizing federal collection of state personal income taxes. Passed 275-122 (R 122-42; D 153-80), June 22. Ford VOTED FOR.

1973. Wage-Price Controls (HR 6168). Bill extending the president's authority to control wages and prices for one year, to April 30, 1974. Passed 293-114 (R 152-31; D 141-83), April 16. Ford VOTED FOR.

1973. Impoundment Control (HR 8480). Bill setting a $267.1-billion ceiling on federal spending in fiscal 1974, providing procedures for either the House or Senate to force the president to release impounded funds and directing the president to impound funds proportionately from controllable federal spending programs to meet the spending ceiling. Passed 254-164 (R 36-150; D 218-14), July 25. Ford VOTED AGAINST.

Transportation

1956. Highways (HR 10660). Bill authorizing a $30-billion, 13-year highway construction program and raising taxes on highway user items such as gasoline and tires over a 16-year period to finance the project. Passed 388-19 (R 188-4; D 200-15), April 27. Ford VOTED FOR.

1970. SST Development (HR 17755). Motion designed to retain in the Department of Transportation appropriations bill for fiscal 1971, funding of $289.9-million for development of the supersonic transport (SST). Agreed to 213-175 (R 105-62; D 108-113), Dec. 8. Ford VOTED FOR.

1973. Mass Transit. (S 502). Amendment to the Federal-Aid Highway Act permitting urban areas to use up to $700-million in each of fiscal years 1974-76 from the Highway Trust Fund for mass transit projects or for roads. Rejected 190-215 (R 70-114; D 120-101), April 19. Ford VOTED FOR.

1973. Mass Transit. (HR 6452). Bill authorizing $800-million for fiscal 1974-75 grants to state and local agencies for urban mass transit operating subsidies and increasing the federal share of assistance for mass transit capital grant programs. Passed 219-195 (R 41-142; D 178-53), Oct. 3. Ford VOTED AGAINST.

Welfare, Housing

1949. Low-Rent Housing (HR 4009). Amendment to Housing Act of 1949 deleting section providing low-rent public housing. Rejected 204-209 (R 140-24; D 64-184), June 29. Ford VOTED FOR.

1961. Housing (HR 6028). Bill authorizing a $4.9-billion housing program over four years. Passed 235-178 (R 25-140; D 210-38), June 22. Ford VOTED AGAINST.

1965. Medicare (HR 6675). Bill providing a basic compulsory health insurance program for the aged, financed primarily by a payroll tax; a supplementary voluntary health insurance program financed by general revenue and contributions from participants; increases in Social Security cash benefits, and expansion of the Kerr-Mills health program, child health-care programs and other federal-state public assistance programs. Passed 313-115 (R 65-73; D 248-42), April 8. Ford VOTED AGAINST.

1965. Rent Supplements (HR 7984). Amendment to the Housing and Urban Development Act, deleting rent supplement payments to low-income families and home improvement grants to homeowners in urban renewal areas. Rejected 202-208 (R 130-4; D 72-204), June 30. Ford VOTED FOR.

1966. War on Poverty (HR 15111). Motion to kill the bill providing $1.75-billion for antipoverty programs in fiscal 1967. Rejected 156-208 (R 107-15; D 49-193), Sept. 29. Ford VOTED FOR.

1966. Urban Renewal (S 3708). Bill providing demonstration city grants for community renewal and other housing programs. Passed 178-141 (R 16-81; D 162-60), Oct. 14. Ford VOTED AGAINST.

1967. Model Cities (HR 9960). Amendment to an appropriations bill for the Department of Housing and Urban Development deleting $225-million in model cities funds, leaving the program with only $12-million in planning funds. Rejected 193-213 (R 141-35; D 52-178), May 17. Ford VOTED FOR.

1967. Antipoverty (S 2388). Amendment reducing funds in the bill authorizing antipoverty funds for fiscal 1968 from $2.1-billion to $1.6-billion. Adopted 221-190 (R 148-28; D 73-162), Nov. 15. Ford VOTED FOR.

1968. Housing Programs (S 3497). Conference report on the bill providing new programs of federal assistance for home ownership and rental housing for low-income families, federal reinsurance for insurance industry riot losses, flood insurance for homeowners, federal assistance for developers of entire new towns and new communities, and extending a number of existing housing and urban development programs. Adopted 228-135 (R 72-92; D 156-43), July 26. Ford VOTED FOR.

1969. Antipoverty (HR 12321). Amendment to the Office of Economic Opportunity authorization bill for fiscal 1970, turning control of the antipoverty program over to the states. Rejected 163-231 (R 103-63; D 60-168), Dec. 12. Ford VOTED FOR.

1970. Family Assistance (HR 16311). Bill replacing the Aid to Families with Dependent Children program with a family assistance plan providing guaranteed federal payments to poor families. Passed 243-155 (R 102-72; D 141-83), April 16. Ford VOTED FOR.

1973. Antipoverty (HR 8877). Amendment to the bill appropriating funds for the Departments of Labor and Health, Education and Welfare reducing the appropriation for the Office of Economic Opportunity from $333.8-million to $141.3-million. Rejected 110-288 (R 90-90; D 20-198), June 26. Ford VOTED FOR.

1974 BUDGET: $268.6-BILLION SPENDING, 12.7-BILLION DEFICIT

President Nixon's fiscal 1974 budget attacked social welfare programs enacted under Democratic Presidents and drew sharp and immediate criticism from congressional Democrats and supporters of the individual programs.

The budget for the year beginning July 1, sent to Congress by the President Jan. 29, proposed federal spending of $268.7-billion. It also continued a Nixon practice of never having submitted a budget without a builtin deficit.

References. *President's budget message, p. 2-A; President's economic report, p. 17-A; budget authority and outlays by function, table p. 42; budget authority and outlays by agency, table p. 45.*

Even with reduction or outright elimination of more than 100 programs, the budget predicted that total federal spending would rise $18.9-billion in fiscal 1974, largely through relatively uncontrollable increases in social and health insurance programs and through maintenance of defense spending levels.

The President offered the budget as "clear evidence of the kind of change in direction demanded by the great majority of the American people," and urged Congress "to join me in a concerted effort to control federal spending" by enacting a rigid $268.7-billion ceiling on fiscal 1974 outlays.

That congressional Democrats did not share the President's view of his re-election mandate was made clear by House Speaker Carl Albert (D Okla.), who vowed that Congress "will not permit the President to lay waste the great programs...which we have developed during the decades past."

Nixon's budget, Albert declared, was "nothing less than the systematic dismantling and destruction of the great social programs and the great precedents of humanitarian government inaugurated by Franklin D. Roosevelt and advanced and enlarged by every Democratic President since then."

The Democratic members of committees that handle social programs echoed Albert's complaint. Senate Labor and Public Welfare Committee Chairman Harrison A. Williams Jr. (D N.J.) termed the budget "contemptuous of the real needs of the American people."

Sen. Warren G. Magnuson (D Wash.), chairman of the Senate Appropriations Subcommittee on Labor, Health, Education and Welfare, promised "a long and hard look at these dismaying proposals."

House Appropriations Committee Chairman George Mahon (D Texas), on the other hand, applauded the President "for facing up to some of the major aspects of the fiscal crisis which continues to confront the country."

Nevertheless, Mahon added, "the improvement is nowhere near as dramatic as it may appear" because the budget still contemplated federal funds deficits (ex-

cluding trust funds) of $34-billion in fiscal 1973 and $29-billion in fiscal 1974.

Nixon Arguments. In arguing his case for budgetary restraint, the President struck three themes: restraint on taxes, restraint on inflation and redistribution of power in the federal system of government.

To fulfill his 1972 re-election campaign pledge of no new taxes, the President counted on a $115-billion rise in gross national product during calendar 1973 to help produce a $31-billion increase in fiscal 1974 revenues—aided by previously enacted Social Security payroll tax boosts.

To mute the budget's stimulative effect on the economy—in hopes of lowering inflationary pressures—the President planned a $12.7-billion fiscal 1974 deficit, down from an estimated $24.8-billion deficit in fiscal 1973. To reduce the deficit to a more acceptable level—it would become a $300-million surplus if the economy were operating at full employment—the President cut potential fiscal 1974 spending by $16.9-billion. That left the over-all increase in outlays $12-billion below the anticipated growth of revenues.

Federal Budget 1954-1974

(in millions of dollars)

Fiscal Year	Receipts	Outlays	Surplus/ Deficit
1954	69,719	70,890	—1,170
1955	65,469	68,509	—,041
1956	74,547	70,460	+4,087
1957	79,990	76,741	+3,249
1958	79,636	82,575	—2,939
1959	79,249	92,104	—12,855
1960	92,492	92,223	+269
1961	94,389	97,795	—3,406
1962	99,676	106,813	—7,137
1963	106,560	111,311	—4,751
1964	112,662	118,584	—5,922
1965	116,833	118,430	—1,596
1966	130,856	134,652	—3,796
1967	149,552	158,254	—8,702
1968	153,671	178,833	—25,161
1969	187,784	184,548	+3,236
1970	193,743	196,588	—2,845
1971	188,392	211,425	·23,033
1972	208,649	231,876	—23,227
1973 est.	224,984	249,796	—24,812
1974 est.	255,982	268,665	—12,683

Note: Figures for years before fiscal year 1969 adjusted to conform to unified budget concept adopted in fiscal 1969

Budget Terminology

The federal budget is a plan of expected receipts and expenditures, a statement of priorities, an accounting of how funds have been and will be spent and a request for authority to spend public money.

The 1974 budget covers the government's fiscal year beginning July 1, 1973, and ending June 30, 1974.

The federal expenditures reported are most frequently outlays: amounts spent, obligated or committed during the year. Examples are funds spent to buy equipment or property, to meet the government's liability under a contract or to pay the salary of an employee. Outlays also include net lending—the difference between disbursements and repayments under government lending programs.

The administration's request to Congress, presented in the form of the budget, is for authority to obligate or lend funds.

Budget authority determines the scope of operations of the government. Congress confers budget authority on a federal agency in general in the form of appropriations.

Appropriations may be for a single year, a specified period of years, or an indefinite number of years, according to the restrictions Congress wishes to place on spending for particular purposes.

Congress also restricts itself in the appropriation process by requiring that an appropriation be preceded by an authorization to appropriate a certain or an indefinite amount of money for a certain purpose over a period of time.

Usually an authorization establishes the scope of a particular program, and Congress appropriates funds within the limits it has previously approved. In the case of authority to enter contract obligations, however, Congress authorizes the administration to make firm commitments for which funds must be appropriated later. Congress also occasionally includes mandatory spending requirements in an authorization, designed to ensure spending at a certain level.

Budget authority often differs from actual outlays. This is because, in practice, funds actually spent or obligated during a year are drawn partly from the budget authority conferred in the year in question and partly from budget authority conferred in previous years.

To reverse the concentration of power in the national government, the President curtailed and canceled programs that had given the federal government major roles in attacking social and economic programs. To redistribute some of that power to state and local governments, he moved to consolidate 70 existing federal grant programs into special revenue sharing funds for education, law enforcement and criminal justice, manpower training and urban development. *(Box, p. 46)*

Spending Increases

By imposing such cutbacks, the President left room under his self-imposed spending limit for increases in the following areas:

• An additional $4.7-billion for defense—mainly for pay and price increases—putting fiscal 1974 defense spending at $81.1-billion, roughly one-third of total spending.

• A $5.7-billion increase in Social Security payments, for a fiscal 1974 total of $54.5-billion, roughly one-fifth of the budget.

• Increases of $2.5-billion for Medicare payments and $900-million for Medicaid.

• A $1.9-billion increase in interest on the national debt, making total interest payments $24.7-billion, about one-tenth of the budget.

Spending Cuts

By cutting $11.2-billion from the $261.1-billion in spending approved by Congress for fiscal 1973, the President maintained, the government could avoid ballooning fiscal 1974 spending to $288-billion and fiscal 1975 outlays to $312-billion.

In a departure from previous budgets, the administration listed savings it intended to make from program reductions and terminations in fiscal 1973-75. The targets: savings of $6.5-billion in fiscal 1973, $16.9-billion in fiscal 1974 and $21.7-billion in fiscal 1975. *(List p. 11-A)*

The fiscal 1973 reductions, all intended to be accomplished without substantive legislation by Congress, included cuts of $1.2-billion in Agriculture Department spending and $3.1-billion in Department of Health, Education and Welfare outlays.

Combined with various administrative actions—including a brief deferment of a $1.5-billion general revenue sharing payment into fiscal 1974 and increased estimates for offshore oil receipts—the $6.5-billion program reduction brought estimated fiscal 1973 spending down $11.2-billion. The result, according to the budget, was a reduction in fiscal 1973 outlays to $249.8-billion from the $261-billion total dictated by congressional budget additions.

Of $16.8-billion in savings proposed for fiscal 1974, only $1.4-billion required substantive legislation by Congress, according to the budget listing. Only $2.1-billion of $21.7-billion in proposed fiscal 1975 savings was listed as requiring congressional action.

The budget list was confusing in several areas, however. Among savings listed as not requiring substantive legislation was substitution of special revenue sharing for federal funding of certain education programs—although Congress still had to act on the education revenue sharing proposal.

The budget also listed substantial savings in all three fiscal years ($2.3-billion for fiscal 1973, $2.7-billion for fiscal 1974 and $4.7-billion for fiscal 1975) to be accomplished by a statutory ceiling on social services grants enacted by Congress in 1972.

Fiscal Policy

In his budget message, the President said a strong economic recovery currently underway required a shift from the economic stimulus provided by large fiscal 1972 and 1973 budget deficits toward smaller budget deficits.

(Continued on p. 44)

FISCAL 1974 BUDGET BY FUNCTION: $268.7-BILLION IN

(in millions of dollars)†

	BUDGET AUTHORITY‡			OUTLAYS		
	1972	1973 est.	1974 est.	1972	1973 est.	1974 est.
NATIONAL DEFENSE						
Military Defense	$ 75,084	$ 77,804	$ 83,481	$ 75,151	$ 74,200	$ 78,200
Military Assistance	2,928	1,916	1,684	806	600	800
Atomic Energy	2,293	2,633	2,429	2,392	2,194	2,374
Defense Related Activities	117	117	91	95	192	83
Deductions for Offsetting Receipts	—108	—751	—382	—108	—751	—382
TOTAL	$ 80,314	$ 81,719	$ 87,303	$ 78,336	$ 76,435	$ 81,074
INTERNATIONAL AFFAIRS AND FINANCE						
Conduct of Foreign Affairs	$ 465	$ 514	$ 536	$ 452	$ 503	$ 538
Economic and Financial Assistance	3,226	2,574	3,159	2,287	2,273	2,408
Foreign Information and Exchange Activities	278	297	329	274	294	312
Food for Peace	1,320	895	654	993	847	766
Deductions for Offsetting Receipts	—280	—574	—213	—280	—574	—213
TOTAL	$ 5,010	$ 3,705	$ 4,465	$ 3,726	$ 3,341	$ 3,811
SPACE RESEARCH AND TECHNOLOGY						
Manned Space Flight	$ 1,639	$ 1,521	$ 1,385	$ 1,740	$ 1,417	$ 1,450
Space Sciences and Applications	900	1,098	899	890	943	966
Space Technology	213	161	122	228	156	139
Aeronautical Technology	236	314	281	227	249	269
Supporting Space Activities	331	324	329	349	307	313
Deductions for Offsetting Receipts	—13	—11	— 1	—13	—11	— 1
TOTAL	$ 3,307	$ 3,407	$ 3,015	$ 3,422	$ 3,061	$ 3,135
AGRICULTURE AND RURAL DEVELOPMENT						
Farm Income Stabilization	$ 5,837	$ 4,525	$ 4,605	$ 5,146	$ 4,251	$ 3,920
Rural Housing and Public Facilities	1,251	1,533	1,086	877	657	717
Agricultural Land and Water Resources	412	450	190	354	394	217
Research and Other Services	901	1,006	1,037	916	1,001	971
Deductions for Offsetting Receipts	—230	—239	—253	—230	—239	—253
TOTAL	$ 8,172	$ 7,275	$ 6,665	$ 7,063	$ 6,064	$ 5,572
NATURAL RESOURCES AND ENVIRONMENT						
Water Resources and Power	$ 2,442	$ 2,840	$ 2,221	$ 2,664	$ 3,065	$ 2,795
Land Management	958	850	822	892	1,008	929
Mineral Resources	132	159	128	112	151	131
Pollution Control and Abatement	2,447	7,421	590	763	1,148	2,128
Recreational Resources	816	720	515	524	641	701
Other Natural Resources Programs	158	182	196	153	174	191
Deductions for Offsetting Receipts	—1,346	—5,310	—3,214	—1,346	—5,310	—3,214
TOTAL	$ 5,608	$ 6,862	$ 1,259	$ 3,761	$ 876	$ 3,663
COMMERCE AND TRANSPORTATION						
Air Transportation	$ 1,687	$ 1,640	$ 2,193	$1,685	$ 1,760	$ 1,877
Water Transportation	1,223	1,588	1,304	1,106	1,200	1,282
Ground Transportation	6,262	8,871	6,119	5,210	5,564	5,536
Postal Service	1,418	1,410	1,373	1,772	1,710	1,373
Advancement of Business	1,212	2,599	1,019	645	1,476	548
Area and Regional Development	948	1,099	755	818	901	1,050
Regulation of Business	177	175	170	168	175	168
Deductions for Offsetting Receipts	—203	—243	—254	—203	—243	—254
TOTAL	$ 12,734	$ 17,138	$ 12,678	$ 11,201	$ 12,543	$ 11,580
COMMUNITY DEVELOPMENT AND HOUSING						
Community Planning, Management and Development	$ 3,081	$ 3,221	$ 569	$ 2,878	$ 2,822	$ 2,590
Low and Moderate Income Housing Aids	1,512	1,918	2,235	1,595	1,120	2,009
Maintenance of Housing Mortgage Market	331	779	1,060	—191	15	332
Deductions for Offsetting Receipts	—*	—*	—*	—*	—*	—*
TOTAL	$ 4,924	$ 5,918	$ 3,863	$ 4,282	$ 3,957	$ 4,931
EDUCATION AND MANPOWER						
Elementary and Secondary Education	$ 3,576	$ 3,385	$ 1,290	$ 3,490	$ 3,262	$ 1,739
Higher Education	1,562	1,788	1,910	1,434	1,496	1,635
Vocational Education	584	554	51	521	557	308

EXPENDITURES, $288.0-BILLION IN SPENDING AUTHORITY

(in millions of dollars)†

	BUDGET AUTHORITY‡			OUTLAYS		
	1972	1973 est.	1974 est.	1972	1973 est.	1974 est.
Education Revenue Sharing	0	0	2,527	0	0	1,693
Other Education Aids	627	950	757	541	749	906
General Science	622	646	583	567	573	586
Manpower Training and Employment Services	3,434	3,229	2,424	2,894	3,486	2,847
Other Manpower Aids	337	412	420	318	393	411
Deductions for Offsetting Receipts	—13	—15	—15	—13	—15	—15
TOTAL	$ 10,729	$ 10,948	$ 9,947	$ 9,751	$ 10,500	$ 10,110
HEALTH						
Development of Health Resources	$ 3,049	$ 2,403	$ 2,381	$ 2,479	$ 2,688	$ 2,722
Providing or Financing Medical Services	14,105	17,198	22,580	14,245	14,707	18,358
Prevention and Control of Health Problems	562	704	1,422	391	602	656
Deductions for Offsetting Receipts	—3	—6	—7	—3	—6	—7
TOTAL	$ 17,712	$ 20,299	$ 26,377	$ 17,112	$ 17,991	$ 21,730
INCOME SECURITY						
Retirement and Social Insurance	$ 57,754	$ 66,619	$ 76,767	$ 52,728	$ 63,023	$ 68,006
Public Assistance	9,278	9,893	10,648	9,313	9,073	10,665
Social and Individual Services	2,725	4,463	3,400	2,838	3,800	3,321
Deductions for Offsetting Receipts	—3	—6	—16	—3	—6	—16
TOTAL	$ 69,754	$ 80,969	$ 90,799	$ 64,876	$ 75,889	$ 81,976
VETERANS BENEFITS AND SERVICES						
Income Security	$ 7,026	$ 7,220	$ 7,065	$ 6,833	$ 7,025	$ 6,814
Education, Training and Rehabilitation	1,931	2,598	2,526	1,960	2,597	2,521
Housing	6	5	4	—317	—449	—269
Hospital and Medical Care	2,499	2,903	2,784	2,428	2,741	2,792
Other Benefits and Services	360	368	359	318	363	360
Deductions for Offsetting Receipts	—491	—482	—486	—491	—482	—486
TOTAL	$ 11,330	$ 12,611	$ 12,253	$ 10,731	$ 11,795	$ 11,732
INTEREST						
On Public Debt	$ 21,849	$ 24,200	$ 26,100	$ 21,849	$ 24,200	$ 26,100
On Refunds and Receipts	182	175	175	182	175	175
On Uninvested Funds	6	5	5	6	5	5
Deductions for Offsetting Receipts	—1,455	—1,573	—1,608	—1,455	—1,573	—1,608
TOTAL	$ 20,582	$ 22,808	$ 24,672	$ 20,582	$ 22,808	$ 24,672
GENERAL GOVERNMENT						
Legislative Functions	$ 387	$ 379	$ 362	$ 311	$ 329	$ 383
Judicial Functions	177	195	207	173	194	206
Executive Direction and Management	84	154	177	68	138	148
Central Fiscal Operations	1,713	1,749	1,854	1,647	1,774	1,852
General Property and Records Management	922	957	594	725	902	917
Central Personnel Management	298	329	343	275	327	347
Law Enforcement and Justice	1,645	1,912	1,977	1,233	1,630	1,877
National Capital Region	509	547	627	450	506	634
Other General Government	380	398	437	345	406	429
Deductions for Offsetting Receipts	—335	—576	—767	—335	—576	—767
TOTAL	$ 5,779	$ 6,044	$ 5,809	$ 4,891	$ 5,631	$ 6,025
GENERAL REVENUE SHARING	$ 0	$ 8,295	$ 6,055	$ 0	$ 6,786	$ 6,035
CONTINGENCIES AND CIVILIAN PAY RAISES	$ 0	$ 750	$ 2,000	$ 0	$ 500	$ 1,750
UNDISTRIBUTED INTRAGOVERNMENTAL TRANSACTIONS	$—7,857	$—8,381	$—9,131	$—7,857	$—8,381	$—9,131
GRAND TOTAL	$248,097	$280,366	$288,029	$231,876	$249,796	$268,665

† Figures may not add to totals due to rounding.
‡ Primarily appropriations.
* Less than $500 thousand.

SOURCE: Office of Management and Budget

Moving in that direction, the budget planned an actual fiscal 1974 deficit of $12.7-billion, down from the $24.8-billion deficit now expected in fiscal 1973. On a full employment basis—calculated as if an economy operating at a 4 per cent unemployment rate were producing additional federal revenues—the fiscal 1974 budget would produce a $300-million surplus, compared to a $2.3-billion deficit in fiscal 1973 under current projections.

The budget figures:

Fiscal Years

(billions of dollars)

	1972 (actual)	1973 (estimate)	1974 (estimate)	1975 (estimate)
Receipts	208.6	225.0	256.0	——
Outlays	231.9	249.8	268.7	——
Deficit	—23.2	—24.8	—12.7	——
Full-employment receipts	225.0	245.0	268.0	290.0
Full-employment outlays	228.9	247.3	267.7	288.0
Full-employment surplus or deficit	—3.9	—2.3	0.3	2.0
Budget authority	248.1	280.4	288.0	313.5

Adjusted to reflect decrease in unemployment benefit payments.

Revenues

In pledging no tax increase for fiscal 1974, the administration relied on continued economic expansion—and previously enacted social security tax increases—in estimating $256-billion in budget receipts. If realized, that total would mean a $31-billion increase over projected fiscal 1973 revenues.

The budget's prediction of $111.6-billion in individual income taxes and $37-billion in corporate income tax receipts was based on a projected $115-billion increase in the gross national product during calendar 1973. Together, personal and corporate income taxes were expected to produce 58 percent of federal receipts during fiscal 1974.

With increases in the taxable earnings base and in the payroll tax rate effective in 1973, social insurance taxes were expected to produce fiscal 1974 revenue of $78.2-billion, 31 percent of total federal receipts and a $13.7-billion increase from fiscal 1973 levels.

According to the budget, the sources of federal receipts during fiscal 1974 as compared to actual fiscal 1972 revenue and estimated fiscal 1973 receipts were:

(billions of dollars)

	1972 (actual)	1973 (estimate)	1974 (estimate)
Individual income taxes	94.7	99.4	111.6
Corporation income taxes	32.2	33.5	37.0
Social insurance taxes and contributions (trust funds)	53.9	64.5	78.2

	1972 (actual)	1973 (estimate)	1974 (estimate)
Excise taxes*	15.5	16.0	16.8
Estate and gift taxes	5.4	4.6	5.0
Customs duties	3.3	3.0	3.3
Miscellaneous receipts*	3.6	4.0	4.1
TOTAL	208.6	225.0	256.0

Includes both federal funds and trust funds.

Unified Budget

Following the unified budget form used since fiscal 1969, the fiscal 1974 budget combined federal funds and trust funds, deducting transactions between them. Under this form, a $27.8-billion federal funds deficit will be partially offset by an expected $15.1-billion trust funds surplus, producing an estimated $12.7-billion fiscal 1974 deficit.

Federal funds are government revenues not earmarked at the source for specific purposes. Raised chiefly from taxes and borrowing, federal funds are available for all government purposes.

Trust funds, on the other hand, are government revenues collected separately and segregated for specific purposes. Primary examples are the Social Security and unemployment compensation trust funds, financed by payroll taxes, and the highway trust fund financed by gasoline taxes. Tax revenues to such trust funds and benefits paid from the funds are included in the unified budget.

A substantial part of the federal funds deficit is due to transactions with trust funds, primarily federal funds payments to social insurance trust funds and interest on federal debt securities held by the trust funds. From 1962 to 1972, for instance, more than $65-billion of a cumulative $152-billion federal funds deficit was attributed to transactions with trust funds.

The fiscal 1974 budget provided the following separate accounting for federal funds and trust funds, along with the total deficit:

Fiscal Years

(billions of dollars)

	1972 (actual)	1973 (estimate)	1974 (estimate)
Federal funds:			
Transactions with the public	—16.2	—13.1	— 7.2
Transactions with trust funds	—12.9	—21.0	—20.6
Total	—29.1	—34.1	—27.8
Trust funds:			
Transactions with the public	— 7.1	—11.7	— 5.4
Transactions with Federal funds	12.9	21.0	20.6
Total	5.9	9.3	15.1
Budget total:			
Federal funds	—29.1	—34.1	—27.8
Trust funds	5.9	9.3	15.1
Unified budget deficit	—23.2	—24.8	—12.7

Budget Authority and Outlays by Agency

(in millions of dollars)

Department or other unit	Budget authority			Outlays		
	1972 actual	1973 estimate	1974 estimate	1972 actual	1973 estimate	1974 estimate
Legislative Branch	$ 577	581	590	487	527	607
The Judiciary	178	194	205	173	192	204
Executive Office of the President	60	111	121	54	96	89
Funds appropriated to the President	7,158	5,756	5,115	4,276	3,872	3,936
Agriculture	12,825	11,532	10,400	10,935	10,124	9,562
Commerce	1,479	1,826	1,242	1,250	1,318	1,431
Defense—Military*	75,084	77,804	83,481	75,151	74,200	78,200
Defense—Civil	1,625	1,881	1,514	1,530	1,753	1,623
Health, Education and Welfare	75,708	87,859	101,880	71,780	83,580	93,822
Housing and Urban Development	4,081	5,048	3,713	3,642	3,364	4,768
Interior	1,652	—2,067	—356	1,256	—2,247	5
Justice	1,571	1,774	1,834	1,180	1,496	1,737
Labor	9,354	9,268	8,952	10,033	9,563	8,115
State	553	683	648	536	621	654
Transportation	8,658	11,327	9,025	7,531	8,042	8,139
Treasury	22,198	32,744	32,612	22,124	31,250	32,577
Atomic Energy Commission	2,293	2,633	2,429	2,392	2,194	2,374
Environmental Protection Agency	2,447	7,420	589	763	1,148	2,127
General Services Administration	790	96	175	589	40	499
National Aeronautics and Space Administration	3,307	3,407	3,015	3,422	3,061	3,135
Veterans Administration	11,292	12,566	12,209	10,710	11,759	11,703
Other Independent Agencies	13,064	15,553	15,765	9,919	11,726	10,738
Allowances for contingencies and civilian agency pay raises	——	750	2,000	——	500	1,750
Undistributed intragovernmental transactions:						
Employer share, employee retirement	—2,768	—2,980	—3,157	—2,768	—2,980	—3,157
Interest received by trust funds	—5,089	—5,401	—5,974	—5,089	—5,401	—5,974
TOTAL	**$248,097**	**280,366**	**288,029**	**231,876**	**249,796**	**268,665**

Includes allowances for all-volunteer force, retirement systems reform and civilian and military pay raises for Department of Defense.

SOURCE: 1974 Budget

Public Debt

The President's budget projected a $32.1-billion increase in the federal debt during fiscal 1974. If the projection is correct, an expected federal debt of $473.3-billion at the end of fiscal 1973 would increase to $505.5-billion by the end of fiscal 1974.

According to fiscal 1974 estimate, federal debt held by the public, including the Federal Reserve System, will rise $16.5-billion to a total of $365.3-billion.

The remaining $15.6-billion of the $32.1-billion fiscal 1974 increase is expected to be held by federal agencies and trust funds.

Role of Congress

The fiscal 1974 budget was submitted amid a growing dispute between Congress and the executive branch over federal spending. The issue, which centered on the President's practice of impounding appropriated funds, involved both the total of government spending and the uses to which the money was put.

In his budget message, the President blamed Congress for exceeding budgetary capacity and called for its cooperation in holding spending down.

"Should the Congress cause the total budgeted outlays to be exceeded, it would inescapably face the
(Continued on p. 48)

President's Special Revenue-Sharing Program . . .

Presenting his fiscal 1974 budget as an instrument for "revitalizing our over-all federal system," President Nixon in his Jan. 29 budget message proposed a $6.9-billion special revenue-sharing program to replace 70 "outmoded, narrower categorical grant programs."

The proposal, a scaled-down version of a special revenue-sharing plan in the President's 1971 State of the Union message, would provide broad-purpose grants for use by state and local governments for four purposes: education, law enforcement and criminal justice, manpower training and urban community development.

The 92nd Congress proved unreceptive to Nixon's initial special revenue-sharing plan, although it did enact a companion $5.3-billion general revenue-sharing program. As proposed in 1971, special revenue sharing would have consolidated 105 grant programs into an $11-billion package providing largely unrestricted grants for six broad purposes.

In renewing the proposal in his 1974 budget message, the President left out two of the 1971 plan's categories: transportation and rural community development. The transportation proposal was dropped because administration officials said they believed its purpose was served by proposals to allocate highway trust fund money for mass transportation development.

For rural development, the administration decided to rely on the Rural Development Act of 1972 to start programs "consistent with the revenue-sharing concept," the budget message said. Despite speculation that many health programs would be turned into a health revenue-sharing category, no such proposal was made in the budget.

The fiscal 1974 budget requests for revenue sharing were $2.8-billion for education, $1.3-billion for manpower and $800-million for law enforcement and criminal justice. The urban community development proposal was deferred until fiscal 1975, with an initial appropriation of $2.3-billion planned.

Education

The administration submitted education revenue-sharing legislation to Congress for a second time. The budget requested $2.8-billion for revenue sharing beginning July 1, 1973

The legislation proposed consolidation of 30 categorical grant programs for elementary and secondary education into five broad areas—elementary and secondary education; federal education impact aid for students whose parents both live and work on federal property (Category A); education for the handicapped; vocational and adult education; and school lunch programs.

In 1971, Nixon requested about $2.8-billion for education revenue sharing, which at that time did not include the school lunch program. Hearings were held on the 1971 proposal, but neither house took any further action.

Nixon requested $2.5-billion for fiscal 1974 for the four education areas and another $244-million for the school lunch programs. The education revenue-sharing legislation was expected to be submitted to Congress by mid-March.

Categorical grant programs to be terminated if education revenue-sharing legislation were approved, and for which there are no fiscal 1974 requests, include most of the programs under the Elementary and Secondary Education Act of 1965; several programs for education of the handicapped; most programs under the Adult Education Act of 1966, and the program for Category B students (those whose parents either lived or worked on federal property) under the federal impact aid authorization. All those programs will expire in fiscal 1973, although there will be an automatic one-year extension of the Elementary and Secondary Education Act.

Manpower

Although the House defeated the administration's manpower revenue-sharing proposal in 1971 and neither a Senate nor a House committee reported the proposal after hearings in 1972, the White House intended to implement the plan anyway under existing law. Labor Department officials said that the program would be authorized in fiscal 1974 by the Manpower Development and Training Act of 1962, the Economic Opportunity Act of 1964, as amended, and the Trade Expansion Act of 1962—legislation under which the categorical manpower programs were administered as well.

The budget authority request for manpower revenue sharing in fiscal 1974 was $1.34-billion. Seventy-four percent of the money would go to states and localities; the rest would cover administrative costs.

Appropriations Committees of both the House and Senate "have urged us in this direction," said the Labor Department officials, explaining the proposed budget's approach to manpower revenue sharing.

Some manpower programs would remain categorical and federal. These include JOBS, which subsidizes on-the-job training provided by private industry; the Work Incentive (WIN) program, which places welfare recipients in jobs; the national division of the Job Corps, which helped disadvantaged youth; in migrant program, which was to be transferred from the terminated Office of Economic Opportunity, and the phase-out period of the Emergency Employment Act, which provided public service jobs.

Other programs to be consolidated under manpower revenue sharing include the local section of the Neighborhood Youth Corps; Operation Mainstream; the Concentrated Employment Program, and the Public Service Careers program.

Under manpower revenue sharing, broad federal performance guidelines would be established. State and local programs would be monitored by the staff of the Manpower Administration in the Labor Department.

. . . 4-Purpose Block Grants, Not Categorical Aid

The House on June 2, 1971, defeated the initial manpower revenue-sharing proposal (HR 8141) by a 184-204 recorded teller vote. Both the House Education and Labor and the Senate Labor and Public Welfare Committees held hearings on the proposal (HR 6181, S 1423) in 1972, but no bill was reported.

Manpower revenue sharing's apparent lack of appeal, a Senate committee aide said, originated with the "no strings" principle. Congress was reluctant to relinquish control over manpower programs, he said.

Law Enforcement

President Nixon on March 2, 1971, set forth his first special revenue-sharing proposal, asking Congress to transform the block grants provided by the Law Enforcement Assistance Administration (LEAA) to state and local governments into revenue-sharing funds for law enforcement. Nixon asked Congress to do this by removing matching, maintenance-of-effort and federal approval requirements applying to the action block grants, which comprised the bulk of LEAA's swelling budget. The 92nd Congress took no action on the proposal.

But on June 30, 1973, the authorizing legislation for LEAA expired. Well before that time, the White House planned to send to Congress a revised law enforcement revenue-sharing measure. In the revised proposal, said administration officials, more of the LEAA functions will be contained: action grants, planning grants, corrections, grants, technical assistance and manpower development funds—totaling $800-million in fiscal 1974. The administration estimated that only $221-million of this annual amount would be spent in the first full year of the revenue-sharing program; it projected continuing annual appropriations of $800-million through fiscal 1978, with outlays reaching that annual level in fiscal 1976. The budget documents stated that LEAA would continue its federal functions—of technical development and dissemination, the development and application of data systems, and management. Under the special revenue sharing, the budget stated that the law enforcement funds would be distributed by formula among the states, with an assured "pass-through" to local governments. It noted also that unnecessarily restrictive federal limitations would be removed from the funds.

Urban Community Development

Urban community development revenue sharing was the only one of the special revenue-sharing proposals that neared enactment in the 92nd Congress. In his fiscal 1974 budget, President Nixon renewed his commitment to this approach and asked for a $2.3-billion program to begin on July 1, 1974—the start of fiscal 1975.

The program as proposed by the President terminated new commitments for categorical grants on Jan.

5 for some programs and would terminate others on June 30. It would allow existing contract obligations for these programs to be spent in fiscal 1974 and would begin the block grant program for cities at the start of fiscal 1975.

Loan programs for open-space land, water and sewer facilities and public facilities were terminated on Jan. 5. Model cities, urban renewal and rehabilitation loan programs would be terminated June 30. A wide range of physical, economic and social community development activities would be eligible under the new program in addition to those funded by the community development categorical programs.

In 1972, the Senate Banking, Housing and Urban Affairs Committee and the House Banking and Currency Committee each included, with some changes, the President's revenue-sharing program in their versions of the 1972 housing bill. But a 1972 housing bill was not enacted, because the House Rules Committee in late September deferred action on it, in effect killing it for the 92nd Congress.

Contrast

The special revenue sharing concept differs to a degree from the general revenue sharing enacted by Congress in 1972.

General revenue sharing provides money to be used at the discretion of local and state officials without requirements or an application. It is distributed according to a formula included in the law.

Special revenue sharing, if enacted, may have a formula, may require an application and the funds must be spent within the broad subject category for which it is intended. No federal approval is required for how the money is spent within each category, such as education or manpower.

The President's budget message said his special revenue sharing plan would eliminate matching state and local fund requirements from most of the programs being replaced. Special revenue sharing funds would be distributed according to "formulas appropriate to each area," the message said.

In the case of manpower revenue sharing, the message said the administration would request a simple extension of existing law and remove existing administrative requirements "so that state and local governments can group manpower services in ways that best meet their own local needs."

The fiscal 1974 budget in its termination statement on a variety of categorical grant programs indicated that the administration expects cities and states will continue the programs with these revenue sharing funds —both general and special.

The National League of Cities and U.S. Conference of Mayors Feb. 3 said the "magnitude" of program cuts in the budget will leave local government "far behind their position last year, before general revenue sharing was enacted."

(Continued from p. 45)

alternatives of higher taxes, higher interest rates, renewed inflation, or all three," the President said. "I oppose these alternatives; with a firm rein on spending, none of them is necessary."

In addition to urging enactment of a statutory budget ceiling, the President's message devoted a section to a critique of the congressional budget procedures.

"Specific changes in congressional procedures, are, of course, the business of the Congress," the President said. "However, the manner in which the Congress reviews and modifies the budget impinges so heavily on the management of the executive branch that I am impelled to suggest a few subjects" for consideration by a special Joint Committee on Budget Reform. The committee was formed in the 93rd Congress to study ways of improving the congressional budgetary process. *(Budget reform, impoundment stories, chapter on Congress and Government.)*

Nixon's suggestions included adoption of a spending ceiling before Congress considers any appropriations bills, an end to "backdoor financing" bypassing the appropriations process, elimination of annual authorizations and early action on all fiscal 1974 appropriations bills.

The budget document made clear that Congress will have only limited control over fiscal 1974 outlays. Of $288-billion in budget authority recommended for fiscal 1974, only $172.8-billion required congressional action.

The remaining $115.2-billion in budget authority already was available under existing laws without further congressional action. That total included $108.5-billion automatically appropriated to trust funds and $26.1-billion appropriated for interest on the public law under a permanent appropriation enacted in 1847.

There was only an indirect relationship, moreover, between the $288-billion in appropriations recommended for fiscal 1974 and the $268.7-billion in outlays planned for fiscal 1974. Of the fiscal 1974 spending total, only $173.9-billion would be funds appropriated in fiscal 1974; the remaining $94.8-billion was from unspent authority enacted in previous years.

The fiscal 1974 spending plan left $114.1-billion in fiscal 1974 authority for outlays in future years. Together with an additional $191.6-billion in unspent authority from previous years, authority to be carried over from fiscal 1974 brought the total of unspent authority available for future years to $305.7-billion.

NEW VICE PRESIDENT, 10 CABINET CHANGES IN 1973

In 1973, for the first time, a vice president was selected under the 25th Amendment to the Constitution. Ratified in 1967, the amendment requires confirmation of the president's nominee to fill a vacancy by a majority of both houses of Congress. House Minority Leader Gerald R. Ford (R Mich.) was confirmed by the Senate Nov. 27 and the House Dec. 6 to become the 40th vice president of the United States. He succeeded Spiro T. Agnew, who resigned Oct. 10 after pleading no contest to a charge of income tax evasion. *(Agnew, Ford stories p. 20, 26)*

Another first in 1973 was the confirmation of Clarence M. Kelley as director of the Federal Bureau of Investigation. The post was made subject to Senate confirmation upon the death in 1972 of J. Edgar Hoover, the only permanent director the organization had ever had.

Administration Shifts. Of the 10 cabinet changes President Nixon made during 1973, three involved Elliot L. Richardson. Richardson left his post as secretary of health, education and welfare in January to become secretary of defense, only to resign that position five months later to become attorney general. Richardson left the administration Oct. 20 when he resigned rather than fire special Watergate prosecutor Archibald Cox. Richardson's successor as attorney general was Sen. William B. Saxbe (R Ohio), who was confirmed Dec. 17 but did not take office until 1974.

Deputy Attorney General William D. Ruckelshaus, also a casualty of the Cox controversy, submitted his resignation Oct. 20. Ruckelshaus previously had served as administrator of the Environmental Protection Agency and as acting director of the FBI—where he succeeded L. Patrick Gray III, who resigned under fire April 27 after his nomination as permanent FBI director was withdrawn.

James R. Schlesinger, chairman of the Atomic Energy Commission since 1971, was confirmed as director of the Central Intelligence Agency (CIA) Jan. 23. Five months later he became secretary of defense, replacing Richardson. Schlesinger's successor as CIA director was William E. Colby, former chief of CIA's clandestine operations.

Nomination Controversies. For the first time since 1950, the Senate in 1973 struck down a nomination to a major independent federal regulatory agency. The Senate June 13 recommitted the nomination of Robert H. Morris to be a member of the Federal Power Commission. Opponents said he was too closely tied to the oil industry. Don S. Smith, a "consumer-oriented" Democrat, was confirmed in his place Nov. 28.

A Senate committee agreed in December to withhold indefinitely any action on President Nixon's nomination of William J. Casey as president of the Export-Import Bank. Casey, under secretary of state for economic affairs since January, previously had served as chairman of

Cabinet Members, 1973

Agriculture. Earl L. Butz (12/2/71-).

Commerce. Peter G. Peterson (2/21/72-1/20/73); Frederick B. Dent (1/20/73-).

Defense. Melvin R. Laird (1/20/69-1/20/73); Elliot L. Richardson (1/29/73-4/30/73); James R. Schlesinger (6/28/73-).

Health, Education and Welfare. Elliot L. Richardson (6/15/70-1/20/73); Caspar W. Weinberger (2/8/73-).

Housing and Urban Development. George W. Romney (1/20/69—1/20/73); James T. Lynn (1/31/73-).

Interior. Rogers C. B. Morton (2/8/71-).

Justice. Richard G. Kleindienst (6/8/72-4/30/73); Elliot L. Richardson (5/23/73-10/20/73); William B. Saxbe (confirmed 12/17/73- ; sworn in 1/4/74).

Labor. James D. Hodgson (6/17/70-1/20/73); Peter J. Brennan (1/31/73-).

State. William P. Rogers (1/20/69-9/3/73); Henry A. Kissinger (9/21/73-).

Transportation. John A. Volpe (1/20/69-1/20/73); Claude S. Brinegar (1/20/73-).

Treasury. George P. Shultz (6/8/72-).

the Securities and Exchange Commission (SEC). Critics alleged that Casey tried during 1972 to shield from congressional investigators SEC files concerning the settlement of an antitrust case against International Telephone and Telegraph Corp. (ITT).

A nomination that was never made also aroused controversy in 1973. Following a June court ruling that Howard J. Phillips, acting director of the Office of Economic Opportunity (OEO), could no longer serve in the job because he never had been confirmed by the Senate, Nixon appointed and the Senate confirmed Alvin J. Arnett as OEO director.

Judicial Nominations. The Senate in 1973 confirmed President Nixon's nominations to 21 federal circuit and district judgeships. During his first five years as president, Nixon made more judicial appointments (198) than any other president. President Franklin D. Roosevelt appointed 194 judges in his 12 years as chief executive. As of Jan. 11, 1974, there were 19 vacancies in the federal courts: two in the circuit courts and 17 in the district courts.

Total Nominations. In the first session of the 93rd Congress, the Senate received 68,080 nominations and confirmed 66,817. President Nixon withdrew 10 nominations which had been submitted to the Senate, and 1,253 nominations remained unconfirmed at the end of the first session.

Confirmations of 1973 Nominations

Listed below are the names of 196 persons named to major federal posts by President Nixon and confirmed by the Senate in 1973. Information is given in the following order: name of office, salary, appointee, voting residence, occupation before appointment, date and place of birth, party affiliation (if known) and date of Senate confirmation. Ambassadorial confirmations are listed only if the appointment was of more than routine interest.

Vice President of the United States

$62,500 and $10,000 for expenses—**Gerald R. Ford;** Grand Rapids, Mich.; U.S. representative (R Mich. 1949-73); July 14, 1913, in Omaha, Neb.; Rep.; Nov. 25 (Senate) and Dec. 6 (House).

Executive Office of the President

Office of Economic Opportunity

Director, $42,500—**Alvin J. Arnett;** Bethesda, Md.; deputy assistant director of OEO (operations); Feb. 6, 1935, in Saylersville, Ky.; Rep.; Sept. 12.

Central Intelligence Agency

Director, $42,500—**James R. Schlesinger;** Arlington, Va.; chairman, Atomic Energy Commission; Feb. 15, 1929, in New York City; Rep.; Jan. 23.

Director, $42,500—**William Egan Colby;** Springfield, Md.; deputy director of CIA (operations); Jan. 4, 1920, in St. Paul, Minn.; Aug. 1.

Council of Economic Advisers

Member, $38,000—**William John Fellner;** New Haven, Conn.; on leave of absence as resident scholar, American Enterprise Institute; May 31, 1905, in Budapest, Hungary; Oct. 18.

Member, $38,000—**Gary L. Seevers;** Jonesville, Mich.; special assistant to chairman, Council of Economic Advisers; May 24, 1937, in Jonesville, Mich.; July 11.

Departments

Agriculture Department

Assistant Secretary (rural development), $38,000—**William W. Erwin;** Bourbon, Ind.; deputy under secretary (rural development); Sept. 28, 1925, in Plymouth, Ind.; Rep.; Jan. 23.

Assistant Secretary (conservation, research and education), $38,000—**Robert W. Long;** Palo Alto, Calif.; senior vice president, Bank of America; Oct. 27, 1922, in Chicago, Ill.; Rep.; March 12.

Assistant Secretary (marketing and consumer services), $38,000—**Clayton Yeutter;** Lincoln, Neb.; midwest regional director and director for agriculture, Committee for the Re-election of the President; Dec. 10, 1930, in Eustis, Neb.; Rep.; Jan. 23.

General Counsel, $38,000—**John A. Knebel;** Annandale Va.; general counsel, Small Business Administration; Oct. 4, 1936, in Tulsa, Okla.; Rep.; Jan. 23.

Commerce Department

Secretary, $60,000—**Frederick B. Dent;** Spartanburg, S.C.; president, Mayfair Mills; Aug. 17, 1922, in Cape May, N.J.; Rep.; Jan. 18.

Under Secretary, $40,000—**John K. Tabor;** Pittsburgh, Pa.; partner in the law firm of Kirkpatrick, Lockhart, John-

son and Hutchison; April 19, 1921, in Uniontown, Pa.; Rep.; June 13.

Assistant Secretary (science and technology), $38,000—**Dr. Betsy Ancker-Johnson;** Seattle, Wash.; academic/science adviser, Boeing Co.; April 27, 1929, in Seattle, Wash.; April 10.

Assistant Secretary (domestic and international business), $38,000—**Tilton H. Dobbin;** Owings Mills, Md.; president, chairman of the executive committee and member of the board of directors of Maryland National Bank; April 9, 1917, in Howard County, Md.; Rep.; June 13.

Assistant Secretary (economic affairs), $38,000—**Dr. Sidney L. Jones;** Ann Arbor, Mich.; director, Bradley Woods and Co.; Sept. 23, 1933, in Ogden Utah; June 27.

Assistant Secretary (administration), $38,000—**Henry B. Turner;** Rolling Mills, Calif.; first vice president, director and manager of corporate finance department of Mitchum, Jones and Templeton, Inc.; Sept. 3, 1936, in New York City; Rep.; April 6.

Assistant Secretary (tourism), $38,000—**C. Langhorne Washburn;** McLean, Va.; Committee for the Re-election of the President; July 14, 1918, in Livermore, Maine; Rep.; April 6.

General Counsel, $38,000—**Karl E. Bakke;** Falls Church, Va.; deputy general counsel, Commerce Department, July 3, 1930, in New Haven, Conn.; Rep.; Aug. 3.

Director, National Bureau of Standards, $36,000—**Richard W. Roberts;** Schenectady, N.Y.; research and development manager for materials, science and engineering, General Electric Co.; Jan. 12, 1935, in Buffalo, N.Y.; Rep.; Feb. 1.

Director, Census Bureau, $36,000—**Vincent R. Barabba;** Los Angeles, Calif.; chairman of the board, Decision Making Information, Inc.; Sept. 6, 1934, in Chicago, Ill.; July 24.

Defense Department

Secretary, $60,000—**Elliot L. Richardson;** Brookline, Mass.; secretary of Health, Education and Welfare Department; July 20, 1920, in Boston, Mass.; Rep.; Jan. 29.

Judgeships as Patronage

The prestige of a federal judgeship is high, and appointment to the judiciary is considered by most attorneys and politicians to be the apex of a legal and public career.

Federal judgeships are lifetime appointments and pay $42,500 in the circuit court and $40,000 in the district court annually. There is no mandatory retirement age, but judges may retire at full salary at age 65 after 15 years or at 70 after 10 years on the bench.

The following list gives the number of confirmed federal circuit and district court judges appointed by President Nixon during his first five years in office and by his five immediate predecessors.

	Democrats	Republicans
Roosevelt	188	6
Truman	116	9
Eisenhower	9	165
Kennedy†	111	11
Johnson	159	9
Nixon (first term)*	12	162
Nixon (1973)‡	——	21

† One New York Liberal also was appointed.
* In addition, one judge was appointed from the New Progressive Party of Puerto Rico and no party affiliation was available for another Puerto Rican appointee.
‡ One Independent was also appointed.

Secretary, $60,000—**James R. Schlesinger**; Arlington, Va.; director, Central Intelligence Agency; Feb. 15, 1929, in New York City; Rep.; June 28.

Deputy Secretary, $42,500—**William P. Clements Jr.**; Dallas, Texas; chairman of the board, SEDCO, Inc.; April 13, 1917, in Dallas, Texas; Rep.; Jan. 23.

Assistant Secretary (manpower and reserve affairs), $38,000—**William Keith Brehm**; Los Angeles, Calif.; assistant secretary (manpower and reserve affairs), U.S. Army; March 29, 1929, in Dearborn, Mich.; Aug. 3.

Assistant Secretary (public affairs), $38,000—**Jerry Warden Friedheim**; Alexandria, Va.; principal deputy assistant secretary (public affairs), Defense Department; Oct. 7, 1934, in Joplin, Mo.; Rep.; April 13.

Assistant Secretary (international security affairs), $38,000—**Robert C. Hill**; Littleton, N.H.; U.S. ambassador to Spain; Sept. 30, 1917, in Littleton, N.H.; Rep.; May 10.

Assistant Secretary (comptroller), $38,000—**Terence E. McClary**; Lynnfield, Mass.; vice president (comptroller and contracts) of Sanders Associates, Inc.; Dec. 1, 1921, in Lincoln, Neb.; Dem.; June 15.

Assistant Secretary (legislative affairs), $38,000—**John O. Marsh Jr.**; Strasburg, Va.; former U.S. representative (D Va. 1963-71); Aug. 7, 1926, in Winchester, Va.; Ind.; April 13.

Assistant Secretary (installations and logistics), $38,000—**Arthur I. Mendolia**; Greenville, Del.; vice president and general manager, Polymer Intermediates Department of E. I. duPont de Nemours Co.; May 6, 1917, in Brooklyn, N.Y.; Rep.; June 15.

Army

Secretary, $42,500—**Howard H. Callaway**; Pine Mountain, Ga.; president, Interfinancial, Inc.; April 2, 1927, in La Grange, Ga.; Rep.; May 10.

Assistant Secretary (research and development), $38,000—**Norman R. Augustine**; McLean, Va.; director of advanced missiles and space systems; Vought Systems Division, LTV Aerospace Inc.; July 27, 1935, in Denver, Colo.; Sept. 13.

Assistant Secretary (installations and logistics), $38,000—**Eugene E. Berg**; Edina, Minn.; executive of interest, Canadian JETS, Univac defense systems division; Feb. 16, 1928, in Marietta, Minn.; Rep.; Nov. 20.

Assistant Secretary (financial management), $38,000—**Hadlai A. Hull**; Wayzata, Minn.; assistant secretary (manpower and reserve affairs), U.S. Army; May 30, 1914, in New London, Conn.; Rep.; March 22.

Assistant Secretary (manpower and reserve affairs), $38,000—**Carl S. Wallace**; Alexandria, Va.; special assistant to the secretary and deputy secretary of Defense Department; Sept. 27, 1918, in Ontario, Wis.; Rep.; March 22.

Under Secretary, $38,000—**Herman R. Staudt**; Fairfax, Va.; vice president for operations, Orlando Aerospace Division of Martin Marietta Corp.; June 29, 1926, in Yonkers, N.Y.; Oct. 8.

Navy

Assistant Secretary (installations and logistics), $38,000—**Jack L. Bowers**; El Cajon, Calif.; president, Electro Dynamic Division of General Dynamics Corp.; Aug. 25, 1920, in Colorado Springs, Colo.; Rep.; June 15.

Assistant Secretary (research and development), $38,000—**David Samuel Potter**; McLean, Va.; director of research, Detroit Diesel Allison Division, General Motors Corp.; Jan. 16, 1925, in Seattle, Wash.; Sept. 13.

Under Secretary, $38,000—**J. William Middendorf II**; Greenwich, Conn.; U.S. ambassador to the Netherlands; Sept. 22, 1924, in Baltimore, Md.; Rep.; July 26.

Air Force

Secretary, $42,500—**John L. McLucas**; Concord, Mass.; under secretary of the Air Force; Aug. 22, 1920, in Fayetteville, N.C.; July 14.

Assistant Secretary (research and development), $38,000—**Dr. Walter B. LaBerge**; McLean, Va.; technical director, Naval Weapons Center, China Lake, Calif.; March 29, 1924, in Chicago, Ill.; Sept. 13.

Assistant Secretary (installations and logistics), $38,000—**Frank A. Shrontz**; McLean, Va.; director of sales operations, Boeing Co.; Dec. 14, 1931, in Boise, Idaho; Oct. 8.

Assistant Secretary (financial management), $38,000—**William W. Woodruff**; Alexandria, Va.; counsel to Senate Appropriations Committee; July 15, 1924, in McDonough, Ga.; March 22.

Under Secretary, $38,000—**James W. Plummer**; Los Altos, Calif.; vice president, Lockheed Aircraft Corp. and Lockheed Missiles and Space Co. and general manager, space systems division; Jan. 29, 1920, in Idaho Springs, Colo.; Rep.; Dec. 14.

Department of Health, Education and Welfare

Secretary, $60,000—**Caspar W. Weinberger**; Hillsborough, Calif.; director, Office of Management and Budget; Aug. 18, 1917, in San Francisco, Calif.; Rep.; Feb. 8.

Under Secretary, $40,000—**Frank C. Carlucci**; Wilkes-Barre, Pa.; director, Office of Economic Opportunity; Oct. 18, 1930, in Scranton, Pa.; Jan. 18.

Assistant Secretary (health), $38,000—**Dr. Charles C. Edwards**; Bethesda, Md.; commissioner of food and drugs; Sept. 16, 1923, in Overton, Neb.; Rep.; April 2.

Assistant Secretary (public affairs), $38,000—**Lewis M. Helm**; Silver Spring, Md.; public information officer, Interior Department; Sept. 9, 1931, in Riverdale, Md.; Rep.; June 15.

Assistant Secretary (planning and evaluation), $38,000—**William A. Morrill**; Alexandria, Va.; assistant director, Office of Management and Budget; April 23, 1930, in Bronxville, N.Y.; June 15.

Assistant Secretary (human development), $38,000—**Stanley B. Thomas Jr.**; Washington, D.C.; deputy assistant secretary (youth and student affairs), HEW; April 28, 1942, in New York City; Rep.; July 24.

General Counsel, $38,000—**John B. Rhinelander**; McLean, Va.; partner in the law firm of Sidley and Austin; June 18, 1933, in Boston, Mass.; Rep.; Oct. 4.

Commissioner of Education, $36,000—**John R. Ottina**; Los Angeles, Calif.; acting commissioner of education and deputy commissioner of education for planning, evaluation and management; Nov. 5, 1931, in Los Angeles, Calif.; July 26.

Commissioner of Social Security, $36,000—**James B. Cardwell**; Rockville, Md.; assistant secretary (comptroller), HEW; Sept. 28, 1922, in Washington, D.C.; Oct. 4.

Department of Housing and Urban Development

Secretary, $60,000—**James T. Lynn**; Cleveland, Ohio; under secretary, Commerce Department; Feb. 27, 1927, in Cleveland, Ohio; Rep.; Jan. 31.

Under Secretary, $40,000—**Floyd H. Hyde**; Fresno, Calif.; assistant secretary (community development), HUD; March 18, 1921, in Fresno, Calif.; Rep.; March 14.

Assistant Secretary (housing management), $38,000—**H. R. Crawford**; Washington, D.C.; vice president, Pollinger-Crawford Corp.; Jan. 18, 1939, in Winston-Salem, N.C.; Dem.; March 14.

Assistant Secretary (housing production and mortgage credit) and Federal Housing Commissioner, $38,000—**Sheldon B. Lubar**; Shorewood, Wis.; chairman and chief executive officer, Mortgage Associates, Inc.; May 21, 1929, in Milwaukee, Wis.; June 30.

Assistant Secretary (community planning and development), **David Olan Meeker Jr.**; Indianapolis, Ind.; deputy mayor of Indianapolis; May 19, 1924, in Clifton, Spring, N.Y.; Rep.; July 28.

Assistant Secretary (legislative affairs), $38,000—**Sol Mosher;** Springfield, Mo.; special assistant to secretary of Commerce for congressional relations; April 14, 1928, in Chicago, Ill.; March 14.

Assistant Secretary (policy development and research), $38,000—**Michael H. Moskow;** Paterson, N.J.; assistant secretary (policy, evaluation and research), Labor Department; Jan. 7, 1938, in Paterson, N.J.; Rep.; March 14.

Assistant Secretary (equal opportunity), $38,000—**Dr. Gloria E. A. Toote;** New York City; assistant director of ACTION and director of ACTION's office of voluntary action Nov. 8, 1931, in New York City; Rep.; June 1.

General Counsel, $38,000—**James L. Mitchell;** Winnetka, Ill.; special assistant to the secretary of Commerce for policy development and director, Office of Policy Development, Commerce Department; May 20, 1937, in Evanston, Ill.; Rep.; March 14.

Interior Department

Under Secretary, $40,000—**John C. Whitaker;** Bethesda, Md.; deputy assistant to the President for environment, natural resources and energy policy; Dec. 29, 1926, in Victoria, B.C., Canada; Rep.; Jan. 18.

Assistant Secretary (management), $38,000—**James T. Clarke;** Grosse Pointe Farms, Mich.; partner in the management consulting firm of Coopers and Lybrand; May 18, 1937, in Harbor Springs, Mich.; Rep.; May 21.

Assistant Secretary (land and water resources), $38,000—**Jack O. Horton;** Saddlestring, Wyo.; co-chairman of Joint Federal-State Land Planning Commission for Alaska; Jan. 28, 1938, in Sheridan, Wyo.; Rep.; March 1.

Assistant Secretary (congressional and public affairs), $38,000—**John H. Kyl;** Bloomfield, Iowa; U.S. representative (R 1959-65, 1967-73); May 9, 1919, in Wisner, Neb.; Rep.; Feb. 20.

Assistant Secretary (program development and budget), $38,000—**Laurence E. Lynn Jr.;** Washington, D.C.; assistant secretary (planning and evaluation), HEW; June 10, 1937, in Long Beach, Calif.; April 17.

Assistant Secretary (energy and minerals), $38,000—**Stephen A. Wakefield;** Houston, Texas; deputy assistant secretary (mineral resources), Interior Department; Oct. 18, 1940, in Olney, Ill.; Rep.; March 22.

Solicitor, $38,000—**Dale Kent Frizzell;** Topeka, Kan.; assistant attorney general (land and natural resources), Feb. 11, 1929, in Wichita, Kan.; Rep.; April 17.

Commissioner of Indian Affairs, $36,000—**Morris Thompson;** Douglas, Alaska; Alaska area director of Bureau of Indian Affairs, Sept. 11, 1939, in Tanana, Alaska; Rep.; Nov. 28.

Justice Department

Attorney General, $60,000—**Elliot L. Richardson;** Brookline, Mass.; secretary of Defense; July 20, 1920, in Boston, Mass.; Rep.; May 23.

Attorney General, $35,000—**William B. Saxbe;** Mechanicsburg, Ohio; U.S. senator (R Ohio 1969-73); June 24, 1916, in Mechanicsburg, Ohio; Rep.; Dec. 17.

Deputy Attorney General, $42,500—**Joseph T. Sneed;** Durham, N.C.; dean, Duke Law School; July 21, 1920, in Calvert, Texas; Feb. 1.

Deputy Attorney General, $42,500—**William D. Ruckelshaus;** Indianapolis, Ind.; acting director, FBI; July 24, 1932, in Indianapolis, Ind.; Rep.; Sept. 13.

Solicitor General, $40,000—**Robert H. Bork;** New Haven, Conn.; professor of law, Yale Law School; March 1, 1927, in Pittsburgh, Pa.; Feb. 1.

Assistant Attorney General (office of legal counsel), $38,000—**Robert G. Dixon Jr.;** Rockville, Md.; professor of law, George Washington University; April 24, 1920, in Canajoharie, N.Y.; Feb. 1.

Assistant Attorney General (land and natural resources), $38,000—**Wallace H. Johnson Jr.;** Vienna, Va.; special as-

sistant for legislative affairs, White House; Oct. 7, 1939, in Cleveland, Ohio; Rep.; April 10.

Assistant Atorney General (office of alien property), $38,000—**James D. McKevitt;** Denver, Colo.; U.S. representative (R Colo. 1971-73); Oct. 26, 1928, in Spokane, Wash.; Rep.; Feb. 1.

Assistant Attorney General (civil rights), $38,000—**J. Stanley Pottinger;** Bethesda, Md.; director, Office of Civil Rights, HEW; Feb. 13, 1940, in Dayton, Ohio; Rep.; Feb. 1.

Commissioner of Immigration and Naturalization, $36,000—**Leonard F. Chapman Jr.;** Alexandria, Va.; commandant of U.S Marine Corps; Nov. 3, 1913, in Key West, Fla.; Nov. 20.

Federal Bureau of Investigation

Director, $40,000—**Clarence M. Kelley;** Kansas City, Mo.; chief of police, Kansas City, Mo.; Oct. 23, 1911, in Kansas City, Mo.; June 27.

Law Enforcement Assistance Administration

Administrator, $40,000—**Donald E. Santarelli;** Alexandria, Va.; associate deputy attorney general; July 22, 1937, in Hershey, Pa.; Rep.; April 10.

Labor Department

Secretary, $60,000—**Peter J. Brennan;** New York City; president, New York City and New York State Building and Construction Trades Councils; May 24, 1918, in New York City; Dem.; Jan. 31.

Under Secretary, $40,000—**Richard F. Schubert;** Easton, Pa.; solicitor, Labor Department; Nov. 2, 1936, in Trenton, N.J.; Rep.; May 16.

Assistant Secretary (employment standards), $38,000—**Bernard E. DeLury;** Floral Park, N.Y.; deputy industrial commissioner, New York State Department of Labor; April 1, 1938, in Brooklyn, N.Y.; Rep.; May 16.

Assistant Secretary (labor-management relations), $38,000—**Paul J. Fasser Jr.;** McLean, Va.; deputy assistant secretary (manpower) and Manpower Administrator; June 15, 1926, in Gary, Ind.; April 6.

Assistant Secretary (occupational safety and health), $38,000—**John H. Stender;** Auburn, Wash.; state senator; July 16, 1916, in Ismay, Mont.; Rep.; April 3.

Solicitor, $38,000—**William Jeffrey Kilberg;** New York City; associate solicitor (labor relations and civil rights), Labor Department; June 12, 1946, in Brooklyn, N.Y.; Rep.; April 6.

State Department

Secretary, $60,000—**Henry A. Kissinger;** Washington, D.C.; special assistant to the President for national security affairs; May 27, 1923, in Furth, Germany; Sept. 21.

Deputy Secretary, $42,500—**Kenneth Rush;** Rye, N.Y.; deputy secretary, Defense Department; Jan. 17, 1910, in Walla Walla, Wash.; Rep.; Feb. 1.

Under Secretary (economic affairs), $40,000—**William J. Casey;** Roslyn Harbor, N.Y.; chairman of Securities and Exchange Commission; March 13, 1913, in Elmhurst, N.Y.; Rep.; Feb. 1.

Under Secretary (coordinating security assistance programs), $40,000—**William H. Donaldson;** New York City; chairman of brokerage house of Donaldson, Lufkin & Jenrette, Inc.; June 2, 1931, in Buffalo, N.Y.; Ind.; Nov. 20.

Under Secretary (political affairs), $40,000—**William J. Porter;** Westport Point, Mass.; chief U.S. delegate to Paris peace talks; Sept. 1, 1914, in Stalybridge, England; Feb. 1.

Assistant Secretary (economic development), $38,000—**William W. Blunt Jr.;** Washington, D.C.; deputy assistant secretary (economic development), Commerce Department; Dec. 19, 1936, in New York City; Sept. 26.

Assistant Secretary (international organization affairs) $38,-000—**William B. Buffum;** Pelham, N.Y.; U.S. ambassador to Lebanon; Sept. 10, 1921, in Binghamton, N.Y.; Dec. 18.

Assistant Secretary (east Asian and Pacific affairs), $38,000—**Robert Stephen Ingersoll;** Winnetka, Ill.; U.S. ambassador to Japan; Jan. 28, 1914, in Galesburg, Ill.; Rep.; Dec. 18.

Assistant Secretary (public affairs), $38,000—**Carol C. Laise;** Putney, Vt.; U.S. ambassador to Nepal; Nov. 14, 1917, in Winchester, Va.; Sept. 19.

Assistant Secretary (international organization affairs), $38,000—**David H. Popper;** Buffalo, N.Y.; U.S. ambassador to the Republic of Cyprus; Oct. 3, 1912, in New York City; June 6.

Assistant Secretary (administration), $38,000—**John M. Thomas;** Ida Grove, Iowa; deputy assistant secretary (operations), State Department; Oct. 12, 1926, in Ida Grove, Iowa; Dec. 20.

Agency for International Development

Administrator, $42,500—**Daniel Parker;** Janesville, Wis.; chairman of the board, Parker Pen Co., June 8, 1925, in Chicago, Ill.; Rep.; Oct. 12.

Assistant Administrator (legislative affairs), $38,000—**Matthew J. Harvey;** Upper Marlboro, Md.; director, Office of Legislative Affairs (AID); Dec. 13, 1924, in Boston, Mass.; Rep.; June 6.

Ambassadors

Salaries for Ambassadors depend upon seniority and station, and range between $36,000 and $42,500 per year. Only those appointments which are of more than routine interest are listed.

At Large—**U. Alexis Johnson;** Washington, D.C.; under secretary of state (political affairs); Oct. 17, 1908, in Falun, Kan.; Feb. 1.

At Large—**Ellsworth Bunker;** Putney, Vt.; U.S. ambassador to Vietnam; May 11, 1894, in Yonkers, N.Y.; Sept. 19.

Argentina—**Robert C. Hill;** Littleton, N.H.; assistant secretary (international security affairs), Defense Department; Sept. 30, 1917, in Littleton, N.H.; Rep.; Dec. 19.

Denmark—**Philip K. Crowe;** Easton, Md.; U.S. ambassador to Norway; Jan. 7, 1908, in New York City; July 12.

Finland—**V. John Krehbiel;** South Laguna, Calif; underwriter, Aetna Life and Casualty Co.; July 29, 1905, in Reno County, Kan.; Rep.; March 26.

France—**John N. Irwin II;** New York City; under secretary of state; Dec. 31, 1913, in Keokuk, Iowa; Rep.; Feb. 1.

Honduras—**Phillip V. Sanchez;** Fresno, Calif.; director, Office of Economic Opportunity; July 28, 1929, in Pinedale, Calif.; Rep.; May 17.

Hungary—**Richard F. Pedersen;** Stockton, Calif.; counselor, State Department; Feb. 21, 1925, in Miami, Ariz.; July 18.

Israel—**Kenneth B. Keating;** New York City; partner in the law firm of Royall, Koegel and Wells; and former member of Congress (R N.Y. House 1946-53, 1956-57; Senate 1958-65); May 18, 1900, in Lima, N.Y.; Rep.; June 15.

Italy—**John A. Volpe;** Winchester, Mass.; secretary of Transportation Department; Dec. 8, 1908, in Wakefield, Mass.; Rep.; Feb. 1.

Kenya—**Anthony D. Marshall;** New York City; U.S. ambassador to Trinidad and Tobago; May 30, 1924, in New York City; Dec. 18.

Luxembourg—**Ruth Lewis Farkas;** New York City; member of the board of directors and executive committee of Alexander's Inc.; Dec. 20, 1906, in New York City; Rep.; March 26.

Morocco—**Robert G. Neumann;** Los Angeles, Calif.; U.S. ambassador to Afghanistan; Jan. 2, 1916, in Vienna, Austria; Rep.; Sept. 19.

NATO—**Donald Rumsfeld;** Wilmette, Ill.; director, Cost of Living Council; July 9, 1932, in Evanston, Ill.; Rep.; Feb. 1.

Netherlands—**Kingdon Gould Jr.;** Laurel, Md.; limited partner in Parking Management Inc.; Jan. 6, 1924, in New York City; Rep.; Sept. 26.

Philippines—**William H. Sullivan;** Cranston, R.I.: deputy assistant secretary of state (east Asian and Pacific affairs); Oct. 12, 1922, in Cranston, R.I.; July 12.

Portugal—**Stuart Nash Scott;** New York City; member of the law firm of Dewey, Bushby, Palmer and Wood; Dec. 6, 1906, in Madison, Wis.; Dec. 18.

Thailand—**William R. Kintner;** Bryn Athyn, Pa.; professor of political science, University of Pennsylvania and director, Foreign Policy Research Institute; April 21, 1915, in Lock Haven, Pa.; Sept. 26.

Turkey—**William B. Macomber Jr.;** Rochester, N.Y.; deputy under secretary of state (management); March 28, 1921, in Rochester, N.Y.; Rep.; March 26.

United Nations—**John A. Scali;** Washington, D.C.; special consultant to the President for foreign affairs; April 27, 1918, in Canton, Ohio; Feb. 1.

U.S.S.R.—**Walter J. Stoessel Jr.;** Santa Monica, Calif.; assistant secretary of state (European affairs); Jan. 24, 1920, in Manhattan. Kan.; Dec. 19.

Transportation Department

Secretary, $60,000—**Claude S. Brinegar;** Rolling Hills, Calif.; senior vice president, Union Oil Co.; Dec. 16, 1926, in Rockport, Calif.; Rep.; Jan. 18.

Under Secretary, $42,500—**John W. Barnum;** New York City; general counsel, Transportation Department; Aug. 25, 1928, in New York City; Rep.; June 28.

Under Secretary, $42,500—**Egil Krogh Jr.;** Washington, D.C.; deputy assistant to the President for domestic affairs; Aug. 3, 1939, in Chicago, Ill.; Rep.; Jan. 18.

Assistant Secretary (congressional and intergovernmental affairs), $38,000—**Robert T. Monagan Jr.;** Tracy, Calif.; member and Republican leader of California Assembly; July 5, 1920, in Ogden, Utah; Rep.; April 6.

General Counsel, $38,000—**Rodney Eugene Eyster;** Chicago, Ill.; partner in the law firm of Sonnenschein, Levinson, Carlin, Nath & Rosenthal; Sept. 21, 1928, in York, Pa.; Dec. 19.

Administrator, Federal Aviation Administration, $42,500—**Alexander P. Butterfield;** Alexandria, Va.; deputy assistant to the President; April 6, 1926, in Pensacola, Fla.; Rep.; March 12.

Administrator, Federal Highway Administration, $40,000—**Norbert T. Tiemann;** Lincoln, Neb.; vice president for corporate finance, First Mid-America Inc.; former governor of Nebraska (R 1967-71); July 18, 1924, in Minden, Neb.; Rep.; May 16.

Administrator, National Highway Traffic Safety Administration, $40,000—**James B. Gregory;** Fullerton, Calif.; retired as manager of environmental sciences, Union Oil Co. of California; April 2, 1925, in Alhambra, Calif.; Aug. 3.

Administrator, Urban Mass Transportation Administration, $40,000—**Frank C. Herringer;** Fairfax, Va.; staff assistant at White House; Nov. 12, 1942, in New York City; Rep.; Jan. 31.

Treasury Department

Deputy Secretary, $42,500—**William E. Simon;** New Vernon, N.J.; partner in the investment banking firm of Salomon Brothers; Nov. 27, 1927, in Paterson, N.J.; Rep.; Jan. 16.

Comptroller of the Currency, $40,000—**James E. Smith;** McLean, Va.; deputy under secretary of the Treasury; Sept. 29, 1930, in Aberdeen, S.D.; Rep.; June 1.

Assistant Secretary (customs, engraving and printing, mint, law enforcement), $38,000—**Edward L. Morgan;** Phoenix, Ariz.; deputy assistant to the President for domestic affairs and assistant director of the Domestic Council; March 6, 1938, in Lorain, Ohio; Rep.; Jan. 16.

General Counsel, $38,000—**Edward C. Schmults;** Chappaqua, N.Y.; partner in the law firm of White & Case; Feb. 6, 1931, in Paterson, N.J.; Rep.; May 17.

Commissioner of Internal Revenue, $40,000—**Donald C. Alexander;** Cincinnati, Ohio; partner in the law firm of Dinsmore, Shohl, Coates and Deupree; May 22, 1921, in Pine Bluff, Ark.; May 17.

Independent Agencies

ACTION

Director, $40,000—**Michael P. Balzano Jr.;** Arlington, Va.; staff assistant, White House; Nov. 6, 1935, in New Haven, Conn., Dem., April 6.

Atomic Energy Commission

Member for the term expiring June 30, 1978, $40,000—**William A. Anders;** McLean, Va.; executive secretary, National Aeronautics and Space Council; Oct. 17, 1933, in Hong Kong; Aug. 2.

Member for the term expiring June 30, 1975, $40,000—**William E. Kriegsman;** Bethesda, Md.; manager, Washington, D.C. office of Arthur D. Little, Inc.; Feb. 22, 1932, in New York City; Rep.; May 31.

Civil Aeronautics Board

Member for the term expiring Dec. 31, 1979, $38,000—**G. Joseph Minetti;** Brooklyn, N.Y.; Reappointment; April 21, 1907, in New York City; Dem.; Dec. 12.

Member for the term expiring Dec. 31, 1974, $38,000—**Richard Joseph O'Melia;** Westmoreland Hills, Md.; director, CAB Bureau of Enforcement; May 24, 1917, in Rhinelander, Wis.; Rep.; Nov. 20.

Member for the term expiring Dec. 31, 1978, $38,000—**Lee R. West;** Ada, Okla.; judge, Oklahoma 22nd Judicial District; Nov. 26, 1929, in Clayton, Okla.; Dem.; Nov. 20.

U.S. Civil Service Commission

Chairman for the term expiring March 1, 1979, $40,000—**Robert E. Hampton;** Bethesda, Md.; reappointment; Sept. 21, 1922, in Chattanooga, Tenn.; Rep.; June 30.

Environmental Protection Agency

Administrator, $42,500—**Russell E. Train;** Washington, D.C.; chairman, Council on Environmental Quality; June 4, 1920, in Jamestown, R.I.; Rep.; Sept. 10.

Deputy Administrator, $40,000—**John R. Quarles;** McLean, Va.; acting deputy administrator, EPA; April 26, 1935, in Boston, Mass.; Rep.; Sept. 20.

Assistant Administrator (planning and management), $38,000—**Alvin L. Alm;** Washington, D.C.; staff director for program development, Council on Environmental Quality; Jan. 27, 1937, in Denver, Colo.; Dem.; July 30.

Assistant Administrator, (enforcement and general counsel), $38,000—**Alan G. Kirk II;** McLean, Va.; acting assistant administrator (enforcement and general counsel), EPA; Dec. 15, 1926, in Rosemont, Pa.; Rep.; Dec.13.

Equal Employment Opportunity Commission

Chairman for the term expiring July 1, 1978, $40,000—**John H. Powell Jr.;** Glen Echo Heights, Md.; general counsel, U.S. Commission on Civil Rights; Feb. 11, 1931, in Mineola, N.Y.; Rep.; Dec. 21.

Federal Home Loan Bank Board

Chairman for the term expiring June 30, 1974, $40,000—**Thomas R. Bomar;** Potomac, Md.; executive vice president, Federal Home Loan Mortgage Corp.; July 16, 1937, in Sherman, Texas; Rep.; June 1.

Member for the term expiring June 30, 1977, $38,000—**Grady Perry Jr.;** Gadsden, Ala.; congressional liaison for Federal Home Loan Bank Board; Feb. 23, 1931, in Fyffe, Ala.; Dem.; June 1.

Federal Maritime Commission

Commissioner for the term expiring June 30, 1978, $38,000 **George Henry Hearn;** Brooklyn, N.Y.; reappointment; July 4, 1927, in Brooklyn, N.Y.; Dem.; Nov. 20.

Federal Mediation and Conciliation Service

Director, $40,000—**Willie J. Usery Jr.;** Macon, Ga.; assistant secretary (labor-management relations), Labor Department; Dec. 21, 1923, in Hardwick, Ga.; Rep.; March 14.

Federal Power Commission

Member for the term expiring June 22, 1978, $38,000—**Don S. Smith;** Little Rock, Ark.; Arkansas public service commissioner; Oct. 9, 1937, in Camden, Ark.; Dem.; Nov. 28.

Member for the term expiring June 22, 1977, $38,000—**William L. Springer;** Champaign, Ill.; U.S. representative (R Ill. 1951-73); April 12, 1909, in Sullivan, Ind.; Rep.; May 21.

Federal Reserve System

Member of the Board of Governors for the term expiring Jan. 31, 1978, $40,000—**Robert C. Holland;** Tekamah, Neb.; executive director of Board of Governors; April 7, 1925, in Tekamah, Neb.; Rep.; June 1.

Federal Trade Commission

Director for the term expiring Sept. 25, 1976, $40,000—**Lewis A. Engman;** Grand Rapids, Mich.; assistant director, Domestic Council; Jan. 6, 1936, in Grand Rapids, Mich.; Rep.; Feb. 7.

Member for the term expiring Sept. 25, 1980, $38,000—**Mary Elizabeth Hanford;** Salisbury, N.C.; deputy director, Office of Consumer Affairs; July 29, 1936, in Salisbury, N.C.; Rep.; Nov. 20.

Member for the term expiring Sept. 25, 1975, $38,000—**Mayo J. Thompson;** Houston, Texas; senior partner in the law firm of Royston, Rayzor, Cook and Vickery; May 12, 1919, in Houston, Texas; Dem.; June 21.

General Services Administration

Administrator, $40,000—**Arthur F. Sampson;** Camp Hill, Pa.; acting administrator, GSA; Oct. 8, 1926, in Warren, R.I.; Rep.; June 20.

Interstate Commerce Commission

Commissioner for the term expiring Dec. 31, 1979, $38,000—**Willard Deason;** Austin, Texas; reappointment; Jan. 3, 1905, in Stockdale, Texas; Dem.; April 6.

Commissioner for the term expiring Dec. 31, 1978, $38,000—**Alfred Towson MacFarland;** Castalian Springs, Tenn.; senior partner in the law firm of MacFarland, Reed and Kinnard; April 23, 1917, in Lebanon, Tenn.; Dem.; April 6.

Commissioner for the term expiring Dec. 31, 1979, $38,000—**A. Daniel O'Neal Jr.;** Seattle, Wash.; transportation counsel to U.S. Senate Commerce Committee; May 15, 1936, in Bremerton, Wash.; Dem.; April 6.

National Labor Relations Board

Member for the term expiring Aug. 27, 1978, $38,000—**Howard Jenkins Jr.;** Washington, D.C.; reappointment; June 16, 1915, in Denver, Colo.; Rep.; Oct. 11.

Member for the term expiring Dec. 16, 1977, $38,000—**John Harold Fanning;** Woodacres, Md.; reappointment; Sept. 19, 1916, in Putnam, Conn.; Dem.; Jan. 31.

National Mediation Board

Member for the term expiring July 1, 1976, $38,000—**David H. Stowe;** Bethesda, Md.; reappointment; Sept. 10, 1910, in New Canaan, Conn.; Dem.; June 7.

Securities and Exchange Commission

Member (chairman) for the term expiring June 5, 1977, $40,000—**G. Bradford Cook;** Chicago, Ill.; director, Division of Market Regulation, SEC; May 10, 1937, in Lincoln, Neb.; Rep.; Feb. 22.

Member (chairman) for the term expiring June 5, 1977, $40,000—**Ray Garrett Jr.;** Winnetka, Ill.; partner in the law firm of Gardner, Carton, Douglas, Children and Waud; Aug. 11, 1920, in Chicago, Ill.; Rep.; July 28.

Member for the term expiring June 5, 1973, $38,000—**John R. Evans;** Murray, Utah; professional staff member, Senate Banking, Housing and Urban Affairs Committee; June 1, 1932, in Bisbee, Ariz.; Rep.; Feb. 22.

Member for the term expiring June 5, 1978, $38,000—**John R. Evans;** Murray, Utah; reappointment; June 1, 1932, in Bisbee, Ariz.; Rep.; June 1.

Member for the term expiring June 5, 1974, $38,000—**Philip A. Loomis Jr.;** Pasadena, Calif.; reappointment; June 11, 1915, in Colorado Springs, Colo.; Rep.; Feb. 22.

Member for the term expiring June 5, 1976, $38,000—**A. A. Sommer Jr.;** Potomac, Md.; partner and chairman of the executive committee, Calfee, Halter, Calfee, Griswold and Sommer; April 7, 1924, in Portsmouth, Ohio; Dem.; July 28.

Selective Service System

Director, $38,000—**Byron V. Pepitone;** Arlington, Va.; deputy director of Selective Service; June 9, 1918, in New Brunswock, N.J.; Rep.; March 26.

United States Information Agency

Director, $42,500—**James Keogh;** Arlington, Va.; free-lance writer; Oct. 29, 1916, in Platte County, Neb.; Rep.; Feb. 8.

Deputy Director, $38,000—**Eugene Paul Kopp;** Alexandria, Va.; assistant director (administration), USIA; Nov. 20, 1934, in Charleston, W. Va.; Rep.; March 26.

United States Tariff Commission

Member for the term expiring June 16, 1979, $36,000—**George M. Moore;** Silver Spring, Md.; reappointment; Dec. 9, 1913, in LaGrange, Ky.; Rep.; June 15.

Judiciary

U.S. Circuit Courts of Appeals

Judge for the third circuit, $42,500—**Leonard I. Garth;** Paterson, N.J.; judge for the district of New Jersey; April 7, 1921, in Brooklyn, N.Y.; Rep.; Aug. 3.

Judge for the third circuit, $42,500—**Joseph G. Weis Jr.;** Pittsburgh, Pa.; judge for the western district of Pennsylvania; March 12, 1923, in Ross Township, Pa.; Rep.; March 14.

Judge for the fifth circuit, $42,500—**Thomas G. Gee;** Austin, Texas; partner in the law firm of Graves, Dougherty, Gee, Hearon, Moody & Garwood; Dec. 9, 1925, in Jacksonville, Fla.; Rep.; July 13.

Judge for the sixth circuit, $42,500—**Albert J. Engel;** Muskegon, Mich.; judge for the western district of Michigan; March 21, 1924, in Lake City, Mich.; Rep.; Dec. 13.

Judge for the eighth circuit, $42,500—**William H. Webster;** St. Louis, Mo.; judge for the eastern district of Missouri; March 8, 1924, in St. Louis, Mo.; Rep.; July 13.

Judge for the ninth circuit, $42,500—**Joseph T. Sneed;** Durham, N.C.; deputy attorney general, Justice Department; July 21, 1920, in Calvert, Texas; Rep.; Aug. 3.

U.S. Court of Customs and Patent Appeals

Associate Judge, $42,500—**Jack R. Miller;** Sioux City, Iowa; U.S. senator (R Iowa 1961-73); June 6, 1916, in Chicago, Ill.; Rep.; June 28.

U.S. District Courts

Judge for the northern district of Alabama, $40,000—**J. Foy Guin Jr.;** Russellville, Ala.; senior partner in the law firm of Guin, Guin, Bouldin & Porch; Feb. 2, 1924, in Russellville, Ala.; Rep.; April 10.

Judge for the northern district of Alabama, $40,000—**James H. Hancock;** Birmingham, Ala.; partner in the law firm of Balch, Bingham, Baker, Hawthorne & Williams; April 30, 1931, in Montgomery, Ala.; Rep.; April 10.

Judge for the middle district of Florida, $40,000—**John A. Reed Jr.;** West Palm Beach, Fla.; chief judge, Florida Fourth District Court of Appeal; June 29, 1931, in Washington, D.C.; Rep.; Aug. 3.

Judge for the northern district of Illinois, $40,000—**Prentice H. Marshall;** Urbana, Ill.; hearing officer, Illinois Fair Employment Practices Commission and professor of law, University of Illinois College of Law; Aug. 7, 1926, in Oak Park, Ill.; Ind.; July 13.

Judge for the southern district of Illinois, $40,000—**Harlington Wood Jr.;** Springfield, Ill.; assistant attorney general (civil), Justice Department; April 17, 920, in Springfield, Ill.; Rep.; July 13.

Judge for the northern district of Indiana, $40,000—**Allen Sharp;** Williamsport, Ind.; judge, Appellate Court of Indiana; Feb. 11, 1932, in Washington, D.C.; Rep.; Oct. 4.

Judge for the district of Massachusetts, $40,000—**Walter Jay Skinner;** Newton, Mass.; partner in the law firm of Wardwell, Allen, McLaughlin & Skinner; Sept. 12, 1927, in Washington, D.C.; Rep.; Dec. 14.

Judge for the eastern district of Michigan, $40,000—**Russell James Harvey;** Saginaw, Mich.; U.S. representative (R Mich 1961-74); July 4, 1922, in Iron Mountain, Mich.; Rep.; Dec. 13.

Judge for the eastern district of Missouri, $40,000—**John F. Nangle;** Brentwood, Mo.; attorney in private practice; June 8, 1922, in St. Louis, Mo.; Rep.; July 13.

Judge for the district of Nebraska, $40,000—**Albert G. Schatz;** Omaha, Neb.; partner in the law firm of Gross, Welch, Vinardi, Kauffman, Schatz & Day; Aug. 4, 1921, in Omaha, Neb.; Rep.; May 10.

Judge for the district of New Jersey, $40,000—**Vincent P. Biunno;** Glen Ridge, N.J.; partner in the law firm of Lum, Biunno & Tompkins; Feb. 2, 1916, in Newark, N.J.; Rep.; April 10.

Judge for the district of New Jersey, $40,000—**Herbert J. Stern;** Newark, N.J.; U.S. Attorney, District of New Jersey; Nov. 8, 1936, in New York City; Rep.; Dec. 19.

Judge for the southern district of New York, $40,000—**William C. Conner;** Dobbs Ferry, N.Y.; member of the law firm of Curtis, Morris & Ssafford; March 27, 1920, in Wichita Falls, Texas; Rep.; Dec. 13.

Judge for the southern district of New York, $40,000—**Richard Owen;** New York City; partner in the law firm of Owen & Turchin; Dec. 11, 1922, in New York City; Rep.; Dec. 13.

Judge for the eastern district of Pennsylvania, $40,000—**Herbert A. Fogel;** Philadelphia, Pa.; partner in the law firm of Obermayer, Rebmann, Maxwell & Hippel; April 20, 1929, in Philadelphia, Pa.; Rep.; March 14.

Judge for the western district of Pennsylvania, $40,000—**Daniel J. Snyder;** Greensburg, Pa.; senior partner in the law firm of Costello, Synder, Berk & Horner; May 2, 1916, in Greensburg, Pa.; Rep.; April 10.

Membership of Federal Regulatory Agencies 1973

Atomic Energy Commission

(Five members appointed for five-year terms; no statutory limitation on political party membership)

Member	Party	Term Expires	Nominated by Nixon	Confirmed by Senate
Clarence E. Larson*	R	6/30/74	6/30/69	8/8/69
William E. Kriegsman*	R	6/30/75	4/13/73	5/31/73
William Offutt Doub*	R	6/30/76	7/21/71	8/6/71
Dixy Lee Ray (C)*	I	6/30/77	7/17/72	8/2/72
William A. Anders*	NA	6/30/78	7/19/73	8/2/73

Civil Aeronautics Board

(Five members appointed for six-year terms; not more than three members from one political party)

Member	Party	Term Expires	Nominated by Nixon	Confirmed by Senate
Richard J. O'Melia*	R	12/31/74	9/7/73	11/20/73
Robert D. Timm* (C)	R	12/31/76	12/14/70	12/16/70
Whitney Gillilland*	R	12/31/77	12/13/71	2/29/72
Lee R. West*	D	12/31/78	3/12/73	11/20/73
G. Joseph Minetti**	D	12/31/79	11/26/73	12/12/73

Federal Communications Commission

(Seven members appointed for seven-year terms; not more than four members from one political party)

Member	Party	Term Expires	Nominated by Nixon	Confirmed by Senate
Robert E. Lee	R	6/30/74		
Dean Burch* (C)	R	6/30/76	9/17/69	10/30/69
Richard E. Wiley*	R	6/30/77	1/24/72	5/30/72
Charlotte T. Reid*	R	6/30/78	7/6/71	7/19/71
Benjamin L. Hooks*	D	6/30/79	4/12/72	8/2/72
2 Vacancies				

Federal Maritime Commission

(Five members appointed for five-year terms; not more than three members from one political party)

Member	Party	Term Expires	Nominated by Nixon	Confirmed by Senate
James V. Day**	R	6/30/74	9/17/69	10/23/69
Helen D. Bentley** (C)	R	6/30/75	5/5/70	6/3/70
Clarence Morse*	R	6/30/76	8/7/71	10/7/71
Ashton C. Barrett**	D	6/30/77	5/11/72	6/30/72
George H. Hearn**	D	6/30/78	9/5/73	11/20/73

Federal Power Commission

(Five members appointed for five-year terms; not more than three members from one political party)

Member	Party	Term Expires	Nominated by Nixon	Confirmed by Senate
Albert B. Brooke Jr.**	R	6/22/74	6/23/69	10/23/69
John N. Nassikas* (C)	R	6/22/75	3/23/70	4/30/70
Rush Moody Jr.*	D	6/22/76	7/20/71	10/8/71
William L. Springer*	R	6/22/77	2/13/73	9/21/73
Don S. Smith*	D	6/22/78	11/2/73	11/28/73

Federal Reserve System, Board of Governors

(Seven members appointed for fourteen-year terms; no statutory limitation on political party membership, but not more than one member may be appointed from each Federal Reserve District. No member may be appointed to serve more than one full term.)

Member	Party	Term Expires	Nominated by Nixon	Confirmed by Senate
J. Dewey Daane	NA	1/31/74		
George W. Mitchell	D	1/31/76		
Robert C. Holland*	R	1/31/78	5/16/73	6/1/73
Andrew F. Brimmer	D	1/31/80		
John E. Sheehan*	R	1/31/82	1/24/72	2/7/72
Arthur F. Burns* (C)	R	1/31/84	10/22/69	12/18/69
Jeffrey M. Bucher*	NA	1/31/86	4/27/72	5/31/72

Federal Trade Commission

(Five members appointed for seven-year terms; not more than three members from one political party)

Member	Party	Term Expires	Nominated by Nixon	Confirmed by Senate
Paul Rand Dixon	D	9/25/74		
Mayo J. Thompson*	D	9/25/75	5/10/73	6/21/73
Lewis A. Engman* (C)	R	9/25/76	1/26/73	2/7/73
David S. Dennison Jr.*	R	9/25/77	9/22/70	10/13/70
Mary E. Hanford*	R	9/25/80	9/5/73	11/20/73

Interstate Commerce Commission

(Eleven members appointed for seven-year terms; not more than six members from one political party)

Member	Party	Term Expires	Nominated by Nixon	Confirmed by Senate
George M. Stafford (C)	R	12/31/73†		
Robert C. Gresham*	R	12/31/74	9/25/69	11/19/69
Kenneth H. Tuggle	R	12/31/75		
William D. Brewer*	R	12/31/76	5/18/70	7/14/70
Virginia Mae Brown*	D	12/31/77	4/14/71	6/30/71
Dale W. Hardin**	R	12/31/77	4/14/71	6/30/71
Rupert I. Murphy**	D	12/31/78	3/23/72	10/5/72
Alfred T. MacFarland*	D	12/31/78	2/7/73	4/6/73
Willard Deason**	D	12/31/79	2/7/73	4/6/73
A. Daniel O'Neal Jr.*	D	12/31/79	3/6/73	4/6/73
Vacancy				

National Labor Relations Board

(Five members appointed for five-year terms; no statutory limitation on political party membership)

Member	Party	Term Expires	Nominated by Nixon	Confirmed by Senate
Edward B. Miller* (C)	R	12/16/74	2/20/70	5/21/70
Ralph E. Kennedy*	R	8/27/75	9/21/70	12/2/70
John A. Penello*	D	8/27/76	1/24/72	2/7/72
John H. Fanning**	D	12/16/77	1/11/73	1/31/73
Howard Jenkins Jr.**	R	8/27/78	9/5/73	10/11/73

National Mediation Board

(Three members appointed for three-year terms; not more than two members from one political party)

Member	Party	Term Expires	Nominated by Nixon	Confirmed by Senate
Kay McMurray* (C)	R	7/1/74	9/11/72	9/26/72
George S. Ives*	R	7/1/75	6/22/72	6/22/72
David H. Stowe**	D	7/1/76	5/11/73	6/7/73

Securities and Exchange Commission

(Five members appointed for five-year terms; not more than three members from one political party)

Member	Party	Term Expires	Nominated by Nixon	Confirmed by Senate
Philip A. Loomis Jr.*	R	6/5/74	2/19/73	2/22/73
A. A. Sommer Jr.*	D	6/5/76	7/20/73	7/28/73
Ray Garrett (C)*	R	6/5/77	7/20/73	7/28/73
John R. Evans*	R	6/5/78	5/29/73	6/1/73
Vacancy				

(C) chairman.
* Nixon appointment.
** Reappointed by Nixon; first appointed in a previous administration.
† Has not been renominated; can serve until successor is appointed.

NIXON SUPPORT IN CONGRESS HITS RECORD LOW IN 1973

President Nixon won 50.6 per cent of the congressional votes on which he took a position during 1973, fewer than any president had won in the 20 years since Congressional Quarterly began measuring presidential support.

Nixon's 1973 support mark was nearly 16 points lower than his 1972 record, and more than 26 points lower than his best score—77 per cent—recorded in 1970. Before 1973, the all-time low was the 52 per cent recorded in 1959, during the Eisenhower administration.

Presidential support actually increased somewhat during the last three months of the year, with both houses taking routine votes on many matters which drew a presidential position but evoked little controversy. This late trend allowed the President to finish the year above the 50 per cent mark, but did not erase the all-time record low.

The study was based on 310 votes that featured a clear-cut presidential position. There were more such votes in 1973 than in any other year in the history of the study, but this was due mainly to an increase in the total number of votes cast. The President took a position on 27 per cent of the votes during the year, well above the 10 per cent he recorded in 1972 but far below the 20-year average of 45 per cent.

Votes were included in the 1973 study only if the President or his aides had made a specific indication of his wishes before the vote was taken.

The two chambers of Congress were about equal in their support of the President during the year, with the Senate backing Nixon 52 per cent of the time, and the House 48 per cent. This was a marked contrast with 1972, when Senate support was 54 per cent but House support was 81 per cent. It was the first time since 1969, Nixon's first year in office, that the Senate supported him more often than the House.

More Than Watergate

In conversations with Congressional Quarterly, members of both houses said the Watergate affair was not the most important reason for the decline in presidential support during 1973. They attributed much of the change to the President's threats in the beginning of the year to dismantle long-standing social programs.

"They cut off disaster aid and rural environmental assistance and rural water-sewer funds," recalled Rep. John M. Zwach (R Minn.). "These were things we were naturally not going to go along with."

Congress sustained the President's vetoes on most of these economic issues, but it expressed its anger by reducing its over-all support score to 43 per cent during the first seven months of the year. Never before had a President lost more support tests in Congress than he had won.

Until U.S. bombing of Cambodia ended in August, the Indochina war had an effect on presidential support in Congress. "One of the major thorns this year was the war," admitted White House lobbyist Max Friedersdorf, "and this was poisoning our whole effort with Congress."

Congressional and White House sources differed on why the President's legislative requests fared better during the last part of the year. "When the White House got in trouble over Watergate," argued Sen. Robert T. Stafford (R Vt.), "they began to work and compromise."

Rep. H. John Heinz III (R Pa.) said the same thing was happening in the House. "The White House wasn't looking for an argument that they would lose," Heinz said. He mentioned compromises on a manpower bill, a health maintenance organization bill, and a northeast railroad bill.

But Friedersdorf said it was Congress that was learning to compromise. "When the House sustained the vetoes," he said, "this had a sobering effect on the Democratic leadership. We could sense the frustration that they felt when they could not win on these issues. This had an effect and helped us."

Others pointed out that the end of the year gave both houses a chance to vote on numerous issues where there was little disagreement, and offered some easy padding for the President's support score.

"Right at the end of the year," said Sen. Richard S. Schweiker (R Pa.), "there were a lot of nominations and the energy thing. We're all for measures to help save energy."

The year-end increase in presidential support also was related to a large number of non-controversial Senate votes on treaties, most of which came after the August recess. Had treaty votes been excluded from the study, the President's support score both for the Senate and for Congress would have been 48 per cent. Nearly all the treaties were approved unanimously.

Support Breakdown

Party Differences. In both chambers, the average Democrat opposed the President a majority of the time. Composite scores show that Democrats in the Senate voted against the President 51 per cent of the time and supported him 37 per cent. This was a switch from 1972, when the average Senate Democrat supported the President more often (44 per cent) than he opposed him (41 per cent). House Democrats showed a similar trend.

The average Republican in both the House and the Senate supported the President nearly two-thirds of the time: 61 per cent in the Senate and 62 per cent in the House. The 1973 Republican scores reflected a slight drop in support from 1972 in both chambers.

State and Regional Averages. As in previous years, southerners were more likely to go along with the President's wishes than those in any other regional bloc. This was true in both parties. The average southern Senate Republican backed the President 69 per cent of the time, while his Democratic counterpart supported Nixon 47 per cent of the time. Southern Republicans in the Senate supported the President more often than members from any other region in either party.

In the Senate, the leading opponents of the President were midwestern Democrats (30 per cent). In the House, that distinction went to Democrats from the East (29 per cent). Among Republicans, easterners were the least frequent Nixon supporters in both chambers (53 per cent in the Senate and 58 per cent in the House).

Members from the East and Far West, Republicans as well as Democrats, supported the President less often in 1973 than in 1972. Republican House members from the South and Midwest, and Democratic senators from the Midwest, all averaged higher over-all in presidential support than they had the previous year.

Senators and representatives from Nebraska had the highest support average of any state delegation in Congress, supporting the President 71 per cent of the time, while opposing him 24 per cent. The Massachusetts delegation was the least supportive, with a support score of 33 per cent and an opposition score of 61. Nebraska's five-member delegation is all Republican; Massachusetts has 10 Democrats and four Republicans.

Individual Scorers. The strongest Nixon supporter in the Senate was Clifford P. Hansen (R Wyo.), who scored 78 per cent. Next came 15 other Republicans, led by party whip Robert P. Griffin (Mich.) with 77 per cent; Jesse A. Helms (N.C.), Dewey F. Bartlett (Okla.), and Strom Thurmond (S.C.), all with 76 per cent; and Paul J. Fannin (Ariz.), Roman L. Hruska (Neb.) and John G. Tower (Texas), all with 75 per cent.

The leading Democratic supporters of the President in the Senate were all southerners. First was James B. Allen (Ala.), who had a 66 per cent score. Behind him were John L. McClellan (Ark.) and Sam Nunn (Ga.) with 56 per cent; and John Sparkman (Ala.) and James O. Eastland (Miss.) with 55. Independent Harry F. Byrd (Va.) had a support score of 63 per cent.

In the House, the Republican leadership ranked at the top in presidential support. First was Barber B. Conable (N.Y.), chairman of the House Republican Policy Committee. He voted with Nixon 86 per cent of the time.

After Conable came Gerald R. Ford (Mich.), who was House minority leader until he was confirmed as Vice President Dec. 6. Ford had an 80 per cent support score. Next came Leslie C. Arends (Ill.), the minority whip, and Samuel L. Devine (Ohio), vice-chairman of the party conference. Both scored 79.

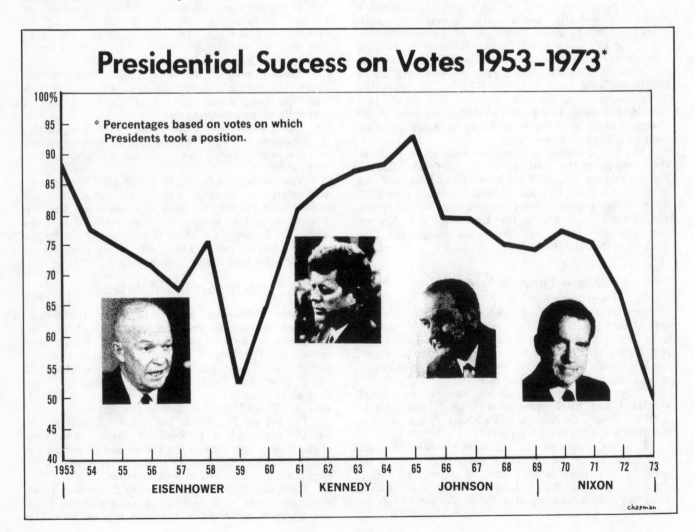

Presidential Success on Votes 1953-1973*

* Percentages based on votes on which Presidents took a position.

EISENHOWER   KENNEDY   JOHNSON   NIXON

chapman

Ground Rules for CQ Presidential Support-Opposition

● **Presidential Issues**—CQ analyzes all messages, press conference remarks and other public statements of the President to determine what he personally, as distinct from other administration spokesmen, does or does not want in the way of legislative action.

● **Borderline Cases**—By the time an issue reaches a vote, it may differ from the original form on which the President expressed himself. In such cases, CQ analyzes the measure to determine whether, on balance, the features favored by the President outweigh those he opposed or vice versa. Only then is the vote classified.

● **Some Votes Excluded**—Occasionally, important measures are so extensively amended on the floor that it is impossible to characterize final passage as a victory or defeat for the President.

● **Motions**—Votes on motions to recommit, to reconsider or to table often are key tests that govern the legislative outcome. Such votes are necessarily included in the Nixon support tabulations.

● **Rules**—In the House, debate on most significant bills is governed by rules that restrict time and may bar floor amendments. These rules must be adopted by the House before the bills in question may be considered. Members may vote for the rule, in order to permit debate, although they intend to vote against the bill. Generally, however, a vote against

a rule is a vote against the bill, and vice versa, since rejection of the rule prevents consideration of the bill. CQ assumes that if the President favored a bill, he favored the rule unless it was a closed rule that would prevent amendments he wanted.

● **Appropriations**—Generally, votes on passage of appropriation bills are not included in the tabulation, since it is rarely possible to determine the President's position on the over-all revisions Congress almost invariably makes in the sums allowed. Votes to cut or increase specific funds requested in the President's budget, however, are included.

● **Failures to Vote**—In tabulating the Support or Opposition scores of members on the selected Nixon-issue votes, CQ counts only "yea" and "nay" votes on the ground that only these affect the outcome. Most failures to vote reflect absences because of illness or official business. Failures to vote lower both support and opposition scores equally.

● **Weighting**—All Nixon-issue votes have equal statistical weight in the analysis.

● **Changed Position**—Presidential Support is determined by the position of the President at the time of a vote even though that position may be different from an earlier position, or may have been reversed after the vote was taken.

Other strong Nixon supporters among House Republicans were James M. Collins (Texas), George A. Goodling (Pa.), David C. Treen (La.) and John Ware (Pa.). All had 77 per cent scores.

John Jarman (Okla.) led House Democrats with a 72 per cent support score. Runners-up were W. C. (Dan) Daniel (Va.), with 66 per cent; Joe D. Waggonner Jr. (La.) and David E. Satterfield (Va.), both with 65; Omar Burleson (Texas), with 64; George Mahon (Texas), with 62; and G. V. (Sonny) Montgomery (Miss.), with 60.

The three most consistent opponents of the President in the House were Democrats Robert W. Kastenmeier (Wis.), Parren J. Mitchell (Md.) and John F. Seiberling (Ohio), each with 73 per cent opposition scores. Five Democrats shared the second highest opposition score of 72 per cent. They were Phillip Burton (Calif.), Ronald V. Dellums (Calif.), Henry Helstoski (N.J.), Joseph M. Gaydos (Pa.) and Paul S. Sarbanes (Md.).

The most persistent opponent in the House from the President's own party was Margaret M. Heckler (Mass.) who opposed Nixon 57 per cent of the time. Behind her were Gilbert Gude (Md.) and Charles W. Whalen Jr. (Ohio), both with 55 per cent; Robert H. Steele (Conn.) and Joseph M. McDade (Pa.), both with 54 per cent; and Paul W. Cronin (Mass.), with 53 per cent.

House Judiciary Committee. The House committee studying the possibility of impeaching President Nixon supported the President about as often as the rest of the House. The average support score for the commit-

tee was 45.7 per cent, while the House as a whole supported the President 47 per cent of the time in 1973.

Democrats on the Judiciary Committee showed less support than Democrats from the whole House. The average Democratic committee member supported the President 31 per cent of the time. The average Democratic member of the House sided with the President 35 per cent of the time.

The average Republican on the committee supported the President more often than the average Republican House member. Republican committee members backed the President 64 per cent of the time. The average Republican House member sided with President Nixon 62 per cent of the time.

Nixon's Wins and Losses

Economic controls, rural programs, energy policy and the Indochina war were the issues over which the President and Congress clashed most often in 1973.

Both chambers began the year with efforts to impose a freeze or roll-back on prices, rents, interest rates and dividends. The President opposed such a move. The Senate was able to defeat him on only three of 13 votes in this area, while the House went along with the President on each of seven occasions.

Farm issues were another battleground, as the President attempted to eliminate or cut back aid programs for rural areas and tried to hold the line on price

State Averages

Following are 1973 presidential support and opposition scores for each state delegation. Ranking is according to combined chambers' support score, carried to the necessary decimal places to break a tie.

	Rank	Both Chambers Support	Both Chambers Opposition	Senate Support	Senate Opposition	House Support	House Opposition
Total Congress		47	43	47	41	47	44
South		52	38	55	32	52	40
Midwest		48	42	41	46	50	41
West		45	44	46	41	44	46
East		42	49	45	45	42	50
Ala.	7	58	33	60	32	56	34
Alaska	29	46	42	42	42	57	39
Ariz.	3	60	23	60	12	61	31
Ark.	38	41	41	41	42	41	40
Calif.	36	43	46	31	54	43	45
Colo.	22	49	44	49	41	49	46
Conn.	39	41	54	44	49	39	56
Del.	15	52	38	50	47	57	41
Fla.	21	49	43	51	40	48	44
Ga.	28	47	44	53	41	45	45
Hawaii	42	40	51	47	41	31	67
Idaho	14	52	38	45	42	63	31
Ill.	18	50	40	40	48	51	39
Ind.	17	51	40	28	56	57	38
Iowa	37	42	49	25	54	49	47
Kan.	4	59	32	56	32	61	32
Ky.	33	44	49	43	47	45	49
La.	25	48	39	42	43	50	38
Maine	49	33	59	28	61	40	57
Md.	24	49	47	55	36	46	52
Mass.	50	33	61	35	53	32	63
Mich.	20	50	39	51	47	50	39
Minn.	41	41	49	29	59	45	46
Miss.	12	53	27	38	16	62	34
Mo.	44	37	55	33	56	38	54
Mont.	46	35	57	31	63	42	48
Neb.	1	71	24	74	19	67	30
Nev.	31	45	46	41	51	57	34
N. H.	11	55	33	49	34	65	32
N. J.	40	41	51	36	55	42	50
N. M.	19	50	43	52	44	46	42
N. Y.	35	43	44	54	27	42	45
N. C.	9	57	38	64	27	55	41
N. D.	26	48	49	48	50	46	46
Ohio	13	52	37	58	18	51	39
Okla.	5	59	31	71	22	52	36
Ore.	23	49	38	51	37	47	39
Penn.	32	45	48	53	42	44	49
R. I.	48	35	58	41	53	24	65
S. C.	6	58	34	59	32	58	35
S. D.	47	35	53	25	60	49	42
Tenn.	10	57	33	63	20	54	38
Texas	27	47	42	60	30	46	44
Utah	30	45	40	50	34	37	50
Vt.	8	57	37	54	39	66	32
Va.	2	68	28	68	26	68	29
Wash.	45	36	56	43	50	33	59
W. Va.	43	37	59	41	56	34	60
Wis.	34	44	52	36	62	47	49
Wyo.	16	52	37	60	27	28	68

supports in the 1973 Agriculture Act. Both chambers delivered 12 defeats to the President on farm and rural issues. The President had only four victories in the Senate and six in the House.

The year-end rush to pass energy legislation left the President with mixed results. Both chambers defeated the President in passing fuel allocation bills, but supported his efforts to establish year-round daylight saving time and reorganize energy research and development.

Each chamber made six attempts to override presidential vetoes. The Senate voted to override three times, but twice the House chose to sustain. The only veto the House voted to override, and the only veto actually overridden in 1973, came on the bill limiting a president's warmaking powers.

Congressional attempts to end all American combat involvement in the Indochina war provided a substantial number of defeats for the President. The House went against Nixon on nine of eleven votes in its effort to cut off funds for American bombing of Cambodia.

Average Scores

Following are composites of Republican and Democratic scores for 1973, compared with those for 1972.

	1973 Dem.	1973 Rep.	1972 Dem.	1972 Rep.
SUPPORT				
Senate	37%	61%	44%	66%
House	35	62	47	64
OPPOSITION				
Senate	51	27	41	20
House	55	30	37	22

Regional Averages

SUPPORT

Regional presidential support scores for 1973; scores for 1972 are in parentheses:

DEMOCRATS

	East	West	South	Midwest
Senate	35% (36%)	35% (40%)	47% (60%)	30% (29%)
House	29 (48)	30 (44)	45 (48)	31 (45)

REPUBLICANS

	East	West	South	Midwest
Senate	53% (63%)	62% (66%)	69% (73%)	62% (64%)
House	58 (70)	61 (63)	66 (58)	65 (63)

OPPOSITION

Regional presidential opposition scores for 1973; scores for 1972 are in parentheses:

DEMOCRATS

	East	West	South	Midwest
Senate	56% (45%)	55% (42%)	39% (25%)	59% (57%)
House	62 (39)	60 (39)	46 (33)	60 (40)

	East	West	South	Midwest
REPUBLICANS				
Senate	36% (30%)	23% (16%)	22% (11%)	25% (16%)
House	35 (19)	30 (17)	27 (28)	28 (23)

High Scorers—Support

Highest individual scorers in Nixon support—those who voted for the President's position most often in 1973.

SENATE

Democrats		Republicans	
Allen (Ala.)	66%	Hansen (Wyo.)	78%
Byrd (Va.)†	63	Griffin (Mich.)	77
McClellan (Ark.)	56	Helms (N.C.)	76
Nunn (Ga.)	56	Bartlett (Okla.)	76
Sparkman (Ala.)	55	Thurmond (S.C.)	76
Eastland (Miss.)	55	Fannin (Ariz.)	75
		Hruska (Neb.)	75
† *Elected as independent*		Tower (Texas)	75
		Curtis (Neb.)	72
		Scott (Va.)	72

HOUSE

Democrats		Republicans	
Jarman (Okla.)	72%	Conable (N.Y.)	86%
Daniel (Va.)	66	Ford (Mich.)	80*
Waggonner (La.)	65	Arends (Ill.)	79
Satterfield (Va.)	65	Devine (Ohio)	79
Burleson (Texas)	64	Treen (La.)	77
Mahon (Texas)	62	Ware (Pa.)	77*
Montgomery (Miss.)	60	Goodling (Pa.)	77*
Haley (Fla.)	59	Collins (Texas)	77
Whitten (Miss.)	59	Rhodes (Ariz.)	76
Mann (S.C.)	59	Dennis (Ind.)	76
Sikes (Fla.)	58	Cederberg (Mich.)	76
Bowen (Miss.)	58	Schneebeli (Pa.)	76*
Casey (Texas)	58	Martin (Neb.)	76

*Not eligible for all recorded votes in 1973.

High-Scorers—Opposition

Highest individual scorers in Nixon opposition—those who voted against the President's position most often in 1973.

SENATE

Democrats		Republicans	
Hathaway (Maine)	68%	Case (N.J.)	57%
Nelson (Wis.)	66	Schweiker (Pa.)	57
Mansfield (Mont.)	64	Brooke (Mass.)	48
McGovern (S.D.)	64	Hatfield (Ore.)	46
Burdick (N.D.)	63	Mathias (Md.)	42
Metcalf (Mont.)	62	Stafford (Vt.)	41
Stevenson (Ill.)	61	Weicker (Conn.)	40

1973 Nixon Issue Votes

Following is a list of all Senate and House recorded votes between Jan. 3 and Dec. 22, 1973, on which the President took a position. The votes, listed by CQ vote number, appear in the roll call chart section of the *Almanac*.

SENATE VOTES (185)

Presidential Victories (97)—1, 2, 3, 4, 14, 34, 44, 46, 48, 49, 50, 52, 56, 57, 58, 59, 60, 64, 69, 70, 72, 74, 100, 118, 136, 141, 145, 164, 165, 180, 221, 228, 234, 235, 236, 239, 240, 243, 251, 252, 253, 254, 275, 289, 315, 352, 359, 360, 361, 362, 363, 364, 366, 375, 383, 392, 394, 396, 397, 400, 407, 410, 412, 413, 415, 416, 417, 418, 425, 427, 428, 429, 430, 431, 432, 435, 455, 456, 457, 458, 459, 463, 470, 493, 495, 496, 499, 508, 527, 530, 532, 536, 568, 580, 582, 586, 587.

Presidential Defeats (88)—5, 6, 8, 9, 16, 20, 21, 24, 26, 29, 31, 32, 36, 37, 45, 55, 65, 66, 79, 84, 85, 87, 98, 111, 112, 113, 114, 117, 121, 126, 127, 144, 154, 162, 163, 166, 167, 168, 169, 170, 171, 188, 191, 209, 210, 211, 218, 219, 224, 230, 231, 232, 233, 237, 238, 241, 242, 255, 258, 259, 267, 268, 291, 299, 303, 346, 254, 355, 356, 357, 358, 372, 373, 376, 409, 421, 422, 426, 451, 462, 465, 525, 528, 531, 551, 552, 553, 577.

HOUSE VOTES (125)

Presidential Victories (60)—15, 38, 39, 46, 52, 54, 55, 56, 57, 59, 68, 79, 85, 93, 95, 96, 103, 110, 118, 123, 131, 147, 148, 150, 155, 173, 190, 212, 215, 220, 221, 224, 226, 230, 233, 250, 257, 272, 302, 306, 325, 328, 329, 336, 341, 364, 409, 421, 437, 441, 442, 468, 472, 475, 477, 479, 480, 489, 525, 531.

Presidential Defeats (65)—10, 13, 19, 25, 26, 30, 41, 42, 66, 71, 73, 87, 88, 89, 90, 91, 94, 112, 119, 120, 121, 122, 124, 125, 127, 129, 134, 157, 172, 189, 192, 198, 199, 200, 201, 218, 225, 227, 228, 229, 231, 232, 241, 249, 258, 259, 277, 310, 366, 367, 382, 395, 402, 404, 407, 412, 417, 418, 420, 425, 444, 463, 471, 473, 474.

Hartke (Ind.)	60	Javits (N.Y.)	39
Byrd (W.Va.)	60	Pearson (Kan.)	38

HOUSE

Democrats		Republicans	
Mitchell (Md.)	73%	Heckler (Mass.)	57%
Seiberling (Ohio)	73	Gude (Md.)	55
Kastenmeier (Wis.)	73	Whalen (Ohio)	55
Burton (Calif.)	72	Steele (Conn.)	54
Dellums (Calif.)	72	McDade (Pa.)	54
Sarbanes (Md.)	72	Cronin (Mass.)	53
Helstoski (N.J.)	72	Biester (Pa.)	52
Gaydos (Pa.)	72	Rinaldo (N.J.)	51

Presidential Support And Opposition: House

1. Support Score, 1973. Percentage of 125 Nixon-issue roll calls in 1973 on which representative voted "yea" or "nay" *in agreement* with the President's position. Failures to vote lower both Support and Opposition scores.

2. Opposition Score, 1973. Percentage of 125 Nixon-issue roll calls in 1973 on which representative voted "yea" or "nay" *in disagreement* with the President's position. Failures to vote lower both Support and Opposition scores.

3. Support Score, 92nd Congress. Percentage of 94 Nixon-issue roll calls in 1971 and 1972 on which representative voted "yea" or "nay" *in agreement* with the President's position. Failures to vote lower both Support and Opposition scores.

4. Opposition Score, 92nd Congress. Percentage of 94 Nixon-issue roll calls in 1971 and 1972 on which representative voted "yea" or "nay" *in disagreement* with the President's position. Failures to vote lower both Support and Opposition scores.

1 Rep. Donald Young (R Alaska) sworn in March 14, 1973, to replace Rep. Nick Begich (D), deceased.
2 Rep. Cardiss Collins (D Ill.) sworn in June 7, 1973, to replace Rep. George W. Collins (D), deceased.
3 Rep. Corinne C. Boggs (D La.) sworn in March 27, 1973, to replace Rep. Hale Boggs (D), deceased.
4 Rep. William O. Mills (R Md.) died May 24, 1973. His scores for 1973 were 68 per cent support and 32 per cent opposition. Rep. Robert E. Bauman (R Md.) sworn in Sept. 5, 1973, to replace Mills.
5 Rep. Gerald R. Ford (R Mich.) resigned Dec. 6, 1973, to become Vice President.
6 Rep. Donald W. Riegle (D Mich.) switched to the Democratic party on Feb. 27, 1973. The 92nd Congress scores reflect Riegle as a Republican. His scores for 1973 as a Republican were 0 per cent support and 66 per cent opposition.
7 Rep. Carl Albert (D Okla.), as Speaker, votes at his own discretion.
8 Rep. John P. Saylor (R Pa.) died Oct. 28, 1973.

- KEY -

†Not eligible for all recorded votes in 1973.
*Not eligible for all recorded votes in 92nd Congress.
—Not a member of 92nd Congress.

	1	2	3	4
ALABAMA				
1 Edwards	73	23	69	17
2 Dickinson	70	22	62	21
3 Nichols	52	38	53	20
4 Bevill	46	50	61	24
5 Jones	39	39	57	31
6 Buchanan	64	24	82	14
7 Flowers	50	40	69	19
ALASKA				
AL Young[1]	57†	39†	—	—
ARIZONA				
1 Rhodes	76	16	81	9
2 Udall	38	57	31	54
3 Steiger	62	25	59	24
4 Conlan	67	26	—	—
ARKANSAS				
1 Alexander	33	53	43	34
2 Mills	26	25	57	23
3 Hammerschmidt	62	32	73	23
4 Thornton	45	52	—	—
CALIFORNIA				
1 Clausen	52	39	80	16
2 Johnson	28	61	66	30
3 Moss	30	63	32	49
4 Leggett	30	58	41	45
5 Burton	25	72	30	66
6 Mailliard	56	28	83	9
7 Dellums	23	72	28	64
8 Stark	24	71	—	—
9 Edwards	21	70	35	63
10 Gubser	61	22	70	3
11 Ryan	25	53	—	—
12 Talcott	62	24	73	14
13 Teague	66†	31†	87	9
14 Waldie	20	58	31	50
15 McFall	42	50	65	28
16 Sisk	37	56	55	34
17 McCloskey	45	48	47	35
18 Mathias	58	34	70	11
19 Holifield	37	56	56	29
20 Moorhead	70	22	—	—
21 Hawkins	20	63	32	45
22 Corman	31	63	36	46
23 Clawson	63	21	60	18
24 Rousselot	58	34	46	32
25 Wiggins	64	13	76	9
26 Rees	30	64	34	54
27 Goldwater	71	19	63	17
28 Bell	40†	35†	62	10
29 Danielson	22	47	50	46
30 Roybal	26	67	32	60
31 Wilson	30	66	49	28
32 Hosmer	70	20	85	5
33 Pettis	61	29	79	13
34 Hanna	28	46	48	30
35 Anderson	30	64	46	47
36 Ketchum	65	26	—	—
37 Burke	15	51	—	—
38 Brown	30	61	—	—
39 Hinshaw	69	26	—	—
40 Wilson	65	23	74	9
41 Van Deerlin	34	62	43	44
42 Burgener	67	25	—	—
43 Veysey	59	20	74	12
COLORADO				
1 Schroeder	29	71	—	—
2 Brotzman	62	34	82	14
3 Evans	38	58	35	46
4 Johnson	43	46	—	—
5 Armstrong	74	23	—	—

	1	2	3	4
CONNECTICUT				
1 Cotter	29	65	48	43
2 Steele	43	54	60	26
3 Giaimo	32	59	49	31
4 McKinney	47	45	63	23
5 Sarasin	53	47	—	—
6 Grasso	31	66	44	38
DELAWARE				
AL DuPont	57	41	78	19
FLORIDA				
1 Sikes	58	33	59	24
2 Fuqua	41	39	59	30
3 Bennett	43	57	54	46
4 Chappell	53	39	59	29
5 Gunter	41	50	—	—
6 Young	63	31	74	22
7 Gibbons	38	53	47	45
8 Haley	59	40	56	34
9 Frey	66	22	71	16
10 Bafalis	66	28	—	—
11 Rogers	50	50	65	33
12 Burke	60	29	62	23
13 Lehman	29	63	—	—
14 Pepper	28	59	63	30
15 Fascell	31	64	53	41
GEORGIA				
1 Ginn	41	58	—	—
2 Mathis	48	42	63	33
3 Brinkley	54	46	65	34
4 Blackburn	62	19	59	22
5 Young	26	71	—	—
6 Flynt	45	44	43	26
7 Davis	43	46	63	20
8 Stuckey	45	50	38	30
9 Landrum	37	36	51	24
10 Stephens	50	42	65	21
HAWAII				
1 Matsunaga	33	63	41	47
2 Mink	29	70	34	60
IDAHO				
1 Symms	58	34	—	—
2 Hansen	69	28	80	6
ILLINOIS				
1 Metcalfe	25	58	30	34
2 Murphy, M.	31	60	45	40
3 Hanrahan	68	29	—	—
4 Derwinski	59	22	51	15
5 Kluczynski	33	53	55	28
6 Collier	66	22	74	15
7 Collins[2]	24	63	—	—
8 Rostenkowski	26	57	51	33
9 Yates	37	62	36	62
10 Young	70	22	—	—
11 Annunzio	32	66	52	33
12 Crane	60	26	50	38
13 McClory	67	27	74	16
14 Erlenborn	67	17	79	6
15 Arends	79	16	82	6
16 Anderson	55	29	84	9
17 O'Brien	71	21	—	—
18 Michel	75	17	66	19
19 Railsback	51†	35†	65	18
20 Findley	58	39	67	16
21 Madigan	69	30	—	—
22 Shipley	34	59	50	37
23 Price	33	66	71	24
24 Gray	26	49	54	33
INDIANA				
1 Madden	34	62	43	53
2 Landgrebe	63	22	62	33
3 Brademas	28	69	38	57
4 Roush	36	58	38	57
5 Hillis	61	32	81	9
6 Bray	72	22	74	18
7 Myers	71	21	71	26
8 Zion	70	22	77	17
9 Hamilton	41	58	52	45
10 Dennis	76	23	67	28
11 Hudnut	72	25	—	—
IOWA				
1 Mezvinsky	34	66	—	—
2 Culver	34	61	32	55
3 Gross	55	40	43	46
4 Smith	38	58	43	48

Democrats *Republicans*

	1	2	3	4
5 Scherle	65	31	56	33
6 Mayne	70	25	72	18
KANSAS				
1 Sebelius	71	26	73	19
2 Roy	40	54	36	60
3 Winn	66	26	78	13
4 Shriver	69	26	83	17
5 Skubitz	61	30	70	16
KENTUCKY				
1 Stubblefield	48	46	56	32
2 Natcher	39	61	60	40
3 Mazzoli	45	54	46	53
4 Snyder	54	44	50	44
5 Carter	44	30	74	15
6 Breckinridge	49	48	—	—
7 Perkins	38	62	54	44
LOUISIANA				
1 Hebert	35	25	47	7
2 Boggs[3]	40†	56†	—	—
3 Treen	77	21	—	—
4 Waggonner	65	31	66	23
5 Passman	54	34	54	24
6 Rarick	51	42	46	43
7 Breaux	37	45	60*	20*
8 Long, G.	42	54	—	—
MAINE				
1 Kyros	27	68	37	55
2 Cohen	53	46	—	—
MARYLAND				
1 Bauman[4]	54†	46†	—	—
2 Long	30	68	32	65
3 Sarbanes	28	72	38	57
4 Holt	69	30	—	—
5 Hogan	67	31	80	17
6 Byron	57	42	77	20
7 Mitchell	22	73	30	62
8 Gude	40	55	47	48
MASSACHUSETTS				
1 Conte	43	49	51	41
2 Boland	36	62	52	45
3 Donohue	28	67	29	44
4 Drinan	33	67	38	62
5 Cronin	37	53	—	—
6 Harrington	29	62	43	56
7 Macdonald	23	66	37	48
8 O'Neill	31	63	47	46
9 Moakley	27	71	—	—
10 Heckler	38	57	44	40
11 Burke	29	70	46	54
12 Studds	30	70	—	—
MICHIGAN				
1 Conyers	20	50	28	54
2 Esch	56	31	50	30
3 Brown	71	25	81	16
4 Hutchinson	75	25	65	33
5 Ford[5]	80†	16†	82	7
6 Chamberlain	72	24	85	11
7 Riegle[6]	25	62	34	47
8 Harvey	50	26	66	26
9 Vander Jagt	58	30	68	18
10 Cederberg	76	21	87	10
11 Ruppe	58	30	50	26
12 O'Hara	31	57	39	50
13 Diggs	24	59	22	33
14 Nedzi	34	62	41	55
15 Ford	28	66	33	51
16 Dingell	21	60	46	47
17 Griffiths	34	46	45	28
18 Huber	68	24	—	—
19 Broomfield	65	29	65	20
MINNESOTA				
1 Quie	68	28	78	21
2 Nelsen	73	21	84	10
3 Frenzel	58	33	61	29
4 Karth	29	68	41	53
5 Fraser	26	67	34	60
6 Zwach	46	44	62	31
7 Bergland	34	63	47	50
8 Blatnik	24	42	29	46
MISSISSIPPI				
1 Whitten	59	34	61	36
2 Bowen	58	37	—	—
3 Montgomery	60	39	65	27

	1	2	3	4
4 Cochran	65	30	—	—
5 Lott	69	29	—	—
MISSOURI				
1 Clay	26	66	16	43
2 Symington	33	60	40	49
3 Sullivan	26	64	41	38
4 Randall	32	60	61	30
5 Bolling	38	43	50	44
6 Litton	37	58	—	—
7 Taylor	60	31	—	—
8 Ichord	51	42	65	21
9 Hungate	34	62	32	54
10 Burlison	45	54	46	50
MONTANA				
1 Shoup	54	38	67	20
2 Melcher	29	58	43	44
NEBRASKA				
1 Thone	55	45	72	23
2 McCollister	71	29	77	23
3 Martin	76	16	63	19
NEVADA				
AL Towell	57	34	—	—
NEW HAMPSHIRE				
1 Wyman	66	29	81	16
2 Cleveland	64	34	79	19
NEW JERSEY				
1 Hunt	62	22	70	20
2 Sandman	44	27	78	16
3 Howard	20	71	34	55
4 Thompson	23	56	31	53
5 Freling-				
huysen	70	18	78	5
6 Forsythe	62	35	70	23
7 Widnall	57	37	70	16
8 Roe	31	64	48	48
9 Helstoski	27	72	36	51
10 Rodino	28	70	41	49
11 Minish	30	66	46	50
12 Rinaldo	48	51	—	—
13 Maraziti	61	34	—	—
14 Daniels	30	62	52	41
15 Patten	32	66	52	45
NEW MEXICO				
1 Lujan	56	35	54	15
2 Runnels	36	50	32	32
NEW YORK				
1 Pike	42	57	52	48
2 Grover	60	31	79	16
3 Roncallo	59	35	—	—
4 Lent	61	28	76	16
5 Wydler	68	24	71	19
6 Wolff	37	59	38	48
7 Addabbo	31	63	40	55
8 Rosenthal	26	70	34	63
9 Delaney	32	54	61	27
10 Biaggi	24	51	44	45
11 Brasco	28	64	40	52
12 Chisholm	23	64	26	56
13 Podell	25	63	39	52
14 Rooney	4	13	51	26
15 Carey	30	54	37	50
16 Holtzman	29	70	—	—
17 Murphy	36	54	56	17
18 Koch	30	62	38	52
19 Rangel	27	65	30	56
20 Abzug	30	69	33	65
21 Badillo	14	46	29	63
22 Bingham	33	66	36	61
23 Peyser	42	43	73	15
24 Reid	18	54	43	46
25 Fish	49	41	71	19
26 Gilman	49	47	—	—
27 Robison	66	29	67	28
28 Stratton	52	38	71	21
29 King	36	10	74*	17*
30 McEwen	67	20	71	15
31 Mitchell	52	34	—	—
32 Hanley	38	58	61	35
33 Walsh	51	37	—	—
34 Horton	63	36	66	24
35 Conable	86	11	85	9
36 Smith	68	26	80	11
37 Dulski	34	57	44	49

	1	2	3	4
38 Kemp	61	29	79	17
39 Hastings	66	27	74	13
NORTH CAROLINA				
1 Jones	52	42	60	35
2 Fountain	47	50	77	21
3 Henderson	43	54	67	30
4 Andrews	42	51	—	—
5 Mizell	70	26	81	16
6 Preyer	49	50	64	34
7 Rose	41	55	—	—
8 Ruth	73	25	78	21
9 Martin	73	25	—	—
10 Broyhill	66	30	76	18
11 Taylor	50	48	65	26
NORTH DAKOTA				
AL Andrews	46	46	68	23
OHIO				
1 Keating	66	22	86	12
2 Clancy	69	25	71	22
3 Whalen	41	55	52	45
4 Guyer	58	34	—	—
5 Latta	72	28	72	23
6 Harsha	57	38	71	22
7 Brown	62	17	82	9
8 Powell	64	24	70	19
9 Ashley	33	50	50	34
10 Miller	54	46	69	31
11 Stanton	71	29	74	16
12 Devine	79	18	69	18
13 Mosher	50	42	50	41
14 Seiberling	25	73	32	60
15 Wylie	75	22	73	20
16 Regula	64	30	—	—
17 Ashbrook	50	23	52	34
18 Hays	34	50	49	44
19 Carney	28	65	46	41
20 Stanton	25	71	47	46
21 Stokes	19	48	26	53
22 Vanik	31	69	41	57
23 Minshall	54†	20†	63	17
OKLAHOMA				
1 Jones	45	48	—	—
2 McSpadden	39	42	—	—
3 Albert[7]				
4 Steed	48	46	60	32
5 Jarman	72	21	63	20
6 Camp	57	22	66	28
OREGON				
1 Wyatt	49	36	69	15
2 Ullman	38	56	46	44
3 Green	36	32	38	39
4 Dellenback	64	34	76	23
PENNSYLVANIA				
1 Barrett	30	58	37	43
2 Nix	23	63	41	53
3 Green	26	67	36	51
4 Eilberg	28	62	39	54
5 Ware	77†	21†	69	22
6 Yatron	25	67	33	53
7 Williams	66	30	84	15
8 Biester	43	52	62	37
9 Shuster	66	34	—	—
10 McDade	40	54	63	28
11 Flood	38	57	69	28
12 Saylor[8]	50†	40†	53	28
13 Coughlin	58	39	64	31
14 Moorhead	24	64	40	49
15 Rooney	27	63	50	46
16 Eshleman	66	30	66	15
17 Schneebeli	76†	20†	67	20
18 Heinz	51	45	60*	36*
19 Goodling	77†	23†	69	27
20 Gaydos	26	72	41	52
21 Dent	19	64	21	40
22 Morgan	26	53	65	26
23 Johnson	72	22	72	13
24 Vigorito	30	63	60	36
25 Clark	26	52	45	19
RHODE ISLAND				
1 St Germain	26	62	44	49
2 Tiernan	22	67	40	47
SOUTH CAROLINA				
1 Davis	41	54	48*	27*

	1	2	3	4
2 Spence	68	30	68	26
3 Dorn	55	34	62	26
4 Mann	59	34	68	22
5 Gettys	55	38	54	27
6 Young	67	22	—	—
SOUTH DAKOTA				
1 Denholm	37	54	20	61
2 Abdnor	61	30	—	—
TENNESSEE				
1 Quillen	69	24	72	16
2 Duncan	66	34	71	29
3 Baker	64	30	62	19
4 Evins	30	57	39	22
5 Fulton	30	61	34	45
6 Beard	63	29	—	—
7 Jones	42	44	48	27
8 Kuykendall	70	22	64	13
TEXAS				
1 Patman	26	36	50	30
2 Wilson	29	58	—	—
3 Collins	77	22	68	28
4 Roberts	56	36	60	26
5 Steelman	58	37	—	—
6 Teague	40	30	53	29
7 Archer	63	34	70	24
8 Eckhardt	28	70	38	55
9 Brooks	34	55	54	37
10 Pickle	50	47	57	33
11 Poage	54	42	50	34
12 Wright	39	45	43	27
13 Price	56	26	65	22
14 Young	49	47	57	34
15 de la Garza	35	54	50	41
16 White	38	54	66	30
17 Burleson	64	34	66	29
18 Jordan	30	66	—	—
19 Mahon	62	34	71	28
20 Gonzalez	26	71	55	44
21 Fisher	32	19	63	26
22 Casey	58	42	67	29
23 Kazen	40	57	59	39
24 Milford	56	34	—	—
UTAH				
1 McKay	42	40	60	36
2 Owens	32	61	—	—
VERMONT				
AL Mallary	66	32	84*	16*
VIRGINIA				
1 Downing	51	40	69	27
2 Whitehurst	72	26	81	18
3 Satterfield	65	30	64	32
4 Daniel, R. W.	72†	25†	—	—
5 Daniel, W.C.	66	34	69	30
6 Butler	75	23	—	—
7 Robinson	75	24	72	26
8 Parris	64†	33†	—	—
9 Wampler	69	30	73	22
10 Broyhill	70	26	65	27
WASHINGTON				
1 Pritchard	48	48	—	—
2 Meeds	30	67	46	44
3 Hansen	26	54	48	26
4 McCormack	23	60	39	40
5 Foley	37	57	59	36
6 Hicks	36	63	48	50
7 Adams	28	66	45	48
WEST VIRGINIA				
1 Mollohan	35	51	56	18
2 Staggers	33	61	55	29
3 Slack	40	58	50	45
4 Hechler	30	70	34	66
WISCONSIN				
1 Aspin	24	65	39	52
2 Kastenmeier	26	73	35	64
3 Thomson	70	28	73	20
4 Zablocki	44	56	74	26
5 Reuss	30	68	38	60
6 Steiger	70	26	76	18
7 Obey	26	70	38	60
8 Froehlich	60	38	—	—
9 Davis	74	17	72	14
WYOMING				
AL Roncalio	28	68	29	57

Democrats *Republicans*

	1	2	3	4
ALABAMA				
Allen	66	33	66	31
Sparkman	55	31	59	16
ALASKA				
Gravel	26	51	20	54
Stevens	57	34	54	31
ARIZONA				
Fannin	75	14	81	12
Goldwater	45	9	56	9
ARKANSAS				
Fulbright	26	47	29	59
McClellan	56	38	53	34
CALIFORNIA				
Cranston	32	56	35	60
Tunney	30	56	37	52
COLORADO				
Haskell	32	56	—	—
Dominick	65	25	67	9
CONNECTICUT				
Ribicoff	37	57	32	56
Weicker	51	40	66	21
DELAWARE				
Biden	30	49	—	—
Roth	71	25	84	16
FLORIDA				
Chiles	39	52	51	40
Gurney	64	28	86	13
GEORGIA				
Nunn	56	40	—	—
Talmadge	50	43	61	34
HAWAII				
Inouye	32	56	31	47
Fong	61	26	71	12
IDAHO				
Church	28	59	31	55
McClure	61	24	—	—
ILLINOIS				
Stevenson	34	61	37	55
Percy	45	36	48	37
INDIANA				
Bayh	30	53	25	50
Hartke	27	60	20	41

	1	2	3	4
IOWA				
Clark	26	50	—	—
Hughes	24	57	29	63
KANSAS				
Dole	71	27	83	10
Pearson	41	38	57	32
KENTUCKY				
Huddleston	30	58	—	—
Cook	56	37	56	28
LOUISIANA				
Johnston	46	38	—	—
Long	48	47	59	23
MAINE				
Hathaway	30	68	—	—
Muskie	26	54	19	42
MARYLAND				
Beall	68	30	77	17
Mathias	43	42	43	44
MASSACHUSETTS				
Kennedy	30	58	27	51
Brooke	39	48	44	48
MICHIGAN				
Hart	24	59	32	59
Griffin	77	15	84	8
MINNESOTA				
Humphrey	34	59	32	45
Mondale	25	58	33	63
MISSISSIPPI				
Eastland	55	31	65	16
Stennis	22	2	72	24
MISSOURI				
Eagleton	33	58	37	52
Symington	33	55	40	56
MONTANA				
Mansfield	29	64	30	55
Metcalf	36	62	26	46
NEBRASKA				
Curtis	72	18	70	13
Hruska	75	19	84	10
NEVADA				
Bible	39	53	54	34
Cannon	42	48	55	26

	1	2	3	4
NEW HAMPSHIRE				
McIntyre	40	55	42	37
Cotton	58	14	74	14
NEW JERSEY				
Williams	29	54	32	59
Case	42	57	44	50
NEW MEXICO				
Montoya	38	59	41	49
Domenici	67	28	—	—
NEW YORK				
Buckley*	70†	14†	78	13
Javits	38	39	46	39
NORTH CAROLINA				
Ervin	53	34	65	28
Helms	76	21	—	—
NORTH DAKOTA				
Burdick	34	63	35	58
Young	63	36	72	19
OHIO				
Saxbe	58†	19†	63	14
Taft	58	17	70*	13*
OKLAHOMA				
Bartlett	76	22	—	—
Bellmon	65	23	70	10
OREGON				
Hatfield	45	46	27	50
Packwood	57	28	63	18
PENNSYLVANIA				
Schweiker	42	57	50	48
Scott	64	26	75	9
RHODE ISLAND				
Pastore	42	50	43	49
Pell	41	56	31	48
SOUTH CAROLINA				
Hollings	43	49	48	31
Thurmond	76	16	77	16
SOUTH DAKOTA				
Abourezk	25	58	—	—
McGovern	25	64	12	39
TENNESSEE				
Baker	57	25	66	13
Brock	68	16	71	13

- KEY -

† Not eligible for all roll calls in 1973.

* Not eligible for all roll calls in 92nd Congress.

	1	2	3	4
TEXAS				
Bentsen	44	47	59	36
Tower	75	14	70	9
UTAH				
Moss	30	58	30	49
Bennett	70	9	69	12
VERMONT				
Aiken	57	37	66	26
Stafford	51	41	49*	35*
VIRGINIA				
Byrd, Jr.**	63	33	72	26
Scott	72	20	—	—
WASHINGTON				
Jackson	47	53	48	20
Magnuson	38	47	39	40
WEST VIRGINIA				
Byrd	40	60	59	34
Randolph	42	53	46	44
WISCONSIN				
Nelson	31	66	29	66
Proxmire	41	59	38	62
WYOMING				
McGee	42	39	56	17
Hansen	78	14	70	13

Democrats   *Republicans*   *Buckley elected as Conservative*   **Byrd elected as independent*

Presidential Support and Opposition: Senate

1. Support Score, 1973. Percentage of 185 Nixon-issue roll calls in 1973 on which senator voted "yea" or "nay" *in agreement* with the President's position. Failures to vote lower both Support and Opposition scores.

2. Opposition Score, 1973. Percentage of 185 Nixon-issue roll calls in 1973 on which senator voted "yea" or "nay" *in disagreement* with the President's position. Failures to vote lower both Support and Opposition scores.

3. Support Score, 92nd Congress. Percentage of 128 Nixon-issue roll calls in 1971 and 1972 on which senator voted "yea" or "nay" *in agreement* with the President's position. Failures to vote lower both Support and Opposition scores.

4. Opposition Score, 92nd Congress. Percentage of 128 Nixon-issue roll calls in 1971 and 1972 on which senator voted "yea" or "nay" *in disagreement* with the President's position. Failures to vote lower both Support and Opposition scores.

CONGRESS APPROVES 31 PER CENT OF NIXON'S REQUESTS

The first session of the Democratic-controlled 93rd Congress approved less than one-third of President Nixon's 1973 legislative proposals before it adjourned Dec. 22.

Although the session was the seventh longest in history—354 days—congressional debate over the Watergate scandal, limitations on the President's power, congressional reform, the energy crisis and confirmation of a new Vice President delayed action on many of the President's proposals. Congress failed to complete action on legislation involving housing, taxation, foreign trade reform and pension reform.

On the other hand, Mr. Nixon's proposals for construction of the Alaskan pipeline, federal aid to establish health maintenance organizations and emergency security assistance to Israel were approved by the Congress. Also granted were presidential requests for year-round daylight savings time and a mandatory speed limit of 55 miles per hour on federally funded highways. Nixon had asked for a 50 mile per hour limit for automobiles and a 55 mile per hour limit for trucks. Congress and the President also approved a bill which the President requested providing federal aid to the handicapped, but only after Nixon had vetoed an earlier version of the bill as too expensive.

As measured by Congressional Quarterly's annual Boxscore, Nixon made 183 specific requests for legislation (including treaties submitted for ratification) in 28 messages to Congress and other public statements. Of these, 57—or about 31 per cent—were enacted into law or ratified.

The Nixon score represents a significant drop from his 44 per cent mark in 1972.

The Boxscore is a survey of specific presidential legislative requests during a calendar year and their fate during that year's session of Congress. It is not a comprehensive review of an administration's legislative accomplishments. Issues are not reflected in the Boxscore unless they were the subject of public statements or messages to Congress by the President himself in 1973. Success in legislative struggles spanning more than one session of a Congress is not recorded in the Boxscore.

For instance, the Boxscore does not include war powers legislation since Mr. Nixon did not make a request on the subject. But congressional action to override the president's veto of legislation placing restrictions on the executive's war-making powers was an important aspect of the legislative year.

Nor does the Boxscore differentiate between major legislation and less significant proposals. (In District of Columbia affairs, however, some minor requests of purely local interest are omitted.) The individual requests are itemized as they were presented in the messages.

Major Proposals. Following is a summary of congressional action on the major aspects of President Nixon's program during 1973:

Foreign Policy. Congress passed the foreign assistance act which authorized funds for fiscal 1974 economic and military aid. Much of this aid was earmarked for the poorest sectors of developing countries.

Congress also passed a measure appropriating nearly $5.8-billion for foreign aid for fiscal 1974, more than $1-billion less than the President had requested. The appropriations measure included the President's $2.2-billion request for aid to Israel and other emergency aid as well as funds for programs authorized in the foreign assistance act. Congress allowed the President $200-million in contract authority to draw down Defense Department stocks for aid to Cambodia.

How the Boxscore Works

The items tabulated in the Boxscore include only the specific legislative requests contained in the President's messages to Congress and other public statements during a calendar year.

Excluded from the Boxscore are proposals advocated by executive branch officials but not specifically by the President; measures endorsed by the President but not specifically requested by him; nominations, and suggestions that Congress consider or study particular topics when legislative action is not requested.

Except for major proposals, presidential requests for District of Columbia legislation also are excluded from the Boxscore tabulation.

Routine appropriation requests, which provide funds for regular, continuing government operations, are excluded. Appropriation requests for specific programs, or requests for substantial budget increases, are included if the President indicated in special messages or other communications that they were important in his over-all legislative program.

Because the Boxscore fundamentally is a tabular checklist of the President's program, presented in neither greater nor less detail than is found in presidential messages, the individual requests necessarily differ considerably from one another in their scope and importance.

Because Congress does not always vote "yes" or "no" on a proposal, CQ evaluates legislative action to determine whether compromises amount to approval or rejection of the President's requests.

Legislative activity on an item must occur in the same year as the presidential request in order to be credited in the Boxscore.

Symbols in the Final Outcome column indicate whether Congress took favorable or unfavorable action on the proposal.

Economic Policy. Congress granted the President's request for a one-year extension of his authority to impose wage and price controls on the nation's economy.

Natural Resources. Congress responded favorably to the President's request for early identification and protection of endangered species. Both houses by overwhelming margins cleared legislation extending protection for species of fish, wildlife and plants considered likely to become extinct in the foreseeable future as well as those facing immediate extinction.

Energy. The first major energy bill to be enacted in 1973 authorized the immediate construction of the long-delayed trans-Alaskan pipeline. The President had called passage of the legislation a matter of the "highest urgency."

Congress failed to complete action on the President's request for additional authority to allocate and ration energy supplies.

Two energy conservation measures requested by the President were approved by Congress. Year-round daylight saving time was imposed and a 55 mile per hour speed limit on all federally aided highways was enacted.

Transportation. Congress passed a bill authorizing $20-billion for federal-aid highway and mass transit purposes. For the first time since the federal highway program was set up in 1956, cities will be permitted by 1976 to finance a portion of urban mass transit projects, including subways, from the Highway Trust Fund under a compromise agreement approved by Congress. The compromise was part of House-Senate conference agreement on the bill extending highway programs, including the interstate system, for three years (1974-76). The President had requested the use of Highway Trust Fund money for mass transit purposes and called the compromise "a significant extension and reform of the federal highway program."

General Welfare. An increase in the hourly minimum wage was blocked when the House Sept. 19 sustained President Nixon's Sept. 6 veto of the minimum wage bill. Nixon vetoed the bill, he said, because he considered it inflationary and because it did not contain a provision allowing employers to pay a lower, or subminimum, wage to youths under 18 years of age.

Congress passed a bill that authorized $1.55-billion in fiscal 1974-75 for the federal rehabilitation program to aid the handicapped. Although the President had requested more federal aid for the handicapped, he had vetoed an earlier version of the bill as too expensive.

Congress approved the President's request to enact the flood disaster protection act which increased flood insurance coverage and included insurance for communities that are flood prone.

District of Columbia. Echoing the sentiments of the President, the Congress passed a bill providing for partial home rule for residents of the District of Columbia.

Crime. A new Drug Enforcement Administration was created within the Justice Department. The President submitted the proposal for the new unit in his Executive Reorganization Plan No. 2 of March 28. Since neither house voted disapproval of the plan within the 60-day period provided by law, the new unit began operations July 1.

Health. In its most important action in the health field, Congress granted the President's request for federal aid to establish about 100 health maintenance organizations (HMOs) over a five year period. HMOs, offering comprehensive health services for a set annual or monthly fee, were considered the major alternative to the traditional fee-for-service medical practice.

Source Key: Nixon's 1973 Legislative Requests

The sources of President Nixon's 1973 legislative requests are listed below, preceded by a letter-symbol. Messages asking Senate consent to treaty ratifications are excluded from this compilation. Page numbers refer to those requests in the text section of this book.

	Source, Message	Date	Page
A	Economic Report	Jan. 31	—
B	American Revolution Bicentennial Celebration	Feb. 1	—
C	Letter to Congress on Foreign Assistance	Feb. 7	—
D	Natural Resources and the Environment	Feb. 15	15-A
E	The American Economy	Feb. 22	17-A
F	Human Resources	March 1	20-A
G	Community Development	March 8	26-A
H	Law Enforcement and Drug Abuse Prevention	March 14	30-A
I	Drug Law Enforcement Reorganization	March 28	35-A
J	Letter to Congress on Import Barriers	March 30	—
K	Trade Reform	April 10	42-A
L	Pension Reform	April 11	48-A
M	Unemployment Insurance System Reform	April 12	57-A
N	Stockpile Disposal	April 16	59-A
O	Energy Policy	April 18	50-A
P	Foreign Assistance Programs	May 1	63-A
Q	Legal Services Corporation	May 11	77-A
R	Federal Election Reform	May 16	65-A
S	The Nation's Economy	June 13	87-A
T	Energy and Natural Resources	June 29	91-A
U	U.S. Financial System	Aug. 3	
V	National Legislative Goals	Sept. 10	70-A
W	Housing Policy	Sept. 19	81-A
X	Patent Reform	Sept. 27	67-A
Y	Emergency Security Assistance for Israel and Cambodia	Oct. 19	88-A
Z	Funds for International Development Association and Asian Development Bank	Oct. 31	
AA	Energy Message	Nov. 8	93-A
BB	Wilderness Preservation	Nov. 28	92-A

PRESIDENTIAL BOXSCORE FOR 1973

Following is a list of President Nixon's specific legislative requests to Congress in 1973 and a summary in tabular form of the action taken on each. A letter in parentheses following each item indicates the presidential statement or message which was the most definitive source of the request. A key to the sources appears on page 332. Each treaty ratification request made during the Nixon administration and pending in 1973 is followed by the date the treaty was originally sent to the Senate.

STATUS KEY

√   Favorable Action

X   Unfavorable Action

   No Action Taken

H   Hearings Held

Congressional Inaction Constitutes Favorable Action.

Foreign Policy

FOREIGN AID

	HOUSE COMMITTEE ACTION	HOUSE FLOOR ACTION	SENATE COMMITTEE ACTION	SENATE FLOOR ACTION	FINAL OUTCOME	PUBLIC LAW NUMBER
	1	2	3	4	5	6
1. Amend the Foreign Assistance Act of 1961 to permit relief assistance to Bangladesh and the Philippines and to authorize appropriations for fiscal 1973 for international security assistance. (C)	√	√	√	√	√	9
2. Authorize emergency security asistance of $2.2-billion for Israel. (Y)	√	√	√	√	√	199
3. Authorize emergency security assistance of $200-million for Cambodia. (Y)	√	√	√	√	√	189
4. Pass the Foreign Assistance Act of 1973 to assist developing countries respond quickly to the ravages of natural disasters, and provide adequate security assistance to friendly governments. (P)	√	√	√	√	√	189
5. Authorize $1-billion in fiscal 1974 for development assistance.	√	√	√	√		189
6. Authorize $1.3-billion in fiscal 1974 for security assistance. (P)	√	√	√	√	√	189
7. Authorize $632-million in fiscal 1974 for the reconstruction effort in Indochina. (P)	√	√	√	√	√	189
8. Authorize for future appropriation $1.5-billion for U.S. contribution to the International Development Association. (Z)	√		H			
9. Authorize an additional $50-million for U.S. contribution to the Asian Development Bank. (Z)	√		H			

TREATIES

Consent to ratification of:

	HOUSE COMMITTEE ACTION	HOUSE FLOOR ACTION	SENATE COMMITTEE ACTION	SENATE FLOOR ACTION	FINAL OUTCOME	PUBLIC LAW NUMBER
1. Renewal of request for convention on prevention and punishment of the crime of genocide. 6/16/49						
2. International Convention Relating to Intervention on the High Seas in Cases of Oil Pollution Casualties. 5/20/70						
3. Protocol for the Prohibition of the Use in War of Asphyxiating, Poisonous or Other Gases, and of Bacteriological Methods of Warfare. 8/19/70						
4. Convention on Psychotropic Substances. 6/29/71						
5. Convention on the Law of Treaties. 11/22/71						
6. International Convention on the Establishment of an International Fund for Compensation for Oill Pollution Damage, and an amendment to the 1954 Convention for the Prevention of Pollution of the Sea. 5/5/72						
7. International Convention on Tonnage Measurement of Ships. 6/15/72						
8. Convention on the Prohibition of the Development, Production and Stockpiling of Bacteriological (Biological) and Toxin Weapons, and on their Destruction. 8/10/72						
9. Convention with Japan for the Protection of Migratory Birds and Birds in Danger of Extinction, and their Environment. 8/18/72			√	√	√	—
10. Treaty simplifying the process of filing and examining patent applications on the same invention in member countries. 9/12/72			√	√	√	—
11. Convention with Poland establishing consular relations. 9/19/72			√	√	√	—

	1	2	3	4	5	6
12. Convention with Romania establishing consular relations. 9/19/72			✓	✓	✓	—
13. Convention with Hungary establishing consular relations. 9/19/72			✓	✓	✓	—
14. Treaty with Republic of Colombia in which U.S. renounces all claims to sovereignty over three uninhabited outcroppings of coral reefs in the Caribbean. 1/9/73						
15. Termination of notes accompanying the Treaty of Amity and Economic Relations between the U.S. and Ethiopia. 2/28/73			✓	✓	✓	—
16. Convention on the Prevention of Marine Pollution by Dumping of Wastes and Other Matter. 2/28/73			✓	✓	✓	—
17. Amendments to the 1966 International Convention on Load Lines, regarding the limits to which ships on international voyages can be loaded 2/22/73			✓	✓	✓	—
18. Strasbourg Agreement establishing an International Patent Classification. 3/22/73			✓	✓	✓	—
19. Convention for the Protection of the World Cultural and Natural Heritage to create international machinery for the identification and protection of natural and cultural areas of outstanding universal value which constitute the common heritage of mankind. 3/28/73			✓	✓	✓	—
20. Convention for the Protection of Producers of Phonograms against Unauthorized Duplication of their Phonograms. 4/11/73			✓	✓	✓	—
21. Convention on International Trade in Endangered Species of Wild Fauna and Flora, designed to establish a system by which countries may control international trade of species which are in danger of becoming extinct because of that trade. 4/13/73			✓	✓	✓	—
22. Amendments to the 1960 Convention for the Safety of Life at Sea to improve the safety of maritime navigation including requiring certain new communication procedures. 5/9/73			✓	✓	✓	—
23. Agreement with Canada for the Promotion of Safety on the Great Lakes. 5/14/73			✓	✓	✓	—
24. Treaty with Uruguay updating extradition relations and adding to the list of extraditable offenses both narcotic violations and aircraft hijacking. 5/21/73			✓	✓	✓	—
25. Amendment to Article 61 of the United Nations Charter increasing the membership of the Economic and Social Council from 27 to 54. 5/21/73			✓	✓	✓	—
26. Treaty with Italy updating extradition relations and adding to the list of extraditable offenses both narcotic violations and aircraft hijacking. 6/27/73			✓	✓	✓	—
27. Protocol amending the 1928 convention concerning international expositions. 7/19/73			✓	✓	✓	—
28. International Coffee Agreement of 1968. 7/23/73			✓	✓	✓	—
29. Convention On the International Transit of Goods. 7/23/73						
30. Protocol amending the Convention on International Civil Aviation increasing to 15 the membership of the Air Navigation Commission. 9/12/73			✓	✓	✓	—
31. Statutes of the World Tourism Organization as an intergovernmental body, replacing the International Union of Official Travel Organizations, a non-governmental organization. 9/12/73			✓	✓	✓	—
32. Treaty with Paraguay updating extradition relations and adding to the list of extraditable offenses both narcotic violations and aircraft hijacking. 9/12/73			✓	✓	✓	—
33. Convention on Matters of Taxation to promote economic and cultural relations with the Soviet Union by eliminating tax barriers. 9/19/73						
34. Treaty with Denmark updating extradition relations and adding to the list of extraditable offenses both narcotic violations and aircraft hijacking. 10/30/73						
35. Protocol amending the 1964 Convention for the International Council for the Exploration of the Sea with respect to the vote required by the council for approving its annual budget. 11/9/73						
36. Convention on the International Regulations for Preventing Collisions at Sea, designed to revise the existing regulations in the light of technological developments and the increased use of the seas. 11/9/73						
37. Customs Convention on Containers and the International Convention for Safe Containers to provide respectively for the temporary importation of containers free of import regulations and specific structural requirements to assure their safe operation. 11/15/73						

TRADE

	1	2	3	4	5	6
1. Pass the Trade Reform Act of 1973 granting the President five-year authority to eliminate, reduce, or increase customs duties in the context of negotiated agreements. (K)	✓	✓				
2. Permit the President to negotiate agreements for the reciprocal reduction of non-tariff barriers subject to a three-month congressional veto procedure. (K)	✓	✓				

	1	2	3	4	5	6

3. Permit the President advanced authority to carry out mutually beneficial agreements concerning specific customs matters primarily involving valuation and the marking of goods by country of origin. (K) — **1:** X

4. Impose a less restrictive text for invoking import restraints. (K) — **1:** ✓ **2:** ✓

5. Provide a new method for determining whether imports actually are the primary cause for serious injury to domestic producers. (K) — **1:** ✓ **2:** ✓

6. Provide readily available assistance to workers unemployed due to import-related causes. (K) — **1:** ✓ **2:** ✓

7. Revise and extend the President's authority to raise barriers against countries which unreasonably or unjustifiably restrict our exports. (K) — **1:** ✓ **2:** ✓

8. Amend antidumping and countervailing duty laws to provide for more expeditious investigations and decisions concerning unfair trade practices. (K) — **1:** ✓ **2:** ✓

9. Amend the current statute concerning patent infringement by subjecting cases involving imports to judicial proceedings and by providing for fair processes and effective action in the event of court delays. (K) — **1:** H

10. Grant the President authority to extent most-favored-nation treatment to countries who do not currently receive such treatment, subject to a three month congressional veto procedure. (K) — **1:** ✓ **2:** ✓

11. Allow the President flexible authority to raise or lower import restrictions on a temporary basis to help correct deficits or surpluses in our balance of payments position. (K) — **1:** ✓ **2:** ✓

12. Authorize the President to reduce or suspend import barriers to restrain inflation. (J) — **1:** ✓ **2:** ✓

13. Permit the U.S. to join with other developed countries in helping to improve the access of poorer nations to the markets of developed countries. (K) — **1:** ✓ **2:** ✓

14. Authorize the President to make limited reductions in our tariffs as a form of compensation to other countries. (K) — **1:** ✓ **2:** ✓

15. Amend the Export Trade Act to make it clear that the act applies not only to the export of goods but also to certain kinds of services such as architecture, construction, engineering, training and management consulting. (K) — **1:** H **3:** H

16. Amend the Federal Trade Commission Act to strengthen our ability to deal with foreign producers whose cartel or monopoly practices raise prices in our markets. (K) — **1:** H **3:** H

17. Allow approval of non-tariff barrier agreements to be covered by a new, optional procedure whereby the President would be required to give Congress 90 days advance notice of such agreements subject to a congressional veto procedure. (K) — **1:** ✓ **2:** ✓

18. Give the President greater flexibility in providing appropriate relief from import problems—including orderly marketing agreements or higher tariffs or quotas. (K) — **1:** ✓ **2:** ✓

19. Authorize the President to offer reductions in particular United States barriers as a means of obtaining significant advantages for American exports. (K) — **1:** ✓ **2:** ✓

20. Clarify the exemption of export associations from our domestic antitrust laws. (K)

Taxes and Economic Policy

TAXES

1. Provide income tax credit for tuition paid to non-public elementary and secondary schools. (E)
2. Amend the tax laws so that earnings from new American investments, which take advantage of tax inducements by foreign countries, will be taxed by the U.S. at the time they are earned. (K)
3. Provide property tax relief for older citizens. (V)

ECONOMIC POLICY

1. Extend the Economic Stabilization Act for one year to give government continued authority to intervene in instances of unreasonable price and wage behavior. (A) — **1:** ✓ **2:** ✓ **3:** ✓ **4:** ✓ **5:** ✓ **6:** 28

2. Pass legislation which would establish the Council on International Economic Policy on a permanent basis. (V) — **1:** ✓ **2:** ✓ **3:** ✓ **4:** ✓ **5:** ✓ **6:** 121

3. Enact an overall spending ceiling for each fiscal year and establish a regular mechanism for deciding how to maintain the ceiling. (E) — **1:** ✓ **2:** ✓ **3:** ✓

4. Permit interest ceilings on time and savings deposits to be removed over a 5½-year period. (U)

	1	2	3	4	5	6
5. Allow expanded deposit services for consumers by federally chartered thrift institutions and banks. (U)						
6. Expand investment and lending alternatives for federally chartered thrift institutions and banks. (U)						
7. Permit federal charters for stock savings and loan institutions and mutual savings banks. (U)						
8. Provide credit unions with greater access to funds. (U)						
9. Remove FHA and VA interest ceilings. (U)						
10. Modify the tax structure for banks and thrift institutions. (U)						

National Security

	1	2	3	4	5	6
1. Authorize the selling of stockpile items which the U.S. no longer needs to keep in reserve in order to protect national security. (N)	✓	✓	✓	✓	✓	212†

Resources and Public Works

ENVIRONMENT

	1	2	3	4	5	6
1. Pass toxic control legislation which would provide adequate testing standards for chemical substances. (D)	✓	✓	✓	✓		
2. Establish federal regulations and standards for the disposal of extremely hazardous wastes. (D)			H			
3. Pass legislation to stimulate greater state and local action to ensure high standards for our drinking water. (D)	H	✓	✓			
4. Allow the federal government to impose a special financial charge on those who produce sulfur oxide emissions. (D)						
5. Require states to establish regulatory programs to control sediment from new construction as a part of their water quality programs. (D)						
6. Permit use of the Highway Trust Fund to help state and local governments achieve air quality, conserve energy and meet other environmental objectives. (D)	✓	✓	✓	✓	✓	87
7. Authorize a $10-million contribution toward the United Nations fund to coordinate and support international environmental programs. (D)	✓	✓	✓	✓	✓	188
8. Enact a National Land Use Policy Act which would impose sanctions on any state which does not establish an adequate land use program. (D)	H	✓	✓			
9. Enact a powerplant siting law which assures that electric power facilities are constructed on a timely basis, but with early and thorough review of long-range plans and specific provisions to protect the environment. (D)						
10. Use federal tax laws to discourage unwise development in wetlands. (D)						
11. Change the tax laws to encourage preservation and rehabilitation of older buildings and provide federal insurance of loans to restore historic buildings for residential purposes. (D)						
12. Pass legislation to enable the secretary of the interior to protect our environmental interest on lands considered to be under public domain. (D)	H	✓	✓			
13. Revise the formula for allocating grant funds to the states from the Land and Water Conservation Fund so that more funds will be channelled to states with large urban populations. (D)						
14. Repeal the 1872 Mining Act. (D)						
15. Pass legislation to regulate abuses of surface and underground mining in a manner compatible with the environment. (D)	H	✓	✓			
16. Provide for early identification and protection of endangered species and make the taking of an endangered animal a federal offense. (D)	✓	✓	✓	✓	✓	205
17. Develop legislation to improve control of predators without endangering other wildlife. (D)	H					
18. Amend legislation that established the Wilderness Preservation System so that more Eastern lands can be included. (D)		✓				
19. Increase funding authority by $20-million for expansion of the national system of wild and scenic rivers. (D)	✓	✓	✓	✓		
20. Pass legislation which would allow the Interior Department to forestall private or commercial development of Florida's Big Cypress Swamp in order to protect the wildlife in that area, and preserve the water supply of Everglades National Park. (D)	H					

† *Also Public Laws 93-214, 216, 218, 219, 220*

	1	2	3	4	5	6

21. Pass legislation to regulate foreign fishing off the U.S. coasts to the fullest extent authorized by international agreements and to regulate domestic fishing in the U.S. fisheries zone and in the high seas beyond that zone. (D)
22. Adopt regulations to minimize any adverse environmental effects resulting from weather control. (D)
23. Add twelve areas consisting of over one million primeval acres of American terrain to the National Wilderness Preservation System. (BB)

ENERGY

1. Pass legislation that would exempt natural gas from new wells from price regulation at the wellhead. (O)
2. Empower the secretary of interior to impose a ceiling on the price of new natural gas when circumstances warrant. (O)
3. Begin construction of the Alaska pipeline. (O)
4. Require that the government act on all completed license applications for nuclear power plants within 18 months after they are received. (O)
5. Extend the investment credit provisions of present tax law so that a credit will be provided for all exploratory drilling for new oil and gas fields. (O)
6. Permit the Department of Interior to issue licenses for deepwater ports beyond the three-mile limit. (O)
7. Create a new central energy fund in the Interior Department to provide more money for non-nuclear research and development. (O)
8. Authorize a 35 per cent increase in funding for our total fusion research and development effort to accelerate experimental programs and to initiate preliminary reactor design studies. (O)
9. Establish a Department of Energy and Natural Resources which would be responsible for administering the national energy policy. (O)
10. Create a new independent Energy Research and Development Administration. (T)
11. Pass legislation that would provide for appropriate settlement for those who are forced to relinquish their leases in the Santa Barbara Channel for environmental reasons. (O)
12. Pass legislation to cancel oil leases in the Santa Barbara Channel and create in that area a National Energy Reserve. (V)
13. Authorize restrictions on public and private consumption of energy. (AA)
14. Reduce speed limit to 50 miles per hour on highways across the country. (AA)
15. Exempt stationary sources from federal and state air and water quality laws and regulations. (AA)
16. Authorize the exemption of steps taken under the proposed energy emergency act from the National Environmental Protection Act. (AA)
17. Provide emergency powers for the federal regulatory agencies involved in transportation to adjust the operations of air, rail, ship and motor carriers in a manner responsive to the need to conserve fuel. (AA)
18. Empower the Atomic Energy Commission to grant a temporary operating license of up to 18 months for nuclear power plants without holding a public hearing. (AA)
19. Authorize the initiation of full production in Naval Petroleum Reserve #1 (Elk Hills, California) and the exploration and further development of other Naval Petroleum Reserves. (AA)
20. Permit Daylight Saving Time to be established on a year-round basis. (AA)
21. Authorize the President, where practicable, to order a power plant or other installation to convert from the use of a fuel such as oil to another fuel such as coal. (AA)
22. Grant the President additional authority to allocate and ration energy supplies. (AA)

Item	1	2	3	4	5	6
Fishing 21	H					
Energy 1			H			
Energy 2			H			
Energy 3	✓	✓	✓	✓	✓	153
Energy 5	H					
Energy 6	H		H			
Energy 7	X					
Energy 8	X					
Energy 9	H		H			
Energy 10	✓	✓	H			
Energy 11	H		H			
Energy 12	H		H			
Energy 13	✓	✓	✓	✓		
Energy 14	✓	✓	✓	✓	✓	239
Energy 16	✓	✓	✓	✓		
Energy 17	H					
Energy 20			✓	✓		
Energy 21	✓	✓	✓	✓	✓	182
Energy 22	✓	✓	✓	✓		
	✓	✓	✓	✓	✓	

Welfare and Urban Affairs

HOUSING

1. Authorize the Federal Housing Administration (FHA) to insure larger housing loans on a low downpayment basis for single and multifamily dwellings. (W)
2. Allow FHA and the Veterans Administration (VA) to insure mortgages carrying market rates of interest. (W)

Item	1	2	3	4	5	6
Housing 1	H		H			
Housing 2	H		H			

	1	2	3	4	5	6
3. Permit the secretary of housing and urban development (HUD) to allow greater flexibility in repayment arrangements for federally insured loans on a experimental basis. (W)	H		H			
4. Allow investors a tax credit on the interest they earn when they put money into residential mortgages. (W)	H		H			
5. Further the development of private mortgage insurance companies by allowing them to purchase inexpensive federal reinsurance. (W)	H		H			
6. Expand experimental programs to test additional techniques for administering the cash assistance approach to lower income families for housing. (W)	H		H			
7. Develop and put into effect the appropriate mechanisms for measuring the cost of safe and sanitary housing in various parts of the country. (W)	H		H			
8. Extend for one year the FHA mortgage insurance programs. (V)	H		H			

TRANSPORTATION

	1	2	3	4	5	6
1. Authorize the expenditure by state and local governments of $3.65-billion over the next three years from the Highway Trust Fund for urban transportation needs, including capital improvements for bus and rapid rail systems. (G)	X		X			
2. Allow states and localities to transfer federal monies earmarked for interstate highway segments to construction of other federal-aid highways and mass transit capital improvements. (G)	✓	✓	✓	✓	✓	87
3. Increase funding for mass transit capital grants by $3-billion, bringing the obligational authority for the mass transit program to $6.1-billion. (G)	✓	✓	✓	✓	✓	87
4. Amend the Urban Mass Transportation Act by increasing the federal share of urban mass transit capital grant assistance programs to 70 per cent. (G)	✓	✓	✓	✓	✓	87
5. Allow local officials to use money from the Highway Trust Fund for mass transit purposes. (O)	✓	X	✓	✓	✓	87
6. Enact the Transportation Improvement Act of 1973 which would release some of the outmoded and excessively restrictive regulatory procedures which affect the entire railroad industry. (V)						
7. Continue the rural highway program at the $1-billion a year level, and provide ample resources to advance the interstate system as it approaches its 1980 funding completion date. (G)	✓	✓	✓	✓	✓	87

INDIANS

	1	2	3	4	5	6
1. Empower any Indian community to take over control of federally-funded and administered programs of the Bureau of Indian Affairs and the Department of Health, Education and Welfare. (F)			H			
2. Pass legislation to foster local Indian self-determination by developing an Interior Department program of bloc grants to federally recognized tribes as a replacement for a number of existing economic and resource development programs. (F)						
3. Provide easier access to loan and credit opportunities for Indian tribal organizations and Indians seeking to enter business. (F)	H		✓	✓		
4. Establish an Indian Trust Counsel Authority to assure independent legal representation for Indians' natural resource rights. (F)	H		H			
5. Establish a new position in the Department of Interior of assistant secretary for Indian and territorial affairs. (F)	✓	✓	✓	✓		

GENERAL WELFARE

	1	2	3	4	5	6
1. Raise the minimum wage in light of cost of living increases. (V)	✓	✓	✓	✓	✓	X†
2. Amend the Vocational Rehabilitation Act to extend and improve job training programs for the handicapped (V)	✓	✓	✓	✓	✓	112‡
3. Enact the Disaster Preparedness and Assistance Act which would encourage the use of insurance before disasters strike, increase the role of state and local officials in determining how federal money would be spent in disaster-stricken communities and automatically release federal funds in the case of major disasters. (V)	H					
4. Enact the Flood Disaster Protection Act which would increase flood insurance coverage from $6- to $10-billion and include insurance for communities that are flood prone. (V)	✓	✓	✓	✓	✓	234
5. Appropriate $200-million in fiscal 1974 for the Administration on Aging. (F)	✓	✓	✓	✓	✓	192

† Vetoed Sept. 6, 1973. (HR 7935)
‡ An earlier vocational rehabilitation measure (S 7) was vetoed March 27. HR 8070 was signed by the President Sept. 26.

General Government

CRIME

	1	2	3	4	5	6
1. Enact a new Heroin Trafficking Act which would increase the sentences for heroin and morphine offenses. (H)						
2. Pass legislation aimed at curbing the manufacture and sale of handguns. (H)						
3. Reform the federal criminal system to provide speedier and more rational criminal trial procedures. (H)			H			
4. Create a Drug Enforcement Administration within the Department of Justice to lead the war against illicit drug traffic. (I)					#	
5. Transfer to the secretary of the treasury all functions currently vested in Justice Department officials to inspect persons, or the documents of persons at ports of entry. (I)	X	X	X	X	X	
6. Reform the federal criminal code to be a fully effective instrument for the administration of criminal justice. (V)			H			
7. Restore the death penalty for treason, assassination, acts of sabotage and espionage and for violations of selected federal laws in which death results. (V)			H			
8. Authorize a $680-million special revenue sharing fund for law enforcement. (H)	X		H X			

DISTRICT OF COLUMBIA
(Major Requests Only)

	1	2	3	4	5	6
1. Strengthen the capability and expand the authority of the District of Columbia government and moderate the federal restraints over its operation. (V)	✓	✓	✓	✓	✓	198

CONSUMER PROTECTION

	1	2	3	4	5	6
1. Establish a Consumer Protection Agency. (V)	H		H			

GOVERNMENT OPERATIONS

	1	2	3	4	5	6
1. Create a new American Revolution Bicentennial Administration with a full-time administrator. (B)	✓	✓	✓	✓	✓	179
2. Create a separate, nonprofit Legal Services Corporation as a means of delivering high quality legal assistance to those who would otherwise be unable to afford it. (Q)	✓	✓	✓			
3. Create a non-partisan Commission on Federal Election Reform, to be charged with examining the entire pattern of campaign practices and recommending comprehensive reforms. (R)	H	✓	✓			
4. Provide legislative authority for ACTION. (V)	✓	✓	✓	✓	✓	113
5. Enact a new Responsive Governments Act to assist state and local governments in strengthening their planning and management capabilities. (G)						
6. Enact the Better Communities Act to provide revenue sharing for community development. (G)	H	H				
7. Pass legislation to convert the United States to the metric system. (V)	✓	✓				
8. Extend the authority of the President to submit reorganization plans to Congress. (V)						
9. Enact the Patent Modernization and Reform Act of 1973. (X)						
10. Expand funds for the National Foundation on the Arts and Humanities to $168-million. (F)	✓	✓	✓	✓	✓	133

Health and Education

EDUCATION

	1	2	3	4	5	6
1. Establish a new program of education revenue sharing such as compensatory education for the disadvantaged, education for the handicapped, vocational education, needed assistance in federally affected areas and supporting services. (F)	X					
2. Channel more higher education support through students themselves, including a new grant program which would increase funds provided to $948-million and the number assisted to over 1,500,000 persons. (F)						

	1	2	3	4	5	6

HEALTH

1. Enact the Health Maintenance Organization Assistance Act which would provide limited federal money to demonstrate the promising innovation of group medical centers. (V)

	1	2	3	4	5	6
Health 1	✓	✓	✓	✓	✓	222

Agriculture and Labor

LABOR

1. Establish a "Rule of 50" formula for vesting pension rights—preserving pension rights of employees even though they leave their jobs before retirement. (L)
2. Pass legislation requiring employers to set aside at least 5 per cent of the unfunded, vested liabilities in a pension plan. (L)
3. Make an individual's contributions to a retirement savings program deductible up to $1,500 per year or 20 per cent of earned income, whichever is less. (L)
4. Raise annual limit for deductable contributions by the self-employed to $7,500 or 15 per cent of income, whichever is less. (L)
5. Amend the tax law to permit the worker who receives a lump-sum payment of retirement benefits before he retires to put the money into another qualified retirement savings program without having to pay a tax on it, or on the interest it earns, until he draws benefits upon retirement. (L)
6. Enact the Employee Benefits Protection Act, establishing an explicit federal requirement to insure proper management, reporting and disclosure of employee benefit plans, and broadening investigative and enforcement powers for the secretary of labor. (L)
7. Allow pension fund participants and beneficiaries to seek remedies for breach of fiduciary duty through class action suits. (L)
8. Enact the Job Security Act of 1973 which would establish minimum benefit standards for the states, extend coverage to most farm employees and set up safeguards to preserve the neutrality of the unemployment insurance system during industrial disputes. (M)
9. Provide that every eligible insured worker, when unemployed, must be paid a benefit equal to at least 50 per cent of his average weekly wage, up to a state maximum which shall be at least two-thirds of the average weekly wage of covered workers in the state. (M)

	1	2	3	4	5	6
Labor 1	H		X	X		
Labor 2	H		✓	✓		
Labor 3	H.		H			
Labor 4	H		✓	✓		
Labor 5	H		H			
Labor 6	✓		✓	✓		
Labor 7	H		✓	✓		

AGRICULTURE

1. Authorize a new system of export controls on food products. (S)

	1	2	3	4	5	6
Agriculture 1	✓	✓	✓			

PRESIDENTIAL MESSAGES

1974 BUDGET: TIGHTER CONTROL AND LOWER SPENDING

Following is the text, as made available by the White House, of President Nixon's Jan. 29 budget message to Congress.

BUDGET MESSAGE OF THE PRESIDENT

To the Congress of the United States:

The 1974 budget fulfills my pledge to hold down Federal spending so that there will be no need for a tax increase.

This is a budget that will continue to move the Nation's economy toward a goal it has not achieved in nearly two decades: a high employment prosperity for American's citizens without inflation and without war.

Rarely is a budget message perceived as a dramatic document. In a real sense, however, the 1974 budget is the clear evidence of the kind of change in direction demanded by the great majority of the American people. No longer will power flow inexorably to Washington. Instead, the power to make many major decisions and to help meet local needs will be returned to where it belongs—to State and local officials, men and women accountable to an alert citizenry and responsive to local conditions and opinions.

The 1974 budget proposes a leaner Federal bureaucracy, increased reliance on State and local governments to carry out what are primarily State and local responsibilities, and greater freedom for the American people to make for themselves fundamental choices about what is best for them.

This budget concerns itself not only with the needs of all the people, but with an idea that is central to the preservation of democracy: the "consent of the governed."

The American people as a whole—the "governed"—will give their consent to the spending of their dollars if they can be provided a greater say in how the money is spent and a greater assurance that their money is used wisely and efficiently by government. They will consent to the expenditure of their tax dollars as long as individual incentive is not sapped by an ever-increasing percentage of earnings taken for taxes.

Since the mid-1950's, the share of the Nation's output taken by all governments in the United States—Federal, State, and local—has increased from a quarter to a third. It need not and should not go higher.

The increase in government claims on taxpayers was not for defense programs. In fact, the defense share of the gross national product declined by one-quarter while the share for civilian activities of all governments grew by three-fourths, rising from 14% of the gross national product in 1955 to about 25% in 1972.

In no sense have Federal civilian programs been starved; their share of the gross national product will increase from 6½% in 1955 to 14% in 1972. Nor will they be starved by the budget that I am proposing. A generous increase in outlays is provided each year by the normal growth in revenues. Higher Federal tax rates are not needed now or in the years ahead to assure adequate resources for properly responsive government—*if* the business of government is managed well. And revenue sharing will help State and local governments avoid higher taxes.

During the past 2 years, with the economy operating below capacity and the threat of inflation receding, the Federal budget provided fiscal stimulus that moved the economy toward full employment. The 1974 budget recognizes the Federal Government's continuing obligation to help create and maintain—through sound monetary and fiscal policies—the conditions in which the national economy will prosper and new job opportunities will be developed. However, instead of operating primarily as a stimulus, the budget must now guard against inflation.

The surest way to avoid inflation or higher taxes or both is for the Congress to join me in a concerted effort to control Federal spending. I therefore propose that before the Congress approves *any* spending bill, it establish a rigid ceiling on spending, limiting total 1974 outlays to the $268.7 billion recommended in this budget.

I do not believe the American people want higher taxes any more than they want inflation. I am proposing to avoid both higher taxes and inflation by holding spending in 1974 and 1975 to no more than revenues would be at full employment.

1975 PROJECTIONS IN THE 1974 BUDGET

This year's budget presents, for the first time, a detailed preview of next year's. I have taken this step to demonstrate that if we stay within the 1974 and 1975 estimated outlays presented in this budget, we will prevent a tax increase—and that the 1974 budget is a sound program for the longer range future, not simply for today. This innovation in budget presentation is a blueprint for avoiding inflation and tax increases, while framing more responsive instruments of government and maintaining prosperity.

Our ability to carry out sound fiscal policy and to provide the resources needed to meet emerging problems has been limited by past decisions. In 1974, $202 billion in outlays, or 75% of the budget, is *virtually uncontrollable* due to existing law and prior-year commitments. But just as every budget is heavily influenced by those that have preceded it, so it strongly influences those that follow.

Control over the budget can be improved by projecting future available resources and the known claims on them, and then making current decisions within the constraints they impose. That is why, in my first budget, I began the practice of showing projections of future *total* revenues and outlays under current and proposed legislation. In the 1973 budget, 5-year projections of the cost of legislative proposals for major new and expanded programs were added.

This budget presents an even closer look at the implications of the 1974 proposals for the 1975 budget. It projects, in agency and functional detail, the outlays in 1975 that will result from the major program proposals in the 1974 budget, including the outlay savings that can be realized from program reductions in 1973 and 1974. In so doing, it takes into consideration the longer range effect of each of our fiscal actions.

Most importantly, this budget shows the narrow margin between projected outlays and full-employment revenues in 1975, despite the economy measures that are recommended. Program reductions and terminations of the scale proposed are clearly necessary if we are to keep control of fiscal policy in the future.

The 1974 budget program implies 1975 full-employment outlays of about $288 billion, $19 billion (7%) more than in 1974. This is within our estimate of full-employment revenues of $290 billion for 1975. There is, however, very little room for the creation of new programs requiring additional outlays in 1975 and *no room for the postponement of the reductions and terminations proposed in this budget.*

The program reductions and terminations I have proposed will result in more significant savings in 1975 and later years than in 1973 and 1974. It is for this reason, too, that I have included the 1975 projections in my budget this year. The Federal spending pipeline is a very long one in most cases, and the sooner we start reducing costs the better for the Nation.

The estimated 1975 outlays for the various Federal agencies are, of course, tentative. The outlay total, however, is the approximate amount that will represent appropriate Federal spending in 1975 if we are to avoid new taxes and inflation. As program priorities change and require increases in some areas, offsetting decreases must be found in others. As the projections indicate, this is necessary for both 1974 and 1975.

FISCAL POLICY AND THE BUDGET PROCESS

Fiscal policy.—In July 1970, I adopted the full-employment budget principle in order to make the budget a tool to promote orderly economic expansion.

Consistent with this principle, the budget that I submitted to the Congress last January proposed fiscal stimulus as part of a balanced economic program that included sound monetary policy and the new economic policy that I launched on August 15, 1971. My confidence that the American economy would respond to sensible stimulus in this context has been fully justified. During 1972, employment increased by 2.3 million persons, real output rose by 7½%, business fixed investment was 14% higher, and the rate of increase in consumer prices declined.

From 1971 through 1973, the full-employment budget principle permitted and called for substantial actual budget deficits. For this reason, some people have forgotten the crucial point that the full-employment principle requires that deficits be reduced as the economy approaches full employment—and that it establishes the essential discipline of an upper limit on spending at all times.

Full Employment Budget—Surplus or Deficit

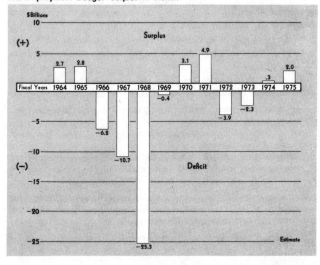

The full-employment budget principle permits fiscal stimulation when stimulation is appropriate and calls for restraint when restraint is appropriate. But it is not self-enforcing. It signals us what course to steer, but requires us to take the actions necessary to keep on course. These steps are not taken for us, and they are rarely easy.

As we look ahead, with the economy on the upswing, the full-employment budget principle—and common sense—prescribe a shift away from fiscal stimulus and toward smaller budget deficits. We *must* do what is necessary to make this shift.

Holding 1973 spending to $250 billion and achieving full-employment balance in 1974 and in 1975 will be difficult. Reduction of some activities and termination of others are necessary and are proposed in this budget. Nonetheless, the budget provides significant increases for many important programs.

If we did not budget with firm restraint, our expenditures in 1973 would be over $260 billion. The ballooning effect of one year's expenditures on the next would in turn have meant that 1974's expenditures would be about $288 billion, far beyond full-employment revenues, and 1975's expenditures would be approximately $312 billion, leading to a huge, inflationary deficit.

If spending is to be controlled, the Congress must establish a spending ceiling promptly. Otherwise, the seeds sown in individual authorization and appropriation actions will produce ever-growing Federal spending not only in the coming fiscal year but in the years beyond.

Should the Congress cause the total budgeted outlays to be exceeded, it would inescapably face the alternatives of higher taxes, higher interest rates, renewed inflation, or all three. I oppose these alternatives; with a firm rein on spending, none of them is necessary.

Reforming congressional budget procedures.—Delay in congressional consideration of the budget is a major problem. Each time I have submitted a budget, the Congress has failed to enact major portions of it before the next budget was prepared. Instead, it has resorted to the device of continuing resolutions to carry on the activities for which it has not made appropriations. Such delay needlessly compounds the complexities of budget preparation, and frustrates the potential of the budget as an effective management and fiscal tool.

The complexity of the budgeting process is another problem. Because of modifications made to reflect the desires of the more than 300

Restraining Outlays

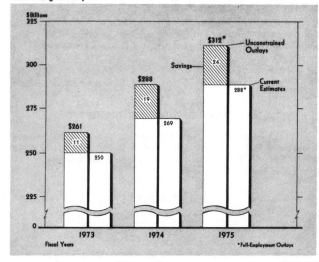

congressional committees and subcommittees that influence it, the process has become more complicated and less comprehensible.

The fragmented nature of congressional action results in a still more serious problem. Rarely does the Congress concern itself with the budget totals or with the effect of its individual actions on those totals. Appropriations are enacted in at least 15 separate bills. In addition, "backdoor financing" in other bills provides permanent appropriations, authority to contract in advance of appropriations, authority to borrow and spend without an appropriation, and program authorizations that require mandatory spending whether or not it is desirable in the light of current priorities.

At the same time, a momentum of extravagance is speeded by requirements created initially by legislative committees sympathetic to particular and narrow causes. These committees are encouraged by special interest groups and by some executive branch officials who are more concerned with expansion of their own programs than with total Federal spending and the taxes required to support that spending. Since most programs have some attractive features, it is easy for the committees and the Congress itself to authorize large sums for them. These authorizations, however, create pressure on the appropriations committees to appropriate higher amounts than the Nation's fiscal situation permits.

Last October, the Congress enacted legislation establishing a joint committee to consider a spending ceiling and to recommend procedures for improving congressional control over budgetary outlay and receipt totals.

I welcome this effort and pledge the full cooperation of my Administration in working closely with the committee and in other efforts of the Congress toward this end.

Specific changes in congressional procedures are, of course, the business of the Congress. However, the manner in which the Congress reviews and modifies the budget impinges so heavily on the management of the executive branch that I am impelled to suggest a few subjects that deserve high priority in the committee's deliberations, including:

—adoption of a *rigid* spending ceiling to create restraint on the total at the beginning of each annual review;

—avoidance of new "backdoor financing" and review of existing legislation of this type;

—elimination of annual authorizations, especially annual authorizations in specific amounts; and

—prompt enactment of all necessary appropriation bills before the beginning of the fiscal year.

The Congress must accept responsibility for the budget *totals* and must develop a systematic procedure for maintaining fiscal discipline. To do otherwise in the light of the budget outlook is to accept the responsibility for increased taxes, higher interest rates, higher inflation, or all three. In practice, this means that should the Congress pass any legislation increasing outlays beyond the recommended total, it must find financing for the additional amount. Otherwise, such legislation will inevitably contribute to undue inflationary pressures and thus will not be in the public interest. And it will be subject to veto.

I will do everything in my power to avert the need for a tax increase, but I cannot do it alone. The cooperation of the Congress in controlling total spending is absolutely essential.

SUMMARY OF THE 1974 BUDGET

The 1974 budget proposes an approximate balance in full-employment terms and an actual deficit that is about one-half the 1973 deficit. The 1975 budget totals I propose here would also yield a balance in full-employment terms.

THE BUDGET TOTALS

[Fiscal years. In billions]

Description	1972 actual	1973 estimate	1974 estimate	1975 estimate
Budget receipts	$208.6	$225.0	$256.0	*
Budget outlays	231.9	249.8	268.7	*
Deficit (−)	−23.2	−24.8	−12.7	*
Full-employment receipts	225.0	245.0	268.0	$290.0
Full-employment outlays ¹	228.9	247.3	267.7	288.0
Full-employment surplus or deficit (−)	−3.9	−2.3	0.3	2.0
Budget authority	248.1	280.4	288.0	313.5

	1971 actual			
Outstanding debt, end of year:				
Gross Federal debt	$409.5	$437.3	$473.3	$505.5
Debt held by the public	304.3	323.8	348.8	365.3
Outstanding Federal and federally assisted credit, end of year:				
Direct loans	53.1	50.1	50.1	51.0
Guaranteed and insured loans ²	118.1	133.1	150.3	164.1
Government-sponsored agency loans ³	38.8	48.9	59.6	71.8

¹ In these estimates, outlays for unemployment insurance benefits and the Emergency Employment Act program are calculated as they would be under conditions of full employment.
² Excludes loans held by Government accounts and special credit agencies.
³ Excludes Federal Reserve banks, but, starting in 1972, includes Export-Import Bank (previously reported as direct loans) and, starting in 1974, includes the newly authorized Environmental Financing Authority.
*Estimates of actual receipts and outlays have not been made at this time.

The full-employment budget balance in 1974 assures support for continuation of the economy's upward momentum without rekindling inflation. Greater stimulus in 1974 would be dangerous, and would put an unsupportable burden on future budgets.

Budget receipts in 1974 are estimated to be $256 billion. This is an increase of $31 billion over 1973, reflecting growing prosperity, higher personal income, and rising corporate profits. The receipts estimates also reflect the impact of tax cuts resulting from the Tax Reform Act of 1969, the new economic policy and the Revenue Act of 1971, as well as the payroll tax increases enacted to finance higher social security benefits.

Budget outlays in 1974 are expected to be $268.7 billion. The total would have been substantially greater—probably about $288 billion—had my Administration not made an extraordinary effort to hold to the fiscal guidelines of a $250 billion maximum in 1973, rather than the nearly $261 billion which otherwise would have occurred, and to full-employment balance in 1974.

Even so, this budget necessarily proposes an increase in outlays of $19 billion, or nearly 8% over the previous year. It provides amply for America's security and well-being in the year ahead.

The 1974 budget program projects full-employment outlays of $288 billion in 1975, which, together with the revenues that would be produced under existing law, will mean full-employment balance in that year.

About $288 billion of *budget authority*—the new authority to make commitments to spend—is requested for 1974. Of the total, about $173 billion will require new action by the Congress.

IMPROVING GOVERNMENT

The role of government.—The last article of the Bill of Rights says:

"The powers not delegated to the United States by the Constitution, nor prohibited by it to the States, are reserved to the States respectively, or to the people."

The philosophy of the Founding Fathers embodied in this amendment is also my philosophy. I believe that a larger share of our national resources must be retained by private citizens and State and local governments to enable them to meet their individual and community needs.

Our goal must not be bigger government, but better government—at all levels. Our progress must not be measured by the amount of money we put into programs, but by the accomplishments which result from them.

One of my first acts as President was to direct that an intensive review be made of our federal system of government. We found that:

—the executive branch was poorly organized to accomplish domestic program objectives;
—State and local governments often could not meet the basic needs of their citizens; and
—Federal programs to assist State and local governments had become a confusing maze, understood only by members of a new, highly specialized occupation—the grantsmen.

My Administration has developed a comprehensive strategy for dealing with these problems through restructuring the executive departments and revitalizing the federal system.

A restructured Federal Government.—A thorough overhaul of the Federal bureaucracy is long overdue, and I am determined to accomplish it.

As the role of government has grown over the years, so has the number of departments and agencies which carry out its functions. Unfortunately, very little attention has been given to the ways in which each new unit would fit in with all the old units. The consequence has been a hodgepodge of independent, organizationally unrelated offices that pursue interrelated goals. As a result, able officials at all levels have been frustrated, public accountability has been obscured, and decentralization and coordination of Federal operations have been impeded. This overlapping of responsibilities has increased the costs of government. It has generated interagency conflict and rivalry and, most importantly, it has imposed inexcusable inconvenience on the public that is supposed to be served.

To help remedy this situation, I proposed to the Congress in 1971 that the executive branch be restructured by consolidating many functions now scattered among several departments and agencies into four new departments. These new departments would be organized around four major domestic purposes of government: community development, human resources, natural resources, and economic affairs—thus consolidating in a single chain of command programs that contribute to the achievement of a clearly stated mission. Under this arrangement, we will be able to formulate policy more responsibly and more responsively and carry out that policy more efficiently and more effectively. I welcome congressional cooperation in this important endeavor and will seek it in the weeks ahead. I plan now to streamline the executive branch along these lines as much as possible within existing law, and to propose similar legislation on departmental reorganization to the 93d Congress.

Meanwhile, I have already taken the first in a series of steps that will increase the management effectiveness of the Cabinet and the White House staff. I hope the smaller and more efficient Executive Office of the President will become a model for the entire executive branch.

Reorganization of the executive branch is a necessary beginning but reorganization alone is not enough.

Increased emphasis will also be placed on program performance. Programs will be evaluated to identify those that must be redirected, reduced, or eliminated because they do not justify the taxes required to pay for them. Federal programs must meet their objectives and costs must be related to achievements.

The Federal Assistance Review program, which I began in 1969, has made important progress in decentralizing and streamlining Federal grant programs. To speed the process of decentralization, improve program coordination, and eliminate unnecessary administrative complications, I have strengthened the Federal Regional Council system. These councils, working with State and local governments, have played an impressive and growing role in coordinating the delivery of Federal services.

A revitalized federal system.—Restructuring of the Federal Government is only one step in revitalizing our overall federal system. We must also make certain that State and local governments can fulfill their role as partners with the Federal Government. Our General Revenue Sharing and special revenue sharing programs can help considerably in achieving this goal. They provide our States and communities with the financial assistance they need—in a way that allows them the freedom and the responsibility necessary to use those funds most effectively.

On October 20, 1972, I signed a program of General Revenue Sharing into law. This program provides State and local governments with more than $30 billion over a 5-year period beginning January 1, 1972. This historic shift of power away from Washington will help strengthen State and local governments and permit more local decisionmaking about local needs.

Although final congressional action was not taken on my special revenue sharing proposals, I remain convinced that the principle of special revenue sharing is essential to continued revitalization of the federal system. I am, therefore, proposing the creation of special revenue sharing programs in the 1974 budget.

These four programs consist of broad-purpose grants, which will provide State and local governments with $6.9 billion to use with considerable discretion in the areas of education, law enforcement and criminal justice, manpower training, and urban community development. They will replace 70 outmoded, narrower categorical grant programs and will, in most cases, eliminate matching requirements.

The funds for special revenue sharing will be disbursed according to formulas appropriate to each area. In the case of manpower revenue sharing, an extension of existing law will be proposed. Current administrative requirements will be removed so that State and local governments can group manpower services in ways that best meet their own local needs.

The inefficiency of the present grant systems makes favorable action on special revenue sharing by the Congress an urgent priority.

SPECIAL REVENUE SHARING, BUDGET AUTHORITY, FIRST FULL YEAR

Description	Billions
Urban community development	2.3
Education	2.5
Manpower training	1.3
Law enforcement	.8
Total	**6.9**

As an important companion to returning responsibility to State and local governments, I proposed to the Congress in 1971 a program to provide funds to help State and local governments strengthen their management capabilities to carry out their expanded role. I am submitting this important proposal again this year.

The federal system is dynamic, not static. To maintain its vitality, we must constantly reform and refine it. The executive branch reorganization and special revenue sharing programs that I am proposing, along with continued decentralization of Federal agencies, are essential to that vitality.

BUILDING A LASTING STRUCTURE OF PEACE

Building a lasting peace requires much more than wishful thinking. It can be achieved and preserved only through patient diplomacy and negotiation supported by military strength. To be durable, peace must also rest upon a foundation of mutual interest and respect among nations. It must be so constructed that those who might otherwise be tempted to destroy it have an incentive to preserve it.

The 1974 budget supports America's efforts to establish such a peace in two important ways. First, it maintains the military strength we will need to support our negotiations and diplomacy. Second, it proposes a sound fiscal policy that, supported by a complementary monetary policy, will contribute to prosperity and economic stability here and abroad.

Our strength, together with our willingness to negotiate, already has enabled us to begin building a structure for lasting world peace and to contribute to a general relaxation of world tensions.

—We have made substantial progress toward ending our involvement in the difficult war in Southeast Asia.

—In the past 4 years, we have concluded more significant agreements with the Soviet Union than in all previous years since World War II, including the historic agreement for limiting strategic nuclear arms.

—We have ended nearly a quarter century of mutual isolation between the United States and the People's Republic of China and can look forward to the development of peaceful cooperation in areas of mutual interest.

In this atmosphere, other nations have also begun to move toward peaceful settlement of their differences.

One of the results of our negotiations, taken together with the success of the Nixon Doctrine, our substantial disengagement from Vietnam, and the increased effectiveness of newer weapons systems, has been a significant but prudent reduction in our military forces. Total manpower has been reduced by about one-third since 1968, and will be further reduced as we end the draft and achieve an All-Volunteer Force. At the same time, our allies are assuming an increasing share of the burden of providing for their defense.

As a result, defense outlays have been kept in line. In 1974, they will be substantially the same as in 1968. During the same period, the total budget has grown by 50%, and nondefense outlays have grown by 91%, or $90 billion. When adjusted for pay and price increases, defense spending in 1974 will be about the same as in 1973 and about one-third *below* 1968.

But, while this Administration has succeeded in eliminating unnecessary defense spending, it is equally determined to spend whatever is necessary for national security. Our 1974 budget achieves this goal. It assures us of sufficient strength to preserve our security and to continue as a major force for peace. Moreover, this strength will be supported, beginning this year, without reliance on a peacetime draft.

A framework for international economic progress is an important part of our efforts for peace. A solid beginning has been made on international monetary reform through our participation in the ongoing discussions of the Committee of Twenty. We will continue to press these efforts during the year ahead.

Our foreign assistance programs also reflect our intention to build a lasting structure of peace through a mutual sharing of burdens and benefits. America will remain firm in its support of friendly nations that seek economic advancement and a secure defense. But we also expect other nations to do their part, and the 1974 budget for foreign assistance is based upon this expectation.

Our goal is a durable peace that is sustained by the self-interest of all nations in preserving it. Our continuing military strength and our programs for international economic progress, as provided for in this budget, will bring us closer to that goal for ourselves and for posterity.

MEETING HUMAN NEEDS

The 1974 budget for human resources programs, like the three that have preceded it under this Administration, reflects my conviction that social compassion is demonstrated not just by the commitment of public funds in hope of meeting a need, but by the tangible betterments those funds produce in the lives of our people. My drive for basic reforms that will improve the Federal Government's performance will continue in the coming fiscal year.

Between 1969 and 1974, outlays for Federal human resources programs have increased 97%, while total budget outlays have grown by only 46%. As a result, human resources spending now accounts for close to half the total budget dollar, compared with just over one-third of the total at the time I took office.

Many solid accomplishments have resulted. Higher social security benefits are bringing greater dignity for the aged and the disabled. Better health care and better education and training opportunities, especially for the disabled, the disadvantaged, and veterans, are helping to raise the social and economic status of millions of individuals and have improved the productive capacity of the Nation as a whole. Expanded food programs are helping to assure adequate nutrition for the needy.

However, disappointments and failures have accompanied these accomplishments. The seeds of those failures were sown in the 1960's when the "do something, do anything" pressure for Federal panaceas led to the establishment of scores of well-intentioned social programs too often poorly conceived and hastily put together. In many respects, these were classic cases of believing that by "throwing money at problems" we could automatically solve them. But with vaguely defined objectives, incomplete plans of operation, and no effective means of evaluation, most of these programs simply did not do the job.

We gave these programs the benefit of every doubt and continued them while we conducted a long-needed, thorough review of all Federal human resources programs. Based on this review, the 1974 budget proposes to reform those programs that can be made productive and to terminate those that were poorly conceived, as well as those that have served their purpose.

We can and will find better ways to make the most of our human resources—through the partnership of a restructured Federal Government and strong State and local governments, and with the help of a socially committed private sector that is bolstered by a revival of individual initiative and self-reliance among our people. But only by halting the unproductive programs here and now can we assure ourselves of the money needed to pursue those programs that will get results.

Income security.—Federal income maintenance programs have expanded dramatically in the last 4 years. Cash benefits under the social security system alone will have grown from $30 billion in 1970 to $55 billion in 1974, an increase of 83%. These benefits will account for about one-fifth of *all* Federal budget outlays. Legislation enacted in calendar year 1972 alone increased these benefits by $10.5 billion, or almost 30% over 1971 benefits.

Beginning on January 1, 1974, under the terms of legislation passed last year, the Federal Government is scheduled to assume responsibility for providing a basic assistance payment for the aged, blind, and disabled. While this would require that we add a very large number of Federal employees to the Social Security Administration, I have ordered this increase held to an absolute minimum, and I will urge the Governors to seek ways of eliminating an equivalent number of positions in their States so that the overall size of government will not grow.

The 1974 budget for income maintenance programs will emphasize:

—intensified efforts to eliminate wasteful and inefficient management of welfare programs; and
—further improvement in the welfare of the aging.

The legislation that established General Revenue Sharing also set a long-needed ceiling on Federal outlays for social services. In 1969, Federal outlays for these services were less than $400 million. By 1972, States had discovered that this ill-defined program could be used to finance most public services and they were planning to make claim on about $5 billion in Federal funds.

This runaway, open-ended program was out of control. The $2.5 billion statutory limit imposed on the program, about seven times the 1969 level, will restore a measure of control. We are now emphasizing efforts to assure that this massive increase in funding is used effectively to meet the real needs of public assistance recipients for useful social services.

Education and manpower training.—Outlays in the 1974 budget for education and manpower, including those for veterans, will be $12 billion. The 1974 program is based upon a reevaluation of the Federal Government's role in these areas. The primary responsibility

for most of these activities, other than those for veterans, rests with State and local governments. The proper Federal role is primarily that of helping State and local governments finance their own activities, while conducting directly those few programs that can be done efficiently and effectively only by the Federal Government.

The 1974 budget supports such a role for the Federal Government. It provides for:

—creation of education and manpower revenue sharing programs to give State and local governments greater power in allocating resources within these vital areas;
—proposed legislation that would provide an income tax credit for tuition paid to nonpublic elementary and secondary schools;
—full funding for Basic Education Opportunity grants to provide assistance for college students;
—continued emphasis on training disadvantaged veterans;
—an increase in the work incentive program to help welfare recipients get jobs; and
—phasedown of the temporary Emergency Employment Assistance program consistent with the increase in new jobs in the private sector.

Health.—My strategy for health in the 1970's stresses a new Federal role and basic program reforms to assure that economical, medically appropriate health services are available when needed. As major elements in this strategy, the 1974 budget provides for:

—a proposal for national health insurance legislation;
—increased funding for cancer and heart disease research;
—initiation of a nationwide system of physician-sponsored Professional Standards Review Organizations to assure quality and appropriateness of care;
—reform of Medicaid and Medicare to reduce financial burdens for aged and disabled patients who experience long hospital stays and to improve program management and increase incentives for appropriate use of services; and
—increased special care units and continued improvement of outpatient and extended care benefits for veterans.

The impact of the 1974 budget will be significant. In 1974, nearly 5 million more poor, aged, and disabled persons will benefit through expanded financial support for health services. There will be continued emphasis on consumer safety. Finally, strengthened cost controls will give Americans greater protection against unreasonable medical cost increases.

Drug abuse control.—During my first term, in order to meet what had become both a crime problem and a health crisis of epidemic proportions, we launched an all-out war on drug abuse. With the 1974 budget, we will continue to press that attack aggressively. Budgeted expenditures of $719 million, an increase of $64 million over 1973, will permit continued strong support for interdiction of drug traffic and for the treatment and rehabilitation of drug users.

Civil rights.—The protection of each citizen's civil rights is one of the highest priorities of my Administration. No American should be denied equal justice and equal opportunity in our society because of race, color, sex, religion, or national origin. Toward this end, the Department of Justice and other Federal agencies will be able under the 1974 budget to increase their civil rights enforcement efforts aimed at upholding this fundamental principle as follows:

—The Department of Justice will expand its efforts to coordinate the enforcement of equal access to and equal benefit from Federal financial assistance programs.
—The Community Relations Service will expand its crisis resolution and State liaison activities.
—The civil rights performance of Federal agencies will be monitored and reviewed throughout the year.
—The Equal Employment Opportunity Commission will receive additional resources to carry out its expanded responsibilities.
—The Civil Service Commission will expand its monitoring of Federal service equal opportunity.
—The Commission on Civil Rights will receive additional resources to carry out its newly granted jurisdiction over sex discrimination.

In addition, the Small Business Administration will expand its loan program for minority business by nearly one-third.

NATURAL RESOURCES AND ENVIRONMENT

The balanced development of our natural resources is essential to a healthy economy and an improved standard of living. Development inevitably brings change to our natural environment which, if not properly controlled, could impair the health and welfare of our citizens and the beauty of our surroundings. Balancing the need for development and growth with the need to preserve and enhance our environment has become a major challenge of our time.

Meeting this challenge is not solely the responsibility of the Federal Government. Heavy responsibilities fall on State and local governments, private industry, and the general public as well. This budget reflects my determination to seek a proper balance between development and preservation. It contemplates neither blind or insensitive exploitation of our natural resources nor acceptance of a no-growth philosophy. It avoids such a spurious choice and plots an orderly and reasoned course toward sensible development and environmental enhancement.

The forward thrust of our environmental programs has not been altered. We will continue vigorous enforcement of laws and Federal regulations. The Environmental Protection Agency has allotted to the States $5 billion of new authorizations to make grants for waste treatment construction. With $5.1 billion in additional funds already available for payment on new projects and projects for which the Federal Government had made prior commitments, a total of $10.1 billion has been set aside in a short period of time for waste treatment facilities. I believe that more funds would not speed our progress toward clean water, but merely inflate the cost while creating substantial fiscal problems.

Major Environmental Quality Programs

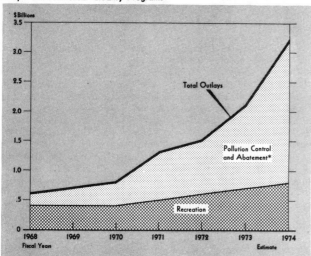

$ Billions

Total Outlays

Pollution Control and Abatement*

Recreation

1968 1969 1970 1971 1972 1973 1974
Fiscal Years   Estimate

*Includes EPA and remedial actions at federal facilities

Adequate supplies of clean energy are a vital concern. The resources devoted in this budget to energy research and development are one important element of the response to this problem. My initiative to demonstrate a large-scale fast breeder reactor by 1980 will be continued; and funds have been significantly increased to develop means of using other energy resources—particularly our abundant coal resources. At the same time, this budget provides funds to carry out a program for regulation of strip mining activities to minimize their adverse environmental impact.

I have long been committed to sound, multiple-use management of public lands consistent with long-term environmental preservation. My 1974 program provides both for development of new outdoor recreation opportunities accessible to our large population centers and for new wilderness areas. In addition, the budget includes funds for a program providing incentives to States to undertake regulation of private land use. This program would encourage establishment at the State level of open decisionmaking processes to insure proper consideration of the long-term environmental implications of major land use decisions.

The role of agriculture.—The American farmer wants to raise high quality products in the most efficient manner, and to receive prices that provide him a fair return on his investment. He wants a minimum of Government regulation, and recognizes the need for some protection from events beyond his control. We are working to create conditions favorable to the American farmer by expanding our world markets, stabilizing the domestic economy, and tailoring farm programs to provide both freedom of choice and reasonable earnings for farmers.

We have made some impressive progress toward these objectives. Farm income has improved; more freedom to plant has been achieved; and the costs of price support are down. Americans and the entire world have benefited from the extraordinary productivity of American agriculture. In the period ahead, we seek to use this productivity in domestic and world marketplaces in order to maintain both high farm income and reasonable consumer prices.

REFORMING COMMUNITY AND AREA DEVELOPMENT PROGRAMS

My deep commitment to providing change that works is, and must be, matched by a total determination to identify and reform or eliminate programs that have not worked. It would be irresponsible to continue spending taxpayers' money for programs that have long since served their purpose, are not working at all, or are not working sufficiently to justify their costs.

I began my efforts in community and area development with proposals for general and special revenue sharing. In 1971, I proposed a reorganization of the executive branch agencies responsible for community and area development programs—to consolidate related functions and thereby assure better management. Substantial progress in furthering community development was made last year when General Revenue Sharing became law.

The 1974 budget reflects my determination to accelerate major reforms of programs for urban development and housing, rural development, transportation, and crime prevention and criminal justice.

Urban development and housing.—During the past 4 years, the private housing industry reached, and has maintained, an unprecedented level of housing production. Early in this period the downward trend in housing production that existed in 1969 was reversed. New housing starts rose 60%, from 1.5 million in calendar year 1969 to nearly 2.4 million in calendar year 1972, a new record. While federally subsidized starts were 11% of the 1972 total, it is clear that our broad fiscal and monetary policies are the dominant factors that determined the overall level of housing production.

Throughout this period, federally assisted housing programs have been plagued with problems and their intended beneficiaries have thus been shortchanged. As a result, new commitments under those programs which have not worked well enough have been temporarily halted, pending a complete reevaluation of the Federal role in housing and of alternative ways to provide housing.

In addition, no new projects will be approved under several outmoded and narrowly focused community development programs which have not produced benefits that justify their costs to the taxpayer. Continuing to channel resources into these programs can only delay the initiation of more effective programs and policies.

The 1974 budget will:

—honor those commitments already made under housing and community development programs;

—continue the evaluation of alternative ways to help the private market satisfy the Nation's need for housing;

—continue to seek congressional approval of the Administration's Urban Community Development Revenue Sharing proposal so that new funds can begin to flow to State and local governments on July 1, 1974; and

—emphasize those programs that help State and local officials strengthen their decisionmaking and management processes, allowing responsibility to be shifted increasingly to these officials, while the Federal Government concentrates on those activities which cannot be accomplished more effectively by the private sector or other levels of government.

Despite the halt in new commitments, federally assisted activity will continue at a high level. Subsidized housing starts in calendar year 1973 will increase over the previous year, totaling 270,000. Approximately 1,800 urban renewal projects will still be active. Federal outlays on these uncompleted housing and community development projects will rise from $4.0 billion in 1973 to $4.9 billion in 1974.

Rural development.—The 1974 budget consolidates and reorients our rural development programs.

While I would have preferred that the Congress enact special revenue sharing for rural development, the Rural Development Act of 1972 provides a basis for beginning efforts consistent with the revenue sharing concept. In particular, State and local officials will have greater control in project decisions. Rural development programs as a whole will increase over last year, with loan programs growing particularly rapidly.

I intend to watch closely our experience with this new approach and then consider whether additional legislation may be needed to make it more effective.

The counterpart to proceeding with the new authorities is the consolidation, termination, or reorientation of older programs. Public works and related economic development programs of the Department of Commerce will be phased out in favor of programs established under the Rural Development Act and Small Business Administration authorities. Loans to improve rural electric and telephone service will be available on an even larger scale—but at reduced cost to taxpayers—through the loan authority of the Rural Development Act and through the new Rural Telephone Bank.

Transportation.—The Federal role in transportation is significant but limited. It must insure that national needs, such as the Interstate Highway System and airway control, are met. Otherwise, the primary responsibilities rest with the States, local governments, and the private sector, while the Federal Government provides financial support.

Last year, the Administration supported legislation that recognized this proper Federal role. It proposed providing flexibility at the State and local level in meeting mass transit and highway needs and avoiding narrow categorical grants. The legislation narrowly failed to be enacted.

I will propose legislation incorporating the same principles again this year. The legislation and this budget propose a broad $1 billion program to aid urban mass transit capital investment and sufficient funds for the Interstate Highway System to insure completion of the system in a reasonable time.

The safety of our transportation systems is a matter of paramount importance. I have directed that Federal safety efforts for all modes of transportation be intensified.

Crime prevention and criminal justice.—Helping State and local criminal justice agencies fight crime in our cities and towns continues to be a major commitment of my Administration.

Outlays for law enforcement activities will be $2.6 billion in 1974, a 7½% increase over 1973. This increase reflects my determination to enforce the laws of this country and protect the safety of all our citizens. We must make certain, however, that the programs which assist State and local criminal justice systems are not only expanded, but reformed, and that we do a better job of reducing crime and rehabilitating criminal offenders. To accomplish these goals, I propose in this budget that:

—the grants to State and local governments for law enforcement assistance be converted to a law enforcement revenue sharing program with additional funding;
—the Law Enforcement Assistance Administration continue and strengthen its national research, demonstration, and dissemination efforts to develop more effective ways of preventing crime; and
—Federal agencies intensify their efforts to fight organized crime.

Further, new and improved measures to prevent airplane hijacking will be put into effect in cooperation with the airlines and airport operators.

CONCLUSION

The respect given to the common sense of the common man is what has made America the most uncommon of nations.

Common sense tells us that government cannot make a habit of living beyond its means. If we are not willing to make some sacrifices in holding down spending, we will be forced to make a much greater sacrifice in higher taxes or renewed inflation.

Common sense tells us that a family budget cannot succeed if every member of the family plans his own spending individually—which is how the Congress operates today. We must set an overall ceiling and affix the responsibility for staying within that ceiling.

Common sense tells us that we must not abuse an economic system that already provides more income for more people than any other system by suffocating the productive members of the society with excessive tax rates.

Common sense tells us that it is more important to save tax dollars than to save bureaucratic reputations. By abandoning programs that have failed, we do not close our eyes to problems that exist; we shift resources to more productive use.

It is hard to argue with these common sense judgments; surprisingly, it is just as hard to put them into action. Lethargy, habit, pride, and politics combine to resist the necessary process of change, but I am confident that the expressed will of the people will not be denied.

Two years ago, I spoke of the need for a new American Revolution to return power to people and put the individual *self* back in the idea of *self*-government. The 1974 budget moves us firmly toward that goal.

JANUARY 29, 1973.   RICHARD NIXON.

OUTLAY SAVINGS

In a departure from previous budgets, the President's fiscal 1974 budget document offered a list of federal programs that would be reduced or terminated to save $6.5-billion in fiscal 1973, $16.9-billion in fiscal 1974 and $21.7-billion in fiscal 1975.

Part of the listed savings, however, came from outlays that could not be made anyway. In 1972, Congress placed a $2.5-billion ceiling on federal social services grants to state and local governments in order to head off growing state and local requests for federal funds on a matching basis.

In its list of savings, the administration claimed reduction of $2.3-billion in fiscal 1973, $2.7-billion in fiscal 1974 and $4.7-billion in fiscal 1975 as results of the ceiling. The fiscal 1974 and 1975 figures, however, were estimates of requests for federal matching funds that could not be made after states reached the limits the ceiling placed on their eligibility for social service funds.

OUTLAY SAVINGS FROM PROGRAM REDUCTIONS AND TERMINATIONS, 1973–75

[Fiscal years. In millions]

Agency and program	Outlay savings		
	1973	1974	1975
PROPOSED ACTIONS REQUIRING SUBSTANTIVE LEGISLATION			
Department of Health, Education, and Welfare			
Eliminate certain optional payment procedures under OASDI	....	310	310
Eliminate Federal financing for low-priority Medicaid services to adults	....	75	100
Reform Medicare cost-sharing and implement effective utilization review	....	616	1,300
Improve structure of public assistance programs	....	158	158
Total, Department of Health, Education, and Welfare	....	1,159	1,868
Veterans Administration			
Eliminate duplicate burial benefits		54	54
Bring pensions into closer alignment with need	....	223	227
Total, Veterans Administration	....	277	281
Total, proposed actions requiring substantive legislation	....	1,436	2,149

PERSPECTIVES

OUTLAY SAVINGS FROM PROGRAM REDUCTIONS AND TERMINATIONS, 1973-75—Con.

[Fiscal years. In millions]

Agency and program	Outlay savings		
	1973	1974	1975

ITEMS NOT REQUIRING SUBSTANTIVE LEGISLATION

Funds appropriated to the President
Foreign economic assistance:

Reduce programs of the Agency for International Development below levels previously budgeted	....	62	170
Arrange for return of amounts advanced previously	242	....	....
Total, foreign economic assistance	242	62	170

Office of Economic Opportunity

Reassign OEO activities and discontinue direct Federal funding of community action organizations leaving support to local decision	62	328	390

Department of Agriculture

Reduce the cost of farm price support programs consistent with rising farm income prospects and achievement of foreign sales agreements:			
—Reducing direct payment to farmers			
—Stopping export subsidies			
—Increasing crop loan interest	656	1,219	1,234
—Terminating old crop loans			
—Tightening storage facility loan eligibility			
Terminate rural water systems and waste disposal grants which are replaced by loans, or to extent consistent with Water Pollution Control Act, EPA financing	50	100	150
Substitute regular loan assistance for emergency loans	365	....	....
Decrease the large interest subsidy by the Rural Electrification Administration through use of Rural Development Act 5% insured loans vice 2% direct loans	84	373	695
Eliminate cost-sharing for installation of soil and water management practices on private lands and make corresponding reductions in technical assistance given through conservation programs	41	258	259
Limit the special milk subsidy to institutions not receiving subsidized milk through free and reduced price child feeding programs	....	59	77
Achieve economies in the Forest Service through tightened management, reduced State forestry support, and shifting construction of forest roads to timber purchasers	39	94	106
Curtail anticipated growth in Agriculture extension programs and reduce Federal support for agricultural research of primarily local benefit and low-national priority	13	34	34
Total, Department of Agriculture [1]	1,248	2,137	2,555

See footnotes at end of table.

Department of Commerce

Phase out Economic Development Administration programs in favor of more focused and consolidated efforts to stimulate economic development	5	35	56
Redirect or defer selected R. & D. programs of the National Oceanic and Atmospheric Administration which are not directly focused on national objectives or not critical now	26	41	....
Limit planned expansion of selected science and technology programs of National Bureau of Standards which could be delayed without significant adverse impact	17	10	7
Modify planned expansion of minority business enterprise program due to recent rapid growth in program and need to evaluate effectiveness	6	....	....
Adjust maritime ship operating subsidies due to delays in Russian grain shipments	17	....	....
Provide planning funds directly to States for support of regional commissions and eliminate Federal participation	....	27	44
Total, Department of Commerce	71	113	107

Department of Defense—Military

Reduce military and civilian personnel and other operations costs	....	1,200	400
Reduce procurement of Safeguard, aircraft, missiles, and ships	....	650	1,300
Limit growth in research, development, test, and evaluation programs	....	200	200
Reduce construction associated with Safeguard deployment, bachelor housing, and family housing	....	50	200
Limit new spending for All-Volunteer Force and other legislation	....	400	500
Tighten operations of revolving and management funds	....	200	100
Total, Department of Defense	....	2,700	2,700

Department of Defense—Civil: Corps of Engineers

Slow scheduling of less critical navigation and flood control projects while meeting essential flood control, power, and water supply demands	102	471	650

Department of Health, Education, and Welfare
Health:

Strengthen Medicare cost controls and eliminate unnecessary advance payments for hospitals	342	277	431
Strengthen Medicaid management	101	175	200

See footnotes at end of table.

Department of Health, Education, and Welfare—Continued
Health—Continued

Rely on Federal health financing mechanisms to pay depreciation charges in place of medical facilities grant program, and achieve quality care objectives through the professional standards review in place of the regional medical program	35	189	206
Phase out, over an 8-year period, Federal financing for local mental health programs	18	63	75
Eliminate duplicative health program grants	16	53	53
Phase out training grants over a 3-year period and control the level of new research grants in selected nonpriority areas	29	57	67
Focus health manpower training support on areas of special need	26	49	54
Education:			
Substitute education revenue sharing for the Federal funding component of certain education programs and discontinue the Federal role in some areas:			
—foreign language and area training programs	....	13	14
—land grant college support	10	10	10
—university community services	9	15	15
—State departments of education	1	36	13
—payments to local school systems for certain federally related students	....	119	120
—public libraries and school library resources	2	49	135
—certain narrowly focused categorical programs	1	53	76
Substitute private market mechanism for Federal capitalization of direct student loans	24	264	288
Income security:			
Limit outlays through the operation of the Administration-supported statutory ceiling on social services grants (already enacted by the Congress)	2,343	2,700	4,700
Adjust the growth rate for vocational rehabilitation program	6	31	26
Limit to 5 years Federal funding responsibility for Cuban refugees	12	58	98
Institute quality control for social services research and training	10	31	62
Eliminate overpayments and payments to ineligible recipients of public assistance and introduce management improvements	129	592	592
Total, Department of Health, Education, and Welfare [2]	3,114	4,834	7,235

Department of Housing and Urban Development

Temporarily suspend new commitments under housing subsidy programs	59	305	612

See footnotes at end of table.

Department of Housing and Urban Development—Continued

Terminate categorical community development programs in favor of urban special revenue sharing:			
Model Cities	....	....	435
Urban Renewal	....	....	180
All other	....	7	130
Total, Department of Housing and Urban Development [3]	59	312	1,357

Department of the Interior

Reduce construction activity on some roads and other capital improvements of relatively low priority in national parks, public lands, and Indian areas to less than anticipated rates in 1973 and 1974	20	10	13
Schedule water resources development construction by Bureau of Reclamation at less than anticipated rates except for hydropower and water supply projects	19	123	113
Reorient saline water program to emphasize research on new technologies and deemphasize construction of large-scale test plants of known technology	2	14	21

Agency and program	Outlay savings		
	1973	1974	1975
Constrain land purchases for Federal recreation and wildlife areas and grants to States for purchase of recreation areas in 1973 and 1974 below anticipated levels	42	61	46
Increase rate of lease sales on Outer Continental Shelf to increase domestic oil production thereby reducing outlays		1,010	510
Reduce other costs not accounted for in program reductions above	10	2	
Total, Department of the Interior	93	1,220	703
Department of Justice			
Review prison construction program for its relationship to State and local facilities and impact of alternatives to incarceration on Federal prison population	8	28	
Return responsibility to functional agencies for Community Relations Service technical assistance program		4	4
Total, Department of Justice	8	32	4
Department of Labor			
Reform manpower training programs administratively to accomplish the purposes of manpower special revenue sharing	123	354	250
Phase down the Emergency Employment Assistance program consistent with the increase in new jobs in the private sector		670	700
See footnotes at end of table.			
Department of Labor—Continued			
Increase efficiency of employment and unemployment insurance services	52	35	35
Tighten the operations and management in the Department	4	10	10
Allocate proper unemployment benefit costs to the Postal Service		26	26
Total Department of Labor	179	1,095	1,021
Department of Transportation			
States are deferring highway projects because of a lack of legislative authority	100	83	
Defer lower priority Coast Guard construction and research contracts	29	14	10
Reschedule FAA equipment purchase and long-range research that are not essential to air safety	35	35	
Delay airport grants due to environmental and other problems	20		
Reorder high-speed rail research and development, placing greater emphasis on near-term needs and deferring projects where results are not required for several years	15	41	5
Reduce operating subsidies for Amtrak	10	27	
Focus UMTA research and development on immediate improvement programs and hold up contracts for some hardware developments awaiting additional studies and evaluations	10	26	5
Rephase intermodal transport research and development, focusing on immediate problems. Reduce selected research and development projects whose results are not required in the near term	10	7	6
Increase efficiencies of Coast Guard operations	28	10	3
Stretch out the termination payments on the SST	17		
Increase efficiencies of FAA operations	21	20	
Total, Department of Transportation	295	263	29
Department of the Treasury			
Delay construction of Federal Law Enforcement Training Center to assure resolution of environmental impact problems	1	12	
Reduce personnel, travel, and related costs	3	9	9
Total, Department of the Treasury	4	21	9
Atomic Energy Commission			
Reduce Plowshare program to permit further economic and environmental study	3	3	3
Reduce space electric power and propulsion programs because of no current mission requirements	6	12	18
See footnotes at end of table.			
Atomic Energy Commission—Continued			
Defer selected lower priority projects in the nuclear materials, weapons, civilian reactor, and research programs	25	21	46
Reduce inventory and working capital requirements	56	−35	
Total, Atomic Energy Commission	90	1	67
Environmental Protection Agency			
Actions related to Federal Water Pollution Control Act amendments of 1972	300	950	1,950

Agency and program	Outlay savings		
	1973	1974	1975
General Services Administration			
Provide more efficient guard service in public buildings		3	3
Require more effective supply practices	15	25	
Reduce new computer procurements by improving utilization of existing equipment	7	9	
Total, General Services Administration	22	37	3
National Aeronautics and Space Administration			
Delay the space shuttle to provide for a more orderly program buildup	18	45	75
Reduce other manned space flight	93	47	10
Defer the High-Energy Astronomy Observatory to allow NASA to study same program objectives at lower cost	7	68	56
Cancel Application Technology Satellite-G because research can be funded by industry without Government support	3	17	16
Reduce nuclear power and propulsion research since prospective applications are in the distant future	9	16	18
Cancel experimental STOL aircraft because of uncertainty on the timing of a commercial market	3	34	20
Reduce other technology and support consistent with the slower pace of the space program	28		
Reduce NASA personnel and administrative expenses consistent with program reductions	18	24	24
Total, National Aeronautics and Space Administration	179	251	219
Veterans Administration			
Reform veterans benefits administratively to align benefits and need		160	160
Reschedule construction activities		55	65
Restructure research in line with current needs	5	13	27
Total, Veterans Administration	5	228	252
See footnotes at end of table.			
Civil Service Commission			
Limit the level of the intergovernmental personnel assistance grant program pending evaluation		1	5
Allocate proper retirement costs to the Postal Service		285	105
Total, Civil Service Commission		286	110
Corporation for Public Broadcasting			
Maintain previous years level of support	10		
National Science Foundation			
Curtail lower priority institutional and also educational programs, pending development of plans to meet new program objectives	20		
Reductions due to effect of the above curtailment and other selective reductions		32	
Total, National Science Foundation	20	32	
Small Business Administration			
Reduce direct business loan program of Small Business Administration as needs are met by increased participation of private banking community through SBA guaranteed loans	42	41	34
Subversive Activities Control Board			
Terminate as a result of court decisions limiting workload		(⁴)	(⁴)
Tennessee Valley Authority			
Slow scheduling of construction activity on projects underway and postpone increases in other programs	10	30	25
Washington Metropolitan Area Transit Authority			
Use bond proceeds to even out level of Federal contribution to subway construction	80	13	
Pay raises for civilian agencies:			
Require absorption of most of January 1973 comparability increase	280		
Total, items not requiring substantive legislation [2]	6,515	15,457	19,590
Total, all savings [2]	6,515	16,893	21,739

[1] Excludes rural housing.
[2] Includes savings accomplished by enactment of administration-supported limitation on open-end social services grant program.
[3] Includes rural housing program of the Farmers Home Administration.
[4] $400,000 in 1974 and 1975.

PRESIDENT NIXON'S RADIO ADDRESS ON 1974 BUDGET

Following is the text, as made available by the White House, of President Nixon's Jan. 28 radio address on the fiscal 1974 budget.

At noon tomorrow, I will send to the Congress one of the most important documents I will sign as President—my budget proposals for the coming fiscal year.

This budget will not require higher taxes. It will not drive prices higher. And it will give us the chance I spoke of in my Inaugural Address to make our new era of peace a new era of progress.

In the last few decades, the cost of government has skyrocketed. For every one dollar we were spending in 1952, we are spending nearly four dollars today. If the budget continues to double every 10 years, it will be over a trillion dollars by the 1990s—20 years from now—or as big as our entire economy is now.

We must resist this trend, for several reasons. The first involves your taxes.

Since 1950, the share of personal income taken for taxes by all levels of government has doubled—to more than 20 percent of your family budget. This growing burden works to dull individual incentive and discourage individual responsibility. As government takes more from people, people can do less for themselves. The only way to restrain taxes is to restrain spending.

In the campaign last fall, I promised I would not propose any new tax increases. By keeping a tight lid on spending, my new budget keeps that promise.

The second reason for resisting bigger government is its impact on our economy. We saw in the 1960 what happens when government spends beyond its means. The result is runaway inflation, the most insidious of all taxes, which begins by picking your pockets, goes on to threaten your very jobs. Not only the size of your tax bill—but also the size of your grocery bill and the security of your job itself—all of these are at stake when we draw up the Federal budget.

Improvements

In the past four years, we have put our economy back on course again. Since 1969, inflation has been cut nearly in half. Jobs increased more rapidly last year than at any time since 1947 —25 years ago. Real spendable weekly earnings—that is what you have left to spend after paying your taxes and after allowing for inflation—showed their greatest improvement since 1955.

Best of all, the prospects for the coming year are very bright. 1973 could be our best year ever, ushering in a new era of prolonged and growing prosperity.

The greatest threat to our new prosperity is excessive government spending. My budget calls for spending $250 billion in the current fiscal year, $269 billion next year, and $288 billion in fiscal year 1975. These are large amounts—but they would be $20 billion higher for each of the next two years if we had just gone about spending as usual. That, in turn, would have meant either an annual budget deficit of $30 billion a year, which would have led to higher prices, or a 15 percent increase in your income taxes.

To keep the totals even this low required a rigorous effort within the Executive Branch. But we cannot do the job alone.

If we are going to keep taxes and prices down, the Congress must keep spending down. That is why it is so important for the Congress to set a firm ceiling on its overall expenditures—so that the Congress will consider not only the particular merits of individual programs, but also what happens to taxes and prices when you add them all together.

The third reason my new budget tries to curb the growth of government is that relying on bigger government is the wrong way to meet our Nation's needs. Government has grown by leaps and bounds since the 1930s; but so have problems—problems like crime and blight and inflation and pollution. The bigger government became, the more clumsy it became, until its attempts to help often proved a hindrance.

The time has come to get rid of old programs that have outlived their time, or that have failed. Whenever the return on our tax dollars is not worth the expenditure, we must either change that program or end it.

Sacred Cows

In the next few days, you will hear about some very sharp reductions in some very familiar programs. Some have been regarded as sacred cows in the past. No matter what their real value, no one dared to touch them. Let me give you just a few examples.

Last year we spent nearly $200 million on the Hill-Burton program to help build more hospitals, but today the shortage of hospital beds which existed through the '50s and the '60s has been more than met. And yet, the Hill-Burton program continues to pour out funds, regardless of need.

Or take some of our urban renewal programs. They have cost us billions of dollars, with very disappointing results. And little wonder. How can a committee of Federal bureaucrats, hundreds or thousands of miles away, decide intelligently where building should take place? That is a job for people you elect at the local level, people whom you know, people you can talk to.

And then there is our aid to schools near Federal facilities. There was a time when this program made sense, when Federal workers were a drain on local resources. Now most Federal workers pay full local taxes. Yet we still have been paying out more than $500 million a year in compensation to these communities, many of which are among the richest in the country, and so I propose we change that program. Let us spend our education dollars where they are really needed.

Our search for waste has led us into every nook and cranny of the bureaucracy. And because economy must begin right at home, we are cutting the number of people who work in the President's own Executive office from 4,200 to 1,700. That is a 60 percent reduction.

We also found we could save $2.7 billion in the projected defense budget for 1974 and $2.1 billion in the projected agricultural budget.

Money Returned

But after talking about these cuts, let's get one thing straight. Cutting back on Federal programs does not mean cutting back on progress. In fact, it means a better way to progress. When we cut a million dollars from a Federal program, that money is not lost and its power to do good things eliminated; rather, that money is transferred to other budgets where its power to do good things is multiplied. Some of it will stay in family budgets where people can use it as they, themselves, see fit.

Much will go back to State and county and municipal governments, back to the scene of the action, where needs are best understood, where public officials are most accessible and, therefore, most accountable.

And finally, some of the money we save will be shifted to other Federal programs—where it can do the most good with least waste for the most people.

I am proposing, for example, to double spending for major pollution control programs. I am asking for an 8 percent increase to fight crime and drug abuse; for a 20 percent increase in research to meet the energy crisis; for a 21 percent increase to fight cancer and heart disease.

In fact, overall spending for human resource programs will be increased to a level almost twice what it was when I first came to office. Instead of spending one-third of our budget on human resources and nearly half of our budget on defense—as we were doing in 1969—we have exactly reversed those priorities.

We can be thankful that with the war in Vietnam now ended, this is a true peacetime budget in every sense of the word.

In the days and weeks ahead, I shall be spelling out my recommendations in much greater detail. My budget will go to the Congress tomorrow; my Economic Report on Wednesday. And instead of delivering just one State of the Union Address, covering a laundry list of programs, I shall present my State of the Union Report this year in a series of detailed messages on specific subjects. Together, these statements will chart a new course for America—a course that will bring more progress by putting more responsibility and money in more places.

In holding down spending, what is at stake is not just a big, impersonal Federal budget. What is at stake is your job, your taxes, the prices you pay, and whether the money you earn by your work is spent by you for what you want, or by Government for what someone else wants.

It is important that the struggle to hold the line against bigger government not become a contest which pits one branch of government against another, but one which joins the President and the Congress in meeting a common challenge. And those in the Congress who enlist in this struggle need your support.

Every Member of the Congress gets enormous pressure from special interests to spend your money for what they want. And so I ask you to back up those Congressmen and those Senators, whether Democrats or Republicans, who have the courage to vote against higher spending. They hear from the special interests; let them hear from you.

It is time to get big government off your back and out of your pocket. I ask your support to hold government spending down, so that we can keep your taxes and your prices from going up.   √

STATE OF THE UNION: SPECIAL REPORTS IN FIVE AREAS

I. OVERVIEW

Following is the White House text of President Nixon's Feb. 2 message to Congress on the state of the union. The message was described by Nixon as an "overview" and was followed by 5 other state of the union messages on specific subject areas:

TO THE CONGRESS OF THE UNITED STATES:

The traditional form of the President's annual report giving "to the Congress Information of the State of the Union" is a single message or address. As the affairs and concerns of our Union have multiplied over the years, however, so too have the subjects that require discussion in State of the Union Messages.

This year in particular, with so many changes in Government programs under consideration—and with our very philosophy about the relationship between the individual and the State at an historic crossroads—a single, all-embracing State of the Union Message would not appear to be adequate.

I have therefore decided to present my 1973 State of the Union report in the form of a series of messages during these early weeks of the 93rd Congress. The purpose of this first message in the series is to give a concise overview of where we stand as a people today, and to outline some of the general goals that I believe we should pursue over the next year and beyond. In coming weeks, I will send to the Congress further State of the Union reports on specific areas of policy including economic affairs, natural resources, human resources, community development and foreign and defense policy.

'A Fresh Approach'

The new course these messages will outline represents a fresh approach to Government: an approach that addresses the realities of the 1970s, not those of the 1930s or of the 1960s. The role of the Federal Government as we approach our third century of independence should not be to dominate any facet of American life, but rather to aid and encourage people, communities and institutions to deal with as many of the difficulties and challenges facing them as possible, and to help see to it that every American has a full and equal opportunity to realize his or her potential.

If we were to continue to expand the Federal Government at the rate of the past several decades, it soon would consume us entirely. The time has come when we must make clear choices —choices between old programs that set worthy goals but failed to reach them and new programs that provide a better way to realize those goals; and choices, too, between competing programs—*all* of which may be desirable in themselves but only *some* of which we can afford with the finite resources at our command.

Because our resources are not infinite, we also face a critical choice in 1973 between holding the line in Government spending and adopting expensive programs which will surely force up taxes and refuel inflation.

Finally, it is vital at this time that we restore a greater sense of responsibility at the State and local level, and among individual Americans.

Where We Stand

The basic state of our Union today is sound, and full of promise. We enter 1973 economically strong, militarily secure and, most important of all, at peace after a long and trying war.

America continues to provide a better and more abundant life for more of its people than any other nation in the world. We have passed through one of the most difficult periods in our history without surrendering to despair and without dishonoring our ideals as a people.

Looking back, there is a lesson in all this for all of us. The lesson is one that we sometimes had to learn the hard way over the past few years. But we did learn it. That lesson is that even potentially destructive forces can be converted into positive forces when we know how to channel them, and when we use common sense and common decency to create a climate of mutual respect and goodwill.

By working together and harnessing the forces of nature, Americans have unlocked some of the great mysteries of the universe. Men have walked the surface of the moon and soared to new heights of discovery. This same spirit of discovery is helping us to conquer disease and suffering that have plagued our own planet since the dawn of time.

By working together with the leaders of other nations, we have been able to build a new hope for lasting peace—for a structure of world order in which common interest outweighs old animosities, and in which a new generation of the human family can grow up at peace in a changing world.

At home, we have learned that by working together we can create prosperity without fanning inflation; we can restore order without weakening freedom.

The Challenges We Face

These first years of the 1970s have been good years for America.

Our job—all of us together—is to make 1973 and the years to come even better ones. I believe that we can. I believe that we can make the years leading to our Bicentennial the best four years in American history.

But we must never forget that nothing worthwhile can be achieved without the will to succeed and the strength to sacrifice. Hard decisions must be made, and we must stick by them.

In the field of foreign policy, we must remember that a strong America—an America whose word is believed and whose strength is respected—is essential to continued peace and understanding in the world. The peace with honor we have achieved in Vietnam has strengthened this basic American credibility. We must act in such a way in coming years that this credibility will remain intact, and with it, the world stability of which it is so indispensable a part.

At home, we must reject the mistaken notion—a notion that has dominated too much of the public dialogue for too long—that ever bigger Government is the answer to every problem.

We have learned only too well that heavy taxation and excessive Government spending are not a cure-all. In too many cases, instead of solving the problems they were aimed at, they have merely placed an ever heavier burden on the shoulders of the American taxpayer, in the form of higher taxes and a higher cost of living. At the same time they have deceived our people because many of the intended beneficiaries received far less than was promised, thus undermining public faith in the effectiveness of Government as a whole.

The time has come for us to draw the line. The time has come for the responsible leaders of both political parties to take a stand against overgrown Government and for the American taxpayer. We are not spending the Federal Government's money, we are spending the taxpayer's money, and it must be spent in a way which guarantees his money's worth and yields the fullest possible benefit to the people being helped.

The answer to many of the domestic problems we face is not higher taxes and more spending. It is less waste, more results and greater freedom for the individual American to earn a rightful place in his own community—and for States and localities to address their own needs in their own ways, in the light of their own priorities.

By giving the people and their locally elected leaders a greater voice through changes such as revenue sharing, and by saying "no" to excessive Federal spending and higher taxes, we can help achieve this goal.

Coming Messages

The policies which I will outline to the Congress in the weeks ahead represent a reaffirmation, not an abdication, of Federal responsibility. They represent a pragmatic rededication to social compassion and national excellence, in place of the combination of good intentions and fuzzy follow-through which too often in the past was thought sufficient.

In the field of economic affairs, our objectives will be to hold down taxes, to continue controlling inflation, to promote economic growth, to increase productivity, to encourage foreign trade, to keep farm income high, to bolster small business, and to promote better labor-management relations.

In the area of natural resources, my recommendations will include programs to preserve and enhance the environment, to advance science and technology, and to assure balanced use of our irreplaceable natural resources.

In developing human resources, I will have recommendations to advance the Nation's health and education, to improve conditions of people in need, to carry forward our increasingly successful attacks on crime, drug abuse and injustice, and to deal with such important areas of special concern as consumer affairs. We will continue and improve our Nation's efforts to assist those who have served in the Armed Services in Viet-Nam through better job and training opportunities.

We must do a better job in community development—in creating more livable communities, in which all of our children can grow up with fuller access to opportunity and greater immunity to the social evils and blights which now plague so many of our towns and cities. I shall have proposals to help us achieve this. I shall also deal with our defense and foreign policies, and with our new approaches to the role and structure of Government itself.

Considered as a whole, this series of messages will be a blueprint for modernizing the concept and the functions of American Government to meet the needs of our people.

Converting it into reality will require a spirit of cooperation and shared commitment on the part of all branches of the Government, for the goals we seek are not those of any single party or faction, they are goals for the betterment of all Americans. As President, I recognize that I cannot do this job alone. The Congress must help, and I pledge to do my part to achieve a constructive working relationship with the Congress. My sincere hope is that the executive and legislative branches can work together in this great undertaking in a positive spirit of mutual respect and cooperation.

Working together—the Congress, the President and the people—I am confident that we can translate these proposals into an action program that can reform and revitalize American Government and, even more important, build a better life for all Americans.

The White House,
February 2, 1973.

Richard Nixon

II. NATURAL RESOURCES
AND ENVIRONMENT

Following is the White House text of the state of the union message on natural resources and the environment sent to Congress Feb. 15.

TO THE CONGRESS OF THE UNITED STATES:

With the opening of a new Congress and the beginning of a new Presidential term come fresh opportunities for achievement in America. To help us consider more adequately the very special challenges of this new year, I am presenting my 1973 State of the Union Message in a number of sections.

Two weeks ago I sent the first of those sections to the Congress—an overview reporting that "the basic state of our Union today is sound, and full of promise."

Today I wish to report to the Congress on the state of our natural resources and environment. It is appropriate that this topic be first of our substantive policy discussions in the State of the Union presentation, since nowhere in our national affairs do we have more gratifying progress—nor more urgent, remaining problems.

There was a time when Americans took our natural resources largely for granted. For example, President Lincoln observed in his State of the Union message for 1862 that "A nation may be said to consist of its territory, its people, and its laws. The territory is the only part which is of certain durability."

In recent years, however, we have come to realize that our "territory"—that is, our land, air, water, minerals, and the like—is not of "certain durability" after all. We have learned that these natural resources are fragile and finite, and that many have been seriously damaged or despoiled.

When we came to office in 1969, we tackled this problem with all the power at our command. Now there is encouraging evidence that the United States has moved away from the environmental crisis that could have been and toward a new era of restoration and renewal. Today, in 1973, I can report to the Congress that we are well on the way to winning the war against environmental degradation—well on the way to making our peace with nature.

Years of Progress

While I am disappointed that the 92nd Congress failed to act upon 19 of my key natural resources and environment proposals, I am pleased to have signed many of the proposals I supported into law during the past four years. They have included air quality legislation, strengthened water quality and pesticide control legislation, new authorities to control noise and ocean dumping, regulations to prevent oil and other spills in our ports and waterways, and legislation establishing major national recreation areas at America's Atlantic and Pacific gateways, New York and San Francisco.

On the organizational front, the National Environmental Policy Act of 1969 has reformed programs and decision-making processes in our Federal agencies and has given citizens a greater opportunity to contribute as decisions are made. In 1970 I appointed the first Council on Environmental Quality—a group which has provided active leadership in environmental policies. In the same year, I established the Environmental Protection Agency and the National Oceanic and Atmospheric Administration to provide more coordinated and vigorous environmental management. Our natural resource programs still need to be consolidated, however, and I will again submit legislation to the Congress to meet this need.

The results of these efforts are tangible and measurable. Day by day, our air is getting cleaner; in virtually every one of our major cities the levels of air pollution are declining. Month by month, our water pollution problems are also being conquered, our noise and pesticide problems are coming under control, our parklands and protected wilderness areas are increasing.

Year by year, our commitment of public funds for environmental programs continues to grow; it has increased four-fold in the last four years. In the area of water quality alone, it has grown fifteen-fold. In fact, we are now buying new facilities nearly as fast as the construction industry can build them. Spending still more money would not buy us more pollution control facilities but only more expensive ones.

In addition to what Government is doing in the battle against pollution, our private industries are assuming a steadily growing share of responsibility in this field. Last year industrial spending for pollution control jumped by 50 percent, and this year it could reach as much as $5 billion.

All nations, regardless of their economic systems, share to some extent in the environmental problem—but with vigorous United States leadership, joint efforts to solve this global problem are showing results. The United Nations has adopted the American proposal for a special U.N. environmental fund to coordinate and support international environmental programs.

Some 92 nations have concluded an international convention to control the ocean dumping of wastes. An agreement is now being forged in the Intergovernmental Maritime Consultative Organization to end the intentional discharge of oil from ships into the ocean. This objective, first recommended by my Administration, was adopted by the NATO Committee on the Challenges of Modern Society.

Representatives of almost 70 countries are meeting in Washington this week at our initiative to draft a treaty to protect endangered species of plant and animal wildlife. The U.S.-USSR environmental cooperation agreement which I signed in Moscow last year makes two of the world's greatest industrial powers allies against pollution. Another agreement which we concluded last year with Canada will help to clean up the Great Lakes.

Domestically, we can also be proud of the steady progress being made in improving the quality of life in rural and agricultural America. We are beginning to break away from the old, rigid system of controls which eroded the farmer's freedom through Government intrusion in the marketplace. The new flexibility permitted by the Agricultural Act of 1970 has enabled us to help expand farm markets and take advantage of the op-

portunity to increase exports by almost 60 percent in just three years. Net farm income is at an all-time high, up from $16.1 billion in 1971 to $19 billion in 1972.

Principles To Guide Us

A record is not something to stand on; it is something to build on. And in this field of natural resources and the environment, we intend to build diligently and well. As we strive to transform our concern into action, our efforts will be guided by five basic principles:

The first principle is that we must strike a balance so that the protection of our irreplaceable heritage becomes as important as its use. The price of economic growth need not and will not be deterioration in the quality of our lives and our surroundings.

Second, because there are no local or State boundaries to the problems of our environment, the Federal Government must play an active, positive role. We can and will set standards and exercise leadership. We are providing necessary funding support. And we will provide encouragement and incentive for others to help with the job. But Washington must not displace State and local initiative, and we shall expect the State and local governments—along with the private sector—to play the central role in making the difficult, particular decisions which lie ahead.

Third, the costs of pollution should be more fully met in the free marketplace, not in the Federal budget. For example, the price of pollution control devices for automobiles should be borne by the owner and the user and not by the general taxpayer. The costs of eliminating pollution should be reflected in the costs of goods and services.

Fourth, we must realize that each individual must take the responsibility for looking after his own home and workplace. These daily surroundings are the environment where most Americans spend most of their time. They reflect people's pride in themselves and their consideration for their communities. A person's backyard is not the domain of the Federal Government.

Finally, we must remain confident that America's technological and economic ingenuity will be equal to our environmental challenges. We will not look upon these challenges as insurmountable obstacles. Instead, we shall convert the so-called crisis of the environment into an opportunity for unprecedented progress.

Controlling Pollution

We have made great progress in developing the laws and institutions to clean up pollution. We now have formidable new tools to protect against air, water and noise pollution and the special problem of pesticides. But to protect ourselves fully from harmful contaminants, we must still close several gaps in governmental authority.

I was keenly disappointed when the last Congress failed to take action on many of my legislative requests related to our natural resources and environment. In the coming weeks I shall once again send these urgently needed proposals to the Congress so that the unfinished environmental business of the 92nd Congress can become the environmental achievements of the 93rd.

Among these 19 proposals are eight whose passage would give us much greater control over the sources of pollution:

Toxic Substances. Many new chemicals can pose hazards to humans and the environment and are not well regulated. Authority is now needed to provide adequate testing standards for chemical substances and to restrict or prevent their distribution if testing confirms a hazard.

Hazardous Wastes. Land disposal of hazardous wastes has always been widely practiced but is now becoming more prevalent because of strict air and water pollution control programs. The disposal of the extremely hazardous wastes which endanger the health of humans and other organisms is a problem requiring direct Federal regulation. For other hazardous wastes, Federal standards should be established with guidelines for State regulatory programs to carry them out.

Safe Drinking Water. Federal action is also needed to stimulate greater State and local action to ensure high standards for our drinking water. We should establish national drinking water standards, with primary enforcement and monitoring powers retained by the State and local agencies as well as a Federal requirement that suppliers notify their customers of the quality of their water.

Sulfur Oxides Emissions Charge. We now have national standards to help curtail sulfur emitted into the atmosphere from combustion, refining, smelting and other processes, but sulfur oxides continue to be among our most harmful air pollutants. For that reason, I favor legislation which would allow the Federal Government to impose a special financial charge on those who produce sulfur oxide emissions. This legislation would also help to ensure that low-sulfur fuels are allocated to areas where they are most urgently needed to protect the public health.

Sediment Control. Sediment from soil erosion and run-off continues to be a pervasive pollutant of our waters. Legislation is needed to ensure that the States make the control of sediment from new construction a vital part of their water quality programs.

Controlling Environmental Impacts of Transportation. As we have learned in recent years, we urgently need a mass transportation system not only to relieve urban congestion but also to reduce the concentrations of pollution that are too often the result of our present methods of transportation. Thus I will continue to place high priority upon my request to permit use of the Highway Trust Fund for mass transit purposes and to help State and local governments achieve air quality, conserve energy, and meet other environmental objectives.

United Nations Environmental Fund. Last year the United Nations adopted my proposal to establish a fund to coordinate and support international environmental programs. May 1974 budget includes a request for $10 million as our initial contribution toward the Fund's five-year goal of $100 million, and I recommend authorizing legislation for this purpose.

Ocean Dumping Convention. Along with 91 other nations, the United States recently concluded an international convention calling for regulation of ocean dumping. I am most anxious to obtain the advice and consent of the Senate for this convention as soon as possible. Congressional action is also needed on several other international conventions and amendments to control oil pollution from ships in the oceans.

Managing The Land

As we steadily bring our pollution problems under control, more effective and sensible use of our land is rapidly emerging as among the highest of our priorities. The land is our Nations' basic natural resource, and our stewardship of this resource today will affect generations to come.

America's land once seemed inexhaustible. There was always more of it beyond the horizon. Until the twentieth century we displayed a carelessness about our land, born of our youthful innocence and desire to expand. But our land is no longer an open frontier.

Americans not only need, but also very much want to preserve diverse and beautiful landscapes, to maintain essential farm lands, to save wetlands and wildlife habitats, to keep open recreational space near crowded population centers, and to protect our shorelines and beaches. Our goal is to harmonize development with environmental quality and to add creatively to the beauty and long-term worth of land already being used.

Land use policy is a basic responsibility of State and local governments. They are closer to the problems and closer to the people. Some localities are already reforming land use regulation—a trend I hope will accelerate. But because land is a national heritage, the Federal Government must exercise leadership in land use decision processes, and I am today again proposing that we provide it. In the coming weeks, I will ask the Congress to enact a number of legislative initiatives which will help us achieve this goal:

National Land Use Policy. Our greatest need is for comprehensive new legislation to stimulate State land use controls. We especially need a National Land Use Policy Act authorizing Federal assistance to encourage the States, in cooperation with local governments, to protect lands of critical environmental concern and to regulate the siting of key facilities such as airports, highways and major private developments. Appropriate Federal funds should be withheld from States that fail to act.

Powerplant Siting. An open, long-range planning process is needed to help meet our power needs while also protecting the environment. We can avoid unnecessary delays with a powerplant siting law which assures that electric power facilities are constructed on a timely basis, but with early and thorough review of long-range plans and specific provisions to protect the environment.

Protection of Wetlands. Our coastal wetlands are increasingly threatened by residential and commercial development. To increase their protection, I believe we should use the Federal tax laws to discourage unwise development in wetlands.

Historic Preservation and Rehabilitation. An important part of our national heritage are those historic structures in our urban areas which should be rehabilitated and preserved, not demolished. To help meet this goal, our tax laws should be revised to encourage rehabilitation of older buildings, and we should provide Federal insurance of loans to restore historic buildings for residential purposes.

Management of Public Lands. Approximately one-fifth of the Nation's land is considered "public domain", and lacks the protection of an overall management policy with environmental safeguards. Legislation is required to enable the Secretary of the Interior to protect our environmental interest on those lands.

Legacy of Parks. Under the Legacy of Parks program which I initiated in 1971, 257 separate parcels of parklands and underused Federal lands in all 50 States have been turned over to local control for park and recreational purposes. Most of these parcels are near congested urban areas, so that millions of citizens can now have easy access to parklands. I am pleased to announce today that 16 more parcels of Federal land will soon be made available under this same program.

We must not be content, however, with just the Legacy of Parks program. New authority is needed to revise the formula for allocating grant funds to the States from the Land and Water Conservation Fund. More of these funds should be channelled to States with large urban populations.

Mining on Public Lands. Under a statute now over a century old, public lands must be transferred to private ownership at the request of any person who discovers minerals on them. We thus have no effective control over mining on these properties. Because the public lands belong to all Americans, this 1872 Mining Act should be repealed and replaced with new legislation which I shall send to the Congress.

Mined Area Protection. Surface and underground mining can too often cause serious air and water pollution as well as unnecessary destruction of wildlife habitats and aesthetic and recreational areas. New legislation with stringent performance standards is required to regulate abuses of surface and underground mining in a manner compatible with the environment.

American Agriculture

Nearly three-fifth of America's land is in the stewardship of the farmer and the rancher. We can be grateful that farmers have been among our best conservationists over the years. Farmers know better than most that sound conservation means better long-term production and improved land values. More importantly, no one respects and understands our soil and land better than those who make their living by the land.

But Americans know their farmers and ranchers best for all they have done to keep us the best-fed and best-clothed people in the history of mankind. A forward-looking agricultural economy is not only essential for environmental progress, but also to provide for our burgeoning food and fiber needs.

My Administration is not going to express its goal for farmers in confusing terms. Our goal, instead, is very simple. The farmer wants, has earned, and deserves more freedom to make his own decisions. The Nation wants and needs expanded supplies of reasonably priced goods and commodities.

These goals are complementary. Both have been advanced by the basic philosophy of the Agricultural Act of 1970. They must be further advanced by Congressional action this year.

The Agricultural Act of 1970 expires with the 1973 crop. We now face the fundamental challenge of developing legislation appropriate to the economy of the 1970's. Over the next several months, the future direction of the farm program must be discussed, debated and written into law. The outcome of this process will be crucial not only to farmers and ranchers, but to consumers and taxpayers as well.

My Administration's fundamental approach to farm policy is to build on the forward course set by the 1970 Act. These principles should guide us in enacting new farm legislation:

• Farmers must be provided with greater freedom to make production and marketing decisions. I have never known anyone in Washington who knows better than a farmer what is in his own interest.

• Government influence in the farm commodity marketplace must be reduced. Old fashioned Federal intrusion is as inappropriate to today's farm economy as the old McCormick reaper would be on a highly sophisticated modern farm.

• We must allow farmers the opportunity to produce for expanding domestic demands and to continue our vigorous competition in export markets. We will not accomplish that goal by telling the farmer how much he can grow or the rancher how much livestock he can raise. Fidelity to this principle will have the welcome effect of encouraging both fair food prices for consumers and growing income from the marketplace for farmers.

• We must reduce the farmer's dependence on Government payments through increased returns from sales of farm products at home and abroad. Because some of our current methods of handling farm problems are outmoded, the farmer has been unfairly saddled with the unflattering image of drinking primarily at the Federal well. Let us remember that more than 93 percent of gross farm income comes directly through the marketplace. Farmers and ranchers are strong and independent businessmen; we should expand their opportunity to exercise their strength and independence.

• Finally, we need a program that will put the United States in a good posture for forthcoming trade negotiations.

In pursuing all of these goals, we will work closely through the Secretary of Agriculture with the Senate Committee on Agriculture and Forestry and the House Committee on Agriculture to formulate and enact new legislation in areas where it is needed.

I believe, for example, that dairy support systems, wheat, feed grains and cotton allotments and bases—some established decades ago—are drastically outdated. They tend to be discriminatory for many farm operators.

It would be desirable to establish, after a reasonable transition period, a more equitable basis for production adjustment in the agricultural economy should such adjustment be needed in the years ahead. Direct Federal payments should, at the end of the transition period, be limited to the amounts necessary to compensate farmers for withholding unneeded land from crop production.

As new farm legislation is debated in the months ahead, I hope the Congress will address this important subject with a deep appreciation of the need to keep the Government off the farm as well as keeping the farmer on.

Protecting Our Natural Heritage

An important measure of our true commitment to environmental quality is our dedication to protecting the wilderness and its inhabitants. We must recognize their ecological significance and preserve them as sources of inspiration and education. And we need them as places of quiet refuge and reflection.

Important progress has been made in recent years, but still further action is needed in the Congress. Specifically, I will ask the 93rd Congress to direct its attention to the following areas of concern:

Endangered Species. The limited scope of existing laws requires new authority to identify and protect endangered species before they are so depleted that it is too late. New legislation must also make the taking of an endangered animal a Federal offense.

Predator Control. The widespread use of highly toxic poisons to kill coyotes and other predatory animals has spread persistent poisions to range and forest lands without adequate foresight of environmental effects. I believe Federal assistance is now required so that we can find better means of controlling predators without endangering other wildlife.

Wilderness Areas. Historically, Americans have always looked westward to enjoy wilderness areas. Today we realize that we must also preserve the remaining areas of wilderness in the East, if the majority of our people are to have the full benefit of our natural glories. Therefore I will ask the Congress to amend the legislation that established the Wilderness Preservation System so that more of our Eastern lands can be included.

Wild and Scenic Rivers. New legislation is also needed to continue our expansion of the national system of wild and scenic rivers. Funding authorization must be increased by $20 million to complete acquisitions in seven areas, and we must extend the moratorium on Federal licensing for water resource projects on those rivers being considered for inclusion in the system.

Big Cypress National Fresh Water Preserve. It is our great hope that we can create a reserve of Florida's Big Cypress Swamp in order to protect the outstanding wildlife in that area, preserve the water supply of Everglades National Park and provide the Nation with an outstanding recreation area. Prompt passage of Federal legislation would allow the Interior Department to forestall private or commercial development and inflationary pressures that will build if we delay.

Protecting Marine Fisheries. Current regulation of fisheries off U.S. coasts is inadequate to conserve and manage these resources. Legislation is needed to authorize U.S. regulation of foreign fishing off U.S. coasts to the fullest extent authorized by international agreements. In addition, domestic fishing should be regulated in the U.S. fisheries zone and in the high seas beyond that zone.

World Heritage Trust. The United States has endorsed an international convention for a World Heritage Trust embodying our proposals to accord special recognition and protection to areas of the world which are of such unique natural, historical, or cultural value that they are a part of the heritage of all mankind. I am hopeful that this convention will be ratified early in 1973.

Weather Modification. Our capacity to affect the weather has grown considerably in sophistication and predictability, but with this advancement has also come a new potential for endangering lives and property and causing adverse environmental effects. With additional Federal regulations, I believe that we can minimize these dangers.

Meeting Our Energy Needs

One of the highest priorities of my Administration during the coming year will be a concern for energy supplies—a concern underscored this winter by occasional fuel shortages. We must face up to a stark fact in America: we are now consuming more energy than we produce.

A year and a half ago I sent to the Congress the first Presidential message ever devoted to the energy question. I shall soon submit a new and far more comprehensive energy message containing wide-ranging initiatives to ensure necessary supplies of energy at acceptable economic and environmental costs. In the meantime, to help meet immediate needs, I have temporarily suspended import quotas on home heating oil east of the Rocky Mountains.

As we work to expand our supplies of energy, we should also recognize that we must balance those efforts with our concern to preserve our environment. In the past, as we have sought new energy sources, we have too often damaged or despoiled our land. Actions to avoid such damage will probably aggravate our energy problems to some extent and may lead to higher prices. But all development and use of energy sources carries environmental risks, and we must find ways to minimize those risks while providing adequate supplies of energy. I am fully confident that we can satisfy both of these imperatives.

Going Forward In Confidence

The environmental awakening of recent years has triggered substantial progress in the fight to preserve and renew the great legacies of nature. Unfortunately, it has also triggered a certain tendency to despair. Some people have moved from complacency to the opposite extreme of alarmism, suggesting that our pollution problems were hopeless and predicting impending ecological disaster. Some have suggested that we could never reconcile environmental protection with continued economic growth.

I reject this doomsday mentality—and I hope the Congress will also reject it. I believe that we can meet our environmental challenges without turning our back on progress. What we must do is to stop the hand-wringing, roll up our sleeves and get on with the job.

The advocates of defeatism warn us of all that is wrong. But I believe they underestimate this Nation's genius for responsive adaptability and its enormous reservoir of spirit.

I believe there is always a sensible middle ground between the Cassandras and the Pollyannas. We must take our stand upon that ground.

I have profound respect for the enormous challenge ahead, but I have even stronger respect for the capacity and character of the American people. Many of us have heard the adage that the last letters of the word, "American," say "I can." I am confident that we can, and we will, meet our national resource challenges.

Richard Nixon

The White House
February 15, 1973

III. THE ECONOMY

Following is the text, as made available by the White House, of President Nixon's Feb. 22 State of the Union message on economic affairs.

TO THE CONGRESS OF THE UNITED STATES:

Today, in this third section of my 1973 State of the Union Message, I wish to report on the state of our economy and to urge the Congress to join with me in building the foundations for a new era of prosperity in the United States.

The state of our Union depends fundamentally on the state of our economy. I am pleased to report that our economic prospects are very bright. For the first time in nearly 20 years, we

can look forward to a period of genuine prosperity in a time of peace. We can, in fact, achieve the most bountiful prosperity that this Nation has ever known.

That goal can only be attained, however, if we discipline ourselves and unite on certain basic policies:

- We must be restrained in Federal spending.
- We must show reasonableness in labor-management relations.
- We must comply fully with the new Phase III requirements of our economic stabilization program.
- We must continue our battle to hold down the price of food.
- And we must vigorously meet the challenge of foreign trading competition.

It is clear to me that the American people stand firmly together in support of these policies. Their President stands with them. And as Members of the 93rd Congress consider the alternatives before us this year, I am confident that they, too, will join in this great endeavor.

Impact of the Economy

This message will present my basic economic recommendations and priorities and will indicate some areas in which further detailed plans will be submitted later.

But I also want to discuss our economic situation in less formal terms: how do statistical measurements, comparisons and projections affect the daily lives of individual Americans and their families?

We build our economy, after all, not to create cold, impersonal statistics for the record books but to better the lives of our people.

Basically, the economy affects people in three ways.

First, it affects their jobs—how plentiful they are, how secure they are, how good they are.

Second, it affects what people are paid on their jobs—and how much they can buy with that income.

Finally, it affects how much people have to pay back to the Government in taxes.

Job Picture Encouraging

To begin with, the job picture today is very encouraging.

The number of people at work in this country rose by 2.3 million during 1972—the largest increase in 25 years. Unemployment fell from the 6 percent level in 1971 to 5 percent last month.

The reason jobs have grown so rapidly is that the economy grew in real terms by 6-1/2 percent last year, one of the best performances in the past quarter century. Our economic advisers expect a growth rate of nearly 7 percent in 1973. That would bring unemployment down to arou..d the 4-1/2 percent level by the end of the year.

Five percent unemployment is too high. Nevertheless, it is instructive to examine that 5 percent figure more closely.

For example:

- Only 40 percent of those now counted as unemployed are in that status because they lost their last job. The rate of layoffs at the end of last year was lower than it has been since the Korean War.
- The other 60 percent either left their last job voluntarily, are seeking jobs for the first time or are re-entering the labor force after being out of it for a period of time.
- About 45 percent of the unemployed have been unemployed for less than five weeks.
- As compared with earlier periods when the overall unemployment rate was about what it is now, the unemployment rate is significantly lower for adult males, household heads and married men. Among married men it is only 2.4 percent. Unemployment among these groups should decline even further during 1973.

This employment gain is even more remarkable since so many more people have been seeking jobs than usual. For example, nearly three million Americans have been released from defense-related jobs since 1969—including over one million veterans.

The unemployment rate for veterans of the Vietnam War now stands at 5.9 percent, above the general rate of unemployment but slightly below the rate for other males in the 20-to-29-year-old age bracket. While much better than the 8.5 percent of a year ago, this 5.9 percent rate is still too high. The employment problems of veterans, who have given so much for their country, will remain high on my list of concerns for the coming year.

Women and young people have also been seeking work in record numbers. Yet, as in the case of veterans, jobs for these groups have been increasing even faster. Unemployment among women and young people has thus declined—but it is also much too high and constitutes a great waste for our Nation.

As we move into a new era of peacetime prosperity, our economic system is going to have room—indeed, is going to have need—for nearly every available hand.

The role of women in our economy thus is bound to grow. And it should—not only because the expansion of opportunities for women is right, but also because America will not be able to achieve its full economic potential unless every woman who wants to work can find a job that provides fair compensation and equal opportunity for advancement.

This Administration is committed to the promotion of this goal. We support the Equal Rights Amendment. We have opened the doors of employment to qualified women in the Federal Service. We have called for similar efforts in businesses and institutions which receive Federal contracts or assistance.

Just last year, we established the Advisory Committee on the Economic Role of Women. This Committee will provide leadership in helping to identify economic problems facing women and helping to change the attitudes which create unjust and illogical barriers to their employment.

Pay and Purchasing Power

The second great question is what people are paid on their jobs and how much it will buy for them.

Here the news is also good. Not only are more people working, but they are getting more for their work. Average per capita income rose by 7.7 percent during 1972, well above the average gain during the previous ten years.

The most important thing, however, is that these gains were not wiped out by rising prices—as they often were in the 1960's. The Federal Government spent too much, too fast in that period and the result was runaway inflation.

While wages may have climbed very rapidly during those years, purchasing power did not. Instead, purchasing power stalled, or even moved backward. Inflation created an economic treadmill that sometimes required a person to achieve a 6 percent salary increase every year just to stay even.

Now that has changed. The inflation rate last year was cut nearly in half from what it was four years ago. The purchasing power of the average worker's take-home pay rose more last year than in any year since 1955; it went up by 4.3 percent—the eqivalent of two extra weekly paychecks.

We expect inflation to be reduced even further in 1973—for several reasons.

A fundamental reason is the Nation's growing opposition to runaway Federal spending. The public increasingly perceives what such spending does to prices and taxes. As a result, we have a good chance now, the best in years, to curb the growth of the Federal budget. That will do more than anything else to protect the family budget.

Other forces are working for us too.

Productivity increased sharply last year—which means the average worker is producing more and can therefore earn more without driving prices higher. In addition, the fact that real spendable earnings rose so substantially last year will encourage reasonable wage demands this year. Workers will not have to catch up from an earlier slump in earnings.

Finally, we now have a new system of wage and price controls—one that is the right kind of system for 1973.

Controls in Force

Any idea that controls have virtually been ended is totally wrong. We still have firm controls. We are still enforcing them firmly. All that has changed is our method of enforcing them.

The old system depended on a Washington bureaucracy to approve major wage and price increases in advance. Although it was effective while it lasted, this system was beginning to produce inequities and to get tangled in red tape. The new system will avoid these dangers. Like most of our laws, it relies largely on self-administration, on the voluntary cooperation of the American people.

But if some people should fail to cooperate, we still have the will and the means to crack down on them.

To any economic interests which might feel that the new system will permit them, openly or covertly, to achieve gains beyond the safety limits we shall prescribe, let me deliver this message in clear and unmistakable terms:

We will regard any flouting of our anti-inflationary rules and standards as nothing less than attempted economic arson threatening our national economic stability—and we shall act accordingly.

We would like Phase III to be as voluntary as possible. But we will make it as mandatory as necessary.

Our new system of controls has broad support from business and labor—the keystone for any successful program. It will prepare us for the day when we no longer need controls. It will allow us to concentrate on those areas where inflation has been most troublesome—construction, health care and especially food prices.

We are focusing particular attention and action on the tough problem of food prices. These prices have risen sharply at the wholesale level in recent months, so that figures for retail prices in January and February will inevitably show sharp increases. In fact, we will probably see increases in food prices for some months to come.

The underlying cause of this problem is that food supplies have not risen fast enough to keep up with the rapidly rising demand.

But we must not accept rising food prices as a permanent feature of American life. We must halt this inflationary spiral by attacking the causes of rising food prices on all fronts. Our first priority must be to increase supplies of food to meet the increasing demand.

We are moving vigorously to expand our food supplies:

• We are encouraging farmers to put more acreage into production of both crops and livestock.

• We are allowing more meat and dried milk to come in from abroad.

• We have ended subsidies for agricultural exports.

• And we are reducing the Government's agricultural stockpiles and encouraging farmers to sell the stock they own.

Measures such as these will stop the rise of wholesale food prices and will slow the rise of retail food prices. Unfortunately, nothing we can do will have a decisive effect in the next few months. But the steps I have taken will have a powerful effect in the second half of the year.

These steps will also help our farmers to improve their incomes by producing more without corresponding price increases. We anticipate that farm prices will be no higher at the end of this year than they were at the beginning.

For all of these reasons, we have a good chance to reduce the overall inflation rate to 2-1/2 percent by the end of 1973.

Holding the Line on Taxes

The third important economic question concerns how much money people pay out in taxes and how much they have left to control themselves. Here, too, the picture is promising.

Since 1950, the share of the average family's income taken for taxes in the United States has nearly doubled—to more than 20 percent. The average person worked less than one hour out of each eight-hour day to pay his taxes in 1950; today he works nearly two hours each day for the tax collector.

In fact, if tax cut proposals had not been adopted during our first term, the average worker's pay increase last year would have been wiped out completely by increased taxes and the taxpayers would have to pay out an additional $25 billion in personal income taxes this year.

The only way to hold the line on taxes is to hold the line on Federal spending.

This is why we are cutting back, eliminating or reforming Federal programs that waste the taxpayers money.

My Administration has now had four years of experience with all of our Federal programs. We have conducted detailed studies comparing their costs and results. On the basis of that experience, I am convinced that the cost of many Federal programs can no longer be justified. Among them are:

• housing programs that benefit the well-to-do but short-change the poor;

• health programs that build more hospitals when hospital beds are now in surplus;

• educational fellowships designed to attract more people into teaching when tens of thousands of teachers already cannot find teaching jobs;

• programs that subsidize education for the children of Federal employees who already pay enough local taxes to support their local schools;

• programs that blindly continue welfare payments to those who are ineligible or overpaid.

Such programs may have appealing names; they may sound like good causes. But behind a fancy lable can lie a dismal failure. And unless we cut back now on the programs that have failed, we will soon run out of money for the programs that succeed.

It has been charged that our budget cuts show a lack of compassion for the disadvantaged. The best answer to this charge is to look at the facts. We are budgeting 66 percent more to help the poor next year than was the case four years ago; 67 percent more to help the sick; 71 percent more to help older Americans and 242 percent more to help the hungry and malnourished. Altogether, our human resources budget is a record $125 billion—nearly double that of four years ago when I came into office.

We have already shifted our spending priorities from defense programs to human resource programs. Now we must also switch our spending priorities from programs which give us a bad return on the dollar to programs that pay off. That is how to show we truly care about the needy.

The question is not whether we help but how we help. By eliminating programs that are wasteful, we can concentrate on programs that work.

Our recent round of budget cuts can save $11 billion in this fiscal year, $19 billion next fiscal year, and $24 billion the year after. That means an average saving of $700 over the next three years for each of America's 75 million taxpayers.

Without the savings I have achieved through program reductions and reforms, those spending totals respectively would be $261 billion, $288 billion and $312 billion—figures which would spell either higher taxes, a new surge of crippling inflation, or both.

To hold the line on Federal spending, it is absolutely vital that we have the full cooperation of the Congress. I urge the Congress, as one of its most pressing responsibilities, to adopt an overall spending ceiling for each fiscal year. I also ask that it establish a regular procedure for ensuring that the ceiling is maintained.

The International Challenge

In recent years, the attention of Americans has increasingly turned to the serious questions confronting us in international trade and in the monetary arena.

This is no longer the era in which the United States, preeminent in science, marketing and services, can dominate world markets with the advanced products of our technology and our advanced means of production.

This is no longer the era in which the United States can automatically sell more abroad than we purchase from foreign countries.

We face new challenges in international competition and are thus in a period of substantial adjustment in our relations with our trading partners.

One consequence of these developments was the step we took last week to change the relative value of the dollar in trading abroad.

We took this step because of a serious trade imbalance which could threaten the mounting prosperity of our people. America has been buying more from other countries than they have been buying from us. And just as a family or a company cannot go on indefinitely buying more than it sells, neither can a country.

Changing the exchange rates will help us change this picture. It means our exports will be priced more competitively in the international marketplace and should therefore sell better. Our imports, on the other hand, will not grow as fast.

But this step must now be followed by reforms which are more basic.

First, we need a more flexible international monetary system, one that will lead to balance without crisis. The United States set forth fundamental proposals for such a system last September. It is time for other nations to join us in getting action on these proposals.

Secondly, American products must get a fairer shake in a more open world trading system—so that we can extend American markets and expand American jobs. If other countries make it harder for our products to be sold abroad, then our trade imbalance can only grow worse.

Responsibility of the Congress

America is assuredly on the road to a new era of prosperity. The roadsigns are clear, and we are gathering more momentum with each passing month. But we can easily lose our way unless the Congress is on board, helping to steer the course.

As we face 1973, in fact, we may be sure that the state of our economy in the future will very much depend upon the decisions made this year on Capitol Hill.

Over the course of the next few months, I will urge prompt Congressional action on a variety of economic proposals. Together, these proposals will constitute one of the most important packages of economic initiatives ever considered by any Congress in our history. I hope—as do all of our people—that the Congress will act with both discipline and dispatch.

Among the items included in my 1973 economic package are:

• **Extension of the Economic Stabilization Program.** Present authority will soon expire, and I have asked the Congress to extend the law for one year to April 30, 1974. I hope this will be done without adding general mandatory standards or prescribing rigid advance decisions—steps that would only hamper sound administration of the program. A highly complex economy simply cannot be regulated effectively for extended periods in that way.

• **Tax Program.** I shall recommend a tax program that builds further reforms on those we achieved in 1969 and 1971.

• **Property Tax Relief.** I shall also submit recommendations for alleviating the crushing burdens which property taxes now create for older Americans.

• **Tax Credit for Nonpublic Schools.** I shall propose legislation which would provide for income tax credit for tuition paid to nonpublic elementary and secondary schools. These institutions are a valuable national resource, relieving the public school system of enrollment pressures, injecting a welcome variety into our educational process, and expanding the options of millions of parents.

• **Trade Legislation.** Another item high on our agenda will be new trade proposals which I will soon send to the Congress. They would make it easier for us not only to lower our trade barriers when other countries lower theirs but also to raise our barriers when that is necessary to keep things fair.

• **Other Reforms.** To modernize and make them more equitable and beneficial, I shall also later submit recommendations for improving the performance of our private pension system, our unemployment compensation program, our minimum wage laws and the manner in which we deal with our transportation systems.

• **Spending Limits.** Finally, but most importantly, I ask the Congress to act this year to impose strict limits on Federal spending.

The cuts I have suggested in this year's budget did not come easily. Thus I can well understand that it may not be easy for the Congress to sustain them, as every special interest group lobbies with its own special Congressional committees for its own special legislation. But the Congress should serve more than the special interest; its first allegiance must always be to the public interest.

We must also recognize that no one in the Congress is now charged with adding all of our Federal expenditures together—and considering their total impact on taxes and prices. It is as if each member of a family went shopping on his own, without knowing how much money was available in the overall family budget or how much other members of the family were spending or charging on various credit accounts.

To overcome these problems, I urge prompt adoption by the Congress of an overall spending ceiling for each fiscal year. This action would allow the Congress to work jointly with me in holding spending to $250 billion in the current fiscal year, $269 billion next year, and $288 billion in fiscal year 1975. Beyond the adoption of an annual ceiling, I also recommend that the Congress consider internal reforms which would establish a regular mechanism for deciding how to maintain the ceiling.

I have no economic recommendation to make to the Congress which is more important to the economic well-being of our people.

I believe that most members of the House and Senate want to hold down spending. Most Congressmen voted for a spending ceiling in principle when the Senate and House approved a ceiling last fall. Unfortunately the two bodies could not get together on a final version. I believe they must get together soon—so that the Congress can proceed this year with a firm sense of budget discipline.

The stakes are high. If we do not restrain spending and if my recommended cuts are reversed, it would take a 15 percent increase in income taxes to pay for the additional expenditures.

The separation of powers between the President and the Congress has become a favorite topic of discussion in recent weeks. We should never, of course, lose our sharp concern for maintaining Constitutional balances.

But we should never overlook the fact we have joint responsibilities as well as separate powers.

There are many areas in which the President and the Congress should and must work together in behalf of all the people —and the level of spending, since it directly affects the pocketbooks of every family in the land, is one of the most critical.

I have fulfilled my pledge that I would not recommend any programs that would require a general tax increase or would create inflationary pressures.

Now it is up to the Congress to match these efforts with a spending ceiling of its own.

Making a Choice

We stand on the threshold of a new era of prolonged and growing prosperity for the United States.

Unlike past booms, this new prosperity will not depend on the stimulus of war.

It will not be eaten away by the blight of inflation.

It will be solid; it will be steady; and it will be sustainable.

If we act responsibly, this new prosperity can be ours for many years to come. If we don't, then, as Franklin Roosevelt once warned, we could be "wrecked on (the) rocks of loose fiscal policy."

The choice is ours. Let us choose responsible prosperity.

RICHARD NIXON

IV. HUMAN RESOURCES

Following is the White House text of the March 1 state of the union message on human resources:

TO THE CONGRESS OF THE UNITED STATES:

"Information of the State of the Union," which our Constitution directs shall be communicated from time to time to the Congress by the President, must consist above all of information about the well-being of the American people.

As the opening words of the Constitution proclaim, America began with "We the People." The people are the Union, and its condition depends wholly on theirs.

While the Nation's land and resources, its communities, its economy, and its political institutions are also vital concerns to be addressed in my reports to the Congress this year, all of these in the final analysis are no more than means to a greater end. For each of them must ultimately be measured according to a single standard: what will serve the millions of individual Americans for whom all public officials serve as trustees.

Too often in the past that standard has not prevailed. Too often public policy decisions have been founded not on the long-run interests of all the people, but on the short-run interests of special groups of people. Programs once set in motion tend to stay in motion—sometimes long after their useful life has ended. They acquire a constituency of their own, even within the Government, and they cannot easily be reformed or stopped. Means come to be regarded as ends in themselves. And no one suffers more than the people they were designed to serve.

Despite all of the factors which conspire to hinder both the executive and the legislative branches in being as objective and analytical as we should be about the soundness of activities that continue from year to year supposedly in the public interest, we can and must discipline ourselves to take a larger view.

As we consider the subject of human resources in this fourth section of my 1973 State of the Union Message, we must not confine ourselves solely to a discussion of the year past and the year ahead. Nor can we be content to frame the choices we face in strictly governmental and programmatic terms—as though Federal money and programs were the only variables that mattered in meeting human needs.

The American Dream

I am irrevocably committed, as Presidents before me have been and as I know each Member of the Congress is, to fulfilling the American dream for all Americans.

But I also believe deeply that in seeking progress and reform we must neither underestimate our society's present greatness, nor mistake the sources of that greatness. To do so would be to run a serious risk of damaging, with unproven panaceas applied in excessive haste and zeal, the very institutions we seek to improve.

Let us begin them, by recognizing that by almost any measure, life is better for Americans in 1973 than ever before in our history, and better than in any other society of the world in this or any earlier age.

No previous generation of our people has ever enjoyed higher incomes, better health and nutrition, longer life-expectancy, or greater mobility and convenience in their lives than we enjoy today. None before us have had a better chance for fulfillment and advancement in their work, more leisure time and recreational opportunities, more widespread access to culture and the arts, or a higher level of education and awareness of the world around them. None have had greater access to and control over the natural and human forces that shape their lives, or better protection against suffering, inhumanity, injustice, and discrimination. And none have enjoyed greater freedom.

Secondly, let us recognize that the American system which has brought us so far so fast is not simply a system of Government helping people. Rather it is a system under which Government helps people to help themselves and one another.

The real miracles in raising millions out of poverty, for example, have been performed by the free-enterprise economy, not by Government anti-poverty programs. The integration of one disadvantaged minority after another into the American mainstream has been accomplished by the inherent responsiveness of our political and social system, not by quotas and coercion. The dramatic gains in health and medical care have come primarily through private medicine, not from federally-operated systems.

Even where the public sector has played a major role, as in education, the great strength of the system has derived from State and local governments' primacy and from the diverse mixture of private and public institutions in the educational process —both factors which have facilitated grassroots influence and popular participation.

We should not tamper lightly, then, with the delicately balanced social, economic, and political system which has been responsible for making this country the best place on earth to live—and which has tremendous potential to rectify whatever shortcomings may still persist.

But we Americans—to our great credit—are a restless and impatient people, a nation of idealists. We dream not simply of alleviating poverty, hunger, discrimination, ignorance, disease, and fear, but of eradicating them altogether—and we would like to do it all today.

During the middle and late 1960's, under the pressure of this impatient idealism, Federal intervention to help meet human needs increased sharply. Provision of services from Federal programs directly to individuals began to be regarded as the rule in human resources policy, rather than the rare exception it had been in the past.

The Government in those years undertook sweeping, sometimes almost utopian, commitments in one area of social concern after another. The State and local governments and the private sector were elbowed aside with little regard for the dislocations that might result. Literally hundreds of new programs were established on the assumption that even the most complex problems could be quickly solved by throwing enough Federal dollars at them.

Well-intentioned as this effort may have been, the results in case after case amounted to dismal failure. It was a classic case of elevating means to the status of ends in themselves. Hard evidence of actual betterment in people's lives was seldom demanded. Ever-larger amounts of funds, new agencies, and increased staff were treated as proof enough of success, simply because the motive was compassionate.

The American people deserve better than this. They deserve compassion that works—not simply compassion that means well. They deserve programs that say yes to human needs by saying no to paternalism, social exploitation and waste.

Protecting and enhancing the greatness of our society is a great goal. It is doubly important, therefore, that we not permit the worthiness of our objective to render us uncritical or careless in the means we select for attaining that objective.

It will increase our greatness as a society, for example, to establish the principle that no American family should be denied good health care because of inability to pay. But it will diminish our greatness if we deprive families of the freedom to make their own health care arrangements without bureaucratic meddling.

It will increase our greatness to ensure that no boy or girl is denied a quality education. But it will diminish our greatness if we force hundreds of thousands of children to ride buses miles away from their neighborhood schools in order to achieve an arbitrary racial balance.

It will increase our greatness to establish an income security system under which no American family will have to suffer for lack of income or break up because welfare regulations encourage it. But it would erode the very foundations of our stability and our prosperity if we ever made it more comfortable or more profitable to live on a welfare check than on a paycheck.

Principles for the 1970's

Consistently since 1969, this Administration has worked to establish a new human resources policy, based on a healthy skepticism about Federal Government omniscience and omnicompetence, and on a strong reaffirmation of the right and the capacity of individuals to chart their own lives and solve their own problems through State and local government and private endeavor. We have achieved a wide variety of significant reforms.

Now the progress made and the experience gained over the past four years, together with the results of careful program reviews which were conducted over this period, have prepared us to seek broader reforms in 1973 than any we have requested before.

In the time since the outlines of these proposals emerged in the new budget, intense controversy and considerable misunderstanding about both their purposes and their effects have understandably arisen among persons of goodwill on all sides.

To provide a more rational, less emotional basis for the national debate which will—and properly should—surround my recommendations, I would invite the Congress to consider four basic principles which I believe should govern our human resources policy in the 1970's:

• Government at all levels should seek to support and nurture, rather than limit, the diversity and freedom of choice which is the hallmark of the American system. The Federal Government in particular must work to guarantee an equal chance at the starting line by removing barriers which might impede an individual's opportunity to realize his or her full potential.

• The Federal Government should concentrate more on providing incentives and opening opportunities, and less on delivering direct services. Such programs of direct assistance to individuals as the Federal Government does conduct must provide evenhanded treatment for all, and must be carefully designed to ensure that the benefits are actually received by those who are intended to receive them.

• Rather than stifling initiative by trying to direct everything from Washington, Federal efforts should encourage State and local governments to make those decisions and supply those services for which their closeness to the people best qualifies them. In addition, the Federal Government should seek means of encouraging the private sector to address social problems, thereby utilizing the market mechanism to marshal resources behind clearly stated national objectives.

• Finally, all Federal policy must adhere to a strict standard of fiscal responsibility. Ballooning deficits which spent our economy into a new inflationary spiral or a recessionary tailspin in the name of social welfare would punish most cruelly the very people whom they seek to help. On the other hand, continued additions to a personal tax burden which has already doubled since 1950 would reduce incentives for excellence and would conflict directly with the goal of allowing each individual to keep as much as possible of what he or she earns so as to permit maximum personal freedom of choice.

The new post of Counsellor to the President for Human Resources, which I have recently created within the Executive Office of the President, will provide a much-needed focal point for our efforts to see that these principles are carried out in all Federal activities aimed at meeting human needs, as well as in the Federal Government's complex relationships with State and local governments in this field. The coordinating function to be performed by this Counsellor should materially increase the unity, coherence, and effectiveness of our policies.

The following sections present a review of the progress we have made over the past four years in bringing each of the various human resources activities into line with these principles, and they outline our agenda for the years ahead.

Health

I am committed to removing financial barriers that would limit access to quality medical care for all American families. To that end, we have nearly doubled Federal outlays for health since the beginning of this Administration. Next year, they will exceed $30 billion.

Nearly 60 percent of these funds will go to finance health care for older Americans, the disabled, and the poor, through Medicare and Medicaid.

But we have taken significant steps to meet other priority needs as well. In the last four years, funding for cancer and heart and lung disease research has more than doubled; it will amount to more than three-quarters of a billion dollars in 1974.

We have supported reform of the health care delivery system and have proposed legislation to assist in the development of health maintenance organizations on a demonstration basis. We have increased funds for programs which help prevent illness, such as those which help carry out our pure food and drug laws and those which promote consumer safety.

We have declared total war on the epidemic problem of drug abuse—and we are winning that war. We have come a long way toward our goal of creating sufficient treatment services so that any addict desiring treatment can obtain it. We are also making substantial investments in research to develop innovative treatment approaches to drug abuse. I will report in greater detail on our anti-drug effort in a later section of this year's State of the Union message.

Strong measures have been taken to ensure that health care costs do not contribute to inflation and price people out of the care they need. The rate of increase in physicians' fees was cut by two-thirds last year alone, and hospital price rises have also been slowed. To build on these gains, controls on the health services industry have been retained and will be strengthened under Phase III of the Economic Stabilization Program.

A major goal of this Administration has been to develop an insurance system which can guarantee adequate financing of health care for every American family. The 92nd Congress failed to act upon my 1971 proposal to accomplish this goal, and now the need for legislation has grown still more pressing. I shall once again submit to the Congress legislation to help meet the Nation's health insurance needs.

Federal health policy should seek to safeguard this country's pluralistic health care system and to build on its strengths, minimizing reliance on Government-run arrangements. We must recognize appropriate limits to the Federal role, and we must see that every health care dollar is spent as effectively as possible.

This means discontinuing federally funded health programs which have served their purpose, or which have proved ineffective, or which involve functions more suitably performed by State and local government or the private sector.

The Hill-Burton hospital grants program, for example, can no longer be justified on the basis of the shortage of hospital facilities which prompted its creation in 1946. That shortage has given way to a surplus—so that to continue this program would only add to the Nation's excess of hospital beds and lead to higher charges to patients. It should be terminated.

We are also proposing to phase out the community mental health center demonstration program while providing funding for commitments to existing arrangements extending up to eight years. This program has helped to build and establish some 500 such centers, which have demonstrated new ways to deliver mental health services at the community level.

Regional Medical Programs likewise can now be discontinued. The planning function they have performed can better be conducted by comprehensive State planning efforts. A second function of these programs, the continuing education of physicians who are already licensed, is an inappropriate burden for Federal taxpayers to bear.

Education

1973 must be a year of decisive action to restructure Federal aid programs for education. Our goal is to provide continued Federal financial support for our schools while expanding State and local control over basic educational decisions.

I shall again ask the Congress to establish a new program of Education Revenue Sharing. This program would replace the complex and inefficient tangle of approximately 30 separate programs for elementary and secondary education with a single flexible authority for use in a few broad areas such as compensatory education for the disadvantaged, education for the handicapped, vocational education, needed assistance in federally affected areas, and supporting services.

Education Revenue Sharing would enlarge the opportunities for State and local decision-makers to tailor programs and resources to meet the specific educational needs of their own localities. It would mean less red tape, less paper work, and greater freedom for those at the local level to do what they think is best for their schools—not what someone in Washington tells them is best.

It would help to strengthen the principle of diversity and freedom in education that is as old as America itself, and would give educators a chance to create fresher, more individual approaches to the educational challenges of the Seventies. At the same time, it would affirm and further the national interest in promoting equal educational opportunities for economically disadvantaged children.

If there is any one area of human activity where decisions are best made at the local level by the people who know local conditions and local needs, it is in the field of primary and secondary education. I urge the Congress to join me in making this year, the third in which Education Revenue Sharing has been on the legislative agenda, the year when this much-needed reform becomes law.

The time has also come to redefine the Federal role in higher education, by replacing categorical support programs for institutions with substantially increased funds for student assistance. My budget proposals have already outlined a plan to channel much more of our higher education support through students themselves, including a new grant program which would increase funds provided to $948 million and the number assisted to over 1,500,000 people—almost a five-fold increase over the current academic year.

These proposals would help to ensure for the first time that no qualified student seeking postsecondary education would be barred from attaining it by a lack of funds and they would at the same time reinforce the spirit of competition among institutions that has made American higher education strong. I urge their prompt enactment.

As we work to eliminate the unnecessary bureaucratic constraints currently hampering Federal education aid, we will also be devoting more attention to educational research and development through the new National Institute of Education. Funding for NIE will increase by almost 50 percent in fiscal year 1974, reaching $162 million.

Finally, in order to enhance the diversity provided by our mixed educational system of public and private schools, I will propose to the Congress legislation to provide a tax credit for tuition payments made by parents of children who attend non-public elementary and secondary schools.

Manpower

The Federal manpower program is a vital part of our total effort to conserve and develop our human resources.

Up to the present time, however, the "manpower program" has been not a unified effort, but a collection of separate categorical activities, many of them overlapping. These activities now include such programs as Manpower Development and Training Act, Institutional Training programs, on-the-job training, Neighborhood Youth Corps, Public Service Careers, Operation Mainstream, and the Concentrated Employment Program. The net effect of several such programs operating in a single city seldom amounts to a coherent strategy for meeting the needs of people in that community.

While many well-run local programs are more than worth what they cost, many other individual projects are largely ineffective—and their failure wastes money which could be used to bolster the solid accomplishments of the rest.

Manpower programs ought to offer golden "second chances" for the less fortunate to acquire the skills and work habits which will help them become self-supporting, fully productive citizens. But as presently organized and managed, these second chance opportunities too often become just another dead-end exercise in frustration, rather than a genuine entree into a good job.

I believe that the answer to much of this problem lies in our program of Manpower Revenue Sharing—uniting several previously fragmented manpower activities under a single umbrella and then giving most of the responsibility for running this effort to those governments which are closest to the working men and women who need assistance. In the next 16 months, administrative measures will be taken to institute this needed reform of the manpower system within the present legal framework.

Manpower Revenue Sharing assistance will be freed from unnecessary Federal constraints, and aimed at developing jobs, equipping unemployed workers with useful work skills, and moving trainees into regular employment.

Welfare

With the failure of the past two Congresses to enact my proposals for fundamental reform of the Nation's public assistance system, that system remains as I described it in a message last year—"a crazy quilt of injustice and contradiction that has developed in bits and pieces over the years."

The major existing program, Aid to Families with Dependent Children (AFDC), is as inequitable, inefficient, and inadequate as ever.

• The administration of this program is unacceptably loose. The latest national data indicate that in round numbers, one of every 20 persons on the AFDC rolls is totally ineligible for welfare; 3 more are paid more benefits than they are entitled to; and another is underpaid. About one-quarter of AFDC recipients, in other words, are receiving improper payments.

• Complex program requirements and administrative red tape at the Federal and State levels have created bureaucracies that are difficult to manage.

• Inconsistent and unclear definitions of need have diluted resources that should be targeted on those who need help most.

• Misguided incentives have discouraged employable persons from work and induced fathers to leave home so that their families can qualify for welfare.

After several years of skyrocketing increases, however, outlays for this program have begun to level off. This results from the strong resurgence of our economy and expansion of the job market, along with some management improvements in the AFDC program and strengthened work requirements which were introduced into the program last year.

Since the legislative outlook seems to preclude passage of an overall structural reform bill in the immediate future, I have directed that vigorous steps be taken to strengthen the management of AFDC through administrative measures and legislative proposals.

Under these reforms, Federal impediments to efficient State administration of the current AFDC system will be removed wherever possible. Changes will be proposed to reduce the complexities of current eligibility and payment processes. Work will continue to be required of all those who can reasonably be considered available for employment, while Federal funds to help welfare recipients acquire needed job skills will increase.

One thing is certain: the welfare mess cannot be permitted to continue. A system which penalizes a person for going to work and rewards a person for going on welfare is totally alien to the American tradition of self-reliance and self-respect. That is why welfare reform has been and will continue to be one of our major goals; and we will work diligently with the Congress in developing ways to achieve it.

Nutrition

During the past four years, Federal outlays for food assistance have increased more than three-fold. Food stamp and food distribution programs for needy families have been extended to virtually every community in the country. More than 15 million persons are now receiving food stamps or distributed foods, more than double the 1969 total. More than 8 million school children are now being provided with free or reduced-price lunches—up from only 3 million in 1969.

We have made great strides toward banishing hunger and malnutrition from American life—and we shall continue building on that progress until the job is done.

Older Americans

One measure of the Nation's devotion to our older citizens is the fact that programs benefitting them—including Social Security and a wide range of other activities—now account for nearly one-fourth of the entire Federal budget.

Social Security benefit levels have been increased 51 percent in the last four years—the most rapid increase in history. Under new legislation which I initially proposed, benefits have also become inflation-proof, increasing automatically as the cost of living increases.

Over 1-1/2 million older Americans or their dependents can now receive higher Social Security benefits while continuing to work. Nearly 4 million widows and widowers are also starting to receive larger benefits—$1 billion in additional income in the next fiscal year. And millions of older Americans will be helped by the new Supplemental Security Income program which establishes a Federal income floor for the aging, blind, and disabled poor.

Nevertheless, we are confronted with a major item of unfinished business. Approximately two-thirds of the twenty million persons who are 65 and over own their own homes. A disproportionate amount of their fixed income must now be used for property taxes. I will submit to the Congress recommendations for alleviating the often crushing burdens which property taxes place upon many older Americans.

I also ask the cooperation of the Congress in passing my 1974 budget request for $200 million to fund the programs of the Administration on Aging—a funding level more than four times that appropriated for AoA programs in fiscal year 1972. Half of this amount will be devoted to nutrition projects for the elderly, with the remainder going to assist States and localities in developing comprehensive service programs for older Americans.

In 1973, we shall continue to carry out the commitment I made in 1971 at the White House Conference on Aging: to help make the last days of our older Americans their best days.

Economic Opportunity

No one who started life in a family at the bottom of the income scale, as I did and as many Members of the Congress did, can ever forget how that condition felt, or ever turn his back on an opportunity to help alleviate it in the lives of others.

We in the Federal Government have such an opportunity to help combat poverty. Our commitment to this fight has grown steadily during the past decade, without regard to which party happened to be in power, from under $8 billion in total Federal anti-poverty expenditures in 1964 to more than $30 billion in my proposed budget for 1974.

And we have moved steadily closer to the goal of a society in which all our citizens, regardless of economic status, will have both the resources and the opportunity to fully control their own destinies.

At the beginning of this period, when Government found itself unprepared to respond to the sharp new national awareness of the plight of the disadvantaged, creation of an institutional structure separate from the regular machinery of Government and specifically charged with helping the poor seemed a wise first step to take. Thus the Office of Economic Opportunity was brought into being in 1964.

A wide range of useful anti-poverty programs have been conceived and put into operation over the years by the Office of Economic Opportunity. Some programs which got their start within OEO have been moved out into the operating departments and agencies of the Government when they matured, and they are thriving there. VISTA, for example, became part of ACTION in 1971, and Head Start was integrated with other activities focused on the first five years of life under HEW's Office of Child Development. OEO's other programs have now developed to a point where they can be similarly integrated.

Accordingly, in keeping with my determination to make every dollar devoted to human resources programs return 100 cents worth of real benefits to the people who most need those benefits, I have decided that most of the anti-poverty activities now conducted by the Office of Economic Opportunity should be delegated or transferred into the Cabinet departments relating to their respective fields of activity. Adhering strictly to statutory procedures, and requesting Congressional approval whenever necessary, I shall take action to effect this change.

This reorganization will increase the efficiency of the various programs by grouping them with other functionally related Federal efforts and by minimizing the overhead costs which in the past have diverted too much money from human needs into staff payrolls and administrative expenses. Funding for the transferred activities will stay level, or in many cases will even increase.

The only major OEO program for which termination of Federal funding is recommended in my budget is Community Action. New funding for Community Action activities in fiscal year 1974 will be at the discretion of local communities.

After more than 7 years of existence, Community Action has had an adequate opportunity to demonstrate its value within the communities it serves, and to build locally based agencies. OEO has taken steps to help Community Action agencies put down local roots through a program of incentives and training, and has incorporated the basic community action concept—participation in programs by the people whom the programs seek to serve—into all Federal anti-poverty activities. Further Federal spending on behalf of this concept, beyond the $2.8 billion which has been spent on it since 1965, no longer seems necessary or desirable.

Legal Services

One other economic opportunity effort deserving special mention is the Legal Services Program. Notwithstanding some abuses, legal services has done much in its seven-year history to breathe new life into the cherished concept of equal justice for all by providing access to quality legal representation for millions of Americans who would otherwise have been denied it for want of funds.

The time has now come to institutionalize legal services as a permanent, responsible, and responsive component of the American system of justice.

I shall soon propose legislation to the Congress to form a legal services corporation constituted so as to permit its attorneys to practice according to the highest professional standards, provided with safeguards against politicization of its activities, and held accountable to the people through appropriate monitoring and evaluation procedures.

Civil Rights

Protecting the civil rights of every American is one of my firmest commitments as President. No citizen should be denied equal justice and equal opportunity in our society because of race, color, sex, religion, or national origin.

This Administration has steadily increased the Federal financial commitment in this field. Outlays for civil rights and equal opportunity in 1974 will pass $3 billion—3-1/2 times what they were when we took office.

We have worked hard—and with good results—to end de jure school segregation, to promote equal job opportunity, to combat housing discrimination, to foster minority business enterprise, to uphold voting rights, to assist minority higher education, to meet minority health problems like sickle cell anemia, and to make progress on many other fronts.

Now that equal opportunity is clearly written into the statute books, the next and in many ways more difficult step involves moving from abstract legal rights to concrete economic opportunities. We must ensure real social mobility—the freedom of all Americans to make their own choices and to go as far and as high as their abilities will take them. Legislation and court decisions play a major part in establishing that freedom. But community attitudes, government programs, and the vigor of the economic system all play large parts as well.

I believe that we have made progress, and we shall continue building on that progress in the coming year:

• The Department of Justice will expand its efforts to guarantee equal access to, and equal benefit from, Federal financial assistance programs.

• The Equal Employment Opportunity Commission will receive additional resources to carry out its expanded responsibilities.

• The Civil Service Commission will expand its monitoring of equal employment opportunities within the Federal Government.

- Efforts to assure that Federal contractors provide equal access to job opportunities will be expanded.
- The Small Business Administration will expand its loan program for minority business by nearly one-third.
- The Commission on Civil Rights will receive additional resources to carry out its newly granted responsibilities.

Additionally, in the year ahead, we will continue to support ratification of the Equal Rights Amendment to the Constitution so that American women—not a minority group but a majority of the whole population—need never again be denied equal opportunity.

The American Indian

For Indian people the policy of this Administration will continue to be one of advancing their opportunities for self-determination, without termination of the special Federal relationship with recognized Indian tribes.

Just as it is essential to put more decision-making in the hands of State and local governments, I continue to believe that Indian tribal governments should assume greater responsibility for programs of the Bureau of Indian Affairs and the Department of Health, Education, and Welfare which operate on their reservations.

As I first proposed in 1970, I recommend that the Congress enact the necessary legislation to facilitate this take-over of responsibility. Also, I recommend that the 1953 termination resolution be repealed. Meanwhile the new statutory provisions for Indian tribal governments under General Revenue Sharing will assist responsible tribal governments in allocating extra resources with greater flexibility.

I shall also propose new legislation to foster local Indian self-determination by developing an Interior Department program of bloc grants to Federally recognized tribes as a replacement for a number of existing economic and resource development programs. The primary purpose of these grants would be to provide tribal governments with funds which they could use at their own discretion to promote development of their reservations.

Indian tribal organizations and Indians seeking to enter business need easier access to loan and credit opportunities; I proposed in 1970 and will again propose legislation to accomplish this objective.

Because Indian rights to natural resources need better protection, I am again urging the Congress to create an Indian Trust Counsel Authority to guarantee that protection.

In the two and one-half years that Indians have been waiting for the Congress to enact the major legislation I have proposed, we have moved ahead administratively whenever possible. We have restored 21,000 acres of wrongfully acquired Government land to the Yakima Tribe. We have filed a precedent-setting suit in the Supreme Court to protect Indian water rights in Pyramid Lake. My fiscal year 1974 budget proposed total Federal outlays of $1.45 billion for Indian affairs, an increase of more than 15 percent over 1973.

To accelerate organizational reform, I have directed the Secretary of the Interior to transfer day to day operational activities of the Bureau of Indian Affairs out of Washington to its field offices. And I am again asking the Congress to create a new Assistant Secretary position within the Interior Department to deal with Indian matters.

Veterans

With the coming of peace, the Nation's inestimable debt to our veterans and their dependents will continue to command a high priority among the human resource efforts of this Administration.

During the past four years, I have twice signed legislation increasing the allowances for educational assistance to veterans.

Nearly 2 million veterans are now in some form of training under the GI Bill for Vietnam veterans.

Pension payments to veterans or their survivors who need income support have also been raised twice and the test of need has been greatly improved, including a more equitable formula for adjusting the VA pension rate when other sources of income, such as Social Security, are increased. The VA pension program now directly benefits over 2 million individuals.

Compensation payments for service-related disabilities have been raised on two occasions, and more than 2 million veterans of all wars now receive this benefit. The service-disabled veteran deserves special concern. In addition to top-priority consideration in medical care, my budget calls for VA outlays to provide disabled Vietnam-era veterans with vocational rehabilitation, housing grants, and specially equipped automobiles to be nearly doubled in 1974 compared to their 1971 level.

Disability compensation is also being intensively reviewed to ensure that disabled veterans will receive compensation payments which fully recognize their earnings impairment.

VA guaranteed home loans for veterans have risen by almost two-thirds since we took office. And high-priority job programs have decreased the unemployment rate among Vietnam-era veterans by almost one-third during the past year alone.

Dramatic progress has been made in the veterans medical care program. A high level of construction and modernization of VA medical facilities has been carried on. The total number of medical care personnel staffing VA facilities has increased by one-sixth since 1969. The total number of veterans treated both in VA facilities and as outpatients—has risen to new highs. Beneficiaries treated as hospital inpatients will go over the million mark in fiscal 1974 for the first time. Outpatient visits will climb to almost 14,000,000—about twice the level of 1969.

Since 1969, there has also been a steady shortening of the average length of stay in VA hospitals, a highly desirable objective from every viewpoint. This means that VA hospitals have fewer patients in bed on an average day, with shorter waiting lists, even though the total number of patients treated has gone up.

Misunderstanding these statistics, some have sought to establish by law a numerical minimum average daily patient census in VA hospitals. But such a fixed daily census would represent a backward step: it would force a sharply increased length-of-stay—an effect that is medically, economically, and socially undesirable.

It is far better that our veterans be restored to their families and jobs as rapidly as feasible, consistent with good medical care. A fixed patient census would tie the hands of those seeking to serve veterans' health needs; I urge the Congress not to enact such a requirement.

The Congress is now studying several bills involving the VA pension program and cemetery and burial benefits for veterans. I hope that the Congress will work to see that the veterans pension program is realistically structured and compatible with other major income maintenance programs.

On the burial benefits question, I urge that legislative action be deferred until completion of a study currently being conducted by the Administration of Veterans Affairs to determine the most equitable approach to improving burial and cemetery benefits for veterans. The Administrator's recommendations will be made available to the Congress in the near future.

Consumer Affairs

The self-reliance and resourcefulness of our people when they enter the marketplace as consumers, the generally high standard of ethics and social responsibility upheld by business and industry, and the restrained intervention of government at various levels as a vigorous but not heavy-handed referee of commerce—that combination of factors, in that order, has been largely responsible for confounding predictions that American capitalism would breed its own downfall · in the 20th century.

We must build on each of these strengths in our efforts to protect the rights of the consumer as well as the vigor of the free enterprise economy in the 1970's.

Early in 1971, after the Congress had failed to act on my "Buyer's Bill of Rights" proposal for a new Office of Consumer Affairs directly under the President, I established such an office by executive order. Under the direction of my Special Assistant for Consumer Affairs, OCA has helped to create a stronger consumer consciousness throughout the executive branch.

This office is now ready to integrate its operations more fully with the line departments of the Government, and has accordingly been transferred into the Department of Health, Education and Welfare—the logical base for an agency concerned with human well-being.

From this new base the Office of Consumer Affairs will continue its policy formation role and educational efforts, and will also take on additional responsibilities, including representing consumer interests in testimony before the Congress and acting as a general ombudsman for the individual consumer.

Voluntary Action

Many thousands of Americans already are volunteering their time to meet human needs in their communities—fighting disease, teaching children to read, working to solve local social problems. But now we must do more to tap the enormous reservoir of energy represented by millions of other potential citizen volunteers.

That is why three years ago I encouraged a number of our leading citizens to create the National Center for Voluntary Action to support private volunteer efforts; that is why two years ago I established the new ACTION agency to strengthen Federal volunteer programs.

We must now continue seeking new avenues of citizen service. As we turn from the concerns of war, may all Americans accept the challenge of peace by volunteering to help meet the needs of their communities—so that we can mobilize a new army of concerned, dedicated, able volunteers across the Nation.

Arts and Humanities

I know that many in the Congress share the concern I have often expressed that some Americans, particularly younger people, lost faith in their country during the 1960's. I believe this faith is now being reborn out of the knowledge that our country is moving toward an era of lasting peace in the world, toward a healthier environment, and toward a new era of progress and equality of opportunity for all our people.

But renewed faith in ourselves also arrives from a deeper understanding of who we are, where we have come from, and where we are going—an understanding to which the arts and the humanities can make a great contribution.

Government has a limited but important function in encouraging the arts and the humanities—that of reinforcing local initiatives and helping key institutions to help themselves. With the approach of our Bicentennial, we have a special opportunity to draw on the enrichment and renewal which cultural activity can provide in our national life. With this in mind, my 1974 budget requests further expansion of the funds for the National Foundation on the Arts and the Humanities, to a new high of $168 million. I ask continued full support from the Congress for this funding.

Saying 'Yes'

Carl Sandburg spoke volumes about this country's past and future in three simple words that became the title for one of his greatest poems: "The People, Yes."

America has risen to greatness because again and again when the chips were down, the American people have said yes—yes to the challenge of freedom, yes to the dare of progress, and yes to the hope of peace—even when defending the peace has meant paying the price of war.

America's greatness will endure in the future only if our institutions continually rededicate themselves to saying yes to the people—yes to human needs and aspirations, yes to democracy and the consent of the governed, yes to equal opportunity and unlimited horizons of achievement for every American.

1973 is a year full of opportunity for great advances on this front. After more than a decade of war, we have successfully completed one of the most unselfish missions ever undertaken by one nation in the defense of another. Now the coming of peace permits us to turn our attention more fully to the works of compassion, concern, and social betterment here at home.

The seriousness of my commitment to make the most of this opportunity is evidenced by the record level of funding for human resource programs proposed in our new budget—$125 billion in all—nearly twice the amount that was being spent on such programs when I took office in 1969.

This is both a generous budget and a reform budget. The reforms it proposes will put muscle behind the generosity it intends. The overall effect of these reforms will be the elimination of programs that are wasteful so that we can concentrate on programs that work. They will make possible the continued growth of Federal efforts to meet human needs—while at the same time helping to prevent a runaway deficit that could lead to higher taxes, higher prices, and higher interest rates for all Americans.

The opportunity is ours, executive and legislative branches together, to lead America to a new standard of fairness, of freedom, and of vitality within our federal system. We can forge a new approach to human services in this country—an approach which will treat people as more than mere statistics—an approach which recognizes that problems like poverty and unemployment, health care and the costs of education are more than cold abstractions in a government file drawer.

We know how tough these problems are, because many of us grew up with them ourselves. But we also know that with the right kind of help and the right kind of spirit they can be overcome.

Let us give all our citizens the help they need. But let us remember that each of us also bears a basic obligation to help ourselves and to help our fellowman, and that no one else can assume that obligation for us—least of all the Federal Government.

If we shirk our individual responsibility, the American dream will never be more than a dream.

But if the people say yes to this challenge, if government says yes to the people—and if all of us in Washington say no to petty quarrels and partisanship and yes to our public trust—then we can truly bring that dream to life for all Americans in the new day of peace that is dawning.

RICHARD NIXON

The White House
March 1, 1973.

V. COMMUNITY DEVELOPMENT

Following is the White House text of President Nixon's March 8 state of the union message on community development:

TO THE CONGRESS OF THE UNITED STATES:

Today, in this fifth report to the Congress on the State of the Union, I want to discuss the quality of life in our cities and towns and set forth new directions for community development in America.

Not long ago we became accustomed to the constant rhetorical drumbeat of the "crisis of our cities." Problems were multiplying so rapidly for our larger urban areas that some observers said our cities were doomed as centers of culture, of commerce, and of constructive change.

Many of these problems still persist, but I believe we have made sufficient progress in recent years that fears of doom are no longer justified.

What is needed today is calm reflection upon the nature of modern community life in the United States, a reassessment of the manner in which we are trying to solve our remaining problems, and a firm resolve to get on with the task.

Community Diversity

America's communities are as diverse as our people themselves. They vary tremendously in size—from massive cities to medium-sized urban and suburban areas, to small towns and rural communities.

Just as importantly, each of our communities has built up strong individual characteristics over the years, shaped by region, climate, economic influences, ethnic origins and local culture.

Of course, communities do share common needs and concerns. People in every community want adequate housing, transportation, and jobs, a clean environment, good health, education, recreation facilities, security from crime and fear, and other essential services. But local priorities differ; the intensity and order of local needs vary.

Clearly, no single, rigid scheme, imposed by the Federal Government from Washington, is capable of meeting the changing and varied needs of this diverse and dynamic Nation.

There is no "best" way, no magic, universal cure-all, that can be dispensed from hundreds or thousands of miles away. What is good for New York City is not necessarily good for Chicago, or San Francisco, much less for smaller communities with entirely different economies, traditions and populations.

Too often in the past we have fallen into the trap of letting Washington make the final decisions for St. Louis, Detroit, Miami and our other cities. Sometimes the decisions were right, and programs have succeeded. Too often they were wrong, and we are still paying the price.

The time has come to recognize the errors of past Federal efforts to support community development and to move swiftly to correct them.

Errors of the Past

The results of past errors form a disturbing catalogue:
• They have distorted local priorities.
• They have spawned a massive glut of red tape.
• They have created an adversary climate between local communities and Washington which has often led to waste, delay and mutual frustration.
• They have contributed to a lack of confidence among our people in the ability of both local and national governments to solve problems and get results.
• They have led to the creation of too many complex and often competing Federal programs.
• Perhaps worst of all, they have undercut the will and the ability of local and State governments to take the initiative to mobilize their own energies and those of their citizens.

The Federal policy that will work best in the last third of this century is not one that tries to force all of our communities into a single restrictive mold. The Federal policy that will work best is one that helps people and their leaders in each community meet their own needs in the way they think best.

It is this policy which binds together the many aspects of our community development programs.

The Better Communities Act

In the near future, I will submit to the Congress the Better Communities Act to provide revenue sharing for community development. Beginning July 1, 1974, this act would provide $2.3 billion a year to communities to be spent as they desire to meet their community development needs. In the interim period before the legislation becomes effective, funds already available to the Department of Housing and Urban Development will be used to maintain and support community development.

The Better Communities Act is intended to replace inflexible and fragmented categorical grant-in-aid programs, and to reduce the excessive Federal control that has been so frustrating to local governments.

Rather than focusing and concentrating resources in a coordinated assault on a set of problems, the categorical system scatters these resources, and diminishes their impact upon the most needy. Excessive Federal influence also limits the variety and diversity of development programs. Local officials should be able to focus their time, their resources and their talents on meeting local needs and producing results, instead of trying to please Washington with an endless torrent of paperwork.

I first proposed such legislation in 1971, and although the Congress failed to enact it, significant support was expressed in both the Senate and the House. Since that time, members of my Administration have been consulting with Congressional leaders, mayors, Governors, other local officials and their representatives. Many constructive suggestions have been received and will be incorporated in my new legislative proposal. As a result, I believe the Better Communities Act will represent our best hope for the future of community development and will deserve rapid approval by the Congress.

Among the most significant features of the Better Communities Act are these:

• **Hold-Harmless Provision:** The flow of money to cities and urban counties is to be based on a formula reflecting community needs, as determined by objective standards. In the years immediately following enactment, funds would be used to assure that no city receives less money for community development than it has received under the categorical grant programs.

• **Assistance for Smaller Communities:** Funding is also to be provided for our smaller communities, recognizing the vital importance of small towns and rural communities to the future of the Nation.

• **The Role of State Government:** State governments have always played an important part in meeting the community development needs of their communities. The Act will recognize this role.

• **Local Decision Making:** While each of the activities now supported by categorical grants may be continued, it would be up to local leaders to determine how that money will be spent.

• **Minimizing Red Tape:** Recipients would be required to show the Federal Government only that they are complying with Federal statutes in the way they are spending their revenue sharing money.

• **Elimination of Matching:** Shared revenues would not have to be matched by local funds.

• **Protection for Minorities:** Under no circumstances could funds provided under the Better Communities Act be used for purposes that would violate the civil rights of any person.

A Department of Community Development

One of the most serious deficiencies in the effort of the Federal Government to assist in community development has been the fragmentation and scattering of Federal programs among a variety of departments and agencies. All too often State or local officials seeking help for a particular project must shuttle back and forth from one Federal office to another, wasting precious time and resources in a bureaucratic wild goose chase.

In order to coordinate our community development activities more effectively, I proposed nearly two years ago that we create a Department of Community Development which would pull under one roof various programs now in the Departments of Housing and Urban Development, Transportation, Agriculture, and other agencies.

After extensive hearings on this proposal, the Committee on Government Operations of the House of Representatives reached this conclusion:

"The Department of Community Development will be a constructive center in the Federal Government for assistance to communities, large and small. It will facilitate rational planning, orderly growth, and the effective employment of resources to build viable communities throughout the United States. It will help to strengthen the physical and institutional bases for cooperative action by Federal, State and local governments."

This Administration fully agrees, of course, and will continue to work with the Congress for the prompt creation of a Department of Community Development.

In the interim, I recently appointed a Presidential Counsellor on Community Development who will coordinate community development programs and policies in the executive branch. But only when the Congress approves the basic departmental reorganization proposed by the Administration can our efforts to eliminate waste, confusion and duplication, and to promote community betterment more efficiently, be fully effective.

The Responsive Governments Act

For nearly 20 years, the Federal Government has provided assistance to State and local governments in order to strengthen their planning and management capabilities.

This aid, provided under the Comprehensive Planning Assistance Program, has always been helpful, but the program itself has several major flaws. It has tended, for instance, to stress one aspect of public administration—planning—without adequately recognizing other essential features such as budgeting, management, personnel administration, and information-gathering. Planning has often been irrelevant to the problems and the actual decisions. State and local governments have also found it difficult to coordinate their planning because of the fragmented way in which funds have been sent from Washington.

This Administration proposed new planning and management legislation to the 92nd Congress, but it was not approved. In the meantime, we took what steps we could to improve the existing program. Some progress has been made, but corrective legislation is still needed.

I shall therefore propose that the 93rd Congress enact a new Responsive Governments Act. I shall also propose that we provide $110 million for this act in fiscal year 1974—almost one-fifth of the entire amount that has been spent under the present law in the last two decades.

This Responsive Governments Act would assist State and local governments in meeting several important goals:

• Developing reliable information on their problems and opportunities;

• Developing and analyzing alternative policies and programs;

• Managing the programs;

• And evaluating the results, so that appropriate adjustments can be made.

The ability to plan and manage is vital to effective government. It will be even more important to State and local governments as they are freed from the restraints of narrow categorical Federal programs and must decide how to spend revenue sharing funds. Thus the Responsive Governments Act is a vitally necessary companion piece to the Better Communities Act.

Housing

This Administration is firmly committed to the goal first set forth for America in the 1949 Housing Act: "a decent home and a suitable living environment for every American family."

While we believe that some of our housing programs have failed and should be replaced, we should never waiver in our commitment.

During the past four years, the Federal Government has provided housing assistance to an additional 1.5 million American families of low and moderate income. This represents more housing assistance than the total provided by the Federal Government during the entire 34-year history of our national housing program preceding this Administration.

In addition, a healthy, vigorous, private housing industry has provided 6 million new unsubsidized units of housing for Americans in the last four years. Housing starts for each of the last three years have reached record high levels,—levels, in fact, that are more than double the average for the preceding 21 years.

Most importantly, the percentage of Americans living in substandard housing has dropped dramatically from 46 percent in 1940 to 37 percent in 1950 to 18 percent in 1960 to 8 percent in 1970. Americans today are better housed than ever before in our history.

At the same time, however, there has been mounting evidence of basic defects in some of our housing programs. It is now clear that all too frequently the needy have not been the primary beneficiaries of these programs; that the programs have been riddled with inequities; and that the cost for each unit of subsidized housing produced under these programs has been too high. In short, we shall be making far more progress than we have been and we should now move to place our housing policies on a much firmer foundation.

That is why we suspended new activity under Federal subsidized housing programs effective January 5th of this year. I would emphasize, however, that commitments that were made under these programs prior to their suspension will be honored. This will mean that approximately 300,000 units of new subsidized housing will be started in 1973.

In pursuing our goal of decent homes for all Americans, we know that better means are needed—that the old and wasteful programs, programs which have already obligated the taxpayer to payments of between $63 billion and $95 billion during the next 40 years, are not the answer.

One of my highest domestic priorities this year will be the development of new policies that will provide aid to genuinely needy families and eliminate waste.

A major housing study is now underway within the Government, under the direction of my Counsellor for Community Development. Within the next six months, I intend to submit to the Congress my policy recommendations in this field, based upon the results of that study.

Transportation

To thrive, a community must provide for the efficient movement of its people and its products. Yet in recent years, the growing separation of the city from its suburbs and changing employment patterns have made transportation more of a community problem than a community asset. To improve community development we must meet the challenge of transportation planning and provide more flexible means for communities to meet their transportation needs.

Without better transportation, our communities will either stagnate or choke.

Four years ago we initiated programs to renew and redirect our transportation systems. We took action to expand the capacity of our airways, to preserve and improve intercity rail passenger service, to continue the Nation's highway program with greater emphasis on safety, and to bring needed progress to our surface public transportation. The Federal commitment has been substantial:

• The enlarged Airport Development Aid Program established under the Airport-Airways Development Act of 1970 has quadrupled Federal assistance to airports to $295 million per year.

• Under the Rail Passenger Service Act of 1970 we have begun to rejuvenate rail service as part of a balanced transportation system.

• From 1970 through 1974 we will have invested some $23 billion in highways. In 1972 alone we committed $3.3 billion to the Interstate system, which is now 80 percent complete. In that same year, $870 million was designated for primary and secondary roads. Equally important, we have emphasized safety on our highways, both in their design and use.

• We have progressively increased the levels of Federal funding for transportation research, development, and demonstration projects. This support focuses on new transportation technology. It is designed to encourage private industry to join aggressively in the search for better transportation.

Concurrent with our programs to improve transportation between our cities, we have undertaken programs to develop freeflowing corridors for people and commerce within our cities.

• Since 1970, when I proposed and the Congress passed the Urban Mass Transportation Assistance Act, we have committed more than 2 billion Federal dollars to preserve and upgrade public transportation. Nationally, urban public transportation has become a billion-dollar-a-year Federal program.

• Over the past four years, Federal dollars have helped 60 American cities to help those who depend on public systems for transportation to jobs, hospitals, shops and recreational centers. Now we must deal even more aggressively with community development challenges in transportation by building on the strong foundations we have laid.

Nothing can do more to lift the face of our cities, and the spirit of our city dwellers, than truly adequate systems of modern transportation. With the best highway system in the world, and with 75 percent of our people owning and operating automobiles, we have more transportation assets per capita than any other people on earth. Yet the commuter who uses a two-ton vehicle to transport only himself to and from work each day is not making the most efficient use of our transportation system and is himself contributing to our transportation and environmental problems.

Good public transportation is essential not only to assure adequate transportation for all citizens, but to forward the common goal of less congested, cleaner and safer communities. As I pointed out a few weeks ago in my message on the environment and natural resources, effective mass transit systems that relieve urban congestion will also reduce pollution and the waste of our limited energy resources.

As we build such systems, we must be aware of the two special challenges in coordinating the needs of the inner city and the suburb and in alleviating potential disruptions which new transportation systems can bring to neighborhood life.

Highway Trust Fund

To further these efforts I again continue to urge Congress to permit a portion of the Highway Trust Fund to be used in a more flexible fashion, thus allowing mass transit capital investments where communities so desire.

I recommend that the Congress authorize the expenditure by State and local governments of $3.65 billion over the next three years from the Highway Trust Fund for urban transportation needs, including capital improvements for bus and rapid rail systems. I also recommend continuing the rural high program at the $1 billion a year level, and providing ample resources to advance the Interstate system as it approaches its 1980 funding completion date. This legislation can meet old needs while at the same time addressing new ones.

Some communities now feel unduly obligated to spend Federal monies on controversial Interstate highway segments in urban areas. I urge the Congress to allow States and localities to transfer such funds to the construction of other Federal-aid highways and mass transit capital improvements. In this way, we can help resolve controversies which have slowed work on a number of Interstate links in urban areas.

It is very important to recognize that this proposal does not represent an arbitrary Federal shift of funds from highways to transit. What it does stress is the right of local governments to choose the best solutions for their urban transportation problems.

This year, in a companion measure to our Federal Highway Bill, I am also proposing that funding for mass transit capital grants be increased by $3 billion, bringing the obligational authority for the mass transit program to $6.1 billion. This provision would maintain a forward looking mass transit program through at least 1977. I am also asking the Congress to amend the Urban Mass Transportation Assistance Act, increasing the Federal share for urban mass transit capital grant assistance programs to 70 percent and thereby achieving parity with Federal aid for urban and rural road building projects.

Rural Development

Community Development is sometimes thought of primarily in terms of urban areas. However, as this Administration has often pointed out—and will continue to emphasize—no element of our national well-being is more important than the health and vitality of our rural communities. Thus, in pursuing a policy of balanced development for our community life, we must always keep the needs of rural America clearly in sight.

Twice in the last two years, I have recommended legislation which would provide new revenues for rural development. Under my latest proposal, loans and guarantees would have been made for projects selected and prepared by the States.

While the 92nd Congress did not enact either of these proposals, it did enact the Rural Development Act of 1972, establishing additional lending authority for rural needs. Like the Administration's proposals, this lending authority provides for insured loans and guaranteed loans which allow maximum participation of the private sector.

Several new programs are proposed to be funded under the Rural Development Act. One is a $200 million loan program to assist communities with a population of less than 50,000 in developing commercial and industrial facilities. A previously existing loan program has been increased by $100 million—to a total of $445 million— and, under the new law, can now be used to construct a wide variety of essential community facilities. In addition, grants and other programs under the act will be funded at a level of $33 million.

This Administration will implement the Rural Development Act in a manner consistent with the revenue sharing concept, allowing major project selections and priority decisions to be made by the State and local governments whenever possible. It is our intent, after fully evaluating the effectiveness of this approach, to seek whatever additional legislation may be needed.

Disaster Assistance

To a community suffering the ravages of a natural disaster, nothing is more important than prompt and effective relief assistance. As our population grows and spreads, each storm, earthquake, drought or freeze affects larger numbers of people.

During the past four years, we have tried to reduce personal injury, deaths, and property damage by emphasizing adequate preventive measures. During the same period, however, I have had to declare 111 major disasters in 39 States and three Territories. This past year alone set a tragic record for major disaster activity, as I had to declare 48 major disasters—43 caused by storms and floodings. There were a number of especially devastating disaster emergencies in this period: the flooding in Buffalo Creek, West Virginia; flash flood in Rapid City, South Dakota; and, of course, Tropical Storm Agnes which rampaged through the eastern United States. Agnes alone caused 118 deaths and some $3 billion in property damage.

Until now, disaster relief efforts have involved a number of different agencies and have been coordinated by the Executive Office of the President. The experience of the past few years has demonstrated that:

• We are not doing nearly enough to prepare in advance for disasters.

• States, local governments and private individuals should assume a larger role in preparing for disasters, and in relieving the damage after they have occurred.

• Responsibility for relief is presently too fragmented among too many authorities.

• At the Federal level, disaster relief should be managed by a single agency.

I intend to make 1973 a turning point in the quality of governmental response to natural disasters.

To achieve this goal, I have already proposed Reorganization Plan Number 1 of 1973, which is now before the Congress. It calls for the delegation of all responsibility for co-ordinating disaster relief to the Secretary of Housing and Urban Development, who is also my Counsellor for Community Development. This transfer of operations would take place at the beginning of the new fiscal year and would be carried out in such a way that the effective relations which now exist with State disaster officials would in no way be harmed, while a new sense of unity and mobility at the Federal level would be fostered.

If the Congress enacts my proposal for a new Department of Community Development, that new department would be responsible for directing all Federal disaster activities, including those of several other agencies which perform disaster roles.

In addition to the improvements I have proposed in Reorganization Plan Number 1, I will shortly submit a new Disaster Assistance Act to the Congress. This new act is designed to improve the delivery of Federal assistance, to provide a more equitable basis for financing individual property losses, and to forge a more balanced partnership for meeting disasters head-on—a partnership not only among governments at all levels but also between governments and private citizens.

Under these proposals, each level of government would accept responsibility for those things it can do best. While the Federal Government would continue to assist with financing, State and local governments would have far more latitude and responsibility in the use of those funds. They would also be encouraged to assert stronger leadership in efforts to minimize the damage of future disasters.

For homeowners, farmers and businessmen who have suffered disaster losses, the Federal Government would continue to provide direct assistance.

I will also recommend to the Congress an expansion of the national flood insurance program to allow participation by more communities in flood-prone areas and to increase the limits of coverage.

Conclusion

As reflected by the proposals set forth here, I believe that we must strike out on broad, new paths of community development in America.

During the last few years, we have taken genuine, measurable strides toward better communities. All of this is good; it is not good enough.

It is clear that we can and should be accomplishing more in the field of community development. There are too many programs that have been tried and found wanting. There are too many programs that strengthen the bureaucracy in Washington but sap the strength of our State and local governments.

People today want to have a real say in the way their communities are run. They want to feel that, once again, they can play a significant role in shaping the kind of world their children will inherit. And they expect their institutions to respond to their needs and aspirations.

That feeling will never flourish if the Federal Government, however vast its financial resources and however good its intentions, tries to direct the pattern of our lives. That feeling

cannot be manufactured in Washington, it must come from within.

But the Federal Government can and should eliminate some of the barriers that have impeded the development of that feeling by returning resources and initiatives to the people and their locally elected leaders. It is in that spirit that I urge the 93rd Congress to give favorable consideration to my proposals for community development.

RICHARD NIXON

The White House
March 8, 1973.

VI. CRIME & LAW ENFORCEMENT

Following is the White House text of President Nixon's March 14 state of the union message on crime and law enforcement:

TO THE CONGRESS OF THE UNITED STATES:

This sixth message to the Congress on the State of the Union, concerns our Federal system of criminal justice. It discusses both the progress we have made in improving that system and the additional steps we must take to consolidate our accomplishments and to further our efforts to achieve a safe, just, and law-abiding society.

In the period from 1960 to 1968 serious crime in the United States increased by 122 percent according to the FBI's Uniform Crime Index. The rate of increase accelerated each year until it reached a peak of 17 percent in 1968.

In 1968 one major public opinion poll showed that Americans considered lawlessness to be the top domestic problem facing the Nation. Another poll showed that four out of five Americans believed that "Law and order has broken down in this country." There was a very real fear that crime and violence were becoming a threat to the stability of our society.

The decade of the 1960s was characterized in many quarters by a growing sense of permissiveness in America—as well intentioned as it was poorly reasoned—in which many people were reluctant to take the steps necessary to control crime. It is no coincidence that within a few years time, America experienced a crime wave that threatened to become uncontrollable.

'All Out Attack'

This Administration came to office in 1969 with the conviction that the integrity of our free institutions demanded stronger and firmer crime control. I promised that the wave of crime would not be the wave of the future. An all-out attack was mounted against crime in the United States.

• The manpower of Federal enforcement and prosecution agencies was increased.

• New legislation was proposed and passed by the Congress to put teeth into Federal enforcement efforts against organized crime, drug trafficking, and crime in the District of Columbia.

• Federal financial aid to State and local criminal justice systems—a forerunner of revenue sharing—was greatly expanded through Administration budgeting and Congressional appropriations, reaching a total of $1.5 billion in the three fiscal years from 1970 through 1972.

These steps marked a clear departure from the philosophy which had come to dominate Federal crime fighting efforts, and which had brought America to record-breaking levels of lawlessness. Slowly, we began to bring America back. The effort has been long, slow, and difficult. In spite of the difficulties, we have made dramatic progress.

In the last four years the Department of Justice has obtained convictions against more than 2500 organized crime figures, including a number of bosses and under-bosses in major cities across the country. The pressure on the underworld is building constantly.

Today, the capital of the United States no longer bears the stigma of also being the Nation's crime capital. As a result of decisive reforms in the criminal justice system the serious crime rate has been cut in half in Washington, D.C. From a peak rate of more than 200 serious crimes per day reached during one month in 1969, the figure has been cut by more than half to 93 per day for the latest month of record in 1973. Felony prosecutions have increased from 2100 to 3800, and the time between arrest and trial for felonies has fallen from ten months to less than two.

Because of the combined efforts of Federal, State, and local agencies, the wave of serious crime in the United States is being brought under control. Latest figures from the FBI's Uniform Crime Index show that serious crime is increasing at the rate of only one percent a year—the lowest recorded rate since 1960. A majority of cities with over 100,000 population shows an actual reduction in crime.

These statistics and these indices suggest that our anti-crime program is on the right track. They suggest that we are taking the right measures. They prove that the only way to attack crime in America is the way crime attacks our people—without pity. Our program is based on this philosophy, and it is working.

Now we intend to maintain the momentum we have developed by taking additional steps to further improve law enforcement and to further protect the people of the United States.

Law Enforcement Special Revenue Sharing

Most crime in America does not fall under Federal jurisdiction. Those who serve in the front lines of the battle against crime are the State and local law enforcement authorities. State and local police are supported in turn by many other elements of the criminal justice system, including prosecuting and defending attorneys, judges, and probation and corrections officers. All these elements need assistance and some need dramatic reform, especially the prison systems.

While the Federal Government does not have full jurisdiction in the field of criminal law enforcement, it does have a broad, constitutional responsibility to insure domestic tranquility. I intend to meet that responsibility.

At my direction, the Law Enforcement Assistance Administration (LEAA) has greatly expanded its efforts to aid in the improvement of State and local criminal justice systems. In the last three years of the previous Administration, Federal grants to State and local law enforcement authorities amounted to only $22 million. In the first three years of my Administration, this same assistance totaled more than $1.5 billion—more than 67 times as much. I consider this money to be an investment in justice and safety on our streets, an investment which has been yielding encouraging dividends.

But the job has not been completed. We must now act further to improve the Federal role in the granting of aid for criminal justice. Such improvement can come with the adoption of Special Revenue Sharing for law enforcement.

I believe the transition to Special Revenue Sharing for law enforcement will be a relatively easy one. Since its inception, the LEAA has given block grants which allow State and local authorities somewhat greater discretion than does the old-fashioned categorical grant system. But States and localities still lack both the flexibility and the clear authority they need in spending Federal monies to meet their law enforcement challenges.

Under my proposed legislation, block grants, technical assistance grants, manpower development grants, and aid for correctional institutions would be combined into one $680 million Special Revenue Sharing fund which would be distributed to States and local governments on a formula basis. This money could be used for improving any area of State and local criminal justice systems.

I have repeatedly expressed my conviction that decisions affecting those at State and local levels should be made to the fullest possible extent at State and local levels. This is the guiding principle behind revenue sharing. Experience has demonstrated the validity of this approach and I urge that it now be fully applied to the field of law enforcement and criminal justice.

Criminal Code Reform Act

The Federal criminal laws of the United States date back to 1790 and are based on statutes then pertinent to effective law enforcement. With the passage of new criminal laws, with the unfolding of new court decisions interpreting those laws, and with the development and growth of our Nation, many of the concepts still reflected in our criminal laws have become inadequate, clumsy, or outmoded.

In 1966, the Congress established the National Commission on Reform of the Federal Criminal Laws to analyze and evaluate the criminal Code. The Commission's final report of January 7, 1971, has been studied and further refined by the Department of Justice, working with the Congress. In some areas this Administration has substantial disagreements with the Commission's recommendations. But we agree fully with the almost universal recognition that modification of the Code is not merely desirable but absolutely imperative.

Accordingly, I will soon submit to the Congress the Criminal Code Reform Act aimed at a comprehensive revision of existing Federal criminal laws. This act will provide a rational, integrated code of Federal criminal law that is workable and responsive to the demands of a modern Nation.

The act is divided into three parts: (1) general provisions and principles, (2) definitions of Federal offenses, and (3) provisions for sentencing.

Part 1 of the Code establishes general provisions and principles regarding such matters as Federal criminal jurisdiction, culpability, complicity, and legal defenses, and contains a number of significant innovations. Foremost among these is a more effective test for establishing Federal criminal jurisdiction. Those circumstances giving rise to Federal jurisdiction are clearly delineated in the proposed new Code and the extent of jurisdiction is clearly defined.

I am emphatically opposed to encroachment by Federal authorities on State sovereignty, by unnecessarily increasing the areas over which the Federal Government asserts jurisdiction. To the contrary, jurisdiction, has been relinquished in those areas where the States have demonstrated no genuine need for assistance in protecting their citizens.

In those instances where jurisdiction is expanded, care has been taken to limit that expansion to areas of compelling Federal interest which are not adequately dealt with under present law. An example of such an instance would be the present law which states that it is a Federal crime to travel in interstate commerce to bribe a witness in a State court proceeding, but it is not a crime to travel in interstate commerce to threaten or intimidate the same witness, though intimidation might even take the form of murdering the witness.

The Federal interest is the same in each case—to assist the State in safeguarding the integrity of its judicial processes. In such a case, an extension of Federal jurisdiction is clearly warranted and is provided for under my proposal.

The rationalization of jurisdictional bases permits greater clarity of drafting, uniformity of interpretation, and the consolidation of numerous statutes presently applying to basically the same conduct.

For example, title 18 of the criminal Code as presently drawn, lists some 70 theft offenses—each written in a different fashion to cover the taking of various kinds of property in different jurisdictional situations. In the proposed new Code, these have been reduced to 5 general sections. Almost 80 forgery, counterfeiting, and related offenses have been replaced by only 3 sections. Over 50 statutes involving perjury and false statements have been reduced to 7 sections. Approximately 70 arson and property destruction offenses have been consolidated into 4 offenses.

Similar changes have been made in the Code's treatment of culpability. Instead of 79 undefined terms or combinations of terms presently found in title 18, the Code uses four clearly defined terms.

Another major innovation reflected in Part One is a codification of general defenses available to a defendant. This change permits clarification of areas in which the law is presently confused and, for the first time, provides uniform Federal standards for defense.

Insanity Defense

The most significant feature of this chapter is a codification of the "insanity" defense. At present the test is determined by the courts and varies across the country. The standard has become so vague in some instances that it has led to unconscionable abuse by defendants.

My proposed new formulation would provide an insanity defense only if the defendant did not know what he was doing. Under this formulation, which has considerable support in psychiatric and legal circles, the only question considered germane in a murder case, for example, would be whether the defendant knew whether he was pulling the trigger of a gun. Questions such as the existence of a mental disease or defect and whether the defendant requires treatment or deserves punishment would be reserved for consideration at the time of sentencing.

Part Two of the Code consolidates the definitions of all Federal felonies, as well as certain related Federal offenses of a less serious character. Offenses and, in appropriate instances, specific defenses, are defined in simple, concise terms, and those existing provisions found to be obsolete or unusable have been eliminated—for example, operating a pirate ship on behalf of a "foreign prince," or detaining a United States carrier pigeon. Loopholes in existing law have been closed—for example, statutes concerning the theft of union funds, and new offenses have been created where necessary, as in the case of leaders of organized crime.

We have not indulged in changes merely for the sake of changes. Where existing law has proved satisfactory and where existing statutory language has received favorable interpretation by the courts, the law and the operative language have been retained. In other areas, such as pornography, there has been a thorough revision to reassert the Federal interest in protecting our citizens.

The reforms set forth in Parts One and Two of the Code would be of little practical consequence without a more realistic approach to those problems which arise in the post-conviction phase of dealing with Federal offenses.

For example, the penalty structure prescribed in the present criminal Code is riddled with inconsistencies and inadequacies. Title 18 alone provides 18 different terms of imprisonment and 14 different fines, often with no discernible relationship between the possible term of imprisonment and the possible levying of a fine.

Part Three of the new Code classifies offenses into 8 categories for purposes of assessing and levying imprisonment and fines. It brings the present structure into line with current judgments as to the seriousness of various offenses and with the best opinions of penologists as the efficacy of specific penalties. In some instances, more stringent sanctions are provided. For example, sentences for arson are increased from 5 to 15 years. In other cases penalties are reduced. For example, impersonating a foreign official carries a three year sentence, as opposed to the 10 year term originally prescribed.

To reduce the possibility of unwarranted disparities in sentencing, the Code establishes criteria for the imposition of sentence. At the same time, it provides for parole supervision after all prison sentences, so that even hardened criminals who serve their full prison terms will receive supervision following their release.

There are certain crimes reflecting such a degree of hostility to society that a decent regard for the common welfare requires that a defendant convicted of those crimes be removed from free society. For this reason my proposed new Code provides mandatory minimum prison terms for trafficking in hard narcotics; it provides mandatory minimum prison terms for persons using dangerous weapons in the execution of a crime; and it provides mandatory minimum prison sentences for those convicted as leaders of organized crime.

The magnitude of the proposed revision of the Federal criminal Code will require careful detailed consideration by the Congress. I have no doubt this will be time-consuming. There are, however, two provisions in the Code which I feel require immediate enactment. I have thus directed that provisions relating to the death penalty and to heroin trafficking also be transmitted as separate bills in order that the Congress may act more rapidly on these two measures.

Death Penalty

The sharp reduction in the application of the death penalty was a component of the more permissive attitude toward crime in the last decade.

I do not contend that the death penalty is a panacea that will cure crime. Crime is the product of a variety of different circumstances—sometimes social, sometimes psychological—but it is committed by human beings and at the point of commission it is the product of that individual's motivation. If the incentive not to commit crime is stronger than the incentive to commit it, then logic suggests that crime will be reduced. It is in part the entirely justified feeling of the prospective criminal that he will not suffer for his deed which, in the present circumstances, helps allow those deeds to take place.

Federal crimes are rarely "crimes of passion." Airplane hi-jacking is not done in a blind rage; it has to be carefully planned. Using incendiary devices and bombs are not crimes of passion, nor is kidnapping; all these must be thought out in advance. At present those who plan these crimes do not have to include in their deliberations the possibility that they will be put to death for their deeds. I believe that in making their plans, they should have to consider the fact that if a death results from their crime, they too may die.

Under those conditions, I am confident that the death penalty can be a valuable deterrent. By making the death penalty available, we will provide Federal enforcement authorities with additional leverage to dissuade those individuals who may commit a Federal crime from taking the lives of others in the course of committing that crime.

Hard experience has taught us that with due regard for the rights of all—including the right to life itself—we must return to a greater concern with protecting those who might otherwise be the innocent victims of violent crime than with protecting those who have committed those crimes. The society which fails to recognize this as a reasonable ordering of its priorities must inevitably find itself, in time, at the mercy of criminals.

America was heading in that direction in the last decade, and I believe that we must not risk returning to it again. Accordingly, I am proposing the re-institution of the death penalty for war-related treason, sabotage, and espionage, and for all specifically enumerated crimes under Federal jurisdiction from which death results.

The Department of Justice has examined the constitutionality of the death penalty in the light of the Supreme Court's recent decision in *Furman v. Georgia*. It is the Department's opinion that *Furman* holds unconstitutional the imposition of the death penalty only insofar as it is applied arbitrarily and capriciously. I believe the best way to accommodate the reservations of the Court is to authorize the automatic imposition of the death penalty where it is warranted.

Under the proposal drafted by the Department of Justice, a hearing would be required after the trial for the purpose of determining the existence or nonexistence of certain rational standards which delineate aggravating factors or mitigating factors.

Among those mitigating factors which would preclude the imposition of a death sentence are the youth of the defendant, his or her mental capacity, or the fact that the crime was committed under duress. Aggravating factors include the creation of a grave risk of danger to the national security, or to the life of another person, or the killing of another person during the commission of one of a circumscribed list of serious offenses, such as treason, kidnapping, or aircraft piracy.

The hearing would be held before the judge who presided at the trial and before either the same jury or, if circumstances require, a jury specially impaneled. Imposition of the death penalty by the judge would be mandatory if the jury returns a special verdict finding the existence of one or more aggravating factors and the absence of any mitigating factor. The death sentence is prohibited if the jury finds the existence of one or more mitigating factors.

Current statutes containing the death penalty would be amended to eliminate the requirement for jury recommendation, thus limiting the imposition of the death penalty to cases in which the legislative guidelines for its imposition clearly require it, and eliminating arbitrary and capricious application of the death penalty which the Supreme Court has condemned in the *Furman* case.

Drug Abuse

No single law enforcement problem has occupied more time, effort and money in the past four years than that of drug abuse and drug addiction. We have regarded drugs as "public enemy number one," destroying the most precious resource we have—our young people—and breeding lawlessness, violence and death.

When this Administration assumed office in 1969, only $82 million was budgeted by the Federal Government for law enforcement, prevention, and rehabilitation in the field of drug abuse.

Today that figure has been increased to $785 million for 1974—nearly 10 times as much. Narcotics production has been disrupted, more traffickers and distributors have been put out of business, and addicts and abusers have been treated and started on the road to rehabilitation.

Since last June, the supply of heroin on the East Coast has been substantially reduced. The scarcity of heroin in our big Eastern cities has driven up the price of an average "fix" from $4.31 to $9.88, encouraging more addicts to seek medical treatment. At the same time the heroin content of that fix has dropped from 6.5 to 3.7 percent.

Meanwhile, through my Cabinet Committee on International Narcotics Control, action plans are underway to help 59 foreign countries develop and carry out their own national control programs. These efforts, linked with those of the Bureau of Customs and the Bureau of Narcotics and Dangerous Drugs, have produced heartening results.

Our worldwide narcotics seizures almost tripled in 1972 over 1971. Seizures by our anti-narcotics allies abroad are at an all-time high.

In January, 1972, the French seized a half-ton of heroin on a shrimp boat headed for this country. Argentine, Brazilian and Venezuelan agents seized 285 pounds of heroin in three raids in 1972, and with twenty arrests crippled the existing French-Latin American connection. The ringleader was extradited to the U.S. by Paraguay and has just begun to serve a 20-year sentence in Federal prison.

Thailand's Special Narcotics Organization recently seized a total of almost eleven tons of opium along the Burmese border, as well as a half-ton of morphine and heroin. Recently Iran scored the largest opium seizure on record—over 12 tons taken from smugglers along the Afghanistan border. Turkey, as a result of a courageous decision by the government under Prime Minister Erim in 1971, has prohibited all cultivation of opium within her borders.

These results are all the more gratifying in light of the fact that heroin is wholly a foreign import to the United States. We do not grow opium here; we do not produce heroin here; yet we have the largest addict population in the world. Clearly we will end our problem faster with continued foreign assistance.

Our domestic accomplishments are keeping pace with international efforts and are producing equally encouraging results. Domestic drug seizures, including seizures of marijuana and hashish, almost doubled in 1972 over 1971. Arrests have risen by more than one-third and convictions have doubled.

In January of 1972, a new agency, the Office of Drug Abuse Law Enforcement (DALE), was created within the Department of Justice. Task forces composed of investigators, attorneys, and special prosecuting attorneys have been assigned to more than forty cities with heroin problems. DALE now arrests pushers at the rate of 550 a month and has obtained 750 convictions.

At my direction, the Internal Revenue Service (IRS) established a special unit to make intensive tax investigations of suspected domestic traffickers. To date, IRS has collected $18 million in currency and property, assessed tax penalties of more than $100 million, and obtained 25 convictions. This effort can be particularly effective in reaching the high level traffickers and financiers who never actually touch the heroin, but who profit from the misery of those who do.

A Balanced Approach

The problem of drug abuse in America is not a law enforcement problem alone. Under my Administration, the Federal Government has pursued a balanced, comprehensive approach to ending this problem. Increased law enforcement efforts have been coupled with expanded treatment programs.

The Special Action Office for Drug Abuse Prevention was created to aid in preventing drug abuse before it begins and in rehabilitating those who have fallen victim to it.

In each year of my Administration, more Federal dollars have been spent on treatment, rehabilitation, prevention, and research in the field of drug abuse than has been budgeted for law enforcement in the drug field.

The Special Action Office for Drug Abuse Prevention is currently developing a special program of Treatment Alternatives to Street Crime (TASC) to break the vicious cycle of addiction, crime, arrest, bail, and more crime. Under the TASC program, arrestees who are scientifically identified as heroin-dependent may be assigned by judges to treatment programs as a condition for release on bail, or as a possible alternative to prosecution.

Federally funded treatment programs have increased from sixteen in January, 1969, to a current level of 400. In the last fiscal year, the Special Action Office created more facilities for treating drug addiction than the Federal Government had provided in all the previous fifty years.

Today, federally funded treatment is available for 100,000 addicts a year. We also have sufficient funds available to expand our facilities to treat 250,000 addicts if required.

Nationwide, in the last two years, the rate of new addiction to heroin registered its first decline since 1964. This is a particularly important trend because it is estimated that one addict "infects" six of his peers. The trend in narcotic-related deaths is also clearly on its way down. My advisers report to me that virtually complete statistics show such fatalities declined approximately 6 percent in 1972 compared to 1971.

In spite of these accomplishments, however, it is still estimated that one-third to one-half of all individuals arrested for street crimes continue to be narcotics abusers and addicts. What this suggests is that in the area of enforcement we are still only holding our own, and we must increase the tools available to do the job.

The work of the Special Action Office for Drug Abuse Prevention has aided in smoothing the large expansion of Federal effort in the area of drug treatment and prevention. Now we must move to improve Federal action in the area of law enforcement.

Drug abuse treatment specialists have continuously emphasized in their discussions with me the need for strong, effective law enforcement to restrict the availability of drugs and to punish the pusher.

Heroin Pushers

One area where I am convinced of the need for immediate action is that of jailing heroin pushers. Under the Bail Reform Act of 1966, a Federal judge is precluded from considering the danger to the community when setting bail for suspects arrested for selling heroin. The effect of this restriction is that many accused pushers are immediately released on bail and are thus given the opportunity to go out and create more misery, generate more violence, and commit more crimes while they are waiting to be tried for these same activities.

In a study of 422 accused violators, the Bureau of Narcotics and Dangerous Drugs found that 71 percent were freed on bail for a period ranging from three months to more than one year between the time of arrest and the time of trial. Nearly 40 percent of the total were free for a period ranging from one-half year to more than one year. As for the major cases, those involving pushers accused of trafficking in large quantities of heroin, it was found that one-fourth were free for over three months to one-half year; one-fourth were free for one-half year to one year; and 16 percent remained free for over one year prior to their trial.

In most cases these individuals had criminal records. One-fifth had been convicted of a previous drug charge and a total of 64 percent had a record of prior felony arrests. The cost of obtaining such a pre-trial release in most cases was minimal; 19 percent of the total sample were freed on personal recognizance and only 23 percent were required to post bonds of $10,000 or more.

Sentencing practices have also been found to be inadequate in many cases. In a study of 955 narcotics drug violators who were arrested by the Bureau of Narcotics and Dangerous Drugs and convicted in the courts, a total of 27 percent received sentences other than imprisonment. Most of these individuals were placed on probation.

This situation is intolerable. I am therefore calling upon the Congress to promptly enact a new Heroin Trafficking Act. The first part of my proposed legislation would increase the sentences for heroin and morphine offenses.

For a first offense of trafficking in less than four ounces of a mixture or substance containing heroin or morphine, it provides a mandatory sentence of not less than five years nor more than fifteen years. For a first offense of trafficking in four or more ounces, it provides a mandatory sentence of not less than ten years or for life.

For those with a prior felony narcotic conviction who are convicted of trafficking in less than four ounces, my proposed legislation provides a mandatory prison term of ten years to life imprisonment. For second offenders who are convicted of trafficking in more than four ounces, I am proposing a mandatory sentence of life imprisonment without parole.

While four ounces of a heroin mixture may seem a very small amount to use as the criterion for major penalties, that amount is actually worth $12-15,000 and would supply about 180 addicts for a day. Anyone selling four or more ounces cannot be considered a small time operator.

For those who are convicted of possessing large amounts of heroin but cannot be convicted of trafficking, I am proposing a series of lesser penalties.

To be sure that judges actually apply these tough sentences, my legislation would provide that the mandatory minimum sentences cannot be suspended, nor probation granted.

The second portion of my proposed legislation would deny pre-trial release to those charged with trafficking in heroin or morphine unless the judicial officer finds that release will not pose a danger to the persons or property of others. It would also prohibit the release of anyone convicted of one of the above felonies who is awaiting sentencing or the results of an appeal.

These are very harsh measures, to be applied within very rigid guidelines and providing only a minimum of sentencing discretion to judges. But circumstances warrant such provisions. All the evidence shows that we are now doing a more effective job in the areas of enforcement and rehabilitation. In spite of this progress, however, we find an intolerably high level of street crime being committed by addicts. Part of the reason, I believe, lies in the court system which takes over after drug pushers have been apprehended. The courts are frequently little more than an escape hatch for those who are responsible for the menace of drugs.

Sometimes it seems that as fast as we bail water out of the boat through law enforcement and rehabilitation, it runs right back in through the holes in our judicial system. I intend to plug those holes. Until then, all the money we spend, all the enforcement we provide, and all the rehabilitation services we offer are not going to solve the drug problem in America.

Finally, I want to emphasize my continued opposition to legalizing the possession, sale or use of marijuana. There is no question about whether marijuana is dangerous, the only question is how dangerous. While the matter is still in dispute, the only responsible government approach is to prevent marijuana from being legalized. I intend, as I have said before, to do just that.

Conclusion

This Nation has fought hard and sacrificed greatly to achieve a lasting peace in the world. Peace in the world, however, must be accompanied by peace in our own land. Of what ultimate value is it to end the threat to our national safety in the world if our citizens face a constant threat to the personal safety in our own streets?

The American people are a law-abiding people. They have faith in the law. It is now time for Government to justify that faith by insuring that the law works, that our system of criminal justice works, and that "domestic tranquility" is preserved.

I believe we have gone a long way toward erasing the apprehensions of the last decade. But we must go further if we are to achieve that peace at home which will truly complement peace abroad.

In the coming months I will propose legislation aimed at curbing the manufacture and sale of cheap handguns commonly known as "Saturday night specials," I will propose reforms of the Federal criminal system to provide speedier and more rational criminal trial procedures, and I will continue to press for innovation and improvement in our correctional systems.

The Federal Government cannot do everything. Indeed, it is prohibited from doing everything. But it can do a great deal. The crime legislation I will submit to the Congress can give us the tools we need to do all that we can do. This is sound, responsible legislation. I am confident that the approval of the American people for measures of the sort that I have suggested will be reflected in the actions of the Congress.

RICHARD NIXON

The White House,
March 14, 1973.

PHASE III ECONOMIC CONTROLS

Following is the text, as made available by the White House Jan. 11, of President Nixon's message to Congress on Phase III controls.

TO THE CONGRESS OF THE UNITED STATES:

During 1969, the annual rate of inflation in the United States was about six percent. During my first term in office, that rate has been cut nearly in half and today the United States has the lowest rate of inflation of an industrial country in the free world.

In the last year and a half, this decline in inflation has been accompanied by a rapid economic expansion. Civilian employment rose more rapidly during the past year than ever before in our history and unemployment substantially declined. We now have one of the highest economic growth rates in the developed world.

In short, 1972 was a very good year for the American economy. I expect 1973 and 1974 to be even better. They can, in fact, be the best years our economy has ever experienced—provided we have the will and wisdom, in both the public and private sectors, to follow appropriate economic policies.

For the past several weeks, members of my administration have been reviewing our economic policies in an effort to keep them up to date. I deeply appreciate the generous advice and excellent suggestions we have received in our consultations with the Congress.

We are also grateful for the enormous assistance we have received from hundreds of leaders representing business, labor, farm and consumer groups, and the general public. These discussions have been extremely helpful to us in reaching several central conclusions about out economic future.

One major point which emerges as we look both at the record of the past and the prospects for the future is the central role of our Federal monetary and fiscal policies. We cannot keep inflation in check unless we keep Government spending in check. This is why I have insisted that our spending for fiscal year 1973 not exceed $250 billion and that our proposed budget for fiscal year 1974 not exceed the revenues which the existing tax system would produce at full employment. I hope and expect that the Congress will receive this budget with a similar sense of fiscal discipline. The stability of our prices depends on the restraint of the Congress.

As we move into a new year, and into a new term for this Administration, we are also moving to a new phase of our economic stabilization program. I believe the system of controls which has been in effect since 1971 has helped considerably in improving the health of our economy. I am today submitting to the Congress legislation which would extend for another year—until April 30 of 1974—the basic legislation on which that system is based, the Economic Stabilization Act.

But even while we recognize the need for continued Government restraints on prices and wages, we also look to the day when we can enjoy the advantages of price stability without the disadvantages of such restraints. I believe we can prepare for that day, and hasten its coming, by modifying the present system so that it relies to a greater extent on the voluntary cooperation of the private sector in making reasonable price and wage decisions.

Under Phase III, prior approval by the Federal Government will not be required for changes in wages and prices, except in special problem areas. The Federal Government, with the advice of management and labor, will develop standards to guide private conduct which will be self-administering. This means that businesses and workers will be able to determine for themselves the conduct that conforms to the standards. Initially and generally we shall rely upon the voluntary cooperation of the private sector for reasonable observance of the standards. However, the Federal Government will retain the power—and the responsibility—to step in and stop action that would be inconsistent with our anti-inflation goals.

I have established as the overall goal of this program a further reduction in the inflation rate to 2½ percent or less by the end of 1973.

Under this program, much of the Federal machinery which worked so well during Phase I and Phase II can be eliminated, including the Price Commission, the Pay Board, the Committee on the Health Services Industry, the Committee on State and Local Government Cooperation, and the Rent Advisory Board. Those who served so ably as members of these panels and their

staffs—especially Judge George H. Boldt, Chairman of the Pay Board, and C. Jackson Grayson, Jr., Chairman of the Price Commission—have my deep appreciation and that of their countrymen for their devoted and effective contributions.

This new program will be administered by the Cost of Living Council. The Council's new Director will be John T. Dunlop. Dr. Dunlop succeeds Donald Rumsfeld who leaves this post with the Nation's deepest gratitude for a job well done.

Under our new program, special efforts will be made to combat inflation in areas where rising prices have been particularly troublesome, especially in fighting rising food prices. Our anti-inflation program will not be fully successful until its impact is felt at the local supermarket or corner grocery store.

I am therefore directing that our current mandatory wage and price control system be continued with special vigor for firms involved in food processing and food retailing. I am also establishing a new committee to review Government policies which affect food prices and a non-Government advisory group to examine other ways of achieving price stability in food markets. I will ask this advisory group to give special attention to new ways of cutting costs and improving productivity at all points along the food production, processing and distribution chain. In addition, the Department of Agriculture and the Cost of Living Council yesterday and today announced a number of important steps to hold down food prices in the best possible way—by increasing food supply. I believe all these efforts will enable us to check effectively the rising cost of food without damaging the growing prosperity of American farmers. Other special actions which will be taken to fight inflation include continuing the present mandatory controls over the health and construction industries and continuing the present successful program for interest and dividends.

The new policies I am announcing today can mean even greater price stability with less restrictive bureaucracy. Their success, however, will now depend on a firm spirit of self-restraint both within the Federal Government and among the general public. If the Congress will receive our new budget with a high sense of fiscal responsibility and if the public will continue to demonstrate the same spirit of voluntary cooperation which was so important during Phase I and Phase II, then we can bring the inflation rate below 2½ percent and usher in an unprecedented era of full and stable prosperity.

RICHARD NIXON

EXECUTIVE OFFICE REORGANIZATION

Following is the text, as made available by the White House, of the President's reorganization plan of Jan. 26, 1973, concerning the abolition of the Office of Emergency Preparedness, Office of Science and Technology and the National Aeronautics and Space Council:

TO THE CONGRESS OF THE UNITED STATES:

On Jan. 5 I announced a three-part program to streamline the executive branch of the federal government. By concentrating less responsibility in the President's immediate staff and more in the hands of the departments and agencies, this program should significantly improve the services of the government. I believe these reforms have become so urgently necessary that I intend, with the cooperation of the Congress, to pursue them with all of the resources of my office during the coming year.

The first part of this program is a renewed drive to achieve passage of my legislative proposals to overhaul the cabinet departments. Secondly, I have appointed three cabinet secretaries as counsellors to the President with coordinating responsibilities in the broad areas of human resources, natural resources, and community development, and five assistants to the President with special responsibilities in the areas of domestic affairs, economic affairs, foreign affairs, executive management, and operations of the White House.

The third part of this program is a sharp reduction in the overall size of the Executive Office of the President and a reorientation of that office back to its original mission as a staff for top-level policy formation and monitoring of policy execution in broad functional areas. The Executive Office of the President should no longer be encumbered with the task of managing or administering programs which can be run more effectively by the departments and agencies.

I have therefore concluded that a number of specialized operational and program functions should be shifted out of the Executive Office into the line departments and agencies of the government. Reorganization plan No. 1 of 1973, transmitted herewith, would effect such changes with respect to emergency preparedness functions and scientific and technological affairs.

When the National Science Foundation was established by an act of the Congress in 1950, its statutory responsibilities included evaluation of the government's scientific research programs and development of basic science policy. In the late 1950's however, with the effectiveness of the U.S. science effort under serious scrutiny as a result of Sputnik, the post of Science Adviser to the President was established.

The White House became increasingly involved in the evaluation and coordination of research and development programs and in science policy matters, and that involvement was institutionalized in 1962 when a reorganization plan established the Office of Science and Technology within the Executive Office of the President, through transfer of authorities formerly vested in the National Science Foundation.

Science Office

With advice and assistance from OST during the past decade, the scientific and technological capability of the government has been markedly strengthened. This administration is firmly committed to a sustained, broad-based national effort in science and technology, as I made plain last year in the first special message on the subject ever sent by a President to the Congress.

The research and development capability of the various executive departments and agencies, civilian as well as defense, has been upgraded. The National Science Foundation has broadened from its earlier concentration on basic research support to take on a significant role in applied research as well. It has matured in its ability to play a coordinating and evaluative role within the government and between the public and private sectors.

I have therefore concluded that it is timely and appropriate to transfer to the Director of the National Science Foundation all functions presently vested in the Office of Science and Technology, and to abolish that office. Reorganization plan No. 1 would effect these changes.

The multi-disciplinary staff resources of the foundation will provide analytic capabilities for performance of the transferred functions. In addition, the director of the foundation will be able to draw on expertise from all of the federal agencies, as well as from outside the government, for assistance in carrying out his new responsibilities.

It is also my intention, after the transfer of responsibilities is effected, to ask Dr. H. Guyford Stever, the current director of the foundation, to take on the additional post of science adviser. In this capacity, he would advise and assist the White House, Office of Management and Budget, Domestic Council, and other entitites within the Executive Office of the President on matters where scientific and technological expertise is called for, and would act as the President's representative in selected cooperative programs in international scientific affairs, including chairing such hoint bodies as the U.S.-U.S.S.R. Joint Commission on Scientific and Technical Cooperation.

In the case of national security, the Department of Defense has strong capabilities for assessing weapons needs and for undertaking new weapons development, and the President will continue to draw primarily on this source for advice regarding military technology. The President in special situations also may seek independent studies or assessments concerning military technology from within or outside the federal establishment using the machinery of the National Security Council for this purpose, as well as the science adviser when appropriate.

Space Council

In one special area of technology—space and aeronautics—a coordinating council has existed within the Executive Office of the President since 1958. This body, the National Aeronautics and Space Council, met a major need during the evolution of our nation's space program. Vice President Agnew has served with distinction as its chairman for the past four years. At my request, beginning in 1969, the Vice President also chaired a special space task group charged with developing strategy alternatives for a balanced U.S. space program in the coming years.

As a result of this work, basic policy issues in the United States space effort have been resolved, and the necessary interagency relationships have been established. I have therefore concluded, with the Vice President's concurrence, that the council can be discontinued. Needed policy coordination can now be achieved through the resources of the executive departments and agencies, such as the National Aeronautics and Space Administration, augmented by some of the former council staff. Accordingly, my reorganization plan proposes the abolition of the National Aeronautics and Space Council.

Emergency Preparedness Office

The organization within the Executive Office of the President which has been known in recent years as the Office of Emergency Preparedness dates back, through its numerous predecessor agencies, more than 20 years. It has performed valuable functions in developing plans for emergency preparedness, in administering federal disaster relief, and in overseeing and assisting the agencies in this area.

OEP's work as a coordinating and supervisory authority in this field has in fact been so effective—particularly under the leadership of Gen. George A. Lincoln, its director for the past four years, who retired earlier this month after an exceptional military and public service career—that the line departments and agencies which in the past have shared in the performance the various preparedness functions now possess the capability to assume full responsibility for those functions. In the interest of efficiency and economy, we can now further streamline the Executive Office of the President by formally relocating those responsibilities and closing the Office of Emergency Preparedness.

I propose to accomplish this reform in two steps. First, reorganization plan No. 1 would transfer to the President all functions previously vested by law in the office or its director, except the director's role as a member of the National Security Council, which would be abolished; and it would abolish the Office of Emergency Preparedness.

The functions to be transferred to the President from OEP are largely incidental to emergency authorities already vested in him. They include functions under the Disaster Relief Act of 1970; the function of determining whether a major disaster has occurred within the meaning of (1) Section 7 of the Act of Sept. 30, 1950, as amended, 20 U.S.C. 241-1, or (2) Section 762 (a) of the Higher Education Act of 1965, as added by Section 161 (a) of the Education Amendments of 1972, Public Law 92-318, 86 Stat. 288 at 299 (relating to the furnishing by the Commissioner of Education of disaster relief assistance for educational purposes); and functions under Section 232 of the Trade Expansion Act of 1962, as amended (19 U.S.C. 1862), with respect to the conduct of investigations to determine the effects on national security of the importation of certain articles.

The Civil Defense Advisory Council within OEP would also be abolished by this plan, as changes in domestic and international conditions since its establishment in 1950 have now obviated the need for a standing council of this type. Should advice of the kind the council has provided be required again in the future, state and local officials and experts in the field can be consulted on an ad hoc basis.

Secondly, as soon as the plan became effective, I would delegate OEP's former functions as follows:

• All OEP responsibilities having to do with preparedness for and relief of civil emergencies and disasters would be transferred to the Department of Housing and Urban Development. This would provide greater field capabilities for coordination of federal disaster assistance with that provided by states and local communities, and would be in keeping with the objective of creating a broad, new Department of Community Development.

• OEP's responsibilities for measures to ensure the continuity of civil government operations in the event of major military attack would be reassigned to the General Services Administration, as would responsibility for resource mobilization including the management of national security stockpiles, with policy guidance in both cases to be provided by the National Security Council, and with economic considerations relating to changes in stockpile levels to be coordinated by the Council on Economic Policy.

• Investigations of imports which might threaten the national security—assigned to OEP by Section 232 of the Trade Expansion Act of 1962—would be reassigned to the Treasury Department, whose other trade studies give it a ready-made capability in this field; the National Security Council would maintain its supervisory role over strategic imports.

Those disaster relief authorities which have been reserved to the President in the past, such as the authority to declare major disasters, will continue to be exercised by him under rapid interagency coordination, the federal response will be coordinated by the Executive Office of the President under the general supervision of the assistant to the President in charge of executive management.

The Oil Policy Committee will continue to function as in the past, unaffected by this reorganization, except that I will designate the Deputy Secretary of the Treasury as chairman in place of the Director of OEP. The Committee will operate under the general supervision of the Assistant to the President in charge of economic affairs.

Declarations

After investigation, I have found that each action included in the accompanying reorganization plan is necessary to accomplish one or more of the purposes set forth in Section 901 (a) of title 5 of the United States Code. In particular, the plan is responsive to the intention of the Congress as expressed in Section 901 (a) (1), "to promote better execution of the laws, more effective management of the executive branch and of its agencies and functions, and expeditious administration of the public business;" and in Section 901 (a) (3), "to increase the efficiency of the operations of the government to the fullest extent practicable;" and in Section 901 (a) (5), "to reduce the number of agencies by consolidating those having similar functions under a single head, and to abolish such agencies or functions as may not be necessary for the efficient conduct of the government."

While it is not practicable to specify all of the expenditure reductions and other economies which will result from the actions proposed, personnel and budget savings from abolition of the National Aeronautics and Space Council and the Office of Science and Technology alone will exceed $2-million annually, and additional savings should result from a reduction of executive pay schedule positions now associated with other transferred and delegated functions.

The plan has as its one logically consistent subject matter the streamlining of the Executive Office of the President and

the disposition of major responsibilities currently conducted in the Executive Office of the President, which can better be performed elsewhere or abolished.

The functions which would be abolished by this plan, and the statutory authorities for each, are:

(1) the functions of the Director of the Office of Emergency Preparedness with respect to being a member of the National Security Council (Sec. 101, National Security Act of 1947, as amended, 50 U.S.C. 402; and Sec. 4, Reorganization Plan No. 1 of 1958);

(2) the functions of the Civil Defense Advisory Council (Sec. 102 (a) Federal Civil Defense Act of 1950; 50 U.S.C. App. 2272 (a)); and

(3) the functions of the National Aeronautics and Space Council (Sec. 201, National Aeronautics and Space Act of 1958; 42 U.S.C. 2471).

The proposed reorganization is a necessary part of the restructuring of the Executive Office of the President. It would provide through the Director of the National Science Foundation a strong focus for Federal efforts to encourage the development and application of science and technology to meet national needs. It would mean better preparedness for and swifter response to civil emergencies, and more reliable precautions against threats to the national security. The leaner and less diffuse Presidential staff structure which would result would enhance the President's ability to do his job and would advance the interests of the Congress as well.

I am confident that this reorganization plan would significantly increase the overall efficiency and effectiveness of the federal government. I urge the Congress to allow it to become effective.

RICHARD NIXON

The White House,
Jan. 26, 1973

Reorganization Plan No. 1 of 1973

Prepared by the President and transmitted to the Senate and the House of Representatives in Congress assembled, Jan. 26, 1973, pursuant to the provisions of Chapter 9 of Title 5 of the United States Code.

Section 1. Transfer of functions to the President. Except as provided in section 3(a)(2) of this reorganization plan, there are hereby transferred to the President of the United States all functions vested by law in the Office of Emergency Preparedness or the Director of the Office of Emergency Preparedness after the effective date of Reorganization Plan No. 1 of 1958.

Section 2. Transfer of functions to the Director, National Science Foundation. There are hereby transferred to the Director of the National Science Foundation all functions vested by law in the Office of Science and Technology or the Director or Deputy Director of the Office of Science and Technology.

Section 3. Abolitions. (a) The following are hereby abolished:

(1) The Office of Emergency Preparedness including the offices of Director, Deputy Director, and all offices of Assistant Director, and Regional Director of the Office of Emergency Preparedness provided for by sections 2 and 3 of reorganization Plan No. 1 of 1958 (5 U.S.C., App).

(2) The functions of the Director of the Office of Emergency Preparedness with respect to being a member of the National Security Council.

(3) The Civil Defense Advisory Council, created by section 102(a) of the Federal Civil Defense Act of 1950 (50 U.S.C. App. 2272(a)), together with its functions.

(4) The National Aeronautics and Space Council, created by section 201 of the National Aeronautics and Space Act of 1958 (42 U.S.C. 2471), including the office of Executive Secretary of the Council, together with its functions.

(5) The Office of Science and Technology, including the offices of Director and Deputy Director, provided for by sec-

tions 1 and 2 of reorganization plan No. 2 of 1962 (5 U.S.C., App).

(b) The Director of the Office of Management and Budget shall make such provisions as he shall deem necessary respecting the winding up of any outstanding affairs of the agencies abolished by the provisions of this section.

Section 4. Incidental transfers. (a) So much of the personnel, property, records, and unexpended balances of appropriations, allocations, and other funds employed, used, held, available, or to be made available in connection with the functions transferred by sections 1 and 2 of this reorganization plan as the Director of the Office of Management and Budget shall determine shall be transferred at such time or times as he shall direct for use in connection with the functions transferred.

(b) Such further measures and dispositions as the Director of the Office of Management and Budget shall deem to be necessary in order to effectuate the transfers referred to in subsection (a) of this section shall be carried out in such manner as he shall direct and by such agencies as he shall designate.

Section 5. Effective Date. The provisions of this reorganization plan shall take effect as provided by section 906 (a) of title 5 of the United States Code, or on July 1, 1973, whichever is later.   √

REHABILITATION ACT VETO

Following is the White House text of the President's veto message on S 7, the Rehabilitation Act of 1972:

TO THE SENATE OF THE UNITED STATES:

I am returning today without my approval S. 7, the "Rehabilitation Act of 1972." This bill is one of several now before the Congress which mask bad legislation beneath alluring labels.

Their supporters would have the American public believe that each of these bills would further an important social cause, but they neglect to warn the public that the cumulative effect of a Congressional spending spree would be a massive assault upon the pocketbooks of millions of men and women in this country. They also fail to warn us that simply throwing money at problems does not solve anything; it only creates poor legislation which frequently misses the target.

As President, it is my duty to sound the warning—and to defend the public interest by vetoing fiscally irresponsible, badly constructed bills that come to my desk from Capitol Hill. S. 7 is such a bill.

Over the past nineteen months, we have made significant headway toward a goal that has eluded America for nearly two decades: full prosperity without war. But all of our economic progress—and all of our hopes—will be washed away if we open the floodgates on the Federal budget.

S. 7, if enacted, would result in an increase in Federal outlays of some $1 billion above my budget recommendations for fiscal years 1973-1975.

To some Members of the Congress, a $1 billion increase in Federal spending may seem only a small crack in the dam. But there are more than a dozen other bills already before the Congress which also carry extravagant price tags. And more seem likely to follow during the remainder of the year.

If we allow the big spenders to sweep aside budgetary restraints, we can expect an increase of more than $50 billion in Federal spending before the end of fiscal year 1975. This would force upon us the unacceptable choice of either raising taxes substantially—perhaps as much as 15 percent in personal income taxes—or inviting a hefty boost in consumer prices and interest rates.

The American people have repeatedly shown that they want to hold a firm line on both prices and taxes. I stand solidly with them. At a time when the world is watching to see if we can demonstrate our willingness to hold down inflation at home while we seek monetary stability abroad, this resolve is more important than ever. I shall therefore veto those big-spending bills which would jeopardize our economic hopes for the future.

I would emphasize that even if S. 7 were not fatally flawed by its large expense, I would have serious reservations about signing it, for it also contains a number of substantive defects. Among them:

● It would further divert the Vocational Rehabilitation program from its original purposes by requiring that it provide new medical services. For instance, it would set up a new program for end-stage kidney disease—a worthy concern in itself; but one that can be approached more effectively within the Medicare program, as existing legislation already provides.

Vocational Rehabilitation has worked well for over half a century by focusing on a single objective: training people for meaningful jobs. We should not dilute the resources of that program or distort its objective by turning it toward welfare or medical goals.

● Secondly, S. 7 would create a hodge-podge of seven new categorical grant programs, many of which would overlap and duplicate existing services. Coordination of services would become considerably more difficult and would place the Federal Government back on the path to wasteful, overlapping program disasters.

● By rigidly cementing into law the organizational structures of the Rehabilitation Services Administration and by confusing the lines of management responsibility, S. 7 would also prevent the Secretary of Health, Education and Welfare from carrying forward his efforts to manage vocational rehabilitation services more effectively.

● Finally, by promising increased Federal spending for this program in such a large amount, S. 7 would cruelly raise the hopes of the handicapped in a way that we could never responsibly hope to fulfill.

Through past increases in funding and by our efforts to find more effective means of providing services, this Administration has demonstrated its strong commitment to vocational rehabilitation. Funding for the Vocational Rehabilitation program will reach $650 million under my budget for the coming fiscal year, an increase of 75 percent over the level of support when I took office.

Two other sources of funding for rehabilitation of the handicapped, the Disability Insurance Trust Fund and the new Supplemental Security Income program, will provide another $100 million. Altogether during the coming fiscal year, the Vocational Rehabilitation program should provide services for about 1.2 million people—an increase of more than 50 percent over the figure of four years ago.

This is a good record and one that provides promise for the future. I shall thus look forward to working with the Congress in developing a more responsible bill that would extend and strengthen the Vocational Rehabilitation program.

This Administration has submitted recommendations to both the 92nd and 93rd Congresses which would accomplish these purposes. The 92nd Congress passed a bill which contained some of my recommendations but was so inordinately expensive that I felt compelled to veto it. In returning S. 7 without my approval, I ask the 93rd Congress now to turn its attention to the substitute recently offered by Rep. Earl Landgrebe.

My decision to disapprove S. 7 should be seen by the Congress as more than just an isolated rejection of a single piece of unwise legislation. It is part of my overall commitment to hold down taxes and prices. I remind the Congress of that determination, I ask the Congress to consider carefully the implications of spend-thrift actions, and I urge the Congress to be more reasonable and responsible in the legislation its passes in the future. √

EXECUTIVE REORGANIZATION

Following is the White House text of the President's reorganization plan and message of March 28, 1973, on federal drug law enforcement activities.

TO THE CONGRESS OF THE UNITED STATES:

Drug abuse is one of the most vicious and corrosive forces attacking the foundations of American society today. It is a major cause of crime and a merciless destroyer of human lives. We must fight it with all of the resources at our command.

This Administration has declared all-out, global war on the drug menace. As I reported to the Congress earlier this month in my State of the Union message, there is evidence of significant progress on a number of fronts in that war.

Both the rate of new addiction to heroin and the number of narcotic-related deaths showed an encouraging downturn last year. More drug addicts and abusers are in treatment and rehabilitation programs than ever before.

Progress in pinching off the supply of illicit drugs was evident in last year's stepped-up volume of drug seizures worldwide—which more than doubled in 1972 over the 1971 level.

Arrests of traffickers have risen by more than one-third since 1971. Prompt Congressional action on my proposal for mandatory minimum sentences for pushers of hard drugs will help ensure that convictions stemming from such arrests lead to actual imprisonment of the guilty.

Notwithstanding these gains, much more must be done. The resilience of the international drug trade remains grimly impressive—current estimates suggest that we still intercept only a small fraction of all the heroin and cocaine entering this country. Local police still find that more than one of every three suspects arrested for street crimes are narcotics abusers or addicts. And the total number of Americans addicted to narcotics, suffering terribly themselves and inflicting their suffering on countless others, still stands in the hundreds of thousands.

A Unified Command

Seeking ways to intensify our counteroffensive against this menace, I am asking the Congress today to join with this Administration in strengthening and streamlining the Federal drug law enforcement effort.

Funding for this effort has increased sevenfold during the past five years, from $36 million in fiscal year 1969 to $257 million in fiscal year 1974—more money is not the most pressing enforcement need at present. Nor is there a primary need for more manpower working on the problem, over 2100 new agents having already been added to the Federal drug enforcement agencies under this Administration, an increase of more than 250 percent over the 1969 level.

The enforcement work could benefit significantly, however, from consolidation of our anti-drug forces under a single unified command. Right now the Federal Government is fighting the war on drug abuse under a distinct handicap, for its efforts are those of a loosely confederated alliance facing a resourceful, elusive, worldwide enemy. Admiral Mahan, the master naval strategist, described this handicap precisely when he wrote that "Granting the same aggregate of force, it is never as great in two hands as in one, because it is not perfectly concentrated."

More specifically, the drug law enforcement activities of the United States now are not merely in two hands but in half a dozen. Within the Department of Justice, with no overall direction below the level of the Attorney General, these fragmented forces include the Bureau of Narcotics and Dangerous Drugs, the Office for Drug Abuse Law Enforcement, the Office of National Narcotics Intelligence, and certain activities of the Law Enforcement Assistance Administration. The Treasury Department is also heavily engaged in enforcement work through the Bureau of Customs.

This aggregation of Federal activities has grown up rapidly over the past few years in response to the urgent need for stronger anti-drug measures. It has enabled us to make a very encouraging beginning in the accelerated drug enforcement drive of this Administration.

But it also has serious operational and organizational shortcomings. Certainly the cold-blooded underworld networks that funnel narcotics from suppliers all over the world into the veins of American drug victims are no respecters of the bureaucratic dividing lines that now complicate our anti-drug efforts. On the contrary, these modern-day slave traders can derive only advantage from the limitations of the existing organizational patchwork. Experience has now given us a good basis for correcting those limitations, and it is time to do so.

I therefore propose creation of a single, comprehensive Federal agency within the Department of Justice to lead the war against illicit drug traffic.

New Agency

Reorganization Plan No. 2 of 1973, which I am transmitting to the Congress with this message, would establish such an agency, to be called the Drug Enforcement Administration. It would be headed by an Administrator reporting directly to the Attorney General.

The Drug Enforcement Administration would carry out the following anti-drug functions, and would absorb the associated manpower and budgets:

• All functions of the Bureau of Narcotics and Dangerous Drugs (which would be abolished as a separate entity by the reorganization plan);

• Those functions of the Bureau of Customs pertaining to drug investigations and intelligence (to be transferred from the Treasury Department to the Attorney General by the reorganization plan);

• All functions of the Office for Drug Abuse Law Enforcement; and

• All functions of the Office of National Narcotics Intelligence.

Merger of the latter two organizations into the new agency would be effected by an executive order dissolving them and transferring their functions, to take effect upon approval of Reorganization Plan No. 2 by the Congress. Drug law enforcement research currently funded by the Law Enforcement Assistance Administration and other agencies would also be transferred to the new agency by executive action.

The major responsibilities of the Drug Enforcement Administration would thus include:

• development of overall Federal drug law enforcement strategy, programs, planning, and evaluation;

• full investigation and preparation for prosecution of suspects for violations under all Federal drug trafficking laws,

• full investigation and preparation for prosecution of suspects connected with illicit drugs seized at U.S. ports-of-entry and international borders;

• conduct of all relations with drug law enforcement officials of foreign governments, under the policy guidance of the Cabinet Committee on International Narcotics Control;

• full coordination and cooperation with State and local law enforcement officials on joint drug enforcement efforts; and

• regulation of the legal manufacture of drugs and other controlled substances under Federal regulations.

The Attorney General, working closely with the Administrator of this new agency, would have authority to make needed program adjustments. He would take steps within the Department of Justice to ensure that high priority emphasis is placed on the prosecution and sentencing of drug traffickers following their apprehension by the enforcement organization. He would also have the authority and responsibility for securing the fullest possible cooperation—particularly with respect to collection of drug intelligence—from all Federal departments and agencies which can contribute to the anti-drug work, including the Internal Revenue Service and the Federal Bureau of Investigation.

My proposals would make possible a more effective anti-drug role for the FBI, especially in dealing with the relationship between drug trafficking and organized crime. I intend to see that the resources of the FBI are fully committed to assist in supporting the new Drug Enforcement Administration.

The consolidation effected under Reorganization Plan No. 2 would reinforce the basic law enforcement and criminal justice mission of the Department of Justice. With worldwide drug law enforcement responsibilities no longer divided among several organizations in two different Cabinet departments, more complete and cumulative drug law enforcement intelligence could be compiled. Patterns of international and domestic illicit drug production, distribution and sale could be more directly compared and interpreted. Case-by-case drug law enforcement activities could be more comprehensively linked, cross-referenced, and coordinated into a single, organic enforcement operation. In short, drug law enforcement officers would be able to spend more time going after the traffickers and less time coordinating with one another.

Such progress could be especially helpful on the international front. Narcotics control action plans, developed under the leadership of the Cabinet Committee on International Narcotics Control, are now being carried out by U.S. officials in cooperation with host governments in 59 countries around the world. This wide-ranging effort to cut off drug supplies before they ever reach U.S. borders or streets is just now beginning to bear fruit.

We can enhance its effectiveness, with little disruption of ongoing enforcement activities, by merging both the highly effective narcotics force of overseas Customs agents and the rapidly developing international activities of the Bureau of Narcotics and Dangerous Drugs into the Drug Enforcement Administration. The new agency would work closely with the Cabinet Committee under the active leadership of the U.S. Ambassador in each country where anti-drug programs are underway.

Two years ago, when I established the Special Action Office for Drug Abuse Prevention within the Executive Office of the President, we gained an organization with the necessary resources, breadth, and leadership capacity to begin dealing decisively with the "demand" side of the drug abuse problem—treatment and rehabilitation for those who have been drug victims, and preventive programs for potential drug abusers. This year, by permitting my reorganization proposals to take effect, the Congress can help provide a similar capability on the "supply" side.

The proposed Drug Enforcement Administration, working as a team with the Special Action Office, would arm Americans with a potent one-two punch to help us fight back against the deadly enemy of drug abuse. I ask full Congressional cooperation in its establishment.

Improving Inspections

No heroin or cocaine is produced within the United States; domestic availability of these substances results solely from their illegal importation. The careful and complete inspection of all persons and goods coming into the United States is therefore an integral part of effective Federal drug law enforcement.

At the present time, however, Federal responsibility for conducting port-of-entry inspections is awkwardly divided among several Cabinet departments. The principal agencies involved are the Treasury Department's Bureau of Customs, which inspects goods, and the Justice Department's Immigration and Naturalization Service, which inspects persons and their papers. The two utilize separate inspection procedures, hold differing views of inspection priorities, and employ dissimilar personnel management practices.

To reduce the possibility that illicit drugs will escape detection at ports-of-entry because of divided responsibility, and

to enhance the effectiveness of the Drug Enforcement Administration, the reorganization plan which I am proposing today would transfer to the Secretary of the Treasury all functions currently vested in Justice Department officials to inspect persons, or the documents of persons.

When the plan takes effect, it is my intention to direct the Secretary of the Treasury to use the resources so transferred—including some 1,000 employees of the Immigration and Naturalization Service—to augment the staff and budget of the Bureau of Customs. The Bureau's primary responsibilities would then include:

- Inspection of all persons and goods entering the United States;
- valuation of goods being imported, and assessment of appropriate tariff duties;
- interception of contraband being smuggled into the United States;
- enforcement of U.S. laws governing the international movement of goods, except the investigation of contraband drugs and narcotics; and
- turning over the investigation responsibility for all drug law enforcement cases to the Department of Justice.

The reorganization would thus group most port-of-entry inspection functions in a single Cabinet department. It would reduce the need for much day-to-day interdepartmental coordination, allow more efficient staffing at some field locations, and remove the basis for damaging inter-agency rivalries. It would also give the Secretary of the Treasury the authority and flexibility to meet changing requirements in inspecting the international flow of people and goods. An important by-product of the change would be more convenient service for travellers entering and leaving the country.

For these reasons, I am convinced that inspection activities at U.S. ports-of-entry can more effectively support our drug law enforcement efforts if concentrated in a single agency. The processing of persons at ports-of-entry is too closely interrelated with the inspection of goods to remain organizationally separated from it any longer.

Both types of inspections have numerous objectives besides drug law enforcement, so it is logical to vest them in the Treasury Department, which has long had the principal responsibility for port-of-entry inspection of goods, including goods being transported in connection with persons. As long as the inspections are conducted with full awareness of related drug concerns it is neither necessary nor desirable that they be made a responsibility of the primary drug enforcement organization.

Declarations

After investigation, I have found that each action included in Reorganization Plan No. 2 of 1973 is necessary to accomplish one or more of the purposes set forth in Section 901(a) of Title 5 of the United States Code. In particular, the plan is responsive to the intention of the Congress as expressed in Section 901 (a) (1): "to promote better execution of the laws, more effective management of the executive branch and of its agencies and functions, and expeditious administration of the public business;" Section 901 (a) (3): "to increase the efficiency of the operations of the Government to the fullest extent practicable;" Section 901(a)(5): "to reduce the number of agencies by consolidating those having similar functions under a single head, and to abolish such agencies or functions as may not be necessary for the efficient conduct of the Government; and Section 901(a)(6): "to eliminate overlapping and duplication of effort."

As required by law, the plan has one logically consistent subject matter: consolidation of Federal drug law enforcement activities in a manner designed to increase their effectiveness.

The plan would establish within the Department of Justice a new Drug Enforcement Administration, to be headed by an Administrator and a Deputy Administrator authorized pursuant to Title 5 of the amended United States Code, Sections 5314 and 5316 respectively.

While it is not practicable to specify all of the expenditure reductions and other economies which may result from the actions proposed, some savings may be anticipated in administrative costs now associated with the functions being transferred and consolidated.

The proposed reorganization is a necessary step in upgrading the effectiveness of our Nation's drug law enforcement effort. Both of the proposed changes would build on the strengths of established agencies, yielding maximum gains in the battle against drug abuse with minimum loss of time and momentum in the transition.

I am confident that this reorganization plan would significantly increase the overall efficiency and effectiveness of the Federal Government. I urge the Congress to allow it to become effective.

RICHARD NIXON

THE WHITE HOUSE,
March 28, 1973.

Reorganization Plan No. 2 of 1973

Prepared by the President and transmitted to the Senate and the House of Representatives in Congress assembled, March 28, 1973, pursuant to the provisions of Chapter 9 of Title 5 of the United States Code.

Law Enforcement In Illicit Drug Activities

Section 1. **Transfers to the Attorney General.** There are hereby transferred from the Secretary of the Treasury, the Department of the Treasury, and any other officer or any agency of the Department of the Treasury, to the Attorney General all intelligence, investigative, and law enforcement functions, vested by law in the Secretary, the Department, officers, or agencies which relate to the suppression of illicit traffic in narcotics, dangerous drugs, or marihuana, except that the Secretary shall retain, and continue to perform, those functions, to the extent that they relate to searches and seizures of illicit narcotics, dangerous drugs, or marihuana or to the apprehension or detention of persons in connection therewith, at regular inspection locations at ports of entry or anywhere along the land or water borders of the United States: Provided, that any illicit narcotics, dangerous drugs, marihuana, or related evidence seized, and any person apprehended or detained by the Secretary or any officer of the Department of the Treasury, pursuant to the authority retained in them by virtue of this section, shall be turned over forthwith to the jurisdiction of the Attorney General; Provided further, that nothing in this section shall be construed as limiting in any way any authority vested by law in the Secretary of the Treasury, the Department of the Treasury, or any other officer or any agency of that Department on the effective date of this Plan with respect to contraband other than illicit narcotics, dangerous drugs, and marihuana: and Provided further, that nothing in this section shall be construed as limiting in any way any authority the Attorney General, the Department of Justice, or any other officer or any agency of that Department may otherwise have to make investigations or engage in law enforcement activities, including activities relating to the suppression of illicit traffic in narcotics, dangerous drugs, and marihuana, at ports of entry or along the land and water borders of the United States.

Sec. 2. **Transfers to the Secretary of the Treasury.** There are hereby transferred to the Secretary of the Treasury all functions vested by law in the Attorney General, the Department of Justice, or any other officer or any agency of that Department, with respect to the inspection at regular inspec-

tion locations at ports of entry of persons, and documents of persons, entering or leaving the United States: Provided, that any person apprehended or detained by the Secretary or his designee pursuant to this section shall be turned over forthwith to the jurisdiction of the Attorney General: and, Provided further, that nothing in this section shall be construed as limiting, in any way, any other authority that the Attorney General may have with respect to the enforcement, at ports of entry or elsewhere, of laws relating to persons entering or leaving the United States.

Sec. 3. **Abolition.** The Bureau of Narcotics and Dangerous Drugs, including the Office of Director thereof, is hereby abolished, and section 3(a) of Reorganization Plan No. 1 of 1968 is hereby repealed. The Attorney General shall make such provision as he may deem necessary with respect to terminating those affairs of the Bureau of Narcotics and Dangerous Drugs not otherwise provided for in this Reorganization Plan.

Sec. 4. **Drug Enforcement Administration.** There is established in the Department of Justice an agency which shall be known as the Drug Enforcement Administration, hereinafter referred to as "the Administration."

Sec. 5. **Officers of the Administration.** (a) There shall be at the head of the Administration the Administrator of Drug Enforcement, hereinafter referred to as "the Administrator." The Administrator shall be appointed by the President by and with the advice and consent of the Senate, and shall receive compensation at the rate now or hereafter prescribed by law for positions of level III of the Executive Schedule Pay Rates (5 U.S.C. 5314). He shall perform such functions as the Attorney General shall from time to time direct.

(b) There shall be in the Administration a Deputy Administrator of the Drug Enforcement Administration, hereinafter referred to as "the Deputy Administrator," who shall be appointed by the President by and with the advice and consent of the Senate, shall perform such functions as the Attorney General may from time to time direct, and shall receive compensation at the rate now or thereafter prescribed by law for positions of level V of the Executive Schedule Pay Rates (5 U.S.C. 5316).

(c) The Deputy Administrator or such other official of the Department of Justice as the Attorney General shall from time to time designate shall act as Administrator during the absence or disability of the Administrator or in the event of a vacancy in the office of Administrator.

Sec. 6. **Performance of transferred functions.** (a) The Attorney General may from time to time make such provisions as he shall deem appropriate authorizing the performance of any of the functions transferred to him by the provisions of this Reorganization Plan by any officer, employee, or agency of the Department of Justice.

(b) The Secretary of the Treasury may from time to time make such provisions as he shall deem appropriate authorizing the performance of any of the functions transferred to him by the provisions of this Reorganization Plan by any officer, employee, or agency of the Department of the Treasury.

Sec. 7. **Coordination.** The Attorney General, acting through the Administrator and such other officials of the Department of Justice as he may designate, shall provide for the coordination of all drug law enforcement functions vested in the Attorney General so as to assure maximum cooperation between and among the Administration, the Federal Bureau of Investigation, and other units of the Department involved in the performance of these and related functions.

Sec. 8. **Incidental transfers.** (a) So much of the personnel, property, records, and unexpended balances of appropriations, allocations, and other funds employed, used, held, available or to be made available in connection with the functions transferred to the Attorney General and to the Secretary of the Treasury by this Reorganization Plan as the Director of the Office of Management and Budget shall determine shall be transferred to the Department of Justice and to the Department of the Treasury, respectively, at such time or times as the Director shall direct.

(b) Such further measures and dispositions as the Director of the Office of Management and Budget shall deem to be necessary in order to effectuate transfers referred to in subsection (a) of this section shall be carried out in such manner as he shall direct and by such Federal agencies as he shall designate.

Sec. 9. **Interim Officers.** (a) The President may authorize any person who, immediately prior to the effective date of this Reorganization Plan, held a position in the Executive Branch of the Government to act as Administrator until the

office of Administrator is for the first time filled pursuant to the provisions of this Reorganization Plan or by recess appointment as the case may be.

(b) The President may similarly authorize any such person to act as Deputy Administrator.

(c) The President may authorize any person who serves in an acting capacity under the foregoing provisions of this section to receive the compensation attached to the office in respect to which he so serves. Such compensation, if authorized, shall be in lieu of, but not in addition to, other compensation from the United States to which such person may be entitled.

Sec. 10. **Effective date.** The provisions of this Reorganization Plan shall take effect as provided by section 906(a) of title 5 of the United States Code or on July 1, 1973, whichever is later. √

TRADE REFORM: NEW TARIFF ADJUSTMENT POWERS ASKED

Following is the White House text of President Nixon's April 10 message to Congress on trade.

TO THE CONGRESS OF THE UNITED STATES:

The Trade Reform Act of 1973, which I am today proposing to the Congress, calls for the most important changes in more than a decade in America's approach to world trade.

This legislation can mean more and better jobs for American workers.

It can help American consumers get more for their money.

It can mean expanding trade and expanding prosperity, for the United States and for our trading partners alike.

Most importantly, these proposals can help us reduce international tensions and strengthen the structure of peace.

The need for trade reform is urgent. The task of trade reform requires an effective, working partnership between the executive and legislative branches. The legislation I submit today has been developed in close consultation with the Congress and it envisions continuing cooperation after it is enacted. I urge the Congress to examine these proposals in a spirit of constructive partnership and to give them prompt and favorable consideration.

This legislation would help us to:

—Negotiate for a more open and equitable world trading system;

—Deal effectively with rapid increases in imports that disrupt domestic markets and displace American workers;

—Strengthen our ability to meet unfair competitive practices;

—Manage our trade policy more efficiently and use it more effectively to deal with special needs such as our balance of payments and inflation problems; and

—Take advantage of new trade opportunities while enhancing the contribution trade can make to the development of poorer countries.

The Structure of Peace

The world is embarked today on a profound and historic movement away from confrontation and toward negotiation in resolving international differences. Increasingly in recent years, countries have come to see that the best way of advancing their own interests is by expanding peaceful contacts with other peoples. We have thus begun to erect a durable structure of peace in the world from which all nations can benefit and in which all nations have a stake.

This structure of peace cannot be strong, however, unless it encompasses international economic affairs. Our progress toward world peace and stability can be significantly undermined by economic conflicts which breed political tensions and weaken security ties. It is imperative, therefore, that we promptly turn our negotiating efforts to the task of resolving problems in the economic arena.

My trade reform proposals would equip us to meet this challenge. They would help us in creating a new economic order which both reflects and reinforces the progress we have made in political affairs. As I said to the Governors of the International Monetary Fund last September, our common goal should be to "set in place an economic structure that will help and not hinder the world's historic movement toward peace."

International Economic Order

The principal institutions which now govern the world economy date from the close of World War II. At that time, the United States enjoyed a dominant position. Our industrial and agricultural systems had emerged from the war virtually intact. Our substantial reserves enabled us to finance a major share of international reconstruction. We gave generously of our resources and our leadership in helping the world economy get back on track.

The result has been a quarter century of remarkable economic achievement—and profound economic change. In place of a splintered and shattered Europe stands a new and vibrant European Community. In place of a prostrate Japan stands one of the free world's strongest economies. In all parts of the world new economic patterns have developed and new economic energies have been released.

These successes have now brought the world into a very different period. America is no longer the sole, dominating economic power. The new era is one of growing economic interdependence, shared economic leadership, and dramatic economic change.

These sweeping transformations, however, have not been matched by sufficient change in our trading and monetary systems. The approaches which served us so well in the years following World War II have now become outmoded; they are simply no longer equal to the challenges of our time.

The result has been a growing sense of strain and stress in the international economy and even a resurgence of economic isolationism as some have sought to insulate themselves from change. If we are to make our new economic era a time of progress and prosperity for all the world's peoples, we must resist the impulse to turn inward and instead do all we can to see that our international economic arrangements are substantially improved.

Momentum for Change

The United States has already taken a number of actions to help build a new international economic order and to advance our interests within it.

—Our New Economic Policy, announced on August 15, 1971, has helped to improve the performance of our domestic economy, reducing unemployment and inflation and thereby enhancing our competitive position.

—The realignment of currencies achieved under the Smithsonian Agreement of December 18, 1971, and by the adjustments of recent weeks have also made American goods more competitive with foreign products in markets at home and abroad.

—Building on the Smithsonian Agreement, we have advanced far-reaching proposals for lasting reform in the world's monetary system.

—We have concluded a trade agreement with the Soviet Union that promises to strengthen the fabric of prosperity and peace.

—Opportunities for mutually beneficial trade are developing with the People's Republic of China.

—We have opened negotiations with the enlarged European Community and several of the countries with which it has concluded special trading agreements concerning compensation due us as a result of their new arrangements.

But despite all these efforts, underlying problems remain. We need basic trade reform, and we need it now. Our efforts to improve the world's monetary system, for example, will never meet with lasting success unless basic improvements are also achieved in the field of international trade.

A Fair and Open Trading World

A wide variety of barriers to trade still distort the world's economic relations, harming our own interests and those of other countries.

—Quantitative barriers hamper trade in many commodities, including some of our potentially most profitable exports.

—Agricultural barriers limit and distort trade in farm products, with special damage to the American economy because of our comparative advantage in the agricultural field.

—Preferential trading arrangements have spread to include most of Western Europe, Africa and other countries bordering on the Mediterranean Sea.

—Non-tariff barriers have greatly proliferated as tariffs have declined.

These barriers to trade, in other countries and in ours, presently cost the United States several billion dollars a year in the form of higher consumer prices and the inefficient use of our resources. Even an economy as strong as ours can ill afford such losses.

Fortunately, our major trading partners have joined us in a commitment to broad, multilateral trade negotiations beginning this fall. These negotiations will provide a unique opportunity for reducing trading barriers and expanding world trade.

It is in the best interest of every nation to sell to others the goods it produces more efficiently and to purchase the goods which other nations produce more efficiently. If we can operate on this basis, then both the earnings of our workers and the buying power of our dollars can be significantly increased.

But while trade should be more open, it should also be more fair. This means, first, that the rules and practices of trade should be fair to all nations. Secondly, it means that the benefits of trade should be fairly distributed among American workers, farmers, businessmen and consumers alike and that trade should create no undue burdens for any of these groups.

I am confident that our free and vigorous American economy can more than hold its own in open world competition. But we must always insist that such competition take place under equitable rules.

Need for Action

The key to success in our coming trade negotiations will be the negotiating authority the United States brings to the bargaining table. Unless our negotiators can speak for this country with sufficient authority, other nations will undoubtedly be cautious and non-committal—and the opportunity for change will be lost.

We must move promptly to provide our negotiators with the authority their task requires. Delay can only aggravate the strains we have already experienced. Disruptions in world financial markets, deficits in our trading balance, inflation in the international marketplace, and tensions in the diplomatic arena all argue for prompt and decisive action. So does the plight of those American workers and businesses who are damaged by rapidly rising imports or whose products face barriers in foreign markets.

For all of these reasons, I urge the Congress to act on my recommendations as expeditiously as possible. We face pressing problems here and now. We cannot wait until tomorrow to solve them.

New Negotiating Authorities

Negotiators from other countries will bring to the coming round of trade discussions broad authority to alter their barriers to trade. Such authority makes them more effective bargainers; without such authority the hands of any negotiator would be severely tied.

Unfortunately, the President of the United States and those who negotiate at his direction do not now possess authorities comparable to those which other countries will bring to these bargaining sessions. Unless these authorities are provided, we will be badly hampered in our efforts to advance American interests and improve our trading system.

My proposed legislation therefore calls upon the Congress to delegate significant new negotiating authorities to the executive branch. For several decades now, both the Congress and the President have recognized that trade policy is one field in which such delegations are indispensable. This concept is clearly established; the questions which remain concern the degree of delegation which is appropriate and the conditions under which it should be carried out.

The legislation I submit today spells out only that degree of delegation which I believe is necessary and proper to advance the national interest. And just as we have consulted closely with the Congress in shaping this legislation, so the executive branch will consult closely with the Congress in exercising any negotiating authorities it receives. I invite the Congress to set up whatever mechanism it deems best for closer consultation and cooperation to ensure that its views are properly represented as trade negotiations go forward.

It is important that America speak authoritatively and with a single voice at the international bargaining table. But it is also important that many voices contribute as the American position is being shaped.

The proposed Trade Reform Act of 1973 would provide for the following new authorities:

First, I request authority to eliminate, reduce, or increase customs duties in the context of negotiated agreements. Although this authority is requested for a period of five years, it is my intention and my expectation that agreements can be concluded in a much shorter time. Last October, the member governments of the European Community expressed their hope that the coming round of trade negotiations will be concluded by 1975. I endorse this timetable and our negotiators will cooperate fully in striving to meet it.

Secondly, I request a Congressional declaration favoring negotiations and agreements on non-tariff barriers. I am also asking that a new, optional procedure be created for obtaining the approval of the Congress for such agreements when that is appropriate. Currently both Houses of the Congress must take positive action before any such agreement requiring changes in domestic law becomes effective—a process which makes it difficult to achieve agreements since our trading partners know it is subject to much uncertainty and delay. Under the new arrangement, the President would give notice to the Congress of his intention to use the procedure at least 90 days in advance of concluding an agreement in order to provide time for appropriate House and Senate Committees to consider the issues involved and to make their views known. After an agreement was negotiated, the President would submit that agreement and proposed implementing orders to the Congress. If neither House rejected them by a majority vote of all members within a period of 90 days, the agreement and implementing orders would then enter into effect.

Thirdly, I request advance authority to carry out mutually beneficial agreements concerning specific customs matters primarily involving valuation and the marking of goods by country of origin.

The authorities I outline in my proposed legislation would give our negotiators the leverage and the flexibility they need to reduce or eliminate foreign barriers to American products. These proposals would significantly strengthen America's bargaining position in the coming trade negotiations.

Agricultural Trade

I am not requesting specific negotiating authority relating to agricultural trade. Barriers to such trade are either tariff or non-tariff in nature and can be dealt with under the general authorities I am requesting.

One of our major objectives in the coming negotiations is to provide for expansion in agricultural trade. The strength of American agriculture depends on the continued expansion of our world markets—especially for the major bulk commodities our farmers produce so efficiently. Even as we have been moving toward a great reliance on free market forces here at home under the Agricultural Act of 1970, so we seek to broaden the role of market forces on the international level by reducing and removing barriers to trade in farm products.

I am convinced that the concerns which all nations have for their farmers and consumers can be met most effectively if the market plays a far greater role in determining patterns of agricultural production and consumption. Movement in this direction can do much to help ensure adequate supplies of food and relieve pressure on consumer prices.

Import Relief

As other countries agree to reduce their trading barriers, we expect to reduce ours. The result will be expanding trade, creating more and better jobs for the American people and providing them with greater access to a wider variety of products from other countries.

It is true, of course, that reducing import barriers has on some occasions led to sudden surges in imports which have had disruptive effects on the domestic economy. It is important to note, however, that most severe problems caused by surging imports have not been related to the reduction of import barriers. Steps toward a more open trading order generally have a favorable rather than an unfavorable impact on domestic jobs.

Nevertheless, damaging import surges, whatever their cause, should be a matter of great concern to our people and our Government. I believe we should have effective intruments readily available to help avoid serious injury from imports and give American industries and workers time to adjust to increased imports in an orderly way. My proposed legislation outlines new measures for achieving these goals.

To begin with, I recommend a less restrictive test for invoking import restraints. Today, restraints are authorized only when

the Tariff Commission finds that imports are the "major cause" of serious injury or threat thereof to a domestic industry, meaning that their impact must be larger than that of all other causes combined. Under my proposal, restraints would be authorized when import competition was the "primary cause" of such injury, meaning that it must only be the largest single cause. In addition, the present requirement that injury must result from a previous tariff concession would be dropped.

I also recommend a new method for determining whether imports actually are the primary cause of serious injury to domestic producers. Under my proposal, a finding of "market disruption" would constitute *prima facie* evidence of that fact. Market disruption would be defined as occurring when imports are substantial, are rising rapidly both absolutely and as a percentage of total domestic consumption, and are offered at prices substantially below those of competing domestic products.

My proposed legislation would give the President greater flexibility in providing appropriate relief from import problems—including orderly marketing agreements or higher tariffs or quotas. Restraints could be imposed for an initial period of five years and, at the discretion of the President, could be extended for an additional period of two years. In exceptional cases, restrictions could be extended even further after a two-year period and following a new investigation by the Tariff Commission.

Adjustment Assistance

Our responsibilities for easing the problems of displaced workers are not limited to those whose unemployment can be traced to imports. All displaced workers are entitled to adequate assistance while they seek new employment. Only if all workers believe they are getting a fair break can our economy adjust effectively to change.

I will therefore propose in a separate message to the Congress new legislation to improve our systems of unemployment insurance and compensation. My proposals would set minimum Federal standards for benefit levels in State programs, ensuring that all workers covered by such programs are treated equitably, whatever the cause of their involuntary unemployment. In the meantime, until these standards become effective, I am recommending as a part of my trade reform proposals that we immediately establish benefit levels which meet these proposed general standards for workers displaced because of imports.

I further propose that until the new standards for unemployment insurance are in place, we make assistance for workers more readily available by dropping the present requirement that their unemployment must have been caused by prior tariff concessions and that imports must have been the "major cause" of injury. Instead, such assistance would be authorized if the Secretary of Labor determined that unemployment was substantially due to import-related causes. Workers unemployed because of imports would also have job training, job search allowances, employment services and relocation assistance available to them as permanent features of trade adjustment assistance.

Pension Reform

In addition, I will submit to the Congress comprehensive pension reform legislation which would help protect workers who lose their jobs against loss of pension benefits. This legislation will contain a mandatory vesting requirement which has been developed with older workers particularly in mind.

The proposed Trade Reform Act of 1973 would terminate the present program of adjustment assistance to individual firms. I recommend this action because I believe this program has been largely ineffective, discriminates among firms within a given industry and has needlessly subsidized some firms at the taxpayer's expense. Changing competitive conditions, after all, typically act not upon particular firms but upon an industry as a whole and I have provided for entire industries under my import relief proposals.

Unfair Trade Practices

The President of the United States possesses a variety of authorities to deal with unfair trade practices. Many of these authorities must now be modernized if we are to respond effectively and even-handedly to unfair import competition at home and to practices which unfairly prejudice our export opportunities abroad.

To cope with unfair competitive practices in our own markets, my proposed legislation would amend our antidumping and countervailing duty laws to provide for more expeditious investigations and decisions. It would make a number of procedural and other changes in these laws to guarantee their effective operation. The bill would also amend the current statute concerning patent infringement by subjecting cases involving imports to judicial proceedings similar to those which involve domestic infringement, and by providing for fair processes and effective action in the event of court delays. I also propose that the Federal Trade Commission Act be amended to strengthen our ability to deal with foreign producers whose cartel or monopoly practices raise prices in our market or otherwise harm our interest by restraining trade.

In addition, I ask for a revision and extension of my authority to raise barriers against countries which unreasonably or unjustifiably restrict our exports. Existing law provides such authority only under a complex array of conditions which vary according to the practices or exports involved. My proposed bill would simplify the authority and its use. I would prefer, of course, that other countries agree to remove such restrictions on their own, so that we should not have to use this authority. But I will consider using it whenever it becomes clear that our trading partners are unwilling to remove unreasonable or unjustifiable restrictions against our exports.

Other Major Provisions

Most-Favored-Nation Authority. My proposed legislation would grant the President authority to extend most-favored-nation treatment to any country when he deemed it in the national interest to do so. Under my proposal, however, any such extension to countries not now receiving most-favored-nation treatment could be vetoed by a majority vote of either the House or the Senate within a three-month period.

This new authority would enable us to carry out the trade agreement we have negotiated with the Soviet Union and thereby ensure that country's repayment of its lend-lease debt. It would also enable us to fulfill our commitment to Romania and to take advantage of opportunities to conclude beneficial agreements with other countries which do not now receive most-favored-nation treatment.

In the case of the Soviet Union, I recognize the deep concern which many in the Congress have expressed over the tax levied on Soviet citizens wishing to emigrate to new countries. However, I do not believe that a policy of denying most-favored-nation treatment to Soviet exports is a proper or even an effective way of dealing with this problem.

One of the most important elements of our trade agreement with the Soviet Union is the clause which calls upon each party to reduce exports of products which cause market disruptions in the other country. While I have no reason to doubt that the Soviet Union will meet its obligations under this clause if the need arises, we should still have authority to take unilateral action to prevent disruption if such action is warranted.

Because of the special way in which state-trading countries market their products abroad, I would recommend two modifications in the way we take such action. First, the Tariff Commission should only have to find "material injury" rather than "serious injury" from imports in order to impose appropriate restraints. Secondly, such restraints should apply only to exports from the offending country. These recommendations can simplify our laws relating to dumping actions by state-trading countries,

eliminating the difficult and time-consuming problems associated with trying to reach a constructed value for their exports.

Balance of Payments Authority. Though it should only be used in exceptional circumstances, trade policy can sometimes be an effective supplementary tool for dealing with our international payments imbalances. I therefore request more flexible authority to raise or lower import restrictions on a temporary basis to help correct deficits or surpluses in our payments position. Such restraints could be applied to imports from all countries across the board or only to those countries which fail to correct a persistent and excessive surplus in their global payments position.

Anti-Inflation Authority. My trade recommendations also include a proposal I made on March 30th as a part of this Administration's effort to curb the rising cost of living. I asked the Congress at that time to give the President new, permanent authority to reduce certain import barriers temporarily and to a limited extent when he determined that such action was necessary to relieve inflationary pressures within the United States. I again urge prompt approval for this important weapon in our war against inflation.

Generalized Tariff Preferences. Another significant provision of my proposed bill would permit the United States to join with other developed countries, including Japan and the members of the European Community, in helping to improve the access of poorer nations to the markets of developed countries. Under this arrangement, certain products of developing nations would benefit from preferential treatment for a ten-year period, creating new export opportunities for such countries, raising their foreign exchange earnings, and permitting them to finance those higher levels of imports that are essential for more rapid economic growth.

This legislation would allow duty-free treatment for a broad range of manufactured and semi-manufactured products and for a selected list of agricultural and primary products which are now regulated only by tariffs. It is our intention to exclude certain import-sensitive products such as textile products, footwear, watches and certain steel products from such preferential treatment, along with products which are now subject to outstanding orders restricting imports. As is the case for the multilateral negotiations authority, public hearing procedures would be held before such preferences were granted and preferential imports would be subject to the import relief provisions which I have recommended above. Once a particular product from a given country became fully competitive, however, it would no longer qualify for special treatment.

The United States would grant such tariff preferences on the basis of international fair play. We would take into account the actions of other preference-granting countries and we would not grant preferences to countries which discriminate against our products in favor of goods from other industrialized nations unless those countries agreed to end such discrimination.

Permanent Management Authorities. To permit more efficient and more flexible management of American trade policy, I request permanent authority to make limited reductions in our tariffs as a form of compensation to other countries. Such compensation could be necessary in cases where we have raised certain barriers under the new import restraints discussed above and would provide an alternative in such cases to increased barriers against our exports.

I also request permanent authority to offer reductions in particular United States barriers as a means of obtaining significant advantages for American exports. These reductions would be strictly limited; they would involve tariff cuts of no more than 20 percent covering no more than two percent of total United States imports in any one year.

International Trading Rules

The coming multilateral trade negotiations will give us an excellent opportunity to reform and update the rules of international trade. There are several areas where we will seek such changes.

One important need concerns the use of trade policy in promoting equilibrium in the international payments system. We will seek rule changes to permit nations, in those exceptional cases where such measures are necessary, to increase or decrease trade barriers across the board as one means of helping to correct their payments imbalances. We will also seek a new rule allowing nations to impose restrictions against individual countries which fail to take effective action to correct an excessive surplus in their balance of payments. This rule would parallel the authority I have requested to use American import restrictions to meet our own balance of payments problem.

A second area of concern is the need for a multilateral system for limiting imports to protect against disruptions caused by rapidly changing patterns of international trade. As I emphasized earlier, we need a more effective domestic procedure to meet such problems. But it is also important that new arrangements be developed at the international level to cope with disruptions caused by the accelerating pace of change in world trade.

We will therefore seek new international rules which would allow countries to gain time for adjustment by imposing import restrictions, without having to compensate their trading partners by simultaneously reducing barriers to other products. At the same time, the interests of exporting countries should be protected by providing that such safeguards will be phased out over a reasonable period of time.

Export Expansion

As trade barriers are reduced around the world, American exports will increase substantially, enhancing the health of our entire economy.

Already our efforts to expand American exports have moved forward on many fronts. We have made our exports more competitive by realigning exchange rates. Since 1971, our new law permitting the establishment of Domestic International Sales Corporations has been helping American companies organize their export activities more effectively. The lending, guaranty and insurance authorities of the Export-Import Bank have been increased and operations have been extended to include a short-term discount loan facility. The Department of Commerce has reorganized its facilities for promoting exports and has expanded its services for exporters. The Department of State, in cooperation with the Department of Commerce, is giving increased emphasis to commercial service programs in our missions abroad.

In addition, I am today submitting separate legislation which would amend the Export Trade Act in order to clarify the legal framework in which associations of exporters can function. One amendment would make it clear that the act applies not only to the export of goods but also to certain kinds of services—architecture, construction, engineering, training and management consulting, for example. Another amendment would clarify the exemption of export associations from our domestic antitrust laws, while setting up clear information, disclosure and regulatory requirements to ensure that the public interest is fully protected.

In an era when more countries are seeking foreign contracts for entire industrial projects—including steps ranging from engineering studies through the supply of equipment and the construction of plants—it is essential that our laws concerning joint export activities allow us to meet our foreign competition on a fair and equal basis.

International Investment

The rapid growth of international investment in recent years has raised new questions and new challenges for businesses and governments. In our own country, for example, some people have feared that American investment abroad will result in a loss of American jobs. Our studies show, however, that such investment on balance has meant more and better jobs for American workers, has improved our balance of trade and our overall balance of payments, and has generally strengthened our economy. Moreover, I strongly believe that an open system for international investment, one which eliminates artificial incentives or impediments here and abroad, offers great promise for improved prosperity throughout the world.

It may well be that new rules and new mechanisms will be needed for international investment activities. It will take time, however, to develop them. And it is important that they be developed as much as possible on an international scale. If we restrict the ability of American firms to take advantage of investment opportunities abroad, we can only expect that foreign firms will seize these opportunities and prosper at our expense.

I therefore urge the Congress to refrain from enacting broad new changes in our laws governing direct foreign investment until we see what possibilities for multilateral agreements emerge.

It is in this context that we must also shape our system for taxing the foreign profits of American business. Our existing system permits American-controlled businesses in foreign countries to operate under the same tax burdens which apply to its foreign competitors in that country. I believe that system is fundamentally sound. We should not penalize American business by placing it at a disadvantage with respect to its foreign competitors.

American enterprises abroad now pay substantial foreign income taxes. In most cases, in fact, Americans do not invest abroad because of an attractive tax situation but because of attractive business opportunities. Our income taxes are not the cause of our trade problems and tax changes will not solve them.

The Congress exhaustively reviewed this entire matter in 1962 and the conclusion it reached then is still fundamentally sound: there is no reason that our tax credit and deferral provisions relating to overseas investment should be subjected to drastic surgery.

On the other hand, ten years of experience have demonstrated that in certain specialized cases American investment abroad can be subject to abuse. Some artificial incentives for such investment still exist, distorting the flow of capital and producing unnecessary hardship. In those cases where unusual tax advantages are offered to induce investment that might not otherwise occur, we should move to eliminate that inducement.

A number of foreign countries presently grant major tax inducements such as extended "holidays" from local taxes in order to attract investment from outside their borders. To curb such practices, I will ask the Congress to amend our tax laws so that earnings from new American investments which take advantage of such incentives will be taxed by the United States at the time they are earned—even though the earnings are not returned to this country. The only exception to this provision would come in cases where a bilateral tax treaty provided for such an exception under mutually advantageous conditions.

American companies sometimes make foreign investments specifically for the purpose of re-exporting products to the United States. This is the classic "runaway plant" situation. In cases where foreign subsidiaries of American companies have receipts from exports to the United States which exceed 25 percent of the subsidiaries' total receipts, I recommend that the earnings of those subsidiaries also be taxed at current American rates. This new rule would only apply, however, to new investments and to situations where lower taxes in the foreign country are a factor in the decision to invest. The rule would also provide for exceptions in those unusual cases where our national interest required a different result.

There are other situations in which American companies so design their foreign operations that the United States treasury bears the burden when they lose money and deduct it from their taxes. Yet when that same company makes money, a foreign treasury receives the benefit of taxes on its profits. I will ask the Congress to make appropriate changes in the rules which now allow this inequity to occur.

We have also found that taxing of mineral imports by United States companies from their foreign affiliates is subject to lengthy delays. I am therefore instructing the Department of the Treasury, in consultation with the Department of Justice and the companies concerned, to institute a procedure for determining inter-company prices and tax payments in advance. If a compliance program cannot be developed voluntarily, I shall ask for legislative authority to create one.

The Challenge of Change

Over the past year, this Administration has repeatedly emphasized the importance of bringing about a more equitable and open world trading system. We have encouraged other nations to join in negotiations to achieve this goal. The declaration of European leaders at their summit meeting last October demonstrates their dedication to the success of this effort. Japan, Canada and other nations share this dedication.

The momentum is there. Now we—in this country—must seize the moment if that momentum is to be sustained.

When the history of our time is written, this era will surely be described as one of profound change. That change has been particularly dramatic in the international economic arena.

The magnitude and pace of economic change confronts us today with policy questions of immense and immediate significance. Change can mean increased disruption and suffering, or it can mean increased well-being. It can bring new forms of deprivation and discrimination, or it can bring wider sharing of the benefits of progress. It can mean conflict between men and nations, or it can mean growing opportunities for fair and peaceful competition in which all parties can ultimately gain.

My proposed Trade Reform Act of 1973 is designed to ensure that the inevitable changes of our time are beneficial changes—for our people and for people everywhere.

I urge the Congress to enact these proposals, so that we can help move our country and our world away from trade confrontation and toward trade negotiation, away from a period in which trade has been a source of international and domestic friction and into a new era in which trade among nations helps us to build a peaceful, more prosperous world.

RICHARD NIXON

WATER-SEWER GRANT VETO

Following is the White House text of President Nixon's April 5 message on the veto of HR 3298, the rural water and sewer grant program.

TO THE HOUSE OF REPRESENTATIVES:

I am returning today without my approval H.R. 3298, an act to restore the rural water and sewer grant program which was terminated earlier this year.

My recent budget proposals to the Congress reflect the results of an intensive effort to identify Federal programs that should be reformed, cut back or eliminated. In each case we asked one simple question: would this program justify an increase in taxes in order to pay for it?

The rural water and sewer program, which was launched eight years ago to assist rural communities in constructing water and sewer lines, failed that test. It forced the Federal taxpayer to pay for services that should be locally financed, and it did so in a most uneven and questionable way. We therefore terminated it on January 1, 1973, as part of our determined effort to hold down taxes and combat inflation.

Now the Congress seeks to revive the program. This is a disservice to the taxpayers of this country which I am not prepared to accept.

For many years, local communities have proudly financed and built their own water and sewer facilities. They have recognized that these services are primarily local in nature and should be primarily a local responsibility—just as local communities pay for their own garbage services and fire protection.

Resurrection of the rural water and sewer program would serve only to undercut that tradition, shoving aside local authorities for the increasingly powerful Federal Government.

This program also enlarges the Federal responsibility in a particularly ineffective and insidious way. Experience has shown that water and sewer grants have been distributed in a totally scattershot fashion. Many rural communities, although qualified under the program, have built their own water and sewage systems without waiting for Federal help. They need no incentive from Washington. Yet, in other cases, the water and sewer grants actually delay construction, as communities which would ordinarily finance the facilities on their own, choose instead to wait in line for Federal subsidies. The result has been a very uneven pattern of distribution. It should also come as no surprise that over time the program has attained a distinct flavor of porkbarrel.

Moreover, by singling out a relatively small group of people to receive Federal grants to help build their private water and sewer lines, this program forces the majority of taxpayers, in effect, to pay double taxes: once to build their own facilities and then again to build the sewers in someone else's backyard.

This double taxation leads to little national good and deseves to be stopped, especially at a time when we are earnestly seeking to hold the line on Federal spending.

In view of the many defects in this program, I am convinced that it should no longer be inflicted on the American taxpayer. Congressional restoration of water and sewer grants at the appropriated level of H.R. 3298 would increase Federal spending by at least $300 million during fiscal years 1973-1975. This would represent a dangerous crack in the fiscal dam that this Administration has constructed to hold back a further flood of inflation or higher taxes, or both.

A grave constitutional question is also raised by H.R. 3298, which purports to mandate the spending of the full amount appropriated by the Congress. The Attorney General has advised me that such a mandate conflicts with the allocation of executive power to the President made by Article II of the Constitution. Thus, H.R. 3298 is objectionable not only in its practical and economic aspects, but on basic legal grounds as well.

In reconsidering this bill, the Congress should bear in mind that my fiscal year 1974 budget already provides $345 million in Rural Development Act loan funds for water supply systems in rural areas which will help local communities borrow at favorable interest rates. In addition, the Environmental Protection Agency will be providing grants of $5 billion in fiscal years 1973 and 1974 for waste disposal facilities across the country. These grants will be awarded in accordance with State-established needs, and may be used in rural areas for high priority projects.

I recognize that despite these programs, some rural communities in need of sewer assistance may still have financing difficulties because of their inability to borrow at reasonable rates. Fortunately, a solution to this problem exists.

If my veto of this bill is sustained, I will use my authority under the Rural Development Act to provide qualified rural communities with loans not only for water facilities but also for the development of sewage facilities. These loans for sewer services will be available in fiscal years 1973 and 1974. This step—taken at a fraction of the cost of the taxpayer required by H.R. 3298—will permit qualified small communities to compete for credit on reasonable terms.

Taken in conjunction with other measures already planned, this loan provision should provide sufficient Federal support to those communities which critically need water and sewage systems without shattering the limits of sound fiscal policy. I therefore urge all thoughtful, responsible Members of the Congress to join with me in preventing this costly, unwise and probably unconstitutional measure from becoming law.

In upholding my veto of the Vocational Rehabilitation Act earlier this week, the Congress demonstrated that it can set aside partisan political considerations in the interest of America's economic well-being. I urge the Members of the Congress to hold to that same resolve in reconsidering this second piece of inflationary, budget-breaking legislation.

Together, we can hold down taxes and inflation for all of the American people. Together, we can also create a climate in which local and State governments will have both the incentive and the means to meet their legitimate responsibilities without undue interference from Washington and without a proliferation of costly and unnecessary Federal programs such as the one which H.R. 3298 would re-establish.

RICHARD NIXON

PENSION REFORM

Following is the White House text, released April 11, of President Nixon's message to Congress on pension plans.

TO THE CONGRESS OF THE UNITED STATES:

A dynamic economic system in a democracy must not only provide plentiful jobs, good working conditions, and a decent living wage for the people it employs; it should also help working men and women to set aside enough of the earnings of their most productive years to assure them of a secure and comfortable income in their retirement years.

This fundamental concept of prudent savings for retirement came under direct public sponsorship in the United States more than a generation ago, with the establishment of the Social Security System. Today, Social Security is the largest system of its kind in the world, and one of the most effective and progressive. Numerous significant improvements have been made in it during the past four years by this Administration in cooperation with the Congress.

In addition, public policy has long given active encouragement to the growth of a second form of retirement income: private pensions which are tailored to the needs of particular groups of workers and help to supplement the Social Security floor. Private pension plans now cover over 30 million workers and pay benefits to another 6 million retired persons.

But there is still room for substantial improvement in Federal laws dealing with private retirement savings. Those workers who are covered by pension plans—about half the total private work force—presently lack certain important types of Government protection and support. The other half of the labor force, those who are not participants in private plans, are not receiving sufficient encouragement from the Government to save for retirement themselves. Self-reliance, prudence, and independence—basic strengths of our system which are reinforced by private retirement savings and which government should seek to foster—are in too many cases not supported, and sometimes actually discouraged, by present practices and regulations.

Sixteen months ago I asked the Congress to enact pension reform legislation to remedy these deficiencies. Since then committees of both the House and the Senate have held useful hearings on reform, and the issue has received wide public discussion. The Administration has also completed studies on some additional facets of the pension question, and we have refined our proposals.

I believe that the time is now ripe for action on those proposals. They will be resubmitted within several days, in the form of two bills, the Retirement Benefits Tax Act and the Employee Benefits Protection Act. This message outlines the specific reforms contained in the legislation.

The Retirement Benefits Tax Act

If working men and women are to have a genuine incentive to set aside some of their earnings today for a more secure retirement tomorrow, they need solid assurances that such savings will not be erased late in their career by the loss of a job, wiped out by insufficient financing of promised benefits, nor penalized by the tax laws. To this end, the Retirement Benefits Tax Act would embody the following five major principles:

1. A minimum standard should be established in law for preserving the retirement rights of employees who leave their jobs before retirement.

Protection of retirement rights, which is essential to a growing and healthy pension system, is ordinarily defined in terms of "vesting." A pension vests when an employee becomes legally entitled upon retirement to the benefits he has earned up to a certain date, regardless of whether he leaves or loses his job before retirement.

Despite some recent movement toward earlier vesting, many private plans still carry overly restrictive requirements for age or length of service or participation before vesting occurs. Thus, the pensions of more than two-thirds of all full-time workers participating in private pension plans are not now vested. All too frequently, the worker who resigns or is discharged late in his career finds that the retirement income on which he has been counting heavily has not vested and hence is not due him.

The legislation this Administration is proposing would meet this problem by requiring that pensions become vested at an appropriate specific point in a worker's career. That point should not be set too. early: if a great many younger, short-term workers acquired vested rights, pension plans would be burdened with considerable extra costs and the level of benefits for retiring workers could be reduced. But neither should too long a wait be required before vesting begins, since many older workers would then receive little if any assistance. To strike the right balance, I urge the Congress to adopt a "Rule of 50" vesting formula, which is moderate in cost and works well to protect older workers.

Under this standard, all pension benefits which have been earned would be considered half vested when an employee's age plus the number of years he has participated in the pension plan equals 50. From this half-vested starting point, an additional ten percent of all of the benefits earned would be vested each year, so that the pension would be fully vested five years later.

For example, someone joining a plan at age 30 would find that his pension would become 50 percent vested at age 40—when his years of participation (10) plus his age (40) would equal 50. Similarly, the pension of an employee joining a plan at age 40 would become 50 percent vested at age 45, and that of an employee joining a plan at age 50 would begin to vest immediately. And in each case, the degree of vesting would increase from 50 percent to 100 percent over the subsequent five-year period of the worker's continued employment.

So that this formula would not discourage employers from hiring older workers, who would have an advantage of more rapid vesting, the legislation would permit a waiting period of up to three years before a new employee must be allowed to join a pension plan, and it would also permit employees hired within five years of normal retirement age to be excluded from participation in a plan.

Under the "Rule of 50," the proportion of full-time workers in private retirement plans with vested pension benefits would increase from 32 percent to 61 percent. Among participants age 40 and older the percentage with vested pension benefits would rise from 40 percent to about 90 percent.

To avoid excessive pension cost increases which might lead to reduction of benefits, this new law would apply only to benefits earned after the bill becomes effective, although the number of years a worker participated in a pension plan prior to enactment would count toward meeting the vesting standard. The average cost increase for plans which now have no vesting provision would be about 1.9 cents per hour for each covered employee; for plans that now provide some vesting it would be even less.

2. Employees expecting retirement benefits under employer-financed defined-benefit pension plans should have the security of knowing that their vested benefits are being adequately funded.

Perhaps the most fundamental aspect of any pension plan is the assurance that when retirement age arrives, pension benefits will be paid out according to the terms of the plan. To give this assurance, it is essential that when an employer makes pension promises he begin putting away the money that will eventually be needed to keep them. Yet Federal regulations at present are lenient on this point, requiring that only a small portion of pension liabilities be put aside or "funded" each year.

My retirement savings proposal would augment this minimal protection with an additional requirement calling for at least 5 percent of the unfunded, vested liabilities in a pension plan to be funded annually. Over time, this rate of funding would build up substantial assets for the payment of pension benefits. It would make the average employee or retiree less dependent for his pension upon the survival of a former employer's business.

By requiring employers to be more forehanded and systematic in preparing to meet their pension obligations, this reform should help to reduce the frequency and magnitude of benefit losses when pension plans terminate. Even now the termination problem is not a major one: a study conducted at my direction last year by the Departments of Labor and the Treasury found that about 3100 retired, retirement-eligible, and vested workers lost pension benefits through terminations in the first 7 months of 1972, with losses totalling some $10 million. To put them in perspective, these losses should be compared with the more than $10 billion in benefits paid annually.

I also recognize, however, that these pension termination losses did work very real injustices and hardships on the individual workers affected, and on their families. Though the stricter funding requirements we are proposing will help to minimize these benefit losses, it has also been suggested that a Government-sponsored termination insurance program should be established to see that no workers or retirees whatever suffer termination losses.

After giving this idea thorough consideration, I am not recommending it at this time. No insurance plan has yet been devised which is neither on the one hand so permissive as to make the Government liable for any agreement reached between employees and employers, nor on the other hand so intrusive as to entail Government regulation of business practices and collective bargaining on a scale out of keeping with our free enterprise system. With new support from the funding standard I am requesting, the private sector will be in a better position than the Federal Government to devise protection against the small remaining termination loss problem, and I encourage employers, unions, and private insurance companies to take up this challenge.

3. Employees who wish to save independently for their retirement or to supplement employer-financed pensions should be allowed to deduct on their income tax returns amounts set aside for these purposes.

Under present law, neither an employer's contribution to a qualified private retirement plan on behalf of his employees, nor the investment earnings on those contributions, are generally subject to taxes until benefits are paid to the retired worker or his family. When an employee contributes to a group plan, the tax liability on investment earnings is similarly deferred—though in this case the contribution itself is taxable when initially received as salary. By contrast, a worker investing in a retirement savings program of his own is actually subject year by year to a double tax blow. He is taxed both on the savings contributions themselves as part of his pay and on the investment income his savings earn.

Employees who want to establish their own retirement plan or to augment an employer-financed plan should be offered a tax incentive comparable to that now given those in group plans. Accordingly, I am proposing that an individual's contributions to a retirement savings program be made tax-deductible up to the level of $1,500 per year or 20 percent of earned income, whichever is less, and that the earnings from investments up to this limit also be tax-exempt until received as retirement income. Individuals could retain the power to control the investment of these funds, channeling them into qualified bank accounts, mutual funds, annuity or insurance programs, government bonds, or other investments as they desire.

The maximum deduction of $1,500 would direct benefits primarily to employees with low and moderate incomes, while preserving an incentive to establish employer-financed plans. The limit is nevertheless sufficiently high to permit older employees to finance a substantial retirement income—a consideration which is of special importance to the 9 million full-time workers in this country who are between 40 and 60 years old and are not participating in private pension plans.

The $1,500 ceiling should be more than adequate for most workers. Supposing for example that a worker in that situation was to start an independent plan at age 40, tax-free contributions of $1,500 a year from then on would be sufficient to provide him an annual pension of $7,500, over and above his basic Social Security benefits, beginning at age 65.

The tax deduction I am proposing would also be available to those already covered by employer-financed plans, but in this case the $1,500 maximum would be reduced to reflect pension plan contributions made by the employer.

4. Self-employed persons who invest in pension plans for themselves and their employees should be given a more generous tax deduction than they now receive.

At present, self-employed people who establish pension plans for themselves and their employees are subjected to certain tax limitations which are not imposed on corporations. Pension contributions by the self-employed are tax-deductible only up to the lesser of $2,500 or 10 percent of earned income. There are no such limits to contributions made by corporations on behalf of their employees.

This distinction in treatment is not based on any difference in reality, since unincorporated entities and corporations often engage in substantially the same economic activities. Its chief practical effect has been to deny to the employees of self-employed persons who do not wish to incorporate benefits which are comparable to those of corporate employees. It has also led to otherwise unnecessary incorporation by persons solely for the purpose of obtaining tax benefits.

To achieve greater equity, I propose that the annual limit for deductible contributions by the self-employed be raised to $7,500 or 15 percent of earned income, whichever is less. This provision would enable the self-employed to provide more adequate benefits for themselves and for their workers, without causing excessive revenue losses.

5. Workers who receive lump-sum payments from pension plans when they leave a job before retirement should be able to defer taxes on those payments until retirement.

In order to avoid the problems of administering funds for the benefit of a former employee, an employer will sometimes give a department employee a lump-sum payment representing all his retirement benefits. Present law requires that the employee pay income tax on that payment even if he intends to put it aside for his retirement. A worker who remains with one employer pays no such tax. This discrimination should be corrected.

The legislation we are proposing would amend the tax law to permit the worker who receives a lump-sum payment of retirement benefits before he retires to put the money into another qualified retirement savings program—either his own or an employer-sponsored plan—without having to pay a tax on it, or on the interest it earns, until he draws benefits upon retirement.

The Employee Benefits Protection Act

An important companion to the five-point reform contained in the Retirement Benefits Tax Act is our proposed legislation to make the Federal Government a tougher watchdog over the administration of the more than $160 billion in private pension and welfare funds benefitting American workers.

Submitted by this Administration more than 3 years ago, this needed reform languished in both the 91st and 92nd Congresses. Each month that it has sat unenacted, the small minority of employee benefit fund officials who are careless or unscrupulous have been permitted to deny hard-working men and women part of their benefits. That is why we are today proposing to the 93rd Congress a strengthened and improved Employee Benefits Protection Act, with an urgent request for prompt action.

Control of pension and welfare funds is shared by employers, unions, banks, insurance companies, and many others. Most pension plans are carefully managed by responsible people, but too many workers have too much at stake for the Government simply to assume that all fund management will automatically meet a high fiduciary standard.

Accordingly, the bill we are proposing would establish for the first time an explicit Federal requirement that persons who control employee benefit funds must deal with those funds exclusively in the interest of the employee participants and their beneficiaries. Certain corrupt practices such as embezzlement and kickbacks in connection with welfare and pension funds are already Federal crimes, but many other types of activity which clearly breach principles of fiduciary conduct are overlooked by present statutes. My proposal would plug these holes in the law to give workers a more solid defense against mishandling of funds.

Present reporting and disclosure requirements would also be broadened to require of benefit plan administrators a detailed accounting of their stewardship similar to that rendered by mutual funds, banks, and insurance companies.

To back up these changes, the new law would give additional investigative and enforcement powers to the Secretary of Labor, and would permit pension fund participants and beneficiaries to seek remedies for breach of fiduciary duty through class action suits.

Finally, the Employee Benefits Protection Act would foster the development of uniform Federal laws in employee benefits protection, complementing but in no way interfering with State laws that regulate banking, insurance, and securities.

Brightening The Retirement Picture

By moving rapidly to enact the pension incentive and protection package I am recommending today, this Congress has the opportunity to make 1973 a year of historic progress in brightening the retirement picture for America's working men and women.

Under the reforms we seek, every participant in a private retirement savings plan could have a better opportunity to earn a pension and greater confidence in actually receiving that pension upon retirement. Those who are not members of an employer pension plan or who have only limited benefits in such a plan would be encouraged to ·obtain individual coverage on their own. The self-employed would have an incentive to arrange more adequate coverage for themselves and their employees. And all participants could have well-deserved peace of mind in the knowledge that their welfare and pension funds were being administered under the strictest fiduciary standards.

The achievements of our private welfare and retirement plans have contributed much to the economic security of the Nation's workers. They are a tribute to the cooperation and creativity of American labor and management. We can be proud of the system that provides them—but we must also be alert to the Government's responsibility for fostering conditions which will permit that system's further development.

I urged at the outset of my second term that in shaping public policy we should "measure what we will do for others by what they will do for themselves." By this standard, few groups in this country are more deserving than the millions of working men and women who are prudently saving today so that they can be proudly self-reliant tomorrow. I urge the Congress to help these citizens help themselves by going forward with pension reform.

RICHARD NIXON

NATIONAL POLICY TO DEAL WITH ENERGY PROBLEMS

Following is the White House text of President Nixon's April 18 message to Congress on energy.

TO THE CONGRESS OF THE UNITED STATES:

At home and abroad, America is in a time of transition. Old problems are yielding to new initiatives, but in their place new problems are arising which once again challenge our ingenuity and require vigorous action. Nowhere is this more clearly true than in the field of energy.

As America has become more prosperous and more heavily industrialized, our demands for energy have soared. Today, with 6 percent of the world's population, we consume almost a third of all the energy used in the world. Our energy demands have grown so rapidly that they now outstrip our available supplies, and at our present rate of growth, our energy needs a dozen years from now will be nearly double what they were in 1970.

In the years immediately ahead, we must face up to the possibility of occasional energy shortages and some increase in energy prices.

Clearly, we are facing a vitally important energy challenge. If present trends continue unchecked, we could face a genuine energy crisis. But that crisis can and should be averted, for we have the capacity and the resources to meet our energy needs if only we take the proper steps—and take them now.

More than half the world's total reserves of coal are located within the United States. This resource alone would be enough to provide for our energy needs for well over a century. We have potential resources of billions of barrels of recoverable oil, similar quantities of shale oil and more than 2,000 trillion cubic feet of natural gas. Properly managed, and with more attention on the part of consumers to the conservation of energy, these supplies can last for as long as our economy depends on conventional fuels.

In addition to natural fuels, we can draw upon hydroelectric plants and increasing numbers of nuclear powered facilities. Moreover, long before our present energy sources are exhausted, America's vast capabilities in research and development can provide us with new, clean and virtually unlimited sources of power. Thus we should not be misled into pessimistic predictions of an energy disaster. But neither should we be lulled into a false sense of security. We must examine our circumstances realistically, carefully weigh the alternatives—and then move forward decisively.

Weighing the Alternatives

Over 90 percent of the energy we consume today in the United States comes from three sources: natural gas, coal and petroleum. Each source presents us with a different set of problems.

Natural gas is our cleanest fuel and is most preferred in order to protect our environment, but ill-considered regulations of natural gas prices by the Federal Government have produced a serious and increasing scarcity of this fuel.

We have vast quantities of coal, but the extraction and use of coal have presented such persistent environmental problems that, today, less than 20 percent of our energy needs are met by coal and the health of the entire coal industry is seriously threatened.

Our third conventional resource is oil, but domestic production of available oil is no longer able to keep pace with demands.

In determining how we should expand and develop these resources, along with others such as nuclear power, we must take into account not only our economic goals, but also our environmental goals and our national security goals. Each of these areas is profoundly affected by our decisions concerning energy.

If we are to maintain the vigor of our economy, the health of our environment, and the security of our energy resources, it is essential that we strike the right balance among these priorities.

The choices are difficult, but we cannot refuse to act because of this. We cannot stand still simply because it is difficult to go forward. That is the one choice Americans must never make.

The energy challenge is one of the great opportunities of our time. We have already begun to meet that challenge, and realize its opportunities.

National Energy Policy

In 1971, I sent to the Congress the first message on energy policies ever submitted by an American President. In that message I proposed a number of specific steps to meet our projected needs by increasing our supply of clean energy in America.

Those steps included expanded research and development to obtain more clean energy, increased availability of energy resources located on Federal lands, increased efforts in the development of nuclear power, and a new Federal organization to plan and manage our energy programs.

In the twenty-two months since I submitted that message, America's energy research and development efforts have been expanded by 50 percent.

In order to increase domestic production of conventional fuels, sales of oil and gas leases on the Outer Continental Shelf have been increased. Federal and State standards to protect the marine environment in which these leases are located are being tightened. We have developed a more rigorous surveillance capability and an improved ability to prevent and clean up oil spills.

We are planning to proceed with the development of oil shale and geothermal energy sources on Federal lands, so long as an evaluation now underway shows that our environment can be adequately protected.

We have also taken new steps to expand our uranium enrichment capacity for the production of fuels for nuclear power plants, to standardize nuclear power plant designs, and to ensure the continuation of an already enviable safety record.

We have issued new standards and guidelines, and have taken other actions to increase and encourage better conservation of energy.

In short, we have made a strong beginning in our effort to ensure that America will always have the power needed to fuel its prosperity. But what we have accomplished is only a beginning. Now we must build on our increased knowledge, and on the accomplishments of the past twenty-two months, to develop a more comprehensive, integrated national energy policy. To carry out this policy we must:

—increase domestic production of all forms of energy—

—act to conserve energy more effectively;

—strive to meet our energy needs at the lowest cost consistent with the protection of both our national security and our natural environment;

—reduce excessive regulatory and administrative impediments which have delayed or prevented construction of energy-producing facilities;

—act in concert with other nations to conduct research in the energy field and to find ways to prevent serious shortages; and

—apply our vast scientific and technological capacities—both public and private—so we can utilize our current energy resources more wisely and develop new sources and new forms of energy.

The actions I am announcing today and the proposals I am submitting to the Congress are designed to achieve these objectives. They reflect the fact that we are in a period of transition, in which we must work to avoid or at least minimize short-term supply shortages, while we act to expand and develop our domestic supplies in order to meet long-term energy needs.

We should not suppose this transition period will be easy. The task ahead will require the concerted and cooperative efforts of consumers, industry, and government.

Domestic Energy Resources

The effort to increase domestic energy production in a manner consistent with our economic, environmental and security interests should focus on the following areas:

Natural Gas. Natural gas is America's premium fuel. It is clean-burning and thus has the least detrimental effect on our environment.

Since 1966, our consumption of natural gas has increased by over one-third, so that today natural gas comprises 32 percent of the total energy we consume from all sources. During this same period, our proven and available reserves of natural gas have decreased by a fifth. Unless we act responsibly, we will soon encounter increasing shortages of this vital fuel.

Yet the problem of shortages results less from inadequate resources than from ill-conceived regulation. Natural gas is the fuel most heavily regulated by the Federal Government—through the Federal Power Commission. Not only are the operations of interstate natural gas pipelines regulated, as was originally and properly intended by the Congress, but the price of the natural gas supplied to these pipelines by thousands of independent producers has also been regulated.

For more than a decade the prices of natural gas supplied to pipelines under this extended regulation have been kept artificially low. As a result, demand has been artificially stimulated, but the exploration and development required to provide new supplies to satisfy this increasing demand have been allowed to wither. This form of government regulation has contributed heavily to the shortages we have experienced, and to the greater scarcity we now anticipate.

As a result of its low regulated price, more than 50 percent of our natural gas is consumed by industrial users and utilities, many of which might otherwise be using coal or oil. While homeowners are being forced to turn away from natural gas and toward more expensive fuels, unnecessarily large quantities of natural gas are being used by industry.

Furthermore, because prices within producing States are often higher than the interstate prices established by the Federal Power Commission, most newly discovered and newly produced natural gas does not enter interstate pipelines. Potential consumers in non-producing States thus suffer the worst shortages. While the Federal Power Commission has tried to alleviate these problems, the regulatory framework and attendant judicial constraints inhibit the ability of the Commission to respond adequately.

It is clear that the price paid to producers for natural gas in interstate trade must increase if there is to be the needed incentive for increasing supply and reducing inefficient usage. Some have suggested additional regulation to provide new incentives, but we have already seen the pitfalls in this approach. We must regulate less, not more. At the same time, we cannot remove all natural gas regulations without greatly inflating the price of gas currently in production and generating windfall profits.

To resolve this issue, I am proposing that gas from new wells, gas newly-dedicated to interstate markets, and the continuing production of natural gas from expired contracts should no longer be subject to price regulation at the wellhead. Enactment of this legislation should stimulate new exploration and development. At the same time, because increased prices on new unregulated gas would be averaged in with the prices for gas that is still regulated, the consumer should be protected against precipitous cost increases.

To add further consumer protection against unjustified price increases, I propose that the Secretary of the Interior be given authority to impose a ceiling on the price of new natural gas when circumstances warrant. Before exercising this power, the Secretary would consider the cost of alternative domestic fuels, taking into account the superiority of natural gas from an environmental standpoint. He would also consider the importance of encouraging production and more efficient use of natural gas.

Outer Continental Shelf. Approximately half of the oil and gas resources in this country are located on public lands, primarily on the Outer Continental Shelf (OCS). The speed at which we can increase our domestic energy production will depend in large measure on how rapidly these resources can be developed.

Since 1954, the Department of the Interior has leased to private developers almost 8 million acres on the Outer Continental Shelf. But this is only a small percentage of these potentially productive areas. At a time when we are being forced to obtain almost 30 percent of our oil from foreign sources, this level of development is not adequate.

I am therefore directing the Secretary of the Interior to take steps which would triple the annual acreage leased on the Outer Continental Shelf by 1979, beginning with expanded sales in 1974 in the Gulf of Mexico and including areas beyond 200 meters in depth under conditions consistent with my oceans policy statement of May, 1970. By 1985, this accelerated leasing rate could increase annual energy production by an estimated 1.5 billion barrels of oil (approximately 16 percent of our projected oil requirements in that year), and 5 trillion cubic feet of natural gas (approximately 20 percent of expected demand for natural gas that year).

In the past, a central concern in bringing these particular resources into production has been the threat of environmental damage. Today, new techniques, new regulations and standards, and new surveillance capabilities enable us to reduce and control environmental dangers substantially. We should now take advantage of this progress. The resources under the Shelf, and on all our public lands, belong to all Americans, and the critical needs of all Americans for new energy supplies require that we develop them.

If at any time it is determined that exploration and development of a specific shelf area can only proceed with inadequate protection of the environment, we will not commence or continue operations. This policy was reflected in the suspension of 35 leases in the Santa Barbara Channel in 1971. We are continuing the Santa Barbara suspensions, and I again request that the Congress pass legislation that would provide for appropriate settlement for those who are forced to relinquish their leases in the area.

At the same time, I am directing the Secretary of the Interior to proceed with leasing the Outer Continental Shelf beyond the Channel Islands of California if the reviews now underway show that the environmental risks are acceptable.

I am also asking the Chairman of the Council on Environmental Quality to work with the Environmental Protection Agency, in consultation with the National Academy of Sciences and appropriate Federal agencies, to study the environmental impact of oil and gas production on the Atlantic Outer Continental Shelf and in the Gulf of Alaska. No drilling will be undertaken in these areas until its environmental impact is deter-

mined. Governors, legislators and citizens of these areas will be consulted in this process.

Finally, I am asking the Secretary of the Interior to develop a long-term leasing program for *all* energy resources on public lands, based on a thorough analysis of the Nation's energy, environmental, and economic objectives.

Alaskan Pipeline. Another important source of domestic oil exists on the North Slope of Alaska. Although private industry stands ready to develop these reserves and the Federal Government has spent large sums on environmental analyses, this project is still being delayed. This delay is not related to any adverse judicial findings concerning environmental impact, but rather to an outmoded legal restriction regarding the width of the right of way for the proposed pipeline.

At a time when we are importing growing quantities of oil at great detriment to our balance of payments, and at a time when we are also experiencing significant oil shortages, we clearly need the two million barrels a day which the North Slope could provide—a supply equal to fully one-third of our present import levels.

In recent weeks I have proposed legislation to the Congress which would remove the present restriction on the pipeline. I appeal to the Congress to act swiftly on this matter so that we can begin construction of the pipeline with all possible speed.

I oppose any further delay in order to restudy the advisability of building the pipeline through Canada. Our interest in rapidly increasing our supply of oil is best served by an Alaskan pipeline. It could be completed much more quickly than a Canadian pipeline; its entire capacity would be used to carry domestically owned oil to American markets where it is needed; and construction of an Alaskan pipeline would create a significant number of American jobs both in Alaska and in the maritime industry.

Shale Oil. Recoverable deposits of shale oil in the continental United States are estimated at some 600 billion barrels, 80 billion of which are considered easily accessible.

At the time of my Energy Message of 1971, I requested the Secretary of the Interior to develop an oil shale leasing program on a pilot basis and to provide me with a thorough evaluation of the environmental impact of such a program. The Secretary has prepared this pilot project and expects to have a final environmental impact statement soon. If the environmental risks are acceptable, we will proceed with the program.

To date there has been no commercial production of shale oil in the United States. Our pilot program will provide us with valuable experience in using various operational techniques and acting under various environmental conditions. Under the proposed program, the costs both of development and environmental protection would be borne by the private lessee.

Geothermal Leases. At the time of my earlier Energy Message, I also directed the Department of the Interior to prepare a leasing program for the development of geothermal energy on Federal lands. The regulations and final environmental analysis for such a program should be completed by late spring of this year.

If the analysis indicates that we can proceed in an environmentally acceptable manner, I expect leasing of geothermal fields on Federal lands to begin soon thereafter.

The use of geothermal energy would be of significant importance to many of our western areas, and by supplying a part of the western energy demand, could release other energy resources that would otherwise have to be used. Today, for instance, power from the Geysers geothermal field in California furnishes about one-third of the electric power of the city of San Francisco.

New technologies in locating and producing geothermal energy are now under development. During the coming fiscal year, the National Science Foundation and the Geological Survey will intensify their research and development efforts in this field.

Coal. Coal is our most abundant and least costly domestic source of energy. Nevertheless, at a time when energy shortages loom on the horizon, coal provides less than 20 percent of our energy demands, and there is serious danger that its use will be reduced even further. If this reduction occurs, we would have to increase our oil imports rapidly, with all the trade and security problems this would entail.

Production of coal has been limited not only by competition from natural gas—a competition which has been artificially induced by Federal price regulation—but also by emerging environmental concerns and mine health and safety requirements. In order to meet environmental standards, utilities have shifted to natural gas and imported low-sulphur fuel oil. The problem is compounded by the fact that some low-sulphur coal resources are not being developed because of uncertainty about Federal and State mining regulations.

I urge that highest national priority be given to expanded development and utilization of our coal resources. Present and potential users who are able to choose among energy sources should consider the national interest as they make their choice. Each decision against coal increases petroleum or gas consumption, compromising our national self-sufficiency and raising the cost of meeting our energy needs.

In my State of the Union Message on Natural Resources and the Environment earlier this year, I called for strong legislation to protect the environment from abuse caused by mining. I now repeat that call. Until the coal industry knows the mining rules under which it will have to operate, our vast reserves of low-sulphur coal will not be developed as rapidly as they should be and the under-utilization of such coal will persist.

The Clean Air Act of 1970, as amended, requires that primary air quality standards—those related to health—must be met by 1975, while more stringent secondary standards—those related to the "general welfare"—must be met within a reasonable period. The States are moving very effectively to meet primary standards established by the Clean Air Act, and I am encouraged by their efforts.

At the same time, our concern for the "general welfare" or national interest should take into account considerations of national security and economic prosperity, as well as our environment.

If we insisted upon meeting both primary and secondary clean air standards by 1975, we could prevent the use of up to 155 million tons of coal per year. This would force an increase in demand for oil of 1.6 million barrels per day. This oil would have to be imported, with an adverse effect on our balance of payments of some $1.5 billion or more a year. Such a development would also threaten the loss of an estimated 26,000 coal mining jobs.

If, on the other hand, we carry out the provisions of the Clean Air Act in a judicious manner, carefully meeting the primary, health-related standards, but not moving in a precipitous way toward meeting the secondary standards, then we should be able to use virtually all of that coal which would otherwise go unused.

The Environmental Protection Agency has indicated that the reasonable time allowed by the Clean Air Act for meeting secondary standards could extend beyond 1975. Last year, the Administrator of the Environmental Protection Agency sent to all State governors a letter explaining that during the current period of shortages in low-sulphur fuel, the States should not require the burning of such fuels except where necessary to meet the primary standards for the protection of health. This action by the States should permit the desirable substitution of coal for low-sulphur fuel in many instances. I strongly support this policy.

Many State regulatory commissions permit their State utilities to pass on increased fuel costs to the consumer in the form of higher rates, but there are sometimes lags in allowing the costs of environmental control equipment to be passed on in a similar way. Such lags discourage the use of environmental control technology and encourage the use of low-sulphur fuels, most of which are imported.

To increase the incentive for using new environmental technology, I urge all State utility commissions to ensure that utilities receive a rapid and fair return on pollution control equip-

ment, including stack gas cleaning devices and coal gasification processes.

As an additional measure to increase the production and use of coal, I am directing that a new reporting system on national coal production be instituted within the Department of the Interior, and I am asking the Federal Power Commission for regular reports on the use of coal by utilities.

I am also stepping up our spending for research and development in coal, with special emphasis on technology for sulphur removal and the development of low-cost, clean-burning forms of coal.

Nuclear Energy. Although our greatest dependence for energy until now has been on fossil fuels such as coal and oil, we must not and we need not continue this heavy reliance in the future. The major alternative to fossil fuel energy for the remainder of this century is nuclear energy.

Our well-established nuclear technology already represents an indispensable source of energy for meeting present needs. At present there are 30 nuclear power plants in operation in the United States; of the new electrical generator capacity contracted for during 1972, 70 percent will be nuclear powered. By 1980, the amount of electricity generated by nuclear reactors will be equivalent to 1.25 billion barrels of oil, or 8 trillion cubic feet of gas. It is estimated that nuclear power will provide more than one-quarter of this country's electrical production by 1985, and over half by the year 2000.

Most nuclear power plants now in operation utilize light water reactors. In the near future, some will use high temperature gas-cooled reactors. These techniques will be supplemented during the next decade by the fast breeder reactor, which will bring about a 30-fold increase in the efficiency with which we utilize our domestic uranium resources. At present, development of the liquid metal fast breeder reactor is our highest priority target for nuclear research and development.

Nuclear power generation has an extraordinary safety record. There has never been a nuclear-related fatality in our civilian atomic energy program. We intend to maintain that record by increasing research and development in reactor safety.

The process of determining the safety and environmental acceptability of nuclear power plants is more vigorous and more open to public participation than for any comparable industrial enterprise. Every effort must be made by the Government and industry to protect public health and safety and to provide satisfactory answers to those with honest concerns about this source of power.

At the same time, we must seek to avoid unreasonable delays in developing nuclear power. They serve only to impose unnecessary costs and aggravate our energy shortages. It is discouraging to know that nuclear facilities capable of generating 27,000 megawatts of electric power which were expected to be operational by 1972 were not completed. To replace that generating capacity we would have to use the equivalent of one-third of the natural gas the country used for generating electricity in 1972. This situation must not continue.

In my first Energy Special Message in 1971, I proposed that utilities prepare and publish long-range plans for the siting of nuclear power plants and transmission lines. This legislation would provide a Federal-State framework for licensing individual plants on the basis of a full and balanced consideration of both environmental and energy needs. The Congress has not acted on that proposal. I am resubmitting that legislation this year with a number of new provisions to simplify licensing, including one to require that the Government act on all completed license applications within 18 months after they are received.

I would also emphasize that the private sector's role in future nuclear development must continue to grow. The Atomic Energy Commission is presently taking steps to provide greater amounts of enriched uranium fuel for the Nation's nuclear power plants. However, this expansion will not fully meet our needs in the 1980's; the Government now looks to private industry to provide the additional capacity that will be required.

Our nuclear technology is a national asset of inestimable value. It is essential that we press forward with its development.

The increasing occurrence of unnecessary delays in the development of energy facilities must be ended if we are to meet our energy needs. To be sure, reasonable safeguards must be vigorously maintained for protection of the public and of our environment. Full public participation and questioning must also be allowed as we decide where new energy facilities are to be built. We need to streamline our governmental procedures for licensing and inspections, reduce overlapping jurisdictions and eliminate confusion generated by the government.

To achieve these ends I am taking several steps. During the coming year we will examine various possibilities to assure that all public and private interests are impartially and expeditiously weighed in all government proceedings for permits, licensing and inspections.

I am again proposing siting legislation to the Congress for electric facilities and for the first time, for deepwater ports. All of my new siting legislation includes provision for simplified licensing at both Federal and State levels. It is vital that the Congress take prompt and favorable action on these proposals.

Encouraging Domestic Exploration. Our tax system now provides needed incentives for mineral exploration in the form of percentage depletion allowances and deductions for certain drilling expenses. These provisions do not, however, distinguish between exploration for new reserves and development of existing reserves.

In order to encourage increased exploration, I ask the Congress to extend the investment credit provisions of our present tax law so that a credit will be provided for all exploratory drilling for new oil and gas fields. Under this proposal, a somewhat higher credit would apply for successful exploratory wells than for unsuccessful ones, in order to put an additional premium on results.

The investment credit has proven itself a powerful stimulus to industrial activity. I expect it to be equally effective in the search for new reserves.

Importing

Oil Imports. In order to avert a short-term fuel shortage and to keep fuel costs as low as possible, it will be necessary for us to increase fuel imports. At the same time, in order to reduce our long-term reliance on imports, we must encourage the exploration and development of our domestic oil and the construction of refineries to process it.

The present quota system for oil imports—the Mandatory Oil Import Program—was established at a time when we could produce more oil at home than we were using. By imposing quantitative restrictions on imports, the quota system restricted imports of foreign oil. It also encouraged the development of our domestic petroleum industry in the interest of national security.

Today, however, we are not producing as much oil as we are using, and we must import ever larger amounts to meet our needs.

As a result, the current Mandatory Oil Import Program is of virtually no benefit any longer. Instead, it has the very real potential of aggravating our supply problems, and it denies us the flexibility we need to deal quickly and efficiently with our import requirements. General dissatisfaction with the program and the apparent need for change has led to uncertainty. Under these conditions, there can be little long-range investment planning for new drilling and refinery construction.

Effective today, I am removing by proclamation all existing tariffs on imported crude oil and products. Holders of import licenses will be able to import petroleum duty free. This action will help hold down the cost of energy to the American consumer.

Effective today, I am also suspending direct control over the quantity of crude oil and refined products which can be imported. In place of these controls, I am substituting a license-fee quota system.

Under the new system, present holders of import licenses may import petroleum exempt from fees up to the level of their 1973 quota allocations. For imports in excess of the 1973 level, a fee must be paid by the importer.

This sytem should achieve several objectives.

First, it should help to meet our immediate energy needs by encouraging importation of foreign oil at the lowest cost to consumers, while also providing incentives for exploration and development of our domestic resources to meet our long-term needs. There will be little paid in fees this year, although all exemptions from fees will be phased out over several years. By gradually increasing fees over the next two and one-half years to a maximum level of one-half cent per gallon for crude oil and one and one-half cents per gallon for all refined products, we should continue to meet our energy needs while encouraging industry to increase its domestic production.

Second, this system should encourage refinery construction in the United States, because the fees are higher for refined products than for crude oil. As an added incentive, crude oil in amounts up to three-fourths of new refining capacity may be imported without being subject to any fees. This special allowance will be available to an oil company during the first five years after it builds or expands its refining capacity.

Third, this sytem should provide the flexibility we must have to meet short and long-term needs efficiently. We will review the fee level periodically to ensure that we are imposing the lowest fees consistent with our intention to increase domestic production while keeping costs to the consumer at the lowest possible level. We will also make full use of the Oil Import Appeals Board to ensure that the needs of all elements of the petroleum industry are met, particularly those of independent operators who help to maintain market competition.

Fourth, the new system should contribute to our national security. Increased domestic production will leave us less dependent on foreign supplies. At the same time, we will adjust the fees in a manner designed to encourage, to the extent possible, the security of our foreign supplies. Finally, I am directing the Oil Policy Committee to examine incentives aimed at increasing our domestic storage capacity or shut-in production. In this way we will provide buffer stocks to insulate ourselves against a temporary loss of foreign supplies.

Deepwater Ports. It is clear that in the foreseeable future, we will have to import oil in large quantities. We should do this as cheaply as we can with minimal damage to the environment. Unfortunately, our present capabilities are inadequate for these purposes.

The answer to this problem lies in deepwater ports which can accommodate those larger ships, providing important economic advantages while reducing the risks of collision and grounding. Recent studies by the Council on Environmental Quality demonstrate that we can expect considerably less pollution if we use fewer but larger tankers and deepwater facilities, as opposed to the many small tankers and conventional facilities which we would otherwise need.

If we do not enlarge our deepwater port capacity it is clear that both American and foreign companies will expand oil transshipment terminals in the Bahamas and the Canadian Maritime Provinces. From these terminals, oil will be brought to our conventional ports by growing numbers of small and medium size transshipment vessels, thereby increasing the risks of pollution from shipping operations and accidents. At the same time, the United States will lose the jobs and capital that those foreign facilities provide.

Given these considerations, I believe we must move forward with an ambitious program to create new deepwater ports for receiving petroleum imports.

The development of ports has usually been a responsibility of State and local governments and the private sector. However, States cannot issue licenses beyond the three-mile limit. I am therefore proposing legislation to permit the Department of the Interior to issue such licenses. Licensing would be contingent upon full and proper evaluation of environmental impact, and would provide for strict navigation and safety, as well as proper land use requirements. The proposed legislation specifically provides for Federal cooperation with State and local authorities.

Conserving Energy

The abundance of America's natural resources has been one of our greatest advantages in the past. But if this abundance encourages us to take our resources for granted, then it may well be a detriment to our future.

Common sense clearly dictates that as we expand the types and sources of energy available to us for the future, we must direct equal attention to conserving the energy available to us today, and we must explore means to limit future growth in energy demand.

We as a nation must develop a national energy conservation ethic. Industry can help by designing products which conserve energy and by using energy more efficiently. All workers and consumers can help by continually saving energy in their day-to-day activities: by turning out lights, tuning up automobiles, reducing the use of air conditioning and heating, and purchasing products which use energy efficiently.

Government at all levels also has an important role to play, both by conserving energy directly, and by providing leadership in energy conservation efforts.

I am directing today that an Office of Energy Conservation be established in the Department of the Interior to coordinate the energy conservation programs which are presently scattered throughout the Federal establishment. This office will conduct research and work with consumer and environmental groups in their efforts to educate consumers on ways to get the greatest return on their energy dollar.

To provide consumers with further information, I am directing the Department of Commerce, working with the Council on Environmental Quality and the Environmental Protection Agency, to develop a voluntary system of energy efficiency labels for major home appliances. These labels should provide data on energy use as well as a rating comparing the product's efficiency to other similar products. In addition, the Environmental Protection Agency will soon release the results of its tests of fuel efficiency in automobiles.

There are other ways, too, in which government can exercise leadership in this field. I urge again, for example, that we allow local officials to use money from Highway Trust Fund for mass transit purposes. Greater reliance on mass transit can do a great deal to help us conserve gasoline.

Government by Example. The Federal Government can also lead by example. The General Services Administration, for instance, is constructing a new Federal office building using advanced energy conservation techniques, with a goal of reducing energy use by 20 percent over typical buildings of the same size. At the same time, the National Bureau of Standards is evaluating energy use in a full-size house within its laboratores. When this evaluation is complete, analytical techniques will be available to help predict energy use for new dwellings. This information, together with the experience gained in the construction and operation of the demonstration Federal building, will assist architects and contractors to design and construct energy-efficient buildings.

Significant steps to upgrade insulation standards on single and multi-family dwellings were taken at my direction in 1971 and 1972, helping to reduce heat loss and otherwise conserve energy in the residential sector. As soon as the results of these important demonstration projects are available, I will direct the Federal Housing Administration to update its insulation standards in light of what we have learned and to consider their possible extension to mobile homes.

Finally, we should recognize that the single most effective means of encouraging energy conservation is to ensure that energy prices reflect their true costs. By eliminating regulations such as the current ceiling on natural gas prices and by ensuring

that the costs of adequate environmental controls are equitably allocated, we can move toward more efficient distribution of our resources.

Energy conservation is a national necessity, but I believe that it can be undertaken most effectively on a voluntary basis. If the challenge is ignored, the result will be a danger of increased shortages, increased prices, damage to the environment and the increased possibility that conservation will have to be undertaken by compulsory means in the future. There should be no need for a nation which has always been rich in energy to have to turn to energy rationing. This is a part of the energy challenge which every American can help to meet, and I call upon every American to do his or her part.

Research and Development

If we are to be certain that the forward thrust of our economy will not be hampered by insufficient energy supplies or by energy supplies that are prohibitively expensive, then we must not continue to be dependent on conventional forms of energy. We must instead make every useful effort through research and development to provide both alternative sources of energy and new technologies for producing and utilizing this energy.

For the short-term future, our research and development strategy will provide technologies to extract and utilize our existing fossil fuels in a manner most compatible with a healthy environment.

In the longer run, from 1985 to the beginning of the next century, we will have more sophisticated development of our fossil fuel resources and on the full development of the Liquid Metal Fast Breeder Reactor. Our efforts for the distant future center on the development of technologies—such as nuclear fusion and solar power—that can provide us with a virtually limitless supply of clean energy.

In my 1971 Energy Special Message to the Congress I outlined a broadly based research and development program. I proposed the expansion of cooperative Government-industry efforts to develop the Liquid Metal Fast Breeder Reactor, coal gasification, and stack gas cleaning systems at the demonstration level. These programs are all progressing well.

My budget for fiscal year 1974 provides for an increase in energy research and development funding of 20 percent over the level of 1973.

My 1974 budget provides for creation of a new central energy fund in the Interior Department to provide additional money for non-nuclear research and development, with the greatest part designated for coal research. This central fund is designed to give us the flexibility we need for rapid exploitation of new, especially promising energy technologies with near-term payoffs.

One of the most promising programs that will be receiving increased funding in fiscal year 1974 is the solvent refined coal process which will produce low-ash, low-sulphur fuels from coal. Altogether, coal research and development and proposed funding is increased by 27 percent.

In addition to increased funding for the Liquid Metal Fast Breeder Reactor, I am asking for greater research and development on reactor safety and radioactive waste disposal, and the production of nuclear fuel.

The waters of the world contain potential fuel—in the form of a special isotope of hydrogen—sufficient to power fusion reactors for thousands of years. Scientists at the Atomic Energy Commission now predict with increasing confidence that we can demonstrate laboratory feasibility of controlled thermonuclear fusion by magnetic confinement in the near future. We have also advanced to the point where some scientists believe the feasibility of laser fusion could be demonstrated within the next several years. I have proposed in my 1974 budget a 35 percent increase in funding for our total fusion research and development effort to accelerate experimental programs and to initiate preliminary reactor design studies.

While we look to breeder reactors to meet our mid-term energy needs, today's commercial power reactors will continue to provide most of our nuclear generating capacity for the balance of this century. Although nuclear reactors have had a remarkable safety record, my 1974 budget provides additional funds to assure that our rapidly growing reliance on nuclear power will not compromise public health and safety. This includes work on systems for safe storage of the radioactive waste which nuclear reactors produce. The Atomic Energy Commission is working on additional improvements in surface storage and will continue to explore the possibility of underground burial for long-term containment of these wastes.

Solar energy holds great promise as a potentially limitless source of clean energy. My new budget triples our solar energy research and development effort to a level of $12 million. A major portion of these funds would be devoted to accelerating the development of commercial systems for heating and cooling buildings.

Research and development funds relating to environmental control technologies would be increased 24 percent in my 1974 budget. This research includes a variety of projects related to stack gas cleaning and includes the construction of a demonstration sulphur dioxide removal plant. In addition, the Atomic Energy Commission and the Environmental Protection Agency will continue to conduct research on the thermal effects of power plants.

While the Federal Government is significantly increasing its commitment to energy research and development, a large share of such research is and should be conducted by the private sector.

I am especially pleased that the electric utilities have recognized the importance of research in meeting the rapidly escalating demand for electrical energy. The recent establishment of the Electric Power Research Institute, which will have a budget in 1974 in excess of $100 million, can help develop technology to meet both load demands and environmental regulations currently challenging the industry.

Historically the electric power industry has allocated a smaller portion of its revenues to research than have most other technology-dependent industries. This pattern has been partly attributable to the reluctance of some State utility commissions to include increased research and development expenditures in utility rate bases. Recently the Federal Power Commission instituted a national rule to allow the recovery of research and development expenditures in rates. State regulatory agencies have followed the FPC's lead and are liberalizing their treatment of research and development expenditures consistent with our changing national energy demands.

I am hopeful that this trend will continue and I urge all State utility commissions to review their regulations regarding research and development expenditures to ensure that the electric utility industry can fully cooperate in a national energy research and development effort.

It is foolish and self-defeating to allocate funds more rapidly than they can be effectively spent. At the same time, we must carefully monitor our progress and our needs to ensure that our funding is adequate. When additional funds are found to be essential, I shall do everything I can to see that they are provided.

International Cooperation

The energy challenge confronts every nation. Where there is such a community of interest, there is both a cause and a basis for cooperative action.

Today, the United States is involved in a number of cooperative, international efforts. We have joined with the other 22 member-nations of the Organization for Economic Cooperation and Development to produce a comprehensive report on long-term problems and to develop an agreement for sharing oil in times of acute shortages. The European Economic Community has already discussed the need for cooperative efforts and is

preparing recommendations for a Community energy policy. We have expressed a desire to work together with them in this effort.

We have also agreed with the Soviet Union to pursue joint research in magnetohydrodynamics (MHD), a highly efficient process for generating electricity, and to exchange information on fusion, fission, the generation of electricity, transmission and pollution control technology. These efforts should be a model for joint research efforts with other countries. Additionally, American companies are looking into the possibility of joint projects with the Soviet Union to develop natural resources for the benefit of both nations.

I have also instructed the Department of State, in coordination with the Atomic Energy Commission, other appropriate Government agencies, and the Congress to move rapidly in developing a program of international cooperation in research and development on new forms of energy and in developing international mechanisms for dealing with energy questions in times of critical shortages.

I believe the energy challenge provides an important opportunity for nations to pursue vital objectives through peaceful cooperation. No chance should be lost to strengthen the structure of peace we are seeking to build in the world, and few issues provide us with as good an opportunity to demonstrate that there is more to be gained in pursuing our national interests through mutual cooperation than through destructive competition or dangerous confrontation.

Federal Energy Organization. If we are to meet the energy challenge, the current fragmented organization of energy-related activities in the executive branch of the Government must be overhauled.

In 1971, I proposed legislation to consolidate Federal energy-related activities within a new Department of Natural Resources. The 92nd Congress did not act on this proposal. In the interim I have created a new post of Counsellor to the President on Natural Resources to assist in the policy coordination in the natural resources field.

Today I am taking executive action specifically to improve the Federal organization of energy activities.

I have directed the Secretary of the Interior to strengthen his Department's organization of energy activities in several ways.

—The responsibilities of the new Assistant Secretary for Energy and Minerals will be expanded to incorporate all departmental energy activities;

—The Department is to develop a capacity for gathering and analysis of energy data;

—An Office of Energy Conservation is being created to seek means for reducing demands for energy;

—The Department of the Interior has also strengthened its capabilities for overseeing and coordinating a broader range of energy research and development.

By Executive order, I have placed authority in the Department of the Treasury for directing the Oil Policy Committee. That Committee coordinates the oil import program and makes recommendations to me for changes in that program. The Deputy Secretary of the Treasury has been designated Chairman of that Committee.

Through a second Executive order, effective today, I am strengthening the capabilities of the Executive Office of the President to deal with top level energy policy matters by establishing a special energy committee composed of three of my principal advisors. The order also reaffirms the appointment of a Special Consultant, who heads an energy staff in the Office of the President.

Additionally, a new division of Energy and Science is being established within the Office of Management and Budget.

While these executive actions will help, more fundamental reorganization is needed. To meet this need, I shall propose legislation to establish a Department of Energy and Natural Resources (DENR) building on the legislation I submitted in 1971, with heightened emphasis on energy programs.

This new Department would provide leadership across the entire range of national energy. It would, in short, be responsible for administering the national energy policy detailed in this message.

Conclusion

Nations succeed only as they are able to respond to challenge, and to change when circumstances and opportunities require change.

When the first settlers came to America, they found a land of untold natural wealth, and this became the cornerstone of the most prosperous nation in the world. As we have grown in population, in prosperity, in industrial capacity, in all those indices that reflect the constant upward thrust in the American standard of living, the demands on our natural resources have also grown.

Today, the energy resources which have fueled so much of our national growth are not sufficiently developed to meet the constantly increasing demands which have been placed upon them. The time has come to change the way we meet these demands. The challenge facing us represents one of the great opportunities of our time—an opportunity to create an even stronger domestic economy, a cleaner environment, and a better life for all our people.

The proposals I am submitting and the actions I will take can give us the tools to do this important job.

The need for action is urgent. I hope the Congress will act with dispatch on the proposals I am submitting. But in the final analysis, the ultimate responsibility does not rest merely with the Congress or with this Administration. It rests with all of us—with government, with industry and with the individual citizen.

Whenever we have been confronted with great national challenges in the past, the American people have done their duty. I am confident we shall do so now.

RICHARD NIXON

UNEMPLOYMENT INSURANCE

Following is the White House text of President Nixon's April 12 message to Congress on unemployment insurance.

TO THE CONGRESS OF THE UNITED STATES:

Difficult as it may be to live by the old saw, a sunny day remains the best time to fix a leaky roof. That is why today—with civilian employment in the American economy at an all-time record high of 83.9 million workers, with a solid business expansion continuing, and with the rate of unemployment down to 5 percent and likely to decline still further this year—I am requesting prompt action by the Congress on several reforms in our unemployment insurance system.

The principles behind my proposals were originally advanced as part of my unemployment insurance package almost four years ago. Most of that package became law in August, 1970, when I signed the far-reaching Employment Security Amendments of 1970. At that time coverage was extended to some 6 million jobs which had never before been eligible for unemployment insurance; a much-needed provision for extended benefits triggered automatically at high unemployment levels was added to the system; and basic financial and administrative improvements were effected. In all, these were the most significant improvements ever made in our system of assistance for persons between jobs since that system was established in 1935.

Left unfulfilled in the 1970 legislation, however, were several important objectives on this Administration's agenda for working Americans. The Job Security Assistance Act of 1973, which

we are proposing to the Congress today would meet those objectives by making three major changes in our unemployment insurance system:

—First, it would establish minimum benefit standards for the States, providing an adequate level of benefits to all workers who are covered by the system.

—It would also extend coverage for the first time to most farm employees.

—Finally, it would set up strong safeguards to preserve the neutrality of the unemployment insurance system during industrial disputes.

Adequate Level of Benefits

A properly designed system of unemployment insurance should serve a dual purpose—both helping to tide individual workers financially over the periods when they are without a job, and stabilizing the economy as a whole by helping make up for wage losses which would otherwise cut consumer purchasing power and accelerate business downturns.

But effective performance of both of these functions depends on the provision of benefits which are adequate in relation to a worker's usual weekly wage. It is generally accepted that unemployment benefits are inadequate unless they are equal to at least half what workers would be earning if employed. Otherwise, families relying on the benefits will too often be unable to meet their basic, nondeferrable living expenses, and communities hit by unemployment will find that aggregate benefits are too little to have a significant counter-recessionary impact.

Under present Federal law, the setting of formulas to determine minimum and maximum benefit levels is largely the province of the individual States. On paper, most States do promise the unemployed worker a benefit equal to one-half his usual weekly wage. But many of them also place unrealistically low ceilings on maximum benefit amounts, rendering the guarantee meaningless for a large percentage of workers, especially family breadwinners. In fact, more than two-fifths of all workers now covered by the unemployment insurance system find their benefits limited by State ceilings at a level below the half-pay ostensibly guaranteed them.

In my July, 1969, unemployment insurance reform proposals to the Congress, I asked for action by the States themselves to remedy this serious deficiency. I suggested that the maximum benefit ceiling in each State be raised to at least two-thirds of the average wage of that State's covered workers. The goal was to provide at least four-fifths of the Nation's insured work force half-pay or better when unemployed.

While many States responded in part to this request, only four States, whose workers comprise less than 3 percent of the national covered work force, actually established the standard I had recommended. However, States comprising more than three-fifths of the national covered work force still have weekly benefit ceilings that are less than half their average weekly wage levels. Without denigrating the good-faith efforts of numerous legislatures to liberalize the benefit structure, we simply cannot be content with this situation any longer. The time has come for Federal action.

My proposed Job Security Assistance Act would therefore amend the Federal Unemployment Tax Act by adding a provision that every eligible insured worker, when unemployed, must be paid a benefit equal to at least 50 percent of his average weekly wage, up to a State maximum which shall be at least two-thirds of the average weekly wage of covered workers in the State.

The decentralization of our national unemployment insurance system is one of its greatest strengths. This decentralization permits more flexible adjustment to local needs and circumstances, and I believe that it should be preserved. I also believe, however, that the States have a responsibility to adhere to the basic principles of the system, and that it is up to the Federal Government to furnish such standards and guidelines as may be necessary to protect those principles. That is why I am now submitting to the Congress the same benefit reform recommendation that I urged the States to adopt in 1969.

Estimates indicate that this new requirement would result in an average increase of 15 percent in costs to State pooled unemployment insurance funds, which would, in turn, affect the costs of employers whose taxes support our unemployment compensation programs. To put this increase in perspective, however, we should note that unemployment insurance is one of the least expensive of all fringe benefits related to employment—accounting for less than a penny in each payroll dollar. Considering the enormous importance of this protection to unemployed workers and to economic stability in general, the relatively small cost of keeping it adequate and up to date is a very sound investment.

When the new Federal benefit standard goes into effect, our unemployment insurance system would begin delivering on its promise to working Americans in a way it has never delivered before. The special programs which in the past have substituted for inadequate State unemployment benefit payments—such as the special allowances provided under the Trade Expansion Act of 1962 for workers who lose their jobs because of foreign imports—would become unnecessary as unemployment benefits are raised to fairer levels.

Upon passage of the unemployment insurance reforms proposed today and of the trade proposals which I outlined to the Congress earlier this week, trade adjustment assistance would be gradually phased out and replaced with a temporary program of Federal supplements to bring up to an adequate level the State unemployment benefits for workers displaced by import trade. When State unemployment payments come up to the half-pay minimum I am seeking, the Federal supplement payments would be discontinued, since all workers would then be eligible under the liberalized State laws for benefits that are reasonably adequate in amount. Some would even be eligible for larger weekly benefits than they can now receive under the Trade Expansion Act adjustment assistance program.

The Job Security Assistance Act would thus make unemployment insurance protection more equitable for everyone, by assisting all workers evenhandedly regardless of the reason for their loss of job. Unemployment is just as costly to an individual and his family whether it results from trade, environmental constraints, fluctuations in government procurement, declines in business activity, or any other cause. The effect of my proposals would be to remove arbitrary distinctions among such causes in protecting workers who are involuntarily out of work.

Unemployment Protection

Agriculture is America's oldest and largest industry—and increasingly it truly is an industry, not just an individual enterprise. A growing percentage of the people engaged in farming no longer are their own bosses but work as someone else's employees. Most of these employees earn relatively low wages, have only precarious job security, and have no termination pay coming if they are laid off. Many are members of disadvantaged minority groups.

For all of these reasons, I consider it of urgent importance that we act at once to extend unemployment insurance coverage to as many agricultural employees as can feasibly be accommodated in the system.

Farmworkers were orginally denied unemployment insurance protection on the ground that it was not administratively feasible to cover many thousands of family-operated farms which kept no payroll records. This objection has since been disproved, however, by the successful extension of income and Social Security taxes to a large number of such enterprises.

In 1970 the Congress postponed action on my recommendations for extending coverage to agricultural labor, directing instead that a study be made on the question. The study was undertaken by the Department of Labor in cooperation with land-grant universities and State employment security agencies,

and the results are now in. They conclusively demonstrate the administrative and financial feasibility of extending unemployment insurance coverage to approximately 66,000 agricultural enterprises employing some 635,000 agricultural workers.

Accordingly, the Job Security Assistance Act which I am recommending to the Congress would modify the present agricultural labor exclusion provisions of the Federal Unemployment Tax Act bringing under the unemployment system any farm operator who employs four or more workers in each of 20 weeks in a calendar year or who pays wages for agricultural labor of at least $5,000 in a calendar quarter. The change would take effect on January 1, 1975, thus allowing State legislatures time to make necessary adjustments in their unemployment compensation laws.

The criterion of payroll size was not included in my 1969 farm coverage proposal. Adding this test strengthens the bill by substantially increasing the number of farm jobs affected. The new bill also includes safeguards to help ensure that migrant workers—who especially need unemployment protection—will not be disqualified because of the special problems associated with record-keeping and tax collection in migrant employment.

The coverage definition I am proposing would provide needed protection to the employees of larger agricultural businesses without needlessly adding to the difficulties of small farm operations. It would achieve coverage for about two-thirds of all hired farm workers while affecting fewer than one in 14 farm employers.

In most States, coverage of the larger agricultural enterprises would be self-financing, with the contributions of these concerns meeting the full cost of benefit payments to their workers who become unemployed. Net increases in benefit costs to State pooled funds should be zero in most cases and negligible in all but two States. Even in these two instances, the net increases would amount to only 20 cents or less per $100 of taxable wages.

I know that many in the Congress share my concern that agricultural employees are too frequently excluded from the rights and protections afforded to workers in other industries, and I hope for prompt Congressional approval of this proposal so that we can begin rectifying the injustice. We cannot in good conscience defer this action any longer.

Maintaining Neutrality

As we move to establish a uniform Federal standard that would ensure adequate State benefit levels, we must also insist on strong safeguards to preserve the neutrality of the unemployment tax which an employer is required to pay was never intended to supplement strike funds of those engaged in a dispute with the same employer. Neither, on the other hand, was the income protection which unemployed workers are guaranteed under the insurance system intended to be interrupted when an innocent bystander is put out of work by someone else's dispute.

I therefore propose that the Federal Unemployment Tax Act be amended to prohibit both the payment of unemployment insurance benefits to strikers and the practice of denying benefits to nonstrikers. A gray area does exist between the clear-cut extremes of strike participation and non-participation, where complex definitional problems can arise. Resolution of these problems can properly be left to the judgment of individual States. But to deal with the clear cases, it is appropriate for the Federal Government to set a uniform standard on which each State can elaborate. This the Job Security Assistance Act would do.

Our unemployment insurance system puts some of America's finest principles into action—including those of prudent provision during times of affluence for times of need; effective compassion for our fellow citizens; creative partnership between the Federal Government and the States; and supportive action by the public sector to help keep our private enterprise system stable, healthy, just, and humane.

The Congress can significantly improve the system's fidelity to each of these guiding principles by enacting the proposed Job Security Assistance Act of 1973. This legislation would bring genuine improvement in the lives of millions of those people on whom the Nation depends most heavily—our working men and women.

RICHARD NIXON

STOCKPILE DISPOSAL

Following is the White House text of President Nixon's April 16 message to Congress on stockpile disposal.

TO THE CONGRESS OF THE UNITED STATES:

In our current fight against rising prices, one weapon which has not yet been effectively employed is our national strategic stockpile. Today I am asking for authority from the Congress to sell those items in the stockpile which we no longer need to keep in reserve in order to protect our national security.

Because the world economy has grown so rapidly, short term demand for many industrial commodities has outpaced short term supplies. As a result, prices for industrial commodities have recently been increasing at unacceptably high rates—in some cases by more than 30 percent in the past 12 months alone.

These increases will eventually be felt in higher prices for the American consumer if we do not act decisively now.

By disposing of unneeded items in the strategic stockpile, we can strike a critical blow for the American consumer.

The purpose of the American strategic stockpile is to ensure an adequate reserve of vital materials in time of war without imposing undue hardships on our civilian population. The basic concept is an old one, dating back to the Strategic and Critical Materials Stock Piling Act of 1946. Ninety-five percent of the current stockpile was acquired before 1959—the bulk of it during the Korean War.

The present strategic stockpile totals $6.7 billion worth of material, ranging from metals, minerals, rubber and industrial diamonds to unusual items such as iodine.

Because our economy and technology are dynamic, our capability to find substitutes for scarce materials is far greater today than in the past. We are now able to meet defense requirements for materials during possible major conflicts without imposing an excessive burden on the economy or relying on an enormous stockpile, as was once necessary.

After a careful and searching review of the current stockpile, I have approved new guidelines that would tailor the kind and quantity of materials in the stockpile to the national security needs of the 1970's. The new stockpile would be substantially reduced, but it would contain the critical materials that we need in quantities fully adequate for our national security requirements.

Our new guidelines would provide the needed commodities to cover our material requirements for the first year of a major conflict in Europe and Asia. In the event of a longer conflict, these 12 months would give us sufficient time to mobilize so that we could sustain our defense effort as long as necessary without placing an intolerable burden on the economy or the civilian population.

Under existing law, the Administration has the authority to sell approximately $1.9-billion worth of stockpile material, including substantial amounts of zinc, aluminum and lead. However, to dispose of the remaining $4.1-billion in unnecessary items, Congressional authorization is needed.

Historically, the sale of each commodity has been subject to individual legislation, but this procedure is time-consuming and redundant. To improve on it, the authorizing legislation I am recommending to the Congress takes the form of a single omnibus bill for all excess stockpile commodities; it includes individual authorizations for 16 major commodities.

At the same time that they fully provide for our national security and economic health in the event of an emergency, our new stockpile guidelines also enhance national efficiency and thrift. Specifically, they would permit us to sell $6-billion in no longer needed stockpile material over the next several years.

I urge the Congress to take prompt and favorable action on the stockpile legislation I am submitting. By doing so, the Congress will demonstrate its willingness to act in positive cooperation with the executive branch in a way that is in the best interests of all Americans.

RICHARD NIXON

STATE OF THE WORLD: NEW CONDITIONS, NEW PERSPECTIVES

Following is the text of the introduction to President Nixon's State of the World message to Congress, released May 2.

In January 1969, America needed to change the philosophy and practice of its foreign policy.

Whoever took office four years ago would have faced this challenge. After a generation, the postwar world had been transformed and demanded a fresh approach. It was not a question of our previous policies having failed; indeed, in many areas they had been very successful. It was rather that new conditions, many of them achievements of our policies, summoned new perspectives.

The World We Found

The international environment was dominated by seemingly intractable confrontation between the two major nuclear powers. Throughout the nuclear age both the fears of war and hopes for peace revolved around our relations with the Soviet Union. Our growing nuclear arsenals were largely directed at each other.

We alone had the capacity to wreak catastrophic damage across the planet. Our ideologies clashed. We both had global interests, and this produced many friction points. We each led and dominated a coalition of opposing states.

As a result, our relationship was generally hostile. There were positive interludes, but these were often atmospheric and did not get at the roots of tension. Accords were reached on particular questions, but there was no broad momentum in our relationship. Improvements in the climate were quickly replaced by confrontation and, occasionally, crisis. The basic pattern was a tense jockeying for tactical advantage around the globe.

This was dangerous and unsatisfactory. The threat of a major conflict between us hung over the world. This in turn exacerbated local and regional tensions. And our two countries not only risked collision but were constrained from working positively on common problems.

The weight of China rested outside the international framework. This was due partly to its own attitude and its preoccupation with internal problems, and partly to the policies of the outside world, most importantly the United States. In any event, this Administration inherited two decades of mutual estrangement and hostility. Here the problem was not one of a fluctuating relationship but rather of having no relationship at all. The People's Republic of China was separated not only from us but essentially from the world as a whole.

China also exemplified the great changes that had occurred in the Communist world. For years our guiding principle was containment of what we considered a monolithic challenge. In the 1960's the forces of nationalism dissolved Community unity into divergent centers of power and doctrine, and our foreign policy began to differentiate among the Communist capitals. But this process could not be truly effective so long as we were cut off from one-quarter of the globe's people. China in turn was emerging from its isolation and might be more receptive to overtures from foreign countries.

The gulf between China and the world distorted the international landscape. We could not effectively reduce tensions in Asia without talking to Peking. China's isolation compounded its own sense of insecurity.

There could not be a stable world order with a major power remaining outside and hostile to it.

Our principal alliances with Western Europe and Japan needed adjustment. After the devastation of the Second World War we had helped allies and former adversaries alike. Fueled by our assistance and secure behind our military shield, they regained their economic vigor and political confidence.

Throughout the postwar period our bonds with Europe had rested on American prescriptions as well as resources. We provided much of the leadership and planning for common defense. We took the diplomatic lead. The dollar was unchallenged. But by the time this Administration took office, the tide was flowing toward greater economic and political assertiveness by our allies. European unity, which we had always encouraged, was raising new issues in Atlantic relations. The economic revival of Europe was straining the Atlantic monetary and commercial framework. The relaxation of tensions with the Communist world was generating new doctrines of defense and diplomacy.

The imperatives of change were equally evident in our Pacific partnership with Japan. Its recovery of strength and self-assurance carried political and psychological implications for our relationship. Its spectacular economic growth had made it the world's third industrial power; our entire economic relationship was undergoing transformation. The earlier paternalism of U.S.-Japanese relations no longer suited either partner.

The Vietnam war dominated our attention and was sapping our self-confidence. Our role and our costs had steadily grown without decisive impact on the conflict. The outlook at the conference table was bleak. The war was inhibiting our policy abroad and fostering dissent and self-doubt at home. There was no prospect of either an end to the fighting or an end to our involvement.

Although the historical imperatives for a new international approach existed independently, the war made this challenge at once more urgent and more difficult. More than any other factor, it threatened to exhaust the American people's willingness to sustain a reliable foreign policy. As much as any other factor, the way we treated it would shape overseas attitudes and American psychology.

The context for our national security policy was fundamentally altered. From the mid-1940's to the late 1960's we had moved from America's nuclear monopoly to superiority to rough strategic balance with the Soviet Union. This created fresh challenges to our security and introduced new calculations in our diplomacy. The U.S. defense effort remained disproportionate to that of our allies who had grown much stronger. The threats from potential enemies were more varied and less blatant than during the more rigid bipolar era. These changes, combined with spiraling military costs and the demands of domestic programs, were prompting reexamination of our defense doctrines and posture. They were underlining the importance of arms control as an element in national security. They were also leading some in this country to call for policies that would seriously jeopardize our safety and world stability.

Around the world, friends were ready for a greater role in shaping their own security and well-being. In the 1950's and 1960's other nations had looked to America for ideas and resources, and they found us a willing provider of both. Our motives were sound, the needs were clear, and we had many successes. By 1969, scores of new nations, having emerged from colonial status or dependency on major powers, were asserting themselves with greater assurance and autonomy.

Four years ago this growing capacity of friends was not reflected in the balance of contributions to security and development. This meant that others could do more, and the United States need do proportionately less, in the provision of material resources. More fundamentally, it meant that increasingly the devising of plans belonged outside of Washington. The sweeping American presence was likely to strain our capabilities and to stifle the initiative of others.

There were new issues that called for global cooperation. These challenges were not susceptible to national solutions or relevant to national ideologies. The vast frontiers of space and the oceans beckoned international exploration for humanity's gain. Pollution of air, sea, and land could not be contained behind national frontiers. The brutal tools of assassination, kidnapping, and hijacking could be used to further any cause in any country. No nation's youth was immune from the scourge of international drug traffic. The immediate tragedies of national disasters and the longer-term threat of overpopulation were humanitarian, not political, concerns.

At home we faced pressures that threatened to swing America from overextension in the world to heedless withdrawal from it. The American people had supported the burdens of global leadership with enthusiasm and generosity into the 1960's. But after almost three decades, our enthusiasm was waning and the results of our generosity were being questioned. Our policies needed change, not only to match new realities in the world but also to meet a new mood in America. Many Americans were no longer willing to support the sweeping range of our postwar role. It had drained our financial, and especially our psychological, reserves. Our friends clearly were able to do more. The Vietnam experience was hastening our awareness of change. Voices in this country were claiming that we had to jettison global concerns and turn inward in order to meet our domestic problems.

Therefore the whole underpinning of our foreign policy was in jeopardy. The bipartisan consensus that once existed for a vigorous American internationalism was now being torn apart. Some of the most active proponents of America's commitment in the world in previous decades were not pressing for indiscriminate disengagement. What was once seen as America's overseas obligation was now seen as our overseas preoccupation. What was once viewed as America's unselfishness was now viewed as our naivete. By 1969 we faced the danger that public backing for a continuing world role might be swept away by fatigue, frustration and over-reaction.

This Administration's Approach

We were determined to shape new policies to deal with each of these problems. But our first requirement was philosophic. We needed a fresh vision to inspire and to integrate our efforts.

We began with the conviction that a major American commitment to the world continued to be indispensable. The many changes in the postwar landscape did not alter this central fact. America's strength was so vast, our involvement so broad, and our concerns so deep, that to remove our influence would set off tremors around the globe. Friends would despair, adversaries would be tempted, and our own national security would soon be threatened. There was no escaping the reality of our enormous influence for peace.

But the new times demanded a new definition of our involvement. For more than a score of years our foreign policy had been driven by a global mission that only America could fulfill —to furnish political leadership, provide for the common defense, and promote economic development. Allies were weak and other nations were young, threats were palpable and American power was dominant.

By 1969, a mission of this scale was no longer valid abroad or supportable at home. Allies had grown stronger and young nations were maturing, threats were diversified and American power was offset. It was time to move from a paternal mission *for* others to a cooperative mission *with* others. Convinced as we were that a strong American role remained essential for world stability, we knew, too, that a peace that depends primarily on the exertions of one nation is inherently fragile.

So we saw the potential and the imperative of a pluralistic world. We believed we could move from an environment of emergencies to a more stable international system. We made our new purpose a global structure of peace—comprehensive because it would draw on the efforts of other countries; durable because if countries helped to build it, they would also help to maintain it.

To pursue this fundamental vision, we had to move across a wide and coordinated front, with mutually reinforcing policies for each challenge we faced.

Peace could not depend solely on the uneasy equilibrium between two nuclear giants. We had a responsibility to work for positive relations with the Soviet Union. But there was ample proof that assertions of good will or transitory changes in climate would not erase the hard realities of ideological opposition, geopolitical rivalry, competing alliances, or military competition. We were determined not to lurch along—with isolated agreements vulnerable to sudden shifts of course in political relations, with peaks and valleys based on atmosphere, with incessant tension and maneuvering. We saw as well that there were certain mutual interests that we could build upon. As the two powers capable of global destruction, we had a common stake in preserving peace.

Thus we decided to follow certain principles in our policy toward the Soviet Union. We would engage in concrete negotiations designed to produce specific agreements, both where differences existed and where cooperation was possible. We would work with Moscow across a broad front, believing that progress in one area would induce progress in others. Through the gathering momentum of individual accords we would seek to create vested interests on both sides in restraint and the strengthening of peace. But this process would require a reduction in tactical maneuvering at each other's expense in favor of our shared interest in avoiding calamitous collision, in profiting from cooperation, and in building a more stable world.

Peace could not exclude a fourth of humanity. The longer-term prospects for peace required a new relationship with the People's Republic of China. Only if China's weight was reflected in the international system would it have the incentive, and sense of shared responsibility, to maintain the peace. Furthermore, the time was past when one nation could claim to speak for a bloc of states; we would deal with countries on the basis of their actions, not abstract ideological formulas. Our own policies could be more flexible if we did not assume the permanent enmity of China. The United States had a traditional interest in an independent and peaceful China. We seemed to have no fundamental interests that need collide in the longer sweep of history. There was, indeed, rich potential benefit for our two peoples in a more normal relationship.

So we launched a careful process of private diplomacy and public steps to engage the People's Republic of China with us and involve it more fully in the world. We did so, confident that a strong, independent China was in our national interest; resolved that such a process need not—and would not—be aimed at any other country; and looking for a reciprocal attitude on the part of the Chinese.

Peace must draw upon the vitality of our friends. Our alliances with Western Europe and Japan would continue as major pillars of our foreign policy, but they had not kept pace with the changed international environment. We thus sought to forge more equal partnerships based on a more balanced contribution of both resources and plans.

American had been the automatic source of political leadership and economic power. Now we needed new modes of action that would accommodate our partners' new dynamism. The challenge was to reconcile traditional unity with new diversity. While complete integration of policy was impossible, pure unilateralism would be destructive.

Before, we were allied in containment of a unified Communist danger. Now Communism had taken various forms; our alliances had stabilized the European and Northeast Asian environments; and we had laid the foundations for negotiation. We had to decide together not only what we were against, but what we were for.

Peace required the ending of an ongoing war. Our approach to the Vietnam conflict and our shaping of a new foreign policy were inextricably linked. Naturally, our most urgent concern was to end the war. But we had to end it—or at least our involvement—in a way that would continue to make possible a responsible American role in the world.

We could not continue on the course we inherited, which promised neither an end to the conflict nor to our involvement. At the same time, we would not abandon our friends, for we wanted to shape a structure of peace based in large measure on American steadiness. So we sought peace with honor—through negotiation if possible, through Vietnamization if the enemy gave us no choice. The phased shifting of defense responsibilities to the South Vietnamese would give them the time and means to adjust. It would assure the American people that our own involvement was not open-ended. It would preserve our credibility abroad and our cohesion at home.

Given the enemy's attitude, peace was likely to take time, and other problems in the world could not wait. So we moved promptly to shape a new approach to allies and adversaries. And by painting on this larger canvas we sought both to put the Vietnam war in perspective and to speed its conclusion by demonstrating to Hanoi that continued conflict did not frustrate our global policies.

Peace needed America's strength. Modifications in our defense policy were required, but one central truth persisted—neither our nation nor peace in the would could be secure without our military power. If superiority was no longer practical, inferiority would be unthinkable.

We were determined to maintain a national defense second to none. This would be a force for stability in a world of evolving partnerships and changing doctrines. This was essential to maintain the confidence of our friends and the respect of our adversaries. At the same time, we would seek energetically to promote national and international security through arms control negotiations.

Peace involved a fresh dimension of international cooperation. A new form of multilateral diplomacy was prompted by a new set of issues. These challenges covered a wide range—the promise of exploration, the pollution of our planet, the perils of crime—but they were alike in going beyond the traditional considerations of doctrine and geography. They required cooperation that reached not only across boundaries but often around the globe. So we resolved to work both with friends and adversaries, in the United Nations and other forums to practice partnership on a global scale.

Above all, peace demanded the responsible participation of all nations. With great efforts during the postwar period we had promoted the revitalization of former powers and the growing assurance of new states. For this changed world we needed a new philosophy that would reflect and reconcile two basic principles: *A structure of peace requires the greater participation of other nations, but it also requires the sustained participation of the United States.*

To these ends, we developed the Nixon Doctrine of shared responsibilities. This Doctrine was central to our approach to major allies in the Atlantic and Pacific.

But it also shaped our attitude toward those in Latin America, Asia, and Africa with whom we were working in formal alliances or friendship.

Our primary purpose was to invoke greater efforts by others—not so much to lighten our burdens as to increase their commitment to a new and peaceful structure. This would mean that increasingly they would man their own defenses and furnish more of the funds for their security and economic development. The corollary would be the reduction of the American share of defense or financial contributions.

More fundamental than this material redistribution, however, was a psychological reorientation. Nations had habitually relied on us for political leadership. Much time and energy went into influencing decisions in Washington. Our objective now was to encourage them to play a greater role in formulating plans and programs. For when others design their security and their development, they make their destiny truly their own. And when plans are their plans, they are more motivated to make them realities.

The lowering of our profile was not an end in itself. Other countries needed to do more, but they could not do so without a concerned America. Their role had to be increased, but this would prove empty unless we did what we must. We could not go from overinvolvement to neglect. A changing world needed the continuity of America's strength.

Thus we made clear that the Nixon Doctrine represented a new definition of American leadership, not abandonment of that leadership. In my 1971 Report, I set forth the need for a responsible balance:

"The Nixon Doctrine recognizes that we cannot abandon friends, and must not transfer burdens too swiftly. We must strike a balance between doing too much and thus preventing self-reliance, and doing too little and thus undermining self-confidence.

"The balance we seek abroad is crucial. We only compound insecurity if we modify our protective or development responsibilities without giving our friends the time and the means to adjust, materially and psychologically, to a new form of American participation in the world.

"Precipitate shrinking of the American role would not bring peace. It would not reduce America's stake in a turbulent world. It would not solve our problems, either abroad or at home."

Peace had a domestic dimension. Steadiness abroad required steadiness at home. America could continue to make its vital contribution in the world only if Americans understood the need and supported the effort to do so. But understanding and support for a responsible foreign policy were in serious jeopardy in 1969. Years of burdens, Cold War tensions, and a difficult war threatened to undermine our constancy.

While new policies were required to meet transformed conditions abroad, they were equally imperative because of the changing climate at home. Americans needed a new positive vision of the world and our place in it. In order to continue to do what only America could, we had to demonstrate that our friends were doing more. While maintaining strong defenses, we also had to seek national security through negotiations with adversaries. And where American families were most directly affected, we had to gain a peace with honor to win domestic support for our new foreign policy as well as to make it credible abroad.

We have thus paid great attention, as in these Reports, to the articulation, as well as the implementation, of our new role in the world.

The Past Year

My previous Reports chronicled our progress during the first three years of this Administration. Despite shifting currents, and recognizing that the calendar cannot draw neat dividing lines, there has been a positive evolution.

In 1969, we defined our basic approach, drawing the blueprint of a new strategy for peace.

In 1970, we implemented new policies, building toward peace.

In 1971, we made essential breakthroughs, and a global structure of peace emerged.

This past year we realized major results from our previous efforts. Together they are shaping a durable peace.

● Three years of careful groundwork produced an historic turning point in our relations with the *People's Republic of China.* My conversations with Chinese leaders in February 1972 reestablished contact between the world's most powerful and the world's most populous countries, thereby transforming the postwar landscape. The journey to Peking launched a process with immense potential for the betterment of our peoples and the building of peace in Asia and the world. Since then we have moved to concrete measures which are improving relations and creating more positive conditions in the region. China is becoming fully engaged with us and the world. The process is not inexorable, however. Both countries will have to continue to exercise restraint and contribute to a more stable environment.

● The May 1972 summit meeting with the leadership of the *Soviet Union* achieved a broad range of significant agreements. Negotiations across a wide front, which set the stage for the meeting, were successfully concluded in Moscow. Progress in one area reinforced progress in others. For the first time two nations agreed to limit the strategic weapons that are the heart of their national survival. We launched cooperative ventures in several fields. We agreed on basic principles to govern our relations. Future areas of cooperation and negotiation were opened up. There has been, in sum, major movement toward a steadier and more constructive relationship. On the other hand, areas of tension and potential conflict remain, and certain patterns of Soviet behavior continue to cause concern.

● The attainment of an honorable settlement in *Vietnam* was the most satisfying development of this past year. Successful Vietnamization and intensive negotiations culminated in the Agreement signed on January 27, 1973. This was quickly followed by a settlement in neighboring Laos in February. The steady courage and patience of Americans who supported our policy through the years were echoed in the moving salutes of our returning men. But the coals of war still glow in Vietnam and Laos, and a ceasefire remains elusive altogether in Cambodia. Much work remains to consolidate peace in Indochina.

● In *Western Europe* the inevitable strains of readjustment persisted as we moved from American predominance to balanced partnerships. Generally these were healthy manifestations of the growing strength of countries who share common values and objectives. With less fanfare, but no less dedication, than in our negotiations with adversaries, we consulted closely with our friends. Such a process may not be as susceptible to dramatic advances, but we believe that we have paved the way for substantial progress in Atlantic relations in the coming months. Major political, security, and economic negotiations are on the agenda. They will test the wisdom and adaptability of our Alliance.

● There was continued evolution toward a more mature and equitable partnership with *Japan.* Confidence in our shared purposes, which appeared shaken in 1971, has since been reaffirmed. Nevertheless we have not yet fully defined our new political relationship, and serious economic problems confront us. Our relations with Tokyo will be an area of prime attention during the coming year.

● In the past year we advanced toward major reform of the *international economic system.* With others we have launched proposals to create a more stable international monetary system, and a more open world trading order through new international trade negotiations. This process of readjustment is not without crises, however, and voices of narrow nationalism are heard on both sides of the ocean. We have a long and difficult way to go.

● The explosive *Middle East* continued in the twilight zone between peace and open conflict. The ceasefire arranged at our initiative lasted into its third year, but no genuine progress was made toward a permanent settlement. Some foreign military forces were withdrawn from the region, but the mix of local animosities and external power still makes the Middle East a most dangerous threat to world peace. Efforts to find political solutions are menaced by the upward spiral of terrorism and reprisal.

• For the *South Asian Subcontinent* it was a year of rebuilding and readjustment after the conflict in 1971. India, Pakistan, and the new nation of Bangladesh made tentative moves toward accommodation. But there is still a long road to the stability and reconcilation that are required if the massive human needs of one-fifth of mankind are to be met.

• In the *Western Hemisphere* the United States followed its deliberate policy of restraint, encouraging others to furnish concepts as well as resources for Hemispheric development. A healthy process of regional initiatives and self-definition is now underway, and the foundations have been established for a more mature partnership with our Latin American friends. The common task of redefining and imparting fresh purpose to our community, however, is far from completed.

• *Asia* has witnessed a settlement of the Vietnam war and major developments in relations among the principal powers. It is there that the Nixon Doctrine has been most extensively applied. There has been positive growth in self-help and regional cooperation. But these nations are entering a period of delicate readjustment and American steadiness will be crucial.

• In *Africa* our goals remained economic development, racial justice, and a stable peace resting on independent states. We continue to recognize, however, that these are largely the tasks of the African nations themselves—and there were both hopeful and discouraging events this past year. Our policies of restraint and economic support are designed to help Africa realize its rich potential.

• We moved down the interrelated paths of *national security,* arms control, and a strong defense. The strategic arms limitation pacts with the Soviet Union were a milestone, but major tasks remain—the extension of limitations on strategic arms and then their reduction; the mutual and balanced reduction of conventional forces in Central Europe. In our defense posture we have maintained a clearly sufficient power, and we reached an all-volunteer army. But we are still searching for doctrines and deployments fully adequate to changing times and surging costs. Our fundamental principle remains keeping America strong enough to preserve our vital interests and promote the prospects of peace.

• We paid increasing attention to *global issues* that more and more demand international solutions. Progress was encouraging in some areas, such as reducing the flow of drugs. The world community still refused to grapple effectively, however, with other issues such as terrorism. The global dimension of diplomacy has been developing unevenly.

* * * * * * * * * *

Since last year's Report, there has been historic progress. A changed world has moved closer to a lasting peace. Many events were colorful, but their true drama is that they can herald a new epoch, not fade as fleeting episodes.

As in any year, however, there were disappointments as well as successes. And wherever there is progress, new challenges are added to an always unfinished agenda.

Shaping a peaceful world requires, first of all, an America that stays strong, an America that stays involved.

But the United States alone cannot realize this goal. Our friends and adversaries alike must share in the enterprise of peace.

The President and the Administration alone cannot pursue this goal. We need the cooperation of the Congress and the support of the American people.

It is to these audiences at home and abroad that this Report is addressed.   √

───────

FOREIGN AID

Following is the White House text of the President's May 1 message to Congress on foreign aid.

TO THE CONGRESS OF THE UNITED STATES:

One of the most important building blocks in erecting a durable structure of peace is the foreign assistance program of the United States. Today, in submitting my proposed Foreign Assistance Act of 1973, I urge the Congress to act on it with a special sense of urgency so that we may continue the important progress we have made toward achieving peace during the past year.

Perhaps the most persuasive reason for a strong foreign assistance program was set forth by President Roosevelt in the days shortly before World War II, when Britain needed help. "Suppose my neighbor's home catches fire," he said, "and I have a length of garden hose four or five hundred feet away. If he can take my garden hose and connect it up with his hydrant, I may help him to put out his fire."

Implicit in Roosevelt's analogy was the mutual benefit of giving assistance, for if the fire in question spread, both neighbors would be in danger. Those clear and simple assumptions underlaid our wartime assistance to our European allies and our postwar policy toward the nations of the Western Hemisphere.

Today, we see the wisdom of this policy on every hand. Western Europe is now a bulwark of freedom in the Atlantic Alliance. In the Pacific, Japan has emerged as a major economic power. The remarkable vigor and talents of her people and the dynamic efficiency of her industry are making significant and increasing contributions to other countries, so that Japan itself now plays an extremely important role in working toward a lasting peace in the Pacific.

In recent years, as we have sought a new definition of American leadership in the world, assistance to other nations has remained a key part of our foreign policy. Under the Nixon Doctrine of shared responsibilities, we have tried to stimulate greater efforts by others. We want them to take on an increasing commitment to provide for their own defenses, their security and their economic development. Most importantly, we hope they will assume greater responsibility for making the decisions which shape their future.

We must not, however, try to shift the full weight of these responsibilities too quickly. A balance must be struck between doing too much ourselves and thus discouraging self-reliance, and doing too little to help others make the most of their limited resources. The latter course would spell defeat for the promising progress of many developing nations, destroy their growing self-confidence, and increase the likelihood of international instability. Thus it is critical that we provide a level of foreign assistance that will help to assure our friends safe passage through this period of transition and development.

The sums I am requesting in the Foreign Assistance Act of 1973 represent the absolute minimum prudent investment which the United States can afford to make if we wish to help create a peaceful and prosperous world. Altogether, authorizations under this bill amount to $2.9 billion for economic and military assistance in the coming fiscal year. During the current fiscal year, some $2.6 billion has been appropriated for such purposes under the strictures of a continuing resolution passed by the Congress.

This new Foreign Assistance Act has several fundamental objectives:

—To help the developing countries achieve a greater measure of self-reliance in their struggle against hunger, disease and poverty;

—To respond swiftly to the ravages of natural disasters;

—To assist friendly governments in building and maintaining the military capability to protect their independence and security;

—And to help South Vietnam, Cambodia, and Laos begin the task of rehabilitating and reconstructing their war-torn countries.

Let us look more closely at each of these objectives.

Development Assistance

Hunger, poverty and disease are still widespread among developing countries, despite their significant progress of recent years. Their economic growth—averaging some 5.5 percent a year over the last decade—as well as rapid improvements in agricultural methods and in health care have not yet overcome many deep-seated problems in their societies. Their current needs represent a moral challenge to all mankind.

In providing assistance, however, we should not mislead ourselves into thinking that we act out of pure altruism. Successful development by friendly nations is important to us both economically and politically. Economically, many of the developing countries have energy resources and raw materials which the world will need to share in coming years. They also could represent larger markets for our exports. Politically, we cannot achieve some of our goals without their support. Moreover, if essential needs of any people go entirely unsatisfied, their frustrations only breed violence and international instability. Thus we should recognize that we assist them out of self-interest as well as humanitarian motives.

While development progress as a result of our aid has been less visible than some would like, I believe it is essential for us to persevere in this effort. I am therefore asking the Congress to authorize some $1 billion for development assistance programs during fiscal year 1974 and approximately the same amount for fiscal year 1975.

Emergency Aid

America's fund of goodwill in the world is substantial, precisely because we have traditionally given substance to our concern and compassion for others. In times of major disaster, American assistance has frequently provided the margin of difference between life and death for thousands. Our aid to victims of disasters—such as the earthquake in Peru and floods in the Philippines—has earned us a reputation for caring about our fellowman.

No nation is more generous in such circumstances. And the American people respond with open hearts to those who suffer such hardships. I am therefore asking the Congress to authorize such amounts as may be needed to meet emergency requirements for relief assistance in the case of major disasters.

Security Assistance

Security assistance has been a cornerstone of U.S. foreign policy throughout the last quarter century. Countries whose security we consider important to our own national interest frequently face military challenges, often prompted by third countries. In order to maintain a stable international order, it is important that these threatened countries not only be economically developed but also be able to defend themselves, primarily through their own resources.

The United States can rightly claim a number of successes in this regard during recent years. Our programs to help South Vietnam and South Korea build capable forces of their own, for instance, have permitted us to withdraw all of our forces—over 500,000 men—from South Vietnam and 20,000 men from South Korea.

It is unrealistic to think we can provide all of the money or manpower that might be needed for the security of friendly nations. Nor do our allies want such aid; they prefer to rely on their own resources.

We can and should, however, share our experience, counsel and technical resources to help them develop adequate strength of their own. It is for this reason that I ask the Congress to authorize $652 million in grant military assistance, $525 million in foreign military sales credits, and $100 million in supporting funds for fiscal year 1974.

This year's foreign aid bill includes for the first time separate authority for a foreign military education and training program. We want to strengthen this program so that we can help friendly governments better understand our policies, while they develop a greater sense of self-reliance and professional capability in their own military services.

Aid for Indochina

The signing of cease-fire agreements in Vietnam and Laos marks the beginning of a trend toward a peaceful environment in Indochina. This change will permit us to turn our attention to the considerable post-war needs of Southeast Asia. To ignore these needs would be to risk the enormous investment we have made in the freedom and independence of the countries of Southeast Asia.

The legislation I am presenting today would authorize the continuation of our economic assistance to South Vietnam, Laos and Cambodia and would provide for a sound beginning in the process of rehabilitation and reconstruction there. I anticipate other nations will join in this effort, as they have elsewhere, to solidify the foundations for a new era of reconciliation and progress in Southeast Asia.

Relief assistance for refugees of the war in Southeast Asia is vital to this effort. These refugees number in the hundreds of thousands. In addition to their resettlement, this Administration proposed a major effort to help restore essential community services in areas which have suffered because of the war.

In this bill, I ask the Congress to authorize $632 million for the reconstruction effort in Indochina in fiscal year 1974.

My present request does not include any assistance for North Vietnam. It is my hope that all parties will soon adhere fully to the Paris agreements. If and when that occurs, I believe that American assistance for reconstruction and development of both South and North Vietnam would represent a sound investment in confirming the peace.

Representatives of the United States have recently been holding discussions with representatives of the Government of North Vietnam to assess economic conditions there and to consider possible forms of United States economic assistance. This assessment has now been suspended, pending clarification of North Vietnam's intentions regarding implementation of the cease-fire. Once Hanoi abandons its military efforts and the assessment is complete, the question of aid for North Vietnam will receive my personal review and will be a subject for Congressional approval.

For a quarter century, America has borne a great burden in the service of freedom in the world. As a result of our efforts, in which we have been joined by increasing numbers of free world nations, the foundation has been laid for a structure of world peace. Our military forces have left Vietnam with honor, our prisoners have returned to their families, and there is a cease-fire in Vietnam and Laos, although still imperfectly observed.

Our foreign assistance program responds to the needs of others as well as our own national needs—neither of which we can afford to ignore.

For our own sake—and for the sake of world peace—I ask the Congress to give these recommendations prompt and favorable consideration.

RICHARD NIXON

DISASTER ASSISTANCE

Following is the White House text of President Nixon's May 8 message to Congress on the Disaster Preparedness and Assistance Act of 1973.

TO THE CONGRESS OF THE UNITED STATES:

I am today submitting for the consideration of the Congress the Disaster Preparedness and Assistance Act of 1973. This legislation has resulted from a comprehensive review of all our disaster assistance activities as called for under Public Law 92-385, enacted last August.

A major objective of this bill is to consolidate the responsibility for disaster assistance, reducing the number of Federal agencies involved in these efforts, eliminating overlapping responsibilities and distributing benefits on a more equitable basis. Reorganization Plan No. 1 of 1973, in which the Congress has already concurred, provides the organizational strucure for achieving this consolidation under the Secretary of Housing and Urban Development. This new legislation would also do a great deal to strengthen the role of State and local governments and of private institutions in meeting this important challenge.

In addition, as its name clearly implies, this bill would place greater emphasis on protecting people and property against the effects of disasters before they occur. In this same connection, I would call once again for prompt enactment of the Flood Disaster Protection Act of 1973 which I submitted to the Congress several weeks ago.

The Disaster Preparedness and Assistance Act of 1973 represents a comprehensive new approach to a very crucial problem. To ease the transition to this new system, I propose that during its first year of operation a special Federal grant of $250,000 be provided to each State to help it increase its disaster preparedness and assistance capabilities.

Last year set a new record for the number of disasters which had to be formally declared by the President of the United States —48 in all. Already this year, spring floods and tornadoes have brought tragedy to many areas of our country.

While we cannot fully control the occurrence and the impact of disasters, we must do all we can to prepare for them, to prevent them, and to mitigate and remedy their effects. The legislation I am submitting today can help us do all these things more efficiently and more effectively and I strongly urge its prompt enactment.

RICHARD NIXON

ELECTORAL REFORM

Following is the White House text of President Nixon's May 16 message to Congress asking for creation of a federal election reform commission:

TO THE CONGRESS OF THE UNITED STATES:

A thorough-going reform of campaign practices in our Federal elections ranks high on our list of national priorities.

Many separate proposals for such reform are now pending before the Congress, in light of recent disclosures of widespread abuses during the Presidential campaign of 1972, many more will doubtless soon be made.

I believe that reform is essential, and urgent; I also believe it is vital that these proposed reforms be carefully considered not singly, but in their relation each to the others, and that this be done in a nonpartisan context.

Therefore, I recommend creation of a Non-partisan Commission on Federal Election Reform, to be established as quickly as possible and to be charged with examining our entire pattern of campaign practices and with recommending a comprehensive set of reforms. A proposed Joint Resolution to accomplish this accompanies this Message.

The Commission I propose would be composed of seventeen members. Eight of these would be chosen by and from the Congress, two Democrats and two Republicans from the Senate and two Democrats and two Republicans from the House of Representatives. It would also include the national chairmen of the two principal political parties, and seven other, public members, to be selected by the President. No more than four of seven public members shall be members of the same political party. To further ensure its complete independence, the chairman and vice-chairman would be selected from among the members of the Commission, by the Commission itself.

The Commission's mandate would be as broad as the Federal election process itself. Nothing would be excluded. It would

be authorized to examine the cost and financing of campaigns, including proposals for alternative methods of financing; laws on reporting and disclosure; the elimination from campaigns of violence and the threat of violence, and infringements on the right of privacy, curbing vote frauds, the length of political campaigns; the use and abuse of techniques such as television commercials, polling and computerized direct mail; methods of curbing the entire range of unfair or unsavory campaign practices; and anything else the Commission might consider desirable for a comprehensive reform of Federal elections and campaign practices.

It would be directed to make its final report to the Congress and the President no later than December 1, 1973. It would also be encouraged to make interim recommendations during the course of its work, in order to expedite their consideration by the Congress.

Because it bears an intimate and vital relationship to campaign reform, I recommend that the Commission also consider the question of whether the length of the terms of office of members of the Senate, of the House of Representatives or of the President should be changed.

If the Commission is to complete its work promptly, in order to allow the Congress time to consider and possibly to act on its recommendations prior to the 1974 Congressional campaigns, it is, of course, essential that the Commission begin its work soon and pursue it expeditiously. For my part, I shall do all that I can to facilitate this, and I urge the Congress to take swift and favorable action on this proposal.

RICHARD NIXON

OMB DIRECTOR VETO

Following is the White House text of President Nixon's May 18 veto message on S 518, a bill requiring Senate confirmation of the director and deputy director of the Office of Management and Budget:

TO THE SENATE OF THE UNITED STATES:

I am today returning without my approval S 518, a bill which would require Senate confirmation of those who serve as Director and Deputy Director of the Office of Management and Budget.

This legislation would require the forced removal by an unconstitutional procedure of two officers now serving in the executive branch. This step would be a grave violation of the fundamental doctrine of separation of powers. In view of my responsibilities, it is my firm duty to veto this bill.

Under present law, the Director and Deputy Director of the Office of Management and Budget are appointed by the President and serve at his pleasure. S 518 would abolish these two positions effective thirty days after enactment and then provide for their immediate reestablishment. If the officers now lawfully occupying these Office of Management and Budget positions were to continue to serve, they would have to be reappointed by the President, subject to the advice and consent of the Senate.

The constitutional principle involved in this removal is not equivocal; it is deeply rooted in our system of government. The President has the power and authority to remove, or retain, executive officers appointed by the President. The Supreme Court of the United States in a leading decision, *Myers v. United States,* 272 U.S. 52, 122 (1926), has held that this authority is incident to the power of appointment and is an exclusive power that cannot be infringed upon by the Congress.

I do not dispute Congressional authority to abolish an office or to specify appropriate standards by which the officers may serve. When an office is abolished, the tenure of the incumbent in that office ends. But the power of the Congress to terminate an office cannot be used as a back-door method of circumventing the President's power to remove. With its abolition of two offices,

S 518 is a device—in effect and perhaps in intent—to accomplish Congressional removal of the incumbents who lawfully hold those offices.

Disapproval of this legislation is also required because of the nature of the positions it would subject to Senate confirmation. For over 50 years the Office of Management and Budget, and its predecessor agency, the Bureau of the Budget, has been headed by a Director appointed by the President without Senate confirmation.

The positions of Director and Deputy Director of the Office of Management and Budget were established in the Executive Office of the President to provide the President with advice and staff support in the performance of his budgetary and management responsibilities. These positions cannot reasonably be equated with Cabinet and subcabinet posts for which confirmation is appropriate.

The responsible exercise of the separate legislative and executive powers is a demonstration of the workability of the American system. But, if it is to remain workable, I must continue to insist on a strong delineation of power and authority, the basis of which is too fundamental to allow to be undermined by S 518. The point was made most succinctly by James Madison in 1789:

> "If there is a principle in our Constitution, indeed in any free constitution more sacred than another, it is that which separates the legislative, executive and judicial powers. If there is any point in which the separation of the legislative and executive powers ought to be maintained with great caution, it is that which relates to officers and offices."

RICHARD NIXON

SUPPLEMENTAL APPROPRIATIONS VETO

Following is the White House text of President Nixon's June 27 message accompanying his veto of HR 7447, the Second Supplemental Appropriations Act of 1973.

TO THE HOUSE OF REPRESENTATIVES:

I am returning today without my approval HR 7447, the Second Supplemental Appropriation Act of 1973.

I am doing so because of my grave concern that the enactment into law of the "Cambodia rider" to this bill would cripple or destroy the chances for an effective negotiated settlement in Cambodia and the withdrawal of all North Vietnamese troops, as required by Article 20 of the January 27 Vietnam agreement.

After more than ten arduous years of suffering and sacrifice in Indochina, an equitable framework for peace was finally agreed to in Paris last January. We are now involved in concluding the last element of that settlement, a Cambodian settlement. It would be nothing short of tragic if this great accomplishment, bought with the blood of so many Asians and Americans, were to be undone now by Congressional action.

The decision to veto is never easy, but in this case there is no other responsible course open to me. To understand this decision, we should all recognize what the full impact would be if we call a total halt to U.S. air operations in Cambodia, as now sought by the Congress:

• A total halt would virtually remove Communist incentive to negotiate and would thus seriously undercut ongoing diplomatic efforts to achieve a ceasefire in Cambodia. It would effectively reverse the momentum towards lasting peace in Indochina set in motion last January and renewed in the four-party communique signed in Paris on June 13.

• The proposed halt would also gravely jeopardize the ability of the Cambodian armed forces to prevent a Communist military victory achieved with the assistance of outside forces and the installation of a Hanoi-controlled government in Phnom Penh.

• A Communist victory in Cambodia, in turn, would threaten the fragile balance of negotiated agreements, political alignments and military capabilities upon which the overall peace in Southeast Asia depends and on which my assessment of the acceptability of the Vietnam agreements was based.

• Finally, and with even more serious global implications, the legislatively imposed acceptance of the United States to Communist violations of the Paris agreements and the conquest of Cambodia by Communist forces would call into question our national commitment not only to the Vietnam settlement but to many other settlements or agreements we have reached or seek to reach with other nations. A serious blow to America's international credibility would have been struck—a blow that would be felt far beyond Indochina.

I cannot permit the initiation of a process which could demolish so substantially the progress which has been made, and the future relationships of the United States with other nations.

However, I must emphasize that the provisions of HR 7447, other than the "Cambodia rider," contain a number of appropriations that are essential to the continuity of governmental operations. It is critical that these appropriations be enacted immediately.

By June 28, nine Government agencies will have exhausted their authority to pay the salaries and expenses of their employees. The disruptions that would be caused by a break in the continuity of government are serious and must be prevented. For example, it will be impossible to meet the payroll of the employees at the Social Security Administration, which will threaten to disrupt the flow of benefits to 25 million persons.

But an even greater disservice to the American people—and to all other peace loving people—would be the enactment of a measure which would seriously undermine the chances for a lasting peace in Indochina and jeopardize our efforts to create a stable, enduring structure of peace around the world. It is to prevent such a destructive development that I am returning HR 7447 without my approval.

RICHARD NIXON

MEDICAL SERVICES VETO

TO THE SENATE OF THE UNITED STATES:

I am returning today without my approval S 504, the "Emergency Medical Services Systems Act of 1973."

At my direction, this Administration has been engaged for the past two years in an effort to demonstrate the effectiveness of various types of emergency medical services which can be utilized by local communities. Some $8 million was budgeted for this purpose last fiscal year, and $15 million should be spent in the current fiscal year. I strongly believe the Federal role should be limited to such a demonstration effort, leaving States and communities free to establish the full range of emergency medical services systems that best suit their varying local needs.

By contrast, S 504 would establish a new Federal grant program which would provide Federal dollars to State and local governments for emergency medical services. The program would be a narrow, categorical one, thrusting the Federal Government into an area which is traditionally a concern of State and local governments and should remain under their jurisdiction.

Instead of providing flexibility for local decisionmaking, a new Federal categorical program of this sort would encourage State and local governments to commit limited funds to federally-defined objectives when their funds might otherwise be spent for local purposes of higher priority.

The bill would authorize appropriations of $185 million for this program over the next three years. This is far in excess of the amounts that can be prudently spent, and S 504 therefore represents a promise of Federal financial assistance that cannot be kept. I believe all of us must avoid actions of this kind which tend to mislead and therefore disappoint the public.

My second objection to this bill is that it requires the continued operation of the inpatient facilities of the eight general hospitals presently maintained by the Public Health Service. These hospitals have a record of service to this Nation, and especially to its merchant seamen, which is long and distinguished. Nevertheless, it is clear that their inpatient facilities have now outlived their usefulness to the Federal Government. The number of individuals they serve is declining and many of the facilities have become old and outmoded.

Accordingly, the Department of Health, Education and Welfare has embarked upon a program of contracting with community hospitals for the care of those now served by Public Health Service hospitals. The patients now cared for in Public Health Service hospitals are entitled to receive the best medical treatment available. The fact is that many of our community hospitals are more modern, better equipped and more conveniently located than the Public Health facilities and thus would provide better medical care. I cannot agree to legislation that would deny these patients that opportunity.

RICHARD NIXON.

PATENT REFORM MESSAGE

Following is the text of the President's Sept. 27 message to Congress calling for enactment of the administration's Patent Modernization and Reform Act of 1973:

TO THE CONGRESS OF THE UNITED STATES:

America's dramatic progress from a small agrarian nation to a great technological and industrial leader has been due, in no small degree, to the inventive genius of its people. Names such as Benjamin Franklin, Eli Whitney, Cyrus McCormick, Thomas Edison, Alexander Graham Bell, Samuel Morse, the Wright Brothers and Henry Ford speak volumes about the character of our Nation.

Our creative history, however, has not been a matter of individual inspiration alone. Our Founding Fathers understood the need for innovative thinking and wrote into the Constitution a means of encouraging invention—the patent system—which has enormously stimulated our progress and prosperity.

The national patent system authorized by the Constitution took on form and substance with enactment of special patent acts in 1790, 1793 and 1836. The act of 1836 provided statutory criteria for the issuance of patents and required the Federal Patent Office to examine applications to determine whether they conformed to those criteria. Although this 1836 law has since been amended, no basic change has been made in its general character and it now forms the basis for our present patent system.

While the patent system has changed only slightly since the nineteenth century, the social and economic structure of our Nation has, of course, undergone profound change. The individual inventor, often working alone and unaided, still makes an important contribution, but the lead role in exploring new frontiers of technology is now played by organized research—sophisticated and highly capable teams funded by our Government, industry and universities.

The changing nature of applied research has understandably raised questions about the adequacy of our patent system. Over the past seven years a number of searching studies have been made of that system, including a report by a special Presidential Commission in 1966. Those studies have shown that a successful patent system should meet at least four basic standards. It should:

• provide an incentive for new inventions by offering a meaningful reward to the inventor and to his supporters;

• promote early public disclosures of new discoveries, so that others may also benefit;

• encourage other researchers to explore alternative solutions to crucial technological problems; and

• through the process of discovery and disclosure, widen the opportunity for consumers to choose products of higher quality and lower price.

In recent years, it has become increasingly clear that our current patent system does not measure up to these standards. The United States Patent Office now examines patent applications in an *ex parte* fashion—a series of hearings involving only Patent Office personnel and the party applying for a new patent. The very nature of the examination process denies the Patent Office much information relevant to its decision about issuance of a new patent because that information is frequently held by those who may be in commercial competition with the patent applicant. Thus the Patent Office may grant a patent to one inventor without knowing that similar information already exists. As a consequence, legal disputes between a new patentee and his competitors have often arisen after the patent has been issued, and, because the courts can develop a more complete factual record, a large number of patents have been declared invalid. This litigation is often protracted and needlessly expensive, both for the patentees and their competitors. In addition, there have been increasing allegations of fraud and inequitable conduct in the procurement of patents. The net result is that public confidence in the reliability of our patent system has been eroded, and we have reached the point where reform is clearly desirable.

Accordingly, I am today proposing that the Congress enact the Patent Modernization and Reform Act of 1973. This legislation, which will today be transmitted to the Congress by the Commerce and Justice Departments, is designed to rid the patent system of many of its existing problems without sacrificing the indispensable stimulus to invention now afforded by that system. Specifically, this bill has four major objectives:

1. Strengthening public confidence in the validity of issued patents;

2. Accelerating and improving the disclosure of new technology revealed by the patents;

3. Simplifying the procedures for obtaining patents; and

4. Enhancing the value of the patent grant.

Strengthening Public Confidence

The single most important objective of reform must be the establishment of examination procedures which ensure that new patents are both sound and reliable. The best way to achieve this objective is to obtain as much information from all sources as is practicable.

To remedy the defects of the present system, I am recommending that we broaden public participation in the review of patent applications, that we strengthen the hand of the patent examiner, and that we require applicants to give greater assistance to the examiner in bringing information to light. If we take these steps, I believe we would not only ensure a more orderly and complete patent examination but also greatly strengthen public confidence in the validity of our patents.

Under the proposed bill, the Patent Office would publish all patent applications that seem worthwhile and would then give the public six months to bring to its attention information relevant to the application. Members of the public would be permitted to present their views to the Patent Office in an adversary proceeding, and new procedures for discovery of information and opportunities for the opposing parties to appeal the decisions of the Patent Office through the courts would be established. The bill also provides for additional manpower for the Patent Office so that opposition proceedings can be conducted effectively.

The patent examiner, a critical figure in the application process, would also be given additional tools to perform his job. These would include, in appropriate cases, authorization to require an adversary examination proceeding and to obtain the assistance from a special patent officer in such a proceeding, as well as access to adequate discovery techniques under the Federal Rules of Civil Procedure.

To further assist the examiner, patent applicants would be required to disclose all pertinent information at the outset of the examination proceeding along with a written memorandum describing why their inventions are patentable. In addition, this legislation spells out in considerable detail the duties of inventors, patent applicants and their attorneys to bring to the attention of the Patent Office all relevant information which comes to their attention during the examination process.

Accelerating and Improving Disclosure

A basic premise of the patent system is that in exchange for commercial protection of his discovery, an applicant will disclose the techniques of his invention so that others may build upon this knowledge. Some critics, however, have suggested that the current patent system is not bringing forth the full and rapid disclosure of technology that it should.

The legislation proposed by the Administration would encourage applicants to expedite the processing of their applications by granting a period of protection 20 years from the date the application is filed rather than the present 17-year period from the day a patent is granted. In addition, this legislation would require that patent claims be drafted with greater precision so that others would have a better understanding of how to use the invention.

Simplifying Procedures

The Administration bill also sets forth several important steps to simplify the procedures for filing and obtaining patents. One reform would permit the owners of an invention, not just the inventor, to file the papers for, and directly obtain, a patent. This step should remove the present procedural hurdles to filing of applications by corporations, universities or other research organizations.

The bill would also simplify troublesome problems of amending applications and would give the Patent Office greater flexibility in examining applications containing more than one invention.

Enhancing the Value of Patents

The legislation I am recommending would also enhance the value of the patent grant. The procedural reforms described above, which are designed to strengthen confidence in the examination process, would do much to achieve this goal. But other, more specific changes are also needed.

Current law leaves the owners of United States process patents unprotected against importers who sell foreign products that have been manufactured by utilizing processes developed in the United States. This law should be changed so that exclusive sales agents or affiliates of foreign competitors who handle such products will be considered patent infringers.

The proposed legislation would also permit the patent owner to settle disputes over the infringement and validity of his patent without resorting to expensive and time-consuming court litigation. Patent owners and those accused of infringing patents may instead, if mutually agreeable, turn to arbitration

for resolution once a dispute arises between them. Where arbitration is not possible, improved disclosure and discovery techniques during the patent application process should reduce the expense and uncertainty of subsequent litigation.

In the event of a dispute over the validity of a patent, the legislation I am recommending would clarify the rights of the patentee or a person who might hold his patent, such as an assignee or licensee. Another provision wuld ensure that the patent laws not be construed to replace or preempt state laws concerning trade secrets so long as those state laws do not interfere with the free flow of ideas in the public domain. Decisions of the Supreme Court in both of these areas would also be left undisturbed.

Preserving the Best of the Present System

The Patent Modernization and Reform Act of 1973 is more than a reform bill. It would preserve and extend some of the best and most important aspects of our current patent system. In prepareing this legislation, the Administration considered and analyzed a great many proposals for changing the present law —but our decision was to adopt only those proposals for change that would significantly improve the system.

We were particularly anxious to maintain present standards for the awarding of patents, including the requirement that inventions serve a useful purpose. One of the virtues of the American patent system is its emphasis upon practicality—its demands that ideas be reduced to a tangible form having a known usefulness before the public should grant a monopoly on the concept to the applicant.

My proposal would also preserve the American concept of giving the patent to the person who is first to invent, because he is the individual most deserving of recognition and encouragement. In doing so, we would reject the approach of certain other countries that award the patent to the first applicant to file for a patent.

In addition, the existing state of case law on antitrust standards for patent licensing that have been determined by the courts would not be changed. Some have argued that this case-by-case approach to patent licensing has increasingly eroded the value and reliability of the patent grant. Earlier this year, I requested that various proposals addressed to this issue be carefully studied and reviewed by the Secretary of Commerce, the Attorney General, and my chief advisers on economic policy. After much study, they concluded that there is no clearly demonstrated need or justification for introduction of any patent licensing proposals at this time. They also concluded that the legislation I recommend today will help counter the loss of public confidence by improving the reliability of patents that are issued.

Conclusion

Benjamin Franklin, a famous inventor as well as a statesman, reflected once that he wished it his destiny "to be born two or three centuries hence" so that he could not only enjoy the conveniences of modern life but also satisfy his curiosity. So long as the spirit of Franklin remains alive in America, we can be confident that our civilization will flourish.

Our patent system should always work to foster that spirit. Unfortunately, our current system does not always serve that end. With the changes I am recommending today, however, we can combine the best parts of our existing system with the most promising proposals for improving it. In that belief, I ask the Congress to give the proposals contained in the Patent Modernization and Reform Act of 1973 prompt and careful consideration.

RICHARD NIXON

THE WHITE HOUSE,
September 27, 1973.

FEDERAL PAY RAISE DELAY

Following is the text of the President's Aug. 31 message to Congress on federal pay raises:

TO THE CONGRESS OF THE UNITED STATES:

At a time when the rising cost of living is a major concern to us all, the Federal Government and its employees have a special obligation to avoid any action that would needlessly fan the flames of inflation. This obligation must not be taken lightly, even in cases when meeting it involves a reasonable element of self-denial.

It is in this spirit, and with the knowledge that the action I am taking will help to hold down the cost of living for all Americans, that I now recommend a sixty day deferral in the pending pay adjustment for Federal employees.

As required by law, I am also transmitting to the Congress an alternative plan designed to meet both the rightful needs of those who serve the Government and the common interest of the general public who must bear the burden of increased inflation.

Under this plan, a pay increase for all Federal employees based upon an appropriate comparability adjustment would become effective on the first pay period beginning on or after December 1, 1973. The level of the comparability adjustment will be determined during the next few weeks. My "agent" on Federal pay, the Director of the Office of Management and Budget and the Chairman of the Civil Service Commission, has recommended an average pay increase of 4.77 percent. This recommendation is now being reviewed by my advisory committee on pay, and this committee will make its own recommendations to me in late September. At that time, I will make my decision on the appropriate comparability adjustment.

I regret asking for this postponement of a Federal pay increase but there can be no doubt of its necessity. At a critical time in the economic health of our Nation, when many are being called on to make sacrifices in order to hold down inflation, no one should enjoy special immunity. Thus far labor and management in the private sector have done their share by acting with commendable restraint in agreeing upon new wage increases. As one of the largest groups of workers in the country, Federal employees can do no less. In fact, Federal employees have a unique role to play in the fight against inflation because every dollar of their pay comes out of the Federal budget. It is especially important this year, as we seek a balanced, noninflationary budget, that Federal spending be held to a minimum.

I urge the Congress to support this action, not because it is politically expedient or the easy thing to do, but because it is in the best interest of all Americans.

The alternative plan is attached.

RICHARD NIXON

THE WHITE HOUSE,
August 31, 1973.

FEDERAL PAY COMPARABILITY ALTERNATIVE PLAN

In consideration of the economic conditions affecting the general welfare, I hereby transmit to the Congress the following alternative plan, as authorized and required by section 5305(c)(1) of title 5, United States Code:

Such adjustments in the rates of pay of each Federal statutory pay system as may be determined, based on the 1973 Bureau of Labor Statistics survey, shall become effective on the first day of the first applicable pay period that begins on or after December 1, 1973. ✓

MINIMUM WAGE VETO

Following is the text of President Nixon's Sept. 6 message to the House of Representatives on his veto of HR 7935, the minimum wage bill.

TO THE HOUSE OF REPRESENTATIVES:

I am returning today, without my approval, H.R. 7935, a bill which would make major changes in the Fair Labor Standards Act.

This bill flows from the best of intentions. Its stated purpose is to benefit the working man and woman by raising the minimum wage. The minimum wage for most workers has not been adjusted for five years and in the interim, as sponsors of this bill recognize, rising prices have seriously eroded the purchasing power of those who are still paid at the lowest end of the wage scale.

There can be no doubt about the need for a higher minimum wage. Both fairness and decency require that we act now—this year—to raise the minimum wage rate. We cannot allow millions of America's low-income families to become the prime casualties of inflation.

Yet in carrying out our good intentions, we must also be sure that we do not penalize the very people who need help most. The legislation which my Administration has actively and consistently supported would ultimately raise the minimum wage to higher levels than the bill that I am today vetoing, but would do so in stages over a longer period of time and thereby protect employment opportunities for low wage earners and the unemployed.

H.R. 7935, on the other hand, would unfortunately do far more harm than good. It would cause unemployment. It is inflationary. And it hurts those who can least afford it. For all of these rasons, I am compelled to return it without my approval.

Adverse Effect on Employment

H. R. 7935 would raise the wage rate to $2.00 for most onfarm workers on November 1 and 8 months later, would increase it to $2.20. Thus in less than a year, employers would be faced with a 37.5 per cent increase in the minimum wage rate.

No one knows precisely what impact such sharp and dramatic increases would have upon employment, but my economic advisors inform me that there would probably be a significant decrease in employment opportunities for those affected. When faced with the decision to increase their pay rates by more than a third within a year or to lay off their workers, many employers will be forced to cut back jobs and hours. And the worker will be the first victim.

The solution to this problem is to raise the minimum wage floor more gradually, permitting employers to absorb the higher labor costs over time and minimizing the adverse effects of cutting back on employment. That is why I favor legislation which would raise the floor to a higher level than H. R. 7935 but would do over a longer period of time. The bill supported by the Administration would raise the minimum wage for most nonfarm workers from $1.60 to $1.90, effective immediately, and then over the next three years, would raise it to $2.30. I believe this is a much more prudent and helpful approach.

Increasing Inflation

Sharp increases in the minimum wage rate are also inflationary. Frequently workers paid more than the minimum gauge their wages relative to it. This is especially true of those workers who are paid by the hour. An increase in the minimum therefore increases their demands for higher wages—in order to maintain their place in the structure of wages. And when the increase is as sharp as it is in H. R. 7935, the result is sure to be a fresh surge of inflation.

Once again, prudence dictates a more gradual increase in the wage rate, so that the economy can more easily absorb the impact.

Hurting the Disadvantaged

Changes in the minimum wage law as required by H. R. 7935 would also hurt those who need help most. The ones who would be the first to lose their jobs because of a sharp increase in the minimum wage rate would frequently be those who traditionally have had the most trouble in finding new employment—the young, members of racial and ethnic minority groups, the elderly, and women who need work to support their families.

Three groups would be especially hard hit by special provisions in this bill:

Youth: One major reason for low earnings among the young is that their employment has a considerable element of on-the-job training. Low earnings can be accepted during the training period in expectation of substantially higher earnings after the training is completed. That is why the Administration has urged the Congress to establish a modest short-term differential in minimum wages for teenagers, coupled with protections against using teenagers to substitute for adults in jobs. H. R. 7935, however, includes no meaningful youth differential of this kind. It does provide marginal improvement in the special wage for students working part-time, but these are the young people whose continuing education is improving their employability anyway; the bill makes no provision at all for the millions of nonstudent teenagers who need jobs most.

Unemployment rates for the young are already far too high, recently averaging three to four times the overall national unemployment rate. H.R. 7935 would only drive that rate higher, especially for young people from minority groups or disadvantaged backgrounds. It thus would cut their current income, delay—or even prevent—their start toward economic improvement, and create greater demoralization for the age group which should be most enthusiastically involved in America's world of work.

Domestic household workers: H. R. 7935 would extend minimum wage coverage to domestic household workers for the first time. This would be a backward step. H. R. 7935 abruptly requires that they be paid the same wages as workers who have been covered for several years. The likely effect would be a substantial decrease in the employment and hours of work of current household workers. This view is generally supported by several recent economic studies.

Employees in small retail and service establishments: By extending coverage to these workers for the first time, H. R. 7935 takes aim at the very businesses least able to absorb sharp, sudden payroll increases. Under the burden of this well-intended but impractical requirement, thousands of such establishments would be forced to curtail their growth, lay off employees, or simply close their doors altogether. A "paper" entitlement to a higher minimum wage would be cold comfort indeed to workers whose jobs were eliminated in this squeeze.

Other Problems

H. R. 7935 would also bring almost all government employees under the Fair Labor Standards Act. For Federal employees, such coverage is unnecessary—because the wage rates of this entire group already meet the minimum—and undesirable, because coverage under the act would impose a second, conflicting set of overtime premium pay rules in addition to those already governing such pay for Federal employees. It would be virtually impossible to apply both laws in a consistent and equitable manner.

Extension of Federal minimum wage and overtime standards to State and local government employees is an unwarranted interference with State prerogatives and has been opposed by the Advisory Commission on Intergovernmental Relations.

Need for Balance and Moderation

In sum, while I support the objective of increasing the minimum wage, I cannot agree to doing so in a manner which would substantially curtail employment of the least experienced and least skilled of our people and which would weaken our efforts to achieve full employment and price stability. It is to forestall these unacceptable effects that I am vetoing H. R. 7935.

I call upon the Congress to enact in its place a moderate and balanced set of amendments to the Fair Labor Standards Act which would be consistent with the Nation's economic stabilization objectives and which would protect employment opportunities for low wage earners and the unemployed and especially nonstudent teenagers who have the most severe unemployment problems. To the millions of working Americans who would benefit from sound and carefully drawn legislation to raise the minimum wage, I pledge the Administration's cooperation with the House and Senate in moving such a measure speedily onto the statute books.

RICHARD NIXON

THE WHITE HOUSE,
   September 6, 1973

NIXON SEEKS ACTION ON LEGISLATIVE PRIORITIES

Following is the White House text of President Nixon's Sept. 10 message to Congress on legislative priorities.

TO THE CONGRESS OF THE UNITED STATES:

As the Congress reconvenes for the closing months of the 1973 legislative season, it returns to a critical challenge.

Our country faces many pressing problems which must be solved with dispatch.

Americans want and deserve decisive action to fight rising prices. And they want every possible step taken now—not a year from now or in the next session of the Congress.

Americans want and deserve decisive action this year to ensure that we will have enough heat for our homes, enough power for our factories, and enough fuel for our transportation.

They want and deserve decisive action this year to combat crime and drug abuse.

The national rate of serious crime is now heading down for the first time in 17 years, and they want that downward spiral to continue.

There is also an immediate need to improve the quality of our schools, reform Federal programs for our cities and towns, provide better job training, revamp our housing programs, institute lasting reforms in campaign practices, and strengthen our position in world markets.

Of transcending importance is America's continuing commitment to building a lasting structure of world peace. Our people are now at peace for the first time in more than a decade, and they expect their leaders to do all that is necessary to maintain the peace, including those actions which preserve the Nation's strong defense posture.

At the same time, it is apparent as the fall legislative season begins that many Members of the Congress wish to play a larger role in governing the Nation. They want to increase the respect and authority which the American people feel for that great institution.

Personally, I welcome a Congressional renaissance. Although I believe in a strong Presidency—and I will continue to oppose all efforts to strip the Presidency of the powers it must have to be effective—I also believe in a strong Congress.

In campaigning for the Presidency in 1968, I called for "national leadership that recognizes the need in this country for a balance of power. We must maintain," I said, "a balance of power between the legislative and the judicial and the executive branches of Government."

I still believe in that division of responsibility. There can be no monopoly of wisdom on either end of Pennsylvania Avenue—and there should be no monopoly of power.

The challenge is thus clear. The problems of the Nation are pressing, and our elected leaders must rise to the occasion. These next four months will be a time of great testing. If the Congress is to play its proper role in guiding the affairs of the Nation, now is the time for it to take swift and decisive action.

In sending this message to the Congress today, I want to refocus attention on more than 50 legislative measures which I proposed earlier this year. These proposals, along with my regular authorization requests, are now of the highest priority if we are to meet our responsibilities.

Frankly, the action taken by the Congress on my proposals so far this year has been far less than I had expected. Commendable progress has been made on some fronts, and I have signed into law several bills which were the result of constructive compromise between the Congress and the Administration. Among them have been a new approach to farm legislation, a Federal highway bill which will also spur the development of mass transit systems, an increase in social security benefits, airport development legislation, amendments to the Rural Electrification Act, the Economic Development Administration and the Law Enforcement Assistance Administration authorizations, an Older Americans bill, an emergency farm loan bill, a national cemeteries bill and a medical care bill for veterans.

Yet the work that lies ahead in the final quarter of the year is far heavier and even more critical than that which has been accomplished so far. Nearly all of the significant proposals that I have submitted to the Congress still await final action. In addition, with more than two months of the new fiscal year already behind us, the Congress has passed only three of thirteen regular appropriations bills, all of which ideally should have been passed before the fiscal year began. I regret that it has also been necessary for me to veto six bills this year. Four of those vetoes have been sustained, and the final disposition on two of them has not yet been determined. I am hopeful that in some of these areas where I have exercised the veto, such as minimum wage legislation, the Congress will pass new legislation this fall which will meet my objections. The Congressional agenda for the next four months is thus long and urgent.

I realize that it will not be possible for the Congress to act this year on all of the legislation which I have submitted. But some of these measures respond directly to the most immediate problems before the country. I will give special attention to them in this message, just as I trust the Congress to give special attention to them before the last gavel falls later this year.

In the spirit of responsible cooperation which must prevail between the Executive and the Congress if we are to make genuine progress this fall, I am fully prepared to work closely with Members of the Congress in hammering out modifications to these bills. Already this year I have met more often with the bipartisan leaders of the Congress than in any other year of my Presidency, and I hope to meet even more frequently with Members of the Congress during the coming weeks. In addition, Cabinet members and all other appropriate members of the Administration will be fully accessible and available. There

are, of course, certain principles of vital national concern which cannot be compromised—the need for budgetary discipline, for a strong national security posture, and for the preservation of the requisite powers of the executive branch. But within these limits I stand ready to find workable compromises wherever possible on solutions to our national problems.

The overriding question, however, is not the degree of compromise which is reached between the executive branch and the Congress, nor is it a matter of who receives the credit. The most important question concerns the results we achieve for the American people. We must work hard and we must work constructively over the next four months to meet the country's pressing needs. It is on that basis that we shall be judged.

The First Goal: A Balanced Budget

No issue is of greater concern to the American public than rising consumer prices. The battle against inflation must be our first priority for the remainder of this year.

The executive branch is already actively engaged in this fight:

• We have imposed a strong, new set of economic controls which should help to bring a reduction in the rate of inflation by the end of this year.

• We have taken a series of measures to expand food supplies, so that production will keep up with growing demands. The farm bill passed by the Congress and signed into law last month will make a significant contribution to this effort.

• Thirdly, the Federal Reserve System has been working to maintain reasonable controls on the flow of money within the economy, which is essential to reducing inflation.

We are moving in the right direction, but we must recognize that we can reach our goal only if we also apply the single most important weapon in our arsenal: control of the Federal budget. Every dollar we cut from the Federal deficit is another blow against higher prices. And nothing we could do at this time would be more effective in beating inflation than to wipe out the deficit altogether and to balance the Federal budget.

Eight months ago I submitted to the Congress a new budget calling for Federal outlays of $268.7 billion during fiscal year 1974. Since that time, the Congress has undertaken a serious and commendable effort to establish its own mechanism for controlling overall expenditure levels. If that effort succeeds, the Congress will have a much more reliable tool for holding spending to acceptable totals.

At the same time, the Administration has been working to increase the efficiency and thus cut the cost of the Government. We now expect to end the current fiscal year with no increase of civilian employees over last year's level and with 80,000 fewer employees than in 1972, despite the fact that the workload has increased. I have also acted to delay a pay increase for all Federal employees for a period of 60 days in order to hold the spending line. Clearly, the men and women in the Federal Government are doing their fair share in the inflation fight.

Yet the battle for essential budgetary discipline is still far from won. Although we are only two months into the new fiscal year, the Congress has already enacted programs which would exceed my total budget by some $2 billion and it is considering additional legislation which, if passed, would add another $4 billion of spending in excess of my budgetary requests. In addition, the Congress has failed to enact specific program reductions I have recommended which amount to nearly $1-1/2 billion. Thus, if the Congress continues to follow its present course, the American taxpayers will soon receive a bill for more than $7 billion in increased spending.

These increases, if allowed to stand, would drive this year's budget over the $275 billion mark. That figure would represent a 12 percent increase over last year's budget level. A continuation of that trend would increase the annual budget burden to some one-half trillion dollars by 1980. Clearly we need to draw the line against this tendency. And the time to draw the line is 1973, when excessive spending packs an inflationary wallop that is particularly dangerous.

The Congress has indicated a strong desire not only to control the total level of governmental outlays but also to determine which programs should be curtailed to achieve those levels. I call upon the Congress to act while there is still time, while vital spending bills are still before it, and while it can still go back and reconsider actions taken earlier this year. A great deal of the recent budget busting has been done not through the conventional appropriations process, but through "backdoor" funding and mandatory spending programs approved by legislative committees—two approaches which need to be carefully reviewed. I am fully prepared to work closely with the Congress in determining the best ways to control expenditures and in discussing the particular programs that should be cut back.

In our joint efforts, however, I continue to be adamantly opposed to attempts at balancing the overall budget by slashing the defense budget. We are already at the razor's edge in defense spending. In constant dollars, our defense spending in this fiscal year will be $10 billion less than we spent in 1964, before the Vietnam war began. Our defense forces are at the lowest level since the days just before the Korean war, and a smaller part of our gross national product is being spent on defense than in any year since 1950. Further cuts would be dangerously irresponsible and I will veto any bill that includes cuts which would imperil our national security.

Some people have become so accustomed to Federal deficits that they think a balanced budget is impossible. But balancing the Federal budget is no pipedream; it is a realistic goal. The figures for fiscal year 1973 show that we held spending more than $3 billion below our target figure—and that the budget was actually in surplus during the last three months of the fiscal year.

This record was achieved in part because of the cooperation of the Congress in certain areas, and I am grateful for that cooperation. In other areas, however, Congressional spending was excessive and I found it necessary to veto certain measures and reserve certain funds. I would have preferred not to have exercised those powers, but the public interest demanded that I take such actions. Should those actions prove necessary again in the months ahead, I will not hesitate to take them.

Strengthening the Economy

The fight against inflation must move ahead on many fronts. Even as we strive to hold the line on Federal spending, we must also take a number of additional actions to strengthen the economy and curb rising prices.

Trade Reform Act

One of the most important of all the bills now before the Congress is my proposed Trade Reform Act of 1973. It is important that final action on this measure be taken in the next four months.

This legislation represents the most significant reform of our approach to world trade in more than a decade. But it builds on a strong tradition, steadily maintained since the days of Franklin Roosevelt, of giving the executive branch the authority it needs to represent the Nation effectively in trade negotiations with other countries.

The weeks and months ahead are a particularly important time in international economic history. This month sees the formal opening of a new and highly important round of trade negotiations in Tokyo and the annual meeting of the International Monetary Fund and World Bank in Nairobi. The Nairobi meeting is highly important to international monetary reform negotiations. Decisions which grow out of both of these meetings will shape the world's economy for many years to come. The United States can be a much more effective participant in

such discussions if the Congress provides the tools contained in my proposed trade reform legislation.

The United States continues to seek a more open trading world. We believe that artificial barriers against trade among nations are often barriers against prosperity within nations. But while the trading system should be more open, it should also be more fair. The trading game must be made equitable for all countries—giving our workers, farmers and businessmen the opportunity to sell to other countries goods which they produce most competitively and, as consumers, to buy goods which their counterparts in other countries produce most competitively. In bargaining for a more open and more equitable trading system, our negotiators must be equipped with authorities comparable to those of their counterparts from other nations.

My trade reform legislation would provide a number of such authorities and thus would strengthen our bargaining position. I emphasize again that the Congress should set up whatever mechanism it deems best for closer consultation and cooperation with the executive branch to ensure that its views are properly represented as trade negotiations go forward.

At the same time, I have also requested actions to ensure that the benefits of expanding international trade are fairly distributed among our own people and that no segment of our economy is asked to bear an unfair burden. My proposals would give us greater flexibility in providing appropriate relief from imports which cause severe domestic problems and would also liberalize our programs of adjustment assistance and other forms of compensation to help workers who are displaced because of rising imports. They would also equip us to deal more adequately with the unfair trading practices of other countries, and through expanded trade, to "sop up" some of the excess dollar credits now held abroad which can play havoc with domestic markets.

Other authorities contained in the bill would give us greater flexibility to use trade policy in fighting inflation, correcting our balance of payments, expanding our exports, and advancing our foreign policy goals. One provision of this bill, authorizing the President to extend Most Favored Nation treatment to those countries which lack that status, would be particularly helpful in carrying out our foreign policy and I continue to give it my strong support.

Altogether, the proposed Trade Reform Act of 1973 represents a critical building block as we seek to construct a durable structure of peace in the world and a vibrant and stable economy at home. In the difficult negotiations which lie ahead, this legislation would enable us to assure more jobs for American workers, better markets for American producers, wider opportunities for American investors and lower prices for American consumers.

Export Administration Act

The Export Administration Act amendment which my Administration proposed on June 13th is another weapon which could be helpful in the fight against rising prices. One of the most important causes of the recent inflationary surge has been the extraordinary boom abroad and the additional demand which it has generated for our products. On the whole, this boom should be seen as a healthy, long-range development for our economy as well as for other countries. But as I said last June, when we have pressing shortages in this country and when we must choose between meeting needs abroad or at home, then "we must put the American consumer first."

This is why I have asked for new and more flexible authority to establish certain controls on food and other exports when and where they are needed. I continue, however, to oppose permanent controls because they can upset and discourage our entire pattern of healthy trade relationships and thus complicate the fight against inflation. Our limited controls on soybeans were changed last Friday to permit full exports on new contracts. This action was taken because we are convinced that stocks and new crop supplies are more than adequate to meet our own needs.

Nevertheless, I still seek the authority I requested last June to be sure we will be able to respond rapidly, if necessary, to new circumstances. I also emphasize that new controls will be imposed only if they are absolutely needed.

Tax Reform

This Administration continues its strong opposition to a tax increase. We want to fight inflation and balance the budget by placing restraints on spending and not by adding to our current tax burdens.

At the same time, I remain vitally interested in finding ways to make our present tax structure fairer and simpler. Tax reform has been under consideration for some time and there is a continuing need for revising and simplifying the tax laws. My Administration has made some specific suggestions to that end and has indicated a willingness to work with the tax writing committees of the Congress in a general review of the Internal Revenue Code. This important task should be undertaken now rather than during an election year when political pressures invariably make such reform more difficult.

I would call special attention to one tax reform measure extensively discussed during the 1972 campaign and now pending before the Congress. That is my recommendation for providing property tax relief for older Americans. Retired people with low incomes bear a crushing and unfair property tax burden in many States. Even though their incomes decline with retirement, the property tax in many cases goes on rising. As a result, the home which should be a symbol of financial independence for older people often becomes another cause of financial strain. I again urge prompt action on the Administration's proposal to provide a special tax credit to help older people with lower incomes pay their property taxes. Simple justice demands it.

Stockpile Disposal Act

Another important action which the Congress can take in the battle against rising prices is to provide the necessary authority for selling part of our national strategic stockpile—materials which are no longer needed for national security. I requested such authority last April with regard to $4 billion worth of goods in our stockpile. Such sales, by allowing us to increase supplies in the marketplace of major commodities, could help provide important relief for hard-pressed American consumers. Further, this bill could help to maintain and provide employment for workers whose jobs are dependent upon the availability of basic commodities such as aluminum, zinc and copper, all of which are in short supply.

Our country's strategic stockpile still reflects the economic and military realities of the 1950's—in fact, 95 percent of the current stockpile was acquired before 1959. In the 1970's, however, our military requirements have changed— and so has our economic capacity to meet them. My proposed new guidelines for the stockpile would carefully protect our national security in the light of these changing realities, while substantially enhancing our economic health.

I regret that this legislation has not moved forward more rapidly during the past few months. In the name of national efficiency, thrift, and price stability, I call again for its prompt and favorable consideration.

Other Economic Legislation

As I indicated in my message to Congress on August 3, I will shortly be submitting my legislation on the restructuring of financial institutions. This is a complex matter which requires thorough but prompt study by the Congress.

I call, too, for speedy enactment of legislation which has now emerged from conference which would establish the Council on International Economic Policy on a permanent basis.

Meeting the Energy Challenge

I have previously stated, and wish to restate in the most emphatic terms, that the gap between America's projected short-term energy needs and our available domestic energy supplies is widening at a rate which demands our immediate attention.

I am taking all appropriate measures within my authority to deal with this problem, seeking to increase our supplies and moderate our demands. Looking to the future, I have announced plans for a large scale increase in our research and development effort, and I have asked my top energy advisor, Governor John Love, to meet with State officials to seek temporary modifications of air quality standards. Such modifications would help to minimize fuel shortages this winter. In addition, I will soon be meeting with members of the Atomic Energy Commission to determine whether we can bring nuclear power plants on line more quicly. But the energy problem requires more than Presidential action; it also requires action by the Congress.

It is absolutely essential that the Congress not wait for the stimulation of energy shortage to provide the legislation necessary to meet our needs. Already we have seen some regional inconveniences this summer with respect to gasoline and this winter we may experience a similar problem with regard to heating fuels.

Over the long term, the prospects for adequate energy for the United States are excellent. We have the resources and the technology to meet our growing needs. But to meet those long-term needs and to avoid severe problems over the short term, we must launch a concentrated effort which mobilizes the Government, American industry and the American people.

I have recently called for passage of seven major energy bills now before the Congress. Not all of those can be acted upon with equal speed, but four of these bills are of the highest urgency and must be acted upon before the end of this year. These four would provide for the construction of the Alaskan pipeline, construction of deepwater ports, deregulation of natural gas and establishment of new standards for surface mining. All four of these bills are addressed to both our short-term and long-term needs.

Alaskan Pipeline

Our first legislative goal—and one that should be achieved this month—is the enactment of an Alaskan pipeline bill. Construction of the pipeline would provide us with up to 2 million barrels of oil per day over which we would have full control and would simultaneously reduce by more than $3 billion per year our need for oil imports. I have proposed legislation to avoid any further delay in the construction of the Alaskan pipeline and I am gratified that both Houses of the Congress have already passed variations of this proposal. I urge the earliest possible attention to these bills by the House-Senate Conference Committee, so that pipeline construction can begin.

Deepwater Ports

Until domestic resources are in full production and technological progress has reached a point where sufficient energy sources are within reach, we will have to rely upon imports of foreign oil. At the present time, however, continental port facilities are inadequate to handle our import requirements.

Because of our limited port capacity, the super-tankers presently used for petroleum transport cannot be off-loaded anywhere on our Atlantic coast. I have therefore proposed measures to authorize the construction and operation of deepwater port facilities in a manner consistent with our environmental priorities and consonant with the rights and responsibilities of the States involved.

We must not delay this important legislation. To do so would further delay the economical import of petroleum and would mean increased costs to the American consumer, unnecessary threats to our coastal environment, and further loss of revenues to Canadian and Caribbean ports which are already capable of off-loading large super-tankers.

Natural Gas

For several years Federal regulation of natural gas has helped to keep the price of that product artificially low. Large industrial consumers have welcomed this system of regulations —it has helped them to hold their fuel costs down, and since natural gas is the cleanest of our fossil fuels, it has also enabled them to meet environmental standards at an artificially low cost. This system of regulation, however, has also had the unfortunate result of discouraging producers from expanding supplies. As a result of high consumption by industrial uses coupled with the reluctance of producers to explore and develop new sources of natural gas, we now face a natural gas shortage.

I have therefore proposed that we begin a gradual move to free market prices for natural gas by allowing the price of new supplies of domestic natural gas to be determined by the competitive forces of the marketplace. This action should provide a secure source of natural gas at a price significantly lower than alternative sources. While there may be an increase in the price of natural gas over the short term that increase should be modest.

Surface Mining

Our most abundant domestic source of energy is coal. We must learn to use more of it, and we must learn to do so in a manner which does not damage the land we inhabit or the air we breathe.

Surface mining is both the most economical and the most environmentally destructive method of extracting coal. The damage caused by surface mining, however, can be repaired and the land restored. I believe it is the responsibility of the mining industry to undertake such restorative action and I believe it must be required of them.

I have proposed legislation to establish reclamation mining in this country. These standards would be enforced by the States. I call again for enactment of this proposal, for it would enable us to increase the supply of a highly economic fuel while avoiding the severe environmental penalties which we have often paid in the past.

Reorganization of Federal Energy Effort

The four energy bills discussed above can and should be passed by the Congress this year. There are three additional measures proposed by the Administration whose early passage is important but not so critical they they require action this year. I would hope that these measures would be near the top of the legislative agenca in the future.

On of these bills provides for reorganization of the Federal energy effort. While energy is one of our Nation's most pressing problems, and while the preservation and effective use of our natural resources is an imperative policy goal, it is presently impossible to administer these related objectives in a coordinated way. Our ability to manage our resources and provide for our needs should not be held hostage to old forms and institutions.

I have noted repeatedly the need for thorough reorganization of the executive branch of the Federal Government. I believe the need for reorganization is especially acute in the natural resource area. I have urged and I urge again the creation of a department of Energy and Natural Resources to permit us to deal with these questions in a more comprehensive and more effective manner.

I also again ask the Congress to create a new, independent Energy Research and Development Administration so that we can make the very best use of our research and development funds in the future. Our research and development effort could produce the most helpful solutions to the energy problem. For that reason, I recently announced plans to initiate a $10 billion Federal effort in this field over the next five years. No legislative action is needed by the Congress this year to provide funding, but it will be necessary for the Congress to approve such funding in the years ahead.

Since regulation of atomic energy resources can be better and more fairly performed if it is disengaged from the question of their development and promotion, I have also included in this reorganization package a separate and independent Nuclear Energy Commission to perform these vital duties.

Siting of Power Plants

One of the solutions to that problem lies in the increased use of nuclear energy. It is estimated that by the year 2000 nuclear power can provide nearly half of this country's electrical production.

One of the solutions to that problem lies in the increased use of nuclear energy. It is estimated that by the year 2000 nuclear power can provide nearly half of this country's electrical production.

We now have adequate safeguards to ensure that nuclear power plants are safe and environmentally acceptable, but the way in which we apply those safeguards sometimes causes unreasonable delays in construction. Similarly, protracted delays have been encountered in the siting of our plants that are powered by fossil fuels, which still must provide the majority of our electric generation capacity over the next three decades. Accordingly, I have proposed legislation which would streamline the process for determining the sites of power plants and transmission lines while continuing to provide full protection for public health and for the environment.

This legislation has been under study for two years, and I am anxious to get it out of committees and onto the statute books.

Santa Barbara Energy Reserve

It is important to the necessary expansion of our domestic energy resources that we make more effective use of the vast oil and gas reserves along our Outer Continental Shelf. That is why I have ordered the Department of the Interior to triple the leasing schedule in this area and have directed the Council on Environmental Quality to study the feasibility of extending Outer Continental Shelf leasing to the waters off our Atlantic Coast and the Gulf of Alaska. I am equally determined, however, that our efforts to expand energy production should not run rough-shod over our valid concern to protect and enhance the natural environment.

I have therefore proposed in the past, and have resubmitted to the Congress this year, legislation to cancel oil leases in the Santa Barbara Channel and to create in that area a National Energy Reserve. Under this legislation, oil from Naval Petroleum Reserve No. 1 in California would be substituted for the oil off Santa Barbara and part of the proceeds from that production would be used to meet the expenses of exploring other potentially vast oil and gas reserves in Naval Petroleum Reserve No. 4 in Alaska. I believe that this legislation would permit us to maintain momentum in exploration and development while at the same time removing the threat of oil spills as a result of the unique geological formations off the Southern California coast.

In view of the present scarcity of fuels, it is important that we act now to draw upon the oil available in the Naval Petroleum Reserve No. 1 (Elk Hills). During the next several days, at my direction, representatives of the Administration will seek the necessary consultations with members of the Congress in order to increase   production of oil from Elk Hills. This increased production should help to meet the fuel needs of the West Coast this winter.

Restoring and Renewing Our Environment

In my message to the Congress on February 15th of this year, I was able to report that our Nation had moved away from an era of environmental neglect into a new era of restoration and renewal. The 92nd Congress helped in this process by enacting a number of important measures in 1971 and 1972.

Unfortunately, that Congress failed to act upon nineteen of my environmental proposals, and the Administration therefore resubmitted them last winter to the new Congress. While most of these measures still await action, I continue to hope that the Congress will turn its attention to them.

Some say we have been the victim of our own success—that we have passed important legislation in the environmental area and that many are now tempted to rest on these laurels. But such lassitude would be dangerous. There are many areas of environmental concern still to be addressed. Three particularly important matters are national land use policy, the regulation of toxic substances, and the assurance of safe drinking water.

National Land Use Policy Act

The management of our lands is an emerging need of the highest priority. I firmly believe that land use policy is, and must remain, a basic responsiblity of State and local governments and that the Federal Government should not usurp their functions. Nevertheless, the Federal Government should exercise leadership concerning the land use decisionmaking process, since our land is part of our national heritage and since decisions about land use often have regional and national consequences. The proposals I have made are designed to strike a careful balance between the setting of general standards at the Federal level and specific enforcement at the State and local level.

We first transmitted the proposed National Land Use Policy Act to the Congress in 1971, but there has been no law enacted since then. I am pleased, however, that the Senate has passed legislation invorporating many of the policies I have roles of the Federal, State and local governments in land use regulation. The Senate bill is deficient, however, in that it imposes an excessive financial burden on the Federal Government. I am hopeful that a responsible compromise can be worked out in the weeks ahead.

Toxic Substances

Because the great quantities of new chemicals now being used by industry pose undefined hazards to human life and the environment, I also asked the Congress again last February for legislation that would set standards for determining whether such chemicals are hazardous.

Such legislation has now passed both Houses of the Congress and is in conference committee. Although the Congressional version differs somewhat from the proposals the Administration has submitted, this new legislation would take the essential step of providing the Environmental Protection Agency with significant new authorities in this area. I am confident that a reasonable solution will be ironed out in conference, and I urge the Congress to move forward as rapidly as possible.

Safe Drinking Water Act

Finally, we must take new steps to protect the purity of our drinking water. The Federal Government's role in this process, however, should not be that of direct regulation but rather that of stimulating State and local authorities to ensure that national standards are met. I have asked that the primary monitoring and enforcement responsibilities for such standards be left with the States and localities.

This legislation has passed the Senate and awaits action in the House. While I urge prompt approval of this important new authority for the Environmental Protection Agency, I caution the Congress not to impinge on State and local powers and not to shift the responsibility for financing this program to the Federal Government and away from the users, where it belongs.

Human Resource Needs

It is an old adage that people are our most precious resource, but our legislative progress so far this year scarcely reflects that belief. Only a handful of bills has been passed in this important field. There are many other human resource measures proposed by the Administration and now pending before the Congress which deserve prompt consideration.

Education

As the Congress resumes its work for the fall legislative session, some 50 million young Americans are returning to elementary and secondary school classrooms all across the country. There they will pursue the education which is so important in broadening their horizons for the future and keeping our country progressive and free. Making sure that real educational excellence is available to all of those children must rank high on any list of human resource priorities for our Nation.

Constructive cooperation between the Administration and the Congress has already produced notable gains on this front over the past several years. The dismantling of dual school systems in the South is now virtually complete and the task of remedying school discrimination elsewhere in the country is proceeding harmoniously with forced busing being kept to a minimum. The National Institute of Education, which was created at my request by the Congress in 1972, is becoming the center for educational reform and innovation we hoped it could be. Total Federal outlays for education will reach $13.8 billion under my 1974 budget proposals—an increase of $4.8 billion over the 1969 level.

Of crucial importance now, however, is whether those funds are being channeled in such a way as to purchase maximum educational benefit for the students they are intended to help. The experience of nearly a decade since the Federal Government shouldered a major school aid role under the Elementary and Secondary Education Act of 1965 indicates that these funds are not being used as effectively and equitably as they should be. Elementary and secondary education grant programs have proved so rigid, narrow, fragmented and encumbered with red tape that reform, consolidation, greater equity and simplification are now essential.

It was to meet this need that I first asked the Congress early in 1971 to shift most Federal education programs from a categorical grant basis to a special revenue sharing approach. The need is still unmet as another school year starts. The best remedy is contained in the principles of the education legislation which the Administration proposed in 1971 and again in March of this year. The principles are more important than the question of how the bill is titled or who gets the credit.

I realize that the Better Schools Act has encountered difficulties in the Congress. I believe, however, that an acceptable proposal can be developed, and I am ready to work closely with the Congress to see that this goal is accomplished.

It will take political courage for the House and Senate to reject proposals which would perpetuate the more than 30 categorical grant programs perennially popular with legislators. But these programs are so tangled that we must move toward streamlining them and toward transferring key decisionmaking power out of the Washington bureaucracy back to the State and local levels where it can be exercised more intelligently. But if the Congress will keep its attention focused on the question of what best serves our school children, I believe it will recognize the need for prompt action.

Another area of renewed interest this fall is busing. My position is well known. I am opposed to compulsory busing for the purpose of achieving racial balance in our schools. I continue to believe in the neighborhood school—in the right of children to attend schools near their homes with friends who live near them. I continue to believe that busing is an unsatisfactory remedy for the inequities and inequalities of educational opportunity that exist in our country, tragic as those discrepancies are. We have been working to end those discrepancies, and we will continue to do so. But we should also place effective and reasonable curbs on busing in a way which would aid rather than challenge the courts. Last year I proposed legislation designed to achieve this goal. I will continue to work with the Congress in an effort to enact legislaton which will end involuntary busing for purposes of racial balance and concentrate our effort on true opportunity in education.

Welfare Reform

Another critical need in the human resource area is to overhaul our welfare system. Earlier this year I directed that vigorous steps be taken to strengthen the management of the welfare program through administrative measures and legislative proposals. I have further directed that the study of legislative proposals include a review not only of the basic welfare program but also its relationship to other ›programs designed to assist low-income families, such as food stamps, public housing and medicaid. That study is now going forward, and I will be reviewing its results in the weeks ahead.

Manpower Training and Related Legislation

A second basic concern of public policy in the area of human resources involves the effort to guarantee to all our people the opportunity and satisfaction of working at a good job for a good wage. The Administration and the Congress have worked together effectively to foster the economic expansion which has now brought our total employment to record levels and has raised real wages significantly. In addition, we have taken important steps to improve the quality of the work environment. These steps have included passage of the landmark Occupational Safety and Health Act of 1970 and a major overhaul of the unemployment insurance system.

But much remains to be done, especially for those workers on the fringes of the labor force whose low skills or other disadvantages leave them "on the outside looking in." Massive Federal aid in the manpower training field, as in education, dates from the 1960's—and here, too, it has become clear from the perspective of the 1970's that reform must be the order of the day. A special revenue sharing approach permitting States and communities to tailor their own programs to local needs will get better results for the dollar than those achieved by inflexible categorical grant programs designed in Washington.

In the face of Congressional rejection of my proposals in this area in 1971 and 1972, I directed the Secretary of Labor last January to implement administratively the principles of manpower revenue sharing, in so far as possible under existing law. That effort is now going forward, but I am certainly prepared to work with the Congress to achieve this same goal through legislation.

Working men and women will also be looking to the Congress this fall for action on three other bills which the Administration is requesting in their interest:

• *The Job Security Assistance Act*, which would establish minimum benefit levels for State unemployment compensation programs and extend coverage to farm workers;

• *The Vocational Rehabilitation Act* amendments, which would extend and improve job training programs for the handicapped, taking the place of an earlier measure whose severe over-spending provisions and program distortions necessitated my veto in March; and

• A constructive measure that would *raise the minimum wage* in light of the cost of living increases since the last such adjustment in 1968. Such legislation is essential to replace an earlier minimum wage bill which I felt compelled to veto last week because it would have hurt low-income workers and would have added to inflationary pressures in the economy.

Pension Reform

For most Americans, there are now two principal ways of providing for retirement. The first is the social security system, which is the largest system of its kind in the world and one of the most effective. The second is the system of private pension plans. Those plans now cover some 30 million workers and pay benefits to another 6 million retired persons.

As private pension plans have developed, certain flaws have also become apparent. The Federal Government should now act to help correct them. I first asked the Congress to enact pension reform legislation in 1971 and, after 16 months of additional study and hearings, I submitted two new bills to the Congress in the spring of this year.

One of these bills, the Retirement Benefits Tax Act, would give each worker greater rights in his pension plan and require that more money be put into it so that he will be more fully protected if he leaves his job before retirement. Unlike some of the alternative bills, it would also maintain strong encouragement for other employers to set up pension plans—an important provision since about half of the total private labor force is not covered at the present time.

The second bill, the Employee Benefits Protection Act, would establish tighter fiduciary standards for the administration of the more than $160 billion now invested in private pension and welfare funds. The unscrupulous activity which has sometimes characterized the administration of these funds in the past convinces me that the Federal Government should play a watchdog role.

I am aware that several other pension proposals have support on Capitol Hill. A reasonable compromise seems in order, and my Administration is anxious to work with the Congress to achieve agreement in the months ahead.

Health Legislation

In the field of health care and medical protection, the Administration remains committeed to a broad national health strategy which will eliminate financial barriers to needed medical help for every American family and will open to all our people the promise of longer, fuller lives with increasing freedom from disease. We have nearly doubled Federal outlays for health since I took office, and we have been mobilizing to conquer cancer and to fight other particularly cruel enemies such as heart disease, and drug abuse.

My number one priority in this field over the long term remains the building of a balanced health insurance partnership in which the public and private sectors join to bring the costs of quality care within every family's reach. However, the present crowded calendars of key Congressional committees make it seem more likely to me that the real push for this reform must come in 1974. We will move forward this fall with the work needed for the introduction of legislaton at an early date.

An attainable goal for these final months of 1973 is passage of the Administration's proposed Health Maintenance Organization Assistance Act, which would provide Federal money to demonstrate the promising innovation of group medical centers where quality care can be maximized and costs minimized. The Senate has passed a bill to further the HMO concept. That bill, however, calls for a full-scale development effort rather than a limited demonstration program. A national development effort would require funding levels far beyond what is needed or what we can afford. The House is presently developing a bill which would be a fiscally responsible demonstration effort. If such a bill is passed by the full Congress, I will support it.

Legal Services Corporation

The Administration will also work closely with the Congress in the weeks ahead to obtain final passage of our bill to establish a Legal Services Corporation which would provide the poor with quality legal representation, would be free from political pressures, and would include safeguards to ensure its operation in a responsible manner. Legal Services legislation has passed the House. Nothing should now stand in the way of prompt Senate action.

Indian Legislation

The steadfast policy of this Administration is to advance the opportunities of American Indians for self-determination without bringing an end to the special Federal relationship with recognized Indian tribes. To that end, there are now six major pieces of legislation pending in the Congress which I proposed as long ago as July of 1970. This legislation would help to foster greater self-determination for the Indians, to expand their business opportunities, and to provide better protection of their natural resources. Many Indian leaders have indicated strong support for this legislaton, and I would hope that the Congress will now act on it with the speed that it so clearly deserves.

Pensions for Veterans

This Administration strongly believes that the Nation owes a special debt to its veterans, and we have tried to fulfill that obligation by supporting a number of improvements in veterans legislation. During the past four years, for instance, I have twice signed bills increasing the educational benefits for veterans and, during the current year, I have signed into law bills covering health care and cemetery benefits. All of those bills were the product of close cooperation between the Congress and the Administration.

The Congress is currently considering new pension legislation for veterans. With certain modifications, this bill would be a good first step toward the full reform which I believe to be necessary and which should be considered during the early days of the next session of the Congress.

Consumer Affairs

Early in 1971, after the Congress had failed to act on my proposal to create an Office of Consumer Affairs, I established such an office by Executive order. The office is now a part of the Department of Health, Education and Welfare. In addition to playing an important role in forming Administration policy on consumer affairs and helping to educate the public on better ways to make consumer choices, the office seeks to represent consumer interests in testimony before the Congress and acts as a general ombudsman for the individual consumer.

I am convinced that we can do a good job for the consumer without excessive Federal intervention which could destroy the freedom of the American marketplace. However, I believe that more sould be done in this field. To that end, I outlined this spring appropriate legislative specifications for establishing a separate Consumer Protection Agency and I am prepared to work further with the Congress on this issue.

Volunteerism

More than two years ago, in order to advance our tradition of voluntary action, I created a new Federal agency called ACTION. That agency is now responsible for directing federally funded domestic volunteer programs as well as the Peace Corps. ACTION has now proved to be an effective way of en-

couraging greater voluntary action here and abroad, and I am now anxious to place it on a more permanent footing. Accordingly, I ask that the Congress act this fall to provide legislative authority for this agency. Appropriate language for this legislation was agreed to prior to the August recess by a bipartisan group of sponsors in the House and Senate and by the Administration. I hope that this legislation will soon be sent to me for signature.

Building Better Communities

As we look back over the past decade, we can take pride in the fact that we have substantially slowed the processes of social upheaval in our cities. Yet by any yardstick, there is a great deal of work ahead if we are to make life in our communities as healthy and enriching as it should be.

It would be reassuring to believe that the expensive Federal Government programs of the past have made great inroads on our urban problems, but that is clearly not the case. Many of the programs designed for this purpose, such as urban renewal and the Model Cities experiment, have not done the job that was expected of them and often have had a counterproductive impact. Consequently, I have recommended they be scrapped. We have learned from experience that we cannot cure our social ills simply by throwing money at them or dictating prescriptions from Washington.

What we are seeking now is a set of new approaches and a set of new programs: we are seeking change that works. My Administration has proposed a series of initiatives which would guide us along a more productive path. I have been keenly disappointed that some Members of the Congress seem so interested in continuing programs that are proven failures that we are unable to gain a full hearing for new approaches that clearly deserve a chance.

So far, the only significant legislative breakthrough this year has been the enactment of a modified highway bill, permitting some of the money in the Highway Trust Fund to be used for vitally needed mass transit systems. This is a concept which I vigorously advocated and I signed it into law with a strong sense of pride and hope. Other Administration initiatives, however, still languish on Capitol Hill. To break the present stalemate, I am prepared to accept something less than the full legislative measures I have proposed. I would hope that in the same spirit some Members of the Congress would drop their insistence upon continuing the programs which have produced such limited social returns.

The Better Communities Act

The Better Communities Act is the centerpiece of the legislative package which my Administration has sent to the Congress this year in the community development field. Embodied in this bill is a fundamentally different approach to the problems of community life. If it were passed, the Federal Government would continue to funnel money into our communities, but essential decisions on how that money was to be spent would no longer be made in Washington but at the local level. Five categorical grant programs and two loan programs which have proven to be inflexible and fragmented would be replaced and local governments would no longer be hamstrung by Washington's red tape.

I am aware that action on this bill has been delayed partly because some Members of the Congress wish to consider the Administration's housing proposals simultaneously. As I indicated in March, I ordered an intensive six-month study of Government housing policies to be conducted before I submitted such proposals. That study has just been completed and I plan to submit shortly a new set of housing policy recommendations to the Congress. When those recommendations arrive, I am hopeful that the Congress will move swiftly on both the Better Communities Act and the housing requests. Final action in 1973 may be an unrealistic goal, but I would certainly hope that we might have new laws on the books by early spring in 1974.

Finally, it is important that the Congress pass the simple one-year extension of the FHA mortgage insurance programs which will expire October 1. Last week the House of Representatives took constructive action by refusing to act on an extension bill which contained several undesirable "Christmas tree" amendments. The Congress should now act swiftly and responsibly in order to prevent a repeat of the month-long gap in FHA insurance activity which occurred early this summer.

Railroads

There can be no doubt that the plight of the rail lines in the 17 States of the Northeast and Midwest presents an immediate and far-reaching transportation problem. Six major railroad lines in this area are now bankrupt and shutdowns are threatened. The danger extends across the country because railroads in other parts of the Nation still use the bankrupt lines. A failure of any significant part of our Nation's railroad system would impair our ability to move freight efficiently and cheaply to all parts of our Nation.

The solution proposed by the Administration would provide for the restructuring of the railroad system so that new, privately-owned and economically viable rail systems could be developed from those now in bankruptcy. The Federal Government would provide some $125 million over an 18-month period to assist in this process. While we are always open to suggestions for improvement in our proposal, I feel that some of the alternatives which have been aired in the Congress—especially those which would merely postpone action or would saddle the Federal Government with a heavy financial burden, or could lead to quasi-nationalization—are beyond the pale of acceptability. Present bankruptcy proceedings and the possibility of liquidation make it imperative that the Congress act promptly to meet the emerging crisis.

I will soon submit to the Congress my Transportation Improvement Act of 1973. This legislation is designed to address some of the outmoded and excessively restrictive regulatory procedures which affect the entire railroad industry. The steps recommended are critical to creating a healthy system of railroads for our Nation—a matter of increased urgency as we face environmental and energy problems. I urge prompt Congressional action on this important legislation.

Disaster Preparedness and Relief

This Administration has had ample opportunity to test our Federal programs for dealing with natural disasters. Since taking office in 1969, I have had to declare 147 major disasters in 42 States and 3 Territories. The year 1972—punctuated by Hurricane Agnes—proved to be a record-setting year in this respect: there were 48 major disasters, accounting in part for the food shortages we have had in 1973.

As a result of these experiences, I am convinced that we can do a better job in preparing for disasters and in providing assistance to those who are hardest hit. I have proposed two major pieces of legislation designed to insure that 1973 will mark a turning point in the story of our disaster programs.

The first of these measures is the proposed Disaster Preparedness and Assistance Act. This bill is based upon a major recent study of all disaster relief activities of the Federal Government. It is designed to provide badly needed emphasis upon preventive measures and to encourage the use of insurance before disasters strike. It would increase the role of State and local officials in determining how Federal money would be spent in assisting disaster-stricken communities—and it would provide for automatic release of Federal funds in the case of major disasters. Red tape, bureaucratic delays, and Federal interference would be substantially reduced, while Federal assistance would be provided more rapidly. The bill also includes generous grant features for those disaster victims unable to repay Govern-

ment loans while continuing grants to help communities restore their public facilities.

To date, this legislation, so vital to our efforts to mitigate disaster damage, has received only one perfunctory hearing in the Congress. It deserves more serious consideration.

The second major Administration initiative in this area is the proposed Flood Disaster Protection Act. Flood insurance is a key part of any disaster assistance program. This will would expand the flood insurance program by increasing insurance coverage from $6 to $10 billion. It would also require participation in the flood insurance program by communities that are known to be flood prone, so that residents of these communities would have more adequate protection and would hlep to bear a reasonable share of the cost.

The Congress has moved rapidly on this bill; but unfortunately, in floor action this past week, the House added a number of amendments that would seriously hamstring the administration of the program and would badly erode its effectiveness. I hope that we can iron out our differences on these crippling amendments in a spirit of constructive compromise that preserves the effectiveness of the bill for those who need it so badly.

Self-Government for the District of Columbia

In 1969 I first proposed a series of actions intended to bring about an orderly transfer of political power to the people of the District of Columbia. I called for a Constitutional Amendment giving the District at least one representative in the House and such other additional representation as the Congress may approve. I proposed, and Congress enacted, legislation providing for an interim non-voting Congressional delegate and for the creation of a Commission on the Organization of the Government of the District of Columbia, the so-called Nelsen Commission.

The Nelsen Commission's recommendations deserve careful consideration. If enacted, these proposals would greatly strengthen the capability and expand the authority of the City's government and moderate the Federal constraints over its operation. Once again, I urge rapid action by the Congress.

As the American Bicentennial dawns, I pledge the Administration to work receptively and cooperatively in this area to achieve true and effective self-government for the District of Columbia.

Fighting Crime and Drug Abuse

In recent years, America's peace officers, with the assistance and encouragement of Federal law enforcement agencies and with the support of far-sighted legislation passed by the Congress, have made commendable inroads against crime. After 17 years of continuous and sometimes shocking increases in the rate of crime, the nationwide rate of serious crime went down in 1972.

But this progress must not be taken as evidence that we can now relent in this struggle. Rather, we must redouble our efforts to restore law and order to America, whether it be in the boardrooms of our corporations, in the halls of our government, or on our city streets. We must do all we can to make the present moment a decisive turning point so that our communities will once again be safe. Three of my legislative proposals are designed to do just that: a bill to modernize and reform the Federal Criminal Code; a heroin trafficking bill to crack down on drug pushers; and a bill to restore the death penalty for certain of the most serious Federal offenses.

Criminal Code Reform

There is a compelling need for greater clarity and consistency in our criminal laws, especially in those which fall within the Federal ambit. The Federal Criminal Code, which dates back to 1790, has never been thoroughly revised. It is no longer a fully effective instrument for the administration of criminal justice—just as the national transport systems of 1790 would no longer be adequate to the demands of 20th century America.

Since 1966, a number of public and private studies have been directed to the development of necessary reforms in the Federal Criminal Code. It is time that such reforms be undertaken. I have submitted a sweeping proposal for reform, based upon a five-year study by a bipartisan national commission. This measure would eliminate a number of inadequate, obsolete, or frivolous statutes from the Code and would re-order other statutes into a rational, integrated Code responsive to the needs of our modern society.

Although extensive consideration has already been given to this matter by public and private commissions, I realize that a prudent Congress will still wish to study this matter carefully. Senator McClellan has also introduced his own proposals for comprehensive Code reform. Certainly the best parts of each set of proposals can be joined as the legislative process goes forward. Fortunately, hearings have already begun in the Senate and I trust that both Houses will move with appropriate dispatch on this complex but vital endeavor.

Heroin Trafficking Act

In spite of our encouraging progress in eliminating the scourge of drug abuse in America, we still have a long way to go in this vital work.

The center of gravity for America's drug problem rests in the area of "hard drugs"—with heroin at the top of the list. Heroin trafficking is involved with the entire spectrum of criminality, ranging from international organized crime to muggings on the street. It is one of the most remunerative areas of criminal activity and we will never be able to cope with it effectively until the sanctions we can bring to bear against it are as severe as its profits are attractive.

Recent studies have shown that tens of thousands of those arrested on narcotics charges are put right back on the street for periods ranging up to a year and more as they successfully play for time against the courts. More alarming still is the fact that many thousands of those convicted on narcotics charges are never sent to jail. Such facts mean that the penalties for hard drug trafficking are an ineffective deterrent when compared with the potential gains from this multi-billion dollar criminal activity.

The conclusion is simple. We must have laws that will enable us to take heroin traffickers off the streets. I have submitted a proposal which would do precisely that. It would provide tough new penalties for heroin traffickers including minimum mandatory prison sentences. It would also allow a judge to consider the danger to the community before releasing arrested heroin raffickers on bail.

Heroin traffic is a clear and present danger, the pernicious effects of which all reasonable men can agree upon. While many of the proposals which I have placed before the Congress may require extended consideration, the need for cracking down on the heroin traffic cannot reasonably be supposed to be among them. I ask therefore that the immediate attention of the Congress be given to legislation which would help us eliminate this market for misery.

Capital Punishment

The death penalty is not a sanction to be empoyed loosely or considered lightly, but neither is it to be ignored as a fitting penalty, in exceptional circumstances, for the purpose of preventing or deterring crime. I wish to reaffirm my conviction that the death penalty should be restored for treason, assassination, acts of sabotage and espionage, which are particularly serious, and for violations of selected Federal laws in which death results.

I am deeply troubled by the fact that our courts are often now deprived of a credible sanction in their efforts against violent crime while prospective criminals are provided with the comfort and encouragement of knowing that they will often suffer only limited and mitigable consequences to themselves. I ask that the Congress continue its efforts to correct this discrepancy.

Reform of Campaign Practices

No subject over the last few months has so stirred public comment and reflection as the question of campaign practices.

For nearly four months now, the Congress has had before it my proposal to establish a Non-Partisan Commission on Federal Election Reform so that we could overhaul our campaign practices in a comprehensive, sound and expeditious manner. In light of the great interest of the public and the Congress in such reform, I am at a loss to understand why only the Senate has acted on this request.

In order to have made any reform effective for the 1974 elections, the Commission should have been established and prepared to submit a report by December 1, as I initially proposed. Unfortunately, this opportunity appears to be slipping by and the American public might well ask whether the interest in reform is restricted to calling for changes rather than making changes.

While the passage of time has already made it unlikely that reforms which spring from the Commission's study could be made effective prior to the 1974 Congressional elections, it is not too late for the Congress to move forward to establish the Commission.

Preparing for the Bicentennial

America is virtually on the eve of its Bicentennial anniversary. Yet a great deal of preparation remains to be accomplished in a relatively short time if our celebration of two hundred years of liberty is to be equal to the importance of the occasion. To this end, I have proposed the creation of an American Revolution Bicentennial Administration to continue and expand upon the work of the present American Revolution Bicentennial Commission. The House has passed a bill in this area and the Senate is moving toward final consideration of its version of the bill.

We are moving rapidly toward a fixed point in time, and we must act swiftly if all agencies of the Federal Government, along with State, local, and private institutions, are to be given the maximum opportunity to prepare properly for the Bicentennial year.

Since the expanded resources of the Arts and Humanities Endowments would be designed in part to aid in these preparations, I am also confident that the House and Senate conferees will soon complete needed action on the authorization bill for these two institutions. It is now widely recognized that both of the endowments are playing an effective role in enriching our cultural and intellectual life, and they continue to deserve our strong support.

Metric Conversion

Americans cherish tradition and our own way of doing things. Having been acculturated from childhood to the concepts of an inch, a mile, or a pound, we are understandably nonplussed when we consider the notion of a centimeter, a kilometer, a gram or a kilo. However, when we realize that the rest of the world is equally confused by our system of measurement, we must conclude, however sadly, that we are the ones who are out of step.

In a world of integrated commerce and increasing personal exchange, it is only prudent for us to adjust our own conceptions and devices for measuring and delineating quantity.

I have recommended to the Congress that it pass legislation to convert America to the metric system. This can be done in a reasonable manner, one which is not abrupt or disconcerting. I am pleased to note that the Administration's proposal is presently before the appropriate House subcommittee. I ask that the Senate give equally expeditious consideration to effecting this necessary change.

Reorganization Authority

The authority of the President to submit Reorganization Plans to the Congress lapsed in April of this year and has not yet been renewed.

This authority permits the President to organize programs and agencies in order to achieve the most effective and efficient performance. It is, therefore, an important executive management tool which provides flexibility and increased capacity to respond to changing needs.

This authority has been made available to every President for more than 25 years. It is essential that it be renewed with great dispatch.

Keeping the Peace

For the first time in more than a decade, America is at peace. Now we must learn how to keep that peace—at task that is at least as demanding and in many ways even more subtle than the struggle to end a war.

There is always a temptation after war to enter into a period of withdrawal and isolation. But surely we have learned from past lessons of precipitate disarmament that this temptation must be resisted. And surely, we have also learned that our progress in securing peace is due in large measure to our continued military strength and to the steadfast, responsible role we have played in the affairs of our world.

Defense Spending

In recent years, it has been fashionable to suggest that whatever we want in the way of extra programs at home could be painlessly financed by lopping 5 or 10 or 20 billion dollars off the defense budget. This approach is worse than foolhardly it is suicidal. We could have the finest array of domestic programs in the world, and they would mean nothing if we lost our freedom or if, because of our weakness, we were plunged into the abyss of nuclear war.

The world's hope for peace depends on America's strength—it depends absolutely on our never falling into the position of being the world's second strongest nation in the world.

For years now we have been engaged in a long, painstaking process of negotiating mutual limits on strategic nuclear arms. Historic agreements have already been reached and others are in prospect. Talks are also going forward this year aimed at a mutual and balanced reduction of forces in Europe. But the point of all these negotiations is this: if peace is to be preserved the limitations and the reductions must be mutual. What one side is willing to give up for free, the other side will not bargain for.

If America's peace and America's freedom are worth preserving, then they are worth the cost of whatever level of military strength it takes to preserve them. We must not yield to the folly of breaching that level and so undermining our hopes and the world's hopes for a peaceful future.

Although my military budget—measured in constant dollars—is down by almost one-third since 1968, the Congress is now threatening further defense cuts which would be the largest since 1949. To take such unilateral action—without exacting similar concessions from our adversaries—could undermine the chances for further mutual arms limitations or reductions. I will therefore actively oppose these cuts.

The arms limitations agreement signed with the Soviet Union last year has at last halted the rapid growth in the numbers of strategic weapons. Despite this concrete achievement, much needs to be done to ensure continued stability and to support our negotiation of a permanent strategic arms agreement. A vigorous research and development program is essential to provide vital insurance that no adversary will ever gain a decisive advantage through technological breakthrough and that massive deployment expenditures will therefore not become necessary. Yet the Congress is in the process of slashing research and development funding below minimum prudent levels, including elimination of our cruise missile and air defense programs. The Trident and B-1 programs, which are critical to maintaining a reliable deterrent into the next decade, are also facing proposals to cut them to the bone.

On top of this, the Senate has approved a staggering and unacceptable cut of 156,000 men in our military manpower. Such action would force us to reduce the number of ships in our Navy while the Soviet Union continues an unprecedented naval build-up and to reduce the size of our Army and Air Force while the Soviet Union and the Chinese continue to maintain far larger forces.

In addition to these cuts, there is also a major Senate proposal requiring substantial unilateral troop withdrawals from Europe, a mistake that could begin a serious unraveling of the NATO alliance. Negotiations for mutual and balanced force reductions begin on October 30. On the very eve of negotiations, the troop cuts in Europe and the reduction in military manpower would destroy our chances of reaching an agreement with the Warsaw Pact countries to reduce troop levels in Europe on a mutual basis. If the Congress were to succeed in making these proposed cuts, the United States would be making far-reaching concessions even before the talks begin.

Cuts in other defense programs are equally unacceptable. It is illogical to cut America's capabilities at the very time the Soviet Union increases hers. And it would be difficult to stabilize delicate situations in the Middle East and Asia if the Congress removes the influential tools which have made stability possible.

Foreign Assistance Act

Another matter of prime concern to me is our commitment to a sound program of bilateral and multilateral foreign aid. Last spring I sent to the Congress reasonable requests for our economic and military assistance programs. These programs represent a central element in America's ability to work with her allies to maintain peace and stability in the world. Unfortunately, the Congress has not treated these requests favorably.

The House has already cut about 25 percent from the military aid program and the Senate has cut it by one-half. Not only have extraordinary cuts been made in the funding, but restrictive amendments have been added in committee and others may be suggested on the floor. I cannot stand by while these crucial programs are gutted in haste and reaction.

Current foreign aid programs are being funded through a continuing resolution which ends on September 30. This approach is unsatisfactory, especially in light of demands resulting from North Vietnamese truce violations in Cambodia. Yet the Congress continues not only to provide smaller dollar amounts but also to make unreasonable requests for access to sensitive information and impose counterproductive conditions on specific programs. Such demands are unacceptable; they would badly compromise our ability to maintain security around the world.

I intend to make every effort to increase the funding for fiscal year 1974 security assistance requirements. I shall also strongly resist efforts by the Congress to impose unreasonable demands upon necessary foreign policy prerogatives of the executive branch. A spirit of bipartisan cooperation provided the steel which saw America through the Cold War and then through Vietnam. We must not jeopardize the great potential for peaceful progress in the post Vietnam era by losing that strong bipartisan spirit.

To build a truly durable structure of peace, our progress in reforming the world's trade and monetary systems must be accompanied by efforts to help the poorer countries share more equitably in the world's growing prosperity. To this end, I ask the Congress to support our fair share of contributions to the multilateral development banks—both the proposed contributions now pending in the Congress and other proposals about which I am currently consulting with the Congress and which will be formally submitted in the near future. Our bilateral assistance programs are also an essential part of our effort to stimulate world development and I urge the Congress to give them full support.

All these efforts represent short-range investments in peace and progress which are of enormous long-range importance. To try to save a few dollars on these programs today could cost us far more tomorrow.

Conclusion

With the Congress, the Administration and the people working together during the coming weeks, we can achieve many of the goals described in this meassage. And we will work together most effectively if we remember that our ultimate responsibility is not to one political party, nor to one philosophical position, nor even to one branch of the Government. Our ultimate responsibility is to the people—and our deliberations must always be guided by their best interests.

Inevitably, we will have different opinions about what those interests demand. But if we proceed in a spirit of constructive partnership, our varying perspectives can be a source of greater creativity rather than a cause of deadlock.

We already know that the year 1973 will be recalled in history books as the year in which we ended the longest war in American history. Let us conduct ourselves in the next four months so that 1973 will also be remembered as the time in which we began to turn the blessings of peace into a better life for all.

RICHARD NIXON

HOUSING PLAN MESSAGE

Following is the White House text of President Nixon's Sept. 19 message to Congress on the administration's new housing plan.

TO THE CONGRESS OF THE UNITED STATES:

Six months ago, in my State of the Union Message on Community Development, I announced a sweeping study of Federal housing policy. I said then that its results would be used in formulating new Administration recommendations in this extremely important field.

That study has been completed—and my recommendations are ready. In keeping with the breadth of the issues involved in housing, both the study and my proposals cover a wide spectrum.

• Some of the actions discussed in this message are designed to ease the tight credit conditions in the current housing market.

• Others are intended to improve prospects for potential homebuyers to obtain mortgages over the longer term.

• Some of these proposals reflect my conviction that the housing needs of lower income families require a different approach than we have taken in the past.

• Still other actions are designed to meet other special needs and to update and improve current Federal programs which have been working.

The measures I suggest today can bring us closer to a long-established goal. As I indicated in my message last March, this Administration will not waver in its commitment to the objective of the Housing Act of 1949: "a decent home and a suitable living environment for every American family." While our Nation has made tremendous strides toward that objective in the quarter-century since it was first enunciated, those very strides have carried us into new terrain, presenting new problems and new opportunities. The nature of the challenge has been changing—and our response must change accordingly.

A Proud Record. The housing record of recent decades should be a source of pride for all Americans. For example, the proportion of our people who live in substandard housing dropped from 43 percent in 1940 to only 7 percent in 1970. During the same period, the proportion of Americans living in houses with more than one person per room dropped from 20 percent to 8 percent and the proportion of our housing which is considered "dilapidated" fell from over 18 percent to less than 5 percent.

To be sure, these indicators are imprecise—and we need to improve the ways we collect housing data. But all of these measures, however crude, point to an inescapable conclusion: very substantial progress has been made in the housing field and the benefits have been shared by Americans of all races and economic groups in all regions of the country.

In recent years, housing production in America has reached unprecedented levels. The average number of housing starts in the last twelve months has more than doubled the average for the previous two decades and we expect the next twelve months to be another excellent year for housing.

The ability of our economy to provide vastly expanded housing has been one of the strongest indications of its fundamental vitality. Our people have been able to match their growing desire for housing with growing purchasing power. Our housing industry has been able to expand its production and update its product. And our credit institutions have been able to finance this massive wave of construction in a way which has enabled a broad cross-section of Americans to participate in its benefits.

The state of America's housing will continue to depend on the state of America's economy more than on any other factor. Specific policies aimed at housing can help. But—as our housing study concludes—the forces which will do the most to shape the future of housing in America will be the forces of the marketplace: families with sufficient real income and sufficient confidence to create an effective demand for better housing on the one hand, and builders and credit institutions able to respond to that demand on the other.

But even as good housing has become a reality for most Americans, it is clear that certain important problems still exist. Two are especially significant. First, we are facing certain problems in providing adequate housing credit—and we must move promptly to resolve them. Second, too many low-income families have been left behind: they still live in substandard, overcrowded and dilapidated housing—and we must help them meet their needs. This message and the legislation I will seek from the Congress focus primarily on these two challenges.

I. Making Homeownership Easier

Credit is the life-blood of housing. Without an adequate supply of credit repayable over an extended period of time at reasonable interest rates, very few families could afford to purchase their own homes. Nor could landlords either develop an adequate supply of rental housing or make it available at reasonable rental charges.

One of the most important actions the Federal Government has taken in the housing field was its decision in the 1930's to restructure our housing credit system. The introduction then of Federal insurance for low downpayment, long-term mortgages—first by the Federal Housing Administration (the FHA), and later by the Farmers Home Administration (the FmHA) and the Veterans Administration (the VA)—encouraged lenders to provide home mortgages on attractive terms to millions of American families.

At the same time, the Federal decision to insure savings deposits meant that billions of additional dollars began to flow into our banks and into thrift institutions, such as savings and loan associations. Other Federal policies led these institutions to invest most of this money in housing loans, creating vast new pools of housing credit.

Although these systems have served us well for a long time, the need for improvement has become increasingly evident in recent years. More and more, we find ourselves facing either feast or famine with respect to housing credit.

When interest rates are relatively stable, we find that we have an abundance of mortgage credit available on reasonable terms, as was true in 1971, 1972 and earlier this year. Whenever interest rates move up rapidly, however, mortgage credit becomes extremely scarce. This occurred in 1966 and 1969 and it has been happening again in recent months. As a result, it has become more difficult for an American family to buy or sell a home. Even where credit is available, the combination of higher interest rates and higher downpayment requirements is pricing too many of our families out of the housing market.

Why does this feast or famine situation exist?

As I pointed out in my message of August 3rd on the reform of financial institutions, one principal reason is the fact that our thrift institutions are unable to compete effectively for depositors' funds when interest rates rise quickly. The problem is a structural one: savings and loan associations are now required to invest most of their deposits in residential mortgages, which carry fixed interest rates over long periods of time. When other interest rates rise rapidly, the interest rates on their mortgage portfolios cannot keep pace—and as a consequence neither can the rates they pay to their depositors. The result is that depositors often draw their savings out of the thrift institutions—or at least cut down their rate of saving—leaving the thrift institutions with much less money to invest in housing. I believe this special problem can be met through the recommendations I described in my message of August 3rd.

But structural difficulties are only part of the problem. A number of additional factors also help explain why mortgage money is becoming so expensive.

One major cause is the housing boom itself, which has led to unprecedented demands for credit—and rising costs for money. In addition, inflationary fears have influenced lenders to raise their interest rates as a matter of self protection. Finally, the Federal Reserve Board has been working to restrict the money supply in order to fight inflation. Such restrictions are important, for without them we might win the immediate battle in housing but lose the long-range war in the rest of the economy, including the housing field.

But even as we pursue a responsible monetary policy, we must avoid choking off the consumer credit which families require to meet their needs. That would also be dangerous to the economy. I am particularly concerned that the burdens of fighting inflation not fall unfairly on those who want to buy a home—or sell one.

We have a delicate and difficult balance to maintain. We cannot relent in the fight against inflation, which is our number one domestic problem. Nor can we expect to insulate housing from the effects of that effort. In fact, all of our measures to control inflation—including our efforts to hold down Federal spending—are essential in keeping down both the price of housing and the price of money in the long run. This requirement necessarily limits what can be prudently done to stimulate housing credit in the short run.

Nevertheless, there are some actions that can be taken on the credit front—and I intend to take them. In fact, we have already launched a number of efforts. The Committee on Interest and Dividends has instituted voluntary guidelines designed to encourage banks to keep up their levels of mortgage lending. The Federal Reserve Board has engaged in similar efforts. The Federal National Mortgage Association has stepped up its mortgage commitment and purchasing operations to free up funds for further lending. The Federal Home Loan Bank Board has lowered the reserve requirements for lending operations of its member institutions and has stepped up its advancement of funds to them.

I am today announcing a number of additional administrative actions and legislative proposals designed to do two things: first, to help alleviate the immediate housing credit problem; and second, to improve for the longer term the supply of housing credit and the ability of our people to use it.

Easing Current Credit Conditions

1. Increasing the incentive for savings and loan associations to finance housing construction.

As money has become tighter, savings and loan institutions have become increasingly reluctant to commit housing construction loans for delivery at future dates. The reason is their uncertainty as to whether they will have enough funds to lend then at the interest rates which exist now.

Accordingly, the Federal Home Loan Bank Board will authorize a new program of "forward commitments" to savings and loan associations, promising to loan money to them at a future date should they need it to cover the commitments they now are making. This authority will cover up to $2.5 billion in loan commitments.

2. Providing interest rate assistance to Federally insured borrowers.

The Department of Housing and Urban Development will also join in the effort to ease the current mortgage credit problem by reinstituting the so-called "Tandem Plan" under the auspices of its Government National Mortgage Association. Under this plan, the GNMA will provide money for FHA-insured mortgages at interest rates somewhat below the market level. To encourage new construction, only mortgages on new housing starts will be eligible for this assistance. Up to $3 billion in mortgages for new housing will be financed under this arrangement, making loans available at attractive rates to tens of thousands of American homebuyers.

3. Increasing the size of mortgages eligible for Federal insurance.

The Federal Government presently encourages lenders to put money into housing by insuring mortgages involving low downpayments and long repayment periods. The Government guarantees, in effect, that lenders will be protected in the event of a default on the loan. Such mortgage insurance, whether it is provided by the Federal Government or by private institutions, is particularly important in making mortgages available to younger families and others who do not have enough savings to make a large downpayment or enough income to make the higher monthly payments that come with shorter mortgage terms.

The Congress periodically sets limits on the size of a mortgage loan which the FHA can insure and adjusts the downpayment requirement. The last time this was done was in 1968. Although realistic then, the current ceiling and downpayment terms are unrealistic in today's housing market. As a result, FHA insurance for multifamily units has been completely cut off and FHA-insured financing is impossible for any home purchase in a large and growing number of areas across the country.

To remedy this problem, I ask the Congress to authorize the FHA to insure larger housing loans on a low downpayment basis both for single and for multifamily dwellings.

Such a change would revive Federal insurance activity in areas where it has been curtailed. In addition, it would permit at least a partial resumption of housing loan activity in certain States where anachronistic usury laws impose interest ceilings lower than current market rates and therefore shut off mortgage lending. Many of these States exempt Federally-insured loans from such interest ceilings—which means that Federal insurance is a prerequisite for obtaining a housing loan in these jurisdictions. This makes it all the more important that the Congress act promptly on my proposal to expand the reach of our Federal mortgage insurance programs.

Making Long-Term Improvements in the Credit System

1. Permitting homebuyers to pay market-level interest rates and still be eligible for Federal insurance.

In an effort to hold down the cost of borrowing, the Congress has limited the interest rates which a home mortgage can carry and still be eligible for FHA and VA insurance. Unfortunately, setting the interest rate below market rates does not accomplish this intended purpose.

The reason is that lenders will simply not make their money available for housing at a lower rate than they can get from a comparable investment elsewhere. If the Government's interest limit for a mortgage is set below the general market level interest rate, the lender who still puts money into housing will supplement this artificially low interest rate by requiring a special additional payment. This payment—which is really prepaid interest—is made in a lump sum at the time the loan is made and is commonly called "points."

Although points are usually charged to the seller of a house, they are generally added to the selling price thus are paid by the buyer just the same.

This practice can have a number of unfortunate side-effects. By raising the overall price of the home, points can also raise the size of the downpayment. Moreover, when the price of a house goes up, so does the cost of insuring that house, of paying property taxes on it and of making monthly mortgage payments. An added inequity arises when a home is resold before the mortgage term has run its course—which is the usual case. Since the points were paid to compensate the lender for what he would lose on interest over the full term of the mortgage, the lender can reap an unfair profit when the mortgage is paid off early.

In short, the ceiling on interest rates does just the reverse of what it was intended to do. To end this practice, I again urge the Congress to allow the FHA and the VA to insure mortgages carrying market rates of interest. This proposal would end the need for charging points; indeed, it would prohibit charging such prepaid interest points on these insured mortgages. Hopefully, those States which also have ceilings on mortgage interest rates will take similar action to eliminate their ceilings.

2. Authorizing more flexible repayment plans under Federally insured mortgages.

Many innovative changes in housing finance have been introduced by the Federal Government. It is important that we continue to pursue such innovation—and one area that is particularly ripe for new experiments involves the schedule for repaying mortgages.

To further such innovation, I will seek legislation permitting the Secretary of Housing and Urban Development to allow greater flexibility in repayment arrangements for Federally insured loans on an experimental basis.

One possibility which would be tested under this authority is that of gearing the level of repayments to expected changes in family income. Rather than making the same flat payment over the life of the loan, families would make smaller payments in the earlier years—when they are hardest pressed—and larger payments later on—when their incomes are higher. This provision could help younger families purchase homes earlier in life than they can today and it could help them make an earlier purchase of the home in which they will eventually live, rather than making frequent moves from one home to another as their incomes rise.

3. Establishing a mortgage interest tax credit.

As another means of ensuring a steady supply of housing credit, I will propose legislation which would allow investors a tax credit on the interest they earn when they put their money into residential mortgages. This proposal would make investment in housing loans more attractive in two ways: first, it would make them more attractive to those institutions which traditionally have provided mortgage money; and second, it would give organizations which pool mortgages a better chance to compete for funds in the so-called "secondary market"—from pension funds, insurance companies, various State institutions and the like.

Under my proposal, a tax credit of up to 3½ percent would be provided on interest earnings to financial institutions which invest a certain percentage of their investment portfolio in residential mortgages. The greater the proportion of the portfolio invested in mortgages, the higher the tax credit on interest earned by all the mortgages in the portfolio. When at least 70 percent of a portfolio was invested in mortgages, the tax credit on the interest those mortgages earn would be 3½ percent—the equivalent, at current interest levels, of an additional interest yield of more than one-half of one percent.

4. Furthering the development of private mortgage insurance companies.

Another significant proposal in the credit area concerns private mortgage insurance companies. These companies perform a function similar to that of the FHA, the VA, and the FmHA—they insure residential mortgages with lower downpayments and for longer terms than would ordinarily be available. However, the premiums they charge for such insurance are much lower than those of the Federal agencies. Such private mortgage insurance companies have become a significant factor in the housing market in recent years and we should encourage their continued development.

To help further this objective, I recommend that the Congress—along with the Administration—consider ways of allowing private mortgage insurance companies to purchase inexpensive Federal reinsurance. To this end, I will submit legislation which can provide a basis for this discussion. Such insurance would provide added protection to the owner of a mortgage and could speed the acceptance of private mortgage insurance, especially in secondary markets. It could thus make available even more sources of low downpayment, long-term home financing for prospective home buyers.

II. The Challenge of Low-Income Housing

Since 1937, the Federal Government has tried to help low income families by providing housing for them. Over the years, nearly $90 billion of the taxpayers' money has been spent or committed for public housing projects and other subsidized housing programs.

These programs have been particularly active during the past few years. Since 1969, the Federal Government has subsidized nearly 1.6 million units of new housing and over 400,000 units of existing and rehabilitated housing. These 2 million units will cost taxpayers an estimated $2.5 billion in each of the next few years and could cost us close to $50 billion altogether.

The Failures of Federal Housing Programs

But what have we been getting for all this money?

Federal programs have produced some good housing—but they have also produced some of the worst housing in America. Our recent study makes this clear—and so does my own experience.

I have seen a number of our public housing projects. Some of them are impressive, but too many are monstrous, depressing places—run down, overcrowded, crime-ridden, falling apart.

The residents of these projects are often strangers to one another—with little sense of belonging. And because so many poor people are so heavily concentrated in these projects, they often feel cut off from the mainstream of American life.

A particularly dramatic example of the failure of Federal housing projects is the Pruitt-Igoe project in St. Louis. It was nominated for all sorts of awards when it was built 17 years ago. It was supposed to house some 2,700 families—but it simply didn't work. In fact, a study of this project was published two years ago with the appropriate subtitle: "Life in a Federal Slum."

Last month, we agreed to tear down this Federal slum—every unit of it. Almost everyone thought it was the best thing we could do.

Pruitt-Igoe is only one example of an all too common problem. All across America, the Federal Government has become the biggest slumlord in history.

But the quality of Federally-assisted housing is by no means the only problem. Our present approach is also highly inequitable. Rather than treating those in equal circumstances equally, it arbitrarily selects only a few low income families to live in Federally supported housing, while ignoring others. Moreover, the few often get a *new* home, while many other families—including those who pay the taxes to support these programs—must make do with inferior older housing. And since recipients often lose their eligibility for public housing when they exceed a certain income level, the present approach can actually reward dependence and discourage self-reliance.

The present approach is also very wasteful, for it concentrates on the most expensive means of housing the poor, new buildings, and ignores the potential for using good existing housing. Government involvement adds additional waste; our recent study shows that it costs between 15 and 40 percent more for the Government to provide housing for people than for people to acquire that same housing themselves on the private market.

One of the most disturbing aspects of the current approach is the fact that families are offered subsidized housing on a "take it or leave it" basis—losing their basic right to choose the house they will live in and the place they will live. Too often they are simply warehoused together wherever the Government puts them. They are treated as a class apart, with little freedom to make their own decisions.

Developing a Better Approach

Leaders of all political persuasions and from all levels of government have given a great deal of thought in recent years to the problem of low-income housing. Many of them agree that the Federally-subsidized housing approach has failed. And many of them also agree on the reasons for that failure.

The main flaw they point to in the old approach is its underlying assumption that the basic problem of the poor is a lack of housing rather than a lack of income. Instead of treating the root cause of the problem—the inability to pay for housing—the Government has been attacking the symptom. We have been helping the builders directly and the poor only indirectly, rather than providing assistance directly to low income families.

In place of this old approach, many people have suggested a new approach—direct cash assistance. Under this approach, instead of providing a poor family with a place to live, the Federal Government would provide qualified recipients with an appropriate housing payment and would then let them choose their own homes on the private market. The payment would be carefully scaled to make up the difference between what a family could afford on its own for housing and the cost of safe and sanitary housing in that geographic area. This plan would give the poor the freedom and responsibility to make their own choices about housing—and it would eventually get the Federal Government out of the housing business.

Not surprisingly, our recent housing study indicates what others have been saying: of the policy alternatives available, the most promising way to achieve decent housing for all of our families at an acceptable cost appears to be direct cash assistance.

Our best information to date indicates that direct cash assistance will in the long run be the most equitable, least expensive approach to achieving our goal of a decent home for all Americans—a goal I am committed to meeting. It appears to be a policy that will work—not a policy where success will always be a mirage. However, it may develop that the advantages we now see for direct cash assistance will be outweighed by other factors not presently foreseen or that such advantages may be obtainable in alternative ways which offer additional advantages. In that event, I would, of course, reexamine the situation in partnership with the Congress before moving ahead. But right

now, in my judgment, our principal efforts should be directed toward determining whether a policy of direct cash assistance—with first priority for the elderly poor—can be put into practical operation.

As we proceed with new policies for aiding lower income families, we must also move with caution. Too often in the past new Federal programs have been launched on a sea of taxpayers' dollars with the best intentions but with too little information about how they would work in practice. The results have been less than what was promised and have not been consistent with the Government's obligation to spend the taxpayers' money as effectively as possible.

One particular problem is that past efforts in one area of assistance have tended to ignore programs in other areas, resulting in an inequitable hodge-podge activity which satisfies no one. In this regard, the relationship between housing programs and welfare payments is particularly critical. We must carefully consider the ways in which our housing programs will relate to other programs which also assist low income persons.

Some field work has already begun with respect to direct cash assistance in the area of housing for those with low incomes. In 1970 the Congress authorized housing allowance experiments involving over 18,000 families and costing over $150 million. We expect preliminary data to emerge from these tests in the coming months and we intend to use these data as we evaluate the possibility of further efforts.

This work should help us answer some important and difficult questions.

What, for example, is the appropriate proportion of income that lower income families should pay for housing? Should this level be higher or lower for different kinds of families—for young families with children, for example, or for the elderly, or for other groups? Should families receiving Federal aid be required to spend any particular amount on housing? If they are, and the requirement is high, what kind of inflationary pressures, if any, would that produce in tight housing markets and what steps could be taken to ease those pressures? In the important case where poor families already own their own housing, how should that fact be weighed in measuring their income level? How should the program be applied in the case of younger families who have parents living with them?

All these questions are critical—and they deserve close examination.

In addition, I am also asking the Congress for authority to take two other steps to help us test the cash assistance approach.

First, we need to expand our experimental programs to test additional techniques for administration.

Second, we need to develop and put into effect the appropriate mechanisms for measuring the cost of safe and sanitary housing in various parts of the country. Sound, reliable cost information of this kind would be of vital importance to a fully operational program.

If these steps can be taken in the near future, then I believe we will have the basic information needed to make a final decision concerning this approach late in 1974 or early in 1975.

A Continuing Need for Limited Construction Programs

During the period in which a new approach is being developed, there will be a continuing need to provide housing for some low income families. We must recognize that in some areas of the country there will simply not be a sufficient supply of housing for the foreseeable future. I therefore propose that the Federal Government continue to assist in providing a limited amount of construction for low income housing—though I would expect to use this approach sparingly.

To eliminate the many tangled problems which attend the delivery of subsidies under current construction programs, I am recommending a new approach to construction assistance by the

Federal Government. Under this approach, the developer would make newly constructed units available at special rents for low income families and the Government in return would pay the developer the difference between such rents and fair market rents.

During the remainder of fiscal year 1974, the Department of Housing and Urban Development will continue to process subsidy applications for units which had moved most of the way through the application process by January 5 of this year. In addition, the Department will process applications in cases where bona fide commitments have been made.

I am advised by the Secretary for Housing and Urban Development that one of the existing construction programs—the Section 23 program under which new and existing housing is leased for low income families—can be administered in a way which carries out some of the principles of direct cash assistance. If administered in this way, this program could also provide valuable information for us to use in developing this new approach.

Accordingly, I am lifting the suspension of January 5 with respect to these Section 23 programs. I am also directing the Secretary of Housing and Urban Development to take whatever administrative steps are available to him to eliminate any abuses from such programs and to bring them into line as closely as possible with the direct cash assistance approach.

Altogether, in order to meet bona fide commitments requiring action during this fiscal year and to carry out the Section 23 program, authorization has now been given to process applications for an additional 200,000 units, 150,000 units of which would be new construction.

Improving the Operation of Present Public Housing

There was a time when the only continuing Federal expense connected with public housing after it was built was paying the debts incurred in building it. Other expenses were met from rental income.

As time went on, however, laws were passed making the Federal Government liable for operating deficits. In recent years, as the operating costs of public housing projects has increased and as the income level and rent payments of their occupants have decreased, the cost of such projects for the Federal Government has gone up at an alarming rate. The Federal bill for operating subsidies has grown more than eightfold since 1969—from $33 million annually to $280 million annually—and an additional $1 billion has been obligated for capital improvements.

Moreover, as efforts have been made in recent years to prevent tenants from paying too much of their incomes for housing, some housing managements have been persuaded that some tenants should pay nothing at all. The Federal Government then pick up a good part of the tab, adding considerably to the costs of maintaining these projects.

This growing financial burden for the Federal Government is only one of many problems relating to public housing. Because the local housing authority is responsible for the management of public housing projects while the Federal Government is responsible for project deficits, including those due to poor management, the local authority has little incentive to improve management standards.

There are also indications that even with improved management and a more realistic approach to rents, current Federal subsidies may need to be adjusted to provide for continued operation and maintenance of these projects.

In view of these many problems, I have asked the Secretary of Housing and Urban Development to develop a set of recommendations addressing each of these problems. One of our goals will be to achieve a more equitable sharing of responsibility among the Federal Government, local communities and residents.

III. Additional Actions to Meet Our Housing Needs

Neighborhood Preservation

Simply providing Federal housing assistance to families without proper regard for the condition of the neighborhood as a whole too often results in unmet expectations for the families, added burdens for the municipality and a waste of the taxpayers' dollars. It is important, therefore, that all of our efforts in the housing and community development field be carried out as a partnership venture of the Federal Government, the local government, local financial institutions and the citizens of the neighborhoods involved.

Added resources such as those which would be available under my proposed $2.3 billion Better Communities Act can provide important support for these efforts. To smooth the transition to the Better Communities Act, I am directing the Department of Housing and Urban Development to make available up to $60 million in Section 312 rehabilitation loans in the current fiscal year. Priority will be given to those communities which need these loans to complete present projects or where complimentary local rehabilitation efforts have already been launched.

In addition, I have directed the Secretary of Housing and Urban Development, using his research and demonstration funds, to pursue promising approaches to neighborhood preservation which might be adopted by communities on a broader basis.

Improving Rural Housing

The problems of providing good housing in our rural areas are especially challenging, not only because the proportion of substandard housing is greater in rural areas but also because these areas often lack the resources to foster greater economic development—and better housing. Of course, many of our housing programs and proposals are designed to assist all families, urban and rural alike. But there is also a special need to address in a special way the rural housing challenge.

Our recent housing study concludes that the basic housing problem in many rural areas is that our major financial institutions are not represented in these areas and that credit is therefore inadequate. The Farmers Home Administration has done a great deal to help change this picture—but further efforts are needed. At my direction, the Department of Agriculture and the Department of Housing and Urban Development will seek additional ways of correcting this situation and increasing credit availability in rural areas.

In my Community Development Message last March 8th, I emphasized that "in pursuing a policy of balanced development for our community life, we must always keep the needs of rural America clearly in sight." I mentioned then my continuing support for a revenue sharing approach for rural development, acknowledging that the Rural Development Act fell short of what I preferred in this regard. I went on to indicate my intention, after fully evaluating the effectiveness of this act, to seek whatever additional legislation may be needed. I repeat that pledge today.

A Suitable Living Environment

The housing we live in and the environment surrounding that housing are inextricably linked. In the final analysis, the quality of housing depends on matters such as transportation, proximity to educational and health services, and the availability of jobs and shopping. It also depends on economic factors which are shaped by the larger community. One important finding of our housing study was that the costs of the land on which new housing is located has risen faster than any other cost component of housing.

The Congress, too, has recognized these relationships in its finding "that Federal programs affect the location of population, economic growth, and the character of urban development (and) that such programs frequently conflict and result in undesirable and costly patterns of urban development which adversely affect the environment and wastefully use our natural resources."

It is clear that housing policy cannot be considered separately from other policies related to the economic, social and physical aspects of community development. The next Report on Urban Growth, which I shall submit to the Congress in 1974, will further address these crucial relationships.

Assuring Equal Opportunity

Over the last several years, great strides have been made toward assuring Americans of all races and creeds equal and unhindered access to the housing of their choice. As I stated in 1971:

"At the outset, we set three basic requirements for our program to achieve equal housing opportunity: It must be aimed at correcting the effects of past discrimination; it must contain safeguards to ensure against future discrimination; and it must be results-oriented so its progress toward the overall goal of increasing housing opportunities can be evaluated.

"The administration is embarked upon this course. It must and will press forward firmly.

"The chief components of such a program include the firm enforcement of laws relating to equal housing opportunity, the development of appropriate equal housing opportunity criteria for participation in programs affecting housing, the development of information programs, and the development of policies relating to housing marketing practices."

Each of these components has been put into operation and we are continuing to move ahead. It is important that all Federal agencies vigorously pursue a wide range of efforts to enforce fair housing and equal opportunity laws—and all members of my Administration will continue to be particularly vigilant in this regard.

The availability of mortgage credit has also been restricted in many instances on the grounds that the applicant's financial resources, which would otherwise have been adequate, were deemed insufficient because the applicant was a woman. These practices have occurred, unfortunately, not only in home mortgage lending but also in the field of consumer credit. I shall therefore work with the Congress to achieve legislation which will prohibit lenders from discriminating on the basis of sex or marital status.

Further Proposals

A number of other proposals which have grown out of our recent housing study are included in the legislation I am today submitting to the Congress. They include efforts to encourage home improvements and to facilitate the purchase of mobile homes; measures to ease the Federal burdens in disposing of the large and still growing number of properties returning to the Government upon default; and steps to streamline and reduce the processing time for FHA applications, including a proposal that would move toward the Veterans Administration technique of coinsurance. I urge their prompt consideration.

The American dream cannot be complete for any of us unless it is within the reach of all of us. A decent home in a suitable living environment is an essential part of that dream.

We have done a great deal as a people toward ensuring that objective for every American family in recent years. Our success should not be a reason for complacency, however; rather, it should reinforce both our determination to complete this work and our confidence that we can reach our goal.

The measures I have discussed in this message can make a significant contribution to that great undertaking. I look forward to working closely with the Congress in advancing these efforts.

RICHARD NIXON

SMALL BUSINESS ADMINISTRATION

Following is the text of President Nixon's Sept. 22 message to the Senate on his veto of S 1672, the bill to increase the lending authority of the Small Business Administration and to restore for two years low-interest loans to victims of natural disasters.

TO THE SENATE OF THE UNITED STATES:

I am returning today without my approval S 1672, a bill to amend the Small Business Act.

The stated purpose of this measure is to improve the legislative authority of the Small Business Administration, and I am in complete accord with that objective. Unfortunately, this legislation is also burdened with several extremely undesirable features—provisions which would represent a backward march for the Federal Government's disaster relief programs—and for that reason, I am compelled to veto it.

Last year our Nation experienced the worst series of natural disasters in recent memory. I visited several of the affected areas and talked with the victims. Many of them pointed out problems they were having with Federal aid.

As a result of those discussions, I ordered a thorough review of all Federal disaster assistance programs, and earlier this year I proposed legislation that would fundamentally restructure them. The purpose of those proposals was simple: to help disaster victims in the fastest, most efficient and most humane way possible—and in a way that would target our assistance on those genuinely in need. The Federal Government has a clear responsibility to help disaster victims who cannot help themselves, especially low-income families, but those who have their own resources should not use the general taxpayer as a crutch.

If I were to sign this bill, we would turn our back on these objectives and reinstate practices that have proven unworthy in the past. In fact, this bill would reopen a leaky financial tap in the Federal Treasury which the Congress itself closed last April.

The provisions of S 1672 which I find unacceptable are these:

• At a large and unnecessary expense to the taxpayer, this bill would provide Federally subsidized loans and grants to all disaster victims regardless of economic need. A wealthy landowner, who could provide for himself through insurance or could easily obtain a private loan, would be entitled to a $2,500 free grant from the Government and an additional loan at only three percent interest. Alternatively, he could forego the grant and obtain a loan for the full amount at only one percent interest. A poor family could qualify for the same aid under this bill, but it is unlikely they would require as large a loan as richer families. The net result would be greater Federal assistance for the well-to-do than the needy, and an even larger bill for the general taxpayer. That is not my idea of good government.

• The cost for the taxpayer of S 1672 would be approximately $400 million in Federal spending for each $1 billion in loans. While we cannot precisely forecast future costs, we do know that if our disaster experiences in the next 12 months are the same as last year, this bill would add $800 million to the Federal budget.

• In addition, this bill would slow the Federal Government's ability to respond to disasters by creating an administrative nightmare for those agencies charged with providing assistance.

My continuing hope is that we can act this year to accomplish the much-needed reforms in our disaster assistance programs. The proposals I sent to the Congress earlier this year are designed to insure that the sincere compassion felt by all Americans for disaster victims can be translated into the most rapid, effective and equitable form of disaster assistance possible. To this end the Administration will continue to work with the Congress to enact these comprehensive reforms and, if need be, to enact a constructive, fiscally responsible and effective interim measure which would serve until more permanent reforms can be made. In the meantime, ongoing programs will continue to be of assistance to disaster victims and will not be affected by my disapproval of S 1672.

RICHARD NIXON

THE WHITE HOUSE,
September 22, 1973.

ECONOMIC CONTROLS ADDRESS

Following is the White House text of President Nixon's June 13 address to the nation on economic controls.

I want to tell you tonight about some strong actions I have ordered today with regard to the American economy—actions which will be important to you in terms of the wages you earn and the prices you pay.

But first, since we have been hearing so much in the past few months about what is wrong with the American economy, let us look at some of the things that are right about our economy. We can be proud that the American economy is by far the freest, the strongest and the most productive economy in the whole world. It gives us the highest standard of living in the world. We are in the middle of one of the biggest, strongest booms in our history. More Americans have jobs today than ever before. The average worker is earning more today than ever before. Your income buys more today than ever before.

Growth

In August, 1971, I announced the New Economic Policy. Since then, the Nation's output has increased by a phenomenal eleven and a half percent—a more rapid growth than in any comparable period in the last 21 years. Four and a half million new civilian jobs have been created—more than in any comparable period ever. At the same time, real per capita disposable income—meaning what you have left to spend after taxes and after inflation—has risen by seven and a half percent. This means that, in terms of what your money will actually buy, in the past year and a half your annual income has increased by the equivalent of four extra weeks' pay. When we consider these facts, therefore, we can see that in terms of jobs, of income, of growth, we are enjoying one of the best periods in our history.

We have every reason to be optimistic about the future. But there is one great problem that rightly concerns every one of us. This is rising prices, and especially rising food prices. By the end of last year we had brought the rate of inflation down to 3.4 percent, giving us the best record against inflation in 1972 of any major industrial nation. But now prices are going up at unacceptably high rates.

The greatest part of this increase is due to rising food prices. This has been caused in large measure by increased demand at home and abroad, by crop failures abroad and by some of the worst weather for crops and livestock here in America that we have ever experienced. Whatever the reasons, every American family is confronted with a real and pressing problem of higher prices. I have decided that the time has come to take strong and effective action to deal with this problem.

Price Freeze

Effective immediately, therefore, I am ordering a freeze on prices. This freeze will hold prices at levels no higher than those charged during the first eight days of June. It will cover all prices paid by consumers. The only prices not covered will be those of unprocessed agricultural products at the farm levels, and rents.

Wages, interest and dividends will remain under their present control systems during the freeze. The reason I have decided not to freeze wages is that the wage settlements reached under the rules of Phase III have not been a significant cause of the increase in prices. As long as wage settlements continue to be responsible and non-inflationary, a wage freeze will not be imposed.

The freeze will last for a maximum of 60 days. This time will be used to develop and put into place a new and more effective system of controls which will follow the freeze. This new, Phase IV set of controls will be designed to contain the forces that have sent prices so rapidly upward in the past few months. It will involve tighter standards and more mandatory compliance procedures than under Phase III. It will recognize the need for wages and prices to be treated consistently with one another.

In addition to food prices, I have received reports from various parts of the country lately of many instances of sharp increases in the price of gasoline. Therefore, I have specifically directed the Cost of Living Council to develop new Phase IV measures that will stabilize both food prices at the retail store and the price of gasoline at the local service station.

Phase IV

In announcing these actions, there is one point I want to emphasize to everyone listening to me tonight: The Phase IV that follows the freeze will not be designed to get us permanently into a controlled economy. On the contrary, it will be designed as a better way to get us out of a controlled economy, and to return us as quickly as possible to the free market system.

We are not going to put the American economy in a strait jacket. We are not going to control the boom in a way that would lead to a bust. We are not going to follow the advice of those who have proposed actions that would lead inevitably to a permanent system of price and wage controls. Such actions would bring good headlines tomorrow and bad headaches six months from now for every American family, in terms of rationing, black markets, and eventually a recession leading to more unemployment.

It is your prosperity that is at stake. It is your job that is at stake. The actions I have directed today are designed to deal with the rise in the cost of living without jeopardizing your prosperity or your job.

Because the key to curb food prices lies in increasing supplies, I am not freezing the price of unprocessed agricultural products at the farm level. This would reduce supplies instead of increasing them, and would eventually result, inevitably, in even higher prices for the foods you buy at the supermarket.

Supply and Demand

Beginning in 1972, we embarked on a comprehensive new program for increasing food supplies. Among many other measures, this has included opening up 40 million more acres for crop production. In the months ahead, as these new crops are harvested, they will help hold prices down. But unfortunately, this is not yet helping in terms of the prices you pay at the supermarket today.

One of the major reasons for the rise in food prices at home is that there is now an unprecedented demand abroad for the products of America's farms. Over the long run, increased food exports will be a vital factor in raising farm income, in improving our balance of payments, and in supporting America's position in the world. In the short term, however—when we have shortages and sharply rising prices of food at home—I have made this basic decision: In allocating the products of America's farms between marketings abroad and those in the United States, we must put the American consumer first.

Therefore, I have decided that a new system for export controls on food products is needed—a system designed to hold the price of animal feed-stuffs and other grains in the American market to levels that will make it possible to produce meat and eggs and milk at prices you can afford.

I shall ask the Congress, on an urgent basis, to give me the new and more flexible authority needed to impose such a system. In exercising such authority, this will be my policy. We will keep the export commitments we have made as a Nation. We shall also consult with other countries to seek their cooperation in resolving the world-wide problem of rising food prices. But we will not let foreign sales price meat and eggs off the American table.

I have also taken another action today to stop the rise in the cost of living. I have ordered the Internal Revenue Service to begin immediately a thorough-going audit of the books of companies which have raised their prices more than 1.5 percent above their January ceilings. The purpose of the audit will be to find out whether those increases were justified by rising costs. If they were not, the prices will be rolled back.

Congress' Role

The battle against inflation is everybody's business. I have told you what the Administration will do. There is also a vital role for the Congress. The most important single thing the Congress can do in holding down the cost of living is to hold down the cost of Government. For my part, I shall continue to veto spending bills that we cannot afford, no matter how noble-sounding their names. If these budget-busters became law, the money would come out of your pocket—in higher taxes, higher prices, or both. There are several specific recommendations I have already made to the Congress that will be important in holding down prices in the future. I again urge quick action on all of these proposals.

Congress should give the President authority to reduce tariffs in selected cases in order to increase supplies of scarce goods and hold down their prices. This action will help on such scarce items as meat, plywood and zinc. In particular, the tariff on imported meat should be removed.

Congress should provide authority to dispose of more surplus commodities held in Government stockpiles.

Congress should let us go ahead quickly with the Alaska pipeline, and so combat the shortage of oil and gasoline. I will also soon send to the Congress a major new set of proposals on energy, spelling out new actions I believe are necessary to help us meet our energy needs and thereby lessen pressures on fuel prices.

In its consideration of new farm legislation, it is vital that the Congress put high production ahead of high prices, so that farm prosperity will not be at the cost of higher prices for the consumer. If the Congress sends me a farm bill, or any other bill, that I consider inflationary, I shall veto such a bill.

Beyond what the Administration can do, and what the Congress can do, there is also a great deal that you can do. The next 60 days can decide the question: whether we shall have a continuing inflation that leads to recession, or whether we deal responsibly with our present problems, and so go forward with a vigorous prosperity and a swift return to a free market.

You can help, by giving your Senators and Congressmen your support when they make the difficult decisions to hold back on unnecessary spending.

You can help, by saying no to those who would impose a permanent system of controls on this great, productive economy of ours which is the wonder of the world.

Temporary Controls

Let there be no mistake: If our economy is to remain dynamic, we must never slip into the temptation of imagining that in the long run controls can substitute for a free economy or permit us to escape the need for discipline in fiscal and monetary policy. We must not let controls become a narcotic—and we must not become addicted.

There are all sorts of seemingly simple gimmicks, that would give the appearance or offer the promise of controlling inflation—but that would carry a dangerous risk of bringing on a recession, and that would not be effective in holding down prices. Rigid, permanent controls always look better on paper than they do in practice.

We have much to be thankful for here in America. We are the best-clothed, best-fed, best-housed people in the world—the envy of every nation. This year, for the first time in 12 years, we are at peace in Vietnam—and our courageous prisoners of war have returned to their homes. This year, for the first time in a generation, no American is being drafted into the armed forces. This year, we find our prospects brighter than at any time in the modern era for a lasting peace, and for the abundant prosperity such a peace can make possible.

Next Monday, I will meet at the summit with General Secretary Brezhnev of the Soviet Union. Based on the months of preparatory work that has been done for this meeting, and based on the extensive consultation and correspondence we have had, I can confidently predict that out of our meetings will come major new progress toward reducing both the burden of arms and the danger of war, and toward a better and more rewarding relationship between the world's two most powerful nations.

Today, in America, we have a magnificent opportunity. We hold the future—our future—in our own hands. By standing together, by working together, by joining in bold yet sensible policies to meet our temporary problems without sacrificing our lasting strengths, we can achieve what America has not had since President Eisenhower was in this office: full prosperity without war and without inflation. This is a great goal, and a goal that together we can reach.   ✓

TEXT OF AID REQUEST FOR ISRAEL

Following is the White House text of President Nixon's Oct. 19 message to Congress requesting an authorization of $2.2-billion for Israel and $200-million for Cambodia for emergency security assistance.

TO THE CONGRESS OF THE UNITED STATES:

I am today requesting that the Congress authorize emergency security assistance of $2.2 billion for Israel and $200 million for Cambodia. This request is necessary to permit the United States to follow a responsible course of action in two areas where stability is vital if we are to build a global structure of peace.

For more than a quarter of a century, as strategic interests of the major powers have converged there, the Middle East has been a flashpoint for potential world conflict. Since war broke out again on October 6, bringing tragedy to the people of Israel and the Arab nations alike, the United States has been actively engaged in efforts to contribute to a settlement. Our actions there have reflected my belief that we must take those steps which are necessary for maintaining a balance of military capabilities and achieving stability in the area. The request I am submitting today would give us the essential flexibility to continue meeting those requirements.

To maintain a balance of forces and thus achieve stability, the United States Government is currently providing military material to Israel to replace combat losses. This is necessary to prevent the emergence of a substantial imbalance resulting from a large-scale resupply of Syria and Egypt by the Soviet Union.

The costs of replacing consumables and lost equipment for the Israeli Armed Forces have been extremely high. Combat activity has been intense, and losses on both sides have been large. During the first 12 days of the conflict, the United States has authorized shipments to Israel of material costing $825 million, including transportation.

Major items now being furnished by the United States to the Israeli forces include conventional munitions of many types, air-to-air and air-to-ground missiles, artillery, crew-served and individual weapons, and a standard range of fighter aircraft ordnance.

Additionally, the United States is providing replacements for tanks, aircraft, radios, and other military equipment which have been lost in action.

Thus far, Israel has attempted to obtain the necessary equipment through the use of cash and credit purchases. However, the magnitude of the current conflict coupled with the scale of Soviet supply activities has created needs which exceed Israel's capacity to continue with cash and credit purchases. The alternative to cash and credit sales of United States military materials is for us to provide Israel with grant military assistance as well.

The United States is making every effort to bring this conflict to a very swift and honorable conclusion, measured in days not weeks. But prudent planning also requires us to prepare for a longer struggle.

I am therefore requesting that the Congress approve emergency assistance to Israel in the amount of $2.2 billion. If the conflict moderates, or as we fervently hope, is brought to an end very quickly, funds not absolutely required would of course not be expended.

Assistance for Cambodia

I am also requesting $200 million emergency assistance for Cambodia. As in the case of Israel, additional funds are urgently needed for ammunition and consumable military supplies. The increased requirement results from the larger scale of hostilities and the higher levels of ordnance required by the Cambodian Army and Air Force to defend themselves without American air support.

The end of United States bombing on August 15 was followed by increased communist activity in Cambodia. In the ensuing fight, the Cambodian forces acquitted themselves well. They successfully defended the capital of Phnom Penh and the provincial center of Kampong Cham, as well as the principal supply routes. Although this more intense level of fighting has tapered off somewhat during the current rainy season, it is virtually certain to resume when the dry season begins about the end of the year.

During the period of heaviest fighting in August and September, ammunition costs for the Cambodian forces were running almost $1 million per day. We anticipate similar average costs for the remainder of this fiscal year. These ammunition requirements, plus minimum equipment replacement, will result in a total funding requirement of $380 million for the current fiscal year, rather than the $180 million previously requested. To fail to provide the $200 million for additional ammunition would deny the Cambodian Armed Forces the ability to defend themselves and their country.

We remain hopeful that the conflict in Cambodia be resolved by a negotiated settlement. A communist military victory and the installation of a government in Phnom Penh which is controlled by Hanoi would gravely threaten the fragile structure of peace established in the Paris agreements.

I am confident that the Congress and the American people will support this request for emergency assistance for these two beleaguered friends.

To do less would not only create a dangerous imbalance in these particular arenas but would also endanger the entire structure of peace in the world.

RICHARD NIXON

THE WHITE HOUSE,
October 23, 1973

✓

USIA VETO MESSAGE

Following is the White House text of President Nixon's Oct. 23 message to the Senate on his veto of S 1317, the bill to authorize fiscal 1974 appropriations for the United States Information Agency.

TO THE SENATE OF THE UNITED STATES:

I am returning today without my approval S 1317, the United States Information Agency Appropriations Authorization Act of 1973.

The major purpose of this bill is to authorize appropriations for operation of the USIA during fiscal year 1974. Unfortunately however, the Congress has injected a separate issue which, in good conscience, I must oppose.

Traditionally, when it is deemed necessary for a Department or Agency to withhold certain confidential information that has been requested by the Congress, the President issues a directive or statement prohibiting the disclosure of such information and explaining the reasons for his action. The two branches then explore means of compromise by which data can be supplied in a way that is consistent with the constitutional obligations of each branch.

Section 4 of S 1317 ignores this precedent. Instead, it would penalize the USIA with a possible cut-off of funds if it failed to meet a demand for confidential internal information made by the Senate Committee on Foreign Relations or the House Committee on Foreign Affairs—however unreasonable that demand might be.

The Justice Department has advised me that section 4 is an unconstitutional attempt on the part of the Congress to undermine the President's constitutional responsibility to withhold the disclosure of information when, in his judgment, such disclosure would be contrary to the public interest. From George Washington on, my predecessors have defended this Presidential responsibility, recognizing that the traditional division of powers and comity between the executive and legislative branches must be maintained. I intend to do no less.

A practical effect of section 4 would be to restrict the USIA access to sensitive foreign policy information essential to carrying out its mission. The Agency could also be forced to disclose internal documents and working papers which do not represent approved policy. Failure of the Congress to respect the confidentiality of such papers would prevent a free and frank exchange of views within the USIA and between it and other parts of the executive branch—an exchange that is vital if the USIA is to function as an effective arm of American foreign policy.

This Administration has invoked Executive privilege to withhold information only in the most compelling circumstances and only after thorough, thoughtful evaluation of the facts. As evidence of our good faith, the USIA has complied as fully as possible with every Congressional request for information during the authorization and appropriations hearings this year, and will continue to do so. For example, it provided the Senate Foreign Relations Committee alone with detailed answers to more than one hundred substantive questions prior to this year's authorization hearings.

If a President failed to take a stand in this instance to protect the division of powers and uphold the doctrine of Executive privilege, the door would be opened to even more serious encroachments on the constitutional system. Already, provisions similar to those in section 4 are contained in two vital bills at very advanced stages in the legislative process—S 2335, the economic foreign assistance authorization bill, and S 1443, the security assistance authorization bill.

The issue at stake is simple. It involves far more than the confidential documents of the USIA or our other foreign affairs and national security agencies. Rather, it involves the preservation of the basic ability of the executive branch to continue to function and perform the responsibilities assigned to it by the Constitution. Unless privacy in the preliminary exchange of views between personnel of the Executive agencies can be maintained, the healthy expression of opinion and the frank, forthright interplay of ideas that are essential to sound policy and effective administration cannot survive.

RICHARD NIXON

THE WHITE HOUSE,
October 23, 1973

WAR POWERS VETO TEXT

Following is the White House text of President Nixon's Oct. 24 message to Congress concerning his veto of the War Powers resolution (H J Res 542).

TO THE HOUSE OF REPRESENTATIVES:

I hereby return without my approval House Joint Resolution 542—the War Powers Resolution. While I am in accord with the desire of the Congress to assert its proper role in the conduct of our foreign affairs, the restrictions which this resolution would impose upon the authority of the President are both unconstitutional and dangerous to the best interests of our Nation.

The proper roles of the Congress and the Executive in the conduct of foreign affairs have been debated since the founding of our country. Only recently, however, has there been a serious challenge to the wisdom of the Founding Fathers in choosing not to draw a precise and detailed line of demarcation between the foreign policy powers of the two branches.

The Founding Fathers understood the impossibility of foreseeing every contingency that might arise in this complex area. They acknowledged the need for flexibility in responding to changing circumstances. They recognized that foreign policy decisions must be made through close cooperation between the two branches and not through rigidly codified procedures.

These principles remain as valid today as they were when our Constitution was written. Yet House Joint Resolution 542 would violate those principles by defining the President's powers in ways which would strictly limit his constitutional authority.

Clearly Unconstitutional. House Joint Resolution 542 would purport to take away, by a mere legislative act, authorities which the President has properly exercised under the Constitution for almost 200 years. One of its provisions would automatically cut off certain authorities after sixty days unless the Congress extended them. Another would allow the Congress to eliminate certain authorities merely by the passage of a concurrent resolution—an action which does not normally have the force of law, since it denies the President his constitutional role in approving legislation.

I believe that both these provisions are unconstitutional. The only way in which the constitutional powers of a branch of the Government can be altered is by amending the Constitution—and any attempt to make such alterations by legislation alone is clearly without force.

Undermining Foreign Policy

While I firmly believe that a veto of House Joint Resolution 542 is warranted solely on constitutional grounds, I am also deeply disturbed by the practical consequences of this resolution. For it would seriously undermine this Nation's ability to act decisively and convincingly in times of international crisis. As a result, the confidence of our allies in our ability to assist them could be diminished and the respect of our adversaries for our deterrent posture could decline. A permanent and substantial element of unpredictability would be injected into the world's assessment of American behavior, further increasing the likelihood of miscalculation and war.

If this resolution had been in operation, America's effective response to a variety of challenges in recent years would have been vastly complicated or even made impossible. We may well have been unable to respond in the way we did during the Berlin crisis of 1961, the Cuban missile crisis of 1962, the Congo rescue operation in 1964, and the Jordanian crisis of 1970—to mention just a few examples. In addition, our recent actions to bring about a peaceful settlement of the hostilities in the Middle East would have been seriously impaired if this resolution had been in force.

While all the specific consequences of House Joint Resolution 542 cannot yet be predicted, it is clear that it would undercut the ability of the United States to act as an effective influence for peace. For example, the provision automatically cutting off certain authorities after 60 days unless they are extended by the Congress could work to prolong or intensify a crisis. Until the Congress suspended the deadline, there would be at least a chance of United States withdrawal and an adversary would be tempted therefore to postpone serious negotiations until the 60 days were up. Only after the Congress acted would there be a strong incentive for an adversary to negotiate. In addition, the very existence of a deadline could lead to an escalation of hostilities in order to achieve certain objectives before the 60 days expired.

The measure would jeopardize our role as a force for peace in other ways as well. It would, for example, strike from the President's hand a wide range of important peacekeeping tools by eliminating his ability to exercise quiet diplomacy backed by subtle shifts in our military deployments. It would also cast into doubt authorities which Presidents have used to undertake certain humanitarian relief missions in conflict areas, to protect fishing boats from seizure, to deal with ship or aircraft hijackings, and to respond to threats of attack. Not the least of the adverse consequences of this resolution would be the prohibition contained in section 8 against fulfilling our obigations under the NATO treaty as ratified by the Senate. Finally, since the bill is somewhat vague as to when the 60 day rule would apply, it could lead to extreme confusion and dangerous disagreements concerning the perogatives of the two branches, seriously damaging our ability to respond to international crises.

Failure to Require Positive Congressional Action. I am particularly disturbed by the fact that certain of the President's constitutional powers as Commander in Chief of the Armed Forces would terminate automatically under this resolution 60 days after they were invoked. No overt Congressional action would be required to cut off these powers—they would disappear automatically unless the Congress extended them. In effect, the Congress is here attempting to increase its policy-making role through a provision which requires it to take absolutely no action at all.

In my view, the proper way for the Congress to make known its will on such foreign policy questions is through a positive action, with full debate on the merits of the issue and with each member taking the responsibility of casting a yes or no vote after considering those merits. The authorization and appropriations process represents one of the ways in which such influence can be exercised. I do not, however, believe that the Congress can responsibly contribute its considered, collective judgment on such grave questions without full debate and without a yes or no vote. Yet this is precisely what the joint resolution would allow. It would give every future Congress the ability to handcuff every future President merely by doing nothing and sitting still. In my view, one cannot become a responsible partner unless one is prepared to take responsible action.

Strengthening Cooperation Between the Congress and the Executive Branches. The responsible and effective exercise of the war powers requires the fullest cooperation between the Congress and the Executive and the prudent fulfillment by each branch of its constitutional responsibilities. House Joint Resolution 542 includes certain constructive measures which would foster this process by enhancing the flow of information from the executive branch to the Congress. Section 3, for example, calls for consultations with the Congress before and during the involvement of United States forces in hostilities abroad.

This provision is consistent with the desire of this Administration for regularized consultations with the Congress in an even wider range of circumstances.

I believe that full and cooperative participation in foreign policy matters by both the executive and the legislative branches could be enhanced by a careful and dispassionate study of their constitutional roles. Helpful proposals for such a study have already been made in the Congress. I would welcome the establishment of a non-partisan commission on the constitutional roles of the Congress and the President in the conduct of foreign affairs. This commission could make a thorough review of the principal constitutional issues in Executive-Congressional relations, including the war powers, the international agreement powers, and the question of Executive privilege, and then submit its recommendations to the President and the Congress. The members of such a commission could be drawn from both parties —and could represent many perspectives including those of the Congress, the executive branch, the legal profession, and the academic community.

This Administration is dedicated to strengthening cooperation between the Congress and the President in the conduct of foreign affairs and to preserving the constitutional prerogatives of both branches of our Government. I know that the Congress shares that goal. A commission on the constitutional roles of the Congress and the President would provide a useful opportunity for both branches to work together toward that common objective.

RICHARD NIXON

THE WHITE HOUSE,
October 24, 1973

ENERGY CRISIS MESSAGE

Following is the White House text of President Nixon's Nov. 8 message to Congress on the energy crisis.

TO THE CONGRESS OF THE UNITED STATES:

As America has grown and prospered in recent years, our demands for energy have begun to outstrip available supplies. Along with other major industrialized nations, we are now faced with the prospect of shortages for several years to come.

Two years ago, in the first energy message ever sent to the Congress by a President of the United States, I called attention to the looming energy problem. Since that time, I have repeatedly warned that the problem might become a full-blown crisis, and seeking to minimize shortages, I have taken a number of administrative steps to increase supplies and reduce consumption. Earlier this year, I also sent more than a half dozen urgent legislative proposals to the Congress. While none of these has yet been enacted, I am hopeful at least several of the measures will be ready for my signature before year's end.

Unfortunately, the energy crisis that one seemed a distant threat to many people is now closing upon us quickly. We had expected moderate shortages of energy this winter, but four weeks ago, when war broke out in the Middle East, most of our traditional suppliers in that area cut off their shipments of oil to the United States. Their action has now sharply changed our expectations for the coming months.

Largely because of the war, we must face up to the stark fact that we are heading toward the most acute shortages of energy since the Second World War. Of the 17 million barrels of oil a day that we would ordinarily consume this winter, more than two million barrels a day will no longer be available to us. Instead of a shortage of approximately 2-3 per cent that we had anticipated this winter, we now expect that our supply of petroleum will be at least 10 percent short of our anticipated demands—and could fall short by as much as 17 percent.

Administration Actions

Faced with this emergency, I believe that we must move forward immediately on two fronts: administrative and legislative.

In a speech to the Nation last night, I announced a number of immediate actions:

First, industries and utilities which use coal—our most abundant resource—will be prevented from converting to oil. Efforts will also be made to convert power plants from the use of oil to the use of coal.

Second, reduced quantities of fuel will be allocated to aircraft. This will lead to a cutback of some 10 per cent in the number of commercial flights, but it should not seriously disrupt air travel nor cause serious damage to the airline industry.

Third, there will be reductions of approximately 15 percent in the supply of heating oil for homes, offices and other establishments. This is a precautionary measure to ensure that the oil now available not be consumed early in the winter, so that we shall have adequate amounts available in the later months. This step will make it necessary for all of us to live and work in lower temperatures. We must ask everyone to lower the thermostat in his home by at least 6 degrees, so that we can achieve a national daytime average of 68 degrees. In offices, factories and commercial establishments we must ask that the equivalent of a 10-degree reduction by achieved by either lowering the thermostat or curtailing working hours.

Fourth, there will be additional reductions in the consumption of energy by the Federal Government, cutting even deeper than the 7 percent reduction that I ordered earlier this year. This new reduction will affect the operations of every agency and department in the Government, including the Defense Department, which has already led the way in previous cutbacks. As one of the steps in the Federal effort, I have ordered that daytime temperatures in Federal offices be reduced to a level between 65 and 68 degrees. I have also ordered that all vehicles owned by the Federal Government be driven no faster than 50 miles per hour except in emergencies. This is a step which I have also asked Governors, mayors, and other local officials to take immediately with regard to vehicles under their authority.

Fifth, I have asked the Atomic Energy Commission to speed up the licensing and construction of nuclear plants, seeking to reduce the time required to bring nuclear plants on line from ten years to six years.

Sixth, I have also asked Governors and mayors to reinforce these actions by taking appropriate steps at the State and local level. Among the steps which I believe would be helpful are these: staggering of working hours, the encouragement of mass transit and carpooling, alteration of school schedules, and elimination of unnecessary lighting. I have also recommended to the Governors that, consistent with safety and economic considerations, they seek to reduce highway speed limits to 50 miles per hour. This step alone could save over 200,000 barrels of oil a day.

Need for Emergency Legislation

As essential as these actions are to the solution of our immediate problem, we must recognize that standing alone, they are insufficient. Additional steps must be taken, and for that purpose, we must have new legislation.

I am therefore proposing that the Administration and the Congress join forces and together, in a bipartisan spirit, work to enact an emergency energy bill. Members of my Administration have been consulting with appropriate leaders of the Congress for more than two weeks on this matter. Yesterday I met with the bipartisan leaders of the House and Senate and found them constructive in spirit and eager to get on with the job. In the same manner, I pledge the full cooperation of my Administration. It is my earnest hope that by pushing forward together, we can have new emergency legislation on the books before the Congress recesses in December.

Based on previous consultations with the Congress, I have decided not to send a specific Administration bill to the Congress on this matter but rather to work with the Members in developing a measure that would be acceptable to both the executive and legislative branches. As part of that process, I think it would be helpful to call attention to those provisions that I think should be included in this emergency bill. At a minimum, I hope that the act would:

• Authorize restrictions on both the public and private consumption of energy by such measures as limitations on essential uses of energy (office hours, for instance) and elimination of non-essential uses (decorative lighting, for example);

• Authorize the reduction to 50 miles per hour of speed limits on highways across the country;

• Authorize the exemption or granting of waivers of stationary sources from Federal and State air and water quality laws and regulations. Such actions would be taken through the Administrator of EPA.

• Provide emergency powers for the Federal regulatory agencies involved in transportation to adjust the operations of air, rail, and ship and motor carriers in a manner responsive to the need to conserve fuel.

• Empower the Atomic Energy Commission to grant a temporary operating license of up to 18 months for nuclear power plants without holding a public hearing. Such actons would be subject to all safety and other requirements normally imposed by the Commission.

• Authorize the initiation of full production in Naval Petroleum Reserve #1 (Elk Hills, California) and the exploration and further development of other Naval Petroleum Reserves, including Naval Petroleum Reserve #4 in Alaska.

• Permit Daylight Saving Time to be established on a year-round basis.

• And authorize the President, where practicable, to order a power plant or other installation to convert from the use of a fuel such as oil to another fuel such as coal and to make such equipment conversions as are necessary.

In addition to the provisions above, all of which I believe must be enacted before December, there are a number of other authorities which should be provided as soon as possible and hopefully will be included in the emergency measure.

One such provision would grant the President additonal authority to allocate and ration energy supplies. Under this new authority, the President could take such actions based solely upon energy considerations. It is my hope that rationing of energy products will never be required, but if circumstances dictate it, there should be no impediments to swift action. For contingency purposes, I have already directed that plans for gasoline rationing be drawn up and held in reserve.

Recognizing that a more efficient use of our transportation resources is necessary, we should also provide additional authority to encourage greater use of funds from the Federal-Aid Highway Act of 1973 for mass transit capital improvements.

In addition, we should provide the Federal Power Commission with authority, during the duration of the energy emergency, to suspend the regulation of prices of new natural gas at the wellhead.

Finally, I believe it would be wise if, on energy grounds, the President were empowered to exercise any authority now contained in the Defense Production Act, the Economic Stabilization Act and the Export Administration Act, even though those acts may have otherwise expired.

Meeting the Long-Term Challenge

As we act to deal with the immediate problem before us, we must not ignore the need for preventing such a crisis from recurring. The lead-time required to meet our long-range energy needs dictate that we must move on them at once.

Legislation authorizing construction of the Alaskan pipeline must be the first of business as we tackle our long-range energy problems. The American people are depending upon the Congress to enact this legislation at the earliest possible moment, and they are depending upon me to approve it. With passage apparently imminent, I would urge the Congress not to burden this legislation with irrelevant amendments. This is no time to hold the Nation's energy future hostage to other controversial interests.

I am also requesting early action on pending legislative proposals to:

• permit the competitive pricing of new natural gas;

• provide reasonable standards for the surface mining of coal;

• provide simplified procedures for the siting and approving of electric energy facilities;

• establish a Department of Energy and Natural Resources;

• and provide procedures for approving construction and operation of deepwater ports.

Because of the critical role which energy research and development will play in meeting our future energy needs, I am requesting the Congress to give priority attention to the creation of an Energy Research and Development Administration separate from my proposal to create a Department of Energy and Natural Resources. This new administration would direct the $10 billion program aimed at achieving a national capacity for energy self-sufficiency by 1980.

This new effort to achieve self-sufficiency in energy, to be known as Project Independence, is absolutely critical to the maintenance of our ability to play our independent role in international affairs. In addition, we must recognize that a substantial part of our success in building a strong and vigorous economy in this century is attributable to the fact that we have always had access to almost unlimited amounts of cheap energy. If this growth is to continue, we must develop our capacity to provide enormous amounts of clean energy at the lowest possible cost. Thus, irrespective of the implications for our foreign policy and with the implicit understanding that our intentions are not remotely isolationist, the increasing costs of foreign energy further contribute to the necessity of our achieving self-sufficiency in energy.

RICHARD NIXON

WILDERNESS AREAS TEXT

Following is the White House text of President Nixon's Nov. 28 message to Congress on wilderness areas.

TO THE CONGRESS OF THE UNITED STATES:

At a time when our Nation is seriously concerned with conserving our energy resources, it is also important that we protect another treasured national resource—our wilderness areas and the many varieties of plant and animal life which thrive uniquely in wilderness environments.

With this goal in mind, and pursuant to the Wilderness Act of 1964, I am today proposing twelve additions to the National Wilderness Preservation System. These additions would cover a total of over 1 million primeval acres of American terrain which still exist today in much the same condition as they existed centuries before the first European set foot in the New World.

Briefly described, they are:

(1) The Joshua Tree National Monument, California—372,700 acres located in the great California Desert. The varied desert terrain included in this tract harbors widely differing plants and animals.

(2) Point Reyes National Seashore, California—10,600 acres on a long narrow peninsula characterized by fine beaches and steep, forested slopes.

(3) Big Bend National Park, Texas—533,900 acres. Encompassing both the lofty Chisos Mountains and large tracts of

desert, this area is host to several wildlife habitats and an unusual diversity of plant and animal life.

(4) Imperial National Wildlife Refuge, Arizona and California—14,470 acres along the Lower Colorado River. The desert uplands which this proposal would set aside provide a home for wild waterfowl, serving in particular as the wintering habitat of Canada geese of the Great Basin flock.

(5) Mesa Verde National Park, Colorado—8,100 acres. The two portions of the park which would be added to the wilderness system are an eastern section with wildlife including mule, deer, cougar, bighorn sheep, wild turkey, and many smaller animals, and a northern area which contains the rugged brow of the Mesa Verde Plateau itself.

(6) Mingo National Wildlife Refuge, Missouri—1,700 acres in a former channel of the Mississippi River. The proposed area contains lowland forest vegetation and a natural swamp environment.

(7) Oregon Islands National Wildlife Refuge, Oregon—346 acres located on 26 islands. Nesting ground for thousands of seabirds, these islands, plus two existing wilderness areas with which they will be consolidated, lie along the beautiful Oregon coast.

(8) White River National Wildlife Refuge, Arkansas—975 acres. Located in an area known as the Scrub Grass Bayou Research area, the recommended acreage comprises bottomland hardwood forest.

(9) Saguaro National Monument, Arizona—42,400 acres. This proposal would set aside splendid stands of the giant saguaro cactus and other desert resources, as well as rugged mountainous areas with regional vegetation and wildlife.

(10) Bandelier National Monument, New Mexico—21,110 acres. The monument was once the home of prehistoric Pueblo Indians. The proposal encompasses many archeological sites and a great deal of rugged terrain providing habitat for deer, bear, mountain lion and other large mammals.

(11) Valentine National Wildlife Refuge, Nebraska—16,317 acres characterized by the sandhill range, an unusual geological formation in need of preservation. The refuge is populated by several threatened bird species and a variety of other wildlife.

(12) Crescent Lake National Wildlife Refuge, Nebraska—24,502 acres which provide a pristine sandhill habitat for mule deer, antelope, and such rare bird species as the bald eagle and golden eagle.

After a review of roadless areas of 5,000 acres or more, the Secretary of the Interior has concluded that two areas are not suitable for preservation as part of the National Wilderness Preservation System. These are the Salt Plains National Wilflife Refuge, Oklahoma, and the Klamath Forest National Wildlife Refuge, Oregon.

In addition to this message, I am transmitting to the Congress today letters and reports from the Secretary of the Interior regarding all of these wilderness proposals. I concur with the recommendation of the Secretary in each case.

I would draw to the attention of the Congress once again the eastern wilderness legislation which we recently submitted. This proposal—which is now embodied in legislation labeled S 2487 and HR 10469—would amend the Wilderness Act to designate 16 acres in eastern national forest lands as wilderness on an immediate basis and would subject 37 other areas to study for possible addition to the wilderness system. I urge the Congress to give early and favorable consideration to this proposal, as well as the wilderness proposals accompanying this message.

RICHARD NIXON

NATIONAL ENERGY POLICY

Following is the White House text of President Nixon's Nov. 25 televised address on the national energy policy.

Good evening. Three weeks ago, I spoke to you about the national energy crisis and our policy for meeting it. Tonight I want to talk with you again to report on our progress and to announce further steps we must take to carry out our energy policy.

When I spoke to you earlier, I indicated that the sudden cut-off of oil from the Middle East had turned the serious energy shortages we expected this winter into a major energy crisis. That crisis is now being felt around the world, as other industrialized nations have also suffered from cutbacks in oil from the Middle East.

Shortages in Europe, for example, are far more critical than they are in the United States. Already seven European nations have imposed a ban on Sunday driving. Fortunately, the United States is not as dependent upon Middle Eastern oil as many other nations. We will not have a ban on Sunday driving, but as you will hear later, we are going to try to limit it. Nevertheless, we anticipate that our shortages could run as high as 17 percent. This means that we must immediately take strong, effective counter-measures.

In order to minimize disruptions in our economy, I asked on November 7th that all Americans adopt certain energy-conservation measures to help meet the challenge of reduced energy supplies. These steps include reductions in home heating, reductions in driving speeds, elimination of unnecessary lighting. The American people, all of you, you have responded to this challenge with that spirit of sacrifice which has made this such a great nation.

The Congress has also been moving forward on the energy front. The Alaska pipeline bill has been passed. I signed it into law nine days ago right here at this desk. The Congress has passed a fuel allocation bill which I will sign into law on Tuesday. An additional emergency bill providing special authority to deal with this problem has now passed the Senate. When the House returns from its recess, I am confident the House will move promptly so that this vital legislation can be signed into law by the middle of December.

And so we have made some encouraging progress, but there is much more to be done, and that is what I want to talk to you about tonight.

I have appointed an Energy Emergency Action Group, under my chief energy adviser, Governor John Love, to analyze our situation on a continuing basis and to advise me of all actions required to deal with it.

Five Steps

And upon the action and the recommendation of this group, I am announcing tonight the following steps to meet the energy crisis:

Heating Oil Supply. First, to increase the supply of heating oil that will be available this winter, we must adjust production schedules and divert petroleum which might normally go for the production of gasoline to the production of more heating oil.

To accomplish this, the amount of gasoline which refiners distribute to wholesalers and retailers will be reduced across the Nation by 15 percent. As we reduce gasoline supplies, we must act to insure that the remaining gasoline available is used wisely, and conserved to the fullest possible extent.

Gas Station Closings. Therefore, as a second step, I am asking tonight that all gasoline filling stations close down their pumps between 9:00 p.m. Saturday night and midnight Sunday every weekend, beginning December 1. We are requesting that this step be taken voluntarily now.

Upon passage of the emergency energy legislation before the Congress, gas stations will be required to close during these hours. This step should not result in any serious hardship for any American family. It will, however, discourage long-distance driving during weekends. It will mean perhaps spending a little more time at home.

This savings alone is only a small part of what we have to conserve to meet the total gasoline shortage. We can achieve substantial additional savings by altering our driving habits. While the voluntary response to my request for reduced driving speeds has been excellent, it is now essential that we have mandatory and full compliance with this important step on a nationwide basis.

50 M.P.H. Limit. And therefore, the third step will be the establishment of a maximum speed limit for automobiles of 50 miles per hour nationwide as soon as our emergency energy legislaton passes the Congress. We expect that this measure will produce a savings of 200,000 barrels of gasoline per day. Intercity buses and heavy duty trucks which operate more efficiently at higher speeds, and therefore, do not use more gasoline, will be permitted to observe a 55 mile per hour speed limit.

Jet Fuel. The fourth step we are taking involves our jet airliners. There will be a phased reduction of an additional 15 percent in the consumption of jet fuel for passenger flights bringing the total reduction to approximately 25 percent.

These savings will be achieved by a careful reduction in schedules, combined with an increase in passenger loads. We will not have to stop air travel, but we will have to plan for it more carefully.

Outdoor Lighting. The fifth step involves cutting back on outdoor lighting. As soon as the emergency energy legislation passes the Congress, I shall order the curtailment of ornamental outdoor lighting for homes and the elimination of all commercial lighting except that which identifies places of business.

In the meantime, we are already planning right here at the White House to curtail such lighting that we would normally have at Christmastime and I am asking that all of you act now on a voluntary basis to reduce or eliminate unnecessary lighting in your homes.

As just one example of the impact which such an initiative can have, the energy consumed by ornamental gas lights alone in this country is equivalent to 35,000 barrels per day of oil and that is enough fuel to heat 175,000 homes.

Heating Oil Allocation

Finally, I want to report to you tonight that we have now developed final plans for allocating reduced quanties of heating oil this winter and all of you know how very important heating oil is, particularly in the wintertime.

These plans, to be published Tuesday, will call for an average reduction of 10 percent of heating oil for industrial use, 15 percent for home use, and 25 percent for commercial use.

The reductions for homeowners alone will result in a savings of some 315,000 barrels of heating oil a day, which is enough to heat over 1½ million homes every day. For the average American family, as I indicated three weeks ago, this cutback in heating oil does not mean severe discomfort for anyone, but it will mean that everyone should lower the thermostat—as it is right here in this office now, and throughout the White House, and throughout every Federal installation—you should lower the thermostat by six degrees below its normal setting so that we can achieve a national daytime average of 68 degrees.

Those who fail to adopt such a cutback risk running out of fuel before the winter is over. While additional actions will be necessary to further offset the anticipated shortage of 17 percent, the steps which I have outlined tonight will relieve about 10 percent of that shortage.

They will make a very substantial contribution to our immediate goal of insuring that we have enough fuel to be adequately warm in our homes this winter, that we are able to get to work, and that we experience no serious disruptions in the normal conduct of our lives.

Cooperation

Above all, every step will be taken to insure that any disruptions to our economy which could cost jobs, will be as brief as possible and that they do not cause serious damage.

Nothing we do can succeed, however, without the full cooperation of the Congress in providing the legislation we must have, without the full cooperation of State and local governments in providing the broad leadership that we must have, and without the full cooperation of each and every one of you, all the American people, in sacrificing a little so that no one must endure real hardship.

For my part, I pledge to do everything in my power to insure that the decisions I have announced will be carried out swiftly and effectively and fairly, and whatever additional action is necessary to achieve our objective will be taken.

I intend to participate personally and on a regular basis, as I have since I last addressed you three weeks ago, in the work of my energy advisers. I intend to advise the congressional leadership regularly of problems and progress. And I intend to see that the persons and organizations having responsibilities and capabilities in this area are fully and regularly informed.

We need new rules if we are to meet this challenge; but most of all, we need sustained and serious action and cooperation by millions of men and women if we are to achieve our objective, and that means millions of Americans across this land listening to me tonight.

Self-Sufficiency

Let me conclude by restating our overall objective. It can be summed up in one word that best characterizes this Nation and its essential nature. That word is "independence." From its beginning 200 years ago, throughout its history, American has made great sacrifices of blood and also of treasure to achieve and maintain its independence. In the last third of this century, our independence will depend on maintaining and achieving self-sufficiency in energy.

What I have called Project Independence-1980 is a series of plans and goals set to insure that by the end of this decade Americans will not have to rely on any source of energy beyond our own.

As far as energy is concerned, this means we will hold our fate and our future in our hands alone. As we look to the future, we can do so confident that the energy crisis will be resolved not only for our time but for all time. We will once again have plentiful supplies of energy which helped to build the greatest industrial nation and one of the highest standards of living in the world.

The capacity for self-sufficiency in energy is a great goal. It is also an essential goal, and we are going to achieve it.

Tonight I ask all of you to join together in moving toward that goal, with the spirit of discipline, self-restraint and unity which is the cornerstone of our great and good country.

Thank you and good evening.   √

URBAN MASS TRANSIT VETO

Following is the White House text of President Nixon's Jan. 3, 1974, veto message of HR 10511, a bill to amend the Urban Mass Transportation Act of 1964.

TO THE CONGRESS OF THE UNITED STATES:

I regret that I cannot approve H.R. 10511, a bill to amend the Urban Mass Transportation Act of 1964. Unfortunately, this bill has evolved so as to become an anti-transit measure.

In its favor is the fact that H.R. 10511 would facilitate the use of Urban Mass Transportation monies for the purchase of buses by allowing such equipment to be used for charter services. Unfortunately, however, the bill would leave in effect the prohibition against using buses purchased with Federal-Aid Highway Act of 1973, the provision giving greater flexibility to States and communities in meeting their transportation problems. This we cannot afford.

(Urban mass transit veto continued on p. 187-A)

PRESIDENTIAL NEWS CONFERENCES

CQ

GOVERNMENT REORGANIZATION

Following are excerpts from a prepared text, as made available by the White House, of a Jan. 5 statement by President Nixon on executive reorganization.

The need to revitalize and streamline the Federal Government in preparation for America's third century is one of the most urgent imperatives confronting this Administration and the Congress as we approach the Bicentennial year that begins less than three years from now....

I trust that the Members of the House and Senate received the same message that I did when we went to the people last fall—the message that Americans are fed up with wasteful, musclebound government in Washington and anxious for change that works—and I hope that both Houses will respond constructively to this new opportunity to work with us in producing such change.

During the past few weeks I have had extensive discussions with outgoing and incoming members of the Cabinet and with many other knowledgeable individuals about how we can do a better job of managing the affairs of government over the next four years. I have also had the benefit of studies prepared by all departmental executives pursuant to my request that each consider ways of improving his own operations.

The principal roadblocks to better government which we have identified in this review process are the same ones that prompted my 1971 reorganization proposals to the Congress. One problem is that most of today's major governmental goals and activities cross existing departmental lines in a way that makes coherent policy formation and effective management extremely difficult. A second major problem is that the creation of several new departments and numerous other agencies and offices over the last 40 years has resulted in more officials reporting directly to the President than any one man can work with regularly on a personal basis.

This tangle must be resolved in a way that will make the advice and recommendations of all these officials available to the President for his use in forming policy and carrying out operations. Bureaucratic bottlenecks must be cleared to facilitate the flow of information and advice within the structure of the executive branch. More effective means must be devised for conveying policy guidance from the President to all operating executives and for making sure that guidance is followed.

Congress' Responsibility

The fundamental responsibility and prerogative for reorganizing the operating departments and agencies rests with the people's elected legislators. The President cannot relieve them of it; but the President can and should do everything within his power to apply on a smaller scale, at the staff levels closest to him, those organizational principles which he asks the Congress to apply on a giant scale across the whole Federal establishment.

Though the actual integration of fragmented departmental operations must wait on Congressional action, the broadening of policy perspectives on the part of top managers and advisers can be achieved at once. Similarly, we can and will begin now to realize, at least within the Executive Office of the President, the increased efficiency and economy which thinned-out organization charts and leaner personnel rolls would bring to the whole executive branch under full-scale reorganization.

I am therefore taking the first of a series of steps aimed at increasing the management effectiveness of both the Cabinet and the White House staff, by reordering the timeworn and in many cases obsolete relationships among top staff and line officials to the full extent of my legal authority to do so.

Reorganization

As far as personalities are concerned, the plans of most key members of the White House staff have already been announced. Though I regret the departure of a number of individuals who rendered outstanding service during the first term, I am pleased to be entering the new term with a team of men and women of the high caliber represented by Anne Armstrong, H. R. Haldeman, John Ehrlichman, Henry Kissinger, Roy Ash, George Shultz, Peter Flanigan, Bill Timmons, and their many capable colleagues.

From a managerial standpoint, the nucleus of this staff will be five Assistants to the President. They will work immediately under me, and at my direction, to integrate and unify policies and operations throughout the executive branch of the Government, and to oversee all of the activities for which the President is responsible. They will be charged with ensuring that full information, candid analysis, and a complete range of recommendations and options flow continuously into the Presidential decision-making process from all of the executives on my Administration team.

These five Assistants, with their areas of responsibility and authority are: administration of the White House Office, Mr. Haldeman; domestic affairs, Mr. Ehrlichman; foreign affairs, Dr. Kissinger; executive management, Mr. Ash; and economic affairs, Mr. Shultz. As previously announced, Mr. Shultz will continue to hold his line position as Secretary of the Treasury, and Mr. Ash will do likewise as Director of the Office of Management and Budget.

Within the field of domestic affairs, in order to achieve some of the same benefits of goal-oriented policy formation and advice to the President which would result from creation by the Congress of unified Departments of Natural Resources, Human Resources, and Community Development, I have decided to ask the heads of three of the present departments to serve simultaneously as Counsellors to the President with coordinating responsibilities in these three broad areas of concern.

Earl L. Butz, Secretary of Agriculture, will take on the additional post of Counsellor for Natural Resources. Caspar Weinberger, Secretary-designate of Health, Education, and Welfare, will become Counsellor for Human Resources. James Lynn, Secretary-designate of Housing and Urban Development, will become Counsellor for Community Development.

To facilitate a close working relationship with the President and the Assistant in charge of domestic affairs, each of these Counsellors will have an office in the Old Executive Office Building next to the White House.

To bring about better operational coordination and more unified policy development within the three subject areas to be supervised by the Counsellors, each will chair a committee of the Domestic Council made up of those department and agency heads having substantial responsibilities in his area. These committees will provide a mechanism for interdepartmental cooperation on the problems of natural resources, human resources, and community development in somewhat the same way as the new Council on Economic Policy (formation of which was announced last month) will do in the economic affairs area under the chairmanship of the Assistant to the President in charge of economic affairs. The specific concerns and organizations falling within each of these subject areas will generally be those assigned to the proposed new departments as described in my revised reorganization proposals.

Unchanged Functions

It should be understood that the functions of all eleven executive departments and of all the independent agencies of the Federal Government will continue under these arrangements precisely as they are at present. Only the passage of legislation or the acceptance of reorganization plans by the Congress can alter those functions. It should also be understood that each department Secretary and agency head will continue to exercise full authority and to bear full responsibility in the management of his or her own organization as prescribed by law. Further, I would emphasize that existing Congressional relationships with these various organizations and with their top officials will remain unchanged.

The individual department heads and the Counsellors will routinely report to me via the appropriate Assistant to the President, but will continue to work directly with me on important policy matters. Here let me state my opinion that the eleven men whom I have chosen as department heads in the new Cabinet are one of the strongest executive combinations ever put together here in Washington, in terms of management ability, personal integrity, and commitment to public service. Each has been selected and has accepted his selection on a basis of complete mutual trust, and of firm conviction that the arrangements announced today will serve every Secretary's own interest as well as the public interest, by enabling all the Secretaries to do a better job. I look forward to working closely with all of them during the next four years.

The Cabinet as a whole will continue to function as it has done during the past four years. The major Cabinet-level work will be done in constituent bodies including the National Security Council, Domestic Council, Council on Economic Policy, and Council on International Economic Policy. The non-Cabinet Council of Economic Advisers and Council on Environmental Quality will continue to carry out the advisory functions prescribed for them by statute.

The non-regulatory independent agencies and offices will, in a few cases, continue to report directly to me, but most will hereafter report to me through the appropriate Counsellor or Assistant, depending upon the degree of the President's statutory responsibility and authority for their operations. The regulatory agencies will hereafter communicate with my office through the Counsel to the President, as appropriate.

The Executive Office

Counsellors Butz, Weinberger, and Lynn, with the support of the committees which they will head, will be able to provide much of the advice and supervision for which Presidents in the past have had to turn to domestic policy establishments within the White House. The Counsellors will also be able to resolve with their colleagues at the Secretarial level many inter-departmental issues which have heretofore required arbitration by the President or his staff.

One consequence is that the staff of the Domestic Council can be cut back by about 55 percent—from 66 people at present to 30 people when the new Cabinet/staff structure is in place. But the Domestic Council is only one part of a large, disparate aggregation of entities that makes up what is called the Executive Office of the President (EOP).

The EOP was created in 1939 to give the President immediate staff assistance and direct control over the management and budget functions of the Government. From an original base of four organizations and 570 people, it has mushroomed more than sevenfold in employment over the past 33 years, as successive Congresses and Presidents have created new ad hoc problem-solving entities under the Chief Executive's immediate control rather than come to grips with the more fundamental need to revitalize the bureaucracy itself as an effective problem-solving instrument.

In order to spur such a revitalization, and to disengage the Executive Office of the President from operational activity so that the President can devote his time and attention to overall policy formation and direction, I am now taking action to cut the total personnel of the Executive Office of the President by well over half, and to reduce substantially the number of organizations which now make up the EOP.

Through a combination of Presidential directives, reorganization plans, and budgetary changes, I shall reassign or propose reassignment of most of the activities currently carried on by a number of organizations within the Executive Office of the President, to appropriate line departments and agencies. Specific changes will be announced as they are effected....

I am confident that these measures will enhance my ability to deliver between now and 1977 what the people voted for in 1972: government that performs what it promises, and 100 cents worth of public services for every tax dollar spent. I believe they will contibute to that "energy in the executive" which Hamilton called "a leading character in the definition of good government."

And as these changes demonstrate their worth, I hope the Congress will accept this practical proof and join me in adopting throughout the executive branch the same concepts on which I am now patterning my own staff and Executive Office.   ✓

INAUGURAL ADDRESS

Following is the text, as made available by the White House, of President Nixon's second inaugural address, given Jan. 20, 1973:

Mr. Vice President, Mr. Speaker, Mr. Chief Justice, Senator Cook, Mrs. Eisenhower, and my fellow citizens of this great and good country we share together.

When we met here four years ago, America was bleak in spirit, depressed by the prospect of seemingly endless war abroad and of destructive conflict at home.

As we meet here today, we stand on the threshold of a new era of peace in the world. The central question before us is: How shall we use that peace?

Let us resolve that this era we are about to enter will not be what other post-war periods have so often been: a time of retreat and isolation that leads to stagnation at home and invites new danger abroad.

Let us resolve that this will be what it can become: a time of great responsibilities greatly borne, in which we renew the spirit and the promise of America as we enter our third century as a Nation.

Peace Efforts

This past year saw far-reaching results from our new policies for peace. By continuing to revitalize our traditional friendships, and by our missions to Peking and to Moscow, we were able to establish the base for a new and more durable pattern of relationships among the nations of the world. Because of America's bold initiatives, 1972 will be long remembered as the year of the greatest progress since the end of World War II toward a lasting peace in the world.

The peace we seek in the world is not the flimsy peace which is merely an interlude between wars, but a peace which can endure for generations to come.

It is important that we understand both the necessity and the limitations of America's role in maintaining that peace. Unless we in America work to preserve the peace, there will be no peace. Unless we in America work to preserve freedom, there will be no freedom.

But let us clearly understand the new nature of America's role, as a result of the new policies we have adopted over these past four years.

International Obligations

We shall respect our treaty commitments. We shall support vigorously the principle that no country has the right to impose its will or rule on another by force.

We shall continue, in this era of negotiation, to work for the limitation of nuclear arms, and to reduce the danger of confrontation between the great powers. We shall do our share in defending peace and freedom in the world. But we shall expect others to do their share.

The time has passed when America will make every other nation's conflict our own, or make every other nation's future our responsibility, or presume to tell the people of other nations how to manage their own affairs.

Just as we respect the right of each nation to determine its own future, we also recognize the responsibility of each nation to secure its own future.

Just as America's role is indispensable in preserving the world's peace, so is each nation's role indispensable in preserving its own peace.

Together with the rest of the world, let us resolve to move forward from the beginnings we have made. Let us continue to bring down the walls of hostility which have divided the world for too long, and to build in their place bridges of understanding —so that despite profound differences between systems of government, the people of the world can be friends.

Let us build a structure of peace in the world in which the weak are as safe as the strong—in which each respects the right of the other to live by a different system—in which those who would influence others will do so by the strength of their ideas and not by the force of their arms.

Let us accept that high responsibility not as a burden, but gladly—gladly because the chance to build such a peace is the noblest endeavor in which a nation can engage; gladly also because only if we act greatly in meeting our responsibilities abroad will we remain a great Nation, and only if we remain a great Nation will we act greatly in meeting our challenges at home.

Domestic Challenges

We have the chance today to do more than ever before in our history, to make life better in America—to ensure better education, better health, better housing, better transportation, a cleaner environment—to restore respect for law, to make our communities more livable—and to ensure the God-given right of every American to full and equal opportunity.

Because the range of our needs is so great—because the reach of our opportunities is so great—let us be bold in our determination to meet those needs in new ways.

Just as building a structure of peace abroad has required turning away from old policies that have failed, so building a new era of progress at home requires turning away from old policies that have failed.

Abroad, the shift from old policies to new has not been a retreat from our responsibilities, but a better way to peace. And at home, the shift from old policies to new will not be a retreat from our responsibilities, but a better way to progress.

Abroad and at home, the key to those new responsibilities lies in the placing and the division of responsibility. We have lived too long with the consequences of attempting to gather all power and responsibility in Washington.

Abroad and at home, the time has come to turn away from the condescending policies of paternalism—of "Washington knows best."

A person can be expected to act responsibly only if he has responsibility. This is human nature. So let us encourage individuals at home and nations abroad to do more for themselves, to decide more for themselves. Let us locate responsibility in more places. And let us measure what we will do for others by what they will do for themselves.

Less Government

That is why today I offer no promises of a purely governmental solution for every problem. We have lived too long with that false promise. In trusting too much in government, we have asked of it more than it can deliver. This leads only to inflated expectations, to reduced individual effort, and to a disappointment and frustration that erode confidence both in what government can do and in what people can do.

Government must learn to take less from people so that people can do more for themselves. Let us remember that America was built not by government, but by people—not by welfare, but by work—not by shirking responsibility, but by seeking responsibility.

In our own lives, let each of us ask—not just what will government do for me, but what can I do for myself? In the

challenges we face together, let each of us ask—not just how can government help, but how can I help?

Your national government has a great and vital role to play. And I pledge to you that where this government should act, we will act boldly and we will lead boldly. But just as important is the role that each and every one of us must play, as an individual and as a member of his own community.

From this day forward, let each of us make a solemn commitment in his own hear: to bear his responsibility, to do his part, to live his ideals—so that together, we can see the dawn of a new age of progress for America, and together, as we celebrate our 200th anniversary as a nation, we can do so proud in the fulfillment of our promise to ourselves and to the world.

Mutual Respect Needed

As America's longest and most difficult war comes to an end, let us again learn to debate our differences with civility and decency. And let each of us reach out for that one precious quality government cannot provide—a new level of respect for the rights and feelings of one another, a new level of respect for the individual human dignity which is the cherished birthright of every American.

Above all else, the time has come for us to renew our faith in ourselves and in America. In recent years, that faith has been challenged.

Our children have been taught to be ashamed of their country, ashamed of their parents, ashamed of America's record at home and its role in the world.

At every turn we have been beset by those who find everything wrong with America and little that is right. But I am confident that this will not be the judgment of history on these remarkable times in which we are privileged to live.

America's record in this century has been unparalleled in the world's history for its responsibility, for its generosity, for its creativity and for its progress.

Let us be proud that our system has produced and provided more freedom and more abundance, more widely shared, than any system in the history of the world.

Let us be proud that in each of the four wars in which we have been engaged in this century, including the one we are now bringing to an end, we have fought not for our selfish advantage, but to help others resist aggression.

A Lasting Peace

And let us be proud that by our bold, new initiatives, by our steadfastness for peace with honor, we have made a breakthrough toward creating in the world what the world has not known before—a structure of peace that can last, not merely for our time, but for generations to come.

We are embarking here today on an era that presents challenges as great as those any nation or any generation has ever faced. We shall answer to God, to history, and to our conscience for the way in which we use these years.

As I stand in this place, so hallowed by history, I think of others who have stood here before me. I think of the dreams they had for America and I think of how each recognized that he needed help far beyond himself in order to make those dreams come true.

Today I ask your prayer that in the years ahead I may have God's help in making decisions that are right for America and I pray for your help so that together we may be worthy of our challenge.

Let us pledge together to make these next four years the best four years in America's history, so that on its 200th birthday America will be as young and as vital as when it began, and as bright a beacon of hope for all the world.

Let us go forward from here confident in hope, strong in our faith in one another, sustained by our faith in God who created us, and striving always to serve His purpose.   √

VIETNAM PEACE AGREEMENT

Following is the text, as made available by the White House, of President Nixon's Jan. 23 nationally televised announcement of the Vietnam peace agreement.

Good evening. I have asked for this radio and television time tonight for the purpose of announcing that we today have concluded an agreement to end the war and bring peace with honor in Vietnam and in Southeast Asia.

The following statement is being issued at this moment in Washington and Hanoi:

At 12:30 Paris time today, January 23, 1973, the agreement on ending the war and restoring peace in Vietnam was initialed by Dr. Henry Kissinger on behalf of the United States, and Special Advisor Le Duc Tho on behalf of the Democratic Republic of Vietnam.

The agreement will be formally signed by the parties participating in the Paris Conference on Vietnam on January 27, 1973, at the International Conference Center in Paris.

The cease-fire will take effect at 2400 Greenwich Mean Time, January 27, 1973. The United States and the Democratic Republic of Vietnam express the hope that this agreement will insure stable peace in Vietnam and contribute to the preservation of lasting peace in Indochina and Southeast Asia.

That concludes the formal statement.

Throughout the years of negotiations, we have insisted on peace with honor. In my addresses to the nation from this room of January 25th and May 8th, I set forth the goals that we considered essential for peace with honor.

In the settlement that has now been agreed to, all the conditions that I laid down then have been met. A cease-fire, internationally supervised, will begin at 7 p.m. this Saturday, January 27th, Washington time. Within 60 days from this Saturday, all Americans held prisoners of war throughout Indochina will be released. There will be the fullest possible accounting for all of those who are missing in action.

During the same 60-day period, all American forces will be withdrawn from South Vietnam.

The people of South Vietnam have been guaranteed the right to determine their own future, without outside interference.

By joint agreement, the full text of the agreement and the protocols to carry it out, will be issued tomorrow.

Throughout these negotiations we have been in the closest consultation with President Thieu and other representatives of the Republic of Vietnam. This settlement meets the goals and has the full support of President Thieu and the Government of the Republic of Vietnam, as well as that of our other allies who are affected.

The United States will continue to recognize the Government of the Republic of Vietnam as the sole legitimate government of South Vietnam.

We shall continue to aid South Vietnam within the terms of the agreement and we shall support efforts by the people of South Vietnam to settle their problems peacefully among themselves.

We must recognize that ending the war is only the first step toward building the peace. All parties must now see to it that this is a peace that lasts, and also a peace that heals, and a peace that not only ends the war in Southeast Asia, but contributes to the prospects of peace in the whole world.

This will mean that the terms of the agreement must be scrupulously adhered to. We shall do everything the agreement requires of us and we shall expect the other parties to do everything it requires of them. We shall also expect other interested nations to help insure that the agreement is carried out and peace is maintained.

As this long and very difficult war ends, I would like to address a few special words to each of those who have been parties in the conflict.

First, to the people and Government of South Vietnam: By your courage, by your sacrifice, you have won the precious right to determine your own future and you have developed the strength to defend that right. We look forward to working with you in the future, friends in peace as we have been allies in war.

To the leaders of North Vietnam: As we have ended the war through negotiations, let us now build a peace of reconciliation. For our part, we are prepared to make a major effort to help achieve that goal; but just as reciprocity was needed to end the war, so, too, will it be needed to build and strengthen the peace.

To the other major powers that have been involved even indirectly: Now is the time for mutual restraint so that the peace we have achieved can last.

Peace with Honor

And finally, to all of you who are listening, the American people: Your steadfastness in supporting our insistence on peace with honor has made peace with honor possible. I know that you would not have wanted that peace jeopardized. With our secret negotiations at the sensitive stage they were in during this recent period, for me to have discussed publicly our efforts to secure peace would not only have violated our understanding with North Vietnam; it would have seriously harmed and possible destroyed the chances for peace. Therefore, I know that you now can understand why, during these past several weeks, I have not made any public statements about those efforts.

The important thing was not to talk about peace; but to get peace and to get the right kind of peace. This we have done.

Now that we have achieved an honorable agreement, let us be proud that America did not settle for a peace that would have betrayed our allies, that would have abandoned our prisoners of war, that would have ended the war for us but would have continued the war for the 50 million people of Indochina. Let us be proud of the 2-1/2 million young Americans who served in Vietnam, who served with honor and distinction in one of the most selfless enterprises in the history of nations. And let us be proud of those who have sacrificed, who gave their lives so that the people of South Vietnam might live in freedom and so that the world might live in peace.

In particular, I would like to say a word to some of the bravest people I have ever met—the wives, the children, the families of our prisoners of war and the missing in action. When others called on us to settle on any terms, you had the courage to stand for the right kind of peace so that those who died and those who suffered would not have died and suffered in vain, and so that where this generation knew war, the next generation would know peace. Nothing means more to me at this moment than the fact that your long vigil is coming to an end.

Just yesterday, a great American, who once occupied this office, died. In his life President Johnson endured the vilification of those who sought to portray him as a man of war. But there was nothing he cared about more deeply than achieving a lasting peace in the world.

I remember the last time I talked with him. It was just the day after New Year's. He spoke then of his concern with bringing peace, with making it the right kind of peace; and I was grateful that he once again expressed his support for my efforts to gain such a peace. No one would have welcomed this peace more than he.

And I know he would join me in asking for those who died and for those who live, let us consecrate this moment by resolving together to make the peace we have achieved a peace that will last.

Thank you and good evening. ✓

ECONOMIC ADDRESS

Following is the White House text of the President's Feb. 21 radio address on the economy, the subject of his state of the union message to Congress of Feb. 22.

Good afternoon. Tomorrow I will send to the Congress the economic section of my State of the Union report.

One fact stands out above all others in this report: For the first time in nearly 20 years, we can look forward to genuine prosperity in a time of peace.

For most people, talking about the economy brings to mind some vast, complicated machine. Today, I want to talk about the economy in personal terms—about its impact on you and your family.

Basically the economy affects you in three ways. First, it affects your jobs, how plentiful they are, how secure they are, how good they are. Second, it affects what you take home from those jobs, and how much you can buy with your income, and finally, it affects how much you can spend on your own and how much you have to pay back to the Government in taxes. Let's look briefly at each of these elements.

Employment Up

To begin with, the job picture today is very encouraging. The number of people at work in this country rose by 2-3/10 million during 1972, the largest increase in 25 years. Unemployment fell from the six percent level in 1971 to five percent last month. This record is even more remarkable since so many more people have been seeking jobs than usual. Nearly three million Americans have been released from defense-related jobs since 1969, including over one million veterans. Women and teenagers have also been looking for work in record numbers. Yet jobs for all these groups have increased even faster.

The reason for this success is that the economy grew by six and one-half percent last year, one of the best performances in the past quarter century. Our economic advisers expect a growth rate of nearly seven percent in 1973. That would bring unemployment down to around the 4-1/2 percent level.

The second great question is how much you take home from your job, how much it will buy for you. Here the news is also good. Not only are more people working, but they are getting more for their work. Average per capita income rose by seven and seven-tenths percent during 1972. That is well above the average gain during the previous 10 years. Most important, however, is that these gains were not wiped out by rising prices, as they often were in the 1960s.

The Federal Government spent too much, too fast, in that period, and the result was runaway inflation. Your wages may have climbed very rapidly during those years, but not your purchasing power. Now that has changed. The inflation rate last year was cut nearly in half from what it was four years ago. The purchasing power of the average worker's take-home pay rose more last year than in any year since 1955. It went up by four and three-tenths percent, the equivalent of two extra weekly paychecks.

Lowering Inflation

We expect to reduce inflation even further in 1973, for several reasons. The fundamental reason is the Nation's growing opposition to big spending. We have a good chance now, the best in years, to curb the growth of the Federal budget. That will do more than anything else to protect your family budget.

Other forces are working for us, too. Productivity increased sharply last year, which means the average worker is producing more and, therefore, can earn more without driving prices higher. In addition, the fact that real spendable earnings rose so substantially last year will encourage reasonable wage demands this year. Workers will not have to catch up from an earlier slump in earnings.

Finally, we now have a new system of wage and price controls, one that is the right kind of system for 1973. The idea that controls have virtually been ended is totally wrong. We still have firm controls. We are still enforcing them firmly. All that is changed is our method of enforcing them.

The old wage and price control system depended on a Washington bureaucracy to approve major wage and price increases in advance. Although it was effective while it lasted, this system was beginning to produce inequities and to get tangled in red tape. The new system will avoid these dangers. Like most of our laws, it relies largely on self-administration, on the voluntary cooperation of the American people. But if some people should fail to cooperate, we have the will and we have the means to crack down on them.

We would like Phase III to be as voluntary as possible, but we will make it as mandatory as necessary. Our new system of controls has broad support from business and labor, the keystone for any successful program. It will prepare us for the day when we no longer need controls. It will allow us to concentrate on those areas where inflation has been most troublesome—construction, health care, and especially food prices.

Food Costs

Let me focus for a moment on food prices. They have risen sharply at the wholesale level in recent months, so that figures for retail prices in January and February, when they are published, will inevitably show sharp increases. In fact, we will probably see increases in food prices for some months to come.

The underlying cause of this problem is that food supplies have not risen fast enough to keep up with the rapidly rising demand. But we must not accept rising food prices as a permanent feature of American life. We must halt this inflationary spiral by attacking the causes of rising food prices on all fronts.

Our first priority must be to increase supplies of food to meet the increased demand. Your Government is already moving vigorously to expand our food supplies. We are encouraging farmers to put more acreage into production of both crops and livestock. We are allowing more meat and dried milk to come in from abroad. We have ended subsidies for agricultural exports, and we are reducing the Government's agricultural stockpiles. We are encouraging farmers to sell the stock they own.

Now, measures such as these will stop the rise of wholesale food prices and will slow the rise of retail food prices. Unfortunately, they cannot do much about prices in the next few months, but they will have a powerful effect in the second half of the year. They will bring relief to the American housewife without damaging the prosperity of our farmers.

Farm income today is higher than ever, and it will go even higher as we increase farm production. For all of these reasons, we have a good chance to reduce the overall inflation rate to 2-1/2 percent or less by the end of 1973. That means your dollars will go further at your local shop or supermarket.

Taxes

The third important economic question concerns how much money you control for yourself and how much you pay out in taxes. Here the picture is also promising.

Since 1950, the share of the average family's income taken for taxes in the United States has nearly doubled, to more than 20 percent. The average person worked less than one hour out of each 8-hour day to pay his taxes in 1950. Today he works nearly 2 hours each day for the tax collector. No wonder someone once described the taxpayer as a person who doesn't have to take a Civil Service examination to work for the Federal Government.

In fact, if tax cuts had not been adopted during our first term, the average worker's pay increase last year would have been wiped out entirely by increased taxes. The only way to stop tax increases is to stop spending more than our present tax rates produce in revenue. That is why we are cutting back on Federal programs that waste the taxpayers' money; for example, on housing programs that benefit the well-to-do but shortchange the poor, health programs that build more hospitals when hospital beds are now in surplus, educational bonuses that attract more people into teaching when tens of thousands of teachers already cannot find jobs.

These old programs may have appealing names, they may sound like good causes, but behind the fancy label often lies a dismal failure. Unless we cut back now on the programs that have failed, we will soon run out of money for the programs that can succeed.

It has been charged that our budget cuts show a lack of compassion for the disadvantaged. The best answer to this charge is to look at the facts.

We are budgeting 66 percent more to help the poor next year than was the case four years ago; 67 percent more to help the sick; 71 percent more to help older Americans, and 242 percent more to help the hungry and malnourished. Altogether, our human resources budget is nearly double that of four years ago when I came into office.

We have already shifted our spending priorities from defense programs to human resources programs. Now we must also switch our spending priorities from programs which give us a bad return on the dollar to programs that pay off. That is how to show we truly care about the needy.

The question is not whether we help, but how we help. By eliminating programs that are wasteful, we can concentrate on programs that work. Our recent round of budget cuts can save $11 billion in this fiscal year, $19 billion next fiscal year, $24 billion the year after. That means an average saving of $700 over the next three years for each of America's 75 million taxpayers.

Let me turn, finally, to one other major economic decision we made last week—our proposal to change the relative value of the dollar in trading abroad.

We took this step because of a serious trade imbalance which could threaten your prosperity. America has recently been buying more from other countries than they have been buying from us. Now, just as a company cannot go on indefinitely buying more than it sells, neither can a country.

Changing the exchange rate will help us change this picture. It means our exports will be priced more competitively in the international marketplace, and they should, therefore, sell better. Our imports, on the other hand, will not grow as fast. But this step must now be followed by reforms which are more basic.

First, we need a more flexible international monetary system, one that will lead to balance without crisis. The United States set forth fundamental proposals for such a system last September. It is time for other nations to join us in getting action on these proposals.

Second, American products must get a fairer shake in world trade so that we can extend American markets and expand American jobs. If other countries make it harder for our products to be sold abroad, then our trade imbalance can only grow worse. That is why I will soon propose to the Congress new trade laws which would make it easier for us not only to lower our trade barriers when other countries lower theirs, but also to raise our barriers when that is necessary to keep things fair.

Our overall goal is to reduce trade and investment barriers around the world, but they cannot decline for one country and remain high for others. My proposals will allow us to work more effectively for a new trading system which is equitable for all.

Even as we reduce the foreign barriers that keep us from competing abroad, we must also strengthen our ability to compete. This means working more efficiently as well as working hard, so that we can increase our productivity. It means taking greater pride in our work. It means fighting harder to slow inflation, and it means keeping Federal spending down.

If we do these things, 1973 can usher in a new era of prolonged and growing prosperity for the United States. Unlike past booms, this new prosperity will not depend on the artificial stimulus of war. It will not be eaten away by the blight of inflation. It will be solid. It will be steady. It will be sustainable.

If we act responsibly, this new prosperity can be ours for many years to come; if we don't, then as Franklin Roosevelt once warned, we could be wrecked on the rocks of loose fiscal policy. The choices are ours. Let us choose responsible prosperity.

Thank you and good afternoon.   √

NATURAL RESOURCES

Following is the White House text of President Nixon's Feb. 14 radio address on natural resources and the environment, the subject of his state of the union message of Feb. 15.

Every year since George Washington's time, the President of the United States has sent a message to the Congress about the state of our American Union and the measures which he felt the legislative and executive branches of government should take in partnership to improve it.

This year, however, I am presenting my State of the Union report not just in one speech but in several messages on individual topics to permit more careful consideration of the challenges we face. And because both the President and the Congress are servants of the people, I am inviting the people to join with us in considering these issues, by discussing them in a series of radio talks.

Today I want to talk with you about the first of these detailed messages, the one on the state of America's natural resources and environment, which I will send to the Congress later this week.

President Abraham Lincoln, whose memory we are honoring this week, observed in his State of the Union message in 1862 that "A nation may be said to consist of its territory, its people, and its laws. The territory," he said, "is the only part which is of certain durability."

In recent years, however, we have come to realize that what Lincoln called our "territory"—that is, our land, air, water, minerals, and the like—is not of "certain durability" after all. Instead, we have learned that these natural resources are fragile and finite, and that many have been seriously damaged or despoiled.

To put it another way, we realized that self-destructive tendencies were endangering the American earth during the 1960's in much the same way as conflicting political forces had endangered the body politic during the 1860's.

'Winning the War'

When we came to office in 1969, we tackled this challenge with all the power at our command. Now, in 1973, I can report that America is well on the way to winning the war against environmental degradation—well on the way to making our peace with nature.

Day by day, our air is getting cleaner. In virtually every one of our major cities, the levels of air pollution are declining. Month by month, our water pollution problems are also being conquered, our noise and pesticide problems are yielding to new initiatives, our parklands and protected wilderness areas are increasing.

Year by year, our commitment of public funds for environmental programs continues to grow. Some people claim that we are not spending enough. But they ignore the fact that Federal spending for protection of our environment and natural resources has increased four-fold in the last four years. In the area of water quality alone, it has grown fifteen-fold. In fact, we are now buying new facilities nearly as fast as the construction industry can build them. Spending still more money would not buy us more pollution control facilities but only more expensive ones.

In addition to what Government is doing in the battle against pollution, our private industries are assuming a steadily growing share of responsibility in this field. Last year industrial spending for pollution control jumped by 50 percent, and this year it could reach as much as $5 billion.

As befits America's world leadership role, we are also moving vigorously with other nations to preserve the global environment. The U.S.-Soviet environmental cooperation agreement which I signed in Moscow last year makes two of the world's greatest industrial powers allies against pollution. Another agreement which we concluded last year with Canada will help to clean up the Great Lakes. The ocean-dumping curbs passed by the Congress at my urging have put this country in the forefront of the international effort to protect the seas.

We can be proud of our record in this field over the past four years. But a record is not something to stand on; it is something to build on. Nineteen important natural resources and environmental bills which I submitted to the last Congress were not enacted. In the coming weeks I shall once again send these urgently needed proposals to the Congress so that the unfinished environmental business of the 92nd Congress can become the first environmental achievements of the 93rd.

Areas of Concern

Let me highlight three of the other major subjects which we will be addressing in 1973: wise land use, energy, and a healthy, expanded farm economy.

Land in America is no longer a resource we can take for granted. We no longer live with an open frontier. Just as we must conserve and protect our air and our water, so we must conserve and protect the land—and plan for its wise and balanced use. Some progress is being made—but antiquated land use laws, overlapping jurisdictions, and outdated institutions are still permitting haphazard development which can spoil both the utility and the beauty of the land.

This is why I will urge passage again this year of legislation designed to encourage States to establish effective means of controlling land use. This is why I will reintroduce my proposals to bring coherence to Federal mining and mineral leasing laws, better management of the Federal lands, and enlightened regulation of surface and underground mining.

The energy crisis was dramatized by fuel shortages this winter. We must face up to a stark fact. We are now consuming more energy than we produce. A year and a half ago I sent to the Congress the first Presidential message ever devoted to the energy question. I shall soon submit a new and far more comprehensive energy message containing wide-ranging initiatives to insure necessary supplies of energy at acceptable economic and environmental costs. In the meantime, to help meet immediate needs, I have temporarily suspended import quotas on home heating oil east of the Rocky Mountains.

Energy policy will continue to be a matter of the highest priority, as shown by my budget proposal to increase funding for energy research and development even in a tight budget year.

One of the most precious natural resources since our earliest days has been American agriculture. Our farmers have kept us the best-fed, best-clothed Nation in the history of mankind, while enabling us to export farm products at a level that will reach an all-time annual record of $10 billion this year. Net farm income last year also reached a record high—over $19 billion, an increase of 30 percent over four years ago.

This Administration has responded to the farmer's desire for less Federal intervention by giving him expanded opportunity in planting his acreage. The day is gone when Washington can enlarge its role on the farm at the expense of the farmer's freedom to make his own decisions. The goal of all our farm policies and programs is just the reverse. We want freer markets and expanded individual responsibility. We want to keep the farmer on his land and the Government off.

I shall recommend a number of additional initiatives to preserve and enhance our national resources in the State of the Union report on this topic to the Congress later in the week.

Guiding Principles

These are the basic principles which should continue to guide all our efforts in environment and natural resources policy in the future.

First, we must strike a balance so that the protection of our irreplaceable heritage becomes as important as its use. The price of economic growth need not and will not be deterioration in the quality of our lives and our surroundings.

Second, because there are no local or State boundaries to the problems of our environment, the Federal Government must play an active, positive role.. We can and will set standards and exercise leadership. We are providing necessary funding support. And we will provide encouragement and incentive for others to help with the job. But Washington must not displace State and local initiative. We shall expect the State and local governments—along with the private sector—to play the central role in this field.

Third, the costs of pollution should be more fully met in the free marketplace, not in the Federal budget. For example, the price of pollution control devices for automobiles should be borne by the owner and the user and not by the general taxpayer. People should not have to pay for pollution they do not cause.

Fourth, we must realize that each individual must take the responsibility for looking after his own home and workplace. These daily surroundings are the environment where most Americans spend most of their time. They reflect people's pride in themselves and their consideration for their communities. Your backyard is not the domain of the Federal Government.

Finally, we must remain confident that America's technological and economic ingenuity will be equal to our environmental challenges. We will not look upon these challenges as insurmountable obstacles. Instead, we shall convert the so-called crisis of the environment into an opportunity for unprecedented progress.

Getting the Job Done

Now is the time to stop the sanctimonious hand-wringing and the roll up our sleeves and get on with the job. Now is the time to reject the doomsday mentality which says we are destined to pollute ourselves out of existence.

The advocates of defeatism warn us of all that is wrong, but I remind them and all Americans of our genius for responsive adaptability and our enormous reservoir of spirit. The destiny of our land, the air we breathe and the water we drink is not in the mystical hands of an uncontrollable agent; it is in our own hands. A future which brings the balancing of our resources—preserving quality with quantity—is a future limited only by the boundaries of our will to get the job done.

Each one of us has a personal stake in the task ahead. The choice is always ours, for better or for worse. Above all, we need pride in this beautiful country of ours and belief in our own strength and resourcefulness.

One of the most memorable experiences I have had as President occurred last year during my visit to the People's Republic of China when the Chinese Army Band played "America the Beautiful." This song of tribute to our Nation was also played at my inauguration four years ago and again this year.

No one will sing "America the Beautiful" with greater feeling than our Prisoners of War as they return home from years of Communist captivity in Indochina.

America is a beautiful country. By our commitment to conservation, restoration and renewal, let us resolve to make America ever more beautiful for the generations to come. ✓

SOUTH CAROLINA ADDRESS

Following are excerpts from the White House text of President Nixon's address to a joint session of the South Carolina legislature Feb. 20. The legislature was the first to pass a resolution supporting the Vietnam peace settlement.

...I would like to turn to the settlement which has been discussed at considerable length, probably, on the Floor of this chamber when the resolution was passed, and also throughout the country since that settlement was announced. I should like to speak to you quite candidly about the settlement in terms of what it really means—what it means to America, what it means to the people of South Vietnam, and what it means to the world.

In referring to that settlement, I think it is important for us to note that I have often used the term "peace with honor." What does peace with honor mean? And here we go back into the long history of this terribly difficult war, the longest in this Nation's history.

Because the war has been so long, and because it has been so difficult, there is a tendency for us to forget how the United States became involved, and why. It would be very easy now, looking back, to point out the mistakes that were made in the conduct of the war, to even question whether or not the United States should have become involved in the first place.

But let us get one thing very clear: When, during the course of President Kennedy's Administration, the first men were sent to Vietnam for combat, when, during the course of President Johnson's Administration others were sent there to continue the activities in the military area, they were sent there for the most selfless purpose that any nation has ever fought a war.

Purpose of War

We did not go to South Vietnam, and our men did not go there, for the purpose of conquering North Vietnam. Our men did not go to South Vietnam for the purpose of getting bases in South Vietnam or acquiring territory or domination over that part of the world. They went for a very high purpose, and that purpose can never be taken away from them or this country. It was, very simply, to prevent the imposition by force of a Communist government on the 17 million people of South Vietnam. That was our goal and we achieved that goal, and we can be proud that we stuck it out until we did reach that goal.

Now the question, of course, will be raised by historians, the instant historians of the present and those who look at it in the future and attempt to evaluate this long and difficult war.

Was the purpose worth it? Was the sacrifice worth it? Only historians in the future, perhaps, will be able to judge that accurately, but we, at this time, and you, as you passed your resolution, must have considered the alternatives.

We had alternatives. I recall when I first became President there were those of my own party who suggested that after all, I had not made the decision that involved the United States with combat troops in Vietnam in the first place and, therefore, from a political and partisan standpoint, the better course of action and the easy course of action was to get out of Vietnam, to bring our men home, and to bring them home and to get our prisoners of war back regardless of what happened to South Vietnam.

That would have been a rather easy position, politically, to take. On the other hand, when we examine it for what it really meant and could have meant to the United States, we can see why I had to reject it and why the people of the United States have supported that rejection during the four years which finally ended with the peace settlement.

If, for example, the North Vietnamese would have accepted the proposition of returning our prisoners of war simply for our getting out our own troops from Vietnam, and that is a highly doubtful proposition, but if they had, let us see what it would have meant.

We would have fought a long war. We would have lost tens of thousands of Americans who were killed in action and we would have fought it for what purpose? Only to get our prisoners of war back. If you wonder whether or not that purpose would have been adequate, let me say that a letter that I received from a mother in California perhaps will answer the question.

"As a mother of a young man who gave his life in this war, I felt very strongly about wanting an honorable peace agreement. Had you agreed to anything less, you would have let down not only the boys remaining in Vietnam, but also those who died in this war. It was difficult enough to accept our son's death, but to know it was all in vain would have been even more a tragedy. We feel that our son James would have felt as we do, and would have supported your policy."

I say to the members of this Assembly gathered here that James did not die in vain, that the men who went to Vietnam and have served there with honor did not serve in vain, and that our POWs, as they return, did not make the sacrifices they made in vain, and I say it because of what we did in Vietnam.

Honoring the Servicemen

It is my firm conviction that the United States can now exercise more effective leadership in the cause of world peace which the Governor has so eloquently described a moment ago. On this occasion, I think it is well for us to think of a number of people whom we should honor today. We, of course, should honor our prisoners of war who have come back after their great ordeal standing tall, proud of their country, proud of their service.

We should honor also those who have died, and in honoring them, let's honor some of the bravest women this Nation has ever seen, the wives, the mothers, not only of the POWs, but of those who died, the mother of a boy like James.

And finally, let us honor the 2½ million men who served, who did not desert America, but who served, served in a difficult war, came back, often not with honor in terms of what they found from their neighbors and friends, but came back to what could have been a rather discouraging reception.

Now that we have brought an end to the war, let us honor them all, and the way to honor them, I say, is for us to work together to build a lasting peace in the world, a peace that can last not only in Southeast Asia, but a peace that the United States can help to build for this whole world in which we live.

Ending a war is not usual or unusual for the United States. After all, in this century we ended World War I, we ended World War II, we ended Korea, and now we have ended the American involvement in Vietnam. The critical question is: How do we end a war and then go from there to build a peace? And I address that question in relationship to this war for just a moment.

Historic Breakthroughs

The year 1972 saw some historic breakthroughs in terms of America's search for peace, along with other nations: The opening of the dialogue with the People's Republic of China, with leaders who represent one-fourth of all the people who live on the face of the globe; the discussions that took place in Moscow last May and early June, discussions which led to a number of agreements, but particularly an agreement between the two superpowers to limit nuclear arms, the first step toward arms limitation, and, of course, more talks will take place this year with the leaders of the Soviet Union.

Now, when we consider those great events, the opening to China, which we are already beginning to develop, as you have noted in your papers recently, the opening with the Soviet Union of the discussions that can lead eventually, we trust, to arms control and perhaps further down the line to reduction of the nuclear arms that burden us, burdens them, and threatens the whole world with destruction.

As we look at those great events, combined with the end of the war in Vietnam, there could be a tendency for us to sit back and assume that we are going to have peace, instant peace, because of these new developments. What we must recognize is that we would not have had the kind of fruitful and constructive discussions that we had with the Soviet Union, and in my view we would not have had the opening of the dialogue with the People's Republic of China unless the United States had been strong—strong not only in its arms, but also unless the United States had been strong in terms of its will, its determination.

Strength and Respect

A nation which is strong militarily and yet is not respected is not a nation that is worth talking to. America is strong militarily, and America has demonstrated by its willingness to stand by a small, weak country, until we achieved an honorable peace, that we deserve, first, the trust of our allies and the respect of our potential adversaries in the world.

And that, again, gives us a reason why we can look back on this long and difficult war and say that American men sacrificed —some their lives, some long imprisonment, and some away from home in a land which most of them did not know—that Americans have made that sacrifice in a cause that was important not just for Vietnam, but for America's position of leadership in the whole world.

Had we taken another course, had we, for example, followed the advice of some of the well intentioned people who said, "Peace at any price. Get our prisoners of war back in exchange for withdrawing," had we taken that course, then respect for America, not only among our allies but particularly among those who might be our potential adversaries, would have been eroded, perhaps fatally.

So I say to you here today as we look to the future, the chances for us to build a peace that will last are better than they have been at any time since the end of World War II. We will continue the dialogue with the Soviet leaders; we will continue the dialogue with the People's Republic of China, and in this year ahead, we will renew discussions that we have been having in the past with our friends in Europe and in other parts of the world, because as we talk to those who have been our adversaries in the past, we must not overlook the vital necessity of strengthening the bonds we have with our allies and our friends around the world.

But as we conduct those discussions, I would urge upon this legislative body what I have often urged upon the Congress of the United States: Let us be sure that as the President of the United States and his representatives negotiate with great powers in the world, let us be sure that he never goes to the negotiating table representing the second strongest nation in the world.

Because America is strong and has been strong, we have been able to negotiate successfully. We must maintain our strength and, of course, we will reduce it, but it must be on a mutual basis and not on a unilateral basis, because reducing unilaterally would remove any incentive for others in the world to reduce their strength at the same time.

Having spoken of military strength, let me also speak briefly of other kinds of strength that we need if we are going to build a world of peace and if America is going to continue the great role that we are destined to play as we near our 200th birthday as a nation.

Responsive Government

It is essential that government—and here in this legislative chamber all of us are participants in the role of government—it is essential that government in America be strengthened in terms of being more responsive to the people.

By that I mean that government must get closer to the grass roots, and by getting closer to the grass roots, what I am very simply suggesting is this: For much too long, power has been flowing from the people, from the cities, from the counties, from the States, to Washington, D.C. And that is why, beginning with an historic move on revenue-sharing, and in other areas, I feel firmly we must turn it around, and that power should flow away from the concentration in Washington back to the States and the people. That is where it belongs and that is where it should stay.

Let us also remember that if America is to play the kind of a role that it must play and we want it to play, we need to be a united country. By being a united country, that doesn't mean that we agree on everything. It means that we have disagreements between parties, disagreements on a number of issues. That is the very essence of a free society.

But let the time be gone when this country is divided region against region, North versus South, race against race, black versus white, one economic group against another, labor versus management, simply because they are members of different groups. Let the time be gone when we divide Americans by age, the old against the young; in terms of what they produce, the cities against the farms.

It does not mean that we all have the same interest. It does not mean that we do not have areas where we disagree. But what it does mean is that this nation, when the great issues are involved—the security of America, the honor of America—let us speak of those issues and speak to those issues as one united people.

In that connection, as I speak for the first time as President of the United States to a legislature in the South, one of the things I am most proud of during the time I have served as President, and during the three times I have had the great honor to run for President, is that I have never divided this country North against South, East against West, one region against the other.

I believe this is one country, and let us all work to make it one country, because it is one United States of America that can lead the world to peace, the kind of peace that all of us want in the years ahead.   ✓

HUMAN RESOURCES

Following is the White House text of President Nixon's Feb. 24 radio address on human resources, the subject of his state of the union message of March 1.

Good afternoon.

At the beginning of each new year, as we reflect on the state of our American Union, we seek again a definition of what America means. Carl Sandburg came close to capturing its real meaning in three simple words that became the title for one of his greatest poems: "The People, Yes."

America has risen to greatness because again and again when the chips were down, the American people have said yes— yes to the challenge of freedom, yes to the dare of progress, and yes to the hope of peace—even when defending the peace has meant paying the price of war.

America's greatness will endure in the future only if our institutions continually rededicate themselves to saying yes to the people—yes to human needs and aspirations, yes to democracy and the consent of the governed, yes to equal opportunity and unlimited horizons of achievement for every American.

It is in this spirit of rededication that I will send to the Congress in the next few days the fourth section of my 1973 State of the Union report—a message on the progress we have made, the steps we now must take, in helping people to help themselves through our federal programs for human resources.

1973 is a year full of opportunity for great advances on this front. After more than ten years of war, we have successfully completed one of the most unselfish missions ever undertaken by one nation in the defense of another, and now the coming of peace permits us to turn our attention more fully to the works of compassion, concern, and social progress at home.

Human Resources Actions

The seriousness of your government's commitment to make the most of this opportunity is evidenced by the record level of funding for human resources programs proposed in our new budget—$125 billion—nearly twice the amount that was being spent on such programs when I took office in 1969.

Let us look behind this impersonal label, "human resources," let us see some examples of the way these programs are helping to provide a better life for the American people.

Social Security cash benefits for the elderly and the disabled in fiscal year 1974 will be twice what they were four years ago. Next year, five million additional poor, aged, and disabled persons will receive increased health benefits.

Hundreds of counties, which previously had no food programs to assure nutrition for the needy, have them now—hunger is being eliminated from American life.

Hundreds of school districts, which were giving black or brown children inferior educations in separate school systems at the time we took office, now give all their children an equal chance to learn together in the same schools.

A new student assistance system is being established to bring higher education within reach of every qualified student in America. We have launched a national drive for the conquest of cancer, we have advanced a workable proposal to provide comprehensive health insurance for every American family.

Health and education benefits for our veterans have been substantially increased, high-priority job programs have decreased the unemployment rate among Vietnam-era veterans by almost one-third during the past year alone.

Sweeping reforms have been set in motion to assure our senior citizens of quality nursing home care and of a better chance to live with dignity in homes of their own. Legislative proposals to increase self-determination and economic opportunity for the American Indian have been laid before the Congress, they will be resubmitted to the Congress this year.

Outlays for civil rights activities in 1974 will be more than $3 billion—that's three and one half times what they were at the beginning of this Administration. With this support, we are closer today than ever before to the realization of a truly just society, where all men—and all women—are equal in the eyes of the law.

These achievements, and others that I will outline in my message to the Congress, constitute a record to be proud of, a good beginning to build on. But there are certain other aspects of the state of our Union's human resources which urgently need reform.

Social Policy Evolution

During the 1960's, the Federal Government undertook ambitious, sometimes almost utopian, commitments in one area of social policy after another, elbowing aside the State and local governments and the private sector, and establishing literally hundreds of new programs based on the assumption that any human problem could be solved simply by throwing enough federal dollars at it.

The intention of this effort was laudable, but the results in case after case amounted to dismal failure. The money which left Washington in a seemingly inexhaustible flood was reduced to a mere trickle by the time it had filtered through all the layers of bureaucrats, consultants, and social workers, and finally reached those whom it was supposed to help. Too much money has been going to those who were supposed to help the needy and too little to the needy themselves. Those who make a profession out of poverty got fat; the taxpayer got stuck with the bill; and the disadvantaged themselves got little but broken promises.

We must do better than this. The American people deserve compassion that works—not simply compassion that means well.

They deserve programs that say yes to human needs by saying no to paternalism, social exploitation, and waste.

In order to bring our programs up to this standard, we have carefully reviewed each of them with three questions in mind:

How can we reform the decision-making process to bring it closer to the people whom these decisions will affect? How can we get more value and productivity out of every tax dollar devoted to human resources? How can we reform our approach to the delivery of services so as to give people the assistance they need without taking away their freedom or decreasing their self-reliance and their self-respect?

Proposed Reforms

Here are some of the reforms we propose:

To give the people served a better and greater voice in education and manpower training programs, we propose to convert them from narrow, fragmented, categorical programs—closely controlled from Washington—into new Special Revenue Sharing programs which will provide federal funds to be used within broad areas as each State and community judges best to meet its own special needs.

To make the federal health care dollar go further, we propose to eliminate programs whose job is done—such as hospital construction subsidies which if continued would only worsen the national oversupply of hospital beds and further inflate medical costs. The savings achieved would help to make possible increases in other areas—such as over $100 million more next year in cancer and heart disease research.

To make the economic opportunity dollar go further, we propose to transfer most of the anti-poverty programs now conducted by the Office of Economic Opportunity into the appropriate Cabinet departments, thereby making them more efficient by linking them with other related federal activities.

Improving Welfare System

To ensure that all of our people are provided with a decent income under circumstances that will increase human dignity rather than eroding such basic values as the family structure and the dignity of work, we will work with the Congress to improve the welfare system.

A system which penalizes a person for going to work and rewards a person for going on welfare is totally alien to the American tradition of self-reliance and self-respect. That is why reforming the present welfare system has been, and will continue to be, one of our major goals.

The overall effect of these reforms will be the elimination of programs that are wasteful so that we can concentrate on programs that work. They will make possible the continued growth of Federal efforts to meet human needs—while at the same time helping to prevent a ballooning budget deficit that could lead to higher taxes, higher prices and higher interest rates for all Americans.

Despite what some people say, fiscal responsibility is not just a rich man's concern. If we were to spend our economy into a tailspin in the name of social welfare, we would only be punishing those we sought to help. Over the course of our history, the free American economy has done more to combat poverty and to raise our standard of living then any government program imaginable. The stable, healthy growth of our economy must remain the cornerstone of all of our human resources policies in the 1970's.

To our great credit we Americans are a restless and impatient people—we are a nation of idealists. We dream of eradicating poverty, and hunger, discrimination, ignorance, disease, and fear, and we would like to do it all today. But in order to reach these goals, we need to connect this warmhearted impatience of ours with another equally American trait—and that is level-headed common sense.

'A New Approach'

We need to forge a new approach to human services in this country—an approach which will treat people as more than just statistics—an approach which recognizes that problems like poverty and unemployment, health care and the costs of education are more than cold abstractions in a government file drawer.

I know how tough these problems are, because I grew up with them. But I also know that with the right kind of help and the right kind of spirit they can be overcome.

I believe that no American family should be denied good health care because of inability to pay. But I also believe that no family should be deprived of the freedom to make its own health care arrangements without bureaucratic meddling.

I believe that no boy or girl should be denied a quality education. But I also believe that no child should have to ride a bus miles away from his neighborhood school in order to achieve an arbitrary racial balance.

I believe that no American family should have to suffer for lack of income, or to break up because the welfare regulations encourage it. But I also believe that we should never make it more comfortable or more profitable to live on a welfare check than on a paycheck.

I believe that Government must be generous and humane. But I also believe that Government must be economically responsible. We must reform or end programs that do not work. We must discontinue those programs that have served their purpose, so that our limited resources can be applied to programs that produce 100 cents worth of human benefits for every tax dollar spent.

Working together to meet human needs and unlock human potential is the greatest adventure upon which any people can embark. I pledge continued, strong federal leadership in this work. But we have learned the hard way that Washington cannot do the whole job by itself. State and local governments, private institutions, and each individual American must do their part as well.

Let us give all our citizens the help they need. But let us also remember that each of us bears a basic obligation to help ourselves and to help our fellowman, and no one else can assume that obligation for us—least of all the Federal Government.

If we shirk our individual responsibility, the American dream will never be more than a dream. But if the people say yes to this challenge, and if government says yes to the people, we can make that dream come true in the lives of all Americans.

Thank you and good afternoon.   √

COMMUNITY DEVELOPMENT

Following is the White House text of the President's March 4 radio address on community development, the subject of his state of the union message of March 8:

I want to report to you today on the quality of life in our cities and towns.

A few years ago we constantly heard that urban America was on the brink of collapse. It was one minute to midnight, we were told, and the bells of doom were beginning to toll. One history of America in the 1960s was even given the title "Coming Apart."

Today, America is no longer coming apart.

One of the most difficult problems of the 1960s was the alarming increase in crime—up 122 percent from 1960 to 1968. Today, the rate of crime is dropping in more than half of our major cities.

Civil disorders have also declined. The air is getting cleaner in most of our major cities. The number of people living in substandard housing has been cut by more than 50 percent since 1960.

The Nation's first new transit system in more than 20 years has just been opened in San Francisco. Another is under construction in Washington, D.C.; others are planned in Atlanta and Baltimore.

City governments are no longer on the verge of financial catastrophe. Once again the business world is investing in our downtown areas.

Crisis Over

What does all this mean for community life in America? Simply this: The hour of crisis has passed. The ship of state is back on an even keel, and we can put behind us the fear of capsizing.

We should be proud of our achievements; but we should never be complacent. Many challenges still remain. In approaching them, we must recognize that some of the methods which have been tried in the past are not appropriate to the 1970s.

One serious error of the past was the belief that the Federal Government should take the lead in developing local communities. America is still recovering from years of extravagant, hastily-passed measures, designed by centralized planners and costing billions of dollars—but producing few results.

I recently learned of a city where $30 million was paid for an urban renewal project. But instead of getting better, the physical condition of the target neighborhood actually got worse.

In one of our huge, high-rise public housing projects, less than one-third of the units are now fit for human habitation and less than one-fifth are even occupied.

In another city, urban renewal was supposed to salvage and improve existing housing. $30 million was spent over 12 years—but the results were so meager that the planners finally gave up and called in the bulldozers. Now almost half of the project's 200 acres lies vacant, unsold.

Some of our programs to help people buy or improve housing are also backfiring. Too many of the owners fail to meet their payments, and the taxpayer gets stuck with the bill. He also gets stuck with the house—and the added expense of looking out for it. As a result, over 90,000 federally subsidized housing units are now owned by the Federal Government—your government—over 14,000 in one metropolitan area alone.

Now these examples are not unusual. This does not mean that the people in charge of these programs were dishonest or incompetent. What it does mean is that they are human—and that no human being, accountable only to an office in Washington, can successfully plan and manage the development of communities which are often hundreds or thousands of miles away.

Changing Approaches

There are too many leaks in the Federal pipeline. It is time to plug them up. That is why we are changing our entire approach to human and community development. We are putting an end to wasteful and obsolete programs and replacing them with ones that work.

Our 1974 budget would eliminate seven outmoded urban development programs. It would suspend four ineffective housing programs.

We are not pulling the rug out from under anyone who has already been promised assistance. Under commitments already made, we will subsidize an estimated 300,000 housing starts this year and will provide housing assistance to more than 2 million low- and moderate-income families.

But we are stopping programs which have failed. We are determined to get a dollar's worth of service out of every dollar's worth of taxes. The high-cost, no-result boondoggling by the Federal Government must end.

This means we will continue to press for greater efficiency and better management in Federal programs. But it also means giving the lead role back to grassroots governments again. The time has come to reject the patronizing notion that Federal planners, peering over the point of a pencil in Washington, can guide your lives better than you can.

Revenue Sharing

Last October, at Independence Hall in Philadelphia, I signed into law a General Revenue Sharing Bill. This bill allocates 30 billion Federal dollars over the next five years for State and local governments to use however they like.

Revenue sharing represents a new Declaration of Independence for State and local governments. It gives grassroots governments a new chance to stand on their own feet.

Revenue sharing money can be used to put more policemen on the beat, to build new schools, to lower property taxes—or for whatever other purpose you and your local leaders think best.

Let me emphasize one point which is often misunderstood. General Revenue Sharing money is new money. It was never intended to replace programs we are now cutting back. To replace those programs, I am asking the Congress to create four new Special Revenue Sharing programs.

One of these new revenue sharing bills, the Better Communities Act, would provide $2.3 billion in its first year of operation. This aid will have no strings attached as long as it is used for community development. Your local leaders can go on spending it the way Washington was spending it if they like. But they would also be free to work out better plans without having to get Washington's approval.

Other Proposals

We have several other proposals which deserve the support of every American taxpayer.

One is our recommendation for a new Department of Community Development. This department will pull together programs which are now scattered among different departments or agencies. It would put them under a single roof. I first made this proposal nearly two years ago. It is time for the Congress to act on it. As a first step toward getting better coordination in this field, I have already appointed a Counsellor to the President for Community Development.

Another key recommendation is our $110 million proposal to help State and local governments build up their administrative skills and planning expertise.

In the field of housing, we must stop programs that have been turning the Federal Government into a nationwide slumlord. One of my highest domestic priorities this year will be the development of new policies that eliminate waste and target aid to genuinely needy families.

One of our highest priorities must be to improve transportation. In the past 20 years, Federal money has helped build the world's best system of modern highways. Our Administration has committed $19 billion to this goal. Now we must concentrate on moving people within our cities as effectively as we move them between our cities. We must help our communities develop urban mass transit systems of which America can truly be proud.

Funding Mass Transit

I propose that our States and communities be given the right to use a designated portion of the Highway Trust Fund for capital improvements in urban public transportation, including improvements in bus and rapid rail systems.

Changing the way we use the Highway Trust Fund should be one of the top items on our national agenda. If we do not act now, our children will grow up in cities which are strangled by traffic, raked by noise, choked by pollution.

By opening up the Highway Trust Fund today, we can open up great new vistas for our cities tomorrow.

I have also asked that Federal funding authority for mass transit capital grants be doubled—from $3 billion to $6 billion. And I have recommended that the Federal share of mass transit projects be raised to 70 percent. All of these steps will help us meet the challenge of mass transit.

Perhaps no program means more to those it helps than does disaster aid. But it is not enough for Government merely to respond to disasters. We should also take actions to prevent disasters or reduce their effect.

I will soon send recommendations to the Congress to revamp and improve disaster aid. I hope the Congress will also support an important proposal I have already made—moving disaster assistance out of the Executive Office of the President and into the Department of Housing and Urban Development, where it can be coordinated with other community aid.

'A Balanced Approach'

Too often, people think of community development solely in terms of the big city. In fact, less than 30 percent of our people live in places with a population of more than 100,000. This is approximately the same number who live in rural America. The proportion of our people living in cities with a population of over 1 million is no greater today than it was 50 years ago.

In an age when people move a great deal, the growth of our great cities and that of our smaller communities are directly linked. A balanced approach to community development must keep small-town America clearly in sight.

Our Administration will use every effective means to help develop smaller communities, to bring new vitality to the American countryside.

Perhaps the most important factor in the crisis mentality of the 1960s was the growing sense on the part of the average individual that the circumstances of his life were increasingly beyond his control. Nothing is more important in improving our communities than giving people a sense of control again, letting them know that they can make a difference in shaping the places where they live.

If the spirit of community means anything, it means a spirit of belonging, a spirit of responsibility, a spirit of participation. Restoring this "spirit of community" is the ultimate purpose of all the community development efforts of our Administration.

"A great city," Walt Whitman wrote, "is that which has the greatest men and women." Only by appealing to the greatness that lies within our people can we build and sustain the kind of communities we want for America.   √

LAW ENFORCEMENT

Following is the White House text of President Nixon's March 10 radio address on law enforcement and drug abuse prevention, the subject of his state of the union message of March 14:

Nothing is so precious to Americans as the freedoms provided in our Constitution. In order that these freedoms may be enjoyed to their fullest, there must be another freedom—freedom from the fear of crime.

The senseless shooting of Senator John Stennis in January gave tragic emphasis to the fact that there is still a high risk of crime on our Nation's streets. These acts of violence are the natural residue of an atmosphere in America that for years encouraged potential lawbreakers.

Americans in the last decade were often told that the criminal was not responsible for his crimes against society; but that society was responsible. I totally disagree with this permissive philosophy. Society is guilty of crime only when we fail to bring the criminal to justice. When we fail to make the criminal pay for his crime, we encourage him to think that crime will pay.

Such an attitude will never be reflected in the laws supported by this Administration, nor in the manner in which we enforce those laws. The jurisdiction of the Federal Government over crime is limited, but where we can act, we will act to make sure that we have the laws, the enforcement agencies, the courts, the judges, the penalties, the correctional institutions and the rehabilitation programs we need to do the job.

Criminal Code Revision

Next week I will propose a revision of the entire Federal Criminal Code, modernizing it and strengthening it, to close the loopholes and tailor our laws to present day needs. When I say "modernize," incidentally, I do not mean to be soft on crime; I mean exactly the opposite.

Our new code will give us tougher penalties and stronger weapons in the war against dangerous drugs and organized crime. It will rationalize the present patchwork guilt of punishments for crime. It will substantially raise current limits on monetary fines and it will restrict the present absurd use of the insanity defense.

I am further proposing that the death penalty be restored for certain Federal crimes. At my direction, the Attorney General has drafted a statute consistent with the Supreme Court's recent decision on the death penalty. This statute will provide capital punishment for cases of murder over which the Federal Government has jurisdiction, and for treason and other war-related crimes.

Contrary to the views of some social theorists, I am convinced that the death penalty can be an effective deterrent against specific crimes. The death penalty is not a deterrent so long as there is doubt whether it can be applied. The law I will propose would remove this doubt.

The potential criminal will know that if his intended victims die, he may also die. The hijacker, the kidnapper, the man who throws a fire bomb, the convict who attacks a prison guard, the person who assaults an officer of the law, all will know that they may pay with their own lives for any lives that they take.

This statute will be a part of my proposed reform of the Federal Criminal Code. However, because there is an immediate need for this sanction, I have directed the Attorney General to submit a death penalty statute as a separate proposal so that the Congress can act rapidly on this single provision.

Drug Abuse

Drug abuse is still Public Enemy No. 1 in America. Let me tell you about some of the tragic letters I have received at the White House from victims of drugs.

One tells about a five-year-old boy hospitalized in Missouri. Someone gave him LSD. One is from a boy 18 years old who had spent 11 months in a mental hospital trying to get rid of his drug addiction. He started with marijuana. He is asking me for help because his 14-year-old brother has begun to use drugs.

Another is from a mother in California. Her son committed suicide. He could not end his drug habit, so he ended his life.

One of the things that comes through so forcefully in these letters is the sense of despair of people who feel they have no place to turn for help, and so they write to the White House. I intend to help them. We have already made encouraging progress in the war against drug abuse. Now we must consolidate that progress and strike even harder.

One area in which I am convinced of the need for more immediate action is that of putting heroin pushers in prison and keeping them there. A recent study by the Bureau of Narcotics and Dangerous Drugs revealed that more than 70 percent of those accused of being narcotics violators are freed on bail for a period of three months to one year between the time of arrest and the time of trial. They are thus given the opportunity to go out and create more misery, generate more violence, commit more crimes while they are waiting to be tried for these same activities.

The same study showed that over 25 percent of the federally convicted narcotics violators were not even sentenced to jail. When permissive judges are more considerate of the pusher than they are of his victims, there is little incentive for heroin pushers to obey the law, and great incentive for them to violate it. This is an outrage. It is a danger to every law-abiding citizen, and I am confident that the vast majority of Americans will support immediate passage of the heroin trafficking legislation I will propose to the Congress next week.

This legislation will require Federal judges to consider the danger to the community before freeing on bail a suspect for heroin trafficking. That is something they cannot legally do now. It will require a minimum sentence of five years in prison for anyone convicted of selling heroin. It will require a minimum sentence of 10 years to life imprisonment for major traffickers in drugs. And for offenders with a prior conviction for a drug felony, those who persist in living off the suffering of others, it will require life imprisonment without parole.

This is tough legislation, but we must settle for nothing less. The time has come for soft-headed judges and probation officers to show as much concern for the rights of innocent victims of crime as they do for the rights of convicted criminals.

Marijuana

In recent days, there have been proposals to legalize the possession and use of marijuana. I oppose the legalization of the sale, possession or use of marijuana. The line against the use of dangerous drugs is now drawn on this side of marijuana. If we move the line to the other side and accept the use of this drug, how can we draw the line against other illegal drugs? Or will we slide into an acceptance of their use, as well?

My Administration has carefully weighed this matter. We have examined the statutes. We have taken the lead in making sanctions against the use of marijuana more uniform, more reasonable. Previously, these sanctions were often unrealistically harsh. Today, 35 States have adopted our model statute on drugs, including marijuana. I hope others will.

But there must continue to be criminal sanctions against the possession, sale or use of marijuana.

Law enforcement alone will not eliminate drug abuse. We must also have a strong program to treat and assist the addict. Two-thirds of my proposed anti-narcotics budget goes for treatment, rehabilitation, prevention and research. We are approaching the point where no addict will be able to say that he commits crimes because there is no treatment available for him.

By providing drug offenders with every possible opportunity to get out of the drug culture, we need feel no compunction about applying the most stringent sanctions against those who commit crimes in order to feed their habits.

The crimes which affect most people most often are not those under Federal jurisdiction, but those in which State and local governments have jurisdiction. But while the Federal Government does not have full jurisdiction in the field of criminal law enforcement, it does have a broad, constitutional responsibility to insure domestic tranquility. That is why I am doing everything I can to help strengthen the capacity of State and local governments to fight crime.

Crime-Fighting Assistance

Since I took office, Federal assistance for State and local law enforcement authorities has grown from over $100 million to over $1 billion. We are training over 40,000 law enforcement officers in the control and prevention of drug abuse.

This year more than 1,200 State and local police officers will graduate from the new FBI Academy, and I plan to increase assistance next year to local law enforcement to over $1,200,000,000.

Crime costs Americans twice. It costs first in lives lost, in injuries, in property loss, in increased insurance rates, in being fearful for your own safety as you go about your work. And second, crime costs in the taxes that go to maintain police forces, courts, jails, other means of enforcement.

It is a breach of faith with those who are paying the cost of crime, human as well as financial, to be lenient with the criminal. There are those who say that law and order are just code words for repression and bigotry. That is dangerous nonsense.

Law and order are code words for goodness and decency in America.

Crime is color blind. Let those who doubt this talk to the poor, the minorities, the inner-city dwellers, who are the most frequent victims of crime. There is nothing disgraceful, nothing to be ashamed of, about Americans wanting to live in a law-abiding country.

'Positive Results'

I intend to do everything in my power to see that the American people get all the law and order they are paying for. Our progress in this effort has been encouraging. The latest FBI figures show that for the first nine months of 1972, the growth rate of serious crime in America was reduced to one percent. That is the lowest rate of increase since 1960.

In 83 of our major cities, serious crime has actually been reduced, and in the District of Columbia it has been cut in half since 1969. Convictions for organized crime have more than doubled in the last four years. The rate of new heroin addiction has dramatically decreased.

These are the positive results of refusing to compromise with the forces of crime, refusing to accept the notion that lawlessness is inevitable in America. We have the freedom to choose the kind of nation we want, and we do not choose to live with crime.

The Federal Government can help provide resources. It can help provide leadership. It can act with its own jurisdiction. But in the end, one of the best resources we have, one of the greatest safeguards to public peace, is the active concern of the law-abiding American citizen. The war against crime is not just the job of the FBI and the State and local police; it is your job, everybody's job. It is the very essence of good citizenship to act when and where we see crime being committed.

Citizens in some high crime areas have gathered together to work with the police to protect lives and property, to prevent crime. They have recognized the simple fact that we are going to have a crime problem as long as we are willing to put up with it, and most Americans are not willing to put up with it any longer.

When I saw and heard the remarks of our returning prisoners of war, so strong and confident and proud, I realized that we were seeing men of tough moral fiber, men who reflected, despite their long absence from America, what America is all about.

Just as they are returning home to America, I believe that today we see America returning to the basic truths that have made us and kept us a strong and a free people. I am encouraged by that vision. It points the way toward a better, safer future for all Americans. It points the way toward an America in which men and women and children can truly live free from fear in the full enjoyment of their most basic rights.

To accept anything less than a nation free from crime is to be satisfied with something less than America can be and ought to be for all our people.

ECONOMY-FOREIGN AFFAIRS

Following is the White House text of the President's March 29 address to the nation on the economy and foreign affairs:

Four years and two months ago, when I first came into this office as President, by far the most difficult problem confronting the Nation was the seemingly endless war in Vietnam. 550,000 American troops were in Vietnam. As many as 300 a week were being killed in action. Hundreds were held as prisoners of war in North Vietnam. No progress was being made in the peace negotiations.

I immediately initiated a program to end the war and win an honorable peace.

Eleven times over the past four years, I have reported to the Nation from this room on the progress we have made toward that goal. Tonight, the day we have all worked and prayed for has come.

For the first time in 12 years, no American military forces are stationed in Vietnam. All of our American POWs are now on their way home. The 17 million people of South Vietnam have the right to choose their own government without outside interference. Because of our program of Vietnamization, they have the strength to defend that right. We have prevented the imposition of a Communist government by force on South Vietnam.

Vietnam Aftermath

There are still some problem areas. The provisions of the agreement requiring an accounting for all mission in action in Indochina, the provisions with regard to Laos and Cambodia and the provisions prohibiting infiltration from North Vietnam into South Vietnam have not been complied with. We have and will continue to comply with the agreement. We shall insist that North Vietnam comply with the agreement. The leaders of North Vietnam should have no doubt as to the consequences if they fail to comply with the agreement.

But despite these difficulties we can be proud of the fact that we have achieved our goal of obtaining an agreement which provides peace with honor in Vietnam.

On this day let us honor those who made this achievement possible: those who sacrificed their lives; those who were disabled; those who made every one of us proud to be Americans as they returned from years of Communist imprisonment, and every one of the two and a half million Americans who served honorably in our Nation's longest war. Never have men served with greater devotion abroad with less apparent support at home.

Let us provide these men with the veterans' benefits and job opportunities they have earned. Let us honor them with the respect they deserve. And I say again tonight, let us not dishonor those who served their country by granting amnesty to those who deserted America.

Tonight, I want to express the appreciation of the Nation to others who helped make this day possible. I refer to you, the great majority of Americans listening to me tonight who, despite an unprecedented barrage of criticism from a small but vocal minority stood firm for peace with honor. I know it was not easy for you to do so.

We have been through some difficult times together. I recall the time in November, 1969, when hundreds of thousands of protesters marched on the White House; the time in April, 1970, when I found it necessary to order attacks on Communist bases in Cambodia; the time in May, 1972, when I ordered the mining of Haiphong and air strikes on military targets in North Vietnam in order to stop a massive Communist invasion of South Vietnam.

And, then perhaps the hardest decision I have made as President, on December 18, 1972, when our hopes for peace were so high and when the North Vietnamese stone-walled us at the conference table, I found it necessary to order more air strikes on military targets in North Vietnam to break the deadlock.

On each of these occasions the voices of opposition we heard in Washington were so loud they at times seemed to be the majority. But across America, the overwhelming majority stood firm against those who advocated peace at any price—even if the price would have been defeat and humiliation for the United States.

Because you stood firm for doing what was right, Colonel McKnight was able to say for his fellow POWs when he returned home, "Thank you for bringing us home on our feet instead of on our knees."

Domestic Problems

Let us turn now to some of our problems at home. Tonight I ask your support in another battle. We can be thankful that this is not a battle in war abroad, but a battle we must win if we are to build a new prosperity without war and without inflation at home.

What I refer to is the battle of the budget. Not just the battle over the Federal budget, but, even more important, the battle of your budget—the family budget of every home in America.

One of the most terrible costs of war is inflation. The cost of living has skyrocketed during and after every war we have been engaged in. We recognized this danger four years ago and have taken strong action to deal with it. As a result of our policies we have cut the rate of inflation in half since it reached a peak in 1969 and 1970. Today our rate of inflation is the lowest of any major industrial nation.

Meat Price Ceiling

But these positive statistics are small comfort to a family trying to make both ends meet. And they are no comfort at all to the housewife who sees meat prices soaring every time she goes to the market. The major weak spot in our fight against inflation is in the area of meat prices. I have taken action to increase imports from abroad and production at home. This will increase the supply of meat and will help bring prices down later this year.

But what we need is action that will stop the rise in meat prices now. That is why I have today ordered the Cost of Living Council to impose a ceiling on prices of beef, pork and lamb. The ceiling will remain in effect as long as is necessary to do the job. Meat prices must not go higher. With the help of the housewife and the farmer, they can and should go down.

This ceiling will help in our battle against inflation. But it is not a permanent solution. We must act on all fronts and here is where the Federal budget comes in. I have submitted to Congress for the next fiscal year the largest budget in our history—$268 billion.

Budget Battle

The amount I have requested in this budget for domestic programs in such fields as health, housing, education, and aid to the elderly, the handicapped and the poor, is twice as big as the amount in my first budget four years ago. However, some members of Congress believe the budget in these areas should be even higher.

If I were to approve the increases in my budget that have been proposed in the Congress it would mean a 15% increase in your taxes, or an increase in prices for every American. That is why I shall veto the bills which would break the Federal budget which I have submitted. If I do not veto these bills, increased prices or taxes would break the family budget of millions of Americans.

This is not a battle between Congress and the President. It is your battle. It is your money and your prices and your taxes I am trying to save.

Twenty-five years ago, as a freshman Congressman, I met President Truman in this office. I remember he had a sign on the desk. It read "The buck stops here." That meant, of course, that a President can't pass the buck to anyone else when a tough decision has to be made. It also means that your buck stops here. If I do not act to stop the spending increases which Congress sends to my desk, you will have to pay the bill.

I admit that there is an honest difference of opinion on the matter of the Federal budget. If you are willing to pay the higher taxes or prices that will result if we increase Federal spending over my budget, as some in Congress have proposed, you should ask your Senators and your Congressman to override my vetoes.

But if you want to stop the rise in taxes and prices, then I have a suggestion to make. I remember when I was a Congressman and a Senator, I always seemed to hear from those who wanted government to spend more and I seldom heard from the people who have to pay the bill—the taxpayer. If your

Congressman or Senator has the courage to vote against more spending so that you won't have to pay higher prices or taxes—let him know you support him.

Winning the battle to hold down the Federal budget is essential if we are to achieve our goal of a new prosperity—prosperity without war and without inflation. I ask tonight for your support in helping to win this vitally important battle.

Defense Spending

Let me turn, finally, tonight to another great challenge we face.

As we end America's longest war, let us resolve we shall not lose the peace. During the past year we have made great progress toward our goal of a generation of peace for America and the world. The war in Vietnam has been ended. After 20 years of hostility and confrontation we have opened a constructive new relationship with the People's Republic of China, a country where one-fourth of all the world's people live. We negotiated last year with the Soviet Union a number of important agreements, including an agreement which takes a major step in limiting nuclear arms.

There are some who say that in view of all this progress toward peace why not cut our defense budget? Let us look at the facts. Our defense budget today takes the lowest percentage of our gross national product in twenty years. There is nothing I would like better than to be able to reduce it further. But we must never forget that we would not have made the progress toward lasting peace that we have made in this past year if we had not had the military strength that commanded respect.

This year we have begun new negotiations with the Soviet Union for further limitations on nuclear arms. We shall be participating later in the year in negotiations for mutual reduction of forces in Europe. If prior to these negotiations we unilaterally reduce our defense budget or reduce our forces in Europe, any chance for successful negotiations for mutual reduction of forces or limitation of arms will be destroyed.

There is one unbreakable rule of international diplomacy. You can't get something in a negotiation unless you have something to give. If we cut our defenses before negotiations begin, any incentive for other nations to cut theirs will be completely removed. If the United States reduces its defenses and others do not, it increases the danger of war. Only a mutual reduction of forces will reduce the danger of war. We must maintain our strength until we get agreements under which other nations will join us in reducing the burden of armaments.

What is at stake is whether the United States shall become the second strongest nation in the world. If that day should ever come, the chances for building a new structure of peace in the world would be irreparably damaged and free nations everywhere would live in mortal danger. A strong United States is not a threat to peace. It is the free world's indispensable guardian of peace and freedom.

I ask for your support tonight for keeping the strength which enabled us to make such great progress toward world peace in this past year and which is indispensable as we continue our bold new initiatives for peace in the years ahead.

A Great Nation

As we consider some of our problems tonight, let us never forget how fortunate we are to be living in America at this time in history. We have ended the longest and most difficult war in our history in a way that maintained the trust of our allies and the respect of our adversaries. We are the strongest and most prosperous nation in the world's history.

Because of our strength, America has the magnificent opportunity to play the leading role of bringing down the walls of hostility which divide the people of the world; in reducing the burden of armaments in the world; and of building a structure of lasting peace in the world. Because of our wealth, we have the means to move forward at home on exciting new programs for progress which will provide better environment, education, housing and health care for all Americans and which will enable us to be more generous to the poor, the elderly, the disabled and the disadvantaged than any nation in history.

These are goals worthy of a great people. Let us, therefore, put aside those honest differences about the war which have divided us and dedicate ourselves to meet the great challenges of peace which can unite us. But, as we do so, let us not overlook a third element more important even than military might or economic power which is essential for greatness in a nation.

The pages of history are strewn with the wreckage of nations which fell by the wayside at the height of their strength and wealth because their people became weak, soft and self-indulgent and lost the character and spirit which had led to their greatness. As I speak to you tonight, I am confident that this will not happen to America. My confidence has been increased by the fact that a war which cost America so much in lives, money and division at home has, as it ended, provided an opportunity for millions of Americans to see again the character and spirit which made America the great Nation it is.

A few days ago, in this room, I talked to a man who had spent almost eight years in a Communist prison cell in North Vietnam. For over four years he was in solitary confinement. He never saw another person except his captors in that time. He lived on two meals a day, usually just a piece of bread and a vegetable soup. All he was given to read was Communist propaganda. All he could hear on the radio was Communist propaganda.

I asked him how he was able to survive it and come home standing tall and proud—saluting the American Flag. He paused a long time before he answered. Then he said, "It isn't easy for me to answer. I am not good at words. But all I can say is—that it was faith—faith in God and faith in my country."

If men who suffered so much for America could have such faith, let us who have received so much from America renew our faith—our faith in God, our faith in America and our faith in ourselves.

If we meet the great challenges of peace that lie ahead with this kind of faith, it will one day be written that this was America's finest hour. ✓

FOREIGN POLICY RADIO TEXT

Following is the White House text of President Nixon's May 3 radio address on foreign policy, the subject of his message to Congress the same day.

The year 1972 was a time of more dramatic progress toward a lasting peace in the world than any other year since the end of World War II. But as encouraging as that progress was, we cannot rest on our laurels now.

1973 and the years to come will test whether America will go forward into a new era of international relations, or whether we will go backward into preoccupation with ourselves, thus allowing the world to slip back into its age-old patterns of conflict.

If we meet this test, the rewards can be great. If we do not, a priceless opportunity may be tragically lost.

It is against this background of hope and danger that I have today submitted to the Congress my fourth annual report on United States foreign policy. Tonight I want to share with you some highlights of that report.

Foreign Relations Progress

Since the time of my last foreign policy review 15 months ago, we have witnessed historic achievements on a number of fronts. After more than two decades of hostility and isolation, we have begun an entirely new relationship with the People's Republic of China when I visited Peking last year.

Travel, exchanges and trade between our two countries are accelerating. This month we shall open liaison offices in each other's capitals, headed by distinguished senior diplomats.

The United States and the Soviet Union have taken a decisive turn away from the confrontation of the past quarter century. At our meeting last May, the Soviet leaders and I established a set of basic principles to govern our relations.

We signed a series of cooperative agreements and we laid the foundation for major increases in trade. Most importantly, we reached an unprecedented agreement limiting the nuclear arsenals that have haunted the world for a generation.

In the early months of 1973, intensive negotiations and a decisive military policy brought us at last to a just settlement of the long and costly war in Vietnam. We achieved our fundamental objectives—a ceasefire, the return of our prisoners, a commitment to account for those missing in action, the honorable withdrawal of our forces, and the right of the people of South Vietnam to determine their own political future.

Asian Peace Fragile

But the peace in Vietnam and the parallel peace in Laos remain fragile because of North Vietnam's continued violations of the peace agreement. A ceasefire still has not been reached in Cambodia. We earnestly hope these problems can be solved at the conference table. We will not turn our back on our friends and allies while Hanoi makes a mockery of its promise to help keep the peace.

During recent months, with less fanfare than in negotiations with our adversaries, but with no less dedication, we have also been working closely with our Atlantic and Pacific partners. In addition, we have moved toward major reform of the international economic system, although the process of readjustment is still marked by crises.

We have continued to share more responsibilities with our friends under the Nixon Doctrine. In sum, recalling the challenges we faced and the goals we set at the outset of this Administration, all Americans can take satisfaction in the record of the recent past.

But our progress in the early 1970's has been more marked in reducing tensions than in restructuring partnerships. That is why we must make 1973 not only the "Year of Europe," as some have called it, but also the year of renewal for all of America's alliances and friendships.

In this spirit, we shall cooperate with our European friends to forge even stronger partnerships, cemented by a new articulation of the goals we share.

Worldwide Goals

There will be the closest collaboration on such major issues as the mutual and balanced reduction of forces in Europe, the European Security Conference, and the current round of strategic arms limitation talks. Before the end of the year, I will visit our Atlantic allies.

We shall also continue to attach the highest priority to our relations with our major Pacific ally, Japan. Prime Minister Tanaka will visit the United States this summer for talks on this subject.

We shall work with all concerned nations to create a stable monetary system and to promote freer trade. To make this possible, I again urge the Congress to pass promptly the crucial trade legislation I submitted last month.

We are also seeking in 1973 to further the positive momentum in our relations with the Soviet Union. I look forward to welcoming the Soviet leadership to this country later in the year. Dr. Kissinger leaves tonight for Moscow to prepare for that visit. New U.S.-Soviet talks are already underway aiming for further amendments on controlling nuclear weapons.

We shall also continue this year to build our promising new relationship with the People's Republic of China.

We shall pay particular attention to our neighbors in this hemisphere. Secretary Rogers is soon to embark on a trip to Latin America, and I look forward to a similar journey myself during my second term.

We shall do our part with others to reduce tensions and increase opportunity in such areas as the Middle East, South Asia and Africa.

New Partnerships

We shall continue building new partnerships of shared responsibilities with all our friends around the globe. Approval of the foreign aid bill which I sent to the Congress this week will be fundamental to this effort.

Our policy in the world for the next four years can be summarized quite simply:

Where peace is newly planted, we shall work to make it thrive. Where bridges have been built, we shall work to make them stronger. Where friendships have endured, we shall work to make them grow.

We shall keep America strong, involved in the world, meeting the responsibilities which no other free nation is able to meet in building a structure of peace.

I said upon taking office more than four years ago that a nation could aspire to no higher honor than the title of peacemaker. America has done much to earn that title since then. Let us resolve to do still more in the years ahead.

Thank you, and good evening.

✓

LEGAL SERVICES

Following is the White House text of President Nixon's May 11 statement on legal services.

Two years ago I proposed the creation of a Legal Services Corporation as a means of delivering high quality legal assistance to those who would otherwise be unable to afford it. The need still exists, and today I am once again asking the Congress to establish this corporation.

I firmly believe that we must provide a mechanism to overcome economic barriers to adequate legal assistance.

Eight years ago a legal services program was initiated as a small experiment within the Office of Economic Opportunity. It grew rapidly and today more than 2,250 lawyers are assisting the needy in about 900 neighborhood law offices.

We have learned many lessons during this time. We have learned, for instance, that any Federally-sponsored effort which runs counter to State and local officials is sure to spark controversy. We have learned that Federal programs with noble social aims must be carefully structured to mitigate abuse by those who run them. But more than anything else, we have learned that legal assistance for the poor, when properly provided, is one of the most constructive ways to help them to help themselves. During this period, we have also learned that justice is served far better and differences are settled more rationally within the system than on the streets. Now is the time to make legal services an integral part of our judicial system.

When I asked the Congress in 1971 to create an independent Legal Services Corporation, I said that my proposal had three major objectives. Those same objectives apply to my proposal today:

> "First, that the corporation itself be structured and financed so that it will be assured of independence; second, that the lawyers in the program have full freedom to protect the best interests of their clients in keeping with the Canons of Ethics and the high standards of the legal profession; and third, that the Nation be encouraged to continue giving the program the support it needs in order to become a permanent and vital part of the American system of justice."

Features

Many of the features of the new legislation are also similar to those in the 1971 proposal:

• The corporation would be non-profit and governed by a board of eleven members appointed by the President, with the advice and consent of the Senate. No more than six members could be of the same political affiliation, and a majority would have to be attorneys.

• The corporation would be authorized to make grants or enter into contracts with individuals, partnerships, firms, organizations, and corporations, as well as with State and local governments for the purpose of providing legal assistance to eligible clients.

The corporation would be authorized to undertake research on the delivery of legal services and to serve as a clearinghouse for information on such services.

• No funds provided by the corporation could be used with respect to criminal proceedings.

• While engaged in legal assistance activities, attorneys would be barred from participating in political activities and from encouraging or participating in strikes, boycotts, picketing and various forms of civil disturbance.

In addition to these provisions, the new legislation contains several features which I believe represent an improvement over my 1971 proposal:

• A nine-member advisory council would be established in each State, to be appointed by the Governor or, if he failed to act, by the national board. The State advisory council would maintain a continuing review of all legal service activities within its State and would report any program abuses to the national board.

• Anyone could qualify for legal assistance under the program so long as his income were less than 200 percent of the poverty level and his lack of income did not result from a refusal to seek or accept a job.

• The corporation would also be charged with responsibility for conducting a study of alternative ways of delivering legal services, such as judicare, vouchers, prepaid legal insurance, and contracts with law firms. A report of this study would be prepared and submitted to the President and the Congress no later than June 30, 1974.

I firmly believe that this bill merits the support of all who believe in a legal services program which gives the poor the help they need, which is free and independent of political pressures and which includes safeguards to ensure that it operates in a responsible manner.

America's system of law now requires equal treatment for all in our courts of criminal justice. It is no less important that equal access be afforded those who seek redress through our civil laws.

We propose no special favors for any group in our society, nor do we seek to mandate the use of the legal system to the exclusion of other social institutions as instruments of social progress. We propose, simply, to protect and preserve a basic right of all Americans.

✓

ELECTION REFORM

Following is the White House text of President Nixon's taped radio address of May 16 on his proposal for a federal election reform commission:

In my televised address to the Nation two weeks ago, I called on the leaders of both political parties, and on citizens everywhere, to join in working toward new ways of ensuring that future elections would be as nearly free of abuse as possible.

To achieve this goal, I have today proposed to the Congress the establishment of a non-partisan, top-level, independent commission charged with making concrete proposals for reform—not only to examine our laws and see what new ones are needed, but also to examine the observance and enforcement of our laws, and those campaign standards and practices not governed by law but rooted in common usage.

This Commission would be composed of seventeen members. Eight would be chosen by and from the Congress—two Democrats and two Republicans from the House, and two Democrats and two Republicans from the Senate. Seven public members would be chosen by the President for their experience, knowledge and perspective in this field—of whom no more than four could be from the same political party. The chairman of the Democratic and Republican National Committees would also serve on the panel. To further ensure the Commission's complete independence, its chairman and vice chairman would be selected from among the members of the Commission by the Commission itself.

Quick Action Asked

I trust the Congress will act swiftly to establish the Commission. Yesterday I met with the bipartisan leadership of the Congress to discuss this matter. The proposal I am making today incorporates suggestions made by them; and my discussions with them have given me reason to believe that swift action is possible. If the Congress does give this proposal its quick approval, then the Commission's report and recommendations can provide the basis for reforms that could be in place in time for the 1974 Congressional elections.

The mandate of the Commission I have proposed will be as broad as the Federal election process itself. Nothing will be excluded.

It will be authorized to examine the costs and financing of campaigns, and look into the various ways in which the costs can be kept down and improper influence or influence-seeking through large campaign contributions can be ended. It can consider limitations on the total amounts candidates can spend, recognizing both the potential for abuse and the heavy burden that high campaign costs impose on both parties. It can look into the laws governing disclosure of campaign funds and how they are spent, and how both those laws and their enforcement might be improved. It can review the tax laws as they relate to the financing of political campaigns and can look into the question of possible public funding of campaigns.

Other areas for inquiry would include the elimination from our election campaigns of violence and the threat of violence; of intimidation; of frauds in the casting and counting of ballots; of the throwing about of misleading or malicious charges; of sabotage and espionage and other infringements on the rights of privacy; and of the whole range of improper campaign practices.

Beyond measures to curb these clearly evident abuses, the Commission will be authorized to examine such matters as the length and structure of our political campaigns, the purposes for which campaign funds are spent, the use and abuse of techniques such as television commercials, polling and computerized direct mail—and whatever else it may consider appropriate to a thorough-going campaign reform.

Terms for Officeholders

There is another matter of crucial importance to our election process, which I am also asking that the Commission consider. That is whether the Constitution should be amended to change the length of the terms of office of members of the House, of the Senate or of the President.

Many political scientists have suggested, for example, that the President should be elected for a single, non-renewable six-year term, instead of being eligible for two four-year terms. The Commission could well consider the merits of this proposal.

Another change it might consider is whether members of the House of Representatives should be elected for terms of four years instead of two.

Personally, I have long favored the four-year term for members of the House, with half of the members elected every two years. Members serving for two-year terms have to spend one of every two years running for re-election, with the result that they serve one year and run one year. This not only places an enormous burden on the member himself; it also can work to the disadvantage of his constituents and of the country. By reducing the extraordinary campaign burden on its members, I believe the House of Representatives could be made a more effective instrument of government.

The Commission will be directed to come up with a comprehensive set of legislative recommendations. It will also be directed to examine whether additional measures, such as voluntary agreements between candidates or party organizations, may be desirable to extend into those areas where legislation cannot appropriately reach.

Because time is of the essence, the Resolution I have proposed would direct the Commission to file a public report no later than December 1 of this year. I believe that with hard work, the members of the Commission can complete their study even before then.

Commission Independence

The Commission will have complete, independent authority to choose its own priorities among the matters to be considered—and, as it proceeds, it will be encouraged to make interim recommendations for action by the Congress without waiting for its final report.

One option I considered was for the Administration itself to prepare a set of proposed reforms and present them at this time. I rejected that course for two reasons:

First, a really comprehensive campaign reform, which I believe we need, must thread its way through enormous complexities, high sensitivities, entrenched interests, and a careful assessment of the possibilities of enactment by the Congress. This will take time. It can be done, but it cannot be done overnight.

Second, I feel it is essential that proposals for reform come not from one political party, not from one Administration, not from one Congress, but from a bipartisan group of recognized experts, working in a non-partisan atmosphere and broadly enough based to give their recommendations the full authority of manifest impartiality.

Let me stress that this new Commission is in no way competitive with the Senate's Ervin Committee. The new Commission will draw on information being developed by the Ervin Committee, and also on other studies of past campaign abuses. But its own central focus will be on the future—on how not only Presidential elections, but also Congressional elections, can most effectively be reformed.

Campaigns have changed drastically in the past century, and even in the past generation. Television, the rise of professional campaign management firms, jet air travel, sophisticated polling techniques, skyrocketing costs, all have had a powerful impact on the way campaigns are conducted. As in so many other areas of our life, the sheer size of modern campaigns has contributed to the size of the problem and to the magnitude of the abuses.

'Sweeping' Reforms Needed

There will be a temptation to attempt reforms piecemeal; this, I believe, would be a mistake. The reforms needed are sweeping rather than scattered, and each should be considered in relation to the others. We should think in terms of nothing less than a complete re-examination of our system of elections and campaign practices.

Scores, perhaps hundreds, of ideas for various election reforms have already been seriously and responsibly put forward. Many are now pending before the Congress. The principal need is to sort through these ideas, to develop such additional ones as may be appropriate, and to design a comprehensive reform of the campaign system so that in its totality it will work, and work fairly and honestly.

It would be premature to predict what a Commission such as the one I propose might recommend. But these are a few examples of the kinds of reform it would certainly consider:

- strict limits on the size of individual campaign contributions;
- strict limits on the size of campaign contributions or the amount of campaign assistance that can be given by business, labor or professional organizations;
- strict limits on cash contributions;
- tightened control over the activities of multiple organizations working for the same candidate;
- shorter election campaigns;
- new disclosure rules that would simplify not only the filing of reports, but also the public discovery of what was important in those reports;
- reducing the cost of reaching the public, as, for example, by making free radio and television time available to candidates, or by revision of the equal time requirements that now restrict broadcasters in their campaign coverage;
- new Federal laws that would make illegal, practices that are now only unethical; and
- the establishment of an independent Federal Elections Commission, with its own enforcement powers.

It is important that these reforms stay within the spirit as well as the letter of the Constitution; that they not unduly infringe either the rights of the States or the First Amendment rights of individuals to freedom of expression and freedom of assembly. It is important that they be fair, effective, realistic and enforceable. Devising such a system of campaign reform will be difficult, but not impossible.

I am convinced a route can be charted that will avoid the obstacles; that wide-ranging reforms are possible and desirable; and that persons of the caliber of those who would be named to this Commission, given a reasonable period of time and also a firm deadline, can come up with a set of proposals that will work, and that will help to restore the faith of the American people in the integrity of their political processes. √

REMARKS TO POWS

Following is the White House text of President Nixon's May 24 remarks to former Vietnam prisoners of war in the State Department auditorium:

Gentlemen, as you can imagine during my term as President of the United States and also before that as Vice President, and in other offices, I have spoken to many distinguished audiences. I can say to you today that this is the most distinguished group I have ever addressed and I have never been prouder than I am at this moment to address this group.

I say that not simply because you are here and because the whole nation shares those views, as you know, some of you, I am sure, who have traveled around the nation since you have returned home, but I say it because I feel very deeply at this moment, when we have a culmination of the program which finally has all of you returned to the United States, that this is one of those critical moments in history that can change the world, and we need your help.

We do not talk to you today, and I do not talk to you today simply in terms of thanking you as I do for what you have gone through for your country, but I think all of you would prefer to think of what you can do now, how more you can serve. We need you, the nation needs you. I want to tell you why.

Before doing so, I want to fill you in for just a moment about the program for the balance of this afternoon and this evening.

The Day's Events

As you probably know, we have a rather large dinner tonight out on the White House lawn. They get the statistics for me, and they tell me it is the biggest sit-down dinner they have ever had at the White House—1,300 people. Let me tell you there are a lot of people mad because they have not been invited, but we are just having you and a few Members from Congress and two or three Cabinet officers and that is all.

The normal custom at a White House dinner, as you know, is for a receiving line, and we considered that. But then I timed that out and if Mrs. Nixon and I were to stand and shake hands with all 1,300 guests—you, your wives or your mothers or the other guests you have with you—it would take exactly three hours and 20 minutes. That is assuming we didn't chat as you went through the line.

Now, by the time we went through three hours and 20 minutes, it would be after dinner. You missed enough meals in Hanoi without missing one in the White House tonight.

I would be delighted, of course, to meet all of your guests. Mrs. Nixon is up on the eighth floor—which, incidentally, is a much more elegant room than this one—with your wives, having tea, and she will meet all of them. I have met many of them, these marvelous, marvelous women, your wives and mothers and others who have waited for you and stood by you and by their nation during the period of your captivity.

And I thought after I finished my remarks, which will be in the nature of a briefing, that to the extent that time permits, I would like to meet those of you who are here.

Now, it will take quite a bit of time, and some of you—of course, I don't think we have any refreshments, it is a little early yet, but coffee maybe—in the meantime, I would like to meet as many of you as I possibly can, because a great number did write and wire me, upon your return, that you would like to drop by the White House and just say hello and there is nothing I would like more.

So, if you have the time, I have the time. Just remember we must get through in time for dinner which begins around 6:30, as far as you are concerned.

Now, let me come to the briefing and why I decided to have a briefing. Incidentally, we had first thought it would be a classified briefing, but while we knew there was no problem insofar as leaks as far as this group was concerned, our friends in the press have vigorously objected and they said, "Look, with 600 there, let us come, too."

So welcome. We are glad to have our members of the press here. This will be on the record.

I will, however, speak quite bluntly about our foreign policy and our defense policy. I will try to tell you as much as I can, without divulging any classified information, and I hope that you will take to heart some of the things that I say, and particularly pick up the challenge that I am going to give you at the conclusion of my remarks today.

I began with the question: Was it worth it? And I look over this group and I remember having talked to a half dozen of you in my office. I think of what you went through and I think of what you have come back to. And when you ask that question, was it worth it, you can think in personal terms, or you can think in much broader terms.

You could say, oh yes, it was worth it because we proved that we could tough it through. And thank God you did, because your faith meant a good deal to us.

But I would like to put it in the larger sense. Your sacrifice of all of your colleagues and comrades who died in Vietnam, and the sacrifice of all who have served in Vietnam, will have been worth it only if we build a world of peace now. That is what it was all about.

We didn't go to Vietnam for the purpose of conquering North Vietnam. We didn't begin this war, we haven't begun any war in this century, as you know. That is the greatness of U.S. foreign policy. We make our mistakes, but we always have as our motives defending peace, not breaking it, defending freedom, not destroying it.

But when we think in terms of whether your sacrifice then was worth it, we have to think then about the broader aspects of peace, whether or not the world you come back to, the America you come back to, is a better world or is it, shall we say, a world that is not as safe as when you went to Hanoi or whatever area you were kept in captivity.

I cannot put it in the context of 6-1/2 or seven years, which some of you, of course, have been away. But I can put it in the context of the years I have been in this office. And perhaps we can see in perspective where we have been and where we are. But more important, where we are going to go.

Four-Year Review

First, when I came into this office 4-1/2 years ago, 300 a week were being killed in action in Vietnam. There was no plan to end the war, no hope that it was going to be ended. Many of you were already prisoners of war. You had no hope.

Looking at the world scene, the United States had no communication whatever, in any meaningful sense, with the leaders of one-fourth of all the people in the world, those who govern the People's Republic of China. We were in constant confrontation with the Soviet Union, the other super power on the earth, with no thought or even hope that there was a chance for arms control, or trade, or a lessening of tension between these two great super powers.

There were other troubled areas in the world. Some of them are still troubled. But looking at those three areas and seeing what has happened since, and then looking at the United States, we see some progress has been made.

Some 4 1/2 years ago, this nation was torn by riots. Hundreds of campuses were in flames. The American people seemed to have lost their way. There was a desire to move away from responsibilities in the world. There was a lack of national pride, a lack of patriotism. I don't mean among all the people, not even among a majority, but it was there. There was a crisis in terms of whether America, the greatest hope for peace in the world today, would dash that hope or whether it would be worthy of that hope. That was the situation 4 1/2 years ago.

Now in describing that situation, I do not speak critically of those who preceded me in this office. President Eisenhower, John Kennedy, Lyndon Johnson loved this country. They worked for peace as I have tried to work for peace. They felt for you as I feel for you.

What I am simply saying is that in January of 1969 we did have a critical situation, and we started to move on it. And how I wish we could have moved faster. I remember the first Christmas in '69. I met with a group of the representatives of the League of Families down in the library and I talked to these wonderful remarkable women, and I saw their faith and their courage and their love of country, and I heard them tell me that their husbands had not gone to Vietnam simply for the purpose of getting back. In other words, they rejected totally the idea of "Get out, if you will give us our prisoners."

They said, in effect, and they didn't put it this way, but one of you put it very well, "Bring our men home, but bring them home on their feet and not on their knees." And that is what we have done.

And so that was our goal over those four years. That is why we couldn't achieve it perhaps quite as fast as we would have liked.

But the year 1972 saw remarkable progress, as you know. The year 1972, moving into 1973, in January, saw the return of all Americans from Vietnam, all of our combat forces, the return of all of our prisoners of war, the end of the American involvement in Vietnam, a peace agreement, which, if adhered to, will mean peace for Vietnam and Southeast Asia.

That was one accomplishment. That is the one that most people talk about. They say, "Thank God that war is over. Thank God we have got peace."

But in a broader sense, other events took place that will have even more meaning to the world and to peace than your return and the end of the war in Vietnam.

China, for example. That initiative, which was undertaken in early 1972, began in '71, the negotiations, has finally started communication between the leaders of the People's Republic of China and the leaders of the United States of America. Oh, it doesn't mean they aren't still Communists and that we are not still people who love freedom, but it does mean that instead of having hanging over us, looking down the road 10, 15, 20 years from now, a possible confrontation with a nation of the most able people in the world, armed with nuclear weapons equal to our own, instead of having that, there is a chance, a very good chance now, that we will have negotiations with them rather than confrontation, and that is the key to peace in the Pacific.

And then the second development was the meetings with the Soviet leaders. This did not happen just over a period of 1972. We worked for the whole four years. But it culminated in the summit in Moscow. You perhaps heard something about it since your return. But looking at that summit agreement, a great deal of emphasis can be placed on the aspects of trade, and our cooperation in space and other areas which are important, but the most significant development, undoubtedly, was the first step, and a very important step, in limiting the arms race in the nuclear field.

We have, therefore, an agreement with the Soviet Union on defensive nuclear weapons, where we are both limited, and we are moving now toward getting a limitation in the offensive field. And so those were the developments that occurred in the year 1972.

Defense Budget

The other day I was talking to a Congressman. He is a Congressman who has always voted for strong national defense. He said, "Mr. President, give me an answer to my constituents to this question. They say, 'Since we have made such great progress towards peace, we have ended the war in Vietnam, we have had this initiative with China and this initiative with the Soviet Union, why can't we now reduce our defenses regardless of what the other side does and turn that money that we take away from defense to the very urgent problems at home?'"

Let me tell you, gentlemen, there is nothing I would like to do more. A President never likes to veto a bill when it is going to help somebody any place in this country. Our schools or our hospitals or anything that you say.

But, on the other hand, when we talk now about national defense, let me tell you what the challenge is—and you can help in this respect—and what the danger is, a mortal danger that we face insofar as reduction of our defenses is concerned.

First, our defense budget has been reduced. With a new volunteer armed force, considering the increased costs and the like, we find that it is approximately a third reduction of what it was in 1968.

But second, we must also look at this situation: When they say, "Now that we have made all this progress in 1972 towards peace, let's reduce our defenses regardless of what the other side does," what you are doing, in effect, is advocating changing a game plan that has worked.

Let me put it this way: We wouldn't have ended the war in Vietnam with honor, we wouldn't have had the initiative with China, and we would not have had, without question, the arms control and other agreements with the Soviet Union, had the United States not been strong and respected.

Strength without respect is meaningless. That was another reason why this war had to be ended on an honorable basis, because otherwise we would have lost respect, not only of our allies and the neutrals, but also of our potential adversaries in the world.

But when we see what has happened then, we find that the Soviet Union, at the present time, is preparing to come to the United States for a return summit visit in just a few weeks. We are going to have some very intensive negotiations. They are even more important than the negotiations we had last year, although those were the first, and therefore, the most newsworthy, because they will move in arms control and other fields of enormous importance to the future of the world.

Disarmament

But gentlemen, let me tell you, in the event that the President of the United States goes into meetings with the Soviet leaders with the Congress of the United States having unilaterally cut our defenses, then all hope for an arms control agreement is completely destroyed. Because when you really get down to it in the field of international diplomacy—and this is true of all fields in life—you can't get something from anybody else unless you have something to give.

And I say to you, we must never send the President of the United States into any negotiation with anybody as the head of the second strongest nation of the world.

Now, gentlemen, if you should go out and make that kind of a statement, you sometimes may find people say to you what they say to me: "Those who are for a strong defense are for war, and those who are for disarmament are for peace." It is just the other way around. Disarmament can lead to peace only if it is mutual. But let the day never come when we disarm and the other side arms, because that will enormously increase the danger of war.

Let me describe it in more specific terms. For example, in the field of offensive nuclear weapons, we are ready, and we believe they are ready for an agreement in which we will mutually agree that we will have a limitation on the development of offensive nuclear weapons.

Troop Reductions

But in the event, before we go into the negotiations, we already have reduced our own strength in that area, then their incentive for making a deal is completely out the window and we are second and they are first.

Let's go further. Many of you have served in Europe, I know, and you know one of the points that is going to come up in this Congress will be the problem with regard to what we do about our forces in Europe, and Americans 25 years after World War II justifiably are concerned about the fact that we carry such a heavy load in Europe.

Very well intentioned men in the House and the Senate, therefore, say it is time for us to bring our men home—half of them, or a third of them or a fourth of them, or what have you—regardless of what the other side does.

But here again, let's look at what would happen. In the fall we are going to have very significant negotiations with the Warsaw Pact countries for a mutual reduction of forces in Europe, a reduction on our side and on theirs. As long as it is a mutual reduction, the stability which is essential for peace in that critical area of the world will be maintained.

But if, on the other hand, before we go into those negotiations this fall, the United States unilaterally reduces its forces, all incentive that the Warsaw Pact forces and that the Soviet Union would have to reduce theirs is gone, and you would create that imbalance which would enormously increase instability and the chances for war.

So what I am saying to you is this: I am for limitation of armaments, and I know every one of you is. I am for, certainly in the nuclear field, doing everything that we can to reduce that danger that is hanging over the world today.

But I also know that it is vitally important that in this field of limitation of armaments that we remember that the United States of America is not a threat to the peace of the world.

I have traveled in most of the countries of the world. I have been to the Communist countries and to the free countries.

I have yet to talk to a world leader who believes that the United States of America threatens his peace or his freedom. A strong United States is a force for peace; a weak United States means that the peace will be threatened.

And so that is why I say at this point, not that we want to be strong in order to dominate anybody else. That period is long gone, if it ever did exist in our own minds. But what we need to recognize is that we now have a balance in the world. We must maintain that balance, and that is why, let us keep our defenses up.

Oh, take the fat off, wherever we possibly can, but keep them up and be sure in negotiations we go down only if the other side goes down, and if we do that, then we contribute to the peace of the world in which we are all so very much interested.

National Security Secrecy

One other subject that is somewhat sensitive that I will touch upon only briefly, that I would like to ask for your support on, is with regard to the security of the kind of negotiations that we have.

I want to be quite blunt. Had we not had secrecy, had we not had secret negotiations with the North Vietnamese, had we not had secret negotiations pior to the Soviet Summit, had we not had secret negotiations over a period of time with the Chinese leaders, let me say quite bluntly, there would have been no China initiative, there would have been no limitation of arms for the Soviet Union and no summit, and had we not had that kind of security, and that kind of secrecy that allowed for the kind of exchange that is essential, you men would still be in Hanoi rather than Washington today.

And let me say, I think it is time in this country to quit making national heroes out of those who steal secrets and publish them in the newspapers.

Because, gentlemen, you see, in order to continue these great initiatives for peace, we must have confidentiality, we must have secret communications. It isn't that we are trying to keep anything from the American people that the American people should know. It isn't that we are trying to keep something from the press that the press should print. But it is that what we are trying to do is to accomplish our goal, make a deal. And when we are dealing with potential adversaries, those negotiations must have the highest degree of confidentiality.

And I can assure you that in my term of office as President in the first four years, and also in this second four years, I am going to meet my responsibility to protect the national security of the United States of America insofar as our secrets are concerned.

And by our secrets, what I am saying here is not that we are concerned about every little driblet here and there, but what I am concerned about is the highest classified documents in our National Security Council files, in the State Department, in the Defense Department, which if they get out, for example, in our arms control negotiations with the Soviets, would let them know our position before we ever got to the table. They don't tell us theirs. They have no problem keeping the secrets.

I don't want, and you don't want, their system and that kind of control, but I say it is time for a new sense of responsibility in this country and a new sense of dedication of everybody in the bureaucracy that if a document is classified, keep it classified.

Now, gentlemen, I turn to the challenge for the future. I have talked about the need for strength if we are going to have a mutual reduction of armaments in the world, and therefore, of the threat to peace in the world. I have talked about the need for national security where our highly classified documents are concerned, so we can continue these enormously important initiatives for peace.

U.S. World Role

I now want to talk about why the United States, after all that it has done for the world in World War II, after the billions that it has poured out since World War II, its sacrifices in Korea, its sacrifices in Vietnam, why we, the American people, have to continue to carry this load.

As I said earlier, believe me, as President, what a relief it would be to say, "Now that we have peace in Vietnam, we have a new relationship with China and Russia, we can simply turn away from the problems of the world and turn to the problems at home."

I can assure you gentlemen that if we were to follow that course, we would find very soon that we would be living in a terribly dangerous world. The world is safer today than it was four and one-half years ago. It can be more safe in the years ahead. But that will only happen provided we follow the course that I have tried to lay out to you here today.

As I look to that future, therefore, it is vitally important that the United States continue to play the world role.

Let's look at just this century. We don't need to go back any further than that. I can imagine some of you in those long hours of captivity were thinking back over several centuries. In any event, looking back just over this century, World War I, the United States could stand aside. After all, there was Britain, there was France, two great powers who thought as we did about the world, and they could carry the load. And then we came in toward the end in World War II. The United States, for a time, could stand aside because Britain was still strong, and France at the beginning had some strength, but eventually we had to come in.

But today, look at the world. Among the free nations of the world there is no one else, not the Japanese, as you well know, even though they have the economic strength, they do not have the military strength, and cannot be allowed to acquire it under their constitution; and not one nation in Europe, by itself, or Europe collectively, has the strength to be the peacemaker in the world.

So it is all right there. It is in America. It is in that Oval Office, whoever is there, and it is there for the foreseeable future. In other words, the United States must maintain its strength in order to play a role between the great powers of the world and among the great powers of the world of reducing the danger of war, because our ideals and our goals—subject as they can be to much criticism as far as tactics are concerned in the world scene—our ideals and our goals are for a world of peace. Our ideals and our goals are for a world in which we reduce the burden of arms, and therefore, it is vitally important that this nation that has that kind of ideals and that kind of goals maintains its strength so that we can play that role.

But maintaining the strength alone is not enough. It must be respected. And that means that we must continue to have a policy which commands respect throughout the world. We must continue to insist on adherence to agreements that are made. We must continue to let the world know that while we have no aggressive intentions any place in the world, we will stand by our treaty commitments wherever they are in the world.

That, you see, is the language of peace rather than the language of bugging out of the world and turning to what people wistfully might think to be a fortress America. But let me tell you, fortress America might have been before World War II a concept that was viable. Today it is ridiculous. We cannot be apart from the world, not when weapons that can destroy us are 30 minutes away.

And so we must play this role, and rather than playing it in terms of whining about it and complaining about it, let us do it proudly, because what greater mission could a people have than to say that in these years—the 70's—of 1971-2-3-4-5 and 6, when we reach our 200th birthday, the United States of America played a great role in the world and made the world safer not only for ourselves but for everybody in the world. That is the stake, that is the challenge we must meet.

Today then, I ask for your support, obviously, for a strong national defense. That is like the preacher talking to the choir. But I know as far as you are concerned, you will be for that, and I hope so many of you will stay in our armed forces. We need you.

Faith and Spirit

But also, beyond that, I ask for your support in helping to develop the national spirit, the faith that we need in order to meet our responsibilities in the world. You have already contributed enormously to that by your statements on your return, by what you have said, what you have done, and I am sure you can contribute more to it in the future.

But the young people of America need to hear the truth. They will believe you. They will believe you because you have suffered so much for this country and have proved that you will do anything that you can to do what is best for America, not just for yourselves.

Because, at this particular point, America is the richest country in the world; militarily, it is the strongest, and will always have that potential because of its wealth. The only question is whether we face up to our world responsibilities, whether we have the faith, the patriotism, the willingness to lead in this critical period.

Gentlemen, by what you did and what you said on your return, you have helped turn this country around. You have helped reinstill faith where there was doubt before. And for what you have done by your faith, you have built up America's faith. This nation and the world will always be in your debt.

Those first four years in the office were not easy ones for me in the international front, fighting for an adequate defense budget, fighting for a responsible foreign policy, but looking toward the balance of the second four years, let me say I feel better, because out in this room, I think I have some allies and I will appreciate your help.

Thank you.   √

ECONOMIC CONTROLS

Following is the White House text of President Nixon's June 13 address to the nation on economic controls:

I want to tell you tonight about some strong actions I have ordered today with regard to the American economy—actions which will be important to you in terms of the wages you earn and the prices you pay.

But first, since we have been hearing so much in the past few months about what is wrong with the American economy, let us look at some of the things that are right about our economy. We can be proud that the American economy is by far the freest, the strongest and the most productive economy in the whole world. It gives us the highest standard of living in the world. We are in the middle of one of the biggest, strongest booms in our history. More Americans have jobs today than ever before. The average worker is earning more today than ever before. Your income buys more today than ever before.

Growth

In August, 1971, I announced the New Economic Policy. Since then, the Nation's output has increased by a phenomenal eleven and a half percent—a more rapid growth than in any comparable period in the last 21 years. Four and a half million new civilian jobs have been created—more than in any comparable period ever. At the same time, real per capita disposable income—meaning what you have left to spend after taxes and after inflation—has risen by seven and a half percent. This means that, in terms of what your money will actually buy, in the past year and a half your annual income has increased by the equivalent of four extra weeks' pay. When we consider these facts, therefore, we can see that in terms of jobs, of income, of growth, we are enjoying one of the best periods in our history.

We have every reason to be optimistic about the future. But there is one great problem that rightly concerns every one of us. This is rising prices, and especially rising food prices. By the end of last year we had brought the rate of inflation down to 3.4 percent, giving us the best record against inflation in 1972 of any major industrial nation. But now prices are going up at unacceptably high rates.

The greatest part of this increase is due to rising food prices. This has been caused in large measure by increased demand at home and abroad, by crop failures abroad and by some of the worst weather for crops and livestock here in America that we have ever experienced. Whatever the reasons, every American family is confronted with a real and pressing problem of higher prices. I have decided that the time has come to take strong and effective action to deal with this problem.

Price Freeze

Effective immediately, therefore, I am ordering a freeze on prices. This freeze will hold prices at levels no higher than those charged during the first eight days of June. It will cover all prices paid by consumers. The only prices not covered will be those of unprocessed agricultural products at the farm levels, and rents.

Wages, interest and dividends will remain under their present control systems during the freeze. The reason I have decided not to freeze wages is that the wage settlements reached under the rules of Phase III have not been a significant cause of the increase in prices. As long as wage settlements continue to be responsible and non-inflationary, a wage freeze will not be imposed.

The freeze will last for a maximum of 60 days. This time will be used to develop and put into place a new and more effective system of controls which will follow the freeze. This new, Phase IV set of controls will be designed to contain the forces that have sent prices so rapidly upward in the past few months. It will involve tighter standards and more mandatory compliance procedures than under Phase III. It will recognize the need for wages and prices to be treated consistently with one another.

In addition to food prices, I have received reports from various parts of the country lately of many instances of sharp increases in the price of gasoline. Therefore, I have specifically directed the Cost of Living Council to develop new Phase IV measures that will stabilize both food prices at the retail store and the price of gasoline at the local service station.

Phase IV

In announcing these actions, there is one point I want to emphasize to everyone listening to me tonight: The Phase IV that follows the freeze will not be designed to get us permanently into a controlled economy. On the contrary, it will be designed as a better way to get us out of a controlled economy, and to return us as quickly as possible to the free market system.

We are not going to put the American economy in a strait jacket. We are not going to control the boom in a way that would lead to a bust. We are not going to follow the advice of those who have proposed actions that would lead inevitably to a permanent system of price and wage controls. Such actions would bring good headlines tomorrow and bad headaches six months from now for every American family, in terms of rationing, black markets, and eventually a recession leading to more unemployment.

It is your prosperity that is at stake. It is your job that is at stake. The actions I have directed today are designed to deal with the rise in the cost of living without jeopardizing your prosperity or your job.

Because the key to curb food prices lies in increasing supplies, I am not freezing the price of unprocessed agricultural products at the farm level. This would reduce supplies instead of increasing them, and would eventually result, inevitably, in even higher prices for the foods you buy at the supermarket.

Supply and Demand

Beginning in 1972, we embarked on a comprehensive new program for increasing food supplies. Among many other measures, this has included opening up 40 million more acres for crop production. In the months ahead, as these new crops are harvested, they will help hold prices down. But unfortunately, this is not yet helping in terms of the prices you pay at the supermarket today.

One of the major reasons for the rise in food prices at home is that there is now an unprecedented demand abroad for the products of America's farms. Over the long run, increased food exports will be a vital factor in raising farm income, in improving our balance of payments, and in supporting America's position in the world. In the short term, however—when we have shortages and sharply rising prices of food at home—I have made this basic decision: In allocating the products of America's farms between marketings abroad and those in the United States, we must put the American consumer first.

Therefore, I have decided that a new system for export controls on food products is needed—a system designed to hold the price of animal feed-stuffs and other grains in the American market to levels that will make it possible to produce meat and eggs and milk at prices you can afford.

I shall ask the Congress, on an urgent basis, to give me the new and more flexible authority needed to impose such a system. In exercising such authority, this will be my policy. We will keep the export commitments we have made as a Nation. We shall also consult with other countries to seek their cooperation in resolving the world-wide problem of rising food prices. But we will not let foreign sales price meat and eggs off the American table.

I have also taken another action today to stop the rise in the cost of living. I have ordered the Internal Revenue Service to begin immediately a thorough-going audit of the books of companies which have raised their prices more than 1.5 percent above their January ceilings. The purpose of the audit will be to find out whether those increases were justified by rising costs. If they were not, the prices will be rolled back.

Congress' Role

The battle against inflation is everybody's business. I have told you what the Administration will do. There is also a vital role for the Congress. The most important single thing the Congress can do in holding down the cost of living is to hold down the cost of Government. For my part, I shall continue to veto spending bills that we cannot afford, no matter how noble-sounding their names. If these budget-busters became law, the money would come out of your pocket—in higher taxes, higher prices, or both. There are several specific recommendations I have already made to the Congress that will be important in holding down prices in the future. I again urge quick action on all of these proposals.

Congress should give the President authority to reduce tariffs in selected cases in order to increase supplies of scarce goods and hold down their prices. This action will help on such scarce items as meat, plywood and zinc. In particular, the tariff on imported meat should be removed.

Congress should provide authority to dispose of more surplus commodities held in Government stockpiles.

Congress should let us go ahead quickly with the Alaska pipeline, and so combat the shortage of oil and gasoline. I will also soon send to the Congress a major new set of proposals on energy, spelling out new actions I believe are necessary to help us meet our energy needs and thereby lessen pressures on fuel prices.

In its consideration of new farm legislation, it is vital that the Congress put high production ahead of high prices, so that farm prosperity will not be at the cost of higher prices for the consumer. If the Congress sends me a farm bill, or any other bill, that I consider inflationary, I shall veto such a bill.

Beyond what the Administration can do, and what the Congress can do, there is also a great deal that you can do. The next 60 days can decide the question: whether we shall have a continuing inflation that leads to recession, or whether we deal responsibly with our present problems, and so go forward with a vigorous prosperity and a swift return to a free market.

You can help, by giving your Senators and Congressmen your support when they make the difficult decisions to hold back on unnecessary spending.

You can help, by saying no to those who would impose a permanent system of controls on this great, productive economy of ours which is the wonder of the world.

Temporary Controls

Let there be no mistake: If our economy is to remain dynamic, we must never slip into the temptation of imagining that in the long run controls can substitute for a free economy or permit us to escape the need for discipline in fiscal and monetary policy. We must not let controls become a narcotic—and we must not become addicted.

There are all sorts of seemingly simple gimmicks, that would give the appearance or offer the promise of controlling inflation—but that would carry a dangerous risk of bringing on a recession, and that would not be effective in holding down prices. Rigid, permanent controls always look better on paper than they do in practice.

We have much to be thankful for here in America. We are the best-clothed, best-fed, best-housed people in the world—the envy of every nation. This year, for the first time in 12 years, we are at peace in Vietnam—and our courageous prisoners of war have returned to their homes. This year, for the first time in a generation, no American is being drafted into the armed forces. This year, we find our prospects brighter than at any time in the modern era for a lasting peace, and for the abundant prosperity such a peace can make possible.

Next Monday, I will meet at the summit with General Secretary Brezhnev of the Soviet Union. Based on the months of preparatory work that has been done for this meeting, and based on the extensive consultation and correspondence we have had, I can confidently predict that out of our meetings will come major new progress toward reducing both the burden of arms and the danger of war, and toward a better and more rewarding relationship between the world's two most powerful nations.

Today, in America, we have a magnificent opportunity. We hold the future—our future—in our own hands. By standing together, by working together, by joining in bold yet sensible policies to meet our temporary problems without sacrificing our lasting strengths, we can achieve what America has not had since President Eisenhower was in this office: full prosperity without war and without inflation. This is a great goal, and a goal that together we can reach. √

EXECUTIVE ORDER

Following is the White House text of President Nixon's June 13 executive order implementing his new plan for price controls.

On January 11, 1973 I issued Executive Order 11695 which provided for establishment of Phase III of the Economic Stabilization Program. On April 30, 1973 the Congress enacted, and I signed into law, amendments to the Economic Stabilization Act of 1970 which extended for one year, until April 30, 1974, the legislative authority for carrying out the Economic Stabilization Program.

During Phase III, labor and management have contributed to our stabilization efforts through responsible collective bargaining. The American people look to labor and management to continue their constructive and cooperative contributions. Price behavior under Phase III has not been satisfactory, however. I have therefore determined to impose a comprehensive freeze for a maximum period of 60 days on the prices of all commodities and services offered for sale except the prices charged for raw agricultural products. I have determined that this action is necessary to stabilize the economy, reduce inflation, minimize unemployment, improve the Nation's competitive position in world trade and protect the purchasing power of the dollar, all in the context of sound fiscal management and effective monetary policies.

NOW, THEREFORE, by virtue of the authority vested in me by the Constitution and statutes of the United States, particularly the Economic Stabilization Act of 1970, as amended, it is hereby ordered as follows:

Section 1. Effective 9:00 p.m., e.s.t., June 13, 1973, no seller may charge to any class of purchaser and no purchaser may pay a price for any commodity or service which exceeds the freeze price charged for the same or a similar commodity or service in transactions with the same class of purchaser during the freeze base period. This order shall be effective for a maximum period of 60 days from the date hereof, until 11:59 p.m., e.s.t., August 12, 1973. It is not unlawful to charge or pay a price less than the freeze price and lower prices are encouraged.

Section 2. Each seller shall prepare a list of freeze prices for all commodities and services which he sells and shall maintain a copy of that list available for public inspection, during normal business hours, at each place of business where such commodities or services are offered for sale. In addition, the calculations and supporting data upon which the list is based shall be maintained by the seller at the location where the pricing decisions reflected on the list are ordinarily made and shall be made available on request to representatives of the Economic Stabilization Program.

Section 3. The provisions of this order shall not extend to the prices charged for raw agricultural products. The prices of processed agricultural products, however, are subject to the provisions of this order. For those agricultural products which are sold for ultimate consumption in their original unprocessed form, this provision applies after the first sale.

Section 4. The provisions of this order do not extend to (a) wages and salaries, which continue to be subject to the program established pursuant to Executive Order 11695; (b) interest and dividends, which continue to be subject to the program established by the Committee on Interest and Dividends and (c) rents which continue to be subject to controls only to the limited extent provided in Executive Order 11695.

Section 5. The Cost of Living Council shall develop and recommend to the President policies, mechanisms and procedures to achieve and maintain stability of prices and costs in a growing economy after the expiration of this freeze. To this end, it shall consult with representatives of agriculture, industry, labor, consumers and the public.

Section 6(a). Executive Order 11695 continues to remain in full force and effect and the authority conferred by and pursuant to this order shall be in addition to the authority conferred by or pursuant to Executive Order 11695 including authority to grant exceptions and exemptions under appropriate standards issued pursuant to regulations.

(b) All powers and duties delegated to the Chairman of the Cost of Living Council by Executive Order 11695 for the purpose of carrying out the provisions of that order are hereby delegated to the Chairman of the Cost of Living Council for the purpose of carrying out the provisions of this order.

Section 7. Whoever willfully violates this order or any order or regulation continued or issued under authority of this order shall be subject to a fine of not more than $5,000 for each such violation. Whoever violates this order or any order or regulation continued or issued under authority of this order shall be subject to a civil penalty of not more than $2,500 for each such violation.

Section 8. For purposes of this Executive Order, the following definitions apply:

"Freeze price" means the highest price at or above which at least 10 per cent of the commodities or services concerned were priced by the seller in transactions with the class of purchaser concerned during the freeze base period. In computing the freeze price, a seller may not exclude any temporary special sale, deal or allowance in effect during the freeze base period.

"Class of purchaser" means all those purchasers to whom a seller has charged a comprable price for comparable commodities or services during the freeze base period pursuant to customary price differentials between those purchasers and other purchasers.

"Freeze base period" means

(a) the period June 1 to June 8, 1973; or

(b) in the case of a seller who had no transactions during that period, the nearest preceding seven-day period in which he had a transaction.

"Transaction" means an arms length sale between unrelated persons and is considered to occur at the time of shipment in the case of commodities and the time of performance in the case of services.

RICHARD NIXON

NIXON-BREZHNEV REMARKS

Following is the White House text of remarks June 18 by President Nixon and Leonid I. Brezhnev, General Secretary of the Central Committee of the Communist Party of the Soviet Union, as Nixon welcomed Brezhnev to the United States on the South Lawn of the White House:

Nixon's Remarks

Mr. General Secretary and all of our distinguished guests:

Mr. Brezhnev, it is a very great honor for me to welcome you on your first visit to the United States. It was just a year ago that we met in Moscow, and on that occasion we entered into a number of agreements that changed the relationship between our two great countries in a very profound way.

What has happened since those agreements have been entered into, and the preparations that have been made over many, many months, the correspondence we have had, and other meetings, led me to conclude that this year at the summit in Washington we will not only build on the foundation that we laid last year, but that we have the opportunity to make even greater progress than we made last year toward the goals that we share in common—the goals of better relations between our two governments, a better life for our people, the Russian people, the American people, and above all, the goal that goes beyond our two countries, but to the whole world—the goal of lifting the burden of armaments from the world and building a structure of peace.

As you know, Mr. General Secretary, these television cameras mean that right now millions in America and millions in the Soviet Union are seeing us as we appear together and as we speak.

I could also add that not only are the Russian people, the Soviet people, and the American people watching, but all the world is watching as we meet on this occasion, because the people of the world know that if the leaders of the two most powerful nations of the world can work together and their governments can work together, the chance for a world peace is infinitely increased.

The hopes of the world rest with us at this time in the meetings that we will have. I am confident, Mr. General Secretary, that in our meetings this week we shall not disappoint those hopes.

We wish you a good stay in our country, but above all, on this, which is a trip of such great significance to our two peoples and to the world, we trust that at the end, not only the Soviet people and the American people, but the people of the world, will look on this event as a great step forward in the goal we all want, not only peace between our two countries, but peace and progress for all the people of the world.

Brezhnev's Reply

Esteemed Mr. President, esteemed Mrs. Nixon, ladies and gentlemen, I am happy to have a new meeting with you, Mr. President, and I thank you for the warm words addressed to us, representatives of the Union of Soviet Socialist Republics.

This is my first visit to your country, my first direct acquaintance with America and the American people. We have made a long journey from Moscow to Washington. Our two capitals are separated by over 6,000 miles.

But international politics has its own concepts of relativity, not covered by Einstein's theory. The distances between our countries are shrinking, not only because we travel aboard modern aircraft following a well-charted route, but also because we share one great goal, which is to ensure a lasting peace for the peoples of our countries, and to strengthen security on our planet.

One year ago, in Moscow, we jointly took a major step in that direction. The results of our first meeting laid a good and reliable foundation for peaceful relations between our two countries.

But even then we both took the view that, building on that foundation, we should move further ahead. During the past year a good beginning has been made in that sense. And now we regard our visit to the United States and the forthcoming meetings with you as an expression of our common determination to make a new contribution to what was jointly initiated.

I and my comrades, who have come with me, are prepared to work hard to ensure that the talks we will have with you, Mr. President, and with other American statesmen, justify the hopes of our peoples and serve the interests of a peaceful future for all mankind.

JOINT COMMUNIQUE TEXT

Following is the White House text of the joint communique issued June 25 at the western White House concerning the week-long sessions between President Nixon and Soviet Communist Party Secretary Leonid I. Brezhnev.

At the invitation of the President of the United States, Richard Nixon, extended during his official visit to the USSR in May 1972, and in accordance with a subsequent agreement, General Secretary of the Central Committee of the Communist Party of the Soviet Union, Mr. Leonid I. Brezhnev, paid an official visit to the United States from June 18 to June 25. Mr. Brezhnev was accompanied by A. A. Gromyko, Minister of Foreign Affairs of the USSR, Member of the Politbureau of the Central Committee, CPSU; N. S. Patolichev, Minister of Foreign Trade; B. A. Bugayev, Minister of Civil Aviation; G. E. Tsukanov and A. M. Aleksandrov, Assistants to the General Secretary of the Central Committee, CPSU; L. I. Zamyatin, General Director of TASS: E. I. Chazov, Deputy Minister of Public Health of the USSR; G. M. Korniyenko, Member of the Collegium of the Ministry of Foreign Affairs of the USSR; G. A. Arbstov, Director of the USA Institute of the Academy of Sciences of the USSR.

President Nixon and General Secretary Brezhnev held thorough and constructive discussions on the progress achieved in the development of U.S.-Soviet relations and on a number of major international problems of mutual interest.

Also taking part in the conversations held in Washington, Camp David, and San Clemente, were:

On the American side William P. Rogers, Secretary of State; George P. Shultz, Secretary of the Treasury; Dr. Henry A. Kissinger, Assistant to the President for National Security Affairs.

On the Soviet side A. A. Gromyko, Minister of Foreign Affairs of the USSR, Member of the Politbureau of the Central Committee, CPSU; A. F. Dobrynin, Soviet Ambassador to the USA; N. S. Patolichev, Minister of Foreign Trade; B. P. Bugayev, Minister of Civil Aviation; A. M. Aleksandrov and G. E. Tsukanov, Assistants to the General Secretary of the Central Committee, CPSU; G. M. Korniyenko, Member of the Collegium of the Ministry of Foreign Affairs of the USSR.

I. The General State of U.S.-Soviet Relations

Both sides expressed their mutual satisfaction with the fact that the American-Soviet summit meeting in Moscow in May, 1972, and the joint decisions taken there have resulted in a substantial advance in the strengthening of peaceful relations between the U.S.A. and the U.S.S.R. and have created the basis for the further development of broad and mutually beneficial cooperation in various fields of mutual interest to the peoples of both countries and in the interests of all mankind. They noted their satisfaction with the mutual effort to implement strictly and fully the treaties and agreements concluded between the U.S.A. and the U.S.S.R., and to expand areas of cooperation.

They agreed that the process of reshaping relations between the U.S.A. and the U.S.S.R. on the basis of peaceful coexistence and equal security as set forth in the basic principles of relations between the U.S.A. and the U.S.S.R. signed in Moscow on May 29, 1972, is progressing in an encouraging manner. They emphasized the great importance that each side attaches to these basic principles. They reaffirmed their commitment to the continued scrupulous implementation and the enhancement of the effectiveness of each of the provisions of that document.

Both sides noted with satisfaction that the outcome of the U.S.-Soviet meeting in Moscow in May, 1972, was welcomed by other States and by world opinion as an important contribution to strengthening peace and international security, to curbing the arms race and to developing businesslike cooperation among States with different social systems.

Both Sides viewed the return visit to the USA of the General Secretary of the Central Committee of the CPSU, L. I. Brezhnev, and the talks held during the visit as an expression of their mutual determination to continue the course toward a major improvement in US-Soviet relations.

Both Sides are convinced that the discussions they have just held represent a further milestone in the constructive development of their relations.

Convinced that such a development of American-Soviet relations serves the interests of both of their peoples and all of mankind, it was decided to take further major steps to give these relations maximum stability and to turn the development of friendship and cooperation between their peoples into a permanent factor for worldwide peace.

II. The Prevention of Nuclear War and the Limitation of Strategic Armaments

Issues related to the maintenance and strengthening of international peace were a central point of the talks between President Nixon and General Secretary Brezhnev.

Conscious of the exceptional importance for all mankind of taking effective measures to that end, they discussed ways in which both Sides could work toward removing the danger of war, and especially nuclear war, between the USA and the USSR and between either party and other countries. Consequently, in accordance with the Charter of the United Nations and the Basic Principles of Relations of May 29, 1972, it was decided to conclude an Agreement Between the USA and the USSR on the Prevention of Nuclear War. That Agreement was signed by the President and the General Secretary on June 22, 1973. The text has been published separately.

The President and the General Secretary, in appraising this Agreement, believe that it constitutes a historical landmark in Soviet-American relations and substantially strengthens the foundations of international security as a whole. The United States and the Soviet Union state their readiness to consider additional ways of strengthening peace and removing forever the danger of war, and particularly nuclear war.

In the course of the meetings, intensive discussions were held on questions of strategic arms limitation. In this connection both Sides emphasized the fundamental importance of the Treaty on the Limitation of Anti-Ballistic Missile Systems and the Interim Agreement on Certain Measures with Respect to the Limitation of Strategic Offensive Arms signed between the USA and the USSR in May 1972 which, for the first time in history, place actual limits on the most modern and most formidable types of armaments.

Having exchanged views on the progress in the implementation of these agreements, both Sides reaffirmed their intention to carry them out and their readiness to move ahead jointly toward an agreement on the further limitation of strategic arms.

Both Sides noted that progress has been made in the negotiations that resumed in November 1972, and that the prospects for reaching a permanent agreement on more complete measures limiting strategic offensive armaments are favorable.

Both Sides agreed that the progress made in the limitation of strategic armaments is an exceedingly important contribution to the strengthening of US-Soviet relations and to world peace.

On the basis of their discussions, the President and the General Secretary signed on June 21, 1973, Basic Principles of Negotiations on the Further Limitation of Strategic Offensive Arms. The text has been published separately.

The USA and the USSR attach great importance to joining with all States in the cause of strengthening peace, reducing the burden of armaments, and reaching agreements on arms limitation and disarmament measures.

Considering the important role which an effective international agreement with respect to chemical weapons would play, the two Sides agreed to continue their efforts to conclude such an agreement in cooperation with other countries.

The two Sides agree to make every effort to facilitate the work of the Committee on Disarmament which has been meeting in Geneva. They will actively participate in negotiations aimed at working out new measures to curb and end the arms race. They reaffirm that the ultimate objective is general and complete disarmament, including nuclear disarmament, under strict international control. A world disarmament conference could play a role in this process at an appropriate time.

III. International Questions: The Reduction of Tensions and Stengthening of International Security

President Nixon and General Secretary Brezhnev reviewed major questions of the current international situation. They gave special attention to the developments which have occurred since the time of the US-Soviet summit meeting in Moscow. It was noted with satisfaction that positive trends are developing in international relations toward the further relaxation of tensions and the strengthening of cooperative relations in the interests of peace. In the opinion of both Sides, the current process of improvement in the international situation creates new and favorable opportunities for reducing tensions, settling outstanding international issues, and creating a permanent structure of peace.

Indochina. The two Sides expressed their deep satisfaction at the conclusion of the Agreement on Ending the War and Restoring Peace in Vietnam, and also at the results of the International Conference on Vietnam which approved and supported that Agreement.

The two Sides are convinced that the conclusion of the Agreement on Ending the War and Restoring Peace in Vietnam, and the subsequent signing of the Agreement on Restoring Peace and Achieving National Concord in Laos, meet the fundamental interests and aspirations of the peoples of Vietnam and Laos and open up a possibility for establishing a lasting peace in Indochina, based on respect for the independence, sovereignty, unity and territorial integrity of the countries of that area. Both Sides emphasized that these agreements must be strictly implemented.

They further stressed the need to bring an early end to the military conflict in Cambodia in order to bring peace to the entire area of Indochina. They also reaffirmed their stand that the political futures of Vietnam, Laos, and Cambodia should be left to the respective peoples to determine, free from outside interference.

Europe. In the course of the talks both Sides noted with satisfaction that in Europe the process of relaxing tensions and developing cooperation is actively continuing and thereby contributing to international stability.

The two Sides expressed satisfaction with the further normalization of relations among European countries resulting from treaties and agreements signed in recent years, particularly between the USSR and the FRG. They also welcome the coming into force of the Quadripartite Agreement of September 3, 1971. They share the conviction that strict observance of the treaties and agreements that have been concluded will contribute to the security and well-being of all parties concerned.

They also welcome the prospect of United Nations membership this year for the FRG and the GDR and recall, in this connection, that the USA, USSR, UK and France have signed the Quadripartite Declaration of November 9, 1972, on this subject.

The USA and the USSR reaffirm their desire, guided by the appropriate provisions of the Joint US-USSR Communique adopted in Moscow in May 1972, to continue their separate and joint contributions to strengthening peaceful relations in Europe. Both Sides affirm that ensuring a lasting peace in Europe is a paramount goal of their policies.

In this connection satisfaction was expressed with the fact that as a result of common efforts by many States, including the USA and the USSR, the preparatory work has been successfully completed for the Conference on Security and Cooperation in Europe, which will be convened on July 3, 1973. The USA and the USSR hold the view that the Conference will enhance the possibilities for strengthening European security and developing cooperation among the participating States. The USA and the USSR will conduct their policies so as to realize the goals of the Conference and bring about a new era of good relations in this part of the world.

Reflecting their continued positive attitude toward the Conference, both Sides will make efforts to bring the Conference to a successful conclusion at the earliest possible time. Both Sides proceed from the assumption that progress in the work of the Conference will produce possibilities for completing it at the highest level.

The USA and the USSR believe that the goal of strengthening stability and security in Europe would be further advanced if the relaxation of political tensions were accompanied by a reduction of military tensions in Central Europe. In this respect they attach great importance to the negotiations on the mutual reduction of forces and armaments and associated measures in Central Europe which will begin on October 30, 1973. Both

Sides state their readiness to make, along with other States, their contribution to the achievement of mutually acceptable decisions on the substance of this problem, based on the strict observance of the principle of the undiminished security of any of the parties.

Middle East. The parties expressed their deep concern with the situation in the Middle East and exchanged opinions regarding ways of reaching a Middle East settlement.

Each of the parties set forth its position on this problem.

Both parties agreed to continue to exert their efforts to promote the quickest possible settlement in the Middle East. This settlement should be in accordance with the interests of all states in the area, be consistent with their independence and sovereignty and should take into due account the legitimate interests of the Palestinian people.

IV. Commercial and Economic Relations

The President and the General Secretary thoroughly reviewed the status of and prospects for commercial and economic ties between the USA and the USSR. Both Sides noted with satisfaction the progress achieved in the past year in the normalization and development of commercial and economic relations between them.

They agreed that mutually advantageous cooperation and peaceful relations would be strengthened by the creation of a permanent foundation of economic relationships.

They recall with satisfaction the various agreements on trade and commercial relations signed in the past year. Both Sides note that American-Soviet trade has shown a substantial increase, and that there are favorable prospects for a continued rise in the exchange of goods over the coming years.

The believe that the two countries should aim at a total of 2-3 billion dollars of trade over the next three years. The Joint US-USSR Commercial Commission continues to provide a valuable mechanism to promote the broad-scale growth of economic relations. The two Sides noted with satisfaction that contacts between American firms and their Soviet counterparts are continuing to expand.

Both sides confirmed their firm intention to proceed from their earlier understanding on measures directed at creating more favorable conditions for expanding commercial and other economic ties between the USA and the USSR.

It was noted that as a result of the Agreement Regarding Certain Maritime Matters signed in October 1972, Soviet and American commercial ships have been calling more frequently at ports of the United States and the USSR, respectively, and since late May of this year a new regular passenger line has started operating between New York and Leningrad.

In the course of the current meeting, the two Sides signed a Protocol augmenting existing civil air relations between the USA and the USSR providing for direct air services between Washington and Moscow and New York and Leningrad, increasing the frequency of flights and resolving other questions in the field of civil aviation.

In the context of reviewing prospects for futher and more permanent economic cooperation, both Sides expressed themselves in favor of mutually advantageous long term projects. They discussed a number of specific projects involving the participation of American companies, including the delivery of Siberian natural gas to the United States. The President indicated that the USA encourages American firms to work out concrete proposals on these projects and will give serious and sympathetic consideration to proposals that are in the interest of both Sides.

To contribute to expanded commercial, cultural and technical relations between the USA and the USSR, the two Sides signed a tax convention to avoid double taxation on income and eliminate, as much as possible, the need for citizens of one country to become involved in the tax system of the other.

A Protocol was also signed on the opening by the end of October 1973 of a Trade Representation of the USSR in Washington and a Commercial Office of the United States in Moscow. In addition a Protocol was signed on questions related to establishing a US-Soviet Chamber of Commerce. These agreements will facilitate the further development of commercial and economic ties between the USA and the USSR.

V. Further Progress in Other Fields of Bilateral Cooperation

The two Sides reviewed the areas of bilateral cooperation in such fields as environmental protection, public health and medicine, exploration of outer space, and science and technology, established by the agreements signed in May 1972 and subsequently. They noted that those agreements are being satisfactorily carried out in practice in accordance with the programs as adopted.

In particular, a joint effort is under way to develop effective means to combat those diseases which are most widespread and dangerous for mankind: cancer, cardiovascular or infectious diseases and arthritis. The medical aspects of the environmental problems are also subjects of cooperative research.

Preparations for the joint space flight of the Apollo and Soyuz spacecraft are proceeding according to an agreed timetable. The joint flight of these spaceships for a rendezvous and docking mission, and mutual visits of American and Soviet astronauts in each other's spacecraft, are scheduled for July 1975.

Building on the foundation created in previous agreements, and recognizing the potential of both the USA and the USSR to undertake cooperative measures in current scientific and technological areas, new projects for fruitful joint efforts were identified and appropriate agreements were concluded.

Peaceful Uses of Atomic Energy. Bearing in mind the great importance of satisfying the growing energy demands in both countries and throughout the world, and recognizing that the development of highly efficient energy sources could contribute to the solution of this problem, the President and General Secretary signed an agreement to expand and strengthen cooperation in the fields of controlled nuclear fusion, fast breeder reactors, and research on the fundamental properties of matter. A Joint Committee on Cooperation in the Peaceful Uses of Atomic Energy will be established to implement this agreement, which has a duration of ten years.

Agriculture. Recognizing the importance of agriculture in meeting mankind's requirement for food products and the role of science in modern agricultural production, the two Sides concluded an agreement providing for a broad exchange of scientific experience in agricultural research and development, and of information on agricultural economics . A US-USSR Joint Committee on Agricultural Cooperation will be established to oversee joint programs to be carried out under the Agreement.

World Ocean Studies. Considering the unique capabilities and the major interest of both nations in the field of world ocean studies, and noting the extensive experience of US-USSR oceanographic cooperation, the two Sides have agreed to broaden their cooperation and have signed an agreement to this effect. In so doing, they are convinced that the benefits from further development of cooperation in the field of oceanography will accrue not only bilaterally but also to all peoples of the world. A US-USSR Joint Committee on Coperation in World Ocean Studies will be established to coordinate the implementation of cooperative programs.

Transportation. The two Sides agreed that there are opportunities for cooperation between the USA and the USSR in the solution of problems in the field of transportation. To permit expanded, mutually beneficial cooperation in this field, the two Sides concluded an agreement on this subject. The USA and the USSR further agreed that a Joint Committee on Cooperation in Transportation would be established.

Contacts, Exchanges and Cooperation. Recognizing the general expansion of US-USSR bilateral relations and, in parti-

cular, the growing number of exchanges in the fields of science, technology, education and culture, and in other fields of mutual interest, the two Sides agreed to broaden the scope of these activities under a new General Agreement on Contacts, Exchanges, and Cooperation, with a duration of six years. The two Sides agreed to this in the mutual belief that it will further promote better understanding between the peoples of the United States and the Soviet Union and will help to improve the general state of relations between the two countries.

Both Sides believe that the talks at the highest level, which were held in a frank and constructive spirit, were very valuable and made an important contribution to developing mutually advantageous relations between the USA and the USSR. In the view of both Sides, these talks will have a favorable impact on international relations.

They noted that the success of the discussions in the United States was facilitated by the continuing consultation and contacts as agreed in May 1972. They reaffirmed that the practice of consultation should continue. They agreed that further meetings at the highest level should be held regularly.

Having expressed his appreciation to President Nixon for the hospitality extended during the visit to the United States, General Secretary Brezhnev invited the President to visit the USSR in 1974. The invitation was accepted.

June 24, 1973

RICHARD NIXON

PRESIDENT OF THE
UNITED STATES
AMERICA

LEONID I. BREZHNEV

GENERAL SECRETARY OF THE
CENTRAL COMMITTEE, CPSU

BREZHNEV ADDRESS

Following is the White House text of a June 24 address by Soviet Communist Party Secretary Leonid I. Brezhnev to the American people. The address was broadcast on nationwide radio and television.

Dear Americans:

I highly appreciate this opportunity of directly addressing the people of the United States on my visit to your country.

I would like, first of all, to convey to all of you the greetings and friendly feelings of millions of Soviet people who are following with great interest my visit to your country and our talks with President Nixon, and who are looking forward to this new Soviet-American summit meeting making a fruitful contribution to better relations between our countries and stronger universal peace.

Our discussions with President Nixon and other United State Government officials have been going on for several days, and they have been very intensive indeed. We came to this country anticipating that these would be responsible negotiations devoted to major questions bearing on the development of Soviet-American relations and to a search for ways in which our two nations could promote the further envigoration of the entire international atmosphere. Today I have every reason to say that those hopes were justified. We are satisfied with the way the talks went and with the results already achieved. New agreements have been signed in Washington, and in many respects they broaden the sphere of peaceful and mutually advantageous cooperation between the United States of America and the Union of Soviet Socialist Republics. Another big step has been taken along the path that we jointly mapped out a year ago during our meeting in Moscow.

Let me say frankly that personally I am also pleased that this visit has given me an opportunity to gain some first-hand impressions of America, to see some aspects of the American way of life, to meet with prominent government and public leaders of your country and to have some contact with the life of Americans.

You are well aware that, in the past, relations between our countries developed very unevenly. There were periods of stagnation, there were ups and downs. But I guess I would not be making a mistake if I said that the significance of good relations between the Soviet Union and the United States has always been quite clear to the more farsighted statesmen. In this connection we have good reason to recall that this is the year of the fortieth anniversary of the establishment of diplomatic relations between our countries on the initiative of President Franklin D. Roosevelt.

In World War II the Soviet Union and the United States became allies and fought side by side against nazism, which threatened the freedom of nations and civilization itself. The jubilant meeting of Soviet and American soldier on the Elbe River at the hour of victory over Hitlerism is well remembered in our country.

The wartime alliance could have been expected to usher in a new era of broad peaceful cooperation between the Soviet Union and the United States. I can tell you with confidence that that is what our country wanted. We wanted to cement and develop the good relations whose foundations had been laid during the war.

Things went differently, however. What came was not peace, but the "cold war," a poor substitute for genuine peace. For a long time it poisioned relations between our countries, an international relations as a whole. Some of its dismal influence can unfortunately be felt in certain things to this day.

Under the circumstances, it was no easy task indeed to make a turn from mutual distrust to detente, normalization and mutually advantageous cooperation. It took courage and political foresight, it took a lot of painstaking work. We appreciate the fact that President Nixon and his Administration joined their efforts with ours to really put Soviet-American relations on a new track.

'Win the Peace'

I have heard that the American political vocabulary includes the expression, "to win the peace." The present moment in history is, I believe, perhaps the most suitable occasion to use that expression. We jointly won the war. Today our joint efforts must help mankind win a durable peace. The possibility of a new war must be eliminated.

The outcome of the two meetings between the leaders of the Soviet Union and the United States and the practical steps taken in the intervening year convincingly show that important results have already been attained. It transpired that a reasonable and mutually acceptable approach to many problems, which previously seemed insoluable, can in fact be found. Not so long ago I suppose it would have been hard even to imagine the possibility of such progress.

Last year's agreements are, on the whole, being successfully implemented. Tangible progress is being made in almost all spheres—and it is a progress secured through joint efforts. The inauguration of a regular passenger shipping line between Leningrad and New York, the establishment of Consulates General in Leningrad and San Francisco, the intiation of friendly ties between Soviet and American cities, and livelier athletic exchanges are all becoming part of the daily lives of the peoples of our two countries today.

The best possible evidence that Soviet-American relations are moving ahead, and not marking time, is provided by the important document signed the other day by President Nixon and myself, the Agreement between the Soviet Union and the United States on the Prevention of Nuclear War. I trust I will not be accused of making an overstatement, if I say that this document is one of historic significance.

Nuclear Agreement

The Union of Soviet Socialist Republics and the United States of America have concluded an agreement to prevent the outbreak of nuclear war between themselves and to do their utmost to prevent the outbreak of nuclear war generally. It is surely clear how important this is for the peace and tranquility of the peoples of our two countries and for the improvement of the prospects for a peaceful life for all mankind.

Even if our second meeting with the President of the United States yielded no other results, it could still be said with full grounds that it will take a fitting place in the annals of Soviet-American relations and in international affairs as a whole. The entire world can now see that, having signed last year the fundamental document entitled "Basic Principles of Relations between the Union of Soviet Socialist Republics and the United States of America," our two nations regard it not as a mere declaration of good intent but as a program of vigorous and consistent action, a program they have already begun to implement, and one which they are determined to go on implementing.

It is also of no little significance that our countries have agreed on the main principles of further work to prepare a new agreement on strategic arms limitation, a broader one this time and of far longer duration. This means that the exceptionally important job begun in May 1972 in Moscow is continuing. It means that political detente is being backed up by military detente. And this is something from which all the peoples and the very cause of peace stand to gain.

The other day representatives of our two Governments also signed new agreements on Soviet-American cooperation in several specific fields. Together the earlier agreements concluded during the past year, they make up an impressive file of documents on cooperation between our two nations and our two great peoples in some widely ranging fields: from the peaceful uses of atomic energy to agriculture, and from outer space to the ocean depths.

Economic Ties

Of course, the Soviet Union and the United States are countries which are, so to speak, self-sufficient. Until recently that was, in fact, how things were in our relations. However, we, as well as many Americans, realize only too well that renunciation of cooperation in the economic, scientific, technological and cultural fields is tantamount to both sides turning down substantial extra benefits and advantages. And, most important, such a renunciation would be so pointless as to defy any reasonable argument. This is particularly true of economic ties. Today, I believe, both you and we would agree that in this area it is not enough simply to overcome such an anomaly generated by the "cold war" as the complete freezing of Soviet-American trade. Life poses questions of far greater importance. I have in mind, above all, such forms of economic relations as stable large-scale ties in several branches of the economy and long-term scientific and technological cooperation, and in our age this is very important. The contacts we have had with American officials and businessmen confirm that it is along these lines that the main prospects for further economic cooperation between our countries can be traced.

It is alleged at times that the development of such cooperation is one-sided and only benefits the Soviet Union. But those who say so are either completely ignorant of the real state of affairs or deliberately turn a blind eye to the truth.

And the truth is that broader and deeper economic cooperation in general, and the long-term and large-scale deals, which are now either being negotiated or have already been successfully concluded by Soviet organizations and American firms, are bound to yield real and tangible benefits to both sides. This is something that has been confirmed quite definitely by American businessmen whom I have had an opportunity to talk with both in this country and, earlier, in Moscow. It was in that context that we discussed the matter with President Nixon, too.

To this I would like to add that both the Soviet leadership and, as I see it, the United States Government attach particular importance to the fact that the development of long-term economic cooperation will also have very beneficial political consequences. It will consolidate the present trend toward better Soviet-American relations generally.

Prospects for the broad development of Soviet-American exchanges in culture and the arts are, as we see it, also good. Both our countries have much to share in this field. To live at peace, we must trust each other, and to trust each other, we must know each other better. We, for our part, want Americans to visualize our way of life and our way of thinking as completely and correctly as possible.

By and large, we can say that quite a lot has already been done to develop Soviet-American relations. Yet we are still only at the beginning of a long road. Constant care is needed to preserve and develop the new shoots of good relationships. Tireless efforts are needed to define the most essential and most suitable forms of cooperation in various fields. Patience is needed to understand the various specific features of the other side and to learn to do business with each other.

Radical Improvement

I believe those who support a radical improvement in relations between the Soviet Union and the United States can look to the future with optimism for this objective meets the vital interests of both our nations and the interests of peaceloving people all over the world.

The general atmosphere in the world depends to no small extent on the climate prevailing in relations between our two countries. Neither economic or military might nor international prestige give our countries any special privileges but they do invest them with special responsibility for the destinies of universal peace and for preventing war. In its approach to ties and contacts with the United States, the Soviet Union is fully aware of that responsibility.

We regard the improvement of Soviet-American relations not as an isolated phenomenon, but as an integral—and very important—part of the wider process of radically improving the international atmosphere. Mankind has outgrown the rigid "cold war" armor which it was once forced to wear. It wants to breathe freely and peacefully. And we will be happy if our efforts to better Soviet-American relations help draw more and more nations into the process of detente—be it in Europe or Asia, in Africa or Latin America, in the Middle or the Far East.

We regard it as a very positive fact that the normalization of Soviet-American relations is contributing to the solution of the great and important problem of consolidating peace and security in Europe and of convening the all-European conference.

The improvement of Soviet-American relations undoubtedly played its useful role in promoting the termination of the long drawn-out war in Vietnam. Now that the agreement ending the Vietnam war has come into effect and both our countries, together with other nations are signatories to the document of the Paris Conference on Vietnam, it seems to us to be particularly important that the achieved success be consolidated and that all the peoples of Indochina be given the chance to live in peace.

There still exist hotbeds of dangerous tension in the world. In our discussions with President Nixon we touched upon the situation in the Middle East, which is still very acute. We belive that in that area justice should be assured as soon as possible and a stable peace settlement reached that would restore the legitimate rights of those who suffered from the war and ensure the security of all the peoples of that region. This is important for all the peoples of the Middle East, with no exception. It is also important for the maintenance of universal peace.

In short, the ending of conflicts and the prevention of new crisis-fraught situations is an essential condition for creating truly reliable guarantees of peace. And our two countries are called upon to make a worthy contribution to that cause. In our discussions President Nixon and I have devoted a great deal of attention to these matters.

I would like to emphasize at this point that in discussing questions of our bilateral relations and international problems of a general nature we invariably took into account the fact that both the Soviet Union and the United States have their own allies and their own obligations toward various other states. It should be stated quite definitely that our talks, both in their spirit and in the letter of the signed agreements, fully take that fact into consideration.

But the main purport of all that we discussed and agreed upon with President Nixon in the field of international affairs is the firm determination of both sides to make good relations between the USSR and the USA a permanent factor of international peace.

Knowing War

In our time—and I am sure you know this—there are still too many people who would rather make noise about military preparations and the arms race, than discuss problems of detente and peaceful cooperation in a constructive spirit.

What can be said on that account?

The Soviet people are perhaps second to none when it comes to knowing what war means. In World War II we won a victory of world-historic significance. But in that war over 20 million Soviet citizens died. 70,000 of our towns and villages were devastated and one-third of our national wealth was destroyed.

The war wounds have now been healed. Today the Soviet Union is a mightier and more prosperous country than ever before. But we remember the lessons of the war only too well, and that is why the peoples of the Soviet Union value peace so highly, that is why they strongly approve the peace policy of our Party and government.

For us peace is the highest achievement to which all men should strive if they want to make their life a worthy one. We believe in reason, and we feel that this belief is shared also by the peoples of the United States and of other nations. If that belief were lost, or if it were obscured by a blind faith in strength alone, in the power of nuclear arms or some other kind of weapon, the fate of civilization—of humanity itself—would be miserable indeed.

Russian Goals

Our path has not been an easy one. Our people are proud that in a historically short period of time, after the victory of the Socialist Revolution, backward Russia transformed itself into a major industrial power and achieved outstanding successes in science and culture. We take pride in having built a new society—a most stable and confidently developing society—which has assured all our citizens of social justice and has made the values of modern civilization the property of all the people. We are proud that dozens of previously oppressed nations and nationalities in our country have become geninely equal, and that in our close-knit family of nations they are developing their economy and culture.

We have great plans for the future. We want to raise considerably the living standards of the Soviet people. We want to make new advances in education and medicine. We want to make our villages and towns more comfortable to live in and more beautiful. We have drafted programs to develop the remote areas of Siberia, the North and the Far East, with their immense natural resources. And every Soviet individual is deeply conscious of the fact that the realization of those plans requires peace and peaceful cooperation with other nations.

Of course, like any other country, we have quite a few problems and quite a few shortcomings. But the solution to all the problems we face requires, as in the case of other nations, not war or an artificial fanning of tensions, but peace and creative labor, which, we are convinced, are the only things that can guarantee well-being and abundance of material and spiritual benefits for all members of society.

I have attempted to give a brief account of the thoughts and plans of the Soviet people and to explain the nature of the Soviet Union's foreign policy. Its peaceful essence stems from the very core of our society. And it is by no mere chance that the very concept of peaceful coexistence, which today is turning more and more into a universally recognized basis for the development of relations between states with different social systems, was evolved by Vladimir Ilylch Lenin, the founder of the Soviet state.

You probably know that two years ago the twenty-fourth Congress of our ruling party, the Communist Party of the Soviet Union, approved the Soviet Peace Program, which is a concrete embodiment of the policy of peaceful coexistence in modern conditions. It is a program of active contribution to international detente and to securing a truly lasting peace on Earth for many generations to come. It expresses not only the convictions and intentions of our people but also, we are sure, the aspirations of millions and millions of peace-loving people all over the world. We are implementing this program, working hand in hand with our friends and allies, the socialist countries. On the basis of this program we seek to build relations of good will and mutually beneficial cooperation with all countries that have a similar desire. And the improvement of Soviet-American relations occupies its rightful place in that program.

Insufficient Time

The importance and complexity of the problems on the agenda of our talks with President Nixon, of our meeting and discussions with members of the Senate Foreign Relations Committee, headed by Senator Fulbright, and with prominent representatives of the American business community, called for a tight work schedule on this visit.

As I have already pointed out, these were fruitful discussions held in a good atmosphere. This gives us a feeling of satisfaction.

At the same time, I do personally regret that the extreme pressure of business has not given me and my colleagues who accompanied me and took part in our work a chance to see more of your country. While still in Moscow, and then here, in the United States, I received many warm letter from various American cities, organizations, companies and private citizens kindly inviting me to visit this or that town, to see plants, farms and universities, or to be a guest in the homes of Americans. I am taking this opportunity to express my sincere gratitude to all those who wrote such letters. I regret that, for the reasons I have just mentioned, I was unable to take up those invitations.

Of course, it would have been interesting to visit New York, and Chicago, and Detroit and Los Angeles, to see some of your industrial projects and farms, to talk to American working people, whose achievements are admired by Soviet people. Perhaps the future will offer such an opportunity, especially since President Nixon and I have definitely agreed that in the future our contacts will be placed on a regular footing. We are looking forward to President Nixon's visit to the Soviet Union next year.

But even though this brief visit did not give me a chance to see as much as I would like to in America, I nevertheless have every reason, when I return home, to tell my colleagues and all Soviet people both about the important political results of the visit and about the atmosphere of good will, and the trend in favor of peace, of detente, and of improving relations between our two countries. It is a trend which we felt during our stay in the United States and during our contacts with government and public leaders of our country, and with many American citizens. I can assure you that these feelings are fully shared by Soviet people.

I do not believe I will be divulging a major secret if I tell you that in my talks with President Nixon over the last few days we not only addressed ourselves to current political problems but also tried to look ahead and to take into account the future interests of the peoples of both our countries. In so doing we proceeded from the assumption that in politics, those who do not look ahead will inevitably find themselves in the rear, among the stragglers. A year ago in Moscow we laid the foundation for improving Soviet-American relations. Now this great and important objective has been successfully brought closer. It

is our hope that this trend will continue, for it meets the interests of our two great peoples and of all mankind.

In conclusion, I want to express my sincere gratitude to the American people, to the President and the Government of the United States for their hospitality, for their kindness and numerous expressions of warm feelings toward the Soviet people and us, their representatives.

Dear Americans, pleace accept my wishes for well-being and happiness to all of you.

Thank you.   ✓

NUCLEAR WAR AGREEMENT

Following is the White House text of a June 22 agreement between the United States and the Soviet Union on the prevention of nuclear war.

The United States of America and the Union of Soviet Socialist Republics, hereinafter referred to as the Parties,

Guided by the objectives of strengthening world peace and international security,

Conscious that nuclear war would have devastating consequences for mankind,

Proceeding from the desire to bring about conditions in which the danger of an outbreak of nuclear war anywhere in the world would be reduced and ultimately eliminated,

Proceeding from their obligations under the Charter of the United Nations regarding the maintenance of peace, refraining from the threat or use of force, and the avoidance of war, and in conformity with the agreements to which either Party has subscribed,

Proceeding from the Basic Principles of Relations between the United States of America and the Union of Soviet Socialist Republics signed in Moscow on May 29, 1972,

Reaffirming that the development of relations between the United States of America and the Union of Soviet Socialist Republics is not directed against other countries and their interests,

Have agreed as follows:

ARTICLE I

The United States and the Soviet Union agree that an objective of their policies is to remove the danger of nuclear war and of the use of nuclear weapons.

Accordingly, the Parties agree that they will act in such a manner as to prevent the development of situations capable of causing a dangerous exacerbation of their relations, as to avoid military confrontations, and as to exclude the outbreak of nuclear war between them and between either of the Parties and other countries.

ARTICLE II

The Parties agree, in accordance with Article I and to realize the objective stated in that Article, to proceed from the premise that each Party will refrain from the threat or use of force against the other Party, against the allies of the other Party and against other countries, in circumstances which may endanger international peace and security. The Parties agree that they will be guided by these considerations in the formulation of their foreign policies and in their actions in the field of international relations.

ARTICLE III

The Parties undertake to develop their relations with each other and with other countries in a way consistent with the purposes of this Agreement.

ARTICLE IV

If at any time relations between the Parties or between either Party and other countries appear to involve the risk of a nuclear conflict, or if relations between countries not parties to this Agreement appear to involve the risk of nuclear war between the United States of America and the Union of Soviet Socialist Republics or between either Party and other countries, the United States and the Soviet Union, acting in accordance with the provisions of this Agreement, shall immediately enter into urgent consultations with each other and make every effort to avert this risk.

ARTICLE V

Each Party shall be free to inform the Security Council of the United Nations, the Secretary General of the United Nations and the Governments of allied or other countries of the progress and outcome of consultations initiated in accordance with Article IV of this Agreement.

ARTICLE VI

Nothing in this Agreement shall affect or impair:

(a) the inherent right of individual or collective self-defense as envisaged by Article 51 of the Charter of the United Nations,

(b) the provisions of the Charter of the United Nations, including those relating to the maintenance or restoration of international peace and security, and

(c) the obligations undertaken by either Party towards its allies or other countries in treaties, agreements, and other appropriate documents.

ARTICLE VII

This Agreement shall be of unlimited duration.

ARTICLE VIII

This Agreement shall enter into force upon signature.

Done at Washington on June 22, 1973, in two copies, each in the English and Russian languages, both texts being equally authentic.

For the United States of America:
Richard Nixon
President of the United States of America

For the Union of Soviet Socialist Republics:
L. I. Brezhnev
General Secretary of the Central Committee, CPSU

OFFENSIVE ARMS LIMITATION

Following is the White House text of the agreement signed June 21 by President Nixon and Communist Party General Secretary Leonid I. Brezhnev concerning the limitation of strategic offensive weapons.

The President of the United States of America, Richard Nixon, and the General Secretary of the Central Committee of the CPSU, L. I. Brezhnev,

Having thoroughly considered the question of the further limitation of strategic arms, and the progress already achieved in the current negotiations,

Reaffirming their conviction that the earliest adoption of further limitations of strategic arms would be a major contribution in reducing the danger of an outbreak of nuclear war and in strengthening international peace and security,

Have agreed as follows:

First. The two Sides will continue active negotiations in order to work out a permanent agreement on more complete measures on the limitation of strategic offensive arms, as well as their subsequent reduction, proceeding from the Basic Principles of Relations between the United States of America and the Union of Soviet Socialist Republics signed in Moscow on May 29, 1972, and from the Interim Agreement between the United States of America and the Union of Soviet Socialist Republics of May 26, 1972 on Certain Measures with Respect to the Limitation of Strategic Offensive Arms.

Over the course of the next year the two Sides will make serious efforts to work out the provisions of the permanent agreement on more complete measures on the limitation of strategic offensive arms with the objective of signing it in 1974.

Second. New agreements on the limitation of strategic offensive armaments will be based on the principles of the American-Soviet documents adopted in Moscow in May 1972 and the agreements reached in Washington in June 1973; and in particular, both Sides will be guided by the recognition of each other's equal security interests and by the recognition that efforts to obtain unilateral advantage, directly or indirectly, would be inconsistent with the strengthening of peaceful relations between the United States of America and the Union of Soviet Socialist Republics.

Third. The limitations placed on strategic offensive weapons can apply both to their quantitative aspects as well as to their qualitative improvement.

Fourth. Limitations on strategic offensive arms must be subject to adequate verification by national technical means.

Fifth. The modernization and replacement of strategic offensive arms would be permitted under conditions which will be formulated in the agreements to be concluded.

Sixth. Pending the completion of a permanent agreement on more complete measures of strategic offensive arms limitation, both Sides are prepared to reach agreements on separate measures to supplement the existing Interim Agreement of May 26, 1972.

Seventh. Each Side will continue to take necessary organizational and technical measures for preventing accidental or unauthorized use of nuclear weapons under its control in accordance with the Agreement of September 30, 1971 between the United States of America and the Union of Soviet Socialist Republics.

Washington, June 21, 1973

For the United States of America:
Richard Nixon
President of the United States of America

For the Union of Soviet Socialist Republics:
L. I. Brezhnev
General Secretary of the Central Committee, CPSU ✓

ENERGY POLICY OFFICE

Following are the White House texts of President Nixon's June 29 statement on the energy crisis and the June 29 executive order establishing an Energy Policy Office.

One of the most critical problems on America's agenda today is to meet our vital energy needs.

Two months ago I announced a comprehensive program to move us forward in that effort. Today I am taking the following additional measures:

First, I am appointing John A. Love, Governor of Colorado, to direct a new energy office that will be responsible for formulating and coordinating energy policies at the Presidential level.

Second, I am asking the Congress to create a new Cabinet-level department devoted to energy and natural resources and a new independent Energy Research and Development Administration.

Third, I am initiating a $10 billion program for research and development in the energy field, which will extend over the next five years.

Finally, I am launching a conservation drive to reduce anticipated personal consumption of energy resources across the Nation by 5 percent over the next twelve months. The Federal Government will take the lead in this effort, by reducing its anticipated consumption by 7 percent during this same period.

America faces a serious energy problem. While we have only 6 percent of the world's population, we consume one-third of the world's energy output. The supply of domestic energy resources available to us is not keeping pace with our ever-growing demand, and unless we act swiftly and effectively, we could face a genuine energy crisis in the foreseeable future.

Progress Since April

On April 18, I submitted a message to the Congress discussing the energy challenge and the steps necessary to meet it. That message emphasized that as we work to conserve our energy demands, we must also undertake an intensive effort to expand our energy supplies. I am happy to report that many of these steps are already underway, and that they are proving effective.

• At least eight oil companies have made firm decisions to undertake significant refinery construction projects. Within the next three years these projects will increase refinery capacity by more than 1.5 million barrels daily—a 10 percent increase over existing capacity.

• We have announced and carried out a voluntary oil allocation program to help provide farmers and essential government and health services, as well as independent refiners and marketers, with an equitable share of available petroleum.

• A great deal of oil from the Outer Continental Shelf and other Federal lands, which has traditionally been retained by the producers, has been allocated to small independent refiners to augment their present supplies. That figure has already reached 100 thousand barrels of oil per day and will increase to 160 thousand by mid-August.

• The Council on Environmental Quality has begun a study of the environmental impact of drilling on the Atlantic Outer Continental Shelf and in the Gulf of Alaska. The study is scheduled for completion by next spring.

• The Senate Committee on Interior and Insular Affairs has reported out legislation which would finally permit the construction of an Alaskan pipeline. Legislation will shortly be reported out in the House of Representatives. Since construction of that pipeline would provide two million barrels of domestic oil a day, I again urge that the Congress give swift approval to this legislation.

• The Office of Energy Conservation and the Office of Energy Data and Analysis have been established at the Department of the Interior. Although not yet fully staffed, they are now beginning to provide information we must have to proceed with our developing energy policy.

• The Commerce Department has proposed regulations covering the labeling of household appliances so that consumers can make comparisons of the efficiency with which the appliances consume energy.

• The Environmental Protection Agency has published information on gasoline mileage for 1973 automobiles.

• The Department of State is taking steps to consult with the major oil-producing nations to develop the cooperative arrangements needed to ensure adequate and stable sources of oil in the future. We are also working closely with the other major oil-consuming nations in studying ways of meeting growing world demand for energy supplies. These include emergency sharing arrangements, as well as stockpile and rationing programs which might lead to more coordinated policies for meeting oil supply shortages should they occur in the future.

Several of the steps which I announced in April were in the form of legislative proposals which will help to increase energy supplies. They called for the Alaskan pipeline, competitive pricing of natural gas, licensing of deepwater ports, streamlining of powerplant siting, and a rational framework for controls over surface mining. Only the pipeline request has been finally acted on in committee. I hope the Congress will now act quickly and favorably on my other requests.

These steps are a beginning. But they are only a beginning.

Reorganization

The acquisition, distribution, and consumption of energy resources have become increasingly complex and increasingly critical to the functioning of our economy and our society. But the organization of the Federal Government to meet its responsibilities for energy and other natural resource policies has not changed to meet the new demands. The Federal Government cannot effectively meet its obligations in these areas under the present organizational structures, and the time has come to change them.

Energy Policy Office

Effective immediately, the duties of the Special Energy Committee and National Energy Office which I set up 2 months ago to advise and assist in the preliminary organizational phases of the Federal response to the energy challenge will be combined in an expanded Energy Policy Office within the Executive Office of the President. This office will be responsible for the formulation and coordination of energy policies at the Presidential level.

This office will be headed by Governor Love, who will be an Assistant to the President as well as Director of the Energy Policy Office. He will spend full time on this assignment and will report directly to me. My Special Consultant on energy matters, Charles DiBona, will continue in his present advisory capacity, working within the new office.

Department of Energy and Natural Resources

Two years ago I sent to the Congress my proposals for a sweeping reorganization of executive departments and independent agencies to provide an executive branch structure more responsive to the basic goals of public policy. One of those proposals called for a Department of Natural Resources.

During the time these proposals have been receiving the consideration of the Congress, my Administration has continued to refine and improve them. It has become increasingly obvious that reorganization is imperative, and nowhere more clearly so than in the areas of natural resources and related energy matters.

I am therefore proposing today the establishment of a new Cabinet-level Department of Energy and Natural Resources, responsible for the balanced utilization and conservation of America's energy and natural resources.

The Department of Energy and Natural Resources would take charge of all of the present activities of the Department of the Interior, except the Office of Coal Research and certain other energy research and development programs, which would be transferred to a new Energy Research and Development Administration. It would also assume the responsibilities of the Forest Service and certain water resources activities of the Soil Conservation Service from the Department of Agriculture; the planning and funding of the civil functions of the Army Corps of Engineers; the duties of the National Oceanic and Atmospheric Administration of the Department of Commerce, the uranium and thorium assessment functions of the Atomic Energy Commission, the functions of the interagency Water Resources Council, and gas pipeline safety functions of the Department of Transportation.

Energy Research and Development Administration

I am further proposing to the Congress that we create an Energy Research and Development Administration.

The new Administration would have central responsibility for the planning, management and conduct of the Government's energy research and development and for working with industry so that promising new technologies can be developed and put promptly to work. The new Administration would be organized to give significant new emphasis to fossil fuels and potential new forms of energy, while also assuring continued progress in developing nuclear power.

In order to create the new Administration, the present functions of the Atomic Energy Commission, except those pertaining to licensing and related regulatory responsibilities, would be transferred to it as would most of the energy research and development programs of the Department of Interior. The scientific and technological resources of the AEC should provide a solid foundation for building a well-conceived and well-executed effort.

Under my proposal, the five-member organization of the AEC would be retained to provide direction for a separate and renamed Nuclear Energy Commission which would carry on the important licensing and regulatory activities now within the AEC. In addition, I have asked that a comprehensive study be undertaken, in full consultation with the Congress, to determine the best way to organize all energy-related regulatory activities of the Government.

Research and Development

While we must rely on conventional forms of fuel to meet our immediate energy needs, it is clear that the answer to our long-term needs lies in developing new forms of energy.

With this necessity in mind, I am taking three steps immediately to enlarge our Federal energy research and development efforts.

First, I am initiating a Federal energy research and development effort of $10 billion over a five-year period, beginning in fiscal year 1975. To give impetus to this drive, I am directing that an additional $100 million in fiscal year 1974 be devoted to the acceleration of certain existing projects and the initiation of new projects in a number of critical research and development areas. At least one-half of the funding for the new initiatives for this coming fiscal year will be devoted to coal research and development with emphasis on producing clean liquid fuels from coal, improving mining techniques to increase coal mining safety and productivity, accelerating our coal gasification program and developing improved combustion systems. The remainder of the $100 million will be for research and development projects on advanced energy conversion systems, environmental control, geothermal steam, conservation, and gas-cooled nuclear reactors. While it is essential that we maintain the present budget ceiling for fiscal year 1974, these vital programs must and can be funded within that ceiling.

Second, I am directing the Chairman of the Atomic Energy Commission to undertake an immediate review of Federal and private energy research and development activities, under the general direction of the Energy Policy Office, and to recommend an integrated energy research and development program for the Nation. This program should encourage and actively involve industry in cooperative efforts to develop and demonstrate new technologies that will permit better use of our energy resources. I am also directing the Chairman, in consultation with the Department of the Interior and other agencies, to recommend by September 1 of this year specific projects to which the additional $100 million would be allocated during fiscal year 1974. By December 1 of this year, I am asking for her recommendations for energy research and development programs which should be included in my fiscal year 1975 budget.

Third, I am establishing an Energy Research and Development Advisory Council reporting to the Energy Policy Office, to be composed of leading experts in various areas of energy research and development from outside the Government.

I feel that these steps will greatly improve and expand our current energy research and development effort and will ensure the development of technologies vital to meeting our future energy needs.

Conservation

The Federal Effort

In my Energy Message of April 18, I announced preliminary steps to conserve America's fuel supplies. I said at that time that while energy conservation is a national necessity, conservation effort could be undertaken on a voluntary basis. I still believe this.

However, public persuasion alone is not sufficient to the challenge confronting us. The Federal Government is the largest consumer of energy in the country and, as such, it has its own unique role to play in reducing energy consumption and thus setting an example for all consumers.

Effective today, I am therefore ordering the Federal Government to achieve a seven percent reduction in its anticipated energy consumption over the next 12 months.

I have directed the heads of all Cabinet departments and other Federal agencies to report by July 31 on the specific steps they will take to meet this target. Secretary Morton will be responsible for monitoring agency efforts and reporting their progress to me.

These conservation measures are to be designed to ensure that no vital services are impaired nor the proper functioning of these departments and agencies curtailed. Exceptions will be permitted only in unique circumstances, such as the program of uranium enrichment at the AEC where a substantial reduction in energy consumption would have a detrimental effect on our efforts to provide new forms of energy.

While the precise means of conserving energy will be left to the discretion of Cabinet and agency heads, I am directing that conservation efforts include the following measures:

• Reduction in the level of air conditioning of all Federal office buildings throughout the summer.

• Reduction in the number of official trips taken by Federal employees.

• Purchase or leasing of automobiles and other vehicles which provide good gasoline mileage.

Each department and agency is expected to review all of its activities to determine how its own demands might be reduced. The Department of Defense, the largest single consumer of energy within the executive branch, has already examined its activities and has taken steps to reduce its energy demands by 10 percent over last year—steps which will in no way jeopardize our military preparedness.

Conservation in the Private Sector

I am also directing all departments and agencies to work closely with Secretary Morton and the Office of Energy Conservation in the development of long-term energy conservation plans and recommendations for both the private and the public sector.

At my request, the Secretary of the Interior, the Secretary of Commerce and Governor Love are to meet with representatives of American industry to discuss ways of cutting back on unnecessary consumption of energy and to urge their active participation in the conservation effort.

Further, I have directed the Secretary of Transportation to work with the Nation's airlines, the Civil Aeronautics Board, and the Federal Aviation Administration to reduce flight speeds, and, where possible, the frequency of commercial air-line flights. This effort is now underway. By effecting only a small reduction in speeds and flights, it is possible to achieve significant reductions in energy consumption.

Placing the Challenge in Perspective

As these measures cover a broad range of activities in the public and private sectors, I want to put both the problem and the proposed conservation measures into perspective. We all need to understand the dimensions of the challenge, as well as the significance of the role every single American has to play in meeting it.

The Department of the Interior estimates that under the conditions of current usage, our available supply of gasoline this summer could fall short of demand by one or two percent and possibly as much as five percent should the most adverse conditions prevail. To overcome this potential shortage, and to reduce pressure on supplies of other energy resources, I am suggesting that a reasonable and attainable national goal is to reduce anticipated energy use by individual consumers by five percent.

We can achieve this goal by making very small alterations in our present living habits, for steps such as those we are taking at the Federal level can be taken with equal effectiveness by private individuals. We need not sacrifice any activities vital to our economy or to our well-being as a people.

Raising the thermostat of an air conditioner by just 4 degrees, for instance, will result in a saving of an estimated 15-20 percent in its use of electricity.

Just as the Government can obtain energy efficient automobiles, private citizens can do the same. Nearly three-quarters of the gasoline used in America is consumed by automobiles.

Those who drive automobiles can also assist by driving more slowly. A car travelling 50 miles per hour uses 20 to 25 percent less gasoline per mile than the same car travelling 70 miles per hour. Carpooling and using public transportation will result in further fuel savings.

In order to help reduce driving speeds, I am today taking the additional step of writing to each of the Nation's Governors, asking them to work with their State legislatures to reduce highway speed limits in a manner consistent with safety and efficiency, as well as with energy needs.

I also continue to urge the Congress to pass highway-mass transit legislation which would provide States and localities flexibility to choose between capital investment in highways or mass transit. Diversion of some commuter traffic from single occupant automobiles to mass transit will result in significant energy and environmental benefits, and at the same time, permit the highways to be operated in the efficient manner for which they were designed.

Energy conservation is not just sound policy for the country, it is also good economics for the consumer.

Changing to a more efficient automobile, for example, could produce savings of as much as one thousand gallons of gas in the course of a year. A savings of one thousand gallons of gas equals a personal savings of approximately $400.

Cutting down on air conditioning and heating, of course, also cuts down on the family gas or electric or oil bill.

Actions to reduce the rate of growth in energy demands will also improve our ability to protect and improve the quality of our environment.

The conservation of existing energy resources is not a proposal; it is a necessity. It is a requirement that will remain with us indefinitely, and it is for this reason that I believe that the American people must develop an energy conservation ethic.

As a matter of simple prudence and common sense, we must not waste our resources, however abundant they may seem. To do otherwise, in a world of finite resources, reflects adversely upon what we are as a people and a Nation.

Conclusion

We face a challenge in meeting our energy needs. In the past, the American people have viewed challenges as an opportunity to improve our Nation, and to move forward. The steps I have outlined above are not meant to be conclusive. They are part of the ongoing process.

I urge the Congress to act with due concern for our energy needs by rapid consideration of all of my legislative proposals in this field, especially my request to clear the way for the Alaskan pipeline.

Over the coming years it is essential that we increase our supplies of energy.

I urge the members of the Federal Government to play their role in meeting the spirit and the letter of my energy-conservation directives.

I urge private industry to respond with all the imagination and resourcefulness that has made this Nation the richest on earth.

But the final question of whether we can avoid an energy crisis will be determined by the response of the American people to their country's needs. In the past, whenever we have been faced with real challenges, the American people have joined together to share in the common interest.

I am confident we will do so now.   ✓

EXECUTIVE ORDER

By virtue of the authority vested in me as President of the United States of America, it is hereby ordered as follows:

Energy Policy Office

Section 1. There is hereby established in the Executive Office of the President an Energy Policy Office. The office shall be under the immediate supervision and direction of a Director of the Energy Policy Office who shall be designated or appointed by the President.

Functions of the Director

Sec. 2(a) The Director shall be the Administration's chief policy officer with respect to energy matters, and shall be the President's principal adviser concerning those matters.

(b) The Director shall also be responsible for—

(1) identifying major problems, present and prospective, in the energy areas;

(2) making policy recommendations to the President with respect to energy matters;

(3) working with executive branch agencies and outside groups in reviewing policy alternatives with respect to energy matters;

(4) reviewing, commenting on, and making separate recommendations on all other energy-related matters which require Presidential attention;

(5) insuring that executive branch agencies develop short- and long-range plans for dealing with energy matters;

(6) monitoring the implementation of approved energy policies with the assistance of the Office of Management and Budget;

(7) providing guidance and direction to the Oil Policy Committee and its Chairman in the performance of its functions;

(8) providing advice to the Cost of Living Council concerning energy matters;

(9) assuring the development of comprehensive plans and programs to assure the availability of adequate and dependable supplies of energy; and

(10) initiating studies to be carried out by the appropriate Government agencies.

Support

Sec. 3(a). Necessary expenses of the Energy Policy Office may be paid from the Emergency Fund of the President or from such other funds as may be available.

(b) The Administrator of General Services shall provide, on a reimbursable basis, such administrative support as may be needed by the Energy Policy Office.

(c) All departments and agencies of the executive branch shall, to the extent permitted by law, provide assistance and information to the Director of the Energy Policy Office.

Sec. 4. The Director of the Energy Policy Office shall make a report to the President, for transmission to the Congress, no later than March 15, 1974, concerning actions that have been taken and actions that should be taken to carry out the purposes of this order.

Supersedure

Sec. 5. Executive Order No. 11712 of April 18, 1973, is hereby superseded and the Special Committee on Energy and the National Energy Office are hereby abolished.

RICHARD NIXON

TEXT OF ECONOMY SPEECH

Following is the White House text of President Nixon's June 30 radio address to the nation on the economy.

Eighteen days ago, I ordered a freeze on prices and announced that this freeze would be followed by a new and stronger set of controls to check inflation.

Today I want to report to you on some of the progress we have made and some of the problems we face.

First, I am pleased to be able to report that Americans generally are cooperating in making the freeze a success. Prices are being held. We are determined that prices will continue to be held.

In terms of long-range stability, however, what is important is not the freeze itself, but what follows it. We might look at the measures we take as being short-term, medium-term and long-term.

Phase IV

The freeze is a short-term measure. Phase IV is a medium-term measure. The more fundamental adjustments and disciplines we are undertaking are long-term measures.

During these past 2-1/2 weeks, we have been putting the freeze machinery in place, and at the same time holding an intensive series of consultations with persons both inside and outside the Government on the design of Phase IV.

By the arbitrariness of its nature, a freeze is bound to create certain inequities. It can also add to the problems of scarcity. We have seen this, for example, in the fact that some broiler producers have had to kill off baby chicks because they could not afford to pay the high feed prices and still sell the broilers at their ceiling prices.

For this reason, we have been determined from the outset to keep the freeze as short as possible. For this reason, also, the Cost of Living Council is taking a hard and continuing look at the problems created by the freeze. These are being monitored closely by teams from the Department of Agriculture and the Department of Commerce. We want to make sure that the freeze is not administered in such a way as to be counter-productive, while recognizing that to be successful it must be rigorous.

Some have asked why we needed the freeze; why, with all the experience we have had with Phase II and Phase III, we could not simply have announced the new rules for Phase IV and put them into effect immediately.

One reason for the freeze was to stop what were becoming runaway price rises in a number of basic items, which in turn were beginning to create inflationary expectations that could have undermined our whole effort to stabilize the price structure.

Beyond this, however, it was vital that we have genuine consultations with a wide range of interested parties before launching Phase IV. Economic conditions are very different today from those of the earlier periods; the rules of Phase IV will, therefore, have to be different. If these consultations had gone forward without a freeze, it would have been an open invitation to push prices up in anticipation of the new rules.

The freeze provides time in which we can hold these consultations, as part of designing a new Phase IV that will be comprehensive and realistic, that will command the support needed to make it a success, and that will provide a basis for returning to free markets.

In recent days, my consumer affairs adviser, Virginia Knauer, has been meeting with the consumer groups; the Council of Economic Advisers has been meeting with professional economists; and we have been in continuing discussion with business and labor leaders. Tomorrow, the Director of the Cost of Living Council, Dr. John Dunlop, is meeting in San Francisco with key executives of the food, paper, electronics and other industries from the West Coast, and also with consumer representatives. Similar meetings will be held in other regional centers.

Meanwhile, at my instructions, a profit and price check is being run on all companies with annual sales of more than $50 million—a total of 3,100 companies. Any whose price increases since January cannot be justified by cost increases will be required to roll back their prices. The information developed in this "profit sweep" is also providing valuable data for use in designing Phase IV.

Gasoline Prices

Gasoline prices are among those that have caused the greatest concern. A special check by the Cost of Living Council has identified more than 1,000 gas stations that have raised their prices above the levels permitted, and those prices have been rolled back. Holding down the price of gasoline and other fuels requires insuring adequate supplies. Last Friday I announced a number of major additional steps to help meet our energy needs.

I appointed Governor John Love head of a new high-level White House energy office. I asked the Congress to create a new Cabinet department devoted to energy and natural resources, and a new independent Energy Research and Development Administration. I announced a new $10 billion program of energy research and development to extend over the next five years. And I ordered a 7 percent reduction in energy consumption by the Federal Government over the next 12 months.

I have already submitted to the Congress a number of essential proposals to help increase energy supplies and thereby keep prices down. These include the Alaska pipeline, competitive pricing of natural gas, licensing of deepwater ports, streamlining of power plant siting, and a rational framework for controls over surface mining. I again urge quick action by the Congress on these proposals.

For several years now there has been a rapid rate of inflation throughout the Western world. For the year ended in April, consumer prices in the United States rose substantially less than they did in Great Britain, France, West Germany, Canada or Japan. With expanding international trade, these inflationary pressures abroad contribute to the inflationary pressures at home: When prices elsewhere rise, scarce goods chase more profitable markets abroad, rather than being offered in the United States.

Food Prices

Within the past year, our agricultural exports alone have increased by 50 percent, from less than $8 billion to nearly $12 billion. At the same time, the Nation's farmers were suffering in 1972 from some of the worst weather for crops and livestock that America has ever experienced. Output is now rising; prospects for this year are generally good.

For example, the wheat crop this year is expected to be the biggest ever. The many measures we have taken to increase the supply of farm commodities—including the release of more than 40 million additional acres for farm production—will eventually bring more farm products to the market, and will provide relief against high food prices. But meanwhile, we are paying in higher food prices for the combination of limited supply and greater worldwide demand.

Therefore, another key element of the package I announced on June 13th was a request to the Congress for new and more flexible authority to impose export controls on goods that are in short supply in the United States, so that we will not price these out of the American market by sending them abroad in search of higher prices caused by shortages and inflation in other countries.

Acting under existing authority, I have imposed controls on exports of soybean products, which are especially critical to the solution of the feed grain shortage, and therefore to bringing down the price of meat and dairy products. Prices of soybean products have already dropped in response to this action. However, the more flexible authority I have requested from the Congress is still necessary. I again urge swift and urgent action by the Congress to provide this authority.

The problems of scarcity that make these export controls necessary are temporary problems. Therefore, I am confident that the need for export controls on agricultural products will also be only temporary. When this year's crops become available in the fall, we expect to be able to restore international access to these products. During the brief period when controls are necessary, we shall do all that we can to insure that our traditional customers suffer as little as possible, and we shall keep before us our continuing goal of progress toward more international trade, rather than less.

Supplies

There is one point this afternoon more than any other that I want to emphasize: Controls can help in the short run, but in the long run, dependence on controls would destroy the economy and demolish our prosperity.

In the long run, the one thing—and the only thing—that will keep prices down is sufficient supply to meet the demand, coupled with responsible fiscal and monetary policies. Controls will not give us that supply; neither will they substitute for fiscal and monetary discipline.

That is why we have taken vigorous measures to encourage an increase in the supply of key commodities. We have been trying to turn farm policies around; turn them from the old way of keeping farm incomes up by restricting supply and raising prices, to a new policy of keeping farm incomes up, but by increasing supply and expanding markets. We have been trying to sell unnecessary stockpiles of industrial materials more rapidly. We have initiated a trade policy which would enable us to import more of the things others produce most efficiently, while exporting more of the things we produce most efficiently. And we are taking measures to raise productivity.

But whatever we do to increase supplies can be overwhelmed unless we also keep the expansion of demand within sustainable limits. That is why we must sternly resist not only wasteful Government spending, but even worthwhile Government spending that we cannot afford. The battle against higher prices begins with the battle of the Federal budget. I will, therefore, continue to support every move to maintain fiscal responsibility and to resist every move to abandon it.

The Federal Reserve's policy of monetary restraint is also essential in checking inflation. In the short run, this policy may have the effect of raising interest rates. But it is better to have higher interest rates for a while than it would be to have more inflation, and, as a consequence, to have higher interest rates forever.

The object of our policies is not simply to have low prices. We could have low prices and nothing to buy at those prices. The object is to have reasonable prices, and also an abundant supply of goods we can buy. The object is to maintain a stable prosperity at a sustainable rate of growth, so that we can enjoy an increasing abundance with job security. The object is to manage the price and wage control system forcefully, but with the goal of getting out of the controls business, rather than getting permanently enmeshed in it.

The road to full prosperity, without war, and without inflation—something that we have not had in the United States since President Eisenhower was President—is not easy. All of us who have lived through the past 10 years know this very well. But I believe that the American people are determined to reach that goal, and I am determined to use all the means of Government to help us get there.   √

PHASE IV ECONOMIC STATEMENT

Following is the text, as made available by the White House, of President Nixon's July 18 statement announcing Phase IV of the economic stabilization program.

The American people now face a profoundly important decision. We have a freeze on prices which is holding back a surge of inflation that would break out if the controls were removed. At the same time the freeze is holding down production and creating shortages which threaten to get worse, and cause still higher prices, as the freeze and controls continue.

In this situation we are offered two extreme kinds of advice.

One suggestion is that we should accept price and wage controls as a permanent feature of the American economy. We are told to forget the idea of regaining a free economy and set about developing the regulations and bureaucracy for a permanent system of controls.

The other suggestion is to make the move for freedom now, abolishing all controls immediately.

While these suggestions are well meant, and in many cases reflect deep conviction, neither can be accepted. Our wise course today is not to choose one of these extremes but to seek the best possible reconciliation of our interests in slowing down the rate of inflation on the one hand, and preserving American production and efficiency on the other.

The main elements in the policy we need are these:

First, the control system must be tough. It has to hold back and phase in gradually a large part of the built-in pressure for higher prices which already exists in the economy.

Second, the system must be selective. It must permit relaxation of those restraints which interfere most with production, and it must not waste effort on sectors of the economy where stability of prices exists. The control system should also be designed to accommodate the special problems of various sectors of the economy under the strains of high use of capacity.

Third, the system must contain sufficient assurance of its termination at an appropriate time to preserve incentives for investment and production and guard against tendencies for controls to be perpetuated.

Fourth, the control system must be backed up by firm steps to balance the budget, so that excess demand does not regenerate inflationary pressures which make it difficult either to live with the controls or to live without them.

We have had in 1973 an extraordinary combination of circumstances making for rapid inflation. There was a decline of domestic food supplies. The domestic economy boomed at an exceptional pace, generating powerful demand for goods and services. The boom in other countries and the devaluation of the dollar, while desirable from most points of view, raised the prices of things we export or import.

These forces caused a sharp rise of prices in early 1973. The index of consumer prices rose at an annual rate of about 8 per cent from December 1972 to May 1973. The freeze imposed on June 13 put a halt to this rapid rise of prices. But many of the cost increases and demand pressures working to raise prices in the early part of the year had not yet resulted in higher prices by the time the freeze was imposed. Thus a certain built-in pressure for a bulge of price increases awaits the end of the freeze. Moreover, aside from this undigested bulge left over by the freeze, the circumstances causing the sharp price increase in early 1973 will still be present, although not on so large a scale. The demand for goods and services will be rising less rapidly than in the first half of the year. The supply of food will be rising, although not fast enough. Our position in international trade is improving and this will lend strength to the dollar.

All in all, the tendency for prices to rise in the remainder of 1973, a tendency which will either come out in higher prices or be repressed by controls, will be less than in the first half of the year but greater than anyone would like. Particularly, there is no way, with or without controls to prevent a substantial rise of food prices. However, by 1974, we should be able to achieve a much more moderate rate of inflation. By that time, the good feed crops in prospect for this year should have produced a much larger supply of food, and total demand should be rising less rapidly than in 1973.

This more satisfactory situation on the inflation front will be reached if three conditions are met:

First, we do not allow the temporary inflationary forces now confronting us to generate a new wage-price spiral which will continue to run after these temporary forces have passed. To do this we must hold down the expression of those forces in prices and wages.

Second, we do not allow the present controls to damp down 1974 production excessively, a problem that is most obvious in the case of meats and poultry.

Third, we do not permit a continuation or revival of excess demand that will generate new inflationary forces. That is why control of the Federal budget is an essential part of the whole effort.

The steps I am announcing or recommending today are designed to create these conditions.

The Phase IV Controls Program

Our decisions about the new control program have been reached after consulting with all sectors of the American society in over 30 meetings and after studying hundreds of written communications. The advice we received was most helpful and I want to thank all those who provided it.

The Cost of Living Council will describe the Phase IV controls program in detail in statements and regulations. These will take effect at various times between now and September 12. They will include special regulations dealing with the petroleum industry, published for comment. Here I will only review the general features of the program, to indicate its basic firmness and the efforts that have been made to assure that production continues and shortages are avoided.

The controls will be mandatory. The success of the program, however, will depend upon a high degree of voluntary compliance. We have had that in the past. Study of the reports on business behavior during Phase III shows that voluntary compliance was almost universal. Nevertheless, the rules we are now proposing are stricter, and it is only fair to those who will comply voluntarily to assure that there is compulsion for the others.

Except for foods, the freeze on prices will remain in effect until August 12. However, modifications of the freeze rules will be made to relieve its most serious inequities.

The fundamental pricing rule of Phase IV is that prices are permitted to rise as much as costs rise, in dollars per unit of output, without any profit margin on the additional costs. Cost increases will be counted from the end of 1972; cost increases which occurred earlier but had not been reflected in prices may not be passed on. In addition to the cost rule, there remains the previous limitation on profit margins.

Large firms, those with annual sales in excess of $100,000,-000, will be required to notify the Cost of Living Council of intended price increases and may not put them into effect for 30 days. During that period, the Council may deny or suspend the proposed increase.

The wage standards of Phase II and Phase III will remain in force. Notification of wage increases will continue to be required for large employment units.

These are, we recognize, tough rules, in some respects tougher than during Phase II. But the situation is also in many ways more difficult than during Phase II. So long as the system is regarded as temporary, however, we believe that business can continue to prosper, industrial peace can be maintained, and production continue to expand under these rules. Machinery will be established in the Cost of Living Council to consider the need for exceptions from these rules where they may be causing serious injury to the economy. And we will be prepared to consider modification of the rules themselves when that seems necessary or possible.

The Special Case of Food

Nowhere have the dilemmas of price control been clearer than in the case of food. In the early part of this year, rising food prices were the largest part of the inflation problem, statistically and psychologically. If price restraint was needed anywhere, it was needed for food. But since the ceilings were placed on meat prices on March 29, and especially since the freeze was imposed on June 13, food has given the clearest evidence of the harm that controls do to supplies. We have seen baby chicks drowned, pregnant sows and cows, bearing next year's food, slaughtered, and packing plants closed down. This dilemma is no coincidence. It is because food prices were rising most rapidly that the freeze held prices most below their natural level and therefore had the worst effect on supplies.

We must pick our way carefully between a food price policy so rigid as to cut production sharply and to make shortages inevitable within a few months and a food price policy so loose as to give us an unnecessary and intolerable bulge. On this basis we have decided on the following special rules for food:

1. Effective immediately processors and distributors of food, except beef, may increase their prices, on a cents-per-unit basis, to the extent of the increase of costs of raw agricultural products since the freeze base period (June 1-8).
2. Beef prices remain under present ceilings.
3. The foregoing special rules expire on September 12, after which time the same rules that apply to other products will apply to foods.
4. Raw agricultural products remain exempt from price control.

To relieve the extreme high prices of feeds, which have an important effect on prices of meat, poultry, eggs, and dairy products, we have placed limitations on the export of soybeans and related products until the new crop comes into the market. These limitations will remain in effect for that period. But permanent control of exports is not the policy of this Government, and we do not intend at this time to broaden the controls beyond those now in force. To a considerable degree, export controls are self-defeating as an anti-inflation measure. Limiting our exports reduces our foreign earnings, depresses the value of the dollar, and increases the cost of things we import, which also enter into the cost of living of the American family. Moreover, limiting our agricultural exports runs counter to our basic policy of building up our agricultural markets abroad. Unless present crop expectations are seriously disappointed, or foreign demands are extremely large, export controls will not be needed. However, reports of export orders for agricultural commodities will continue to be required. Our policy must always be guided by the fundamental importance of maintaining adequate supplies of food at home.

The stability of the American economy in the months and years ahead demands maximum farm output. I call upon the American farmer to produce as much as he can. There have been reports that farmers have been reluctant to raise livestock because they are uncertain whether Government regulations will permit them a fair return on their investment, and perhaps also because they resent the imposition of ceilings on food prices. I hope that these reports are untrue. In the past year real net income per farm increased 14 per cent, a truly remarkable rise. I can assure the American farmer that there is no intention of the Government to discriminate against him. The rules we are setting forth today should give the farmer confidence that the Government will not keep him from earning a fair return on his investment in providing food.

The Secretary of Agriculture will be offering more specific advice on increasing food production and will be taking several steps to assist, in particular he has decided that there will be no Government set-aside of land in 1974 for feed grains, wheat and cotton.

I am today initiating steps to increase the import of dried skim milk.

When I announced the freeze, I said that special attention would be given, in the post-freeze period, to stabilizing the price of food. That remains a primary objective. But stabilizing the price of food would not be accomplished by low price ceilings and empty shelves, even if the ceilings could be enforced when the shelves are empty. Neither can stabilization be concerned only with a week or a month. The evidence is becoming overwhelming that only if a rise of food prices is permitted now can we avoid shortages and still higher prices later. I hope that the American people will understand this and not be deluded by the idea that we can produce low-priced food out of Acts of Congress or Executive Orders. The American people will continue to be well-fed, at prices which are reasonable relative to their incomes. But they cannot now escape a period in which food prices are higher relative to incomes than we have been accustomed to.

The Process of Decontrol

There is no need for me to reiterate my desire to end controls and return to the free market. I believe that a large proportion of the American people, when faced with a rounded picture of the options, share that desire. Our experience with the freeze has dramatized the essential difficulties of a controlled system—its interference with production, its inequities, its distortions, its evasions, and the obstacles it places in the way of good international relations.

And yet, I must urge a policy of patience. The move to freedom now would most likely turn into a detour, back into a swamp of even more lasting controls. I am impressed by the unanimous recommendation of the leaders of labor and business who constitute the Labor-Management Advisory Committee that the controls should be terminated by the end of 1973. I hope it will be possible to do so and I will do everything in my power to achieve that goal. However, I do not consider it wise to commit ourselves to a specific date for ending all controls at this time.

We shall have to work our way and feel our way out of controls. That is, we shall have to create conditions in which the controls can be terminated without disrupting the economy, and we shall have to move in successive stages to withdraw the controls in parts of the economy where that can be safely done or where the controls are most harmful.

To work our way out of controls means basically to eliminate the excessive growth of total demand which pulls prices up

faster and faster. The main lesson of that is to control the budget, and I shall return to that critical subject below.

But while we are working our way to that ultimate condition in which controls are no longer useful, we must be alert to identify those parts of the economy that can be safely decontrolled. Removing the controls in those sectors will not only be a step towards efficiency and freedom there. It will also reduce the burden of administration, permit administration resources to be concentrated where most needed, and provide an incentive for other firms and industries to reach a similar condition.

During Phase II firms with 60 employees or fewer were exempt from controls. That exemption is now repeated. We are today exempting most regulated public utilities, the lumber industry (where prices are falling), and the price of coal sold under long-term contract. The Cost of Living Council will be studying other sectors for possible decontrol. It will also receive applications from firms or industries that can give assurance of reasonably non-inflationary , behavior without controls. In all cases, of course, the Cost of Living Council will retain authority to reimpose controls.

Balancing the Budget

The key to success of our anti-inflation effort is the budget. If Federal spending soars and the deficit mounts, the control system will not be able to resist the pressure of demand. The most common cause of the breakdown of control systems has been failure to keep fiscal and monetary policy under restraint. We must not let that happen to us.

I am assured that the Federal Reserve will cooperate in the anti-inflation effort by slowing down the expansion of money and credit. But monetary policy should not, and cannot, be expected to exercise the needed restraint alone. A further contribution from the budget is needed.

I propose that we should now take a balanced budget as our goal for the present fiscal year. In the past I have suggested as a standard for the Federal budget that expenditures should not exceed the revenues that would be collected at full employment. We are meeting that standard. But in today's circumstances, that is only a minimum standard of fiscal prudence. When inflationary pressure is strong, when we are forced to emergency controls to resist that pressure, when confidence in our management of our fiscal affairs is low, at home and abroad, we cannot afford to live by that minimum standard. We must take as our goal the more ambitious one of balancing the actual budget.

Achieving that goal will be difficult, more difficult than it seems at first. My original expenditure budget for fiscal 1974 was $268.7-billion. Since that budget was submitted economic expansion, inflation and other factors have raised the estimated revenues to about the level of the original expenditure estimate. However, while that was happening the probable expenditures have also been rising as a result of higher interest rates, new legislation enacted, failure of Congress to act on some of my recommendations, and Congressional action already far advanced but not completed.

It is clear that several billion dollars will have to be cut from the expenditures that are already probable if we are to balance the budget. That will be hard, because my original budget was tight. However, I regard it as essential and pledge myself to work for it.

We should remember that a little over a year ago I set as a goal for fiscal 1973 to hold expenditures within a total of $250 billion. There was much skepticism about that at the time, and suggestions that the number was for political consumption only, to be forgotten after the election. But I meant it, the people endorsed it and the Congress cooperated. I am able to report today that the goal was achieved, and total expenditures for Fiscal Year 1973 were below $249 billion.

I will take those steps that I can take administratively to reach the goal of a balanced budget for Fiscal Year 1974. I shall start by ordering that the number of Federal civilian personnel at the end of Fiscal Year 1974 total below the number now budgeted. The Office of Management and Budget will work with the agencies on this and other reductions. I urge the Congress to assist in this effort, Without its cooperation achievement of the goal cannot be realistically expected.

* * * * *

Despite the difficult conditions and choices we now confront, the American economy is strong. Total production is about 6½ percent above a year ago, employment has risen by 3 million, real incomes are higher than ever. There is every prospect for further increases of output, employment and incomes. Even in the field of inflation our performance is better than in most of the world. So we should not despair of our plight. But we have problems, and they are serious in part because we and the rest of the world expect the highest performance from the American economy. We can do better. And we will, with mutual understanding and the support of the American people.

PHASE IV EXECUTIVE ORDER

Following is the text, as made available by the White House, of President Nixon's July 18 executive order on Phase IV of the economic stabilization program.

On June 13, 1973, I ordered a freeze for a maximum period of 60 days on the prices of all commodities and services offered for sale except the prices charged for raw agricultural products. At that time, I stated that the freeze period would be used to develop a new and more effective system of controls to follow the freeze. Planning for the Phase IV program has proceeded rapidly and I have, therefore, decided that the freeze on food, except for beef, should be removed and more flexible controls substituted in a two-stage process in the food industry. The first stage will be effective at 4:00 p.m., e.s.t., July 18, 1973. The freeze in other sectors of the economy will continue through August 12, 1973. I am also directing the Cost of Living Council to publish for comment now, proposed plans for Phase IV controls in other sectors of the economy. I have determined that this action is necessary to stabilize the economy, reduce inflation, minimize unemployment, improve the Nation's competitive position in world trade and protect the purchasing power of the dollar, all in the context of sound fiscal management and effective monetary policies.

NOW, THEREFORE, by virtue of the authority vested in me by the Constitution and statutes of the United States, particularly the Economic Stabilization Act of 1970, as amended, it is hereby ordered as follows:

Section 1. Executive Order 11723 establishing a freeze on prices effective 9:00 p.m., e.s.t., June 13, 1973, for a maximum period of 60 days is hereby superseded except as herinafter provided. Under the provisions of Executive Order 11695, the freeze regulations issued by the Cost of Living Council, pursuant to the authority of Executive Order 11723 remain in effect except as the Chairman of the Cost of Living Council may modify them. The price freeze established by Executive Order 11723 remains in effect until 11:59 p.m., e.s.t., August 12, 1973, except to the extent the Chairman of the Cost of Living Council may modify it.

Section 2. All orders, regulations, circulars, rulings, notices or other directives issued and all other actions taken by any agency pursuant to Executive Order 11723, and in effect on the date of this order are hereby confirmed and ratified, and shall remain in full force and effect unless or until altered, amended, or revoked by the Chairman of the Cost of Living Council.

Section 3. This order shall not operate to defeat any suit, action, prosecution, or administrative proceeding, whether heretofore or hereafter commenced, with respect to any right possessed, liability incurred, or offense committed prior to this date.

Section 4. Executive Order 11695 continues to remain in full force and effect.

RICHARD NIXON

REMARKS ON ENERGY

Following is a White House text of remarks made by President Nixon to the press Sept. 8 after a meeting with his energy advisers.

THE PRESIDENT: Won't you be seated, ladies and gentlemen.

As you know, we have just completed a two hour meeting in the Cabinet Room of the major Administration officials having responsibilities in the field of energy. Governor Love presided over the meeting at my direction and gave a report with regard to the programs that he has initiated and that had been initiated prior to his taking over this assignment.

I would like to summarize for the members of the press, before having the Governor answer your specific questions in this field, the problem as I see it at this time.

We have heard a lot about a crisis. I do not use that term because we do not face a crisis in that sense of the word. I would simply say that in the short-term we face a problem, a problem with regard to energy, heating, for example, this winter, just as we thought we faced a problem of gasoline this summer, and the possibility of brown-outs.

We are not Pollyannish about solving that problem, but insofar as the short-term problem is concerned, Governor Love has a program which he is working on and one which is designed to meet the problem and to deal with it.

So I would summarize by saying that short-term we face a problem. But long-term, and this is the important thing for us to remember, the prospects for adequate energy for the United States are excellent. I would say the prospects for adequate energy for the United States are as good as they are for any industrial nation in the world and perhaps better, better because of our enormous research capabilities.

This morning we addressed both the short-term problem and the long-term problem and the legislative problem and the administrative problem.

In my press conference a couple of days ago, I mentioned seven pieces of legislation. Today we have moved down to four pieces of legislation that we consider to be of the highest urgency and that must be acted upon before the end of the year. These pieces of legislation deal with both the short-term problem and address themselves particularly, however, to the long-term problem.

One is the Alaska pipeline which is presently in conference and, of course, where the prospects are excellent. The second is the deep water ports. The longer we wait here, the longer we are going to have to wait to have the capacity to bring in the products from abroad that we need to meet our energy needs. The third is the deregulation of gas. This we must act upon now because only through deregulation can the new construction, which is essential, the new construction, the drilling, et cetera, and refineries be undertaken. And the fourth is the legislation with regard to strip mining.

The strip mining legislation, as we know, has elements of controvercy because of conflict with the environmentalists. But Mr. Train was here at the meeting this morning, at our request, and he has been participating in all of these meetings and he believes that the legislation that we have presented to the Congress, properly administered, is one that can be consistent with our environmental goals.

So much for what the Congress should do. These four pieces of legislation the Congress should consider on a high priority basis, because failing to act means that we could have very serious problems, not just this year, but particularly in the years ahead.

The other points that I would make are with regard to what we can do and have done and are doing from an administrative standpoint, that do not require legislation.

One is the relaxation of emission standards. Governor Love is calling together several Governors who have particular interest in this area and he will be meeting with them either next week or early in the following week. The relaxation of emission standards will have the effect of dealing with the immediate problem, the problem we face this winter and unless those standards are relaxed, we could have a very serious problem this winter. That is why the Governor is moving in this particular area. This can be done, incidentally, administratively, but it requires the cooperation of the Governors because the Governors have, in many instances, as a result of our asking them to do so, had their legislators adopt standards at the State level which presently are State law. It will be necessary for those to be modified.

A second area where administrative action is possible is with regard to the Elk Hills Naval Reserve. Here consultation with the Congress is required and we will institute that kind of consultation that is necessary, particularly with the Armed Services Committee. But developing the Elk Hills Reserves is essential in terms of providing, from our domestic sources, for the needs that we have.

And consequently, we are moving next week in the consultative process so that we can go forward with the Elk Hills development.

And then further, and this looks down the road, we gave the go-ahead this morning for a sharp step up in the development of peaceful uses of nuclear energy.

Now, there are many old wives' tales and horror stories that are told about nuclear plants and all the rest. Russell Train was there, I asked him about the effect on the environment, to separate out the fears from what actually the facts were. He came down on the side of going forward with the program, the development of nuclear power, not only having in mind our present technology, but also research which would allow us to develop nuclear energy in much more exciting ways, looking to the future, for peaceful purposes.

And in this field, I will be meeting myself next week with members of the Atomic Energy Commission, along with the Governor and with Russel Train so that we can give new impetus to that program of the development of nuclear power for peaceful purposes.

We were the first to make the breakthrough in nuclear power for military purposes. We have lagged behind in peaceful uses. Some nations abroad, while they certainly do not have our technology, at least have more thrust here, they have more drive here in this area than we have. But the development of nuclear power for peaceful purposes is to be a major Administration initiative from now on through the balance of our term here.

In the field of research also—this relates clear back to the strip mining a moment ago—is the area of research with regard to the use of coal. Secretary Morton pointed out in our meeting this morning that when we think of the energy sources for the United States, that four percent, only four percent presently in the ground come from oil, three percent potentially from natural gas and 91 percent from coal.

The United States, at the present time, has almost half of the coal reserves of the world. And the problem only is to get the coal out in a way that is not too destructive to the environment, but also to find the uses for coal, liquification programs, other programs which the Governor is quite familiar with and I am not, but which he will be glad to fill you in on.

I would simply summarize in this way. The other day in our press conference—the Governor and I did discuss this and I have asked him, once he does have the time, to perhaps travel abroad and have an opportunity to survey the situation in some of these countries himself—I was asked about the developments in the Mideast and what that meant to us.

The United States would prefer to continue to import oil, petroleum products from the Mideast, from Venezuela, from Canada, from other countries, but also we are keenly aware of the fact that no nation, and particularly no industrial nation, must be in the position of being at the mercy of any other nation by having its energy supplies suddenly cut off.

We are going to do the very best we can to work out problems with the Mideastern countries or any other countries that

may develop, so that we can continue to have a flow of imports into the United States of oil products particularly.

On the other hand, the programs that I have discussed here today, for the most part, as you know, deal with developing within the United States itself, the capability of providing for our energy resources. We can develop those resources. It can be done within a matter of a very few years. I am not going to put a timetable on it, but it can be done. Because the United States, as a great industrial nation, the most advanced industrial nation of the world, must be in a position and must develop the capacity so that no other nation in the world that might, for some reason or another, take an unfriendly attitude toward the United States, has us frankly in a position where they can cut off our oil, or basically more important, cut off our energy.

I would like to say finally that Governor Love in his brief time here has done a superb job of trying to pull all the various agencies of the government together. The conversation within the Cabinet Room was quite spirited. There were disagreements in certain areas and finally, however, we did agree on the program that I have outlined here today.

The Governor will be able to answer technical questions about propane and other things, where I am not, frankly, quite knowledgeable.

So, Governor, the ladies and gentlemen are yours.   ✓

LEGISLATIVE GOALS

Following is the White House text of President Nixon's Sept. 9 nationwide radio address on his legislative goals. The address was broadcast the day before Nixon sent his message on the same subject to Capitol Hill.

Good afternoon.

Now that the Congress has returned from its August recess, it is important that we focus our attention on what the Congress and the Administration can do together to improve the well-being of all the American people.

Tomorrow, I shall send to the Congress an extensive special message highlighting more than 50 major legislative proposals which this Administration has urged, and which still await final Congressional action. Each of these messages is a measure in which you have a stake, because the needs it addresses are your needs.

Today, I want to share with you some thoughts about these proposals, and about the way in which together we can best advance the business of the people.

In these few minutes I shall not run through all the details, or even all the proposals. Those will be spelled out in tomorrow's message. What I do want to do is to focus on some of the highlights, to explain why I believe action is needed promptly, and to indicate how you can help get that action.

Together, the Congress and the Administration have a heavy legislative workload in these remaining months of 1973. We were elected less as Republicans or Democrats than as public officials charged with a public responsibility. The work to be done is your work, and every week's delay is a week of your time lost.

In considering the work before us here at home, there is a lesson in our achievements internationally.

We have ended America's longest and most difficult war. By working together, we now can build America's longest and best peace.

This year, for the first time in 12 years, Americans are not at war anywhere in the world—and our courageous prisoners of war have returned to their homes.

This year, for the first time in a generation, no American is being drafted into the Armed Forces.

In these past four and a half years, we have set the Nation on a new course internationally—and we have laid the foundation for a structure of peace that can last far into the future.

The particular lesson I would stress today is this: we were able to achieve this because we sought to turn the world away from those things that divide it, and to build a new pattern of relationships on the basis of those things that can unite nations and peoples whatever their differences.

By the same token, the time has come to focus here at home on those great goals that can unite all Americans, that affect all Americans, and in which all Americans have a direct and personal stake.

Today, for example, we face urgent needs in six major areas that affect all of the people, and in which the Congress has an opportunity to take actions that will help all the people.

We all share a common interest in establishing a stable prosperity without inflation.

We all share a common interest in ensuring that the Nation's energy needs are met.

We all share a common interest in building better and more livable communities.

We all share a common interest in making full use of our Nation's human resources, and ensuring greater opportunity for all.

We all share a common interest in combating the scourge of crimes and drugs.

We all share a common interest in maintaining a level of national defense that will enable us to maintain the peace.

In all of these six areas, as well as in the other areas of important common interest which I shall also stress in tomorrow's message, legislative proposals now before the Congress can have a significant impact on the life of each of you.

The Economy

Of these six major areas, the one that affects all of us most urgently and most directly is the Nation's economy.

Our goal is to achieve what America has not enjoyed since the days of President Eisenhower—full prosperity, without inflation and without war.

We have already made substantial progress toward this goal and because of this progress, the average American family today—despite inflation—has a higher level of real spendable income than ever before. For the first time in 16 years, unemployment in peacetime is below five percent.

However, we still face a major challenge. We must check the rise in prices.

We must move on four fronts at once if we are to win the battle against inflation. We must expand production. We must exercise monetary restraint. For as long as controls are necessary, we must make sure they are effective.

We are doing all these things. The tough new Phase IV controls come into full force this month. The Federal Reserve is checking the growth in the Nation's money supply. We have moved vigorously to expand production, especially food production, and so to reduce the pressure on food prices.

But we could succeed on these three fronts that I have mentioned and we still would lose the battle against inflation unless we prevail also on the fourth front and that is, we must hold the line on Federal spending.

We still face the prospect of strong new inflationary pressures as a result of overspending by the Federal Government.

Programs which the Congress either has already passed or is now considering would produce an additional deficit of $6 billion, and in addition, the Congress has not yet made nearly a billion and a half dollars of cuts that I have recommended. If these actions by the Congress stand, the result will be higher prices for every American family.

The Federal budget is your budget. It is your budget because you pay for it with your taxes; it is also your budget because it determines whether the prices of what you buy allow you to stay within your family budget.

The most important contribution the Congress can make toward holding down the cost of living is to hold down the cost of government. But we cannot expect the Congress to do this without your help; without your support in those difficult decisions every Member of Congress faces when confronted with a vote on a bill that would help some of the people, but that would raise the cost of living for all the people.

The stable prosperity we seek depends also on our full participation in an increasingly prosperous world. A unique and historic opportunity now exists to negotiate an open and equitable world of trade. Most nations have declared their readiness to join in this endeavor. To give us the tools we need for this full participation in this effort, I urge the Congress to act promptly on the Trade Reform Act of 1973 which I proposed in April. This legislation will enable us, in the difficult negotiations which lie ahead, to assure jobs for American workers, markets for American products, opportunities for American investors and lower prices for American consumers.

Energy

Assuring sufficient energy supplies, now and in the future, is another area of urgent national concern. We had a gasoline scare this summer. We could have serious shortages of heating oil this winter. Unless we take prompt and effective action, we can expect little relief from fuel scarcity in the years ahead.

We have taken important administrative actions already to relieve the situation, and we will take additional steps in the next few weeks. But the solution to the energy problem in the long run requires action by the Congress and action now.

There are seven important proposals now before the Congress, designed to help meet our energy needs, on which I am awaiting action. To avoid a major energy crisis in the years ahead, it is vitally important that the Congress act on these seven proposals before it recesses this year. These proposals include, among others, measures to expand the supply of natural gas by deregulating prices; to open the way for creation of the deep-water ports needed for modern oil tankers; to improve our organization to meet energy needs; and, of particular importance, to give the go-ahead for building the Alaska pipeline, which already has been delayed too long and which is vital for making the enormous oil reserves of Alaska available to all of the American people.

I call upon all of you to join me in urging decisive action by the Congress on energy legislation, so that we will have enough heat for our homes, enough fuel for our transportation, enough energy to run the factories that produce our goods and provide our jobs.

Better Communities

Making our towns and cities more livable affects each of us individually, and all of us as a Nation—and so does the plain fact that the time has passed for the old, paternalistic, Washington-knows-best ways of doing things. We need new and better ways of meeting our social needs, ways that place the power and resources where the problems are, that enlist the energies of the people and the communities themselves—and that recognize that not all wisdom is in Washington.

This Administration has submitted to the Congress a landmark Better Communities Act, which would greatly enhance the ability of all of our communities to make effective use of Federal assistance and to shape their own future. Within the next 10 days, I shall send to the Congress new housing policy recommendations, based on an intensive six-months study of the strengths and failures of the old legislation, and of the changing pattern of the Nation's needs. Vital transportation legislation also awaits action—including a measure to keep the bankrupt railroads serving the Northeast and Midwest in operation without saddling an undue share of the burden on the taxpayer.

America's greatest resource is its people themselves—you, your family, your neighbors. In the area of human resources, among the measures awaiting action is a Better Schools Act which would help concentrate Federal education dollars where the needs are greatest, for example, on education for the disadvantaged, for the handicapped, and on vocational education—education to prepare people for jobs. Most important what we need is a measure which would have the decisions affecting your child's education made by your State, by your local school board, rather than by social planners in Washington, D.C.

Also pending are important proposals in the areas of pension reform, job training, health and others that can go far toward expanding opportunity for millions of Americans, and thus make this a better Nation for all of us.

Crime

After nearly twenty years of continuous and sometimes shockingly dramatic increases in the rate of crime, the figures for 1972—released just last month—show that we have finally turned the tide in our battle for a safer America. For the first time in 17 years, serious crime in 1972 was down from the year before.

Much of the credit goes to the new crime legislation that has been enacted during the past four years. Much of the credit goes to local law enforcement officials and much of the credit goes to a changed public attitude toward crime and criminals— away from the era of permissiveness, and toward a renewed respect for law, order and justice.

We must now step up our efforts to ensure that this will be a decisive turning point, and that we can continue to make our communities safer once again for law-abiding citizens. Three of the legislative measures on which I urge swift action are designed to do just that: a heroin trafficking bill, to tighten enforcement against heroin pushers; a bill to restore the death penalty for certain of the most serious offenses; and a bill to modernize and reform the entire Federal Criminal Code.

National Defense

Finally, we come to an area of transcendant importance: that of national defense. In recent years, it has been fashionable to suggest that whatever we want in the way of extra programs at home could be painlessly financed by just lopping $5 or $10 or $20 billion out of the defense budget. This approach is worse than foolhardly; it is suicidal. Because we could have the finest array of domestic programs in the world and they would mean nothing if because of our weakness we lost our freedom or we were plunged into the abyss of nuclear war.

The world's hope for peace depends on America's strength—it depends absolutely on our never falling into the position of being the second strongest nation in the world.

For years now, we have been engaged in a long, painstaking process of negotiating mutual limits on strategic nuclear arms. Historic agreements have already been reached; others are in prospect. Talks are also going forward this year aimed at a mutual and balanced reduction of forces in Europe. But the point of all these negotiations is that if peace is to be preserved, the limitations and the reductions of arms must be mutual. What one side is willing to give up for free, the other side will not bargain for.

If America's peace and America's freedom are worth preserving, they are worth the cost of whatever level of military strength it takes to preserve them—and we must not yield to the folly of breaching that level and so undermining our hopes and the world's hopes for peace now and in the future.

Bipartisan Goals

The questions at issue in achieving these various goals are not ones of partisanship—of Republicans versus Democrats. And neither, for the most part, are they ones of the President versus the Congress.

In some cases, there are real philosophical differences over how best to meet the needs that we face. The American tradition has always been that we argue these differences out, we compromise some, we settle others by a test of strength. But it is important that we act, that we decide, that we get on with the business of Government—that we not let whatever may be our disagreements over the means of achieving these goals bar us from the achievement.

It is important, on all sides, that we approach this legislative season with a willingness to make those reasonable adjustments that are necessary to reach a common objective.

Within that spirit, there are three basic principles which I feel are esssential.

We must maintain a national defense sufficient to safeguard us from attack, and to provide an incentive for mutual reductions in the burden of armaments for all the world.

We must hold down the total of our expenditures, so that new programs will not be bought at the cost of losing the war against higher prices and higher taxes.

We must recognize that the American system requires both a strong Congress and a strong Executive; and we threefore must not place limits on Presidential powers that would jeopardize the capacity of the President, in this and in future Administrations, to carry out his responsibilities to the American people.

There is still enough time to make 1973 a year in which we not only ended the longest war in America's history, but in which we laid the foundation for turning the blessings of peace into a better life for all.

With the Congress, the Administration and the people working together toward this goal, we can achieve it. It means using to the fullest the days and weeks remaining in this year 1973. It means a willingness on the part of both the Executive and the Congress to cooperate, and to seek solutions that are in the common interest.

It also means holding the spotlight of public attention and public debate on those issues that directly and personally affect you and your lives. For it is your attention—your participation in the debate and discussion—that in the final analysis will determine whether and how well these goals are achieved.

It means that the Congress should join the Executive in making up for the precious time lost this year in failing to act on those measures which vitally affect every American by going into extra session, if necessary, to complete the people's business before the year ends.

It will take all of us together—the Congress, the Administration and the public—but we can make this a year of achievement of which we can all be proud. I ask for your best efforts, and I pledge you mine.

Thank you and good afternoon.   ✓

ENERGY EMERGENCY

Following is the White House text of President Nixon's Nov. 7 address to the nation on the energy emergency. The address was carried on nationwide radio and television.

Good evening.

I want to talk to you tonight about a serious national problem, a problem we must all face together in the months and years ahead.

As America has grown and prospered in recent years, our energy demands have begun to exceed available supplies. In recent months, we have taken many actions to increase supplies and to reduce consumption. But even with our best efforts, we knew that a period of temporary shortages was inevitable.

Unfortunately, our expectations for this winter have now been sharply altered by the recent conflict in the Middle East. Because of that war, most of the Middle Eastern oil producers have reduced overall production and cut off their shipments of oil to the United States. By the end of this month, more than 2 million barrels a day of oil we expected to import into the United States will no longer be available.

We must, therefore, face up to a very stark fact. We are heading toward the most acute shortages of energy since World War II. Our supply of petroleum this winter will be at least 10 percent short of our anticipated demands, and it could fall short by as much as 17 percent.

Now, even before war broke out in the Middle East, these prospective shortages were the subject of intensive discussions among members of my Administration, leaders of the Congress, Governors, Mayors and other groups. From these discussions has emerged a broad agreement that we, as a Nation, must now set upon a new course.

In the short run, this course means that we must use less energy—that means less heat, less electricity, less gasoline. In the long run, it means that we must develop new sources of energy which will give us the capacity to meet our needs without relying on any foreign nation.

The immediate shortage will affect the lives of each and every one of us. In our factories, our cars, our homes, our offices, we will have to use less fuel than we are accustomed to using. Some school and factory schedules may be rearranged, and some jet airplane flights will be canceled.

This does not mean that we are going to run out of gasoline or that air travel will stop, or that we will freeze in our homes or offices anyplace in America. The fuel crisis need not mean genuine suffering for any American. But it will require some sacrifice by all Americans.

We must be sure that our most vital needs are met first—and that our less important activities are the first to be cut back. And we must be sure that while the fat from our economy is being trimmed, the muscle is not seriously damaged.

To help us carry out that responsibility, I am tonight announcing the following steps:

Six Steps

First, I am directing that industries and utilities which use coal—which is our most abundant resource—be prevented from converting from coal to oil. Efforts will also be made to convert power plants from the use of oil to the use of coal.

Second, we are allocating reduced quantities of fuel for aircraft. Now, this is going to lead to a cutback of more than 10 percent of the number of flights, and some rescheduling of arrival and departure times.

Third, there will be reductions of approximately 15 percent in the supply of heating oil for homes and offices and other establishments. To be sure that there is enough oil to go around for the entire winter, all over the country, it will be essential for all of us to live and work in lower temperatures. We must ask everyone to lower the thermostat in your home by at least 6 degrees, so that we can achieve a national daytime average of 68 degrees.

Incidentally, my doctor tells me that in a temperature of 66 to 68 degrees, you are really more healthy than when it it is 75 to 78, if that is any comfort. In offices, factories and commercial establishments, we must ask that you achieve the equivalent of a 10-degree reduction by either lowering the thermostat or curtailing working hours.

Fourth, I am ordering additional reductions in the consumption of energy by the Federal Government. We have already taken steps to reduce the Government's consumption by 7 percent. The cuts must now go deeper, and must be made by every agency and every department in the Government. I am directing that the daytime temperatures in Federal offices be reduced immediately to a level of between 65 and 68 degrees, and that means in this room, too, as well as in every other room in the White House. In addition, I am ordering that all vehicles owned by the Federal Government—and there are

over a half-million of them—travel no faster than 50 miles per hour except in emergencies. This is a step which I have also asked Governors, Mayors and local officials to take immediately with regard to vehicles under their authority.

Fifth, I am asking the Atomic Energy Commission to speed up the licensing and construction of nuclear plants. We must seek to reduce the time required to bring nuclear plants on line, nuclear plants that can produce power, to bring them on line from 10 years to 6 years, reduce that time lag.

Sixth, I am asking that Governors and Mayors reinforce these actions by taking appropriate steps at the State and local level. We have already learned, for example, from the State of Oregon, that considerable amounts of energy can be saved simply by curbing unnecessary lighting and slightly altering the school year. I am recommending that other communities follow this example and also seek ways to stagger working hours, to encourage greater use of mass transit and car pooling.

Cooperation for Change

How many times have you gone along the highway or the freeway, wherever the case may be, and seen hundreds and hundreds of cars with only one individual in that car. This we must all cooperate to change.

Consistent with safety and economic consideration, I am also asking Governors to take steps to reduce highway speed limits to 50 miles per hour. This action alone, if it is adopted on a nationwide basis could save over 200,000 barrels of oil a day—just reducing the speed limit to 50 miles per hour.

Now, all of these actions will result in substantial savings of energy. More than that, most of these are actions that we can take right now without further delay.

The key to their success lies, however, not just here in Washington, but in every home, in every community across this country. If each of us joins in this effort, joins with the spirit and the determination that have always graced the American character, then half the battle will already be won.

But we should recognize that even these steps, as essential as they are, may not be enough. We must be prepared to take additional steps, and for that purpose, additional authorities must be provided by the Congress.

Emergency Energy Act

I have therefore directed my chief adviser for energy policy, Governor Love, and other Administration officials, to work closely with the Congress in developing an emergency energy act.

I met with the leaders of the Congress this morning and I asked that they act on this legislation on a priority urgent basis. It is imperative that this legislation be on my desk for signature before the Congress recesses this December.

Because of the hard work that has already been done on this bill by Senators Jackson and Fannin, and others, I am confident that we can meet that goal, and I will have the bill on this desk and will be able to sign it.

This proposed legislation would enable the Executive Branch to meet the energy emergency in several important ways:

First, it would authorize an immediate return to Daylight Saving Time on a year-round basis.

Second, it would provide the necessary authority to relax environmental regulations on a temporary case-by-case basis, thus permitting an appropriate balancing of our environmental interests, which all of us share, with our energy requirements, which, of course, are indispensable.

Third, it would grant authority to impose special energy conservation measures such as restrictions on the working hours for shopping centers and other commercial establishments.

And fourth, it would approve and fund increased exploration, development and production from our Naval Petroleum Reserves. These reserves are rich sources of oil. From one of them alone—Elk Hills in California—we could produce more than 160,000 barrels of oil a day within two months.

Fifth, it would provide the Federal Government with authority to reduce highway speed limits throughout the Nation.

And finally, it would expand the power of the Government's regulatory agencies to adjust the schedules of planes, ships, and other carriers.

If shortages persist, despite all of these actions and despite inevitable increases in the price of energy products, it may then become necessary—may become necessary—to take even stronger measures.

It is only prudent that we be ready to cut the consumption of oil products, such as gasoline, by rationing, or by a fair system of taxation, and consequently, I have directed that contingency plans, if this becomes necessary, be prepared for that purpose.

Now, some of you may wonder whether we are turning back the clock to another age. Gas rationing, oil shortages, reduced speed limits—they all sound like a way of life we left behind with Glenn Miller and the war of the 1940s. Well, in fact, part of our current problem also stems from war—the war in the Middle East. But our deeper energy problems come not from war, but from peace and from abundance. We are running out of energy today because our economy has grown enormously and because in prosperity what were once considered luxuries are now considered necessities.

How many of you can remember when it was very unusual to have a home air conditioned? And yet, this is very common in almost all parts of the Nation.

As a result, the average American will consume as much energy in the next seven days as most other people in the world will consume in an entire year. We have only six percent of the world's people in America, but we consume over 30 percent of all the energy in the world.

Now, our growing demands have bumped up against the limits of available supply and until we provide new sources of energy for tomorrow, we must be prepared to tighten our belts today.

Long-Range Plans

Let me turn now to our long-range plans.

While a resolution of the immediate crisis is our highest priority, we must also act now to prevent a recurrence of such a crisis in the future. This is a matter of bipartisan concern. It is going to require a bipartisan response.

Two years ago, in the first energy message any President has ever sent to the Congress, I called attention to our urgent energy problem. Last April, this year, I reaffirmed to the Congress the magnitude of that problem, and I called for action on seven major legislative initiatives. Again in June, I called for action. I have done so frequently since then.

But thus far, not one major energy bill that I have asked for has been enacted. I realize that the Congress has been distracted in this period by other matters. But the time has now come for the Congress to get on with this urgent business—providing the legislation that will meet not only the current crisis, but also the long-range challenge that we face.

Our failure to act now on our long-term energy problems could seriously endanger the capacity of our farms, and of our factories, to employ Americans at record-breaking rates—nearly 86 million people are now at work in this country—and to provide the highest standard of living we, or any other nation, has ever known in history.

It could reduce the capacity of our farmers to provide the food we need. It could jeopardize our entire transportation system. It could seriously weaken the ability of America to continue to give the leadership which only we can provide to keep the peace that we have won at such great cost, for thousands of our finest young Americans.

That is why it is time to act now on vital energy legislation that will affect our daily lives, not just this year, but for years to come.

We must have legislation now which will authorize construction of the Alaska pipeline—legislation which is not burdened with irrelevant and unnecessary provisions.

We must have legislative authority to encourage production of our vast quantities of natural gas, one of the cleanest and best sources of energy.

We must have the legal ability to set reasonable standards for the surface mining of coal.

And we must have the organizational structures to meet and administer our energy programs.

And therefore, tonight, as I did this morning in meeting with the Congressional leaders, I again urge the Congress to give its attention to the initiatives I recommended six months ago to meet these needs that I have described.

Research and Development

Finally, I have stressed repeatedly the necessity of increasing our energy research and development efforts. Last June, I announced a five-year, $10 billion program to develop better ways of using energy and to explore and develop new energy sources. Last month I announced plans for an immediate acceleration of that problem.

We can take heart from the fact that we in the United States have half the world's known coal reserves. We have huge, untapped sources of natural gas. We have the most advanced nuclear technology known to man. We have oil in our continental shelves. We have oil shales out in the Western part of the United States and we have some of the finest technical and scientific minds in the world. In short, we have all the resources we need to meet the great challenge before us. Now we must demonstrate the will to meet that challenge.

In World War II, America was faced with the necessity of rapidly developing an atomic capability. The circumstances were grave. Responding to that challenge, this Nation brought together its finest scientific skills and its finest administrative skills in what was known as the Manhattan Project. With all the needed resources at its command, with the highest priority assigned to its efforts, the Manhattan Project gave us the atomic capacity that helped to end the war in the Pacific and to bring peace to the world.

Twenty years later, responding to a different challenge, we focused our scientific and technological genius on the frontiers of space. We pledged to put a man on the moon before 1970, and on July 20, 1969, Neil Armstrong made that historic "giant leap for mankind" when he stepped on the moon.

The lessons of the Apollo project, and of the earlier Manhattan Project, are the same lessons that are taught by the whole of American history: Whenever the American people are faced with a clear goal and they are challenged to meet it, we can do extraordinary things.

Today the challenge is to gain the strength that we had earlier in this century, the strength of self-sufficiency. Our ability to meet our own energy needs is directly limited to our continued ability to act decisively and independently at home and abroad in the service of peace, not only for America, but for all nations in the world.

I have ordered funding of this effort to achieve self-sufficiency far in excess of the funds that were expended on the Manhattan Project, but money is only one of the ingredients essential to the success of such a project.

We must also have a unified commitment to that goal. We must have unified direction of the effort to accomplish it. Because of the urgent need for an organization that would provide focused leadership for this effort, I am asking the Congress to consider my proposal for an Energy Research and Development Administration separate from any other organizational initiatives, and to enact this legislation in the present session of the Congress.

'Project Independence'

Let us unite in committing the resources of this Nation to a major new endeavor, an endeavor that in this bicentennial era we can appropriately call "Project Independence." Let us set as our national goal, in the spirit of Apollo, with the determination of the Manhattan Project, that by the end of this decade we will have developed the potential to meet our own energy needs without depending on any foreign energy sources.

Let us pledge that by 1980, under Project Independence, we shall be able to meet America's energy needs from America's own energy resources.

In speaking to you tonight in terms as direct as these, my concern has been to lay before you the full facts of the Nation's energy shortage. It is important that each of us understands what the situation is and how the efforts we, together, can take to help to meet it are essential to our total effort.

No people in the world perform more nobly than the American people when called upon to unite in the service of their country. I am supremely confident that while the days and weeks ahead may be a time of some hardship for many of us, they will also be a time of renewed commitment and concentration to the national interest.

We have an energy crisis, but there is no crisis of the American spirit. Let us go forward, then, doing what needs to be done, proud of what we have accomplished together in the past, and confident of what we can accomplish together in the future.

Let us find in this time of national necessity a renewed awareness of our capacities as a people, a deeper sense of our responsibilities as a Nation, and an increased understanding that the measure and the meaning of America has always been determined by the devotion which each of us brings to our duty as citizens of America.

'I Have No Intention...'

I should like to close with a personal note.

It was just one year ago that I was re-elected as President of the United States of America. During this past year we have made great progress in achieving the goals that I set forth in my re-election campaign.

We have ended the longest war in America's history. All of our prisoners of war have been returned home. And for the first time in 25 years, no young Americans are being drafted into the Armed Services. We have made progress toward our goal of a real prosperity, a prosperity without war. The rate of unemployment is down to 4-1/2 percent, which is the lowest unemployment in peacetime that we have had in 16 years, and we are finally beginning to make progress in our fight against the rise in the cost of living.

These are substantial achievements in this year 1973. But I would be less than candid if I were not to admit that this has not been an easy year in some other respects, as all of you are quite aware.

As a result of the deplorable Watergate matter, great numbers of Americans have had doubts raised as to the integrity of the President of the United States. I have even noted that some publications have called on me to resign the office of President of the United States.

Tonight I would like to give my answer to those who have suggested that I resign.

I have no intention whatever of walking away from the job I was elected to do. As long as I am physically able, I am going to continue to work 16 to 18 hours a day for the cause of a real peace abroad, and for the cause of prosperity without inflation and without war at home. And in the months ahead, I shall do everything that I can to see that any doubts as to the integrity of the man who occupies the highest office in this land, to remove those doubts where they exist.

And I am confident that in the months ahead, the American people will come to realize that I have not violated the trust that they placed in me when they elected me as President of the United States in the past, and I pledge to you tonight that I shall always do everything that I can to be worthy of that trust in the future.

Thank you and good night.   ✓

STATEMENT ON TAPES

Following is the text of a Nov. 12 statement by President Nixon on tape recordings and other materials related to White House conversations:

As a consequence of the public disclosure, two weeks ago, that two conversations of the President were not recorded on the White House recording system, doubts have arisen about just what happened to these conversations and why they were not recorded. The purpose of this statement is to help dispel those doubts and to spell out certain steps I will take to offer information to the Court that will help determine the substance of all nine conversations subpoenaed by the Court.

First, there are no missing tapes. There are two conversations requested by the Courts which were not recorded. The first is a four-minute conversation with the former Attorney General, John Mitchell, on June 20, 1972. The second is a meeting of 55 minutes with John Dean, late in the evening of Sunday, April 15, 1973.

There is no question in my mind but that the open Court hearing, now being conducted, will demonstrate to the Court's satisfaction the truth of our statements that these two conversations were never recorded. In fact there is no affirmative evidence to the contrary. I believe that when the Court concludes its evaluation of the testimony and documentary evidence, public doubt on this issue will be completely and satisfactorily removed.

In the meantime, I believe it important to make a statement about this proceeding so that misconceptions about this matter do not persist simply because certain basic facts are not presented to the American public.

No Committee Subpoena. First, the Senate Select Committee did not subpoena the substance of the two unrecorded conversations. That material was requested only by the Special Prosecutor, and the Court, who believed the substance of nine presidential conversations was necessary for completion of the Watergate investigation.

We are complying fully with the Federal Court decision. In seven of nine instances, the actual recording of the conversation is being submitted; this includes 5 conversations in which John Dean participated—September 15, 1972, March 13, 1973, two on March 31, 1973, one on March 22, 1973. For all nine conversations covered by the subpoena, such contemporaneous notes and memoranda as were made of the conversations are being provided in accordance with the Court order.

Chronological Perspective. Before discussing these matters, the issue of when and why the recorded conversations were listened to by me, and by others on my behalf, should be placed in chronological perspective.

On June 4, 1973, I listened to the tape recordings of a number of conversations I had with John Dean in order to refresh my memory of those discussions. All of the conversations to which I listened that day had taken place prior to March 21, 1973. My purpose in reviewing the recordings of my conversations with Mr. Dean was to confirm my recollection that he had not reported certain facts to me prior to March 21, 1973. In late April, 1973, I asked H. R. Haldeman to listen and report on the conversation of March 21, 1973, in which he had been present for a substantial portion of time. My primary purpose in having Mr. Haldeman listen to this tape was to confirm my recollection that March 21, 1973, was the date on which John Dean had first reported certain facts to me.

There had been rumors and reports to the contrary—one of them suggesting that John Dean and I had met 30 to 40 times to discuss Watergate—and I wanted to refresh my recollection as to what was the precise and entire truth.

On September 29, 1973, I began a review of the tape recordings subpoenaed by the Special Prosecutor for the grand jury and by the Senate Select Committee. The reason was it had been my deliberate intention to litigate the matter up to the Supreme Court, if necessary, to protect the right of confidentiality and the related principle of separation of powers. By late September, however, I had come to the conclusion that the national interest would be better served by a reasonable compromise.

Thus, in late September, I began to consider various approaches which led to what has come to be known as the "Stennis Compromise"—turning over to both the Senate Committee and the Court the full substance of the relevant recorded conversations, leaving the verification of the precision and accuracy of that substance to Senator Stennis. That compromise offer, accepted by the Senate Committee Chairman and Vice Chairman, proved unacceptable to the Special Prosecutor.

Unrecorded Conversations. It was during this process that I first became aware of the possibility that two of the ten conversations in question had not been recorded.

I proceeded with a review of the eight recorded conversations and subsequently ordered a further search for recordings of the two conversations in question and an investigation into the circumstances which caused the conversations not to be recorded. The search and investigation were not finally completed until October 27.

One of the conversations for which no recording could be found was a four-minute telephone call I made to John Mitchell on the evening of June 20, 1972. The only telephone calls which were recorded in the residence of the White House were those made in the Lincoln Sitting Room which I use as an office. Telephone conversations in the family quarters have never been recorded during this Administration. The telephone call with John Mitchell was one that I made on the telephone in the family quarters just before going in to dinner, and consequently it was not recorded.

My conversation with John Dean on Sunday evening, April 15, 1973, was not recorded because the tape on the recording machine for my Executive Office Building office was used up and ran out earlier in the day. The tape which was on the operating recorder on Sunday, April 15, 1973, contains recordings of the conversations in my Executive Office Building office on Saturday, April 14, 1973. It also contains a portion of the first conversation I had in that office on Sunday, April 15, 1973, which was with Attorney General Kleindienst. During that conversation the tape ran out. Normally, I see very few people in my Executive Office Building office on the weekends. However, on the weekend of April 14 and 15, the activity in my Executive Office Building office was unusual and unanticipated. Certain reports made to me by my staff early in the morning of April 14, 1973, led me to have lengthy discussions with staff members during the day in my office in the Executive Office Building. In addition, international developments required a lengthy meeting with my Assistant for National Security Affairs late that morning.

On Sunday, April 15, 1973, I began another series of meetings in my Executive Office Building office at about one o'clock, p.m. The first meeting was with Attorney General Kleindienst. Thereafter the meetings continued until late in the evening with the exception of a break of about two hours for dinner. I did not meet with John Dean until approximately nine o'clock that evening. Since the tape on the recorder for my Executive Office Building office had run out during my afternoon meeting with Attorney General Kleindienst, the Dean meeting was not recorded.

Search for Records. It should be pointed out that the Court order calls for evidentiary materials such as notes and memoranda in addition to recordings of specified conversations. The Court order spells out a detailed procedure for turning materials over for Judge Sirica's private review. In recent days, in an effort to locate materials for the Court, a diligent search has been made for materials that might shed further light on the substance of the conversations in question, including the unrecorded conversations with John Mitchell on June 20, 1972, and with John Dean, on the evening of April 15, 1973.

Since I have been in office, I have maintained a personal diary file which consists of notes which I have personally taken during meetings and of dictation belts on which I record recollections. The dictation belts and notes are placed in my personal diary file by my secretary. They are sealed under specific instructions that they not be transcribed.

In the course of searching my personal diary files, I have located a dictation belt that I dictated at 8:30 p.m. on June 20, 1972, on which, among other activities of the day, I referred to a telephone call with John Mitchell. The portion of the belt relating to the conversation with John Mitchell will be submitted to the Court.

We have also located the dictation belt of my recollections of the conversations in question for March 21, 1973; and the relevant portions of these recollections, together with the actual recordings of the conversations, of course, will also be submitted to the Court in compliance with its order.

No Dictation Belt. Over the weekend of November 4 and 5, 1973, upon checking my personal diary file for April 15, 1973, to locate information to be produced in accordance with the Court's order, I found that my file for that day consists of personal notes of the conversation held with John Dean the evening of April 15, 1973, but not a dictation belt. My original handwritten notes, made during my meeting with John Dean on the evening of April 15, 1973, will be submitted to the Court.

On June 11, 1973, the Special Prosecutor requested a tape of a conversation I had with John Dean on April 15, 1973, (which I had previously offered to let Assistant Attorney General Petersen hear).

As has been pointed out, my personal diary file consists of notes of conversations and dictation belts of recollections, and I believed in June that I had dictated my recollections of April 15, 1973, of conversations which occurred on that day. The response to the Special Prosecutor made on June 16, 1973, referred to such a dictation belt. At that time, however, I did not review my file to confirm that it contained the belt.

April 16 Dean Meeting. I have made a diligent search for other evidentiary materials that might shed light on the substance of my conversation with John Dean on the evening of April 15, 1973. Other than my contemporaneous notes of that meeting mentioned above, I have found no such evidence. However, I did meet with John Dean on Monday, April 16, 1973, on two occasions. The first was in the morning in the Oval Office; the second was in the afternoon in the Executive Office Building office. This was my final meeting with Mr. Dean before he left the White House staff. Both of these conversations were recorded on the White House recording system. I recently reviewed the recordings of these conversations. A comparison of my notes of the April 15, 1973 meeting and the recording of the conversation with Mr. Dean on the morning of April 16, 1973, shows both conversations covered much the same subject matter. There are references throughout the conversation on the morning of April 16 to the conversation held the evening before.

I shall voluntarily submit to the Court, under the procedures applicable to recordings of conversations already covered by the Court order, these recordings of my two conversations with John Dean on April 16, 1973.

Other Records. In addition, as stated above and consistent with the Court order, the Court will be provided with:

(1) The portion of the dictation belt containing my recollection of the June 20, 1973 conversation with Mr. Mitchell.

(2) The portion of the dictation belt of my recollections of the meetings with Mr. Dean on March 21, 1973.

(3) Contemporaneous notes from the April 15, 1973 conversation with Mr. Dean.

(4) All other materials covered by the Court order.

I have also authorized my Counsel to make available to the Court certain tape recordings not covered by the Court order to assist the Court in verifying that the two conversations in question were not recorded. The additional tape recordings to be provided are (a) the full reel of telephone recordings covering the period of June 20, 1972, and (b) the two reels of tape which were on the recorders for my Executive Office Building office on April 15, 1973. This will permit the Court to check the sequence of the conversations against my daily logs of meetings and telephone conversations already provided to the Court, and thus further demonstrate that the Mitchell and Dean conversations in question were not recorded.

Expert Examination. I have also agreed that a group of Court-approved independent experts employing the most advanced technological methods shall examine all tapes in question for any evidence of alterations to the tapes.

It is my hope that these steps will clear up this aspect of the Watergate matter once and for all.   ✓

NATIONAL ENERGY POLICY

Following is the White House text of President Nixon's Nov. 25 televised address on the national energy policy.

Good evening. Three weeks ago, I spoke to you about the national energy crisis and our policy for meeting it. Tonight I want to talk with you again to report on our progress and to announce further steps we must take to carry out our energy policy.

When I spoke to you earlier, I indicated that the sudden cut-off of oil from the Middle East had turned the serious energy shortages we expected this winter into a major energy crisis. That crisis is now being felt around the world, as other industrialized nations have also suffered from cutbacks in oil from the Middle East.

Shortages in Europe, for example, are far more critical than they are in the United States. Already seven European nations have imposed a ban on Sunday driving. Fortunately, the United States is not as dependent upon Middle Eastern oil as many other nations. We will not have a ban on Sunday driving, but as you will hear later, we are going to try to limit it. Nevertheless, we anticipate that our shortages could run as high as 17 percent. This means that we must immediately take strong, effective counter-measures.

In order to minimize disruptions in our economy, I asked on November 7th that all Americans adopt certain energy-conservation measures to help meet the challenge of reduced energy supplies. These steps include reductions in home heating, reductions in driving speeds, elimination of unnecessary lighting. The American people, all of you, you have responded to this challenge with that spirit of sacrifice which has made this such a great nation.

The Congress has also been moving forward on the energy front. The Alaska pipeline bill has been passed. I signed it into law nine days ago right here at this desk. The Congress has passed a fuel allocation bill which I will sign into law on Tuesday. An additional emergency bill providing special authority to deal with this problem has now passed the Senate. When the House returns from its recess, I am confident the House will move promptly so that this vital legislation can be signed into law by the middle of December.

And so we have made some encouraging progress, but there is much more to be done, and that is what I want to talk to you about tonight.

I have appointed an Energy Emergency Action Group, under my chief energy adviser, Governor John Love, to analyze our situation on a continuing basis and to advise me of all actions required to deal with it.

Five Steps

And upon the action and the recommendation of this group, I am announcing tonight the following steps to meet the energy crisis:

Heating Oil Supply. First, to increase the supply of heating oil that will be available this winter, we must adjust production schedules and divert petroleum which might normally go for the production of gasoline to the production of more heating oil.

To accomplish this, the amount of gasoline which refiners distribute to wholesalers and retailers will be reduced across the Nation by 15 percent. As we reduce gasoline supplies, we must act to insure that the remaining gasoline available is used wisely, and conserved to the fullest possible extent.

Gas Station Closings. Therefore, as a second step, I am asking tonight that all gasoline filling stations close down their pumps between 9:00 p.m. Saturday night and midnight Sunday every weekend, beginning December 1. We are requesting that this step be taken voluntarily now.

Upon passage of the emergency energy legislation before the Congress, gas stations will be required to close during these hours. This step should not result in any serious hardship for any American family. It will, however, discourage long-distance driving during weekends. It will mean perhaps spending a little more time at home.

This savings alone is only a small part of what we have to conserve to meet the total gasoline shortage. We can achieve substantial additional savings by altering our driving habits. While the voluntary response to my request for reduced driving speeds has been excellent, it is now essential that we have mandatory and full compliance with this important step on a nationwide basis.

50 M.P.H. Limit. And therefore, the third step will be the establishment of a maximum speed limit for automobiles of 50 miles per hour nationwide as soon as our emergency energy legislation passes the Congress. We expect that this measure will produce a savings of 200,000 barrels of gasoline per day. Inter-city buses and heavy duty trucks which operate more efficiently at higher speeds, and therefore, do not use more gasoline, will be permitted to observe a 55 mile per hour speed limit.

Jet Fuel. The fourth step we are taking involves our jet airliners. There will be a phased reduction of an additional 15 percent in the consumption of jet fuel for passenger flights bringing the total reduction to approximately 25 percent.

These savings will be achieved by a careful reduction in schedules, combined with an increase in passenger loads. We will not have to stop air travel, but we will have to plan for it more carefully.

Outdoor Lighting. The fifth step involves cutting back on outdoor lighting. As soon as the emergency energy legislation passes the Congress, I shall order the curtailment of ornamental outdoor lighting for homes and the elimination of all commercial lighting except that which identifies places of business.

In the meantime, we are already planning right here at the White House to curtail such lighting that we would normally have at Christmastime and I am asking that all of you act now on a voluntary basis to reduce or eliminate unnecessary lighting in your homes.

As just one example of the impact which such an initiative can have, the energy consumed by ornamental gas lights alone in this country is equivalent to 35,000 barrels per day of oil and that is enough fuel to heat 175,000 homes.

Heating Oil Allocation

Finally, I want to report to you tonight that we have now developed final plans for allocating reduced quantities of heating oil this winter and all of you know how very important heating oil is, particularly in the wintertime.

These plans, to be published Tuesday, will call for an average reduction of 10 percent of heating oil for industrial use, 15 percent for home use, and 25 percent for commercial use.

The reductions for homeowners alone will result in a savings of some 315,000 barrels of heating oil a day, which is enough to heat over 1½ million homes every day. For the average American family, as I indicated three weeks ago, this cutback in heating oil does not mean severe discomfort for anyone, but it will mean that everyone should lower the thermostat—as it is right here in this office now, and throughout the White House, and throughout every Federal installation—you should lower the thermostat by six degrees below its normal setting so that we can achieve a national daytime average of 68 degrees.

Those who fail to adopt such a cutback risk running out of fuel before the winter is over. While additional actions will be necessary to further offset the anticipated shortage of 17 percent, the steps which I have outlined tonight will relieve about 10 percent of that shortage.

They will make a very substantial contribution to our immediate goal of insuring that we have enough fuel to be adequately warm in our homes this winter, that we are able to get to work, and that we experience no serious disruptions in the normal conduct of our lives.

Cooperation

Above all, every step will be taken to insure that any disruptions to our economy which could cost jobs, will be as brief as possible and that they do not cause serious damage.

Nothing we do can succeed, however, without the full cooperation of the Congress in providing the legislation we must have, without the full cooperation of State and local governments in providing the broad leadership that we must have, and without the full cooperation of each and every one of you, all the American people, in sacrificing a little so that no one must endure real hardship.

For my part, I pledge to do everything in my power to insure that the decisions I have announced will be carried out swiftly and effectively and fairly, and whatever additional action is necessary to achieve our objective will be taken.

I intend to participate personally and on a regular basis, as I have since I last addressed you three weeks ago, in the work of my energy advisers. I intend to advise the congressional leadership regularly of problems and progress. And I intend to see that the persons and organizations having responsibilities and capabilities in this area are fully and regularly informed.

We need new rules if we are to meet this challenge; but most of all, we need sustained and serious action and cooperation by millions of men and women if we are to achieve our objective, and that means millions of Americans across this land listening to me tonight.

Self-Sufficiency

Let me conclude by restating our overall objective. It can be summed up in one word that best characterizes this Nation and its essential nature. That word is "independence." From its beginning 200 years ago, throughout its history, America has made great sacrifices of blood and also of treasure to achieve and maintain its independence. In the last third of this century, our independence will depend on maintaining and achieving self-sufficiency in energy.

What I have called Project Independence-1980 is a series of plans and goals set to insure that by the end of this decade Americans will not have to rely on any source of energy beyond our own.

As far as energy is concerned, this means we will hold our fate and our future in our hands alone. As we look to the future, we can do so confident that the energy crisis will be resolved not only for our time but for all time. We will once again have plentiful supplies of energy which helped to build

the greatest industrial nation and one of the highest standards of living in the world.

The capacity for self-sufficiency in energy is a great goal. It is also an essential goal, and we are going to achieve it.

Tonight I ask all of you to join together in moving toward that goal, with the spirit of discipline, self-restraint and unity which is the cornerstone of our great and good country.

Thank you and good evening.   √

STATEMENT ON FINANCES

Following is the White House text, released Dec. 8, of President Nixon's statement on his financial disclosures:

With the documents and papers released today, I am making a full disclosure of my financial affairs as President of the United States. No previous President, to my knowledge, has ever made so comprehensive and exhaustive a disclosure as I am making today, with regard to assets and liabilities, expenses and income, during his tenure of office.

The purpose of my release of these papers is to answer questions that have arisen, to remove doubts that have been raised and to correct misinformation that currently exists about what I have earned, and what I own.

To the open-minded, the papers and documents provided today, the facts they contain and the figures they reveal, will lay to rest such false rumors as that campaign contributions were converted to my personal use, that campaign funds were used in the purchase of my home in San Clemente, that I have hidden away a secret $1 million investment portfolio, that I sheltered the income on which my daughter, Tricia, should have paid taxes, and that $10 million in Federal funds was spent on my homes in Key Biscayne and San Clemente.

In conducting my private affairs in public office, I have proceeded in a manner I thought both prudent and in the best interests of my family. And even though both American law and tradition protect the privacy of the papers I am releasing today, these documents are being made public—because the confidentiality of my private finances is far less important to me than the confidence of the American people in the integrity of the President.

Questions and controversies may continue as a consequence of these disclosures. Even the men who have advised me in these matters and who have prepared my financial records, statements and tax returns have disagreements of professional opinion among themselves. But most of the questions outstanding in the public mind today should be put to rest with the publication of these documents.

With regard to my tax returns—the contents of which will be made public today—the accountants who prepared them listed all of the deductions to which they believed I was entitled, and only those deductions—as any accountant would and should do on behalf of his client.

The following are among the papers being released today:
• The figures from the Federal Income tax returns which my wife and I filed for the years 1969, 1970, 1971 and 1972.
• An independent audit of my private financial affairs, since January 1, 1969, conducted by one of the nation's largest and most respected accounting firms, Coopers & Lybrand of New York City.
• The significant documents relating to the major financial transactions since my first Inauguration, including the purchase of my home in San Clemente, and the sale of stock and real estate owned at the time I became President.

TAX REVIEW BY CONGRESSIONAL COMMITTEE

Even with these disclosures, there may continue to be public questions about the tax consequences of two of the transactions shown. One is the gift of my papers to the United States Government in 1969. As permitted by the Internal Revenue Code, I have taken tax deductions for the value of that gift, but some have asked whether the procedures used to make the donation met the technical requirements of the gift law. The second transaction was the sale in 1970 of a large portion of the beneficial interest my wife and I held in our property at San Clemente. No capital gain was declared on that sale for tax purposes, and there has been speculation in the press that the transaction was inaccurately reported.

The tax lawyers and accountants who assisted me in the preparation of my Federal Income tax returns advised me that both of these items were correctly reported to the Internal Revenue Service. My tax attorneys today are giving me similar advice. Furthermore, when it conducted an examination of my tax returns for 1971 and 1972, the Internal Revenue Service reviewed both items and advised me that they were correctly reported.

Nevertheless, questions will continue on these matters and because they are complex transactions, it will not be easy to resolve public doubts without an independent review. For that reason, I have asked the members of the Joint Congressional Committee on Internal Revenue Taxation to examine the procedures relating to both matters and to decide whether, in their judgment, my tax returns should have shown different results. I will abide by the Committee's judgment.

GOVERNMENT SPENDING AT SAN CLEMENTE

Another concern of mine has been the degree of public misunderstanding about Government expenditures at my home in San Clemente.

The perception is now widespread that the Government spent anywhere from $6 million to $10 million on improvements at my home. One myth breeds another, so many observers also believe that the Government improvements have vastly enriched me personally.

Those views are grossly inaccurate. More than 20,000 man-hours have now been expended by the General Services Administration to track down every penny of spending. Their findings establish three points:

• Total GSA spending on my San Clemente home was $68,000. That money was spent almost entirely on fire and smoke detection systems, interior electrical systems for protection and security, and the installation of an electric heating system that the Secret Service thought necessary for safety purposes.

• The GSA spent approximately $635,000 on the grounds surrounding my home. That work consisted largely of the installation of lighting and alarm systems for security purposes, construction of walls and guard posts, and extensive re-landscaping to restore areas torn up when the protective devices were installed.

• By comparison, almost $6 million has been spent by the military services to construct and maintain the Western White House Office complex. That complex is not on my property, but on Government property, and when it is not in use for the White House staff, it is frequently employed as a conference center for public and civic groups.

Unfortunately, the American people have been misled into believing that the funds for the office complex were spent on my home. The fact that the total spent on my home was $68,000 has been ignored; the fact that my wife and I spent ourselves three times as much as that, $187,977 out of our own funds, for real improvements to our homes, has been lost altogether. I trust that with the release of these documents the impressions can be erased and the truth of this matter firmly established.

FUTURE OF THE WESTERN WHITE HOUSE

As public misunderstandings over San Clemente expenditures pass away in the future, we should recognize that the Western White House complex will continue to be a valuable asset for the Nation.

I have always been concerned that over the course of a single man's eight years in office, the country probably will not derive from that complex benefits proportional to the Government investment there. The office facility would, of course, remain available for public use after my term ends, but the usefulness of San Clemente as a conference center, guest facility for visiting foreign dignitaries, and working base for future Presidents would be far greater in the coming decades if what is now my private residence, La Casa Pacifica, could also be part of that complex.

Accordingly, at the time of my death or that of my wife, which ever is later, we intend to make a gift to the people of the United States of my home at San Clemente.

I have directed my attorneys to take the necessary steps to accomplish this, so that future Administrations and future generations can take advantage of this beautiful Western setting to help maintain a truly national perspective for the Presidency.

FINANCIAL SUMMARY

Following is the White House text, released Dec. 8, of a statement on the finances of President and Mrs. Nixon for the period Jan. 1, 1969—May 31, 1973:

I. INTRODUCTION

President Nixon today is releasing to the public more than fifty documents which provide a detailed review of his private financial transactions since taking office in 1969. Contained here is a summary of the major points made in those documents as well as a list of the documents that appear to be relevant to each transaction.

II. PRESIDENT NIXON'S NET ASSETS UPON TAKING OFFICE

As of January 1, 1969, President Nixon's net worth was $307,141. More than half of his assets were in real estate, and a majority of the rest were in stocks, cash and receivables. Nearly all of his liabilities related to his real estate holdings. The following chart, taken from working papers prepared by Coopers & Lybrand, spells out the details:

**THE PRESIDENT AND MRS. NIXON'S
STATEMENT OF ASSETS AND LIABILITIES
JANUARY 1, 1969**

Assets	
Cash in banks	$ 59,752
Due from Mudge, Rose, Guthrie & Alexander	128,611
Due from estate of Hannah Nixon	13,577
Cash value of life insurance and civil service pension fund deposit	44,593
Investment in stock of Fisher's Island, Inc. (at cost)	199,891
Investment in real estate (at cost)	539,367
Miscellaneous accounts receivable	2,718
Total Assets	$988,509
Liabilities	
Mortgages, notes and loans payable	609,869
Due to Tricia Nixon	20,000
Federal income tax payable	37,987
State income tax payable	7,351
Accounts payable and accrued liabilities	6,161
Total Liabilities	681,368
Net Assets	$307,141

III. CHANGES IN THE PRESIDENT'S ASSETS

A. SALES

Since taking office, President Nixon has engaged in three sales that have liquidated part of the assets that he had on January 1, 1969: the sale of his remaining stock in 1969, the sale of his New York City apartment in 1969, and the sale of two vacant lots in Florida in 1972. His proceeds from these three transactions were $771,396.

1. Sale of Stock in Fisher's Island, Inc.

The only stock that President Nixon owned upon taking office was in Fisher's Island, Inc. Fisher's Island, Inc. is a corporation in Florida formed in 1957 for the purpose of acquiring and developing Fisher's Island in Biscayne Bay. Mr. Nixon bought 199,891 shares in the company in 1967 and prior years for $199,891. After he became President, Mr. Nixon decided to limit his investments to real estate, Government bonds and cash or its equivalent. President Nixon transferred 14,000 shares for $13,000 net to fulfill options given by him to others in 1967. He sold 185,891 shares of Fisher's Island stock back to the company on May 22, 1969 for $371,782. His 1969 Federal income tax return shows a capital gain from that sale of $184,891 and tax paid on that amount.

2. Sale of New York City Apartment

When President Nixon was first elected, he and his family maintained a private residence at 810 Fifth Avenue in New York City, purchased in 1963. The cost of the apartment, including improvements, was $166,860.

After the 1968 election, Mr. and Mrs. Nixon decided to replace the New York City dwelling, with a new home in California. They therefore sold the apartment on May 31, 1969 for $312,500. Expenses of the sale amounted to $2,728 and the purchasers reimbursed Mr. and Mrs. Nixon $1,252 of the apartment's maintenance fee. Thus the net proceeds amounted to $311,023. At settlement, the net proceeds were first applied to pay a note of $100,000 to the First National Bank of Miami and accrued interest to the same bank of $3,750. The balance of $207,274 was deposited in his personal checking account at the Key Biscayne Bank and Trust.

A profit of $142,912 was realized on the sale, but under the law, capital gains tax was deferred because of the subsequent purchase of a new residence in California.

3. Sale of Florida Land

In April, 1967, Mr. Nixon bought two undeveloped lots in Florida, as an investment, from Cape Florida Development Company for a total consideration of $38,080.

In May, 1967, Mr. Nixon entered into an oral agreement with his daughter Tricia, who had recently turned 21 and who had received the proceeds of a trust fund which had been set up for her by a family friend, Mr. Elmer Bobst, when Tricia was 12. Pursuant to this agreement, Tricia loaned $20,000 to her father, in return for a demand note for $20,000 and a 40 percent participation in any profit from the real estate venture. Miss Nixon was to have no management or control over the property and would receive the $20,000 back from her father regardless of whether the venture proved successful.

Then on December 28, 1972, the properties were sold to William Griffin for $150,000. Sales expenses were $650, leaving a balance of $149,350 and a total profit of $111,270.

At closing on December 28, 1972, Mr. Griffin paid $38,500 and delivered two purchase money notes, one in the amount of $95,850, due and payable on January 10, 1973; and one in the amount of $15,000, due and payable on December 13, 1973. The first note was paid when due. The second note has recently been paid. Total proceeds received to May 31, 1973 amounted to $134,350.

Under the prior arrangement with his daughter, President Nixon paid her 40 percent of the profit, which amounted to $44,508, plus the original $20,000. The aggregate transfers of funds were rounded up from $64,508 to $65,000, with the difference of $492 treated as a gift from the President to Tricia.

Mrs. Cox declared in her 1972 tax return, filed jointly with her husband, that she had realized a capital gain of $11,617 in 1972, while President Nixon showed in his 1972 tax return that he had realized a gain of $17,424. Earlier this year, payments were made on the final installment so that the 1973 Federal income tax returns for Mr. and Mrs. Cox should reflect a gain of $32,891, and the returns for President and Mrs. Nixon should reflect a gain of $49,338.

Thus, as the documents show, there has been no attempt by the President to shield his daughter from the income taxes that she owes on the sale of this Florida property.

Additional details on these transactions can be found in the following documents made public today:

• Letter from Arthur Blech, accountant to Edward F. Cox dated November 26, 1973, showing the allocation of the capital gain between the President and Mrs. Cox and attaching the relevant schedule from the Coxes' tax return for 1972 reporting her forty percent share of the gain.

• Demand note dated June 28, 1967 from Richard M. Nixon to Patricia Nixon at 6 percent interest, evidencing her investment in Cape Florida lots transaction.

B. PURCHASES

President and Mrs. Nixon now own residences in two locations: Key Biscayne, Florida and San Clemente, California. The Key Biscayne properties were purchased before the President took office and the San Clemente property was purchased in the first year of his Presidency. Details on these acquisitions were compiled by Coopers & Lybrand and released by the White House on August 27, 1973. The President has directed that the earlier report and a general summary be presented again.

1. Key Biscayne Residential Properties

On December 19, 1968, when he was President-elect, Mr. Nixon bought two adjacent residential properties at Key Biscayne, Florida. One of the residences, located at 500 Bay Lane, was purchased from Senator and Mrs. George A. Smathers for $125,527. The second, located next door at 516 Bay Lane, was purchased from Manuel Arca, Jr. and Evora Bonet de Arca for $127,800. The total price for the two purchases was $253,455.

In order to finance these purchases, Mr. Nixon on the same day in December borrowed $65,000 from the First National Bank of Miami, and then made down payments on the two properties of $63,740 and to meet the balance of the purchase price, assumed or entered into mortgages totaling $189,966 (a price reflecting closing costs at settlement of $251). These transactions are spelled out in greater detail in the Coopers & Lybrand property report of August 20, 1973.

After becoming President, Mr. Nixon on June 13, 1969 refinanced two mortgages that were coming due by borrowing $100,000 from the Greater Miami Federal Savings and Loan Association and giving a mortgage for that amount. In paying off the existing mortgages the President paid $11,100 from his own funds. On September 4, 1969, also drawing upon his own funds, the President repaid the $65,000 loan that he had obtained the previous December from the First National Bank of Miami.

As a result of monthly payments on his mortgages since 1968, the President had by May 31, 1973, reduced the total balance of his mortgages on both properties to approximately $161,000. As of that same date, as the Coopers & Lybrand report shows, the President had paid $76,421 from his personal funds for improvements to the two properties, including furniture and remodeling.

Additional details can be found in the following documents made public today:

• Letter of August 7, 1973, from Wakefield, Hewitt & Webster, to Coopers & Lybrand describing the acquisition of the two houses of President and Mrs. Nixon at 500 and 516 Bay Lane, Key Biscayne, and the purchase and sale of two lots at Cape Florida. Title papers and mortgages relating to these transactions are attached to the letter.

2. San Clemente
a.   Purchase of the Property

The homesite that the Nixons chose in California was part of the Old Cotton property in San Clemente, halfway between Los Angeles and San Diego.

The Nixons wanted to buy only 5.9 acres of a 26-acre tract, but the sellers insisted that the tract be sold as a single unit. A trust was formed to enable the trustee to take title on behalf of President and Mrs. Nixon to the entire 26-acre tract.

On April 24, 1969, the Nixons created the trust and named as trustee the Title Insurance and Trust Company of Los Angeles. In order to finance the down payments, the President borrowed $450,000 from a close friend, Mr. Robert Abplanalp. The loan, made on July 11, 1969, carried an 8 percent interest rate.

On July 15, 1969, the trust bought the entire 26-acre tract for $1,400,100 and held it in trust for the Nixons. The trust made a down payment of $399,609 and paid $491 in settlement costs with funds supplied by the Nixons. The trust also issued a promissory note for the remaining $1 million. The note (called the "Cotton note") was to be paid back in five years and carried an annual interest rate of 7.5 percent.

On October 13, 1969, in order to provide better access and privacy for the Nixons, the trust acquired from the Elmore family an additional parcel of 2.9 acres immediately adjacent to the Old Cotton property. The total cost of this purchase was $100,054. To finance it, the trust made a down payment of $20,054 with funds supplied by the President and the trustee gave a promissory note (called the "Elmore note") for the remaining $80,000. This remainder was to be paid back in five annual installments at 7.5 percent annual interest.

b.   Initial Mortgage Payments

In July, 1970, the Nixons paid $175,000 to the trustee which in turn paid $175,000 on the Cotton note, of which $100,000 was for principal. That entire payment was financed by a second loan of $175,000 from Mr. Abplanalp to the President. This Abplanalp loan also carried an 8 percent interest rate.

In October, 1970, through the trustee, the President made the first payment on the Elmore note—$22,000, of which $16,000 was for principal. The $22,000 was paid from the President's own funds.

c.   Sale to B&C Investment Company

On December 15, 1970, following up on their original desire to own only a portion of the Cotton property and to sell the rest to a compatible buyer, President and Mrs. Nixon sold to the B&C Investment Company a portion of their interest in trust, representing a large part of the Cotton property and all of the Elmore property. The two co-partners of the partnership were Mr. Abplanalp and C. G. Rebozo; in August of 1973, Mr. Rebozo sold his entire interest in the partnership to Mr. Abplanalp.

The sale was for the amount of $1,249,000. As consideration, the B&C Investment Company (1) cancelled the two loans that Mr. Nixon owed to Mr. Abplanalp, which amounted to $625,000; (2) assumed the entire principal amount of the Elmore note, which was then $64,000; and (3) assumed $560,000 of the principal amount of the Cotton note, which was then outstanding in the amount of $900,000.

As a result of the sale, the Nixons now retain the beneficial interest in 5.9 acres of land at San Clemente that they wanted originally, including the home and the improvements thereon. The B&C Investment Company has the beneficial interest in the remaining 23 acres of land. The President's interest in the property remained subject to the mortgage for $340,000.

Section IV below contains a discussion of the tax aspects of the sale.

d.   Present Status of San Clemente

The Coopers & Lybrand audit report shows that as of May 31, 1973, the unpaid balance of the Nixons' obligation on the Cotton note amounted to $264,400, payable in two annual installments at 7.5 percent interest. One of those installments,

totaling $37,780, was paid on July 15, 1973. The second installment, totaling $226,660, is due on July 15, 1974.

Further details of the San Clemente transaction may be found in the Coopers & Lybrand property report, released by the White House on August 27, 1973, with accompanying documents, including the letter of instruction for establishment of the trust and the sales agreement with the B&C Investment Company. In addition, the White House is making public today the following documents:

• $1,000,000 promissory note of July 10, 1969, to Cotton heirs signed by the trustee, Title Insurance and Trust Company of Los Angeles.

• $80,000 promissory note of September 11, 1969, to the Elmore family signed by the trustee.

• 8 percent promissory notes of July 15, 1969 and July 15, 1970 for $450,000 and $175,000 to Robert Abplanalp signed by Richard and Patricia Nixon, which were the source of the cash originally converted by the Nixons in the San Clemente property.

• Abplanalp checks dated July 9, 1969 and July 14, 1970 in the amounts of $450,000 and $175,000, respectively. The first was deposited in the Kalmbach client trust account at the Security Pacific National Bank set up for the purpose of the acquisition and operation of the San Clemente property and the second in the Key Biscayne Bank.

• Audit by Arthur Blech & Company, Certified Public Accountants, of Kalmbach client trust account at Security Pacific National Bank through December 31, 1969, showing deposit of Abplanalp loan of $450,000, the down payment on the Cotton purchase of $399,609, the down payment on the Elmore purchase of $20,054 and expenditures for improvements, furniture, taxes and maintenance at San Clemente.

• Statements of gross income and gross expenditures of B&C Investment Company for 1971 and 1972, and statement of C. G. Rebozo's investment therein from January 1, 1971 through December 31, 1972.

IV. THE PRESIDENT'S TAXES

A. PREPARATION OF THE PRESIDENT'S TAX RETURNS

In 1969, President Nixon retained, for tax advice, the law firm of Kalmbach, DeMarco, Knapp & Chillingworth, a firm with offices in Los Angeles and Newport Beach, California.

In turn, the Kalmbach firm engaged Arthur Blech & Company, Certified Public Accountants in Los Angeles, to maintain the President's financial books and records and to assist in the preparation of his tax returns.

Federal income tax returns for President and Mrs. Nixon for the years 1969, 1970, 1971, and 1972 were all prepared by the Blech firm and then checked and approved by the Kalmbach firm.

In 1973, the Internal Revenue Service audited President and Mrs. Nixon's returns for the years 1971 and 1972. This investigation included a review of the sale he made of part of his interest in San Clemente in 1970, and the gift of his papers in 1969. Upon completion of that examination, the District Director of the Internal Revenue Service in Baltimore, where the President's returns were examined, wrote a letter to President Nixon on June 1, 1973, stating: "Our examination of your income tax returns for the years 1971 and 1972 revealed that they are correct. Accordingly, these returns are accepted as filed...."

Documents made public today which relate to the preparation and examination of the tax returns are as follows:

• Letter from William D. Waters, District Director of Internal Revenue Service to President Nixon, dated June 1, 1973.

• Income tax data from President and Mrs. Nixon's joint returns for the years 1969, 1970, 1971 and 1972, including copies of the returns as well as summaries of the information shown in the returns.

B. PAYMENT OF TAXES

The documents released by the President today show the following amount of Federal income tax paid by the President from 1969 through 1972:

FEDERAL TAX RETURN TOTALS
FOR THE PRESIDENT AND MRS. NIXON

(1969 - 1972 TAX RETURNS)*

	1969	1970	1971	1972
Total Income	$328,161.52	$262,942.56	$262,384.75	$268,777.54
Deductions	178,535.10	307,181.92	255,676.69	247,569.77
Exemptions	1,800.00	- 0 -	1,350.00	1,500.00
Taxable Income	147,826.42	- 0 -	5,358.06	19,707.77
Net Tax Paid	72,682.09	792.81**	878.03	4,298.17

President and Mrs. Nixon, like most other individual taxpayers, file their Federal income tax returns on the cash basis. This means that a taxpayer reports items of income in the year he receives the related cash and that he reports items of expense in the year when they are paid in cash. On the other hand, the financial statements included in the Coopers & Lybrand audit report are prepared on a different basis, accrual accounting, which is required to conform with generally accepted accounting principles. (See the American Institute of Certified Public Accountants publication entitled "Audits of Personal Financial Statements.") Under accrual accounting, items of income should be included in the year when they become receivable even though the cash may be collected at a later time. Also, items of expense should be included in the year they are incurred even though related payment may occur at a later time.

** As required by the Internal Revenue Code, a "minimum tax" was paid in 1970 even though there was no taxable income. The net tax amount shown above for 1970 does not include payment of $659 made in that year with respect to an underpayment of taxes in 1968.

The table above shows that in each year, the amount of the President's income that was taxable was substantially reduced by deductions permitted under the Internal Revenue Code. There have been three major sources of these deductions: interest payments in his properties, totaling $257,376; property taxes, totaling $81,255; and deductions for the President's gift to the United States of his papers, totaling $482,019.

THE PRESIDENT AND MRS. NIXON
DETAILS OF TOTAL INCOME AND DEDUCTIONS

(1969 - 1972 TAX RETURNS)

	1969	1970	1971	1972
Wages and expense allowance	$236,468.86	$250,000.00	$250,000.00	$250,000.00
Interest	3,913.79	10,250.56	17,733.04	16,292.94
Income other than wages and interest	87,778.89	2,692.00	(5,348.29)	2,484.60
Total Income	$328,161.54	$262,942.56	$262,384.75	$268,777.54
Deductions				
Taxes	$ 22,453.36	$ 27,797.79	$ 18,153.18	$ 24,663.77
Charitable contributions	98,448.45	131,471.28	131,192.37	134,388.77
Interest	25,594.32	109,054.19	67,003.25	55,724.39
Medical expenses	150.00	150.00		
Miscellaneous	31,888.97	38,708.60	39,327.89	32,792.84
Total Deductions	$178,535.10	$307,181.92	$255,676.69	$247,569.77

Because questions have been publicly raised about two items in the President's tax returns—the gift of his papers and the sale of a partial interest in the San Clemente property in 1970—they are discussed here in some detail.

1. Gift of Papers

In 1969, President Nixon directed his lawyers to take all necessary steps to make a gift of part of his papers to the United States of America through the National Archives. On March 27, 1969, large crates of his papers were delivered to the Archives. Included were a large volume of paper, books and other memorabilia of his career prior to becoming President, including many of his Vice Presidential papers. On April 8 and 9, 1969, Mr. Ralph Newman, a recognized appraiser of documents, visited the Archives and made a final appraisal of a fair market value of the papers comprising the gift, setting the value at $576,000.

In making the gift, President Nixon was following the tradition of his six predecessors—Hoover, Roosevelt, Truman, Eisenhower, Kennedy and Johnson—all of whom made a gift of their papers to the United States.

A question has arisen in the case of President Nixon, however, because in December, 1969, an amendment was passed retroactive to July 25, 1969, disallowing such deductions and some critics question whether technical requirements relating to the intended gift were sufficiently completed before the expiration date.

President Nixon was and is advised by his attorneys that the gift met the deductibility requirements of the law. Accordingly, in the tax years 1969-1972, he has taken deductions totaling approximately $482,019. As the gift is valued at $576,000, he is still entitled to additional deductions of $93,981.

The examination conducted earlier this year by the Internal Revenue Service of President and Mrs. Nixon's returns for the years 1971 and 1972 included a review of the gift. Upon completing this review, the IRS raised no questions about the deductions taken. Nevertheless, because questions have been raised about the procedures followed in making the gift of the papers to the United States, the President is asking the Joint Committee on Internal Revenue Taxation to review those procedures and to pass upon the validity of his tax deductions. The President will abide by the decision of that Committee.

Additional details relating to the gift transaction can be found in the following documents being released today:

• Appraisal by Ralph G. Newman, President of Abraham Lincoln Book Shop of Chicago, Illinois, of papers of Richard Milhous Nixon, consisting of 600,000 items, as of March 27, 1969 at a valuation of $576,000, supported by Newman affidavit and statement of his qualifications as an authority in the field of such appraisals.

• Letter from Kalmbach, DeMarco, Knapp & Chillingworth to Coopers & Lybrand stating their opinion regarding the deductibility for tax purposes of the President's gift of pre-Presidential papers.

2. Tax Aspects of San Clemente Sale in 1970

On December 15, 1970, President and Mrs. Nixon sold their interest in 23 acres of property in San Clemente to the B&C Investment Company.

In determining whether a capital gain had been realized for tax purposes, the President's tax accountant, Mr. Arthur Blech, C.P.A., first had to decide how the original cost of the entire property, including both the Cotton and Elmore parcels, should be allocated between the property sold to the B&C Investment Company and the property retained by the Nixons. The regulations of the Commissioner of the Internal Revenue Service provide in Section 1.61-6:

"...When a part of a larger property is sold, the cost or other basis of the entire property shall be equitably apportioned among the several parts, and the gain realized or loss sustained on the part of the entire property sold is the difference between the selling price and the cost or other basis allocated to such part. The sale of each part is treated as a separate transaction and gain or loss shall be completed separately on each part. This gain or loss shall be determined at the time of sale of each part and not deferred until the entire property has been disposed of...."

It is clear that the apportionment of the cost of the property between the portion sold and the portion retained involved matters of judgment.

Drawing upon his knowledge of the values of property in Orange County, California, where the San Clemente property is located, Mr. Blech determined that as of the date of sale in 1970, the property retained by President and Mrs. Nixon had a fair market value of $376,000. From this amount of $376,000, he deducted the cost of improvements made by the Nixons from the time they purchased their San Clemente property in 1969 until the time of the sale in 1970. Those improvements amounted to $96,000. By subtracting the cost of the improvements from the fair market value, he concluded that the original cost to be allocated to the retained property should be approximately $280,000.

Having determined the original cost that should be allocated to the property *retained,* Mr. Blech could determine the cost that should be allocated to the property *sold.* The Nixons' total purchase cost for the Cotton and Elmore properties was $1,529,447, including $29,293 in acquisition costs. By subtracting $280,000 from that total, Mr. Blech determined that the original cost that should be allocated to the property sold was approximately $1,249,000.

In the sale negotiations which took place in 1970, the B&C Investment Company agreed to buy the beneficial interest in the entire Elmore parcel and a large part of the Cotton property parcel for the price of $1,249,000, as shown by the Coopers & Lybrand audit report.

Based upon that sales price and upon the evaluations made by Mr. Blech, the sale was reported in President and Mrs. Nixon's Federal income tax returns for 1970 as follows:

	Sales Price	Cost	Gain or Loss
Cotton	$1,148,946.40	$1,148,946.40	0
Elmore	100,053.60	100,053.60	0

The Coopers & Lybrand audit report reaches a different conclusion. It reports that the cost basis of the property retained by the Nixons in 1970 should have been approximately $397,817 and that, as a result, a gain of $117,370 was realized upon the sale. The figure of $397,817 was determined from a consideration of the cost incurred, as well as valuations made by independent appraisers at the time the Cotton property was acquired, a customary practice used for accounting purposes.

Even if a gain of $117,370 had been reported in the 1970 Federal income tax return, no tax would have been payable in that year because the President's declared deductions exceeded his income by $44,239, and he could have taken an additional deduction for the gift he made of his papers in 1969 (recognizing, of course, that the larger deduction in 1970 would have reduced the deduction carryover available to him in later years).

The President was and is advised by his attorneys that his method of reporting was accurate for tax purposes and in full accordance with the law. The Internal Revenue Service has also reviewed the transaction and has not challenged it.

Nevertheless, because questions have been publicly raised about the method of reporting, the President has asked the Joint Committee on Internal Revenue Taxation to review the procedures followed and to give him their judgment on what gain, if any, should have been declared. He will abide by their decision.

V. NET ASSETS IN 1973

As shown by the Coopers & Lybrand audit report, the net assets of President and Mrs. Nixon as of May 31, 1973, totaled $988,522.

Their major assets were their cash holdings, amounting to approximately $430,000 (including $250,000 of certificates of deposit), and their investments in land, buildings, and furnishings, amounting to approximately $964,000. Their largest single asset was the San Clemente property which the President has today announced will be conveyed to the Government as a gift.

Their major liabilities were the payments they owe on their residential properties. As of the May 31 date, some $206,241 was still owed on mortgage notes in Key Biscayne and Whittier, California, and $264,440 was owed on the Cotton note.

It is worth noting in conclusion that while the President's net assets, according to the Coopers & Lybrand audit report, have increased from approximately $307,141 in 1969 to $988,522 in 1973, those assets will be substantially reduced by the eventual transfer to the United States of the San Clemente property, now carried in the Coopers & Lybrand net worth statement at a cost of $571,167.

The balance sheet taken from the Coopers & Lybrand audit report shows the following assets and liabilities for the President and Mrs. Nixon as of May 31, 1973:

THE PRESIDENT AND MRS. NIXON
STATEMENT OF ASSETS AND LIABILITIES

May 31, 1973

ASSETS

Cash in Banks		
Key Biscayne Bank, Key Biscayne, Florida including $250,000 of certificates of deposit, due June 21, 1973	$426,313	
Other banks	6,561	$ 432,874
Accounts and note receivable		28,609
Income tax withheld in excess of estimated taxes		19,816
U.S. Savings Bonds, Series E, at cost (face amount $5,300)		3,975
Cash value of life insurance and Civil Service Pension Fund deposit		63,519
Land, buildings and furnishings, at cost, less accumulated depreciation:		
Residential properties:		
Key Biscayne, Florida	311,929	
Casa Pacifica, San Clemente, California	571,167	
Improved real estate, Whittier, California	77,515	
Office furniture, Washington, D.C.	3,553	964,164
		$1,512,957

LIABILITIES

Withholding tax payable	355
Accrued interest and real estate taxes	20,399
Deferred income tax accrued	33,000
Mortgages payable	206,241
Obligation for note payable issued by Trust for San Clemente property	264,440
	524,435
Net Assets	$ 988,522 ✓

MAJOR PRESIDENTIAL
STATEMENTS

JAN. 31

Prisoner Return

Following is the text, as made available by the White House, of President Nixon's Jan. 31 news conference:

THE PRESIDENT: Won't you be seated.

In view of the announcement that has already been made this morning, I know that you will have questions on that and other matters, so we will go right to the questions. I think Miss Thomas has the first question.

Q: Can you tell us whether you are going to meet with President Thieu some time this spring and also give us a better feel on Dr. Kissinger's trip, the purpose and so forth?

THE PRESIDENT: At some time this spring I do plan to meet with President Thieu. I have discussed the matter with him in correspondence and I also discussed it yesterday in my meeting with the Foreign Minister. It will be at a time mutually convenient.

The UPI story, incidentally, was on the mark except for the location. The location we have agreed on will be the Western White House this spring.

As far as Dr. Kissinger's trip is concerned, this is a matter that we feel is very important in terms of developing the post-war relationship with North Vietnam. When we look at this very intricate agreement, which Dr. Kissinger so brilliantly briefed for the members of the press, and if you have read it, you will see why I use the word intricate, we can see that insofar as its terms are concerned, if the agreement is kept, there is no question about the fact that we will have peace in not only Vietnam, but in Indochina for a very long period of time. But the question is whether both parties, in fact, all parties involved, have a will to peace, if any have incentives to peace, if they have desire to peace.

Now, on this particular point, it is necessary, of course, for us to talk to the South Vietnamese as we are. It is also vitally important that we have a direct communication with the North Vietnamese. And Dr. Kissinger will be going to Hanoi to meet with the top leaders of the Government of the DRV. There he will discuss the post-war relationship. He will, of agreement which we have made and he will also discuss, in terms of post-war relationships, the matter of the reconstruction program for all of Indochina.

As the leaders probably reported after my meeting with them, the day after I announced the cease fire agreement, I raised with the leaders the point that the United States would consider for both North Vietnam and South Vietnam and the other countries in the area a reconstruction program.

I, of course, recognized in raising this with the leaders that there would have to be Congressional consultation and Congressional support. In terms of this particular matter at this time, Dr. Kissinger will be having an initial conversation with the North Vietnamese with regard to this whole reconstruction program.

I should also say that I have noted that many Congressmen and Senators and many of the American people are not keen on helping any of the countries in that area, just as they are not keen on foreign aid in general. As far as I am concerned, whether it is with the North or the South or the other countries in the area, I look upon this as a potential investment in peace, to the extent that the North Vietnamese, for example, participate with us and with other interested countries in the reconstruction of North Vietnam, they will have a tendency to turn inward to the works of peace rather than turning outward to the works of war.

This, at least, is our motive, and we will know more about it after Dr. Kissinger completes his talks with them, which we think will be quite extensive and very frank since he has already, obviously, paved the way for it.

Q: Mr. President, Dr. Kissinger is going to Vietnam and is due there in Hanoi on February 10. Is this related in any way with the first prisoners of war to come out of Hanoi?

THE PRESIDENT: Not at all.

Q: I mean, is the date a coincidence?

THE PRESIDENT: The date is a pure coincidence, and Dr. Kissinger will not be meeting with the prisoners of war. Incidentally, speaking of the POW question, I have noted some speculation in the press, and it isn't speculation, I should say, that is justified because I understand there was a Defense Department report to this effect, that I was going to go out to Travis Air Force Base to meet the first POWs when they came in.

I do not intend to do so. I have the greatest admiration for the prisoners of war, for their stamina and their courage and the rest, and also for their wives and their parents and their children who have been so strong during this long period of their vigil.

This is a time that we should not grandstand it; we should not exploit it. We should remember that it is not like astronauts coming back from the moon after what is, of course, shall we say, a very spectacular and dangerous journey, but these are men who have been away sometimes for years. They have a right to be home with their families just as quickly as they possibly can, and I am going to respect that right, of course, to the extent that any of them or their families desiring to visit the White House can be sure that they will be very high on the list.

Q: Mr. President, do you have anything specifically in mind to help heal the wounds in this country, the divisions over the war, and specifically, anything down the road much farther in terms of amnesty?

THE PRESIDENT: Well, it takes two to heal wounds, and I must say, when I see that the most vigorous criticism or, shall we say, the least pleasure out of the peace agreement comes from those who were the most outspoken advocates of peace at any price, it makes one realize whether some want the wounds healed. We do.

We think we have taken a big step toward ending a long and difficult war which was not begun while we were here, and I am not casting any aspersions on those Presidents who were in office who can no longer be here to speak for themselves, for the causes of the war. I am simply saying this: that as far as this Administration is concerned, we have done the very best that we can against very great obstacles, and we finally have achieved a peace with honor.

I know it gags some of you to write that phrase, but it is true, and most Americans realize it is true, because it would be peace with dishonor had we—what some have used, the vernacular—"bugged out" and allowed what the North Vietnamese wanted: the imposition of a Communist Government or a coalition Communist Government in South Vietnam. That goal they have failed to achieve. Consequently, we can speak of peace with honor and with some pride that it has been achieved.

Now, I suppose, Mr. Sheldon, that your question with regard to amnesty may deal with the problems of healing the wounds. Certainly I have sympathy for any individual who has made a mistake. We have all made mistakes. But also, it is a rule of life, we all have to pay for our mistakes.

One of the most moving wires I received, of the many thousands that have come in to the White House since the peace announcement, was from a man who was in prison in Michigan, I believe it is, and he spoke about a group of his fellow inmates. They are in a work camp, so I suppose they are being rehabilitated to come out.

He wrote very emotionally about what we had done and he felt it was an achievement they were very proud of. I feel sorry for that man; on the other hand, it is not my right, and I should not exercise such a right, because he so wrote to me, to say "Now you are forgiven for what you did."

Now, as far as amnesty is concerned, I have stated my views, and those views remain exactly the same. The war is over.

Many Americans paid a very high price to serve their country, some with their lives, some as prisoners of war for as long as six to seven years, and, of course, 2-1/2 million, 2 to 3 years out of their lives, serving in a country far away in a war that they realize had very little support among the so-called better people, in the media and the intellectual circles, and the rest, which had very little support, certainly, among some elements of the Congress, particularly the United States Senate, but which fortunately did have support among a majority of the American people, who some way, despite the fact that they were hammered night after night, and day after day, with the fact that this was an immoral war, that America should not be there, that they should not serve their country, that morally what they should do was desert their country.

Certainly as we look at all of that, there might be a tendency to say now, to those few hundreds who went to Canada or Sweden or someplace else, and chose to desert their country because they had a higher morality, we should now give them amnesty.

Now, amnesty means forgiveness. We cannot provide forgiveness for them. Those who served paid their price. Those who deserted must pay their price, and the price is not a junket in the Peace Corps, or something like that, as some have suggested. The price is a criminal penalty for disobeying the laws of the United States. If they want to return to the United States they must pay the penalty. If they don't want to return, they are certainly welcome to stay in any country that welcomes them. Mr. Theis.

Post-War Reconstruction

Q: Do you have any floor or ceiling dollar figure in mind for the rehabilitation of North Vietnam or the rest of Indochina?

THE PRESIDENT: Mr. Theis, that is a matter that the Members of the Congress raised with me, as you might imagine, and they raised it not only with regard to North Vietnam, but with regard to South Vietnam and Cambodia and Laos in this period as we move into the cease-fire and, we hope, peacetime reconstruction.

I cannot give you that figure now, because it is a matter that has to be negotiated and it must be all part of one pattern. The figure, of course, will come out. The figures will come out, but they must first be discussed with the bipartisan leadership because, with all of this talk about the powers of the Presidency, let me say I am keenly aware of the fact that even though I might believe that a program of reconstruction for North Vietnam, as well as South Vietnam, is an investment in peace, the Congress has to believe it. The Congress has to support it. And this is going to be one of the more difficult assignments I have had as President, but I think we can make it if the Congress sees what the stakes are.

Q: Mr. President, sir, Senator Hollings said on a recent trip to Southeast Asia he discovered that we are letting some countries, including Japan, have 2 percent money, yet we have denied our own farmers in rural cooperatives 2 percent money. We are telling them they have to have their loans at 5 percent. Would you comment on this and how this might relate to your upcoming program of aid to Southeast Asia?

THE PRESIDENT: Well, as far as the program of aid is concerned and the percentage of interest that is paid, we will, of course, have in mind the interest of the American people. We want to be fair, of course, to those who have been our allies and in the great tradition of America when it fights wars to those who have been our enemies, like Germany and Japan, who, with America's help now have become our two greatest competitors in the free world.

Now, when you get down to whether the percentage will be 2 percent or 5 percent or 3 percent, that is a matter to be negotiated, but we will be fair and we will see that our farmers also are treated fairly.

Let me say, if I could, with regard to REA—and Miss Mc-Clendon, because you are somewhat of an expert on this—I have always supported REA because I used to represent the old 12th District. When I lived there and represented it, it was primarily agricultural, orange groves; now it is primarily people, subdivided. But as one who came from that area, I naturally had a great interest in this matter of REA and the rest, and supported it.

But what I have found is that when I first voted for REA, 80 percent of the loans went for the purpose of rural development and getting electricity to farms. Now 80 percent of this 2 percent money goes for country clubs and dilettantes, for example, and others who can afford living in the country. I am not for 2 percent money for people who can afford 5 percent or 7.

Relations With Europe

Q: Mr. President, you and people in your Administration have been quoted as calling 1973 the year of Europe. Could you tell us exactly what that means to you, and specifically, will you be making a trip to Europe in the next month or so?

THE PRESIDENT: I will not be making any trips to Europe certainly in the first half of this year. Whether I can make any trips later on remains to be seen. As a matter of fact, so that all of you can plan not to take shots, I plan no trips whatever in the first half of this year outside the United States. The meeting with President Thieu, if it does work out, at a time mutually convenient, will take place in the spring.

Now, the fact that I don't take a trip to Europe does not mean that this will not be a period when there will be great attention paid to Europe, because it just happens as we complete the long and difficult war in Vietnam, we now must turn to the problems of Europe. We have been to the People's Republic of China. We have been to the Soviet Union. We have been paying attention to the problems of Europe, but those problems will be put on the front burner.

There is the problem of trade, for example. There is the problem of the European Security Conference which we must discuss. There is the problem of mutual balanced force reduction. All of this will require consultation with our European allies, and in that connection that is one of the reasons that the Heath visit is so enormously important.

I am spending more time with Mr. Heath than I have with some other visitors. I mean by that not that time proves everything, but not only will we have the usual dinners and luncheions and so forth, but I am spending a full day with him at Camp David because I want to get his thoughts about what the position of the United States and our European friends should be with regard to the European Security Conference, with regard to the MBFR, and, of course, what the position of the United States should be and the new, broader European Community should be in this period when we can either become competitors in a constructive way or where we can engage in economic confrontation that could lead to bitterness and which would hurt us both.

We want to avoid that, even though it has been predicted by some in this country who really fear the new Europe. I do not fear it if we talk to them and consult at this time.

Q: Mr. President.

THE PRESIDENT: Mr. Deakin.

Q: You are quoted as telling a recent visitor that you believe Governor Connally will be the Republican nominee of 1976. Is that correct?

THE PRESIDENT: I had thought we had just completed an election. (Laughter)

Q: Just a little foresight there.

THE PRESIDENT: Having just completed one, let me give some advice, if I can, to all of those who may be thinking of becoming candidates in 1976.

I have a considerable amount of experience in getting nominations and winning elections and also losing them. So, consequently, I would suggest that as far as the Presidential candidate is concerned, he is out of his mind if he allows any activity in his behalf or participates in any activity in his behalf, running for the nomination before the elections of 1974 are concluded.

If I were advising people who are interested in becoming and running for President, for the nomination in either party, I would say the best way to get the nomination now is not to be out seeking it. The best way to get it is to work as hard as you can for the success of the candidates of your party, be they for the House or the Senate or Governor and do it in a selfless way until after 1974 and immediately after 1974 take off and run as fast as you can. And I have always done that and with mixed results. (Laughter)

But as far as Governor Connally is concerned, you all know my very high respect for him. I have stated my belief that he could handle any job that I can think of in this country or in the world for that matter, but I would be out of my mind if I were to be endorsing anybody for the Presidency at the present time when there are a number of people who have indicated or whose friends have indicated—that they might have an interest in the position and that is just fine.

You have Governor Connally, and, of course, many have suggested that the Vice President would be interested. I assume that several Governors might be interested. In fact, one of these days, perhaps right after the '74 elections, I will give you my list and it will be quite a long one because I am not going to make my choice until after they have been through a few primaries.

Stennis Shooting

Q: Can you give us your reaction to the shooting of Senator Stennis?

THE PRESIDENT: Well, I called Mrs. Stennis last night, as I am sure many others of his friends did, and it is just one of those senseless things that happens, apparently. When she told me that all they got was his billfold, she said it didn't have much in it, and his Phi Beta Kappa key and also his watch, apparently. So, it is one of those things that happens in our cities today. Fortunately not happening as much as it did previously.

The point that I would make with regard to Senator Stennis, and this is what I told her, is that I just hope that the doctors did the most superb job they have ever done. I hope that his spirit would see him through this physically and in every other way, because of all the Senators in the United States Senate, Democrat or Republican, in terms of our being able to achieve the honorable peace we have achieved, John Stennis was the most indispensible.

Gun Control

Q: Mr. President, I would like to ask you, along those lines, you said it was such a senseless thing. The White House, this Administration has not spoken out very strongly against gun controls, particularly hand guns. I would like to know perhaps if maybe you are going to have second thoughts about that now?

THE PRESIDENT: Well, as you know, the problem with that is not so much the White House speaking out on hand guns, and Saturday night specials, which I think this may have been. I haven't seen the latest reports, but the doctor last night told me it was a .22 caliber cheap gun kind of a thing and Mrs. Stennis said it sounded like firecrackers. Obviously if they had had a .45, he would be dead.

We have, and I have, as you know, advocated legislation to deal with what we call the Saturday night specials which can be acquired by anybody, including juveniles, and apparently there are some suggestions that juveniles were those involved in this case. I am not charging that, incidentally, I am saying what I read in the papers, most of which, as you know, is true.

So, under the circumstances, I feel that Senator Hruska, who introduced the bill before and then it came a cropper in the Senate Judiciary Committee, will now work with the Judiciary Committee in attempting to find the formula which will get the support necessary to deal with this specific problem, with-

out, at the same time, running afoul of the rights of those who believe that they need guns for hunting and all that sort of thing.

Let me say personally, I have never hunted in my life, I have no interest in guns and so forth. I am not interested in the National Rifle Association or anything from a personal standpoint, but I do know that in terms of the United States Congress, what we need is a precise definition which will keep the guns out of the hands of the criminals and not one that will impinge on the rights of others to have them for their own purposes in a legitimate way.

Incidentally, the legislation that we originally suggested or that we discussed with Senator Hruska, I thought precisely dealt with the problem, but it did not get through the Senate. My guess is that Senator Stennis—everything perhaps has a down side and an up side; I guess everything really does. But the very fact that Senator Stennis was the victim of one of these things—we thought this was the case when Governor Wallace was—but in this instance, it was apparently one of these small hand guns that most people, most reasonable people, except for the all-out opponents of any kind of legislation in this field—most reasonable people believe it should be controlled. Perhaps we can get some action . I hope the Senate does act.

I have asked the Attorney General—had asked incidentally before this happened—as one of his projects for this year to give us a legislative formula, not one that would simply speak to the country, and not get through, but one that can get through the Congress. That is the problem.

Q: Mr. President.

THE PRESIDENT: Mr. Mollenhoff.

Executive Privilege

Q: Did you approve of the use of executive privilege by Air Force Secretary Seamans in refusing to disclose the White House role in the firing of air cost analyst Fitzgerald?

It came up yesterday in the Civil Service hearings. He used executive privilege. You had stated earlier that you would approve all of these uses of executive privilege, as I understood it, and I wondered whether your view still prevails in this area or whether others are now entitled to use executive privilege on their own in this type of case?

THE PRESIDENT: Mr. Mollenhoff, your first assumption is correct. In my dealings with the Congress—I say mine, let me put it in a broader sense—in the dealings of the Executive with the Congress, I do not want to abuse the executive privilege proposition where the matter does not involve a direct conference with or discussion within the Administration, particularly where the President is involved. And where it is an extraneous matter as far as the White House is concerned, as was the case when we waived executive privilege for Mr. Flanigan last year, as you will recall, we are not going to assert it.

In this case, as I understand it—and I did not approve this directly, but it was approved at my direction by those who have the responsibility in the White House—in this case it was a proper area in which the executive privilege should have been used.

On the other hand, I can assure you that all of these cases will be handled on a case by case basis and we are not going to be in a position where an individual, when he gets under heat from a Congressional committee, can say, "Look, I am going to assert executive privilege." He will call down here, and Mr. Dean, the White House counsel, will then advise him as to whether or not we approve it.

Q: I want to follow one question on this.

THE PRESIDENT: Sure.

Q: This seems to be an expansion of what executive privilege was in the past and you were quite critical of executive privilege in 1948 when you were in the Congress—

THE PRESIDENT: I certainly was.

Q: You seem to have expanded it from conversation with the President himself to conversation with anyone in the Executive Branch of the Government and I wonder can you cite any law or decision of the courts that supports that view?

THE PRESIDENT: Well, Mr. Mollenhoff, I don't want to leave the impression I am expanding it beyond that. I perhaps have not been as precise as I should have been. And I think yours is a very legitimate question because you have been one who has not had a double standard on this. You have always felt that executive privilege, whether I was complaining about its use when I was an investigator, or whether I am now defending its use when others are doing the investigating—I understand that position.

Let me suggest that I would like to have a precise statement prepared which I will personally approve so that you will know exactly what it is. I discussed this with the Leaders and we have talked, for example—the Republicans, like Senator Javits and Senator Percy, are very interested in it; not just the Democrats, and I understand that. But I would rather, at this point, not like to have just an off-the-top of my head press conference statement delineate what executive privilege will be.

I will simply say the general attitude I have is to be as liberal as possible in terms of making people available to testify before the Congress, and we are not going to use executive privilege as a shield for conversations that might be just embarrassing to us, but that really don't deserve executive privilege.

Q: The specific situation with regard to Fitzgerald, I would like to explore that. That dealt with a conversation Seamans had with someone in the White House relative to the firing of Fitzgerald and justification or explanations. I wonder if you feel that that is covered and did you have this explained to you in detail before you made the decision?

THE PRESIDENT: Let me explain. I was totally aware that Mr. Fitzgerald would be fired or discharged or asked to resign. I approved it and Mr. Seamans must have been talking to someone who had discussed the matter with me. No, this was not a case of some person down the line deciding he should go. It was a decision that was submitted to me. I made it and I stick by it.

Impoundment of Funds

Q: Mr. President, how do you respond to criticism that your impoundment of funds abrogates power or authority that the Constitution gave to Congress?

THE PRESIDENT: The same way that Jefferson did, and Jackson did and Truman did.

When I came in on this, Mr. Mollenhoff—he is one of the few old timers around here who will remember it—you remember when Senator Symington, who has now turned the other way on this, but you remember when we were talking about the 70 group air force. You remember that on that case I voted as a Congressman to override President Truman's veto. I think it was 70 wing or 70 group air force, where we insisted on a 70 group air force and he said the budget would only provide for 48.

Despite the fact that the Congress spoke not just as the Leaders spoke to me the other day, but by veto, overwhelming in both Houses, President Truman impounded the money. He did not spend it. And he had a right to. The constitutional right for the President of the United States to impound funds and that is not to spend money, when the spending of money would mean either increasing prices or increasing taxes for all the people, that right is absolutely clear.

The problem we have here is basically that the Congress wants responsibility, they want to share responsibility. Believe me, it would be pleasant to have more sharing of responsibility by the Congress. But if you are going to have responsibility, you have to be responsible, and this Congress and some of the more thoughtful Members of Congress and that includes most of the Leadership, in the very good give-and-take we had the other day—this Congress has not been responsible on money. We simply had this.

There is a clear choice. We either cut spending or raise taxes and I made a little check before the Leaders' meeting. I checked on the campaigns of everybody who had run for office across this country, Democrat and Republican. I didn't find one Member of Congress, Liberal or Conservative who had campaigned on the platform of raising taxes in order that we could spend more.

The point is that the Congress has to decide does it want to raise taxes in order to spend more or does it want to cut, as the President is trying to cut. The difficulty, of course, and I have been a Member of Congress, is that the Congress represents special interests.

The Interior Committee wants to have more parks and the Agriculture Committee wants cheap REA loans and the HEW Committee or the Education and Labor Committee wants more for education and the rest, and each of these wants we all sympathize with, but there is only one place in this Government where somebody has got to speak not for the special interests which the Congress represents but for the general interest.

The general interest of this country, the general interest whether it be rich or poor or old, is don't break the family budget by raising the taxes or raising prices, and I am going to stand for that general interest. Therefore, I will not spend money if the Congress overspends, and I will not be for programs that will raise the taxes and put a bigger burden on the already overburdened American taxpayer.

Prisoners in China

Q: Mr. President, there are two American flyers still being held prisoner in China, and they are sort of in limbo—well, three Americans but two flyers. I wonder if you could give us their status, and do you expect them to be returned with the other prisoners?

THE PRESIDENT: This matter we discussed when we were in the People's Republic of China, and we have every reason to believe that these flyers will be released on the initiative of the People's Republic of China as the POW situation is worked out in Vietnam. I won't go beyond that because this is a matter that should be left to the People's Republic of China, but we have, we believe, every assurance that will happen.

Q: Downey, also?

THE PRESIDENT: Downey is a different case, as you know. Downey involves a CIA agent. His sentence of 30 years has been, I think, commuted to five years, and we have also discussed that with Premier Cho En-Lai. I would have to be quite candid. We have no assurance that any change of action, other than the commutation of the sentence, will take place, but we have, of course, informed the People's Republic through our private channels that we feel that would be a very salutary action on his part.

That is a matter where they must act on their own initiative, and it is not one where any public pressures or bellicose statements from here will be helpful in getting his release.

THE PRESS: Thank you, Mr. President.

MARCH 2

Following is the White House text of President Nixon's March 2 press conference:

THE PRESIDENT: I have one announcement for those who are members of the traveling press. We have now set the date for the San Clemente meeting with President Thieu, and it will be April 2nd and 3rd. Those of you who desire to go should make your plans, if you could, to leave on the Friday before, because I am going to California to attend a dinner on that occasion for John Ford on Saturday night and the meetings will start the following Tuesday and will be concluded that week.

I will take any other questions you have.

Laotian Accord

Q: Mr. President, there has been considerable speculation in the interpretation of the Laos cease-fire pact to the effect that the Communists gained more out of that than they did out of the Geneva Accords, and also a situation in Cambodia that no one seems to be able to interpret. Originally you hinged your peace settlement on all of Indochina. What is your expectation in these areas, and how much confidence do you have that stability will be maintained?

THE PRESIDENT: Mr. Sheldon, first with regard to Laos, the agreement there was made by the Royal Laotian Government, and it is an agreement which, of course, we supported and we accept. I have noted that various elements within Laos have questioned the decision by Souvanna Phouma to make the agreement that he did, but the key to that agreement, and what makes the cease-fire work is an unequivocal provision in the agreement that we made; that is, for the withdrawal of all foreign forces from Laos. We expect that to be adhered to, and when that is adhered to, we believe that the chances for peace in Laos will be very considerable, and considerably more than after the '54 accords.

As I have pointed out, and as Dr. Kissinger has also pointed out, the situation in Cambodia is more complex because you don't have the governmental forces there that can negotiate with each other. However, there has been an attempt on the part of the Cambodian Government to have a unilateral cease-fire that has not been reciprocated on the part of the opposition forces in that area. Once a cease-fire is agreed to or adhered to, we will observe it. Until it is adhered to, we, of course, will provide support for the Cambodian Government.

I would want to indicate that the prospects in Cambodia are not as, shall we say, positive as those in Laos, but we do believe that there, too, the withdrawal of the North Vietnamese forces, which has been agreed to in our agreement with the North Vietnamese, from Cambodia is the key thing.

If those forces are out and if the Cambodians then can determine their own future, we believe the chances for a viable cease-fire in Cambodia will be very substantial.

Aid to North Vietnam

Q: Mr. President, could I ask you whether aid to North Vietnam was a condition of the cease-fire agreement? There seems to be some confusion about that.

THE PRESIDENT: No, Mr. Lisagor, it was not. The provision for assistance to North Vietnam on the economic side is one that we believe is in the interest of creating lasting peace and stability in the area.

That is a provision which, of course, we will have to have Congressional support for. We realize, as I pointed out previously in the meeting with you, ladies and gentlemen of the press, there is considerable opposition to aid to North Vietnam. It is rather reminiscent to me of what I went through when I first came to the Congress and you, Mr. Lisagor, covered in the Congress.

The opposition to aiding Germany and aiding Japan—Japan being the most militaristic and most aggressive force in Asia and Germany being the most militaristic force in Europe at that time—the opposition was very substantial.

I remember at that time I polled my own District, that is when the Congress started polling their Districts, and it was 68 percent against aid for any of our former enemies. I voted for it, even though it was submitted by a Democratic President, because I was convinced that the chances for having peace in Asia and the chance for having peace in Europe would be considerably increased if the Germans and the Japanese, the two strongest, most vigorous people in those two respective areas, were turned towards peaceful pursuits, rather than being left in a position of hopelessness, which would lead to frustration and another war or confrontation.

I think that that decision was right. I don't mean that the situation with regard to North Vietnam is on all fours with it, but I do say that if the North Vietnamese, after 25 years of war, continue to think that their future will only be meaningful if they engage in continuing war, then we are going to continue to have war in that part of the world and it would not only threaten South Vietnam; Cambodia, Laos, the Philippines, the whole area.

If, on the other hand, the people in North Vietnam have a stake in peace, then it can be altogether different and so we believe that once the Congress, both Democrats and Republicans, considers this matter—we want them to consider it, give their judgment on it—that they will decide, as they did 25 years ago, based on that precedent and what happened then, that the interest of peace will be served by providing the aid.

The costs of peace are great, but the costs of war are much greater and, incidentally, with regard to costs, I know that some of you have raised a question that I would like to address myself to as to whether whatever assistance we eventually do agree to and that we do present to the Congress, whether or not that assistance will require a cutting back on domestic programs.

The answer is no. As far as any assistance program is concerned, it will be covered by the existing levels for the budget which we have in for national security purposes. It will not come out of the domestic side of the budget.

Q: Mr. President.

THE PRESIDENT: By national security, I mean the whole area of defense and foreign assistance.

Q: Is this the area that the money for North Vietnam will come out of, the defense budget?

THE PRESIDENT: It will come out of the national security budget, which will mean the area of foreign assistance and defense both. As you know, the two are interlocked because the Defense Department has some foreign aid programs, but the whole national security area will absorb all of the assistance programs which we may agree to.

Q: Can you say how much it will be?

THE PRESIDENT: No, that is something to be negotiated.

Mr. Alexander was on his feet.

Q: Mr. President, I apologize for this question before I ask it.

THE PRESIDENT: Nobody else does. (Laughter)

Nixon and Blacks

Q: The only reason I do so is because I think you should have a chance to answer it, but I was in Richmond shortly after your re-election and a State Senator, who was a Negro, got up and asked me when is President Nixon going to stop kicking the blacks around.

THE PRESIDENT: Well, I could not stop unless I started it, and I have not, I believe.

I think it is very important, Mr. Alexander, that the people who happen to be black Americans in this country understand that the President of this nation is one who first would not, of course, ever say that he would ever admit, and I trust there would be nothing in the record to indicate that he had kicked any group in the population around and particulary one that deserved far better than that because of what they have been exposed to through the years.

The second point I would make is that there has been some speculation I know in some of the press and particularly in the black press to the effect that because I did not get a substantial number of black votes, although greater than in 1968, that therefore now we don't owe anything to them.

Let me say that is not the issue at all. The issue is doing what is right. This nation owes something to all of its people and it owes something particularly to those who have been disadvantaged.

We, I believe, have done a very effective job in that respect in terms of what we have done, maybe not in terms of what we have said so well, and we are going to continue to do well and we hope eventually that our citizens will recognize that we have done so.

Prisoners of War

Q: Mr. President, could you give us your own delineation of what really entered into the recent agreement on the POW return and the resumption of troop withdrawal?

THE PRESIDENT: Well, Mr. Theis, I don't think that any useful purpose would be served by indicating what the content of the various messages were which went between the governments involved at that time. Just let me say that Mr. Ziegler covered that, after a consultation with me, when he was first asked that question.

As far as the POWs are concerned, that provision and the withdrawal provision cannot be linked to anything else. The suggestion, for example, that what brought about the POW return was some action on the part of the United States or some assurance on the part of the United States that we would do something with regard to getting better compliance with the cease-fire, that suggestion is completely wrong. That provision stands on its own, too. It is in our interest and we are doing everything we can to get both parties, North and South, to comply with the cease-fire, but as far as the POWs are concerned, the agreement clearly provides that in return for withdrawal, the POWs will be returned. We expect that agreement to be complied with.

We made our position known publicly very clearly and privately very clearly. We accomplished our goal, and now to go into how we did it, I don't think, would be helpful.

I want to say, too, that I have noted that in the morning press there was some concern expressed about the 30 POWs that are held by the PRG (Provisional Revolutionary Government—Viet Cong). I am not going to speculate about how that is to be accomplished, except to say that we had been assured that within 48 hours from yesterday that the POWs held by the North, this particular group, and the segment by the PRG, would be released.

Now, where they will be released and how is something else again, but we expect them to be released with the time frame and I will not comment about what we will do if they are not, because we expect that they will comply.

Q: Mr. President—

THE PRESIDENT: Yes, Mr. Deakin.

Q: After your last press conference, Senator Scott suggested to some of us that we ask you again about the question of amnesty for draft evaders, as opposed to those who deserted military service after being inducted. Have you something further to tell us on your stand on amnesty?

THE PRESIDENT: No. I think I made my position abundantly clear. I realize that many people disagree with it. I would suggest, incidentally, if Members of the Senate and House disagree with it that they should put it up for a vote in the House and Senate. I think that the Members of the Senate and the House would overwhelmingly approve my position.

Let me say it is not said with any sense of vengeance; it is not said with any lack of compassion. But I take this position because these men have broken the law, and if, at the end of the war, we broke every precedent that this country has had, this will be the first time in history that amnesty was provided for those who deserted or evaded the draft, broke the law rather than complied with it as conscientious objectors. If we did that, we could not have a viable force in the future.

I would also say I can think of no greater insult to the memories of those who have fought and died, to the memories of those who have served, and also to our POWs, to say to them that we are now going to provide amnesty for those who deserted the country or refused to serve. We are not going to do so, and I do not intend to change my position.

John B. Connally

Q: Mr. President, are you going to send John Connally on a mission around the world?

THE PRESIDENT: Well, he has been traveling around the world a great deal already, as you know, and I want you to know, Miss McClendon, seriously, that as Secretary Connally has traveled around the world, he, of course, has been traveling in his private capacity as an attorney, but he has, at my request, undertaken some informal discussions with leaders in various parts of the world.

Secretary Connally, as you know, is very knowledgeable in the field of energy, and without getting involved in anything involving his client-attorney relationship, he is studying the situation with regard to energy from the private sector, and is making recommendations to me and to our energy group.

As far as any future trips are concerned, there are none officially planned, but if he travels privately, and if I can prevail upon him to take a mission that would be semi-public in purpose, I can think of no better man to undertake it.

Q: Mr. President,—

Q: Mr. President, Mr. Weinberger yesterday—I am sorry.

THE PRESIDENT: Either one. You start.

Q: Mr. Weinberger—

THE PRESIDENT: I will always get his; don't worry.

Family Assistance Plan

Q: —said that the Administration was never comfortable about the Family Assistance Plan, and he seemed to include you in that. I wonder if you could give us your views on that, and why you introduced it in the first place if you were not comfortable with it.

THE PRESIDENT: Mr. Weinberger is expressing, I think, the views that we had after we ran into a situation in the Senate which clearly indicated that we were up against an impossible legislative problem.

First, with regard to Family Assistance, I thought at the time that I approved it—and this view has not changed—that it was the best solution to what I have termed, and many others have termed before me, the welfare mess. I believe that it is essential that we develop a new program and a new approach to welfare in which there is a bonus not for welfare but a bonus, if there is to be one, for work.

That may be over-simplifying, but basically, in our welfare system today, because of varying standards and because the amounts for food stamps and other fringes have gone up so much, we find in area after area of this country it is more profitable to go on welfare than to go to work. That is wrong. It is unfair to the working poor. The Family Assistance Program I thought then, and I think now, is the best answer.

Now, there are many who object to it, and because of those objections there is no chance—and we have checked this out. I have made my own judgment of the political situation and I have talked to MacGregor and I have talked to Timmons and I have talked to Bryce Harlow about it. There is no chance that we can get it through the Senate because of the objections, on the one side, to any Family Assistance Program at all, on principle, and to objections, on the other side, if we put up the program to raise the price tag so high that we could not possibly afford it.

So we have to find a different way. I have told Secretary Weinberger, therefore, to go back to the drawing board and also to go to the Members of the Senate on both sides and to bring me back a program which will stop this unconscionable situation where people who go on welfare find it more profitable to go on welfare than to go to work, and I think we will find an answer. The family assistance may be part of that answer, but I know we are going to have to change it in order to get a vote; a proposition that will get the votes.

Now Mr. Mollenhoff.

Confirmation of FBI Chief

Q: Mr. President, Mr. Gray has been up before the Senate Judiciary Committee and he has been under attack for political speeches in 1972 and there is a controversy about those that are or are not political speeches. I wonder if you have looked at those, whether you have a view on that and it seemed to me the most vulnerable point was a memo from Patrick O'Donnell from the White House that was distributed to all the surrogates for the President that went to Pat Gray on the Cleveland situation and it involved a setting out of how crucial Ohio was in the campaign in 1972 and I wonder if you felt that was a breach of your instructions relative to the politics of Pat Gray and whether you had investigated this.

THE PRESIDENT: Well, Mr. Mollenoff, that is a very proper question. I mean I would not suggest other questions are improper, but it is a very proper question because when I appointed Mr. Gray, as you remember, I said I was not going to send his name last year because I felt that we should wait until we got past the political campaign so that the Senate could consider it in a non-political and non-partisan atmosphere, and the Senate is now doing that.

As far as Mr. Gray is concerned—and not the individual, but the Director of the FBI—he must be, as Mr. Hoover was before him, a non-partisan figure. He should not be involved in making political statements and that does not mean, if we look at Mr. Hoover's record, that he will not say some things that will not sound political at times, but it means that he must not become involved in partisan politics, supporting a candidate, opposing a candidate, and Mr. Gray, on the basis of what I have seen, had no intention of doing so. If there was anything indicating that during the campaign that we were trying to enlist him in that, it certainly didn't have my support and would not have it now.

I would also say, too, that the current Senate investigation or hearing, I should say, of Mr. Gray, is altogether proper. They should ask him all these questions. I want the people of this country to have confidence in the Director of the FBI. I had confidence in him when I nominated him.

I believe that the Senate will find, based on his record since he was nominated, that he has been fair, he has been efficient and that he will be a good, shall we say, law man in the tradition of J. Edgar Hoover and I am sure that the Senate will overwhelmingly approve him.

Q: Mr. President, do you think it is fair and efficient for Mr. Gray and the FBI not to question Mrs. Mitchell when they think there was cause to because her husband was a former Attorney General and campaign official of yours?

THE PRESIDENT: With regard to other questions on Mr. Gray, it has always been my practice, as you ladies and gentlemen know, not to comment on a hearing while it is in process. This is a matter that was brought up in the hearing.

I am sure that if the Members of the Senate feel that that was an improper activity on his part, they will question him about it and he will answer on it, but whether it is this hearing or any other hearing, I will not comment on a hearing while it is in process.

My answer to Mr. Mollenhoff stated a principle. Your question goes to a matter that the committee has a right to look into and the answer should come from the committee.

U.S. Hostages in Sudan

Q: Mr. President, we have a crisis, of course, in the Sudan where the U.S. Ambassador is being held hostage and one of the ransom demands is that Sirhan Sirhan be released. I wonder if you have any comment on this, particularly on that demand?

THE PRESIDENT: Last night I was sitting by the wife of Mr. Rabin and we were saying that the position of Ambassador, once so greatly sought after, now, in many places, becomes quite dangerous.

As you know, we had a problem in Latin America last year, we have one here this year. I don't mean to suggest it is that hazardous everyplace, but it is a problem and it is a risk that an Ambassador has to take.

As far as the United States as a government giving in to blackmail demands, we cannot do so and we will not do so.

Now, as to what can be done to get these people released, Mr. Macomber is on his way there for discussions. The Sudanese Government is working on the problem. We will do everything that we can to get them released, but we will not pay blackmail.

Vietnam Cease-Fire

Q: Mr. President, are you disappointed or are you concerned that the cease-fire agreement in Vietnam has not been observed as scrupulously as you might have liked up to now?

THE PRESIDENT: Well, let's look at what has happened. A cease-fire agreement is always difficult. You may recall I have mentioned that on occasion, that it is particularly difficult in the case of a guerrilla war. I have often been, as some of you gentlemen and ladies have, at the demarcation line in Korea. Many people forget that 20 years after the Korean cease-fire where you have a demarcation line, a clear line between the one side and the other where they have no guerrilla war, there are still incidents, not many, but there are still incidents. They were running as high three years ago as 100 a month—I mean 100 a year.

Now, in Vietnam, where you have a guerrilla war situation, where the lines are not so clearly drawn as to which side is held by the PRG and which side is held by the Vietnamese, there will continue to be violations until the situation becomes settled between the two sides.

What is important, however, is to note that the number of violations, the intensity of the fighting, has been reduced. It is not zero yet. I doubt if it will become zero in any time in the foreseeable future because of the fact that a guerrilla war having been fought for 25 years, off and on, is not going to be ended by one agreement, not in one month, not in two months, but the main point is it is going down and we expect adherence to the agreement from both sides. We will use our influence on both sides to get adherence to the agreement.

Phase III

Q: Mr. President, may I ask you about the 5.5 percent wage settlement. The leaders of labor seem to feel that that 5.5 percent ceiling is now more flexible in Phase III than it was in Phase II, but Secretary Shultz and the Director of the Cost of Living Council, Mr. Dunlop, the other day told us it is not more flexible, that it is just as hard a ceiling as it was before. Could you straighten this out for us?

THE PRESIDENT: What we have here as most important is not the 5.5, but the bottom line, which is 2.5. Now on that there is unanimity. The leaders of labor, the leaders of management, this very prestigious and powerful committee representing strong elements in both areas, agreed to a goal toward which we would work in our wage-price discussions this year to achieve an inflation level at the consumer level, retail level, of 2.5.

Now, in order to get to that level, it is going to be necessary that wage demands be within the ball park which will reach that level. As far as the wage guidelines are concerned, and the price guidelines, the same guidelines are in effect now as were before January 11th. However, what we have done is to recognize what we found in Phase II.

In Phase II, actually the wage settlements in all of the various settlements, and I have examined them, a great number of them, you had very few that were 5.5. Some were as high as 7. Some were as low as 3. But what mattered was that in the end, the average worked out so that we almost achieved our goal of 3 percent. We got to 3.4.

Now what we are concerned about is to see that in the negotiations in the year 1973 that those negotiations are undertaken with enough flexibility—some will go a little higher; some will go a little lower—but with enough flexibility so that we don't have a wage-price push which would destroy the goal that everybody unanimously agrees we should try to achieve of 2.5 at the end of the year at the retail level. I am sure that confuses you.

Q: Mr. President, what kind of trouble is the American dollar in in Europe, in your judgment?

THE PRESIDENT: Well, the American dollar, I think, is being attacked by international speculators. I know that when I use that term my sophisticates in the Treasury Department shudder, because they believe these great forces are not determined by speculation and unrest, but as I look at the American economy, as I look at the American rate of inflation, I would say that the dollar is a good bet in the world markets today.

The United States has the lowest rate of inflation of any major industrial country. The United States has certainly the strongest economy of the major industrial countries. The United States also has a program, which we believe is going to work, for continuing controlled inflation. We have a varied type budget, or I should say a responsible budget. Let me point out, it is not a budget which is cut; it is a budget, however, which does not go up as much as some would want it to go, and therefore, one that will continue to cool the inflationary fires.

And, of course, under these circumstances, we believe that the dollar is a sound currency and that this international attack upon it by people who make great sums of money by speculating—one time they make a run on the mark and the next time it is on the yen, and now it is on the dollar. We will survive it.

Let me say there will not be another devaluation. I would say, second, we are going to continue our program of fiscal responsibility so that the dollar will be sound at home and, we trust as well, abroad, and we also are going to continue our efforts to get the other major countries to participate more with us in the goal that we believe we should all achieve, which we set out at the time of the Smithsonian and the other agreements, and that is of getting an international monetary system which is flexible enough to take care of these, what I believe are, temporary attacks on one currency or another.

Q: Can we do anything to bring the speculators under control?

THE PRESIDENT: We cannot, because I would say for the most part they are operating in the international area, and all that we can do is to keep our dollar as sound as we can at home, to keep our economy as sound as we can, to be as responsible as we can so that the run on the dollar does not mean a weakness of the American economy or of the dollar, in fact, that we spend here at home.

Q: Mr. President, are you possibly giving any thought to reviving the Rent Control Board?

THE PRESIDENT: No, we are not. Rent controls have an enormous public appeal, particularly when you see some of the gouging that goes on in individual cases. The difficulty with rent control, however, and any of you who have visited Paris or some of the other major cities which have had rent control almost since World War II and see what has happened to rents, particularly of new dwellings, know what I am talking about.

The difficulty with rent control, if you put a rent control ceiling on that is not economically viable so that the builders and those who will rent apartments and so forth cannot and will not make their investment, all that happens is that you get a shortage of housing, the pressures go up, and also you find that the landlords don't keep up the places.

No, I do not think that rent controls is the right answer. I think the answer to the problem of rents is production of housing which will deal with it.

Watergate Case

Q: Mr. President, now that the Watergate case is over, the trial is over, can you give us your view on the verdict and what implications you see in the verdict on public confidence in the political system?

THE PRESIDENT: No, it would not be proper for me to comment on the case when it not only is not over, but particularly when it is also on appeal.

I will simply say with regard to the Watergate case what I have said previously that the investigation conducted by Mr. Dean, the White House counsel, in which, incidentally, he had access to the FBI records on this particular matter because I directed him to conduct this investigation, indicates that no one on the White House staff, at the time he conducted the investigation—that was last July and August—was involved or had knowledge of the Watergate matter and, as far as the balance of the case is concerned, it is now under investigation by a Congressional committee and that committee should go forward, conduct its investigation in an even-handed way, going into charges made against both candidates, both political parties and if it does, as Senator Ervin has indicated it will, we will, of course cooperate with the committee just as we cooperated with the Grand Jury.

Q: Mr. President, yesterday at the Gray hearings, Senator Tunney suggested he might ask the committee to ask for John Dean to appear before that hearing to talk about the Watergate case and the FBI-White House relationship. Would you object to that?

THE PRESIDENT: Of course.

Q: Why?

THE PRESIDENT: Well, because it is Executive Privilege. I mean you can't—I, of course—no President could ever agree to allow the Counsel to the President to go down and testify before a committee.

On the other hand, as far as any committee of the Congress is concerned, where information is requested that a member of the White House staff may have, we will make arrangements to provide that information, but members of the White House staff, in that position at least, cannot be brought before a Congressional committee in a formal hearing for testimony. I stand on the same position every President has stood on.

Q: Thank you, Mr. President.

Q: Mr. President, on that particular point, if the Counsel was involved—

THE PRESIDENT: He also gets two.

Q: —if the Counsel was involved in an illegal or improper act and the prima facie case came to light, then would you change the rules relative to the White House Counsel?

THE PRESIDENT: I do not expect that to happen and if it should happen I would have to answer that question at that point.

Let me say, too, that I know that, since you are on your feet, Clark, that you had asked about the Executive Privilege statement and we will have that available toward the end of next week or the first of the following week, for sure, because obviously, the Ervin Committee is interested in that statement and that will answer, I think, some of the questions with regard to how information can be obtained from a member of the White House staff, but consistent with Executive Privilege.

THE PRESS: Thank you again.

MARCH 15

Following is the White House text of President Nixon's March 15 press conference:

THE PRESIDENT: Be seated, please.

Ladies and gentlemen, I have an announcement with regard to our liaison office in Peking.

The office will open approximately on May 1, and Ambassador David Bruce will be the Chief of the Liaison Office. In the office will be approximately a total complement of 20, of whom 10 will be what we call the expert level; the others, of course, for the support level.

The two top assistants, top deputies to Ambassador Bruce—however, we should note I call him Ambassador, but his title will be Chief of the Liaison Office—will be Mr. Jenkins from the State Department, who, as you know, is one of our top experts on Chinese-American relations in State; and Mr. Holdridge from NSC, who is the top man in NSC advising in that area there.

We selected these two men because Mr. Jenkins and Mr. Holdridge not only are experts in Chinese, they are bilingual, incidentally, in both Chinese and American; speak it well. I remember both assisted in translations when I have been there. But in addition to that, they are men who have from the beginning been participating in the new initiatives between the People's Republic and the United States. They have accompanied Dr. Kissinger on his trips.

A word about why Ambassador Bruce was selected. We call him out of retirement because I thought it was very important to appoint a man of great stature to this position. The Chinese accepted that view themselves, and we expect soon to hear from them as to the appointment of the man they will have as his opposite number here in Washington. Another reason that I selected Ambassador Bruce was because of his great experience. All of you know that he has been Ambassador to Britain and Ambassador to Germany, Ambassador to France, and also headed our delegation in Paris on the Vietnam talks in 1971 and '72, in the early parts of '72.

A third reason, perhaps, has even greater significance. Many of you in this room were on the trip to China, and sometimes I suppose the feeling must have developed, "Well, this is a one-shot deal." I never considered it that, and all of you who reported on it did not consider it that. It was the beginning, we trust, of a longer journey; a journey in which we will have our differences, but one in which the most populous nation in the world and the United States of America can work together where their interests coincide for the cause of peace and better relations in the Pacific and in the world.

It is necessary that this be, therefore, a bipartisan enterprise in the highest sense of the word.

Mr. Bruce, as you know, while he has not been engaged in partisan politics, as such, is a Democrat. He has served four Presidents with equal distinction, Democratic Presidents as well as Republicans, and we believe that appointing him as head of the delegation indicates our intention that this initiative will continue in the future, whether the Presidency is occupied by a Democrat or a Republican. Of course, I am not making any predictions as to what will happen when I leave.

But that is the end of my announcement. We will now go to your questions. Mr. Risher.

FBI Nomination

QUESTION: Mr. President, do you plan to stick by your decision not to allow Mr. Dean to testify before the Congress, even if it means the defeat of Mr. Gray's nomination?

THE PRESIDENT: I noted some speculation to the effect that the Senate might hold Mr. Gray as hostage to a decision on Mr. Dean. I cannot believe that such responsible Members of the United States Senate would do that, because as far as I am concerned, my decision has been made.

I answered that question rather abruptly, you recall, the last time it was asked by one of the ladies of the press here. I did not mean to be abrupt, I simply meant to be firm.

Mr. Dean is Counsel to the White House. He is also one who was counsel to a number of people on the White House staff. He has, in effect, what I would call a double privilege, the lawyer-client relationship, as well as the Presidential privilege.

And in terms of privilege, I think we could put it another way. I consider it my constitutional responsiblity to defend the principle of separation of powers. I recognize that many Members of the Congress disagree with my interpretation of that responsibility.

But while we are talking on that subject—and I will go on at some length here because it may anticipate some of your other questions—I am very proud of the fact that in this Administration we have been more forthcoming in terms of the relationship between the Executive, the White House and the Congress, than any Administration in my memory. We have not drawn a curtain down and said that there could be no information furnished by members of the White House staff because of their special relationship to the President.

All we have said is that it must be under certain circumstances, certain guidelines, that do not infringe upon or impair the separation of powers that are so essential to the survival of our system.

In that connection, I might say that I had mentioned previously that I was once on the other side of the fence, but what I am doing here in this case is cooperating with the Congress in a way that I asked the then President, Mr. Truman, to cooperate with a committee of the Congress 25 years ago and in which he refused.

I don't say that critically of him now, he had his reasons, I have mine. But what we asked for in the hearings on the Hiss case—and all of you who covered it like Bill Theis and others will remember—what we asked for was not that the head of the FBI or anybody from the White House staff testify. There was very widespread information that there was a report of an investigation that had been made in the Administration about the Hiss case. We asked for that report. We asked for the FBI information with regard to that report.

And Mr. Truman, the day we started our investigation, issued an Executive Order in which he ordered everybody in the Executive department to refuse to cooperate with the committee under any circumstances. The FBI refused all information. We got no report from the Department of Justice and we had to go forward and break the case ourselves.

We did and to the credit of the Administration, after we broke the case, they proceeded to conduct the prosecution and the FBI went into it.

I would like to say, incidentally, that I talked to Mr. Hoover at that time. It was with reluctance that he did not turn over that information. Reluctance, because he felt that the information, the investigation they had conducted, was very pertinent to what the committee was doing.

Now, I thought that decision was wrong and so when this Administration has come in, I have always insisted that we should cooperate with the Members of the Congress and with the committees of the Congress and that is why we have furnished information, but, however, I am not going to have the Counsel to the President of the United States testify in a formal session before the Congress. However, Mr. Dean will furnish information when any of it is requested, provided it is pertinent to the investigation.

QUESTION: Mr. President, would you then be willing to have Mr. Dean sit down informally and let some of the Senators question him, as they have with Dr. Kissinger?

THE PRESIDENT: No, that is quite a different thing. In fact, Dr. Kissinger, Mr. Ehrlichman, as you know, not only informally meet with Members of the Congress on matters of substance, the same is true with members of the press, as you know, Dr. Kissinger meets with you ladies and gentlemen of the press and answers questions on matters of substance.

In this case, where we have the relationship that we have with Mr. Dean and the President of the United States, his Counsel, that would not be a proper way to handle it. He will, however, the important thing is, he will furnish all pertinent information. He will be completely forthcoming. Something that other Administrations have totally refused to do until we got here and I am very proud of the fact that we are forthcoming and I would respectfully suggest that Members of the Congress might look at that record as they decide to test it.

Cease-Fire Violations

QUESTION: Mr. President, can you say, sir, how concerned you are about the reports of cease-fire violations in Vietnam?

THE PRESIDENT: Well, I am concerned about the cease-fire violations. As you ladies and gentlemen will recall, I have consistently pointed out in meetings with you, that we would expect violatiins because of the nature of the war, the guerrilla nature, and that even in Korea, in which we do not have a guerrilla war, we still have violations. They recede each year, but we still have them. Long, 15, 20 years, after the war is over.

In the case of these violations, we are concerned about them on two scores. One, because they occur, but two, we are concerned because of another violation that could lead to, we think, rather serious consequences. We do not believe it will. We hope that it will not. And that is the reports that you ladies and gentlemen have been receiving from your colleagues in Vietnam with regard to infiltration.

You will note that there have been reports of infiltration by the North Vietnamese into South Vietnam of equipment exceeding the amounts that were agreed upon in the settlement.

Now, some equipment can come in. In other words, replacement equipment, but no new equipment, nothing, which steps up the capacity of the North Vietnamese or the Viet Cong to wage war in the South. No new equipment is allowed under the agreement.

Now, as far as that concern is concerned, particularly on the infiltration, that is the more important point, rather than the cease-fire violations which we think, over a period of time, will be reduced—but in terms of the infiltration, I am not going to say publicly what we have said.

I only suggest this: That we have informed the North Vietnamese of our concern about this infiltration and what we believe it to be, a violation of the cease-fire, the cease-fire and the peace agreement. Our concern has also been expressed to other interested parties and I would only suggest that based on my actions over the past four years, that the North Vietnamese should not lightly disregard such expressions of concern, when they are made, with regard to a violation. That is all I will say about it.

QUESTION: Mr. President, in connection with this matter, there is a report also that not just equipment, but a new infusion of North Vietnamese combat personnel have been introduced into South Vietnam, which is apart from just equipment. Can you confirm this? Is this partly what you are talking about?

THE PRESIDENT: Mr. Theis, the reports that we get with regard to infiltration, as you know, are always either too little or too late or too much. And I am not going to confirm that one, except to say that we have noted the report having been made. We, however, are primarily concerned about the equipment, because as far as the personnel are concerned, they could be simply replacement personnel.

QUESTION: Mr. President.

THE PRESIDENT: Go ahead, you are up in front.

QUESTION: Sir, why have we not gone through the ICCS to complain about this infiltration?

THE PRESIDENT: The ICCS is being used. As you know, there are some problems there. The Canadians have expressed considerable concern about the fact they don't want to be on a commission which is not being effectively used and we will continue through the ICCS and any other body that we can

effectively appeal to, to attempt to get action there. I can only answer in that way at this point.

FBI Files

QUESTION: Mr. President, are you concerned, sir, that any of the confidential FBI interviews that were conducted in their Watergate investigation were in any way compromised by Pat Gray's having given information to John Dean or talked about to John Ehrlichman or others.

THE PRESIDENT: No, I am not concerned about that. I would say that there is no possibility whatever that any information from the FBI, that may have been provided in the line of their duties to a member of the White House staff, would be bandied about in the press.

I would express concern on another point. In my long-time association with Mr. Hoover, he always was hard line in dealing with the Members of the Congress and with Congressional committees in terms of what he called "raw files," and when I first came into this office, he showed me a "raw file." I had not seen any before.

And when I saw the gossip, the hearsay, and unsubstantiated kind of slanderous statements, libelous, in this case, because they were in writing, having been made orally and transmitted into writing. I was really shocked.

Mr. Hoover, after showing me the "raw file", gave me an appraisal by the FBI of what could be believed and what could not be believed. And in the case of this particular individual— the reason I saw the file, it involved a check of an individual who I was nominating for a position and I needed to get the facts and, of course, I always have access to those files—what we found was that every charge that had been made against the individual was false.

Now, for the FBI, before a full committee of the Congress, to furnish "raw files" and then to have them leak out to the press, I think could do innocent people a great deal of damage. I understand why Mr. Gray did, because his hearing was involved. But I would say that should not be a precedent for the future.

The way Mr. Hoover handled it with Members of the Congress was that he would show the "raw files," for example, to Mr. Eastland, the Chairman of a committee, and the ranking Minority member, where a judge was up for a confirmation, but nothing ever leaked from those files and the sanctity of those files must be maintained and I believe that the practice of the FBI furnishing "raw files" to full committees must stop with this particular one.

Strategic Stockpiles

QUESTION: Mr. President, have you decided to sell materials from the strategic stockpiles and, if so, what are the safeguards from a security standpoint?

THE PRESIDENT: We have examined the stockpile question over the past four years. I have long felt that these stockpiles were really irrelevant to the kind of a world situation we presently confront. The stockpile numbers were set up at a time that we were thinking of a very different kind of conflict than we presently might be confronted with in the world.

Under the circumstances, after very full evaluation and discussion within the Administration, I have found that it will be safe for the United States to very substantially reduce our stockpiles and we are going to go forward and do that.

Now, there are going to be some squeals, but while the complaints will be made on the basis of national security, let me just say, I have made the decision on the basis of national security. The complaints will be, and I understand this, from those who produce and sell some of the materials in which we are going to sell the stockpiles, but we are going to do this, first, because the government doesn't need this much for its national security and, second, because in this particular period, we need to take every action we possibly can to drive down prices, or at least to drive down those particular elements that force prices up and selling the stockpiles in certain areas will help.

Watergate Incident

QUESTION: Mr. President, one of the revelations made by Mr. Gray during the course of the hearings has been that Mr. Kalmbach was involved with Mr. Chapin in the hiring of Mr. Segretti for amounts up to $40,000. Can you tell us, sir, did you know of that relationship, and did you know of that transaction, and if not, can you tell us your opinion of it now that it has been revealed by Mr. Gray?

THE PRESIDENT: This gives me an opportunity to not only answer that question, but many others that I note you have been asking Mr. Ziegler.

First,—and incidentally, I am not complaining about the fact you are asking the question of me or Mr. Ziegler. It is a very proper question. A Senate committee is conducting investigations. These investigations will go on, I understand, over a period of many months. I respect the right of the Senate to conduct those investigations. We will cooperate; we will cooperate fully with the Senate, just as we did with the Grand Jury, as we did with the FBI, and as we did with the courts when they were conducting their investigations previously in what was called the Watergate matter.

As far as these investigations are concerned, there are all kinds of information, charges, et cetera, et cetera, that have been made and will be made in the future. I could comment upon them. Mr. Ziegler could in the future. I will not. He will not. And the reason that we will not is that when the committee completes its investigation, we will then have comments, if we consider it appropriate to do so. But it is the right of the committee to conduct the investigation; all the facts can come out.

I have confidence in all of the White House people who have been named. I will express that confidence again. But I am not going to comment on any individual matter that the committee may go into.

Let me say, with regard to the committee, too, I do not intend to raise questions about its conduct. I have been very pleased to note that Senator Ervin—at least this is the way I read what he says—has indicated that the investigation will be bipartisan; that it will look into charges that have been made against both election campaigns, and that is as it should be. He has also indicated that he, as a great constitutional lawyer, will accept no hearsay; that he will not tolerate any guilt by innuendo; he will not tolerate any guilt by association.

As long as the committee conducts its investigations with those very high guidelines—guidelines I tried to follow, incidentally, in the Hiss case; not perhaps as well as I might have, but I did what many thought was pretty well—but in any event, as long as it is conducted that way, I do not intend to make any statements with regard to matters before the committee. That is for the committee to look into.

Travel Plans

QUESTION: Mr. President, can you tell us your travel plans outside of the United States during 1973?

THE PRESIDENT: Well, I have previously indicated that I had no immediate travel plans outside the United States. I have received recommendations from the State Department and from the NSC for what they consider to be urgent travel, one to Europe, because of our interest in NATO, second to Latin America because I have not yet had the opportunity to go to Latin America, and third to Africa because I have not traveled there.

I do not mean to suggest by that that travel by the President to these places is absolutely indispensable to foreign policy; but I think this is the concern that many of our foreign policy experts in the State Department and the NSC, the concern they have. They feel that the enormous interest that has been

created by going to Peking and going to Moscow indicates that we don't care about our neighbors in the Western Hemisphere, we don't care about our friends in Africa, and we do not care about our friends in Europe as well. Incidentally, Japan is another on the list.

Now, how we will be able to work some of these trips, in, I do not know. I would suggest that we are considering the possibility of a trip sometime during the summer or shortly before the summer begins, but we have not yet made a decision because there are so many other things on and there will probably be a trip in the fall, but how we select among these, I have not yet determined.

Narcotics Offenses

QUESTION: Mr. President, less than three years ago you signed into law a bill that removed mandatory prison terms for Federal narcotics convictions, as recommended by an earlier President's Crime Commission, and since then 73 percent of those convicted in Federal cases have received prison terms. What evidence is there that causes you now to go the other way, to ask for a restoration of mandatory prison terms for narcotics traffic?

THE PRESIDENT: We have examined this situation very carefully. Here is what we have found with regard to this whole attitude in terms of the restoration of the death penalty, for example, and the mandatory prison terms in cases of narcotics offenders: Let me point out that the mandatory sentences, as you know, only apply to hard drugs, heroin. It does not apply to marijuana. It does not apply to soft drugs, et cetera, et cetera.

Criminologists have honest differences of opinion on this, as to whether it will be more effective or less effective. We have examined it. We have, as you have already indicated, accepted a recommendation and we were moving in one direction at one time and now we have looked at the record since then and we have looked at the record over the past 10 years. I will simply summarize it for this year.

During the '60s, the United States went far down the road of the permissive approach to those charged with crime, and we reaped a terrible harvest, the greatest increase in crime that this country has ever had, explosive to the point that law and order, so-called, became a great issue in '68. It was still a great issue in '72.

Now, under these circumstances, I believe that it is essential that we have not a permissive approach, but an approach where certain major crimes are concerned that the penalties will be ones that will deter those crimes. It is my belief that they will.

Let me suggest, also, that my discussions with criminologists bears that out. We will find some disagreement. I understand there is a commission that will, in a couple of weeks, recommend that we move in the other direction. But I will take the responsibility.

As far as I am concerned, I oppose, as you know, the legalization of marijuana, although I have advocated a more equitable type of punishment which will fit the crime. I am for the mandatory criminal penalties with regard to hard drugs because I think we have to move vigorously in this area. And in terms of the capital punishment, I do not think the Secretary of State of the United States can make a statement to the effect that terrorists in the Sudan should be executed when, if somebody picks up some diplomat in the United States, we would give him perhaps 20 years, 30 years, and then have him out on parole in five years.

So under these circumstances, I am taking this line. I realize many honestly disagree. I respect the disagreement. But that is what I believe. If it doesn't work, we will try something else.

QUESTION: Mr. President, Mr. President—

THE PRESIDENT: I thought that was your voice.

QUESTION: I think you recognized the voice. (Laughter)

THE PRESIDENT: You had three questions last time. I have got to give the St. Louis Post-Dispatch one. You are still with the Post-Dispatch?

QUESTION: Yes. The last time I looked.

Food Price Controls

There is a published report that the Administration, despite what has been publicly said, is considering at least the possibility of controls on meat prices, possibly on other raw agriculture products. We have housewives' strikes now against these tremendous increases in food prices. When are you going to be in a position to offer the American consumer some kind of assurance that this is going to be stopped, this price spiral in food?

THE PRESIDENT: The difficulty with offering rigid price controls on meat prices and food prices is that it would not stop, in the opinion of those whose judgment I value, would not stop the rise in prices. It might stop them momentarily, but as a result of discouraging increased production, we would reap the consequences of greater upward pressure on prices later.

You can be very sure that if I thought that price controls on farm products and on food prices would work, I would impose them instantly.

But the point is, that every bit of evidence that has been presented shows that it would discourage supply, it would lead to black market and we would eventually have to come to rigid price controls, wage controls and rationing and I don't think the American people want that. I think there is a better way.

The better way is, one, to open our imports to the greatest extent that we possibly can. For example, we have already taken some action in that on dairy products. We have already taken some action on beef products. I found, at a meeting with the Cost of Living Council, that we still have a three percent tariff on imported beef. I have asked the Department of Agriculture to give me a legal opinion as to whether the President can remove that tariff. If I can, I will act. If I can't, I am going to ask the Congress to do it, because there shouldn't be any tariff on an item that is in short supply in the United States. That is on the import side.

On the supply side, we are, of course, reducing our stockpiles, whatever stockpiles are left and there are some in which we are able to act, provided we can get the transportation. That is the reason the Secretary of Transportation sat in the meeting with the Cost of Living Council, because we need flatcars and a number of other items in order to get it moved.

Finally, there is the production side and on the production side, as you know, our new farm policy is designed to increase production. We are continuing to examine the situation. If any further action can be taken that will work, we will do it. But I can assure you that I consider it the highest priority to get the pressure on prices down.

Let me say one word about the housewives. I had a letter from one the other day saying, "Should I boycott?" I am not going to suggest to American housewives or to any group of Americans to join in boycotts and so forth. I generally do not feel that that is an effective use of what we call "people power."

On the other hand, I would suggest that the greatest and most powerful weapon against high prices in this country is the American housewife. Her decisions, as she buys, whether she buys something that is more expensive or less expensive, have a far greater effect on price control than anything we do here. And I would suggest that the fact that some of the pressure on prices may be lessening now, as a result of housewives buying more carefully, may have some good effect.

Executive Privilege

QUESTION: Mr. President, does your offer to cooperate with the Ervin committee include the possibility that you would allow your aides to testify before his committee, and if it does not, would you be willing to comply with a court order, if Ervin

went to court to get one, that required some testimony from White House aides?

THE PRESIDENT: In answer to your first part of the question, the statement that we made yesterday answered that completely—not yesterday, the 12th I think it was, my statement on Executive Privilege. Members of the White House staff will not appear before a committee of Congress in any formal session. We will furnish information under the proper circumstances, we will consider each matter on a case-by-case basis.

With regard to the second point, that is not before us. Let me say, however, that if the Senate feels at this time that this matter of separation of powers, where as I said, this Administration has been more forthcoming than any Democratic Administration I know of, if the Senate feels that they want a court test, we would welcome it. Perhaps this is the time to have the highest court of this land make a definitive decision with regard to this matter.

I am not suggesting that we are asking for it. But I would suggest that if the Members of the Senate, in this wisdom, decide that they want to test this matter in the courts, we will, of course, present our side of the case, and we think that the Supreme Court will uphold, as it always usually has, the great constitutional principle of separation of powers rather than to uphold the Senate.

QUESTION: Mr. President, isn't there an essential difference really between your investigation of the Hiss case and the request of this subcommittee to Mr. Dean to appear? In the former foreign affairs was involved and possibly security matters, where here they only wish to question Mr. Dean about the breaking into the Watergate?

THE PRESIDENT: Yes, I would say the difference is very significant. As a matter of fact, when a committee of Congress was investigating espionage against the Government of this country, that committee should have had complete cooperation from at least the Executive Branch of the Government in the form that we asked. All that we asked was to get the report that we knew they had already made of their investigation.

Now, this investigation does not involve espionage against the United States. It is, as we know, espionage by one political organization against another. And I would say that as far as your question is concerned, that the argument would be that the Congress would have a far greater right and would be on much stronger ground to ask the Government to cooperate in a matter involving espionage against the Government than in a matter like this involving politics.

QUESTION: Mr. President, you have talked about the responsibility within the White House and responsibility between Congress and the White House. Where do you feel your responsibility for the Committee to Re-elect the President begins and ends, Mr. Mitchell or any other people who were working for them?

THE PRESIDENT: Well, the responsibility there, of course, is one that will be replied to by Mr. Mitchell, Mr. Stans and all of those in due course. None of them have the privilege, none of them, of course, will refuse to testify, none has when he is asked to, and I am sure they will give very good accounts of themselves, as they have in the court matters that they have been asked to.

Arms Aid

QUESTION: Mr. President, I want to ask you about peace. You have concentrated on peace in your Administration. Don't you find an inconsistency there with continuing to give arms to India and Pakistan and perhaps a hundred other countries around the world?

THE PRESIDENT: First, we are not giving them, we are selling them.

QUESTION: Isn't that worse? That is even worse.

THE PRESIDENT: I just wanted to be sure that we understood the difference, because of all the concern about aid. But the point that is involved in the India-Pakistan thing has been

(March 15 text continued on p. 187-A)

AUGUST 22

Following is an unofficial text of President Nixon's Aug. 22 news conference at San Clemente, Calif.:

Opening Statement

First, gentlemen, I have an announcement before going to your questions.

It is with the deep sense of not only official regret but personal regret that I announce the resignation of Secretary of State William Rogers, effective Sept. 3.

A letter which will be released to the press after this conference will indicate my appraisal of his work as Secretary of State.

I will simply say at this time that he wanted to leave at the conclusion of the first four years.

He agreed to stay on because we had some enormously important problems coming up including the negotiations which resulted in the end of the war in Vietnam, the Soviet summit, the European Security Conference as well as in other areas, Latin America and in Asia where the Secretary of State as you know has been quite busy over these past eight months.

As he returns to private life we will not only miss him in terms of his official service but I shall particularly miss him because of his having been through the years a very close personal friend and adviser. That personal friendship and advice, however, I hope still to have the benefit of and I know that I will.

As his successor I shall nominate and send to the Senate for confirmation the name of Dr. Henry Kissinger.

Dr. Kissinger will become Secretary of State, assume the duties of the office after he is confirmed by the Senate.

I trust the Senate will move expeditiously on the confirmation hearings because there are a number of matters of very great importance that are coming up. There are, for example, some matters that might even involve some foreign travel by Dr. Kissinger that will have to be delayed in the event that the Senate hearings are delayed.

Dr. Kissinger's qualifications for this post I think are well known by all of you ladies and gentlemen as well as those looking to us and listening to us on television and radio.

He will retain the position, after he becomes Secretary of State, of assistant to the President for national security affairs. In other words he will have somewhat a parallel relationship to the White House which George Shultz has. George Shultz as you know is Secretary of the Treasury but is also an assistant to the President in the field of economic affairs.

The purpose of this arrangement is to have a closer coordination between the White House and the departments and in this case between the White House and the National Security Affairs, the N.S.C. and the State Department, which carries a major load in this area.

And also another purpose is to get the work out in the departments where it belongs and I believe that this change in this respect of Dr. Kissinger moving in as Secretary of State and still retaining the position as Assistant to the President for National Security Affairs will serve the interest not only of coordination but also of the interests of an effective foreign policy.

I will simply say finally with regard to Secretary Rogers that he can look back on what I think and I suppose it is a self-serving statement, but I will say it about him rather than about myself at the moment, one of the most successful eras of foreign policy in any Administration in history, an era in which we ended a war, the longest war in America's history, an era in addition in which we began to build a structure of peace, particularly involving the two great powers, the People's Republic of China and the Soviet Union, where before there had been nothing but ugly and at sometimes very, very difficult confrontation.

We still have a long way to go. There are trouble spots in the area of the Mideast, others, Southeast Asia which we could go into in detail. But as Secretary Rogers looks back on his years, four and a half years of service as Secretary of State, he can be very proud that he was one of the major architects of what I think was a very successful foreign policy.

And now we'll go to the question. I think, A.P.

Questions

White House Tapes

Nixon: A.P., Miss Lewin, has the first question.

Q. On Watergate you have said that disclosure of the tapes could jeopardize and cripple the posture of the presidency. Question. If disclosure carries such a risk, why did you make the tapes in the first place and what is your reaction to surveys that show three out of four Americans believe you were wrong to make the tapes?

A. Well, with regard to the questions as to why Americans feel we were wrong to make the tapes, that is not particularly surprising. I think that most Americans do not like the idea of the taping of conversations and, frankly, it is not something that particularly appeals to me. As a matter of fact that is why when I arrived in the White House and saw this rather complex situation set up where there was a taping capacity not only in the President's office, the room outside of his office, but also in the Cabinet room and at Camp David and in other areas, that I had the entire system dismantled.

It was put into place again in June of 1970 because my advisers felt it was important in terms particularly of national security affairs to have a record for future years that would be an accurate one, but a record which would only be disclosed at the discretion of the President, or according to directives that he would set forth.

As you know, of course, this kind of capability not only existed during the Johnson administration, it also existed in the Kennedy Administration, and I can see why both President Johnson and President Kennedy did have the capability because, not because they wanted to infringe upon the privacy of anybody but because they felt that they had some obligation particularly in the field of foreign policy and some domestic areas to have a record that would be accurate.

As far as I'm concerned, we now do not have that capability and I am just as happy that we don't. As a matter of fact, I have a practice whenever I'm not too tired at night, of dictating my own recollections of the day. I think that perhaps will be the more accurate record of history in the end. I think we'll go to the U.P. now and then we'll come to the television....

Gray Warning

Q. On July 6, 1972 you were warned by Patrick Gray you were being mortally wounded by some of your top aides. Can you explain why you didn't ask who they were, and why, what was going on?

A. Well, in the telephone conversation that you refer to that has been, of course, quite widely reported in the press as well as on television, Mr. Gray said that he was concerned that as far as the investigation that he had responsibility for, that some of my top aides were not cooperating. Whether the term used was "mortally wounded" or not, I do not know. Some believe that it was. Some believe that it wasn't. That is irrelevant. He could have said that.

The main point, however, I asked him whether or not he had discussed this matter with General Walters because I knew that there had been meetings between General Walters representing the C.I.A. to be sure that the C.I.A. did not become involved in the investigation and between the director of the F.B.I. He said that he had. He told me that General Walters agreed that the investigation should be pursued and I told him to go forward with a full press on the investigation, to which he has so testified. It seemed to me that with that kind of directive to Mr. Gray that was adequate for the purpose of carrying out the responsibilities. As far as the individuals were concerned, I assume that the individuals that he was referring to involved this operation with the C.I.A.

That's why I asked him the Walters question. When he cleared that up, he went forward with the investigation and he must have thought that it was a very good investigation because when I sent his name down to the Senate for confirmation the next year, I asked him about his investigation and he said he was very proud of it and he said it was the most thorough investigation that had ever taken place since the assassination of President Kennedy, that he could defend it with enthusiasm and that under the circumstances, therefore, he had carried out the directive that I had given him on July 6. So there was no question about Mr. Gray having direct orders from the President to carry out an investigation that was thorough.

Mr. Jarriel.

Haldeman's Access

Q. Assistant Attorney General Henry Petersen has testified that on April 15th of this year he met with you and warned you at that time there might be enough evidence to warrant indictments against three of your top aides, Messrs. Ehrlichman, Haldeman, and Dean. You accepted their resignations on April 30 calling Mr. Haldeman and Mr. Ehrlichman two of the finest public servants you have known. After that you permitted Mr. Haldeman after he had left the White House to hear confidential tapes of conversations you had had in your office with Mr. Dean. My question is why did you permit a man who you knew might be indicted to hear those tapes which you now will not permit the American public or the Federal prosecutors handling the case to listen to.

A. The only tape that has been referred to, that Mr. Haldeman has listened to, he listened to at my request and he listened to that tape that was the one on Sept. 15th, because he had been present and was there. I asked him to listen to it in order to be sure that as far as any allegations that had been made by Mr. Dean with regard to that conversation, I wanted to be sure that we were absolutely correct in our response.

That's all he listened to. He did not listen to any tapes in which only Mr. Dean and I had participated. He listened only to the tape on Sept. 15, this is after he left office, in which he had participated in the conversation throughout.

Firm on Tapes

Q. Mr. President, one of the lingering doubts about your denial of any involvement in (Watergate), is concerning your failure to make the tapes available, either to the Senate committee or the special prosecutor. You've made it perfectly clear you don't intend to release those tapes.

A. Perfectly clear?

Q. Perfectly clear, but is there any way that you could have some group listen to tapes and give a report so that that might satisfy the public mind?

A. I don't believe first that it would satisfy the public mind, and it shouldn't. The second point is that as Mr. Wright, who argued the case, I understand, very well before Judge Sirica this morning, has indicated to have the tapes listened to—he indicated this also in his brief—either by a prosecutor or by a judge or *in camera* or in any way would violate the principle of confidentiality, and I believe he is correct.

That is why we are standing firm on the proposition that we will not agree to the Senate committee's desires to have, for

example, its chief investigator listen to the tapes or the specɪ prosecutor's desire to hear the tapes, and also why we will oppose, as Mr. Wright did in this argument this morning, any compromise of the principle of confidentiality. Let me explain very carefully that the principle of confidentiality either exists or it doesn't exist. And once it is compromised, once it is known that a conversation that is held with the President can be subject to a subpoena by a Senate committee, by a grand jury, by a prosecutor, and be listened to by anyone, the principle of confidentiality is thereby irreparably damaged.

Incidentally, let me say that now that tapes are no longer being made I suppose it could be argued what difference does it make now, now that these tapes are also in the past. What is involved is not only the tapes, what is involved, as you ladies and gentlemen well know, is the request on the part of the Senate committee and the special prosecutor as well, that we turn over Presidential papers, in other words, the record of conversations with the President made by his associates. Those papers and the tapes as well cannot be turned over without breaching the principle of confidentiality. It was President Truman that made that argument very effectively in his letter to a Senate committee for his response to a Congressional committee, a House committee, it was, in 1953 when they asked him to turn over his papers. So whether it is a paper or whether it's a tape, what we have to bear in mind is that for a President to conduct the affairs of this office and conduct effectively, he must be able to do so with the principle of confidentiality intact.

Otherwise, the individuals who come to talk to him, whether it's his advisers or whether it's a visitor in the domestic field or whether it's someone in a foreign field, will always be speaking in a eunuch-like way, rather than laying it on the line. It has to be laid on the line if you're going to have the creative kind of discussions that we have often had and have been responsible for some of our successes in the foreign policy period, particularly in the past few years.

Magruder and MacGregor

Q. Mr. President, could you tell us who you personally talked to in directing that investigations be made both in June of '72 after the Watergate incident and last March 21, when you got new evidence and ordered a more intensive investigation?

A. Certainly. In June I of course talked to Mr. MacGregor first of all who was the new chairman of the committee. He told me that he would conduct a thorough investigation as far as his entire committee staff was concerned. Apparently that investigation was very effective except for Mr. Magruder who stayed on, but Mr. MacGregor does not have to assume responsibility for that, I say not responsibility for it because basically what happened there was that he believed Mr. Magruder and many others had believed him, too. He proved, however, to be wrong.

In the White House, the investigation's responsibility were given to Mr. Ehrlichman at the highest level and, in turn, he delegated them to Mr. Dean, the White House counsel, something of which I was aware and of which I approved. Mr. Dean, as White House counsel, therefore sat in on the F.B.I. interrogations of the members of the White House staff because what I wanted to know was whether any member of the White House staff was in any way involved. If he was involved, he would be fired.

And when we met on Sept. 15 and again throughout our discussions in the month of March, Mr. Dean insisted there was not—and I used his words—a "scintilla of evidence" indicating that anyone on the White House staff was involved in the planning of the Watergate break-in.

Now in terms of after March 21st, Mr. Dean first was given the responsibility to write his own report but I did not rest it there—I also had a contact made with the Attorney General himself, and Attorney General Kleindienst told him—this was on the 27th of March—to report to me directly anything that he found in this particular area, and I gave the responsibility to Mr. Ehrlichman on the 29th of March to continue the investigation that Mr. Dean was unable to conclude, having spent a week at Camp David and unable to finish the report.

Mr. Ehrlichman questioned a number of people in that period at my direction, including Mr. Mitchell, and I should also point out that as far as my own activities were concerned I was not leaving it just to them.

I met at great length with Mr. Ehrlichman, Mr. Haldeman, Mr. Dean, Mr. Mitchell on the 22d. I discussed the whole matter with them. I kept pressing for the view that I had had throughout, that we must get this story out, get the truth out, whatever and whoever it's going to hurt, and it was there that Mr. Mitchell suggested that all the individuals involved in the White House appear in an executive session before the Ervin committee.

We never got that far. But at least that was, that's an indication of the extent of my own investigation.

I think we'll go to Mr. Lisagor now.

Mitchell Testimony

Q. Mr. President, you have said repeatedly that you tried to get all facts and just now you mentioned a March 22nd meeting. Yet former Attorney General John Mitchell said that if you had ever asked him at any time about the Watergate matter he would have told you the whole story chapter and verse. Was Mr. Mitchell not speaking the truth when he said that before the committee?

A. Now Mr. Lisagor, I'm not going to question Mr. Mitchell's veracity. And I will only say that throughout I had confidence in Mr. Mitchell. Mr. Mitchell, in a telephone call that I had with him immediately after it occurred, expressed great chagrin that he had not run a tight enough shop and that some of the boys, as he called them, got involved in this kind of activity, which he knew to be very, very embarrassing to—apart from its illegality—to the campaign.

Throughout I was expecting Mr. Mitchell to tell me, in the event that he was involved or that anybody else was. He did not tell me. I don't blame him for not telling me. He's given his reasons for not telling me. I regret that he did not; because he's exactly right—had he told me I would have blown my stack. Just as I did at Ziegler the other day.

We'll get you next, Mr. Rather.

Responsibility

Q. Mr. President. How much personal blame do you accept for the climate in the White House and of the re-election committee for the abuses of Watergate?

A. I accept it all.

Judge Byrne

Q. Mr. President, I want to state this question with due respect to your office but also as directly as....

A. That would be unusual.

Q. I'd like to think not. It concerns....

A. Only...you're always respectful, Mr. Rather.

Q. It concerns the events surrounding Mr. Ehrlichman's contact and on one occasion your own contact with the judge in the Pentagon paper case, Judge Byrne. As I understand your own explanation of events in putting together your statement with Mr. Ehrlichman's testimony and what is currently said, what happened here is sometime late in March, on March 17, I believe he said, you first found out about the break-in at the psychiatrist's office of Mr. Ellsberg, that you asked to have that looked into and that you later, I think in late April, talked with Attorney General Kleindienst to inform the judge. Now, my question is this, that while the Pentagon papers trial was going on, Mr. Ehrlichman secretly met once with the judge in that case, you secretly met another time the judge with Mr. Ehrlichman, now,

you're a lawyer and given the state of the situation and what you did, could you give us some reason why the American people shouldn't believe that that was at least a subtle attempt to bribe the judge in that case and it gave at least the appearance of a lack of moral leadership?

A. Well I would say the only part of your statement that is perhaps accurate is that I'm a lawyer. Now, beyond that, Mr. Rather, let me say with regard to the secret meeting that we had with the judge that as he said, I met the judge briefly—after all, I had appointed him to the position—I met him for perhaps one minute outside my door here in full view of the whole White House staff and everybody who wanted to see.

I asked him how he liked his job. We did not discuss the case. And he went on with his meeting with Mr. Ehrlichman. Now why did the meeting with Mr. Ehrlichman take place. Because we had determined that Mr. Gray could not be confirmed, as you will recall. We were on a search for a director of the F.B.I. Mr. Kleindienst had been here, and I asked him what he would recommend with regard to a director and I laid down certain qualifications.

I said I wanted a man preferably with F.B.I. experience and preferably with prosecutor's experience. And preferably, if possible, a Democrat, so that we would have no problem on confirmation. He said the man for the job is Byrne. He says he's the best man. I said, are you, would you recommend him? He said, yes. Under those circumstances, then, Mr. Ehrlichman called Mr. Byrne. He said under no circumstances will we talk to you, he, Ehrlichman will talk to you, unless if he felt that it would in any way compromise his handling of the Ellsberg case.

Judge Byrne made the decision that he would talk to Mr. Ehrlichman, and he did talk to him privately, here. And on that occasion he talked to him privately. The case was not discussed at all. Only the question of whether or not at the conclusion of this case Mr. Byrne would like to be considered as director of the F.B.I.

I understand, incidentally, that he told Mr. Ehrlichman that he would be interested. Of course, the way the things broke, eventually we found another name with somewhat the same qualifications, although in this case, not a judge, in this case, a chief of police with former F.B.I. experience.

Now, with regard to the Ellsberg break-in, let me explain that in terms of that I discussed that on the telephone with Mr. Henry Petersen on the 18th of April. It was on the 18th of April that I learned that the grand jury was going away from some of its Watergate investigation and moving into national security areas.

I told Mr. Petersen at that time about my concern about the security areas and particularly about the break-in as far as the Ellsberg case was concerned. And then he asked me a very critical question, which you as a nonlawyer will now understand, and lawyers probably will too. He said, was any evidence developed out of this investigation, out of this break-in, and I said, no, it was a dry hole. He said, good. Now what he meant by that was that in view of the fact that no evidence was developed as the result of the break-in, which is incidentally, illegal, unauthorized as far as I was concerned, and completely deplorable, but since no evidence was developed, there was no requirement that it be presented to the jury that was hearing the case.

That was why Mr. Petersen, a man of impeccable credentials in the law enforcement field, did not at that time, on the 18th, at a time when I told him about, that I had known about the Ellsberg break-in, say, 'Let's present it then to the grand jury' because nothing had been accomplished, nothing had been obtained that would taint the case.

It was approximately 10 days later that Mr. Kleindienst came in and said that after a review of the situation in the prosecutor's office in Washington in which Mr. Petersen had also participated that they believed that it was best that we bend over backwards in this case and send this record of the Ellsberg break-in even though there was no evidence obtained from it that could have affected the jury one way or another, send it to the judge.

When they made that recommendation to me I directed that it be done instantly. It was done. Incidentally, the prosecutor argued this case just the way that I've argued it to you, and whether or not it had an effect on the eventual outcome, I do not know. At least as far as we know, Mr. Ellsberg went free, this being one of the factors, but that is the explanation of what happened, and obviously you in your commentary tonight can attach anything you want to it. I hope you will be just as fair and objective as I try to be in giving you the answer. But I know you will be, sir.

Confidence in Agnew

Q. Mr. President, what is the state of your confidence in your Vice President at this point in time?

A. I noted some press speculation to the effect that I have not expressed confidence in the Vice President and therefore I welcome this question, because I want to set the record straight.

I had confidence in the integrity of the Vice President when I selected him as Vice President when very few knew him, as you may recall, back in 1968, knew him nationally.

My confidence in his integrity has not been shaken, and in fact it has been strengthened by his courageous conduct and his ability even though he's controversial at times, as I am, over the past four and a half years and so I have confidence in the integrity of the Vice President and particularly in the performance of the duties that he has had as Vice President, and as a candidate for Vice President.

Now obviously the question arises as to charges that have been made about activities that occurred before he became Vice President.

He would consider it improper, I would consider it improper for me to comment on those charges and I shall not do so. But I will make a comment on another subject that I think needs to be commented upon and that is the outrageous leak in information from either the grand jury or the prosecutors or the Department of Justice or all three—and incidentally I'm not going to put the responsibility on all three till I have heard from the Attorney General who at my request is making a full investigation of this at the present time.

I'm not going to put the responsibility—but the leak of information with regard to charges that have been made against the Vice President and leaking them all in the press, convicting an individual, not only trying him but convicting him in the headlines and on television before he's had a chance to present his case in court is completely contrary to the American tradition. Even a Vice President has a right to some, shall I say consideration in this respect, let alone the ordinary individual.

And I will say this, and the Attorney General I know has taken note of this fact, any individual in the Justice Department or in the prosecutor's office who is in the employ of the United States, who has leaked information in this case, to the press or to anybody else, will be summarily dismissed from Government service. That's how strongly I feel about it and I feel that way because I would make this ruling whether it was the Vice President or any individual.

We have to remember that a hearing before a grand jury and that determination in the American process is one that is supposed to be in confidence, because all kinds of charges are made which will not stand up in open court, and it's only when the case gets to open court that the press and the TV have a right to cover it. Well, they have a right to cover it, but I mean, have a right, it seems to me to give such broad coverage to the charges.

Resignation Possibility

Q. Mr. President, did at any time during the Watergate crisis have you ever considered resigning? Would you consider resigning if you felt that your capacity to govern had been seriously weakened? And in that connection, how much do you think your capacity to govern has been weakened?

A. The answer to the first two questions is no. The answer to the third question is that it is true that as far as the capacity to govern is concerned, that to be under a constant barrage—12 to 15 minutes a night on each of the three major networks for four months—tends to raise some questions in the people's minds with regard to the President; and it may raise some questions with regard to the capacity to govern.

But I also know this: I was elected to do a job. Watergate is an episode that I deeply deplore; and, had I been running the campaign—other than trying to run the country, and particularly the foreign policy of this country at this time—it would never have happened. But that's water under the bridge. Let's go on now.

The point that I make now is, that we are proceeding as best we know how to get all those guilty brought to justice in Watergate. But now we must move on from Watergate to the business of the people—the business of the people is continuing with initiatives we began in the first Administration.

Watergate Obsession

Q. Mr. President— —

A. Just a moment. We've had 30 minutes of this press conference. I have yet to have, for example, one question on the business of the people. Which shows you are—how we're consumed with it.

I'm not criticizing the members of the press; because you naturally are very interested in this issue. But let me tell you, years from now people are going to perhaps be interested in what happened in terms of the efforts of the United States to build a structure of peace in the world. They are perhaps going to be interested in the efforts of this Administration to have a kind of prosperity that we haven't had since 1955—that is, prosperity without war and without inflation.

Because, throughout the Kennedy years and throughout the Johnson years, whatever prosperity we had was at the cost of either inflation or war, or both.

I don't say that critically of them. I'm simply saying, we've got to do better than that.

Now our goal is to move forward then—to move forward to build a structure of peace. And when you say, have I—do I consider resigning: the answer is no. I shall not resign. I have three and a half years to go, or almost three and a half years, and I'm going to use every day of those three and a half years trying to get the people of the United States to recognize that whatever mistakes we have made that in the long run this Administration, by making this world safer for their children, and this Administration, by making their lives better at home for themselves and their children, deserves high marks rather than low marks.

Impeachment

Q. Mr. President, as long as we're on the subject of the American tradition and following up Mr. Rather's questions, what was authorized even if the burglary of Dr. Fielding's office wasn't, what was authorized was the 1970 plan which by your own description permitted illegal acts, illegal breaking and entering, mail surveillance and the like. Now, under the Constitution you swore an oath to execute the laws of the United States faithfully. If you were serving in Congress, would you not be considering impeachment proceedings and discussing impeachment possibility against an elected public official who had violated his oath of office?

A. I would if I had violated the oath of office. I would also, however, refer you to the recent decision of the Supreme Court or at least an opinion that even last year which indicates inherent power in the Presidency to protect the national security in cases like this. I should also point to you that in the three Kennedy years and the three Johnson years through 1966 when burglarizing of this type did take place, when it was authorized, on a very large scale there was no talk of impeachment and it was quite well known.

I should also like to point out that when you ladies and gentlemen indicate your great interest in wiretaps and I understand that the heights of the wiretaps was when Robert Kennedy was Attorney General in 1963. I don't criticize him, however. He had over 250 in 1963 and of course the average in the Eisenhower Administration and the Nixon Administration is about 110.

But if he had had 10 more and as a result of wiretaps had been able to discover the Oswald plan it would have been worth it.

So, I will go to another question.

Ehrlichman and Haldeman

Q. Mr. President, do you consider Haldeman and Ehrlichman two of the finest public servants you have ever known?

A. I certainly do. I look upon public servants as men who've got to be judged by their entire record—not by simply parts of it. Mr. Ehrlichman, Mr. Haldeman for four and a half years served with great distinction, with great dedication and, like everybody in this deplorable Watergate business, at great personal sacrifice and with no personal gain.

We admit the scandalous conduct. Thank God, there's been no personal gain involved. That would be going much too far, I suppose.

But the point that I make with regard to Mr. Haldeman and Mr. Ehrlichman is that I think, too, that if all the facts come out, that—and when they have an opportunity to have their case heard in court, not simply to be tried before a committee, and tried in the press and tried in television—they will be exonerated.

Conversation With Dean

Q. Mr. President, could you tell us your recollection of what you told John Dean on March 21 on the subject of raising funds for the Watergate defendants?

A. Certainly. Mr. Haldeman has testified to that, and his statement is accurate.

Basically, what Mr. Dean was concerned about on March 21 was not so much the raising of money for the defendants but the raising of money for the defendants for the purpose of keeping them still. In other words so-called hush money.

The one would be legal, in other words raising the defense funds for any group, any individual, as you know is perfectly legal and is done all the time. But you raise funds for the purpose of keeping an individual from talking, that's obstruction of justice.

Mr. Dean said also, on March 21, that there was an attempt to, as he put it, to blackmail the White House, to blackmail the White House by one of the defendants; incidentally, that defendant has denied it, but at least this is what Mr. Dean declared, and that unless certain amounts of money were paid, I think it was $120,000 for attorneys' fees and other support, that this particular defendant would make a statement, not with regard to Watergate but with regard to some national security matters in which Mr. Ehrlichman had particular responsibility.

My reaction very briefly was this: I said as you look at this, I said isn't it quite obvious, first, that if it is going to have any chance to succeed, that these individuals aren't going to sit there in jail for four years, they're going to have clemency. Isn't that correct?

He said yes.

I said we can't give clemency.

He agreed.

Then I went to another point. The second point is that isn't it also quite obvious, as far as this is concerned, that while we could raise the money, and he indicated in answer to my question that it would probably take a million dollars over four years to take care of this defendant and others on this kind of a basis, the problem was, how do you get the money to them. And also,

how do you get around the problem of clemency because they're not going to stay in jail simply because their families are being taken care of.

And so that was why I concluded, as Mr. Haldeman recalls, perhaps, and did testify very effectively, when I said "John, it's wrong, it won't work, we can't give clemency, and we've got to get this story out. And therefore I direct you and I direct Haldeman and I direct Ehrlichman and I direct Mitchell to get together tomorrow and then meet with me as to how we get this story out."

And that's how the meeting on the 22d took place.

Coordinating Defense

Q. Mr. President, earlier in the news conference you said that you gave Mr. Haldeman the right to listen to one tape because you wanted to be sure "that we are correct." And I think I'm quoting you correctly. Now, you have indicated that you still feel that Mr. Haldeman and Mr. Ehrlichman are two of the finest public servants that you've ever know. You have met with their lawyer at least twice that we know of. Are you and Mr. Haldeman and Mr. Ehrlichman coordinating their and your defense and if so why.

A. No, no. As far as my defense is concerned, I make it myself. As far as their defense is concerned, their lawyer demonstrated very well before the committee that he can handle it very well without any assistance from me.

Agnew Resignation

Q. Mr. President, a follow-up question on the Agnew situation. You have said in the past that any White House official who was indicted would be suspended and that anyone convicted would be dismissed. Should Vice President Agnew be indicted, would you expect him to resign or somehow otherwise stand down temporarily until cleared?

A. Well Mr. Theis, a perfectly natural question and one that any good newsman as you are would ask. But as you know it's one that would be most inappropriate for me to comment upon. The Vice President has not been indicted. Charges have been thrown out by innuendo and otherwise, which he has denied to me personally and which he has denied publicly. And the talk about indictment and the talk about resignation even now. I'm not questioning your right to ask the question, understand. But for me to talk about it would be totally inappropriate that I make no comment in answer to that question.

Check on President

Q. Mr. President.

A. I'll take the big man.

Q. Thank you, Mr. President.

A. I know my troubles if I don't take him—or if I do.

Q. Looking to the future on executive privilege, there are a couple of questions that come to mind.

A. I thought we just passed the point.

Q. Well we speak here of the future.

A. All right.

Q. Where is the check on authoritarianism by the executive that the President is to be the sole judge of what the executive branch makes available and suppresses? And you obey a Supreme Court order if you are asked and directed to produce the tapes or other documents for the Senate committee or for the special prosecutor? And if this is not enough, is there any limitation on the President, short of impeachment to compel the production of evidence of a criminal nature?

A. Is there anything else?

Q. No. I think that will be enough.

A. No, I was not being facetious; but I realize it's a complicated question. The answer to the first question is that there's a limitation on the President in almost all fields like this.

There's, of course, the limitation of public opinion; and, of course, congressional and other pressures that may arise.

As far as executive privilege is concerned in the Watergate matter—and I must say the I.T.T. file, etc.—that this Administration has, I think, gone further in terms of waiving executive privilege than any Administration in my memory. Certainly a lot further than Mr. Truman was willing to go when I was on the other side, as you recall, urging that he waive executive privilege.

Now, with regard to what the Supreme Court will do, or say —the White House press secretary, assistant secretary—Mr. Warren—has responded to that already. I won't go beyond that. And particularly I won't make any statement on that matter at this time, while the matter is still being considered by Judge Sirica.

I understand his decision will come down on Wednesday, and then we will make a comment. As far as the statement that Mr. Warren has made with regard to the President's position of complying with a definitive order of the Supreme Court is concerned, that statement stands.

Exploiters of Watergate

Q. Mr. President, sir, last week in your speech you referred to those who would exploit Watergate to keep you from doing your job. Could you specifically detail who those are?

A. I would suggest that where the shoe fits, people should wear it. I would think that some political figures, some members of the press perhaps, some members of the television, perhaps, would exploit it. I don't impute, interestingly enough, motives, however, that are improper interests, because here's what is involved.

There are a great number of people in this country that would prefer that I do resign. There are a great number of people in this country that didn't accept the mandate of 1972. After all, I know that most of the members of the press corps were not enthusiastic. And I understand that about either my election in '68 or '72. That's not unusual. Frankly, if I had always followed what the press predicted or the polls predicted, I would have never been elected President.

But what I am saying is this. People who did not accept the mandate of '72, who do not want the strong America that I want to build, who do not want to give, who do not want to cut down the size of this Government bureaucracy that burdens us so greatly and to give more of our Government back to the people, people who do not want these things naturally would exploit any issues. If it weren't Watergate, anything else in order to keep the President from doing his job.

And so I say I have no improper motives to them. I think they would prefer that I failed. On the other hand, I'm not going to fail. I'm here to do a job, and I'm going to do the best I can, and I'm sure the fair-minded members of this press corps, and that's most of you, will report when I do well, and I'm sure you'll report when I do badly.

Wiretaps

Q. Mr. President, you recently suggested that if the late Robert Kennedy had initiated 10 more wiretaps, he would have been able to discover the Oswald plan, as you described it, and thereby presumably prevent the assassination of President Kennedy.

A. Let me correct you, sir. I want to be sure that the assumption is correct. I said if 10 more wiretaps could have found the conspiracy, if it was a conspiracy, or the individual, then it would have been worth it. As far as I'm concerned, I'm no more of an expert on that assassination than anybody else, but my point is that wiretaps in the national security area were very high in the Kennedy Administration for a very good reason.

Because there were many threats on the President's life, because there were national security problems, and that is why that in that period of 1961 to '63 there were wiretaps on news organizations, on news people, on civil rights leaders and on other people. And I think they were perfectly justified and I'm sure that President Kennedy and his brother, Robert Kennedy, would never authorize them, unless he thought they were in the national interest.

Q. Do you think, then, that threats to assassinate the President merit more national security, wiretaps particularly?

A. No, no, as far as I'm concerned, I was only suggesting that in terms of those times that to have the Oswald thing happen just seemed so unbelievable that it—with his record, with his record, that it, with everything that everybody had on him, that that fellow could have been where he was in a position to shoot the President of the United States seems to me to be, to have been a terrible breakdown in our protective security areas. I would like to say, however, that as far as protection generally is concerned, I don't like it. And my family doesn't like it. Both of my daughters would prefer to have no Secret Service. I discussed it with the Secret Service. They say they have too many threats and they have to have it. My wife doesn't want to have Secret Service. And I would prefer and I recommended this just three days ago, to cut my detail by one third because I noticed there were criticisms of how much the Secret Service is spending.

Let me say, that we always are going to have threats against the President. But I frankly think that one man, probably, is as good against a threat as a hundred, and that's my view, but my view doesn't happen to be in a majority there and it doesn't happen to agree with the Congress, so I will still have a great number of Secret Service around me, more than I want, more than my family wants.

Q. Mr. President, during March and April you received from your staff, on several occasions, information about criminal wrongdoing and some indication that members of your staff might have been involved. The question, sir, is why didn't you turn this information over immediately to the prosecutors, instead of having your own staff continue to make these investigations?

A. Well, for the very obvious reason that in March, for example, the man that was in constant contact with the prosecutors was my counsel, Mr. Dean. Mr. Dean was talking to Mr. Petersen. I assumed that anything he was telling me, he was telling the prosecutors.

And in April, after Mr. Dean left the investigation, Mr. Ehrlichman was in charge. I would assume—and, incidentally, Mr. Ehrlichman did talk to Mr. Kleindienst—that is why it was done that way.

The President doesn't pick up the phone and call the Attorney General every time something comes up on a matter. He depends on his counsel, or whoever he's done the job to—or, given that assignment to—to do the job. And that is what I expected in this instance.

Q. Following on that, Mr. President— A. You've had one now, you don't—you've had three. Go ahead.

Q. Mr. President, in your Cambodian invasion—in your Cambodian invasion speech of April, 1970, you reported to the American people that the United States had been strictly observing the neutrality of Cambodia. I'm wondering if you, in light of what we now know, that there were 15 months of bombing of Cambodia previous to your statement, whether you owe an apology to the American people?

A. Certainly not, and certainly not to the Cambodian people. Because, as far as this area is concerned, the area of approximately 10 miles—which was bombed during this period— no Cambodians had been in it for years. It was totally occupied by the North Vietnamese Communists. They were using this area for the purpose of attacking and killing American marines and soldiers by the thousands.

The bombing was taking—took place against those North Vietnamese forces in enemy-occupied territory.

And as far as the American people are concerned, I think the American people are very thankful that the President ordered what was necessary to save the lives of their men and shorten this war—which he found when he got here, and which he ended.

SEPTEMBER 5

Following is the text of President Nixon's Sept. 5 news conference in the East Room of the White House:

Opening Statement

Ladies and gentlemen, before going to your questions, I have a brief announcement that I think will be of interest not only to our listeners and to you, but also to the Congress.

The Congress is returning today from its August recess, as I am, and as I look over the record of accomplishment this year, I find it is very disappointing in terms of the Administration initiatives, those initiatives that I believe are bipartisan in character and are of vital importance to all of the American people.

Consequently, I will be sending what is in effect a new State of the Union message, one which will concentrate on the measures presently before the Congress which have not been acted upon and which I consider urgent to be acted upon before the end of this year.

I am not trying to present to the Congress an impossible task; consequently, I will not cover the whole waterfront, but it is important that in several areas that actions be taken or it will be too late to act for the interests of the people.

In my statement today, I will cover four or five areas that will be included in that message, which will be distributed to you on Sunday night and delivered to the Congress Monday at the time of the opening of business.

The first is the very high priority area of fighting inflation. As you know, we are going into a new set of tough controls on September 13th. In addition to that, the Federal Reserve is tightening up on the money supply and we are moving on the supply fronts, particularly in the field of agriculture, so that we can eventually look forward to halting the rise in food prices, and we trust, eventually lowering them.

These three areas are vitally important in fighting inflation, but the three alone are not enough without the fourth area. Inflation must be fought on four fronts at all times. The fourth area, of course, is the Federal budget. It is very disconcerting to note that already before the Congress are spending proposals, which, if enacted, would bust the budget to the tune of at least $6 billion. These proposals I do not look forward to vetoing and to go through the agony of having to fight with the Congress on the veto.

I trust that the Congress, in the spirit that Mr. Tip O'Neill suggested, may work with the Executive in this instance in finding a way to control the spending so that we do not break the budget and raise the prices of the family budget for every American.

The second area has to do with the area of national defense. I have noted that several members of the Congress have suggested that the way to balance the budget is to add to the domestic budget to whatever amount they would like and to take it out of defense. This would be a fatal mistake because we can have the finest domestic programs in the world and it isn't going to make any difference if we don't have our freedom and if we are not around to enjoy them.

At the present time, we are in negotiations with regard to the reduction of our forces in Europe. The Soviet Union, as you note, is moving forward in the modernization of its own weapon system, which they have a right to do under the present SALT agreement, but we are looking forward in the next summit meeting, in which preparations are already going forward, to limiting nuclear arms, including MIRVs which, of course, will add a new dimension to their strength as well as to ours; limiting nuclear arms and thereby reducing not only the burden of armament, but the danger of war for the whole world.

This great effort will be destroyed in the event that the Congress reduces the Federal budget for defense in a sub-

stantial amount. It means that we will go into these negotiations in a second-class position and there will be no incentive whatever for the Soviet Union or others involved to negotiate with us for the material reduction, which is the only way to assure that we can have peace as well as limiting the burden of arms.

The third area is one that many of you ladies and gentlemen have been writing about for some months and with very good reason, the area of energy. We were lucky this summer. We didn't have some of the things happen that we had feared would happen with regard to brown-outs, et cetera, although there were some problems in some cities. But the prospect for the future could be very dangerous.

This Saturday, I am calling a meeting in which Governor Love will report to top Administration officials with regard to the whole energy problem. But essential to our success in meeting the energy needs for this winter and particularly for the future is congressional action.

There are seven major proposals, including the Alaska pipeline, which you have all written about, including, for example, research and development in the field of coal and other areas, including the deregulation of gas produced in the United States. There are seven of these proposals in the energy field which the Congress has not yet acted upon. If the Congress does not act upon these proposals, it means that we will have an energy crisis, not perhaps just this winter, but perhaps, certainly later on as well.

And if the Congress does not act upon these proposals, which in effect, have as their purpose, increasing the domestic capacity of the United States to create its energy, it means that we will be at the mercy of the producers of oil in the Mid-East.

All of you ladies and gentlemen very properly have been writing of your concern about the developments in the Mid-East which might cut off, or at least reduce, the supply of oil that goes to Europe and to the United States. Under these circumstances, to meet the problem of energy, it is essential that we move in these energy areas that I have mentioned.

Finally, there is the area that I could perhaps generally describe in the words of Mr. Mel Laird as being the whole domestic group of programs: The Better Schools Act, the Better Communities Act, and a new housing proposal that I will be sending to the Congress within the next two weeks. These are only three of several. I mention them because I think they are of vital importance and I am going to urge the Congress to act on these proposals so that the country, in this period of peacetime, can begin to move forward on what are these, really, achievements and dividends for peace.

I could mention a number of other areas, but the message will speak for itself. I am simply suggesting in conclusion at this time that we have had this year, as far as the Congress is concerned, a disappointing performance so far. I am not placing individual blame on that. I am simply saying we have three months left and I know that the Congress is usually a last quarter team. In that last quarter, we have to score a lot of points.

The Executive, the White House, all the agencies of the Government will work with the leaders of the Congress to move forward on these initiatives for the people. But it is time for us to turn to these initiatives that are in the interests of all the people and turn to them on an urgent basis.

Questions

Agnew Meeting

Nixon: I think Miss Thomas has the first question.

Q. Mr. President, you met with the Vice President for two hours on Saturday. One, can you tell us what you talked about? Two, will you have any part in any future legal moves against the Vice President? And three, did you call John Connally afterwards, as was reported?

A. Let us start, Miss Thomas, with the third part of the question. It is easier to remember the end of the question than the first.

As far as the third question, no, I have not talked to Governor Connally as reported, and I have not talked to him for the past several weeks. Nothing should be made of that one way or another because I enjoy talking to the Governor, and it is very possible I may be talking to him in the future about energy or about a trip that he is going to be making abroad to various parts of the world, including the Mid-East and possibly the Soviet Union.

Second, with regard to the Vice President, we did meet for two hours. It, of course, is not appropriate for me to discuss what the subject was. We went over a number of matters of mutual interest in which he has major responsibilities.

I will say, finally, that with regard to the Vice President and all other questions that may relate to him, when I last met with you ladies and gentlemen in the sun in California—as distinuished from the sun in the East Room—I recall very well that there were several questions about the Vice President, what would happen in the event that this happened or that, in the event that he were indicted, et cetera.

Let me say that I tried to respond to those questions then. I expressed my confidence in the Vice President's integrity during the period that he has served as Vice President and during which I have known him, but I declined to comment on those questions which were purely hypothetical and which would be a grave infringement upon the rights of the Vice President to comment upon what would happen if/and certain things were to occur in the course of an investigation that is presently going on, I understand, in Baltimore in a grand jury.

I will simply say this: As far as such questions are concerned, you are welcome to ask them, but I will not dignify such questions with regard to charges that I have been made by innuendo or otherwise against the Vice President, I will not dignify them with an answer. It would be an infringement on his rights.

Arab Oil and Mideast

Q. Mr. President, you alluded to this a moment ago, but what exactly are you doing to meet these threats from the Arab countries to use oil as a club for us to force a change in the Middle East policy?

A. Mr. Cormier, that has been a subject of major concern, and what we are doing, some can be talked about, and some cannot. Obviously, we are having discussions with some of the companies involved. Obviously, as far as some of the nations involved—for example, Libya—our relations are not that close that we could have too much influence.

With regard to Saudi Arabia, perhaps the relations with the United States as with Saudi Arabia might lead to more influence there.

What I would suggest is this: In a broader context, that the answer to the problem of oil that we presently depend upon in the Middle East, we depend upon it not, of course, nearly as much as Europe, but we are all in the same bag when you really come down to it.

The problem that we have here is that as far as the Arab countries are concerned, the ones that are involved here, is that it is tied up with the Arab-Israeli dispute. That is why in talking to Dr. Kissinger, both before I nominated him and since, that we have put at the highest priority moving toward making some progress toward the settlement of that dispute. That is one side of it.

The other problems, of course, are the radical elements that presently seem to be on ascendency in various countries in the Mid-East, like Libya, Those elements, of course, we are not in position to control, although we may be in a position to influence them, influence them for this reason: Oil without a market, as Mr. Mossadegh learned many, many years ago, does not do a country much good.

We, and Europe, are the market and I think that the responsible Arab leaders will see to it that if they continue to up the price, if they continue to expropriate, if they do ex-

propriate without fair compensation, the inevitable result is that they will lose their markets, and other sources will be developed.

Tax Audit

Q. Mr. President, there have been some conflicting reports about your real estate dealings in California, and I would like to ask about that. Several different versions have been released by the White House, both as to your own personal financial involvement and as to the Government's expenditures in San Clemente and Key Biscayne, and your auditors, I understand from news reports, say that the entire audit has not been released on your financial dealings out there.

I would like to ask you why we have had so many conflicting reports to start with, and second, one of the questions that is raised by the only partial release of the audit is have you paid the taxes on the gain realized from the sale of the land to Mr. Rebozo and Mr. Abplanalp at San Clemente?

A. Of course, whatever a President does in the field of his property is public knowledge, and questions of that sort I do not resent at all. I do resent, I might say, the implications, however, first, that whether at Key Biscayne or in San Clemente my private property was enriched because of what the Government did.

As a matter of fact, what the Government did in San Clemente reduced the value of the property. If you see three Secret Service gazebos and if you see some of the other fences that block out the rather beautiful view to the hills and the mountains that I like, you would realize that what I say is quite true, it reduces its value as far as a residential property is concerned.

The second point is this: At rather considerable expense, and a great deal of time on my part, I ordered an audit, an audit by a firm highly respected, Coopers and Lybrand of New York. That audit has been completed. It covered at my request not simply the last year, but it covered the years 1969, 1970, 1971 and 1972.

The audit has been completed, and the audit gave the lie to the reports that were carried usually in eight-column heads in most of the papers of this country—and incidentally the retractions ended up back with the corset ads for the most part—but on the other hand, it gave the lie to the charge that there was $1 million worth of campaign funds, that that is how I acquired the property in San Clemente.

It also gave the lie to any other charges that as far as my acquisitions in Florida are concerned, or in California, that there was any money there except my own.

Now, I would make two or three other points briefly about it that I think all laymen could understand. I borrowed the money to acquire the property, and I still owe it. I own no stocks and no bounds—I think I am the first President in this office since Harry Truman. I don't own a stock or a bond. I sold everything before I came into office.

All that I have are the two pieces of property in Florida which adjoin each other, the piece of property in San Clemente with which you are familiar, and a house on Whittier Boulevard in which my mother once lived. I have no other property, and I owe money on all of them.

Third, as far as the capital gain matter, which is a technical matter that you have mentioned, I should point out—and maybe this is good news for people who wonder if Presidents are exempt from what the IRS does—the IRS has had a full field review or audit of my income tax returns for 1971 and 1972, and included in its audit is the transaction which you refer to, in which some argue there was a capital gain and some argue that there was not. It is a matter of difference between accountants.

The IRS, after its audit, did not order any change. If it had, I would have paid the tax. It did not order a change.

Now, with regard to the audit itself is concerned, the results of that audit insofar as the acquisition of the property

have been put out. That is all that is going to be put out because I think that is a full disclosure.

I would simply say finally that in this particular case I
realize that naturally there is a suspicion that a President,
because he has the great power of this office and because he
has the benefit of the Secret Service and GSA and all the rest
to protect him, that he some way or other is going to profit from
all of that security that is provided for him.

As I pointed out in my press conference two weeks ago, I'd
far less rather have the security than have my privacy, but
that just can't be done.

Inflation

Q. Mr. President, a couple of economic questions, please.
You said in your opening statement that you hope eventually
that inflation will be stopped. Can you define "eventually"
more specifically? Furthermore, what, if anything, should be
done now to free up mortgage money for home purposes?

A. I am afraid I cannot be any more perceptive than my
economic advisers have been, and their guesses, as you know,
with regard to the numbers insofar as inflation this year have
not been very good. I do not blame them, however, because, as
you know, we have had the problems of weather in the United
States and abroad, an unprecedented demand abroad which
was unforeseen as far as we were concerned, that gave the impetus to food prices, and there were other factors which led to
the inflationary pressures which our economic advisers did not
foresee.

I cannot set a date on it, no. I mean, if I were to try to, I
would be misleading the public, the people, as to when they
could expect that inflation would start to recede. I do say this,
however: We are doing everything that we think should be done,
and that can be done, to stop the inflation without bringing on a
recession, and that is the name of the game.

It is very easy to turn the crank so tight that you have a
hard landing, and we don't want a hard landing. We have had
too many experiences like that, as you know, since World
War II. So, what we have then is a system of controls, as I have
indicated earlier. We are tightening up on the Federal Reserve, we are—Arthur Burns, in his independent capacity with
the board members are, I should say—and in addition to that
we are, of course, increasing supplies on the food front.

My economic advisers tell me that over the next few months
we should begin to see some of the benefits from this, and that
is as far as I will go in terms of indicating what that situation
would be.

Tax Structure

Q. Mr. President?
A. Mr. Theis.
Q. In that connection, do you now feel that the tax
structure should be altered in any way to help strengthen the
economy and, if so, how?

A. Mr. Theis, a number of my advisers, including, incidentally, Arthur Burns, have strongly recommended that the
answer to this whole problem of inflation is the tax structure,
you know, or there is this gimmick and that one. By saying
"gimmick," I don't mean to say anything disrespectful to Arthur Burns because he is very important to us at this moment,
or to Wilbur Mills, who has talked about some of these things.

For example, there has been the suggestion, as you know,
insofar as the investment credit is concerned, to have it in the
power of the President to move it from three percent to 15 percent. I think that is an excellent idea, but there isn't a chance
that Congress is ever going to give the President that power.

President Kennedy found that out—Wilbur Mills told me
about the conversation in a very amusing dialogue we had in
the office a few weeks ago—when he asked for the power of the
President, then, even when the Congress was, the members, in

control of his own party, to move taxes up and down, depending
upon the needs of the economy.

So, what I would say, Mr. Theis, is this: I think a number of
suggestions have been made on the tax front which might be
helpful in the control of inflation but there isn't a chance that
a responsible tax bill would be passed by this Congress in time
to deal with that problem.

Tapes: Definitive Ruling

Q. Mr. President?
A. Mr. Jarriel?
Q. Mr. President, in association with the legal dispute
going on over possession of the Presidential tapes relating to
Watergate conversations in your office, you and your attorneys
have said you would abide only by a definitive ruling of the
Supreme Court in this case. As it moves along, the definitive
ruling, an interpretation of definitive ruling takes on great
importance. Would you elaborate for us what you mean by a
"definitive ruling"?

A. No, Mr. Jarriel, that would not be appropriate. I
discussed this with White House Counsel, and, as you know,
the matter is now on appeal and the appellate procedure will
now go to the Circuit Court of Appeals in the District of Columbia and, if necessary, further on. The matter of definitive ruling
is one that will be discussed in the appeal procedure and for
me, in advance of the discussion, the briefs, the oral arguments,
to discuss that would be inappropriate.

I think it should come to Mr. Rather now.

Tapes : Above the Law

Q. Mr. President, if I may follow on to my colleague
Tom Jarriel's question, while I can understand—
A. It shows the two networks working together.
Q. No, not always, Mr. President.
A. Thank heaven you are competitors.
Q. This is a question that we find a lot of people ask us.
A. Surely.
Q. As you know, President Lincoln said, "No man is above
the law." Now, for most, if not every other American, any Su-
preme Court decision is final, whether the person, in terms of
the decision, finds it definitive or not. Would you explain to us
why you feel that you are in a different category? Why, as it
applies to you, that you will abide only by what you call a
definitive decision and that you won't even define "definitive"?

A. Well, Mr. Rather, with all due deference to your
comment with regard to President Lincoln, he was a very
strong President and, as you may recall, he indicated several
times during his presidency that he would move in the national
interest in a way that many thought was perhaps in violation
of law, the suspension of the writ of *habeas corpus*, for example, during the Civil War for 15,000 people, and other items,
to mention only one.

As far as I am concerned, I am simply suggesting—saying
that the President of the United States, under our Constitution,
has a responsibility to this office to maintain the separation
of power and also maintain the ability of not only this President but future Presidents to conduct the office in the interests
of the people.

Now, in order to do that, it is essential that the confidentiality of discussions that the President has with his advisers, with members of Congress, with visitors from abroad,
with others who come in, that those discussions be uninhibted,
that they be candid, they be free-wheeling.

Now, in the event that Presidential papers, or in the event
that Presidential conversations as recorded on tapes, in my
opinion, were made available to a court, to a judge *in camera*, or
to a committee of Congress, that principle would be so seriously
jeopardized that it would probably destroy that principle—

the confidentiality which is so essential and indispensable for the proper conduct of the presidency.

That is why I have taken the hard line that I have taken with regard to complying with the lower court's order.

Now, when we come to the Supreme Court, the key there is what kind of an order is the Supreme Court going to issue, if any. And as I have said, in answer to Mr. Jarriel, it would not be appropriate for me to comment on whether an order would be definitive or not. I will simply say that as far as I am concerned, we are going to fight the tape issue. We believe, my Counsel believe, that we will prevail in the appellate courts.

And so, consequently, I will not respond to your question until we go through the appellate procedure.

March 21 Investigation

Q. Mr. President, to follow up on that Watergate question, you have referred repeatedly to having ordered a new Watergate investigation on the 21st of March of this year. Several high officials of your Administration, Mr. Petersen, Mr. Gray and Mr. Kleindienst, have testified before the Senate committee that they didn't know anything about it, this investigation that you referred to. And I wonder if you could explain how it is that they apparently didn't know anything about this new investigation?

A. Well, because I had ordered the investigation from within the White House itself. The investigation, up to that time, had been conducted by Mr. Dean, and I thought by him, working as he had been in close communication with the Justice Department.

I turned the investigation—asked Mr. Dean to continue his investigation as I, as you remember, said last week, two weeks ago, in answer to a similar question. When he was unable to write a report, I turned to Mr. Ehrlichman. Mr. Ehrlichman did talk to the Attorney General, I should remind you, on the 27th of March, I think it was the 27th of March. The Attorney General was quite aware of that and Mr. Ehrlichman, in addition, questioned all of the major figures involved and reported to me on the 14th of April; and then, at my suggestion, direction, turned over his report to the Attorney General on the 15th of April. An investigation was conducted in the most thorough way.

Rebuilding Confidence

Q. Mr. President, you listed several areas of domestic concern—

A. Now we have the three networks.

Q. You listed several areas of domestic concern in the message you are going to send to Congress, but it has also been written that one of the major problems facing your Administration now is rebuilding confidence in your leadership.

Do you share that view and, if so, how do you plan to cope with it?

A. Mr. Valeriani, that is a problem, it is true. It is rather difficult to have the President of the United States on prime time television—not prime time, although I would suppose the newscasters would say the news programs are really the prime time—but for four months to have the President of the United States by innuendo, by leak, by, frankly, leers and sneers of commentators, which is their perfect right, attacked in every way without having some of that confidence being worn away.

Now, how is it restored? Well, it is restored by the President not allowing his own confidence to be destroyed; that is to begin. And, second, it is restored by doing something. We have tried to do things. The country hasn't paid a great deal of attention to it, and I may say the media hasn't paid a great deal of attention to it because your attention, quite understandably, is in the more fascinating area of Watergate.

Perhaps that will now change. Perhaps as we move in the foreign policy initiatives now, having ended one war, to build

a structure of peace, moving not only with the Soviet Union and with the PRC where Dr. Kissinger incidentally will go, after he is confirmed by the Senate, which I hope will be soon, but as we move in those areas and as we move on the domestic front, the people will be concerned about what the President does, and I think that that will restore the confidence. What the President says will not restore it, and what you ladies and gentlemen say will certainly not restore it.

Tapes: Nothing Inconsistent

Q. Mr. President, to follow up on the tapes question, earlier you have told us that your reasons are based on principle—separation of powers, Executive privilege, things of this sort. Can you assure us that the tapes do not reflect unfavorably on your Watergate position, that there is nothing in the tapes that would reflect favorably?

A. There is nothing whatever. As a matter of fact, the only time I listened to the tapes, to certain tapes—and I didn't listen to all of them, of course—was on June the 4th. There is nothing whatever in the tapes that is inconsistent with the statement that I made on May 22 or of the statement that I made to you ladies and gentlemen in answer to several questions, rather searching questions I might say, and very polite questions two weeks ago, for the most part, and finally nothing that differs whatever from the statement that I made on the 15th of August. That is not my concern.

My concern is the one that I have expressed and it just does not cover tapes, it covers the appearance of a President before a Congressional Committee which Mr. Truman very properly turned down in 1953 although some of us at that time thought he should have appeared. This was after he had left the Presidency but it had to do with matters while he was President. It covers papers of the President written for him and communications with him and it covers conversations with the President that are recorded on tape. Confidentiality once destroyed cannot in my opinion be restored.

Minimum Wage Veto

Q. Mr. President, do you intend to veto a Minimum Wage Bill, sir?

A. Yes. With very great regret my Secretary of Labor, Mr. Brennan, has urged me to sign it. As a team player he however recognizes some of the arguments that I have made for not signing it. What it has to do is not my dedication to the minimum wage. I have always voted for it in the past and I have signed several bills in this Administration, at least two. The difficulty is that the Minimum Wage Bill which is presently before me on my desk would raise the minimum wage by 38 percent. It would deny employment opportunities to unskilled and younger workers who at present are in the highest numbers and the highest percentage of unemployment, it would increase unemployment. And it would give an enormous boost to inflation. Therefore, I am going to ask the Congress in my veto message to write a new bill, to send one down that will not be inflationary and that will not cost jobs for those who need jobs among the unskilled and the younger workers.

Arab Oil Pressure

Q. Mr. President, I would like to check the Arab oil pressure if I may again. Is it possible that the threat of limiting the supply of oil would cause a moderation in U.S. support of Israel?

A. I think that that question is one that has been understandably speculated about a great deal in the press but obviously for the President of the United States in answer to such a question to suggest that we are going to relate our policy toward Israel which has to do with the independence of that country to which we are dedicated to what happens on Arab oil I think would be highly inappropriate. I will say this and I will put it in another context, however. Israel simply can't wait for the dust to settle and the Arabs can't wait for the dust to settle in the Mid-East. Both sides are at fault. Both sides need to start negotiating. That is our position.

We are not pro-Israel and we are not pro-Arab and we are not any more pro-Arab because they have oil and Israel hasn't. We are pro-peace and it is the interest of the whole area for us to get those negotiations off dead center and that is why we will use our influence with Israel and we will use our influence, what influence we have, with the various Arab States, and a non-Arab State like Egypt, to get those negotiations off.

Now one of the dividends of having a successful negotiation will be to reduce the oil pressure.

Mr. Horst.

New Bipartisanship

Q. Sir, you mentioned a while ago Representative O'Neill's proposal that the Democratic leadership of Congress and the President get together on some bipartisan areas. Can you suggest some bills or some measures of vital concern which a new bipartisanship in his format would work out?

A. Well, I would suggest, Mr. terHorst, the ones I mentioned in my opening statement would all fit in that category with the possible exception of those that I said were in Mr. Laird's particular responsibility—better schools, better housing, and also the Better Communities Act. Those do involve basic philosophic differences and bipartisanship may not be possible, but on the other hand holding the budget down so that we don't have inflation is a bipartisan concern.

Maintaining a national defense that is adequate so that the United States is not in a second position in dealing with the Soviet Union or any other country in the world is a bipartisan concern. Seeing to it that we have adequate energy supplies. In fact, some of the best conversations I have had and the best suggestions I have had in the field of energy have come from Democrats, Senator Jackson among them. I think that we should get a bipartisan policy going with regard to dealing with the problems of energy, and there could be others.

Tapes: Dispelling Doubts

Q. Mr. President, could I ask you one more question about the tapes. If you win the case in the Supreme Court—

A. That's the fifth one.

Q. —and establish the right of confidentiality for Presidents, then would you be willing voluntarily to disclose the tapes to dispel the doubt about their content?

A.: Well, again I would like to respond to that question in a categorical way but I shall not due to the fact that when the matter as it is at the present time is actually in the appeal process, White House counsel advise that it would not be appropriate to comment in any way about what is going to happen during that process. You put that question to me a little later, I will be glad to respond to it.

THE PRESS. Thank you, Mr. President. ✓

OCT. 3

Following is the text, as made available by the White House, of President Nixon's Oct. 3 news conference in the White House briefing room:

Opening Statement

THE PRESIDENT: Won't you be seated, ladies and gentlemen. I guess I should say all those who can find seats.

Dr. Kissinger, as you know from an announcement that I understand got out about 30 minutes ago from Peking, will visit Peking on October 26 to 29. This is part of the continuing dialogue between the People's Republic of China and the United States which began with my visit to China last year.

The subjects that will be discussed include those that have been discussed on previous occasions, trade, for example, where, it is interesting to note, that the amount of bilateral trade between the two countries, which was approximately $6 million in 1971, will be an estimated $800 million in 1973. Scientific and cultural exchanges will be a major subject for discussion and, of course, other matters of mutual concern to the two nations.

In addition, Dr. Kissinger has been invited by the Foreign Minister of Japan, Mr. Ohira, to stop in Japan on his visit to the Far East. He will do so. The timing of that visit, however, has not yet been agreed upon and will be announced as soon as we hear from the Japanese.

Incidentally, I learned that 12 to 15 members of the press will be invited, if they desire to go, to go on the trip with the Secretary of State, and if you would put in your applications at the State Department, in this instance, I think that they will be honored in the order in which they are received.

Now, I will be glad to take question on other subjects, since I understand Mr. Warren has been rather busy with his briefings lately.

The Agnew Case

Q: Mr. President, would you tell us why you sent Bryce Harlow out to Arizona last month just after the Vice President and Mr. Goldwater conferred?

A: I didn't send him to Arizona, as far as I know. I think he went to Oklahoma.

Q: He was reported to have gone to Phoenix.

A: Well, he might have. He might have. I think that what had happened was that Senator Goldwater had indicated an interest in the status of the situation with regard to the Vice President's case and Mr. Harlow, being somewhat familiar with that matter, was the best man to provide that information for him.

Q: Mr. President, do you think that the Vice President should resign if he is indicted?

A: Well, the Vice President has addressed that question and his answer is an altogether proper one. The Vice President is in a different position, for example, than a member of the President's Cabinet or a member of his staff. I have indicated that if a member of the President's Cabinet or his staff is indicted, he would have to resign pending the outcome of the trial.

However, the Vice President, like the President, is elected by all the people. He holds that office in his own right and the decision as to whether he should resign is for him to make. He has indicated that he will not resign if indicted and, therefore, that decision on his part should be respected.

Q· Mr. President, have you ever asked for him to consider resigning?

A: No, I have not. I have noted the lively discussion about resignation here in the press room and I understand that. But let me say that in all the conversations I have had with the Vice President, I have never asked him to resign. I have always told him and he understands this position, that this matter is one for him to decide.

I would say further that as far as our discussions are concerned, they are privileged and I will not go further than that other than to say that we both agreed that we could make public the fact that the charges that have been made against him and which he has denied publicly, he has denied to me privately on three occasions.

San Clemente

Q: Mr. President, at your last press conference you said that some of the government work done at San Clemente had diminished the value of the property for use as a home. I would like to ask about two items that are in the GSA reports on it.

First, do you think that the $13,500 electrical heating system that was installed diminished its value? And, second, do you think when the GSA hired a local landscape architect to redesign the flower beds on the west side of the residence four times a year, that they were spending the taxpayer's money wisely?

A: Well, I can plow that ground again, I guess. If any of you have lived in California, you will know that gas heat costs less than electric heat. I preferred the first, gas heat. For security reasons, apparently, they decided it presented a fire hazard which could not be tolerated. And so that decision was made.

With regard to the other matters that have been brought up, I think full statements have been made over and over again on this, and I really think anything I would say in answer to your question, in view of the way you have already presented it as a statement, would not convince you or anybody else.

Unfilled Jobs

Q: Mr. President, may I ask you two questions in one, because both relate to—

A: You are like Mr. Mollenhoff. You can ask three if you like.

Q: I will just ask a double-header, all right? Both are related to unfilled jobs. That is why I am putting them together.

We have not had an Ambassador in the Soviet Union now for going on to nine months, and the Chairman of your Commission on Civil Rights, that job has been unfilled about eight or nine months, also. What are your plans on that?

A: The Ambassador to the Soviet Union is a very important post, and, as a matter of fact, I discussed that with Dr. Kissinger just yesterday. I think we will have an announcement on it within the next two or three weeks.

With regard to the other position, that is one also that we consider to be very important and it is at present being considered within the Domestic Council. I am sure a recommendation will be made to me soon and we will try to fill it.

The main thing about these appointments, as I am sure you all know, is to get the right person, man or woman, for the job rather than to do it in too much of a hurry.

Percy and the Presidency

Q: Mr. President.

A: Mr. Beckman.

Q: Mr. President, can you tell us if you will actively oppose Senator Percy's efforts to win the 1976 Republican nomination, and if you will not, can you tell us what has changed since February when you suggested that you might?

A: Well, I have noted, particularly in the Chicao papers, not only the Tribune, but the Sun Times and the News—and is there another one there, too?

Q: Today?

A: Today, that there has been much speculation about my meeting with Senator Percy. It was a very candid discussion. I did say at one point, due to a misunderstanding, that I thought that Senator Percy should not be a candidate in 1976 and as I told him when we met, that statement was made because I had understood that he had opposed Elliot Richardson for Attorney General right after I had announced that I was sending his name to the Senate, which I thought was a highly irresponsible thing to do, in view of the fact that both Elliot Richardson and Senator Percy are in what we call the more liberal wing of the Republican Party.

Senator Percy, however, later explained that his resolution in that respect that would have affected Elliot Richardson had been misinterpreted, that he had actually introduced it prior to the time that I made my announcement.

Now, so much for the statement that was made in February. Second, to put it all in perspective, whether it is Senator Percy on the one side, or one of several Governors or former Governors who might be a candidate, the Mayor of Indianapolis, or a number of Senators and one or two House Members, all of them have a right to seek the Presidency if they so desire.

As far as I am concerned, I will make no decision with regard to supporting or opposing any one of these candidates until they have been tried in the field of battle. I think that we learned in the year 1972 that when an individual moves from the Senate—and I am referring now to the primaries—to the big leagues, or when he moves from the Governorship to the big leagues, and we learned this in other years, that sometimes he can't hit the big league pitching. And I would like to see how these various potential candidates handle themselves in the primaries before making any decision with regard to who should be the candidate.

I am not saying now incidentally, categorically that I will endorse a candidate before the Convention. I reserve the right to make that decision at a later time. But certainly, I would say finally, that Senator Percy has been a vigorous campaigner for the Senate, an articulate spokesman, not always on the side of the Administration, but I respect differences of opinion, and he has every right to seek the Presidency. He will not be opposed at this time and should he prove to be the strongest candidate, he will not be opposed, certainly if he receives the nomination. I will support whoever receives that nomination.

Vice Presidential Planning

Q: Mr. President.

A: Mr. Jarriel.

Go ahead. I am sorry.

Q: Mr. Risher.

A: Gene Risher. You look like Jarriel though. (Laughter)

Q: Thank you, Mr. President.

A: You are not paid as much as he is though. (Laughter)

Q: I know. (Laughter)

A: UPI please notice—a raise in salary.

Q: Could you tell us, Mr. President, if you have done any contingency planning about a possible Vice President in the event that Vice President Agnew leaves office for any reason?

A: Mr. Risher, certainly not. It would be highly inappropriate to have any contingency planning with regard to what should happen if the Vice President leaves office.

As far as the Vice President is concerned, I have said in my statement of the 25th of September that he has denied the charges that have been made against him, that he is entitled to the presumption of innocence, which is the right of every American citizen and I urge all of my fellow Americans to give him that presumption of innocence, as I certainly do, and particularly that presumption of innocence, I think, should be underlined in view of his years of distinguished service as Vice President; having in mind, too, the fact that the charges that have been made against him do not relate in any way to his activities as Vice President of the United States.

I would say further in that respect that I would hope that in this rather white hot atmosphere, which I understand, has developed since the Vice President's case came to public attention, that he will not be tried and convicted in the press and on television by leaks and innuendos and the rest. There is nothing really that is more harmful to the rights of an individual than to be tried and convicted in the press before he has an opportunity to present his case and I would urge all of you ladies and gentlemen, because I know you want to be responsible in this respect, to make your statements on the basis of all the evidence, not on the basis—

Q: Mr. President—

A: Let me finish.

—make your judgment on the basis of all the evidence and not simply on the basis of a unilateral charge that is made, not under oath—

Q: Mr. President—

Leaks from Justice Department

A: Mr. Mollenhoff, yes, you.

Q: —on that particular point, you have been briefed in some detail on the evidence in the Agnew problem. You are also a lawyer with some expertise. You could tell us—

A: Some would question that.

Q: —whether there is any substance to Mr. Agnew's charges that this is a frivolous investigation, that it is a frame-up, and that it is in fact a smear.

A: Mr. Mollenhoff, when you say that I have been briefed on the charges, I should respond to that by saying that I have not heard the witnesses. I have only been briefed on what it is believed the witnesses might testify to.

As far as the charges are concerned, they are serious and not frivolous. The Vice President's complaint, as you know, is that the leaks that have come out on this particular matter have convicted him in advance and it is that particular point that concerns him and it concerns me as well.

As a matter of fact, in the strongest terms I have spoken to the Attorney General about this matter. He shares my view. He has taken personal charge of the investigation with regard to leaks, and, incidentally, he has assured me, Mr. Mollenhoff, that the Assistant Attorney General, Mr. Petersen, who, as you recall, I praised rather highly in my 22nd of August press conference in San Clemente, was in no way—neither he nor members of his office in the Justice Department—involved in the leaks involving the Vice President.

Q: Mr. President, if I may follow up, please.

A: Yes, you may follow up.

Q: Thank you.

In view of that remark do you then still support Mr. Petersen's handling of the investigation?

A: If I did not support Mr. Petersen's handling of the investigation, he would have been removed at this time. But it would be a disservice to an individual who has served both Administrations with distinction for many, many years, to remove him from handling the investigation unless there was clear evidence that he had been guilty of an indiscretion and I have taken this matter up quite directly with the Attorney General.

The Attorney General assures me that his investigation—his, the Attorney General's investigation—indicates that Mr. Petersen has handled this investigation without prejudice in advance and without, of course, engaging in what, in my view, is the totally inexcusable and inappropriate conduct of leaking information on a Grand Jury investigation.

Foreign Travel

Q: Mr. President.

A: Mr. Theis.

Q: In view of your sidewalk remark the other night about travel plans, can you pinpoint for us any better your timing of your trip to Europe?

A: Mr. Theis, it is difficult to pinpoint the timing of a trip to Europe, but in order that all of you can make your plans a little better, the trip to Europe will be made within the next few months and the timing will be based on these factors: First, the progress which is made on the discussions now going on with regard to a declaration of principles with regard to the Alliance, and with regard to economic matters as well.

The latter, as you know, I discussed with Mr. Ortoli when he was here. That progress is going on, incidentally, well ahead of schedule according to Dr. Kissinger. As soon as those prelimi-

nary negotiations are completed and as soon as it is clear on both sides of the Atlantic that this will be a trip not for protocol purposes, but one that will have real substance in it, then we will work out a date.

Now the second factor, however, which enters into this is the Congressional schedule. I cannot take a trip to Europe or any place else at a time when there are matters before the Congress of very great significance. That is why I cannot pinpoint this in terms of saying that just as soon as the Europeans are ready we will go.

If the Europeans are ready at a time that we have a heavy calendar in Congress, I shall have to postpone the trip until that.

But I would say I am thinking in terms of the next three or four months, but it might be sooner than that; probably not much later.

Now, with regard to Japan, I agreed with Mr. Tanaka, when he was here, that I would visit Japan before the end of 1974. We will, of course, make those plans again consistent with our developments on the bilateral side and at a time when we think that there is a matter of substance to be discussed or matters of substance to be discussed and at a time which is consistent with my responsibilities on the domestic front.

Q: Could I ask, Mr. President—

A: This lady is—

Q: Thank you, Mr. President.

A: You don't mind a lady going ahead of you, do you?

Q: No, sir.

Q: Thank you, sir.

Russian Emigrants

Do you have any comment to make on the Austrian decision to close the Russian emigrant facilities?

Q: Excuse me.

Q: The Austrian decision to close the Russian emigrant facilities.

A: I heard your question, but I wanted the radio to hear it, too.

Q: Oh, thank you.

A: Yes, I have. The Austrians are in a very difficult position here. As you know, I stopped in Austria on my way to Moscow and for the first time—no, the second time, met the Prime Minister, Mr. Kreisky, and anybody who knows his background knows that he is certainly not anti-Semitic, but Austria is in the eye of a hurricane and Austria, therefore being a relatively small country and relatively weak, militarily, et cetera, is making a very, what I am sure for Mr. Kreisky, painful decision in this respect.

I recall, for example, that at the time of the Hungarian revolution, Austria opened its arms very generously to thousands of refugees and I know that is the Austrian tradition and custom. I would hope—and I would express this—I would hope that the Prime Minister would reconsider his decision, even though I know he has even lately reiterated it, reconsider it for this fundamental reason that goes far beyond his country and even ours, and that is that we simply cannot have governments, small or large, give in to international blackmail by terrorist groups. That is what is involved.

Not to mention, of course, the fact that we all have a concern for the emigres. They must have a place to come. So, on humanitarian grounds and on geopolitical grounds of the highest order, I believe that that decision should be reconsidered, but naturally, I am not going to put my friend, Mr. Kreisky, in the position of trying to dictate to him what it should be.

Now, you go ahead with your question.

Watergate Tapes

Q: Sir, there is at least the possibility that if you don't give up the Watergate tapes, some of the cases or potential cases against your former aides might be aborted. I wonder if you are concerned about this, and further, whether you might see some room for compromise in the Appellate Court suggestion?

A: Well, since the Appellate Court is still considering the matter, it would be inappropriate for me to talk about what should be done with regard to compromise. As you know, discussions, extended discussions, took place between Mr. Buzhardt and the Special Prosecutor in this respect, and they agreed to disagree.

As far as the tapes are concerned, I have stated my position, and I restate it again today. The position is that the confidentiality of Presidential discussions must be maintained and whether it is a Presidential paper, a memorandum of conversation prepared by a member of his staff after meeting with the President, or whether it is a tape of a conversation, it is the responsibility of the President, with regard to the separation of powers principle, to defend the integrity of those conversations so that Presidents in the future will be able to conduct freewheeling, extended conversations with no holds barred with foreign visitors and, of course, with those who come to see him from the United States.

Inflation

Q: Mr. President, do you agree with the proposition put forth by your CEA nominee, Mr. Fellner, that the country will have to abandon its goal of four percent unemployment and move to five percent, or perhaps higher, to fight inflation?

A: I noticed Mr. Fellner's rather, shall we say, outspoken comments, and also his comments with regard to Phase IV where he said he thought we should apparently—at least the press indicated that he thought that we should junk Phase IV pretty soon, or sooner than we certainly intend to do so.

Before answering that question, let me say that I have found that economists are the most independent breed of human species, except for members of the press. (Laughter) And the reason for that is that the American economy is highly unpredictable. It is a free economy.

I have found that my economic advisers are not always right, but they are always sure in everything that the recommend. (Laughter)

Now as far as Mr. Fellner is concerned, whether the goal should be four percent or five percent is not really the point. The main thing is to get unemployment down as low as we can.

At the present time this economy is going at full bore ahead —that is on the plus side—despite the unacceptable rate of inflation, and unemployment is, we trust, going to either stay where it is or come down.

But I am not going to say that we are going to abandon IV or go to V or go to VI. Our goal is to see that every American who wants to work and who is qualified to work can get a job. That is one that we must never give up on, and the percentages are not the main factor.

Relations With Japan

Q: Mr. President, just a point of clarification.

A: Sure.

Q: In your discussion of the declaration of principles, there was an intention to include Japan as well as the European communities. Is that still the case or has that been changed?

A: Let me explain what we feel now with regard to including Japan.

I have told all of our foreign visitors, Chancellor Brandt, and, of course, Prime Minister Heath, President Pompidou, that it is vitally important that Japan—which is now the second major economic power in the world, and, of course, in the Pacific a potential very great force for peace and stability—that Japan not be out of the club.

Now, they all agree. The difficulty is in writing a declaration with regard to the Atlantic Alliance which fits Japan, the difficulty is, is writing one with regard to the European Economic Community which fits Japan.

So what we are presently thinking of is three declarations, one for the Atlantic Alliance, one for the economic community and then a more general declaration to which the Japanese might be willing to adhere.

Now, I have gone beyond what we have worked out, but that is what we can expect.

Let me say finally, that in that respect, I know that these declarations may not seem too important when we consider the domestic problems that presently obsess us, but it is essential at a time that we are having negotiations with the Soviets and with the People's Republic of China, it is essential that we breathe new life and new purpose and new spirit into the American Atlantic Alliance and into the free world community, which includes Japan, and unless we do so, unless, for example, the Atlantic Alliance speaks to our times rather than to the times 25 years ago, it is going to fragment. Our European friends realize this and I am glad to note that even the economic experts like Ortoli recognize it, too.

THE PRESS: Thank you, Mr. President.

OCT. 26

Following is the White House text of President Nixon's Oct. 26 news conference.

THE PRESIDENT: Will you be seated, please?

Ladies and gentlemen, before going to your questions, I have a statement with regard to the Mideast which I think will anticipate some of the questions, because this will update the information which is breaking rather fast in that area, as you know, for the past two days.

The cease-fire is holding. There have been some violations, but generally speaking it can be said that it is holding at this time. As you know, as a result of the U.N. resolution which was agreed to yesterday by a vote of 14 to 0, a peacekeeping force will go to the Mideast, and this force, however, will not include any forces from the major powers, including, of course, the United States and the Soviet Union.

The question, however, has arisen as to whether observers from major powers could go to the Mideast. My up-to-the-minute report on that, and I just talked to Dr. Kissinger five minutes before coming down, is this: We will send observers to the Mideast if requested by the Secretary General of the United Nations, and we have reason to expect that we will receive such a request.

With regard to the peacekeeping force, I think it is important for all of you ladies and gentlemen, and particularly for those listening on radio and television, to know why the United States has insisted that major powers not be part of the peacekeeping force, and that major powers not introduce military forces into the Mideast. A very significant and potentially explosive crisis developed on Wednesday of this week. We obtained information which led us to believe that the Soviet Union was planning to send a very substantial force into the Mideast, a military force.

When I received that information, I ordered, shortly after midnight on Thursday morning, an alert for all American forces around the world. This was a precautionary alert. The purpose of that was to indicate to the Soviet Union that we could not accept any unilateral move on their part to move military forces into the Mideast. At the same time, in the early morning hours, I also proceeded on the diplomatic front. In a message to Mr. Brezhnev, an urgent message, I indicated to him our reasoning and I urged that we not proceed along that course, and that, instead, that we join in the United Nations in supporting a resolution which would exclude any major powers from participating in a peacekeeping force.

As a result of that communication, and the return that I received from Mr. Brezhnev—we had several exchanges, I should say—we reached the conclusion that we would jointly support the resolution which was adopted in the United Nations.

We now come, of course, to the critical time in terms of the future of the Mideast. And here, the outlook is far more hopeful than what we have been through this past week. I think I could safely say that the chances for not just a cease-fire, which we presently have and which, of course, we have had in the Mideast for some time, but the outlook for a permanent peace is the best that it has been in 20 years.

The reason for this is that the two major powers, the Soviet Union and the United States, have agreed—this was one of the results of Dr. Kissinger's trip to Moscow—have agreed that we would participate in trying to expedite the talks between the parties involved. That does not mean that the two major powers will impose a settlement. It does mean, however, that we will use our influence with the nations in the area to expedite a settlement.

The reason we feel this is important is that first, from the standpoint of the nations in the Mideast, none of them, Israel, Egypt, Syria, none of them can or should go through the agony of another war.

The losses in this war on both sides have been very, very high. And the tragedy must not occur again. There have been four of these wars, as you ladies and gentlemen know, over the past 20 years. But beyond that, it is vitally important to the peace of the world that this potential troublespot, which is really one of the most potentially explosive areas in the world, that it not become an area in which the major powers come together in confrontation.

What the developments of this week should indicate to all of us is that the United States and the Soviet Union, who admittedly have very different objectives in the Mideast, have now agreed that it is not in their interest to have a confrontation there, a confrontation which might lead to a nuclear confrontation and neither of the two major powers wants that.

We have agreed, also, that if we are to avoid that, it is necessary for us to use our influence more than we have in the past, to get the negotiating track moving again, but this time, moving to a conclusion. Not simply a temporary truce, but a permanent peace.

I do not mean to suggest that it is going to come quickly because the parties involved are still rather far apart. But I do say that now there are greater incentives within the area to find a peaceful solution and there are enormous incentives as far as the United States is concerned, and the Soviet Union and other major powers, to find such a solution.

Turning now to the subject of our attempts to get a cease-fire on the home front, that is a bit more difficult.

Today White House Counsel contacted Judge Sirica. We tried yesterday but he was in Boston, as you know, and arrangements were made to meet with Judge Sirica on Tuesday to work out the delivery of the tapes to Judge Sirica.

Also, in consultations that we have had in the White House today, we have decided that next week the Acting Attorney General, Mr. Bork, will appoint a new special prosecutor for what is called the Watergate matter. The special prosecutor will have independence. He will have total cooperation from the Executive Branch, and he will have as a primary responsibility to bring this matter which has so long concerned the American people, bring it to an expeditious conclusion, because we have to remember that under our Constitution it has always been held that justice delayed is justice denied. It is time for those who are guilty to be prosecuted, and for those who are innocent to be cleared. I can assure you ladies and gentlemen, all of our listeners tonight, that I have no greater interest than to see that the new special prosecutor has the cooperation from the Executive Branch and the independence that he needs to bring about that conclusion.

And now I will go to Mr. Cormier.

Role of New Prosecutor

Q: Mr. President, would the new special prosecutor have your go-ahead to go to court if necessary to obtain evidence from your files that he felt were vital?

A: Mr. Cormier, I would anticipate that that would not be necessary. I believe that as we look at the events which led to the dismissal of Mr. Cox, we find that these are matters that can be worked out and should be worked out in cooperation and not by having a suit filed by a special prosecutor within the Executive Branch against the President of the United States.

This, incidentally, is not a new attitude on the part of a President. Every President since George Washington has tried to protect the confidentiality of Presidential conversations and you remember the famous case involving Thomas Jefferson where Chief Justice Marshall, then sitting as a trial judge, subpoenaed the letter which Jefferson had written which Marshall thought or felt was necessary evidence in the trial of Aaron Burr. Jefferson refused to do so but it did not result in a suit. What happened was, of course, a compromise in which a summary of the contents of the letter which was relevant to the trial was produced by Jefferson and the Chief Justice of the United States, acting in his capacity as Chief Justice, accepted that.

That is exactly, of course, what we tried to do in this instant case.

I think it would be well if I could take just a moment, Mr. Cormier, in answering your question to point out what we tried to do and why we feel it was the proper solution to a very aggravating and difficult problem.

The matter of the tapes has been one that has concerned me because of my feeling that I have a Constitutional responsibility to defend the Office of the Presidency from any encroachments on confidentiality which might affect future Presidents in their abilities to conduct the kind of conversations and discussions they need to conduct to carry on the responsibilities of this Office. And, of course, the special prosecutor felt that he needed the tapes for the purpose of his prosecution.

That was why, working with the Attorney General, we worked out what we thought was an acceptable compromise, one in which Judge Stennis, now Senator Stennis, would hear the tapes and would provide a complete and full disclosure, not only to Judge Sirica, but also to the Senate Committee.

Attorney General Richardson approved of this proposition. Senator Baker, Senator Ervin approved of the proposition. Mr. Cox was the only one that rejected it.

Under the circumstances, when he rejected it and indicated that despite the approval of the Attorney General, and, of course, of the President and of the two major Senators on the Ervin Committee, when he rejected the proposal, I had no choice but to dismiss him.

Under those circumstances, Mr. Richardson, Mr. Ruckelshaus felt that because of the nature of their confirmation that their commitment to Mr. Cox had to take precedence over any commitment they might have to carry out an order from the President.

Under those circumstances, I accepted with regret the resignations of two fine public servants.

Now we come to a new special prosecutor. We will cooperate with him, and I do not anticipate that we will come to the time when he would consider it necessary to take the President to court. I think our cooperation will be adequate.

Prosecutor and Presidential Documents

Q: This is another way of asking Frank's question, but if the special prosecutor considers that information contained in Presidential documents is needed to prosecute the Watergate case, will you give him the documents, beyond the nine tapes which you have already turned over?

A: I have answered that question before. We will not provide Presidential documents to a special prosecutor. We will provide, as we have in great numbers, all kinds of documents from the White House, but if it is a document involving a conversation with the President, I would have to stand on the principle of confidentiality. However, information that is needed from such documents would be provided. That is what we have been trying to do.

Congressionally Mandated Prosecutor

Q: Mr. President, you know in the Congress there is a great deal of suspicion over any arrangement which will permit the Executive branch to investigate itself or which will establish a special prosecutor which you may fire again. As 53 Senators, a majority, have now co-sponsored a resolution which would permit Judge Sirica to establish and name an independent prosecutor, separate and apart from the White House Executive branch, do you believe this arrangement would be constitutional and would you go along with it?

A: I would suggest that the action that we are going to take of appointing a special prosecutor would be satisfactory to the Congress, and that they would not proceed with that particular matter.

Response to Impeachment Talk

Q: Mr. President, I wonder if you could share with us your thoughts and tell us what goes through your mind when you hear people who love this country, and people who believe in you, say reluctantly that perhaps you should resign or be impeached.

A: Well, I am glad we don't take the vote of this room, let me say. And I understand the feelings of people with regard to impeachment and resignation. As a matter of fact, Mr. Rather, you may remember when I made the rather difficult decision, I thought the most difficult decision of my first term on December 18th, the bombing by B-52s of North Vietnam, that exactly the same words were used on the networks—I don't mean by you, but they were quoted on the networks—that are used now: tyrant, dictator, he has lost his senses, he should resign, he should be impeached.

But I stuck it out, and as a result of that, we not only got our prisoners of war home, as I have often said, on their feet rather than on their knees, but we brought peace to Vietnam, something we haven't had and didn't for over 12 years.

It was a hard decision, and it was one that many of my friends in the press who had consistently supported me on the war up to that time disagreed with. Now, in this instance I realize there are people who feel that the actions that I have taken with regard to the dismissal of Mr. Cox are grounds for impeachment.

I would respectfully suggest that even Mr. Cox and Mr. Richardson have agreed that the President had the right, constitutional right, to dismiss anybody in the Federal Government; and second, I should also point out that as far as the tapes are concerned, rather than being in defiance of the law, I am in compliance with the law.

As far as what goes through my mind, I would simply say that I intend to continue to carry out, to the best of my ability, the responsibilities I was elected to carry out last November. The events of this past week—I know, for example, in your head office in New York, some thought that it was simply a blown-up exercise; there wasn't a real crisis. I wish it had been that. It was a real crisis. It was the most difficult crisis we have had since the Cuban confrontation of 1962.

But because we had had our initiative with the Soviet Union, because I had a basis of communication with Mr. Brezhnev, we not only avoided a confrontation, but we moved a great step forward toward real peace in the Mideast.

Now, as long as I can carry out that kind of responsibility, I am going to continue to do this job.

Cox Motives

Q: Mr. President.

A: Mr. Lisagor.

Q: There have been reports that you felt that Mr. Cox was somehow out to get you. I would like to ask you if you did feel that, and if so, what evidence did you have?

A: Mr. Lisagor, I understand Mr. Cox is going to testify next week under oath before the Judiciary Committee, and I would suggest that he perhaps would be better qualified to answer that question.

As far as I am concerned, we had cooperated with the Special Prosecutor. We tried to work out in a cooperative way this matter of the production of the tapes. He seemed to be more interested in the issue than he was in a settlement, and under the circumstances, I had no choice but to dismiss him. But I am not going to question his motives as to whether or not he was out to get me. Perhaps the Senators would like to ask that question.

'Vicious, Distorted Reporting'

Q: Mr. President, in 1968, before you were elected, you wrote that too many shocks can drain a nation of its energy and even cause a rebellion against creative change and progress. Do you think America is at that point now?

A: I think that many would speculate. I have noted a lot on the networks particularly and sometimes even in the newspapers. But this is a very strong country, and the American people, I think, can ride through the shocks they have.

The difference now from what it was in the days of shocks, even when Mr. Lisagor and I first met 25 years ago, is the electronic media. I have never heard or seen such outrageous, vicious, distorted reporting in 27 years of public life. I am not blaming anybody for that. Perhaps what happened is what we did brought it about, and therefore, the media decided that they would have to take that particular line.

But when people are pounded night after night with that kind of frantic, hysterical reporting, it naturally shakes their confidence. And yet, I should point out that even in this week, when many thought that the President was shell-shocked, unable to act, the President acted decisively in the interest of peace, in the interest of the country, and I can assure you that whatever shocks gentlemen of the press may have, or others, political people, these shocks will not affect me in my doing my job.

Mideast Alert

Q: Mr. President, getting back to the Middle East crisis for a moment, do you consider that the crisis is over now and how much longer will the American forces be kept on alert around the world?

A: With regard to the alert, the alert has already been discontinued with regard to NORAD, that is the North American Command, and with regard to SAC. As far as other forces are concerned, they are being maintained in a state of readiness and obviously, Soviet Union forces are being maintained in a state of readiness.

Now, as far as the crisis in the Mideast is concerned, I don't want to leave any impression that we aren't going to continue to have problems with regard to the cease-fire. There will be outbreaks because of the proximity of the antagonistic forces and there will be some very, very tough negotiating in attempting to reach a diplomatic settlement. But I think now that all parties are going to approach this problem of trying to reach a settlement with a more sober and a more determined attitude than ever before, because the Mideast can't afford, Israel can't afford, Egypt can't afford, Syria can't afford another war. The world cannot afford a war in that part of the world, and because the Soviet Union and the

United States have potentially conflicting interests there, we both now realize that we cannot allow our differences in the Mideast to jeopardize even greater interests that we have, for example, in continuing a detente in Europe, in continuing the negotiations which can lead to a limitation of nuclear arms and eventually reducing the burden of nuclear arms, and in continuing in other ways that can contribute to the peace of the world.

As a matter of fact, I would suggest that with all of the criticism of detente, that without detente, we might have had a major conflict in the Middle East. With detente, we avoided it.

Mideast Oil

Q: Mr. President, the question from the electronic medium related to the Middle East—

A: Radio.

Q: —radio. I have heard there was a meeting at the State Department this afternoon of major oil company executives on the fuel shortage.

Whether or not you confirm that, has this confrontation in the Middle East caused a still more severe oil problem and is there any thinking now of gasoline rationing?

A: Well, we have contingency plans for gasoline rationing and so forth which I hope never have to be put into place.

But, with regard to the oil shortage, which you referred to, one of the major factors which gave enormous urgency to our efforts to settle this particular crisis was the potential of an oil cut-off.

Let me say that I have also noted that in the State Department or from the State Department today a statement raised a little difficulty in Europe to the effect that our European friends hadn't been as cooperative as they might have been in attempting to help us work out the Middle East settlement or at least the settlement to the extent that we have worked it out as of the resolution of yesterday.

I can only say on that score that Europe which gets 80 percent of its oil from the Mideast would have frozen to death this winter unless there had been a settlement and Japan, of course, is in that same position.

The United States, of course, gets only approximately 10 percent of its oil from the Mideast.

What I am simply suggesting is this: That with regard to the fuel shortage potentially in the United States and in the world, it is indispensable at this time that we avoid any further Mideast crisis so that the flow of oil to Europe, to Japan and to the United States can continue.

Mideast Brezhnev Message

Q: Mr. President, against this background of detente, Mr. Brezhnev's note to you has been described as rough or perhaps brutal by one Senator. Can you characterize it for us and for history in any way you can mention?

A: Yes, I could characterize it, but, Mr. Theis, it wouldn't be in the national interest to do so. My notes to him he might characterize as being rather rough. However, I would rather—perhaps it would be best to characterize it. Rather than saying, Mr. Theis, that his note to me was rough and brutal, I would say that it was very firm and it left very little to the imagination as to what he intended.

And my response was also very firm and left little to the imagination of how we would react. And it is because he and I know each other and it is because we have had this personal contact, that notes exchanged in that way result in a settlement rather than a confrontation.

Rebozo-Hughes Contribution

Q: Mr. President.

A: Yes, Mr. Deakin.

Q: Is it credible, can the American people believe that your close friend, Mr. Rebozo, for three years, during which time you saw him weekly sometimes, kept from you the fact that he had $100,000 in cash from Mr. Howard Hughes?

Is that credible, is it credible that your personal attorney, Mr. Kalmbach, knew about this money for at least a year and never told you about it?

And, if this was a campaign contribution, as your press secretaries say, who authorized Mr. Rebozo to collect campaign contributions for your reelection or for the Republican Party?

What campaign committee was he an official of?

A: Well, it is obviously not credible to you, and I suppose that it would sound incredible to many people who did not know how I operate. In terms of campaign contributions, I have had a rule, Mr. Deakin, which Mr. Stans and Mr. Kalmbach and Mr. Rebozo and every contributor will agree has been the rule—I have refused always to accept contributions myself. I have refused to have any discussion of contributions. As a matter of fact, my orders to Mr. Stans were that after the campaign was over, I would then send notes of appreciation to those that contributed, but before the election, I did not want to have any information from anybody with regard to campaign contributions.

Now, with regard to Mr. Rebozo, let me say that he showed, I think, very good judgment in doing what he did. He received a contribution. He was prepared to turn it over to the Finance Chairman when the Finance Chairman was appointed. But in that interlude, after he received the contribution, and before the Finance Chairman was appointed, the Hughes company, as you all know, had an internal fight of massive proportions, and he felt that such a contribution to the campaign might prove to be embarrassing.

At the conclusion of the campaign, he decided that it would be in the best interests of everybody concerned rather than to turn the money over then, to be used in the '74 campaigns, to return it intact. And I would say that any individual, and particularly a banker who would have a contribution of $100,000 and not touch it—because it was turned back in exactly the form it was received—I think that is a pretty good indication that he is a totally honest man, which he is.

Tapes: No Public Disclosure

Q: Mr. President, after the tapes are presented to Judge Sirica and they are processed under the procedure outlined by the U.S. Court of Appeals, will you make those tapes public?

A: No, that is not the procedure that the court has ordered, and it would not be proper. Judge Sirica, under the Circuit Court's order, is to listen to the tapes, and then is to present to the Grand Jury the pertinent evidence with regard to its investigation. Publication of the tapes has not been ordered by the Circuit Court of Appeals, and Judge Sirica, of course, would not do anything that would be in contravention of what the Circuit Court of Appeals has ordered.

Bearing Up Under Stress

Q: Mr. President—

A: Mr. ter Horst.

Q: Mr. President, Harry Truman used to talk about the heat in the kitchen—

A: I know what he meant. (Laughter)

Q: —and a lot of people have been wondering how you are bearing up emotionally under the stress of recent events. Can you discuss that?

A: Those who saw me during the Middle East crisis thought I bore up rather well, and, Mr. ter Horst, I have a quality which is—I guess I must have inherited it from my Midwestern mother and father—which is that the tougher it gets, the cooler I get. Of course, it isn't pleasant to get criticism. Some of it is justified, of course. It isn't pleasant to find, for example, that, speaking of my friend Mr. Rebozo, that despite the fact that those who printed it, and those who said it, knew it was untrue—said that he had a million-dollar trust fund for me that he was handling—it was nevertheless put on one of the networks, knowing it was untrue. It isn't pleasant, for example, to hear or read that a million dollars in campaign funds went into my San Clemente property, and even after we had a complete audit, to have it repeated.

Those are things which, of course, do tend to get under the skin of the man who holds this office. But as far as I am concerned, I have learned to expect it. It has been my lot throughout my political life, and I suppose because I have been through so much, that may be one of the reasons that when I have to face an international crisis, I have what it takes.

Watergate and Mideast

Q: Mr. President, I would like to ask you a question about the Mideast. To what extent do you think your Watergate troubles influenced Soviet thinking about your ability to respond in the Mideast, and did your Watergate problems convince you that the U.S. needed a strong response in the Mideast to convince other nations that you have not been weakened?

A: Well, I have noted speculation to the effect that the Watergate problems may have led the Soviet Union to miscalculate. I tend to disagree with that, however.

I think Mr. Brezhnev probably can't quite understand how the President of the United States wouldn't be able to handle the Watergate problems. He would be able to handle it all right, if he had them. (Laughter) But I think what happens is that what Mr. Brezhnev does understand is the power of the United States. What he does know is the President of the United States.

What he also knows is that the President of the United States, when he was under unmerciful assault at the time of Cambodia, at the time of May 8, when I ordered the bombing and the mining of North Vietnam at the time of December 18, still went ahead and did what he thought was right; the fact that Mr. Brezhnev knew that regardless of the pressures at home, regardless of what people see and hear on television night after night, he would do what was right. That is what made Mr. Brezhnev act as he did.

Television Anger

Q: Mr. President, you have lambasted the televison networks pretty well. Could I ask you, at the risk of reopening an obvious wound, you say after you have put on a lot of heat that you don't blame anyone. I find that a little puzzling. What is it about the television coverage of you in these past weeks and months that has so aroused your anger?

A: Don't get the impression that you arouse my anger. (Laughter)

Q: I'm afraid, sir, that I have that impression. (Laughter)

A: You see, one can only be angry with those he respects.

Regaining Confidence

Q: Mr. President, businessmen are increasingly saying that many chief executive officers of corporations do not get the latitude you have had, if they have the personnel problems that you have had, to stay in the job and correct them. You have said you are going to stay. Do you have any plan set out to regain confidence of people across the country, and these businessmen who are beginning to talk about this matter? Do you have any plans, besides the special prosecutor, which looks backward, do you have any plan that looks forward for regaining the confidence of the people?

A: I certainly have. First, to move forward in building a structure of peace in the world, in which we have made enormous progress in the past and which we are going to make more progress in in the future: our European initiative, our continued initiative with the Soviet Union, with the People's Republic of China. That will be the major legacy of this Administration.

Moving forward at home in our continuing battle against the high cost of living, in which we are now finally beginning to make some progress, and moving forward also on the matters that you referred to, it is true that what happened in Watergate, the campaign abuses, were deplorable. They have been very damaging to this Administration; they have been damaging certainly to the country as well.

Let me say, too, I didn't want to leave an impression with my good friend from CBS over here that I don't respect the reporters. What I was simply saying was this: That when a commentator takes a bit of news and then, with knowledge of what the facts are, distorts it, viciously, I have no respect for that individual.

Executive Privilege

Q: Mr. President—

A: You are so loud, I will have to take you.

Q: I have to be, because you happen to dodge my questions all of the time.

A: You had three last time.

Q: Last May you went before the American People and you said, "Executive privilege will not be invoked as to any testimony concerning possible criminal conduct or discussing of possible criminal conduct, including the Watergate affair and the alleged cover-up."

If you have revised or modified this position, as you seem to have done, could you explain the rationale of a law-and order Administration covering up evidence, prima facie evidence, of high crimes and misdemeanors?

A: I should point out that perhaps all of the other reporters in the room are aware of the fact that we have waived Executive privilege on all individuals in the Administration. It has been the greatest waiver of Executive privilege in the whole history of this Nation.

And as far as any other matters are concerned, the matters of the tapes, the matters of Presidential conversations, those are matters in which the President has a responsibility to defend this office, which I shall continue to do.

THE PRESS: Thank you, Mr. President. ✓

NOV. 17

Following is the White House text of President Nixon's question-and-answer session Nov. 17 at a conference of the Associated Press Managing Editors Association in Walt Disney World, near Orlando, Fla. The session was nationally televised.

THE PRESIDENT: President Quinn and ladies and gentlemen: When Jack Horner, who has been a correspondent in Washington and other places around the world, retired after 40 years, he once told me that if I thought the White House Press Corps answered (asked) tough questions, he (I) should hear the kind of questions the managing editors asked him. Consequently, I welcome this opportunity tonight to meet with the managing editors of the nation's newspapers.

I will not have an opening statement because I know, with 400 of you, it will be hard to get through all of the questions you have, and I understand the president has a prerogative of asking the first question.

Mr. Quinn.

Q: This morning, Gov. Askew of Florida addressed this group and recalled the words of Benjamin Franklin. When leaving the constitutional convention he was asked, "What have you given us, sir, a monarchy or a republic?" Franklin answered, "A republic, sir, if you can keep it."

Mr. President, in the prevailing pessimism of the larger matter we call Watergate, can we keep that republic, and how?

A: Mr. Quinn, I would certainly not be standing here answering these questions unless I had a firm belief that we could keep the republic; that we must keep it, not only for ourselves, but for the whole world. I recognize that because of mistakes that were made, and I must take responsibility for those mistakes, whether in the campaign or during the course of an administration, that there are those who wonder whether this republic can survive. But I also know that the hopes of the whole world for peace, not only now, but in the years to come, rests on the United States of America. I can assure you that as long as I am physically able to handle the position to which I was elected, and then re-elected last November, I am going to work for the cause of peace in the world, for the cause of prosperity without war and without inflation at home, and also to the best of my ability to restore confidence in the White House and in the President. It is a big job, but I think it can be done, and I intend to do it.

Delays on Non-Existent Tapes

Q: Mr. President, I am George Gill of the *Louisville Courier-Journal*. Would you please tell us, sir, when did you personally discover that two of the nine subpoenaed White House tapes did not exist, and why did you apparently delay for a matter of weeks disclosing this matter to the federal court and to the public?

A: Well, the first time that the fact that there were no recordings of the two conversations to which you referred—that they did not exist—came to my attention on approximately Sept. 29 or Sept. 30.

At that time, I was informed only that they might not exist because a search was not made because seven of the nine recordings requested did exist, and my secretary, listening to them for me and making notes for me, proceeded to go through those seven tapes.

I should point out, incidentally, that the two which did not exist, which there were no tape recordings of the conversations, were not ones which were requested by the Senate committee and consequently, we felt we should go forward with the ones requested, both by the Senate committees and the others.

When we finally determined that they could not be in existence was on Oct. 26 of this year. And we learned it then when I directed the White House counsel, Mr. Buzhardt, to question the Secret Service operatives as to what had happened to make sure there might not be a possibility, due to the fact that the mechanism was not operating properly, that we might find them in some other place.

He questioned them for two days and reported on the 27th that he could not find them. He then, having had a date made—and he asked for the date sooner with Judge Sirica, he asked for the date on Thursday; you may recall I pointed that out in the press conference on the 26th—Judge Sirica saw him on Tuesday *in camera*. The White House counsel reported to Judge Sirica that the two tapes did not exist and gave him the reasons for it.

The judge decided, and I think quite properly, that the reasons for the tape not existing should be made public and those involved with access to the tapes and those who operated the machines should be questioned so that there would be no question of the White House, somebody around the President or even the President, himself, having destroyed evidence that was important, even though the Senate committee had not, as I have

already pointed out, subpoenaed either of these two tapes. And since we are on this subject, and I do not want to be taking all of the time on it except I know there is going to be enormous interest in it, not only among this audience here, but among our television viewers, let me point this out.

I have done everything I possibly can to provide the evidence that would have existed had we found the tapes.

June 20 Tape. First, with regard to the tape of June 20, as you may recall, it was a five-minute telephone conversation with the former attorney general, John Mitchell, who had just left as campaign manager or was planning to leave as campaign manager at that time.

I have a practice of keeping a personal diary. I can assure you not every day. Some times you are too tired at the end of a day to either make notes or dictate it into a dictabelt.

On that particular day I happened to have dictated a dictabelt and on the dictabelt for June 20, which I found, I found that I had referred to the conversation to John Mitchell, and I think it is fair to disclose to this audience what was there, because it will be disclosed to the court. It has already been offered to the court and eventually I assume will be made public.

It said, first, that I called John Mitchell to cheer him up because I knew he was terribly disheartened by what had happened to the so-called Watergate matter. Second, he expressed chagrin to me that the organization over which he had control could have gotten out of hand in this way. That was what was on that tape.

Turning now to the one on April 15, I thought that I might have a Dictabelt of that conversation as well. Let me tell you first why the telephone conversation was not recorded, not because of any deliberate attempt to keep the recording from the public, but because the only telephones in the residence of the White House which are recorded, the only telephone, there is only one, the one that is in the office, the Little Lincoln sitting room right off the Lincoln bedroom. The call I made to John Mitchell was made at the end of the day at about 6:30 just before going in to dinner from the family quarters, and no telephones in the family quarters ever were recorded. That is why the recording did not exist.

April 15 Tape. Turning to April 15, the conversation referred to there was at the end of the process in which Mr. Dean came in to tell me what he had told U.S. attorneys that day. He saw me at 9 o'clock at night, Sunday night. There should have been a record. Everybody thought there probably was a recording. The reason there was not a recording is that the tape machines over the weekend only can carry six hours of conversation, and usually that is more than enough, because I do not use the EOB office, that is the Executive Office Building office rather than the Oval Office over the weekend to that extent.

But that weekend I was in the EOB for a long conversation with Dr. Kissinger on foreign policy matters. I was there for two other hours, or two or three other hours, and the tape ran out in the middle of a conversation with Mr. Kleindienst in the middle of the afternoon, Sunday afternoon.

A later conversation I had, the rest of Kleindienst's conversation, a later conversation I had also with Mr. Petersen, and the conversation at 8 o'clock at night with Mr. Dean was not there.

So I tried to find whatever recording whatever record that would help the prosecutor in this instance to reconstruct the evidence, because it was the evidence that I was after and not just this tape.

What I found was not a Dictabelt. What I found was my handwritten notes made at the time of the conversation. I have turned those over to or authorized my counsel to turn those notes over to the judge, so that he can have them checked for authenticity, and I understand there are ways that he can tell that they were written at that time.

Those handwritten notes are available, and then I did one other thing which I think will also be helpful. The next day I had a conversation with Mr. Dean in the morning at 10 o'clock. That conversation was recorded, and in that conversation there are repeated references to what was said the night before, and when compared with my handwritten notes it is clear that we are discussing the same subjects.

That entire tape, as well as the conversation I had in the Mr. Dean for about 20 minutes will be made available to the court even though the court has not subpoenaed it.

Inadequate Recording System. I would just simply say in conclusion you can be very sure that this kind of a subject is one that is a difficult one to explain. It appears that it is impossible that when we have an Apollo system that we could have two missing tapes when the White House is concerned. Let me explain for one moment what the system was. This is no Apollo system. I found that it cost—I just learned this—$2,500. I found that instead of having the kind of equipment that was there when President Johnson was there, which was incidentally much better equipment, but I found—and I am not saying that critically—but I found that in this instance it was a Sony, a little Sony that they had, and that what they had are these little lapel mikes in my desk, and as a result the conversation in the Oval Office, the conversation in the cabinet room, and particularly those in the EOB, those are the three rooms only, only those three rooms where they recorded. For example, the Western White House has no recording equipment, and my houses in Key Biscayne and San Clemente had none, but as far as those particular recordings are concerned, the reason that you have heard that there are difficulties in hearing them is that the system itself was not a sophisticated system.

Points to be Proven. I do not mean to suggest by that that the judge, by listening to them, will not be able to get the facts, and I would simply conclude by saying this: I think I know what is on these tapes from having listened to some, those before March 21, and also from having seen from my secretary's notes the highlights of others. I can assure you that those tapes, when they are presented to the judge, and I hope eventually to the grand jury, and I trust in some way we can find a way at least to get the substance to the American people, they will prove these things without question:

One, that I had no knowledge whatever of the Watergate break-in before it occurred. Two, that I never authorized the offer of clemency to anybody and, as a matter of fact, turned it down whenever it was suggested. It was not recommended by any member of my staff but it was, on occasion, suggested as a result of news reports that clemency might become a factor. Third, as far as any knowledge with regard to the payment of blackmail money, which you recall was the charge that was made that Mr. Hunt's attorney had asked for $120,000 in money to be paid to him or he would tell things about members of the White House staff, not about Watergate, that might be embarrassing.

Testimony had been given before the Senate committee that I was told that before the 21st of March, actually told it on the 13th of March. I know I heard it for the first time the 21st of March, and I will reveal this much of the conversation. I am sure the judge wouldn't mind.

I recall very well Mr. Dean, after the conversation began, telling me, "Mr. President, there are some things about this I haven't told you. I think you should know them."

And then he proceeded then for the first time to tell me about that money. Now, I realize that some will wonder about the truth of these particular statements that I have made. I am going to hand out later—I won't hand them out, but I will have one of your executives hand out my May 21 statement, my Aug. 15 statement and one with regard to these two tapes, you can believe them if you want.

I can tell you it is the truth, because I have listened to or have knowledge of, from someone I have confidence in, as to what is in the tapes.

Personal, Political Reaction

Q: Mr. President, Richard Tuttle, *Democrat and Chronicle,* Rochester, N.Y. Could you tell us your personal reaction and your political reaction—within that word I mean your credibility

with the American people—your reaction to the discovery that the Dean and Mitchell tapes do not exist?

A: Well, my personal reaction was one of great disappointment, because I wanted the evidence out, and I knew that when there was any indication that something didn't exist, immediately there would be the impression that some way, either the President, or more likely, perhaps somebody on the President's staff, knew there was something on those tapes that it wouldn't be wise to get out. But let me point out again, while I was disappointed, let me say I would have been a lot more disappointed if the tapes that had been considered important by both Mr. Cox, the special prosecutor and the Ervin committee, if any one of those had been missing, because I should point out that the tape of Sept. 15 which, as you recall, has been testified that I was first informed there was a cover-up—that, of course, is there.

The tape of March 13, where is has been testified, as I pointed out in the answer to *the Louisville Courier-Journal,* where it has been testified that I was informed then of the demands for money for purposes of blackmail, that is available. And the tape of March 21, where we discussed this in great detail, as well as three other tapes in which Mr. Dean participated, three other conversations, are all available.

But as far as these two tapes are concerned, even though they were not considered by the Ervin committee to be an indispensable part of their investigation, the fact that they were not there was a great disappointment, and I just wish we had had a better system.

I frankly wish we hadn't had a system at all. Then maybe I wouldn't have to answer this question.

Ellsberg Case

Q: Mr. President, when did you decide to stay out of the Ellsberg case and if you did, why, and do you think that the new special prosecutor should be kept from investigating the Ellsberg case?

A: I have never spoken to Mr. Cox at all, as a matter of fact; however, I did talk to Mr. Petersen about it, before Mr. Cox took over.

I told Mr. Petersen that the job that he had, and I would have said the same thing to Mr. Cox, was to investigate the Watergate matter, that national security matters were not matters that should be investigated, because there were some very highly sensitive matters involved, not only in Ellsberg but also another matter so sensitive that even Sen. Ervin and Sen. Baker have decided that they should not delve further into them.

I don't mean by that that we are going to throw the cloak of national security over something because we are guilty of something. I am simply saying that where the national security would be disserved by having an investigation, the President has the responsibility to protect it, and I am going to do so.

Plans to Inform People

Q: Albert L. Abbott from *The Detroit News.* Are you personally satisfied, sir, that the investigation of the Watergate matter is complete, to your satisfaction, and if so, could you tell us what your plans are to tell the American people about the facts of the case with regard, again, to your credibility on this matter?

A: First, with regard to whether the investigation is complete, as you know, there is now a new special prosecutor, Mr. Jaworski. He is a Democrat. He has always supported the Democratic ticket. He is a highly respected lawyer, former president of the ABA in the year 1971. I may have met him. I have never talked to him personally and certainly never talked to him about this matter. I refuse to, because I want him to be completely independent.

He cannot be removed unless there is a consensus of the top leadership Of the House and Senate, Democrat and Republican. The speaker and majority and minority leaders of the House and the president pro tem, the majority and minority leaders of the

Senate and the ranking two members of the Judiciary Committees of both the House and Senate, which, incidentally, gives you, as you can see, a very substantial majority, as far as the Democrats are concerned.

The second point, and the point I am trying to make is, one, he is qualified; two, he is independent, and will have cooperation; and three, he will not be removed unless the Congress, particularly the leaders of the Congress, and particularly the Democratic leaders who have a strong majority of this group I have named, agree that he should be removed, and I do not expect that that time will come.

As to what I can tell the American people, this is one forum, and there may be others. As to what the situation is as to when it can be done, it is of course, necessary to let the grand jury proceed as quickly as possible to a conclusion and I should point out to you, as you may recall, Mr. Petersen testified before the Ervin committee when he was removed from his position—you recall he was removed in April and a special prosecutor was put in—that the case was 90 per cent ready. For six months, under the special prosecutor then appointed, the case has not been brought to a conclusion.

And I think that now, after six months of delay, it is time that the case be brought to a conclusion. If it was 90 per cent finished in April, they ought to be able to finish it now.

Those who are guilty, or presumed to be guilty, should be indicted. Those who are not guilty at least should get some evidence of being cleared, because in the meantime, the reputations of men, some maybe who are not guilty, have been probably irreparably damaged by what has happened in the hearings they have appeared before publicly. They have already been convicted and they may never recover. That isn't our system of government.

The place to try a man or woman for a crime is in the court and not to convict them either in the newspaper or on television before has a fair trial in the courts.

Attitude Toward Haldeman, Ehrlichman

Q: Bob Haiman from *The St. Petersburg Times* in St. Petersburg, Fla. When Mr. Ehrlichman and Mr. Haldeman left your administration, you said they were guiltless in the Watergate affair, and you referred to them as two of the finest public servants you have ever known. After what has transpired and been revealed since then, do you still feel the same way about both men and both statements?

A: First, I hold that both men and others who have been charged are guilty until we have evidence that they are not guilty, and I know every newspaper man and newspaper women in this whole audience would agree with that statement. That is our American system. Second, Mr. Haldeman and Mr. Ehrlichman had been and were dedicated fine public servants, and I believe, it is my belief based on what I know now, that when these proceedings are completed that they will come out all right.

On the other hand, they have appeared before the grand jury before, they will be appearing again, and as I pointed out in answer to an earlier question, it probably does not make any difference, unfortunately, whether the grand jury indicts them or not, whether they are tried or not, because unfortunately they have already been convicted in the minds of millions of Americans by what happened before a Senate committee.

Role in Ellsberg Break-In

Q: Mr. President, this is Ed Heins from *The Des Moines Register and Tribune*. At the time you gave Egil Krogh approval for the Dr. Ellsberg project, was there any discussion of surreptitious entry to any premises and was there any discussion of legality or illegality in that situation?

A: I think, sir, that you have made an assumption that Mr. Krogh and others have not testified to, but I am not saying that critically. But I think I do remember what the evidence is. I don't think Mr. Krogh has said, or Mr. Ehrlichman or anybody

else, that I specifically approved or ordered the entrance into Dr. Ellsberg's psychiatrist's office. As a matter of fact, on the other hand, I learned of that for the first time on the 17th of March, which I have stated in my Aug. 15 statement, which will be available to the members of the press when this meeting is concluded.

Second, with regard to such activities, I personally thought it was a stupid thing to do, apart from being an illegal thing to do, and third, I should also point out that in this particular matter, the reason Mr. Krogh and others were engaged in what we call the "plumbers" operation was because of our concern at that time about leaks out of our government, the Pentagon Papers, which as you recall is what Ellsberg was all about, as well as other leaks which were seriously damaging to the national security, including one that I have pointed out—that was so serious that even Sen. Ervin and Sen. Baker agreed it should not be disclosed. That is what they were working on.

Nixon's Tax Payments

Q: Joe Ungaro of *The Providence Evening Bulletin.*

The Providence Evening Bulletin and *The Journal* on Oct. 3 reported that you paid $792 in federal income tax in 1970 and $878 in 1971. Are these figures accurate, and would you tell us your views on whether elected officials should disclose their personal finances?

A: Well, the answer to the second question is I have disclosed my personal finances, and an audit of my personal finances will be made available at the end of this meeting, because obviously you are all so busy that when these things come across your desk, maybe you don't see them. I can simply point out that that audit I paid for—I have not gotten the bill yet but I know it is several thousand dollars, and I think that that audit is one that is a pretty good one. That audit, however, deals with the acquisition of my property and knocks down some of the ideas that have been around. But since this question has been raised, let me, sir, try to respond to it as fully as I can.

I paid $79,000 in income tax in 1969. In the next two years, I paid nominal amounts. Whether those amounts are correct or not, I do not know, because I have not looked at my returns, and obviously *The Providence Journal* has much better sources than I have to find such returns. I congratulate you, sir, for having such a lively staff.

Now, why did I pay this amount? It was not because of the deductions for, shall we say, a cattle ranch or interest or all of these gimmicks that you have got where you can deduct from, which most of you know about, or if you don't, your publishers do. But the reason was this. Lyndon Johnson came in to see me shortly after I became President, and he told me that he had given his presidential papers, or at least most of them, to the government, and he told me that under the law, up until 1969, presidential or vice presidential papers given to the government were a deduction, and should be taken, and could be taken as a deduction from the tax.

And he said, "You, Mr. President, ought to do the same thing." I said, "I don't have any presidential papers." He said, "You have got your vice presidential papers."

I thought of that a moment and said, "All right, I will turn them over to the tax people." I turned them over. They appraised them at $500,000. I suppose some wonder how could the Vice President's papers be worth that. Well, I was, shall we say, a rather active Vice President. All of my personal notes, including matters that have not been covered in my book—which I don't advise other people to write, but in any event I wrote one and I will stand by it—all of my papers on the Hiss case, on the famous fund controversy in 1952, on President Eisenhower's heart attack, on President Eisenhower's stroke, on my visit to Caracas when I had a few problems in 1968, and on my visit with Khrushchev, all of those papers, all of my notes, were valued, many believed conservatively, at that amount.

So the tax people who prepared it, prepared the returns, and took that as a deduction. No question has been raised by the

Internal Revenue about it but if they do, let me tell you this: I will be glad to have the papers back, and I will pay the tax, because I think they are worth more than that.

I can only say we did what we were told was the right thing to do and, of course, what President Johnson had done before and that doesn't prove, certainly, that it was wrong, because he had done exactly what the law required.

Since 1969, of course, I should point out, presidents can't do that. So I am stuck with a lot of papers now that I have got to find a way to give away, or otherwise my heirs will have a terrible time trying to pay the taxes on things people aren't going to want to buy.

Q: Mr. President, may I suggest you may have misspoke yourself when you said that you assumed Haldeman and Ehrlichman are considered guilty until proven not guilty.

A: Yes, I certainly did, if I said that. Thank you for correcting me.

Sharing Presidential Responsibilities

Q: Richard Smyser, *The Oak Ridge,* Oak Ridge, Tenn. Sen. Mark Hatfield said recently that we demand so much of a president, we ask him to play so many roles, that no man can hold that kind of responsibility without having to share that responsibility with all Americans. To what extent do you think that this explains possibly how something like Watergate can occur?

A: I could stand here before this audience and make all kinds of excuses, and most of you probably would understand because you are busy also. Seventy-two was a very busy year for me. It was a year when we had the visit to China, it was a year when we had the visit to Moscow and the first limited nuclear ban on defensive weapons, you recall, as well as some other very significant events.

It was a year, too, when we had the very difficult decisions on May 8, the bombing and mining of Haiphong and then the negotiations and then in December, of course, the very, very difficult—perhaps the most difficult—decision I made of the December bombing, which did lead to the break-through and the uneasy peace, but it is peace with all of the Americans home, all of our POWs home, and peace at least for a while in that period.

Now, during that period of time, frankly, I didn't manage the campaign. I didn't run the campaign. People around me didn't bring things to me that they probably should have, because I was frankly just too busy trying to do the nation's business to run the politics.

My advice to all new politicians, incidentally, is always run your own campaigns. I used to run mine and I was always criticized for it, because you know whenever you lose you are always criticized for running your own campaign, but my point is Sen. Hatfield is correct, whether you are a senator or a congressman, you are sometimes very busy, you don't watch these things. When you are president, you don't watch them as closely as you might. On that, I say if mistakes are made, however, I am not blaming the people down below. The man at the top has got to take the heat for all of them.

Let me just respond, if I could, sir, before going to your question—I will turn left and then come back to the right; I don't want to tilt either way at the moment, as you can be sure (laughter)—since the question was raised a moment ago about my tax payments, I noted in some editorials and perhaps in some commentaries on television, a very reasonable question.

Property Investments. They said, you know, how is it that President Nixon could have a very heavy investment in a fine piece of property in San Clemente and a big investment in a piece of property in Florida, in which I have two houses, one which I primarily use as an office and the other as a resident and also an investment in what was my mother's home, not very much of a place, but I do own it, those three pieces of property.

I want to say first, that is all I have. I am the first President since Harry Truman who hasn't owned any stock since ever I have been President. I am the first one who has not had a blind

trust since Harry Truman. That doesn't mean those who owned stocks or had blind trusts did anything wrong, but I felt that in the presidency it was important to have no question about the President's personal finances, and I thought real estate was the best place to put it.

But then the question was raised by good editorial writers—and I want to respond to it because some of you might be too polite to ask such an embarrassing question—they said, "Now, Mr. President, you earned $800,000 when you were President. Obviously, you paid at least half that much or could have paid half that much in taxes or a great deal of it. How could you possibly have had the money? Where did you get it?"

Then, of course, overriding all of that is the story to the effect that I had a million dollars in campaign funds which was broadly printed throughout this country with retractions not quite getting quite as much play as the printing of the first, and particularly not on television. The newspapers did much better than television in that respect, I should point out.

And second, they said, how is it that as far as this money is concerned, how is it possible for you to have this kind of investment when all you earned was $800,000 as President?

Personal Finances. Well, I should point out I wasn't a pauper when I became President. I wasn't very rich as presidents go. But you see, in the eight years that I was out of office—first, just to put it all out, and I will give you a paper on this, we will send it around to you, and these figures I would like you to have, not today, but I will have it in a few days—when I left office after four years as a congressman, two years as a senator and eight years at $45,000 a year as Vice President, and after stories had been written, particularly in *The Washington Post,* to the effect that the President had purchased a mansion in Wesley Heights and people wondered where the money came from, you know what my net worth was? It was $47,000 total, after 14 years of government service, and a 1958 Oldsmobile that needed an overhaul.

Now, I have no complaints. In the next eight years, I made a lot of money. I made $250,000 from a book—and the serial rights which many of you were good enough to purchase—also, in the practice of law—and I am not claiming I was worth it, but apparently the former vice presidents or presidents are worth a great deal to the law firms—and I did work pretty hard.

But also in that period, I earned between $100,000 and $250,000 every year. So that when in 1968, I decided to become a candidate for president, I decided to clean the decks and to put everything in real estate. I sold all my stock for $300,000. That is all I owned. I sold my apartment in New York for $300,000 —I am using rough figures here. And I had $100,000 coming to me from the law firm.

So that is where the money came from. Let me just say this: I want to say this to the television audience—I made my mistakes, but in all of my years of public life, I have never profited, never profited from public service. I have earned every cent. And in all of my years of public life, I have never obstructed justice. And I think, too, that I could say that in my years of public life, that I welcome this kind of examination, because people have got to know whether or not their President is a crook. Well, I am not a crook. I have earned everything I have got.

Tap on Donald Nixon's Phone

Q: Mr. President, Harry Rosenfeld of *The Washington Post.* Sir, there have been reports that the Secret Service was asked, at your direction or authorization, to tap the telephone of your brother, Donald Nixon. Is this true, sir, and if so, why?

A: That, of course, is a question that has been commented upon before. It will not take long to respond to it.

The Secret Service did maintain a surveillance. They did so for security reasons, and I will not go beyond that. They were very good reasons, and my brother was aware of it.

And may I say, too, to my friend from *The Washington Post,* I like your sports page. And make sure that Shirley Povich doesn't get paid too much for what I said there. (Laughter)

Q: Edward D. Miller, *Call-Chronicle Newspapers,* Allentown, Pa. Was your brother aware before or after the fact of the surveillance?

A: He was aware during the fact, because he asked about it, and he was told about it. And he approved of it. He knew why it was done.

Q: Excuse me. Does it make any sense to conduct surveillance when somebody knows about it?

A: Does it make any sense? Certainly. The surveillance involved not what he was doing. The surveillance involved what others who were trying to get him, perhaps, to use improper influence and support might be doing, and particularly anybody who might be in a foreign country.

Q: Is some of this full story that you can't state today because of national security? Have you told that to congressmen or anyone else? Will this story come out in the next few weeks, as you present more of the facts?

A: Yes, as a matter of fact, I should tell all of the editors—and I don't want to leave any implication that you have not tried to publish as much as you could—you have just got so much room in your newspapers, but I do want you to know that—well, since you haven't raised some of these subjects, I will raise them myself—ITT; how did we raise the price of milk—I wish someone would ask me that one; and who else wanted it raised?

What about the situation with regard to the $1-million secret stock portfolio that you have; a few of those things. I think all of those things need to be answered, and answered effectively, and I think the best way to answer them is twofold:

One, obviously through the medium of a televised conference like this; but two, through sending to the editors of the nation's newspapers, all 10,000 of them, the facts. I trust that you will use them. If you don't believe them, I don't mean—what I mean, I am not suggesting that you wouldn't believe them, but if you feel you need more information, write to me and I will give it to you. I want the facts out, because the facts will prove that the President is telling the truth.

Shield Law for the Press

Q: Mr. President, John Finnegan, *St. Paul Dispatch-Pioneer Press.* I know the Watergate situation has raised questions of executive privilege, and a recent Gallup Poll indicated that 62 per cent of the American people favor a confidential news source law if adopted by Congress. There is a two-tiered law before the Judiciary Committee which would provide an absolute privilege in case of investigative or grand jury hearings, and a qualified shield in case of a civil or criminal case. If such a law were passed, would you sign it or veto it?

A: Well, you are talking about shield laws in general, are you not?

Q: Yes.

A: Well, my attitude toward the shield laws briefly is this: First, I share the objective. I believe that reporters, if you are going to have a free press, ought to have some kind of a shield, except, of course, if they are involved in criminal activities, and then I don't think the shield law that any of you have suggested would cover those. As I understand, if there are criminal activities involved in by a reporter, obviously a shield law can't protect them.

The second point has to do with the particular legislation and how it reaches my desk, and I will have to take a look at it when it gets there to see if it is proper. If it is proper, I will sign it. But I think that a shield law which would have the effect of providing to reporters what the general public felt after they had a chance to consider it all, provide for them privileges that went beyond what the general public thought was in the national interest, then I would have to take a second look.

Incidentally, I should point out, too, that I followed your editorials—not yours in just the *St. Paul Pioneer Press,* but by

others around the country—and the newspapers of the country are not united on this. So on the shield law I am not trying to duck the question. It is an open question.

But I will answer one thing that I think is important. The new attorney general, Mr. Saxbe, under my direction, will follow this practice: Any federal case involving a reporter will not be brought unless it comes expressly to the attorney general and he approves it, and in that way, that is a pretty good shield, I think.

Executive Privilege

Q: May I ask one other question, sir?

A: Sure.

Q: Do you feel that the executive privilege is absolute?

A: I, of course, do not. I have waived executive privilege with regard to all of the members of my staff who have any knowledge of or who have had any charges made against them in the Watergate matter. I, of course, voluntarily waived privilege with regard to turning over the tapes, and so forth.

Let me point out it was voluntary on my part, and deliberately so to avoid a precedent that might destroy the principle of confidentiality for future presidents, which is terribly important.

If it had gone to the Supreme Court—and I know many of my friends argued, "Why not carry it to the Supreme Court and let them decide it?"—that would, first, have had a confrontation with the Supreme Court, between the Supreme Court and the President. And second, it would have established very possibly a precedent, a precedent breaking down constitutionality that would plague future presidencies, not just this President.

I can say in that respect, too, that I have referred to what I called the Jefferson Rule. It is the rule that I think we should generally follow, a President should follow with the courts when they want information, and a President should also follow with committees of Congress, even when they want information from his personal files. Jefferson, as you know, in that very, very famous case, had correspondence which it was felt might bear upon the guilt or innocence of Aaron Burr. Chief Justice Marshall, sitting as a trial judge, said that Jefferson, as President, had to turn over the correspondence. Jefferson refused.

What he did was to turn over a summary of the correspondence, all that he considered was proper to be turned over for the purposes of the trial.

Then Marshall, sitting as chief justice, ruled for the President.

Now, why did Jefferson do that? Jefferson didn't do that to protect Jefferson. He did that to protect the presidency. That is exactly what I will do in these cases. It isn't for the purpose of protecting the President; it is for the purpose of seeing that the presidency, where great decisions have to be made, and great decisions cannot be made unless there is very free flow of conversation, and that means confidentiality, I have a responsibility to protect that presidency.

At the same time, I will do everything I can to cooperate where there is a need for presidential participation.

THE PRESIDENT: I will go to you next.

Gasoline Rationing

Q: Murray Light, *Buffalo Evening News.* The American people, sir, are very interested in one subject other than Watergate. Is gas rationing imminent?

THE PRESIDENT: Really? (Laughter) I didn't hear the last, I am sorry.

Q: Is gas rationing imminent?

A: I will tell you a little about my career that I didn't put in my campaign folders when I ran for Congress in 1946. I was once in OPA and I was in tire rationing. I suppose they put me in tire rationing—this is just before I went into the service. I was waiting for my service call—because I had worked in a service station, but I didn't know anything about tire rationing, and neither did the man above me, who I don't think had ever been in a service station, but we put out the rationing regulations on tires, and we were as fair as we could be. But also I found that if you get a bunch of government bureaucrats—and in order to have rationing you would have to have thousands of them—making decisions with regard to who is going to get this much, this much, this much in rationing, if you are going to try to do that in peacetime when you do not have what we had in war-time, you know, support, for, you know—"Don't use a C ration card when you are only entitled to an A"—then you are sort of disloyal or something, or unpatriotic. If you do not have that behind it, I can assure you that a rationing system in peacetime, run by a group of well-intentioned but being bureaucrats that they are, gaining and feeling their power, would be something that the American people would resent very, very much.

Now, what we have asked the Congress for is for a contingency plan in the event that rationing becomes necessary, but in the meantime let me tell you, our goal is to make it not necessary. I am not going to pledge to this audience and I am not going to pledge to the television audience that rationing may never come. If you have another war in the Mideast, if you have a complete cut-off and not a resumption of the flow of oil from the Mideast or some other disaster occurs, rationing may come, but if on the other hand the things that I recommended in my message of a week ago for immediate action, if the voluntary cooperation of keeping the speed down to 50 miles an hour—and I am going to talk to the governors about that on Tuesday in Memphis, urging that every state do exactly the same thing—if we cut back on the aircraft flights, and we have done that—and, for example, I came down here in a plane today, Air Force One. I asked them if I couldn't take the Jetstar. They said, "No, it doesn't have communication." So I had to take the big plane. But we did one thing that saved half the cost: We didn't have the back-up plane. The Secret Service didn't like it, Communication didn't like it, but I don't need a back-up plane. If this one goes down, it goes down, and then they don't have to impeach. (laughter)

Relations with Mitchell

Q: Mr. President, Larry Allison from *The Long Beach* (Calif.) *Independent Press-Telegram*. Back to Watergate. Former Attorney General John Mitchell has testified the reason he did not give you details on the Watergate problems was that you did not ask him. Now, I realize that you were very busy at that time, as you said, but there were reports in newspapers that linked people very high in your staff with Watergate problems. Could you tell us, sir, why you did not ask Mr. Mitchell what he knew?

A: For the very simple reason that when I talked to Mr. Mitchell—and I saw him often in that period—that I had every reason to believe that if he were involved, if he had any information to convey, he would tell me. I thought that he would. As a matter of fact, when I called him on the telephone, what did he say—he expressed chagrin that anything like that could have happened in his organization.

Looking back, maybe I should have cross-examined him and said, "John, did you do it?" I probably should have asked him, but the reason I didn't is that I expected him to tell me, and he had every opportunity to do so and decided he wouldn't apparently. At least—now, that doesn't mean to tell me that he was involved, because you understand that is still a matter that is open. The question is whether he could have told me about other people that might be involved where he had information where members of my staff did not have information.

Yes, sir.

ANTICIPATING THE ENERGY CRISIS

Q: I am Joe Shoquist, *Milwaukee Journal*. Why didn't the administration anticipate the energy crisis several years ago, formulate a positive action plan to do something about it?

A: You walked into one there. And that is a great paper, incidentally, as is *The Milwaukee Sentinel*, but, anyway, seriously, you see what happened was that I sent the first energy message ever sent to the Congress. I sent it to the Congress over two years ago. I saw this thing coming, and you know why I saw it coming? Not because of the Mideast or the Alaska pipeline and the rest, but because this world with all of its problems is getting richer. Oh, I don't mean there aren't a lot of hungry people, not only in America, too many here, but if you want to see hungry people, go to India or go to some of the countries in Latin America or upper Brazil, et cetera, et cetera. Generally, as the world gets richer, there is more air conditioning, there is more need for power and there is more need for energy. That is why I sent the message two years ago and asked at that time that the Congress consider a program so that the United States should become self-sufficient in energy. All right, I followed that up this year in April before we even knew there might be or had any idea of the Mideast crisis, which made a serious problem, a serious crisis. I asked them for seven pieces of legislation to deal with energy. One has reached my desk, the Alaska pipeline. I signed it. The other six I hope they act before they go home for Christmas.

Now, I am not saying here the Congress is to blame. The President should have done something. What I do say is that the President warned about it and the Congress did not act even though he warned them two years ago. The President warned in April; the Congress did not act; and now, it is time for the Congress to getaway from some of these other diversions if they have time and get on to this energy crisis.

Let me—since that question has come up, I would like to point out, though, how we should react, because the question about rationing is one that your average reader is going to be interested in.

I am interested in it, too, because I remember how we all went through it, the car pools and all that sort of thing. There are a few of you here old enough to remember a car pool, I am sure. Taxicabs in Washington: you couldn't get one unless five of you rode in one, you remember.

We don't want that. But if we look at this energy crisis as simply the crisis of this year, we could not make a greater mistake. If there never had been a Mideast war, there would have been an energy crisis eventually. That is why I have set as a goal for the American people, and I trust all of you will subscribe to it, what I call Project Independence 1980.

Why 1980, and why not 1976? Because, in checking with the experts, I find it will not be possible doing everything that we can do to become self-sufficient in energy until 1980. But if the Congress cooperates, if the nation cooperates, this nation in 1980 can have all of the energy we need.

Areas of Cooperation. Let us just briefly tell you what areas of cooperation are needed.

One, coal. We have half of the coal in the world, and yet we have conversions from coal to oil. Why? Because coal is not a clean fuel. Coal can be made a clean fuel. Coal can be mined in a way that does not despoil the landscape. It will be argumentative, I am sure. Some of the environmentalists—and I am an environmentalist along with anybody who cares about the landscape for our children—but we have got to get that coal out of the ground and we have to develop the shale oil, for example, that exists in Colorado and some of our western states. That will solve part of the problem.

And second, you have to deregulate natural gas. Some protection for the consumer, yes, but you have got wells in Louisiana, and other places, that are shut down and many that are not being explored, because the price is held at a price too low to make the explorer a profit. Therefore, he isn't going to do it. And natural gas, as you know, is one of the cleanest fuels we can possibly have.

And then, third, the most exciting of all, nuclear power. Now, don't write an editorial on that—you are really going to catch it from your readers if you do, because it scares people.

Nuclear power—they think of the bomb. They think of the possibility that one of them is going to blow up. My house in San Clemente is just 12 miles from the Southern California Edison Company's nuclear power plant. It is safe. It produces good power. It is clean power. And the United States, which first found the secret of the atom, is behind where it ought to be in the development of nuclear power.

If we go all out in developing our coal resources, our natural gas resources, as well as of course our oil from Alaska, which will provide one-third—I said incorrectly the other day in talking to a group not one-third of all of our oil needs, but one-third of all of our oil imports—and if we add to that nuclear power, the United States in 1980 can be self-sufficient. Just closing that off, let me tell you why that is so terribly important. The Arabs, they say, "Well, the Arabs, maybe they are irrational and we shouldn't depend on them anyway."

Need for Independence. Let me tell you, when you are in trouble, don't depend on anybody but yourself. Venezuela. What is going to happen in Venezuela? They send us a lot of oil, but they could change their minds under a radical government, and they could get one some day. I don't think so, but they could.

What about Canada, our great friend to the north? A lot of Canadians are listening here, but I can tell you, your present minister of the interior, or whoever is in charge of oil, he is a tough guy, and they drive hard bargains, and I guess we would, too, if we were Canadians.

My point is, the United States of America, as the greatest industrial power of the world, with 7 per cent of the world's people, and using 30 per cent of the world's energy, shouldn't have to depend on any other country for energy that provides our jobs and transportation and our light and our heat. We can become self-sufficient. This is a great project, and I am going to push it.

Post-Presidency Plans

Q: Mr. President, I am John Chandley of *The Kansas City Times.* Not being a member of the Washington press corps, I am not going to ask when you are going to retire, but I am going to ask you when you do leave the White House, what do you plan to do?

A: I think it depends on when I leave. (Laughter)

No, seriously, I know that this group has asked very good questions and very appropriate ones. I was hoping you would ask me about the milk. Would you mind asking me about the milk?

Q: I don't know anything about the milk.

A: I will answer this, and then I will go to the milk, and then I will go to the man in the back.

As far as retirement, at that time I understand I will be 63 years of age, and I am relatively healthy at present. I don't know how healthy I will be then.

Among these I will not do: I will not practice law. I won't go on any board of directors. I will tell you, after being president, you never want to sit at any other end of the table, and being on a board of directors, it pays well, but it is rather boring. That is what I found when I was Vice President, and not out of any conceit or anything, it is just a fact that boards of directors are fine, but not for former presidents.

What I will try to do is do a little writing. I will not do any speaking. I have made enough speeches in a year to last most people for a lifetime, particularly my audiences.

And so, under the circumstances, what I will probably do is some writing, and perhaps contribute to bettering the political process. Let me say this: Neither party is without fault in the campaign of 1972. There was quite a bit of violence on the other side, and I never spoke anyplace without getting a pretty good working over.

Neither party was without fault with regard to the financing. They raised $36-million and some of that, like some of ours, came from corporate sources and was illegal, because the law had been changed, and apparently people didn't know it.

As far as congressmen and senators are concerned, they will all tell you with the new laws and so forth, there ought to be some changes.

I think if we can't get the Congress to act on the proposal I gave to them six months ago to provide a commission to set up new rules for campaign procedures, then after I leave office, I am going to work for that, because I don't want to be remembered as the man who maybe brought peace for the first time in 12 years, who opened to China, who opened to Russia, maybe avoided a war in the Mideast, maybe if we can continue it, cut unemployment down for the first time in 18 years, for the first time in peacetime it is down to 4½ per cent. It was never at that level, never below 5 per cent in the '60s, any time in the '60s, neither the Kennedy or Johnson administration except during the war years.

I want to be remembered, I would trust, as a President that did his best to bring peace, and also did his best to bring a degree of prosperity, perhaps a contribution in the energy field, in the environmental field, but also one who did his best, when his own campaign got out of hand, to do everything possible to see that other campaigns didn't get out of hand in the future.

Milk Price Supports

Now we will go to the milk case.

Q: Mr. President, APME would like to ask you about the milk, but our 60-minute commitment of time has run out. APME appreciates your appearance.

A: I will take the time. Television, keep me on just a minute. (Laughter)

Q: Thank you.

A: It is a lousy movie anyway tonight. (Laughter)

The reason the milk case question—and this will be the last one I will take—ought to be asked is that just some awful nice people are getting a bad rap about it. And I am not referring about myself. I am referring about people in the administration. They have had John Connally down. They have run him around the track. I guess they are going to have Cliff Hardin down, and Pete Peterson and all the rest.

The whole charge is basically this: That this administration, in 1971, raised the support price for milk as a quid pro quo for a promise by the milk producers that they would contribute substantial amounts, anywhere from $100,000 to $2-million to $10-million, to our campaign.

Now that is just not true. I will tell you how it happened. I was there. Cliff Hardin, in the spring of that year, came in and said, "The milk support prices are high enough." I said, "All right, Cliff, that is your recommendation, the Department of Agriculture?" He said, "Yes." Within three weeks after he had made that announcement, Congress put a gun to our head.

Let me tell you what it was. Republicans? Uh-uh. One hundred and two members of Congress signed a petition demanding not 85 per cent of parity, but a 90 per cent support price, and 28 members of the Senate, most of them Democrats, including Sen. McGovern, signed a petition demanding—a petition, or signed a bill, which would have made the milk support price between 85 and 90 per cent.

So I talked to my legislative leaders and I said, "Look here, what I am concerned about, what I am concerned about is what people pay for that milk, and I don't want to have that price jigged up here if we can keep it and get the supply with the present support price." You know what I was told. They said, "With the kind of heat that we are getting from the Congress, there is no way that you are not going to get on your desk a bill—and they will be able to override your veto—that will raise he support price probably to 90 per cent." So we said 85 per cent.

And that is why it was done, and that is the truth.

Thank you very much, gentlemen. I guess that is the end. ✓

(March 15 text continued from p. 161-A)

a very difficult one for this Administration, because it involves commitments that were made before we got here. Those commitments were made during the Johnson Administration. I do not criticize the fact that they were made, but they were made.

As far as we were concerned, once the war between India and Pakistan began, we cut them off, as you recall. We stopped all economic assistance—not all, but some economic assistance to India, and we stopped all military assistance to Pakistan.

Let's look at the numbers: $83 million in economic assistance to India and $14 million in military assistance to Pakistan. We have maintained that embargo up to this point. The difficulty was that there were contracts that had been made, the materials had already been, in effect, sold, and under the circumstances, we felt that it was time to clean the slate.

So what we have done, the Indians are getting their $83 million in economic assistance; the Pakistanis are being allowed to go through with their purchases of the arms, non-lethal arms and spare parts.

Now as far as the whole, the major problem—and Miss McClendon, you have put your finger on the major problem—and that is peace in the area. This in no way, in no way jeopardizes the peace in the area.

After the war that broke Pakistan in half, India's superiority is so enormous that the possibility of Pakistan being a threat to India is absurd. All we are trying to do is to seek good relations with both, and we trust in the future that our aid to both can be ones that will turn them towards peace rather than war.

I should also say in India's case—while our aid there, our $83 million, was economic—India, as you know, purchases quite significant amounts of arms from the Soviet Union, and also has an arms capability itself. So there is no problem in terms of creating conditions which could lead to another outbreak of war by providing for simply keeping a commitment that the United States had made for the sale of spare parts and non-lethal arms to Pakistan.

THE PRESS: Thank you, Mr. President.   √

(Urban mass transit veto continued from p. 94-A)

I strongly supported legislation which applied uniformly to both the Federal-Aid Highway program. The Senate version of the bill provided flexibility, encouraging bus purchases from mass transit companies can use their buses to produce badly needed charter revenues, and I will continue to press for this balanced flexibility.

As we face gasoline shortages and an increasing demand for public transportation, we should do all we can to afford local officials genuine flexibility to use Federal-Aid Highway funds to improve mass transit if they so desire. I am withholding my signature from H.R. 10511 because this legislation would work directly against that objective.

I urge the Congress to act early in the next session to relax the charger prohibitiion uniformly with respect to both the Federal-Aid Highway program and the Urban Mass Transportation program. If this action is taken promptly, our mass transit systems need not suffer any adverse consequences.

RICHARD NIXON

INDEX TO PRESIDENTIAL TEXTS

49820

Highway trust fund - 29-A, 106-A
Mass transit - 105-A, 106-A
Urban mass transit veto (1-31-74) -
94-A

U

Unemployment. *See* Economy.
**United States Information Agency
veto** (10-23) - 89-A
Urban Mass Transit veto (1-3-74) -
94-A
Urban Renewal - 105-A

V

Veterans
State of the union - 25-A
Veto
Threat of - 109-A, 117-A
Vetoes
OMB director veto - 65-A
Rehabilitation Act of 1972 - 38-A

United States Information Agency
(10-23) - 89-A
Urban mass transit (1-3-74) - 94-A
War powers (10-24) - 90-A
Water-sewer grant program - 47-A
Vietnam
Cease-fire - 98-A, 110-A
Dec. 18, 1972, bombing - 108-A
End of war - 108-A
Fragile peace - 110-A
Mining of Haiphong - 108-A
Purpose of war - 102-A
Remarks to returned POWs - 113-A
Soviet view - 121-A
Vietnamization - 108-A
Vietnam Peace Agreement
Cease-fire violations - 159-A
Observation of - 156-A
Paris conference on Vietnam - 98-A
South Carolina address - 102-A

W

Wage and Price Controls. *See* Economy
Warpowers Veto (10-24) - 90-A

Warsaw Pact - 115-A
Watergate
Comment on investigations - 159-A
Coordinating defense - 166-A
Cox motives - 177-A
Dean meeting - 141-A
Effect on public confidence - 157-A
Ellsberg case - 181-A
Exploitation of - 167-A
FBI involvement - 159-A
FBI post offered to Judge Byrne -
164-A
Haldeman tape - 163-A
Impeachment discussion - 165-A
Resignation possibility - 165-A
March 21 investigation - 171-A
Mideast relation - 179-A
Mitchell testimony - 164-A
New investigation ordered - 163-A
Press obsession with - 165-A
Special Prosecutor
Right to documents - 176-A
Role of - 176-A
Tapes
Content of tapes - 171-A
'Definitive ruling' - 170-A

Delays on - 180-A
Public disclosure - 178-A
Questions - 162-A
Statement (11-12) - 140-A
Willingness to disclose - 172-A
Water-Sewer Grant Program Veto -
47-A
Welfare. *See also* Human Resources.
Family Assistance Plan - 155-A
Legal services - 111-A
Office of Economic Opportunity
(OEO) - 104-A
State of the Union (3-1) - 23-A
Welfare reform - 104-A
Wiretaps - 166-A, 183-A

X, Y, Z

'Year of Europe.' *See* International
Affairs.

DATE DUE

JUL 28 '78			
GAYLORD			PRINTE